MUSIC THEORY REMIXED

A Blended Approach for the Practicing Musician

Kevin Holm-Hudson

New York   Oxford
OXFORD UNIVERSITY PRESS

Oxford University Press is a department of the University of Oxford. It furthers the University's objective of excellence in research, scholarship, and education by publishing worldwide. Oxford is a registered trademark of Oxford University Press in the UK and certain other countries.

Published in the United States of America by Oxford University Press
198 Madison Avenue, New York, NY 10016, United States of America.

Library of Congress Cataloging-in-Publication Data

Names: Holm-Hudson, Kevin.
Title: Music theory remixed : a blended approach for the practicing musician
 / by Kevin Holm-Hudson.
Description: Oxford ; New York : Oxford University Press, [2017] | Includes
 index.
Identifiers: LCCN 2016019356 | ISBN 9780199330560 (alk. paper)
Subjects: LCSH: Music theory—Textbooks.
Classification: LCC MT6.H5736 M87 2017 | DDC 781—dc23 LC record available at
https://lccn.loc.gov/2016019356

9 8 7 6 5 4 3 2 1
Printed by LSC Communications, United States of America

CONTENTS

TO THE STUDENT

As the guitarist Robert Fripp has remarked, "The musician has three instruments: the hands, the head, and the heart." Practicing music disciplines your hands (or your voice), but this is only part of an effective musical education; technique is acquired after hours—years—of practice, but it is of course entirely possible to perform music with technical proficiency but without emotion or formal understanding. The emotional or expressive element of music can be learned with a good teacher, or by listening to good performances of music, but it still does not help us get to the question of *why* or *how* music affects us emotionally, or how to arouse similar emotional responses in others.

Music theory helps to integrate the other two domains—head and heart—into the picture. First, the study of music theory gives us a *mechanical* understanding of music's inner workings). It is this activity—the terminology of musical elements, the labeling of intervals, keys, chords, forms, and so forth—that often comes to mind when thinking of music theory. While this activity is useful—we need a common language of terms when we describe music so that other musicians know what we are talking about—it is just as important to acquire an *emotional* understanding of how and why music is expressive, and how its elements may be used to further musical expression. Once we get past the basics of labeling musical elements, we begin to understand how these elements work together—in progressions, in larger structures. This enhances our understanding, and consequently our appreciation, of music.

Music Theory Remixed aims to blend hands, head, and heart into an integrated approach to music theory. It also mixes together musical genres, from the classic works of Western art music to jazz, rock, film and Broadway music, techno, and world music. This eclectic repertoire not only highlights the common features of the "classical" and popular styles, but also illuminates their crucial differences in harmonic syntax.

Many music theory textbooks have a dry writing style that can be off-putting, making it difficult for many students to connect the content of these books with their activities as performers and listeners. Often what is missing from these texts is the practical application of part-writing *principles*, shown in the context of score analysis. *Music Theory Remixed* emphasizes these principles where possible and shows how those principles manifest themselves as compositional choices. In addition, the text invites you to ponder questions such as: How does one know the key area of a given passage in a musical work? How does the composer treat dissonance? Why did the composer choose to violate the "rules" of part-writing practice in this particular passage? What is the expressive effect of compositional choices?

About the Format of This Book

Music Theory Remixed is organized into four parts, each of which roughly corresponds to a semester of study (your instructor may choose a different order for working through the text). Each chapter begins with a brief summary overview presenting an introduction to the chapter topic. After each major section of a chapter, **Level Mastery** exercises offer low-risk opportunities for you to assess what you have learned. End-of-chapter exercises include **Self-Tests**, which are similar to Level Mastery exercises but tend to be cumulative for the chapter, and **Apply This!** exercises. The Apply This! exercises provide practical application for the concepts learned in each chapter, addressing the activities of **Analysis** (head), **Composition** (heart), and **Improvisation** (hands). There are also **Web Features** online for many chapters, providing more detailed study about particular pieces or topics addressed within a chapter. Please browse through these Web Features as well. These are designed to work together in integrating the hands, head, and heart in your musical training.

There is an old story about the classical guitarist Andrés Segovia. The master was performing an intricate piece by Bach when he reportedly had a memory lapse. However, he was so familiar with Bach's harmonic language and compositional gestures that he did not stop—he simply improvised in the style of Bach until he got to a point in the music that he remembered. Only his students, who had heard him play that piece many times, realized what had happened. The critics wrote that Segovia performed masterfully. One might say that Segovia had integrated the disciplines of the head, hands, and heart so thoroughly that it was second nature for him. It is my hope that this text will make the field of music theory, and its practical applications in music-making, second nature for you.

TO THE INSTRUCTOR

Music Theory Remixed balances popular and classical approaches to music theory, while also balancing the analytical aspects of music theory with its practical or pragmatic aspects. This particular philosophy is drawn from over 20 years of using popular music as an integral part of the undergraduate music theory curriculum with great success.

- Our current entering undergraduates are more media-savvy than ever before, and their musical backgrounds are likely to draw upon a wide variety of popular, jazz, and film music.
- Many students are primarily aural learners; while they may know how to read music, they may still learn music more through guided or focused listening than by studying musical notation alone.
- Today's students are as pluralistic in their music consumption as they are voracious. A student's computer or smartphone is likely to contain selections of rock, rap, classical music, country, Broadway show tunes, jazz, and world music, often programmed to "shuffle" format in a virtual world where Beethoven, the Beatles, and Beyoncé coexist in seemingly happy equality.

This text, by placing "popular" and "classical" works together, often for side-by-side comparisons of elements of musical structure, draws upon the way that many music students already listen to music. The variety of examples used throughout—from Beethoven's Fifth Symphony to *The Sound of Music*, John Williams to Radiohead, "techno" electronic music to Javanese gamelan—enables the student to make tantalizing, meaningful, and never predictable connections among diverse musical practices. All of the examples have been selected for their useful pedagogical applications; some of the "pop" music examples are older, but I believe it is more important that the examples are useful and easily understood in a teaching context than that they are by the latest popular artists.

A crucial tenet of *Music Theory Remixed* is that the study of music theory should be practical. Meeting students where they are, as performers and listeners engaged in a wide range of music, the text introduces students to the tools of listening to music—*any* music—analytically, with an ear for the structural tools of musical expression. While not skimping on analytical depth, the text uses jargon and specialized terms only to the extent that they are necessary (widely used in the field), and the tone of the writing is accordingly aimed at the student's already acquired musical experience. Along the way, students are also introduced to material that could be analyzed in more than one way, with ample opportunity for discussion. Subjects are thus treated with clarity, but not simplistically. In this way the student is equipped to be a fluent, cognizant musician.

Music Theory Remixed offers an approach to harmony that goes beyond atomistic chord-by-chord vertical analysis. It uses a "chunking" approach to harmonic progression wherein chords are learned not in isolation but as elements in hierarchical harmonic patterns. Students are introduced to hierarchies of harmonic function and prolongation in a user-friendly way that eschews more formal jargon (Schenkerian analytical terminology, for example) while illustrating the more practical applications of prolongation based on passing motion, neighboring motion, arpeggiation, and pedal point in the bass. Chords are taught as elements in a linear progression rather than as context-less entities. Not only will the students come away with a better understanding of how harmonic function contributes to structure and meaning in music, but by recognizing and predicting these patterns, they will be better sight-readers and more expressive performers. (They will also understand the expressive or formal significance of when such predictive patterns are delayed or denied.)

The book is organized into four parts, each approximately corresponding to a semester's study (instructors will of course adjust the order of chapters somewhat to reflect teaching preferences and course structures).

Part 1 guides the student to the basics of diatonic harmony and the fundamentals of music theory: musical tone (keyboard and octave registers, clefs and other aspects of staff notation, accidentals and enharmonic spellings, and scales); intervals, consonance, and dissonance; and duration, rhythm, and meter, and so forth. The elements of pitch and interval are then integrated into the basic components of harmony and tonality: chord quality and spelling of triads and seventh chords, figured bass, pop chord symbols, and the nomenclature of Roman numerals and inversion symbols. Chapter 6 introduces the student to counterpoint, including the soprano-bass framework that will serve as a template for filling in harmonies. Voice leading and types of motion (contrary, oblique, similar, and parallel) are also introduced, along with first, second, and third species counterpoint. Later, more elaborate forms of contrapuntal technique are left for further study in a specialized counterpoint course; the genres of canon and fugue are introduced later, in Chapter 19.

Chapters 7 through 10 focus on different aspects of part writing. Chapter 7 introduces the student to tendency tones and cadences; the principles underlying tendency tone resolutions are generalized in Chapters 8 through 10, which show common part-writing procedures involving root-position, first-inversion, and second-inversion chords respectively. Chapter 10 also examines the different contextual functions of second-inversion chords, preparing the student for longer harmonic progressions and the introduction of prolongation in Chapter 13.

Part 2 introduces the student to elements of musical form (phrase/period structures, prolongation, sequence), and also introduces chromatic harmony (initially through mode mixture and tonicization). Part 3 builds on the content of Part 2 more extensively, as chromatic harmony is deepened through modulation (Chapters 17 and 18) and a survey of the various classic forms in Chapters 19 through 23. Chromaticism is revisited in Chapter 24, introducing the Neapolitan chord and augmented sixth chords (and related sonorities).

Part 4 continues in advanced chromaticism (Chapters 25–26) and later varieties of modulation (Chapter 27) before moving on to contemporary compositional techniques in Chapters 28 through 30. Chapter 28 focuses primarily on Impressionism and other styles of tonal-centric music that foregoes traditional functional tonality, whereas Chapter 29 examines atonality (beginning with twelve-tone technique, since that provides a structured introduction to the concepts explored more liberally in free atonality and set theory) and Chapter 30 considers indeterminacy, minimalism, and musical postmodernism.

In Chapter 31, students are introduced to musical intertextuality and narrativity—topics not usually addressed in undergraduate music theory texts, but awareness of which can ultimately have great impact on students' skills and understanding as listeners and performers. The chapter begins with an exploration of intertextuality and stylistic borrowing/quotation in popular music before spinning into a consideration of examples of intertextuality in earlier art music, from Clara Schumann and Erik Satie. The chapter also considers the topic of musical narrativity, beginning with a consideration of music *and* narrative, or music's capacity to support or amplify an external narrative. This is followed by music *as* narrative, in which music's capacity to "tell a story" in an abstract, evocative sense is explored. With this chapter, the groundwork is laid for more detailed analytical courses.

At the end of each chapter, students are provided with terms for review and a number of self-test questions, answers to which are provided in an online appendix (www.oup.com/us/holm-hudson). In addition, *Music Theory Remixed* also offers the student opportunities for score analysis, composition, and improvisation, using the concepts introduced in that chapter. These activities, an important part of National Association of Schools of Music requirements, are a fundamental component of student mastery. Here, students are able to engage with and creatively apply what they have learned.

Throughout the text a "spiral" approach is used for certain pieces (both "classical" and "non-classical"), returning to familiar works to introduce new concepts.

This allows students to engage with a work on successively deeper levels. If needed, a number of the classical works may be found in their entirety in currently available anthologies, or through online repositories such as the International Music Score Library Project (www.imslp.org). Identifying captions for the popular-music examples all include chronological timestamps, making it easy for students to locate and hear the passages illustrated in the absence of a detailed score. (Because of copyright restrictions, examples sometimes use reductive or analytical diagrams rather than full-score transcriptions; this provides the additional benefit of being able to hear the structural skeleton of more elaborate passages.)

Music Theory Remixed begins and ends with an emphasis on listening. In the opening "Prelude" chapter, before notation is even addressed, students are presented with several aural examples—ranging from Robert Schumann to Xenakis and John Lee Hooker—along with questions and discussion points to ponder. Texture is also introduced in this chapter, again with an emphasis on listening; examples come from sources as diverse as a Bach partita for solo violin and Moroccan folk music. The final chapter contains two extended aural analyses: Emmylou Harris's "Goodbye" and Pink Floyd's "Comfortably Numb."

Additional materials are available to the student and instructor in the various Web Features found on the *Music Theory Remixed* website **www.oup.com/us/holm-hudson**. An indication to the student is found at appropriate points in the text that the material may be supplemented by consulting a Web Feature. Instructors are also encouraged to make use of these materials, especially for advanced or honors classes, or in "Comprehensive Musicianship" programs where music theory is more closely integrated with parallel study in musicology.

—Kevin Holm-Hudson
University of Kentucky

ACKNOWLEDGMENTS

I would like to thank those teachers who instilled in me a passion for teaching music: Aline Brugmann, Dolce Bohn, Scott Shuler, Brian Israel, Daniel Godfrey, William Brooks, and John Buccheri. I also wish to thank my colleagues past and present at the University of Kentucky—Michael Baker, Karen Bottge, Richard Domek, and Rob Schultz—for using early versions of the text during its development in their teaching over the last six years, and to my colleagues Chuck Lord and Kate Covington for their early advice and encouragement. My endless gratitude is due to Richard Carlin for his unwavering faith in this project and his patience to see it through. I would also like to thank the editorial and production team at Oxford University Press, particularly Erin Janosik, Jacqueline Levine, Keith Faivre, and Elizabeth Bortka for their guidance. This text also benefited from the helpful suggestions made by the reviewers:

Allison Brewster Franzetti, *Rutgers University*
Benjamin Steege, *Columbia University*
Deanna Weber, *Albany State University*
Debbie Benoist, *Alvin Community College and San Jacinto College South*
Gregory Hoepfner, *Cameron University*
Laura Pollie McDowell, *Brevard College*
Mark McFarland, *Georgia State University*
Megan Fogle, *Claflin University*
Rusty Jones, *Butler University*
Sidney Marquez Boquiren, *Adelphi University*
Victoria Malawey, *Macalester College*
Ya-Hui Cheng, *University of South Florida*
Nathan Baker, *Casper College*
Janet E. Greene, *Hamline University*
Junko Oba, *Hampshire College*
David N. Patterson, *University of Massachusetts–Boston*
Elaine Rendler, *George Mason University*
Nicholas L. Wallin, *Lake Forest College*
Kristin Wendland, *Emory University*
David Heinick, *Crane School of Music, SUNY–Potsdam*
Vincent P. Benitez, *The Pennsylvania State University*
Mark Zanter, *Marshall University*
Timothy Lane, *University of Wisconsin–Eau Claire*
. . . and 10 anonymous reviewers

Finally, I want to thank my loving family—Karen, Miranda, and Toby—for their support and encouragement during the long time it took to bring this book to fruition. I love you all so much. You refresh the music in my heart.

ABOUT THE AUTHOR

KEVIN HOLM-HUDSON is Associate Professor of Music Theory and Coordinator of the Division of Music Theory and Composition at the University of Kentucky. Prior to joining the faculty at the University of Kentucky he was on the faculty of Northwestern University, where he also directed the National High School Music Institute's composition program. He holds a doctoral degree in composition (with an ethnomusicology emphasis) from the University of Illinois at Urbana-Champaign. He is also the author of *Genesis and the Lamb Lies Down on Broadway* (Ashgate, 2008) and the editor of *Progressive Rock Reconsidered* (Routledge, 2002).

PART 1

FUNDAMENTALS AND DIATONIC HARMONY

SETTING THE STAGE
Listening

OVERVIEW

What is music theory? How can it make you a better listener, a better performer . . . a better musician? In this introductory chapter we focus on listening and what it can tell us about musical structure. We will also learn about texture—the interaction of musical elements. Whether there is one line, several lines at once, a melody taking prominence over a supporting accompaniment, or even multiple, slightly different versions of the same melodic line overlapping all at once, sound can be arranged in different ways.

INTRODUCTION: KNOWING THE SECRETS

We are fortunate to live in a time when we are able to hear more music, of more varieties, more often—and *on demand*—than at any other time in history. We can download a song to our computer or our MP3 player instantly, day or night; performances are increasingly streamed online, allowing people around the world to watch in real time. Such variety, and immediate availability, was unthinkable even a few years ago.

At the same time, we may have become spoiled by our instant access to so much music. It has become such a constant part of our lives that it has become an extra background noise alongside the radio, TV, and cell phone. You may even "multitask" various media when you study. This is quite different from the way music was experienced in earlier generations. In nineteenth-century Europe, for example, many people would never have had the opportunity to hear a Beethoven symphony if they had not heard Franz Liszt perform his own solo piano transcriptions of them; hearing an orchestra play Beethoven was a rare experience if one did not live in a large city. How carefully do you think you would listen to a piece of music if you had never heard it before and there was a very real possibility that you would never hear it played again?

This is a book about music theory, but it is also about ways of listening, and changes in compositional style and performance. One way of looking at the history of musical style could go something like this: Changes in a musical style are brought about by performers and composers who try something new, like what they hear, and incorporate it into their special sound. Only later, after the practices have become rather widespread, do theorists account for what has been going on as guidelines for later musicians who want to know the great musicians' secrets. Thus, while it may seem that music theory consists of a number of "rules" to memorize for properly writing chords and so on, they often summarize common musical *principles*.

"Knowing the secrets," then, is not only valuable for composers who would follow the great models while adding their own personal stamp on the art, but for performers who can, through mindful performance, convey the surprise, the humor, and the full spectrum of emotion in their playing in a way that can be experienced by the listener. Think of what it would be like to hear an actor in a Shakespearean comedy who had studied nothing of the language and customs of Shakespeare's time; as a result he or she would have no idea as to which lines were supposed to be humorous. Such an actor may have all of the words memorized perfectly, but the sense isn't there—as a result, the performance is lifeless. Without an understanding of music theory, then—of the norms of a style and how a composer uses rhythm, harmony, form and so forth to communicate their ideas—a musical performance can also be technically perfect but deadly dull.

Music is popularly associated with musical tones or **pitches**, arranged either as consecutive single pitches in a **melody** or into combinations of pitches called **harmony**. For many people, tones or pitches are the very essence of music, even though of course it is possible to have "music" that is not made of pitched material (as, for example, in music for percussion ensemble).

Pitch is a way of labeling the highness or lowness of a sound, based upon the **frequency**—the number of vibrations (or **cycles**) per second—of a sounding body (for example, the note that an oboe player sounds to tune a symphony orchestra before a concert usually sounds at 440 cycles per second); the greater the number of vibrations per second, the higher the pitch.

THREE LISTENING STUDIES

We will have plenty of opportunity for *looking* at musical notation; for now, let's begin our journey into music theory with *listening*, in the form of three carefully chosen sound studies (an additional example is available as a supplementary Web Feature online). All of the examples in this book are available through music download services such as iTunes or Spotify; many, of course, can also be found on video sites such as YouTube. If you do not get the opportunity to listen to these in class, you should listen to them and discuss them with a friend—then you can share your impressions.

SOUND EXAMPLE PRL.1: SCOTT JOHNSON (B. 1952), *JOHN SOMEBODY—PT. 1*

Listen to just the first six seconds or so of this piece (stop the recording at [0:06] if you can). Would you say that this is an example of singing or speech? Most listeners would probably say that this would be an example of speech.

Now, from where you stopped, listen a little more until about [0:25]. The speech material is obviously treated to some compositional arrangement; the fragment "uh, he was a, he was sort of a" is looped onto itself to form a repeating, rhythmic pattern.[1] We might be more inclined to call this music—or at least a text collage—because there has obviously been some degree of human intervention—composition—applied to the result.

Now, notice what happens at [0:28]. A bank of electric guitars enters to accompany the speech tapes. Suddenly, the spoken words become melodies.

We are not always aware of it, but speech has a "melodic contour" all its own—the rise and fall of vocal inflection, as we emphasize certain words, ask questions, or raise our voices while arguing or cheering for our favorite sports team. When speech is cut into fragments and loops, as Johnson did in arranging his taped material, our ears are fooled into thinking the speech has become a melody with its own underlying rhythmic pulse—even though the "notes" of Johnson's friend's voice are not exactly in tune with their musical setting. (Another composer, Steve Reich, has used this technique in his pieces *Different Trains* and *WTC 9/11*.)

In fact, sometimes the boundary between speech and song can be very blurry indeed. In some Islamic cultures, for example, the outdoor prayer (or *adhan*) of the *muezzin* is generally considered to be speech, not music—even though it has been shown to have numerous melodic qualities—because in those cultures music is considered too sensual, too morally suspect. For another example, hip-hop often contains recurring pitch contours, certain repeated rhythms, and so on, giving it a level of formal unity on par with more "melodic" musical styles.

---

[1] The Society for Music Theory's "SMT-V" videocast "Repetition and Musicality," Episode 1.1, examines how speech is turned into music through repetition. https://vimeo.com/120517523

Have you ever thought about where music came from? One idea is that music is a kind of heightened or exaggerated speech. Music came about in this way, for example, dramatized and elevated by a sacred ritual in incantations; "musically" intoned words also carried over a greater distance when called out across a field.

SOUND EXAMPLE PRL.2: IANNIS XENAKIS (1922–2001), *CONCRÈT PH*

Another theory of musical origin suggests that music came about from humans' efforts to replicate sounds they heard in nature, such as the buzzing of insects, bird songs, the calls of wolves and growls of bears, and the sound of thunder. All of these sounds were very mysterious, thought to contain magical power.

This piece is based on a very tiny natural sound—the crackling and pinging of smoldering charcoal. It is an example of *musique concrète*, an electronic music genre that relies on recorded source materials from the natural and urban environment (rather than synthesized electronic tones).

Does this sound like a piece of music to you? It certainly does not have any recognizable elements of melody, or harmony. The sounds of the charcoal are rhythmic in a way, but it doesn't exactly make you want to tap your feet. And yet, this was a "composed" piece of music, performed for thousands of people who visited the Brussels World's Fair in 1958. Perhaps because pieces like this have been created and called musical works by a composer, and because they have been recognized as music by audiences, the British ethnomusicologist John Blacking came up with the definition of music as "humanly organized sound." Even so, the "organization" in this piece is not all that obvious, although Xenakis did apply some electronic processing to the recorded charcoal sounds. And, of course, there are "environment" recordings of crickets, thunderstorms, waterfalls, etc., which are recorded with no human intervention whatsoever; do such recordings become "music" just because someone has packaged them with a title and a purchase price?

SOUND EXAMPLE PRL.3: ROBERT SCHUMANN (1810–1856), *ARABESKE IN C MAJOR, OP. 18*

This piece is a much more conventional example of what we would probably call "music." It has a melody, a repetitive rhythmic pattern, and a chord progression that seems to proceed to a goal or point of repose. Notice how the performer slows down ever so slightly at those points of arrival; this is called *rubato*, and skilled performers know just when to slow down—and just how much—to enhance the emotional expression of a piece and give it some formal coherence. This piece, in particular, we will come to know very well in later chapters.

You may have thought that this piano piece by Schumann sounded much more "normal," more "musical," than the electronic composition by Xenakis. Have you considered, however, how this piano piece would sound to someone from another culture who had never heard a piece of "classical" piano music—or even a piano? Suppose this piece were played to a person who had had no contact with Western music whatsoever. How would you imagine they would respond to the music of Robert Schumann? Would it be much like our response to hearing an ancient tribal song for the first time?

Web Feature PRL.1 may be investigated at this time.

WEAVING THE SONIC TAPESTRY: TEXTURE

One of the great universals we can observe about music is that it is a social activity. Although it is certainly possible to perform music when you are alone solely for your own amusement, it seems to be more rewarding when it is shared with others. Even if you are listening to a recording in the privacy of your room, it is possible to imagine, in some "virtual" sense, that that artist or ensemble is playing for you.

Of course, there are different varieties of social organization and interaction. A drum circle, a jazz band, and a symphony orchestra are all musical ensembles, but their social structures are very different. In a drum circle, for example, everyone plays together to create a musical fabric that is a complex, interlocking whole. Everyone is playing together, responding to each other's rhythms, but no one usually steps forward for a "solo" or dominates the group. In a jazz group, there may be a "leader," but generally the players take turns playing solos while the rest of the ensemble tastefully supports the soloist. The assignment of who plays a solo and when may be worked out in advance or simply determined spontaneously with a glance or nod in a player's direction. Finally, a symphony orchestra most definitely has a leader—the conductor. The conductor determines how slow or how fast to play a passage, interpreting the composer's (sometimes vague) indications, and how loud or soft the music should be. Sometimes the conductor has to cede control to a soloist, as in a cadenza during a concerto, but the conductor's authority is generally unquestioned (though performers may grumble about the conductor's decisions!). We might liken a drum circle to a commune, a jazz band to a democracy (the solos being something like an elected official's term of office), and a symphony orchestra to a monarchy (hopefully with a benevolent ruler!).

These different social patterns are also found within pieces of music. **Texture** refers to the interaction of parts, or players, within a musical work. There are four general types of texture: **monophony** (a single line), **homophony** (a melody with accompaniment), **polyphony** (more than one part, interacting independently and with roughly equal importance), and **heterophony** (a single line, but with many individual variations).

Some of the following musical examples have a written score, but again at this point it would be best to just listen actively and consider the following observations for each example.

Monophony: Jean Ritchie (1922–2015), "Barbary Allen (Barbara Allen)" and Johann Sebastian Bach (1685–1750), Minuet II from Suite no. 1 in G major for solo cello, BWV 1007

Any time that a piece of music is played or sung as a single melody by one performer (or many performers, playing or singing the exact same thing), without accompaniment, the result is **monophony**. The earliest Western art music that we know of—Gregorian chant—is monophonic. Some of the earliest music we heard—nursery songs, lullabies—are examples of monophony.

Working in a monophonic context does not mean that the composer ignores harmony (the simultaneous sounding of more than one pitch). Jean Ritchie's rendition of the Appalachian folk ballad "Barbary Allen" is unaccompanied, but once one is familiar with the song it would certainly be possible to improvise a suitable accompaniment. You may already hear an *implied* harmony that would fit with the melody; a classmate, however, might add a different pattern of harmonies to support the melody, however, and it could still fit. Some composers, such as Johann Sebastian Bach, made several differently harmonized settings of the same melody.

Bach's Minuet II from his Suite no. 1 for solo cello, BWV 1007, is another example of monophonic music that is altogether more complex than "Barbary Allen." You may find yourself more readily hearing an underlying harmony to this piece, or even more than one "part" within the single line. Composers can create a kind of "dialogue of parts" within the melodic line through the rapid alternation of **register**—the relative "highness" or "lowness" of pitches within the **range** of a work—the overall distance from the lowest to the highest pitch in the piece. When more than one melody is heard in a monophonic texture in this way, it is called **compound melody**. At the beginning of this piece, Bach uses quick changes of register to create the impression that there is more than one line, or voice, in the texture. Later in the piece, Bach does not change register so drastically. In what other ways might a composer create variety, especially over a lengthy period of time, using a single melodic line in a piece for a single performer?

Homophony: Fréderic Chopin (1810–1849), Prelude in B minor, op. 28 no. 6

Homophony describes any musical texture that involves a melody with an accompaniment. Most Western "classical" and popular music employs this texture.

Although the melodic line is usually in a higher register than its accompaniment, this is not always the case. In Fréderic Chopin's Prelude in B minor, the melodic line is in a lower register, evoking the sound of a cello. The accompaniment is repetitive and serves mainly to provide a harmonic and rhythmic backdrop for the sweeping arcs of the melody.

Polyphony: Johann Sebastian Bach, Invention no. 6 in E major, BWV 777

Polyphony describes a texture in which more than one part is heard to carry mutually independent roles of more or less equal importance. While one part may seem to be "subservient" to another, that situation is not permanent—sooner or later, the parts switch roles, with the subservient voice emerging as the focal part in the texture.

Listen carefully to this Bach example. At the outset, Bach presents us with two ideas—an ascending line in the low register, and a descending line in the high register. The lines appear to be converging. The equal status of the two parts in this polyphonic texture is affirmed when Bach switches the two main ideas; the ascending line appears above the descending line, and the two parts seem to separate again. In other words, the lower part is not a mere accompaniment for the upper part; the two parts continually change roles.

Most polyphony will contain between two and four parts; more than that will usually be too intricate for the listener to keep track of all at once. (The Renaissance composer Thomas Tallis [1505–1585], however, composed a choral work, *Spem in Allium*, which has forty different parts!)

Heterophony: Master Musicians of Jajouka featuring Bachir Attar, "El Medahey"

Imagine for a moment that you are at a large outdoor sporting event. Before the game begins, the crowd rises in the stands for the National Anthem. Suppose that the crowd of several thousand decide to sing along. It is likely that, because of the outdoor acoustics, the lack of trained singers, and the general giddiness caused by the beverages consumed before the game, the crowd will not be completely in synchronization with the soloist. Now, suppose that the soloist is an opera singer, or perhaps a rhythm-and-blues stylist like Mariah Carey. In those genres, the soloist is likely to add his or her own personal ornaments to the vocal line, which the carousing crowd in the stands would certainly not duplicate. The result is **heterophony**, which may be described as a single melodic line that is doubled by an ensemble with varying degrees of ornament and precision.

The Master Musicians of Jajouka originate from the village of Jajouka near Ksar-el-Kebir in the southern Rif mountains of northern Morocco. Their music is connected with the Sufi tradition of Islam, and before that to the god Pan (a Jajouka legend recalls that centuries ago the goat-man Boujeloud appeared to one of the musicians and bestowed to him the gift of flute music—this event is re-enacted annually).

"El Medahey" was composed by Jajouka musician Hadj Abdesalam Attar. The ensemble heard here consists of flutes called *liras*, with goatskin drums—the lower drum, played with two wooden sticks, is called a *tebel* and the higher drum, capable of more elaborate virtuosic playing, is called a *tarija*. After an introduction on solo *lira* (accompanied by an ensemble of *liras* providing a drone), the drums enter at 1:44 and the *liras* begin playing a series of short melodic figures. As you listen, notice that not everyone seems to be "together"—there are occasional "clusters" of differing ornamentation (especially noticeable at 2:09–2:17 and 2:31–2:49). You may also notice that changes from one melodic cell to another are often triggered by the leader, with the others quickly joining in (again often with differing ornamentations).

CONCLUSION

We have listened to and examined several pieces of music in this chapter, each with a different style and each offering its own entry points for study. Each chapter will contain at least one listening example, with additional web features online for deeper study. Each example will be presented in a framework for active listening couched in a series of questions and observations, much like the ones found in this chapter. When you are studying for a quiz or testing your mastery of a chapter with the self-test materials at the end of each chapter, be sure to listen to the pieces again to aid in your study.

Hopefully you have enjoyed this little musical survey and have come out of this chapter not only knowing a little more about each example, but also having a better idea about what can be involved in the study of music theory. You may have already learned, for example, something about clefs, intervals, and scales, and thought that music theory involved studying that kind of information. You may have even learned about chords and how they may be labeled in a piece you are learning to play or sing. But there is so much more to music theory than harmony. Rhythm (including the larger rhythm of phrases and sections within a form), timbre, register, the markers of musical style, the way conceptions of musical structure are manifested in a culture (as in for example texture), the way your brain processes musical information—all of these things are also part of the discipline of music theory, which is as rich and varied as the music of the world.

Workbook Exercises PRL.1 and PRL.2 may be done at this time.

Terms to Know

compound melody	homophony	polyphony
cycle	melody	range
frequency	monophony	register
harmony	pitch	texture
heterophony		

CHAPTER 1

DIMENSIONS OF PITCH

Notation, Scales, and Key Signatures

OVERVIEW

This chapter introduces the raw materials of musical notation and how to represent pitch: the grand staff, clefs, the major scale, and the different forms of the minor scale. We then move on to key signatures and how key relationships are shown on the circle of fifths.

CHAPTER OUTLINE

THE KEYBOARD, PITCH, AND PITCH CLASS

In Western music, pitches are named with the letters A, B, C, D, E, F, and G. Before we go further, we need to become familiar with where these notes are found on a keyboard. If you look at a piano, organ, or synthesizer keyboard, you will notice that the raised black keys are organized in alternating groups of two and three keys. Find the group of two keys closest to the center of the keyboard. The white key immediately to the *left* of the two black keys is called "middle C" (see Example 1.1). Any two *adjacent* keys on the keyboard (such as E and F in Example 1.1) make what is called a **half step**; if there are two keys with one in between (for example, two white keys with a black key in between, as with C and D in Example 1.1), the distance is a **whole step**.

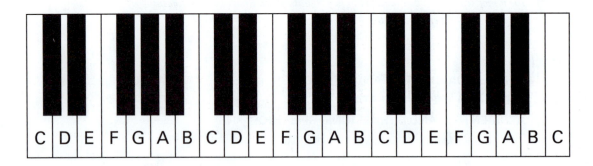

Example 1.1. Keyboard layout with white keys labeled.

Now, find the next group of two black keys to the right, and play the white key immediately to the left of that two-key group. You should notice that this note sounds similar to the first one; in fact, if you play them simultaneously, they may appear to "fuse" into sounding like one tone rather than two. Both of these keys are Cs. The distance between them is called an **octave**; the higher C vibrates at twice the frequency as the lower C. Because each of the Cs—each of the white keys found immediately to the left of the two-black-key groups on the keyboard—sounds similar, each C is a member of the same **pitch class**. The term "pitch class" refers to all of the Cs in all octaves (or all of the As, or all of the Gs, etc.); a **pitch**, on the other hand, refers to a specific note at a specific frequency. Thus, middle C is a pitch, one of (usually) eight Cs on the keyboard that belongs to the same pitch class. The fact that each C, though it is a different pitch, nevertheless sounds "similar" to the others illustrates the principle of **octave equivalence**.

Pitches are often referred to using labels devised by the Acoustical Society of America (ASA). In the ASA system, middle C is labeled C4, because it is the fourth C found ascending up the keyboard; each of the following notes in that octave also have the "4" designation, with C starting the octave (notes below C1—usually the third white key from the lowest end of the keyboard—have a "0" designation). For example, the note that an oboe player sounds to tune a symphony orchestra before a concert is A4, because it is in the octave between C4 and C5 (the next C up the keyboard).

CLEFS AND THE GRAND STAFF

In Western music, pitches are usually written as note symbols on a **staff** (plural: *staves*) made up of five lines and four spaces. Every staff has a **clef** at its far left, which provides a frame of reference for the pitches. There are three types of clefs. The **treble clef** uses G4 (the G above middle C) as its reference point, indicated by the way the clef curls around the G line (the second line of the staff, starting from the bottom).[1] The **bass clef** uses F3 (the F below middle C) as its reference point, shown by the two dots on either side of the F line (the fourth line of the staff, starting from the bottom).[2] Often, as in piano music, one will find the treble clef above the bass clef, joined by a **brace**; this is called a **grand staff** (see Example 1.2).

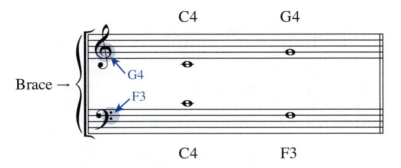

Example 1.2. Grand staff, with F3, G4, and middle C (C4) shown.

The **C clefs** are centered upon a line that represents middle C (C4) itself (Example 1.3). These are less common than the treble and bass clefs; the two most commonly used varieties are the **alto clef**, characteristic of viola parts, and the **tenor clef**, which is sometimes found in higher-register passages for instruments that usually use bass clef, such as the cello or bassoon. The tenor clef is sometimes used in these higher passages to avoid the use of too many **ledger lines**, lines that extend the range of the staff in either direction. Example 1.4 shows the opening phrase of the folk hymn "Amazing Grace" in both bass and tenor clefs.

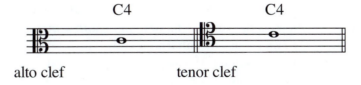

Example 1.3. Alto clef and tenor clef, with middle C shown on each.

---

[1] Historically, the treble clef is an example of a **G clef**. In all G clefs, the curlicue on the clef encloses a line that represents G4. The treble clef—which has a curlicue enclosing the *second line from the bottom* of the staff—is by far the most common variety of G clef.

[2] Historically, the bass clef is an example of an **F clef**. In all F clefs, the two dots after the clef straddle a line that represents F3. The bass clef—whose two dots straddle the *second line from the top of the staff*—is by far the most common variety of F clef.

Example 1.4. "Amazing Grace" in both bass and tenor clefs.

When a small "8" is added below a clef, it means that the notes sound an octave lower than notated.

If specific pitch is not an issue (for example, if writing music for percussion with no definite pitch), one will also encounter **percussion clef**. This is shown in Example 1.5. Usually in percussion clef, different lines and spaces are used for different instruments (such as bass drum, snare drum, and cymbal in a drum kit).

percussion clef →

Example 1.5. Percussion clef.

ACCIDENTALS AND ENHARMONIC SPELLINGS

So far, we have confined our musical exploration to the white keys on the keyboard. However, of course, we also have the raised black keys at our disposal. These pitches are notated using **accidentals**, symbols that raise or lower the pitch. A **sharp** (♯) is used to raise the pitch, whereas a **flat** (♭) lowers the pitch. The black key between C and D, then, can be labeled as C♯ (a raised C) or as D♭ (a lowered D). C♯ and D♭ are **enharmonic spellings** of the same pitch, meaning that they both refer to the same sounding pitch. The two pitches are **enharmonically equivalent**.

Another common accidental is the **natural** (♮). The natural sign restores a note to its original "white key" pitch name. "G natural," then, is the same as "G." The natural may raise or lower the pitch depending on its context. (If a note in a scale is usually G♭, a G♮ would raise that pitch; on the other hand, if the note in the scale is usually G♯, a G♮ would lower that pitch.)

Occasionally, further alterations are necessary. A double sharp (𝄪) modifies a pitch by raising it twice; F𝄪, for example, raises the F to F♯ and then raises the F♯ one more step, making it enharmonically equivalent to G. A double flat (♭♭) is used to lower a pitch twice. B♭♭ lowers the pitch B to B♭ and then lowers the B♭ again, making it enharmonically equivalent to A.

If there are two (or more) ways of notating a pitch, which one should be used? The proper spelling depends on the musical context; *sharped (raised) pitches* tend to proceed *upward to a higher pitch*, whereas *flatted (lowered) pitches* tend to proceed *downward*. In a melody, then, C♯ would usually be followed by D, and D♭ would usually be followed by C. Enharmonic spellings are thus "the same yet different," in the way that, for example, "your" and "you're" are pronounced the same way yet are used differently in a sentence. Just as correct spelling is important when communicating your written ideas to strangers, choosing the right spelling for a note says much about your "musical literacy" when you are writing or arranging music for other musicians. Try reading and playing the passage in Example 1.6. Is there a way to notate this that would be easier to read?

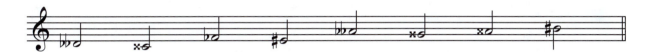

Example 1.6. An example of excessive enharmonic spelling.

LEVEL MASTERY 1.1.

Self-Tests 1.1 and 1.2 may be done at this time.

Workbook Exercises 1.1 and 1.2 may be done at this time.

Write the pitches indicated by their ASA labels in the indicated clefs.

1.	2.	3.	4.	5.	6.	7.	8.
A4, treble clef	B1, bass clef	F♯3, alto clef	G♯4, tenor clef	E♭2, bass clef	C♯6, treble clef	F♭4, bass clef	A×4, alto clef

9.	10.	11.	12.	13.	14.	15.	16.
E♭3, tenor clef	A♭5, treble clef	B♭4, alto clef	G♭♭3, bass clef	F×6, treble clef	B♭2, tenor clef	C♯5, alto clef	F2, bass clef

17.	18.	19.	20.	21.	22.	23.	24.
A♭1, bass clef	D♯3, alto clef	D♭2, tenor clef	E5, treble clef	G♭5, alto clef	B×4, treble clef	D♭3, bass clef	D♯4, tenor clef

Provide all possible enharmonic spellings for the indicated pitches, in the specified clefs.

Self-Test 1.3 may be done at this time.

Workbook Exercise 1.3 may be done at this time.

NOTATION ON THE STAFF

Certain conventions should be followed when writing music, in order to make your music easier to read.

NOTEHEADS. Noteheads may be open (hollow) or closed (solid), depending on their duration. The head of a note is not simply a circle, but rather an oval at about a 30-degree slant from lower left to upper right. Be mindful that your notehead is not too large or too small. If the notehead is too large, it can confuse the reader as to whether it falls on a line or a space; if it is too small, it can be difficult to see. Make sure that noteheads are properly "centered" on the appropriate line or within the appropriate space.

ACCIDENTALS. Accidentals are *always* placed to the left of the notehead they affect, and they must be centered on the same line or space as the notehead (Example 1.7). Be careful not to write accidentals too small.

Example 1.7. Correct and incorrect notation of accidentals.

STEMS. Stems go *up* on all notes below the middle line, and *down* on all notes above the middle line. Notes on the middle line can go either way, depending on the other notes in the measure (especially later in the measure).

If two parts (say, soprano and alto) are found on a single staff, the upper part will always have stems that extend up, and the lower part will always have stems extending down (Example 1.8).

In general, stems extend about an octave in the correct direction from the notehead. However, if the notehead is two or more ledger lines above or below the staff, the stem should reach from the note to the middle line.

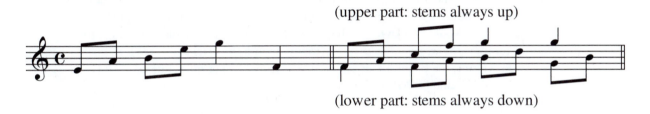

Example 1.8. Correct use of stems, in one and two parts.

In the case of chords written with stems, look at the highest and lowest notes and how they relate to the middle line. The stem will come *from* the note furthest away from the middle line.

THE HARMONIC SERIES AND TIMBRE

Notating a pitch on a staff does not completely communicate to us how it sounds. A pitch played on a clarinet, for example, sounds different from the same pitch played on an oboe. This is because a musical tone is almost never "pure," but rather it is actually a complex combination of simultaneous vibrations at various frequencies, which are called **harmonics** or **overtones**. The proportion of harmonics present in a sound makes up its **timbre**, or "tone color."

Try this experiment, if you have access to a stringed instrument (a guitar works best, as its harmonic positions are marked, but this exercise would also work on a fretless string instrument such as a violin). Lightly mute a low string by resting your fingertip at the midpoint of the string, then pluck or bow the string. (Make sure you are not pushing the string down with your finger.) You should hear a pitch an octave higher than the string would normally sound. Next, slide your finger toward the end of the string while plucking or bowing that string repeatedly. You should hear a whole spectrum of other, higher pitches, in relation to the pitch of the open string. Each of these higher pitches are already present in the string's tone, but your muting the string at its various **nodes** brings out those individual harmonics.

The lowest note in the series—the **fundamental**—is also the strongest in **amplitude** (intensity), and for that reason we hear that tone as the pitch. Different instruments have these harmonics in greater or lesser proportions, contributing to their distinctive timbre. Timbre is also a factor in musical style; among singers, for example, a country singer's voice has a stronger proportion of higher overtones, providing that rich "twang" that one would not hear in, for example, a singer of Gregorian chant. In some cultures, such as the *Hoomi* of Mongolia, singers learn to isolate higher overtones over a droned fundamental to create lively, whistling melodies.

The harmonic series is infinite. Each successive overtone is higher in frequency and weaker in amplitude, however, and the distance between successive higher harmonics also gets smaller and smaller. As a result, most listeners are not able to discern many harmonics beyond the eleventh or twelfth harmonic. The first eleven harmonics above the fundamental are shown in Example 1.9. Note that two of these harmonics—the sixth and tenth—are slightly "out of tune" with their corresponding pitches as they would be played on the piano. This is because the piano is tuned to **equal temperament**, a tuning that artificially divides the octave into twelve equal steps. As a result, the B♭ and F♯, as played on the piano, do not quite line up with the overtones of "B♭" and "F♯" that occur naturally above a C fundamental. (Sometimes, however, the sixth harmonic is used as a "blue note" in popular music and jazz.)

harmonics or overtones

fundamental

Example 1.9. The first eleven harmonics of the harmonic series, over a C2 fundamental.

THE MAJOR SCALE AND ITS SCALE DEGREES

If you start on middle C (C4) and play each key—white and black—upward until you reach the next C (C5), you have played a **chromatic** scale, consisting of twelve pitches. Most pieces of music do not feature all twelve pitches equally (there are some twentieth- and twenty-first-century pieces that do); usually a scale will have no more than seven pitches, in a specific pattern of whole steps and half steps encompassing an octave.

For example, if we start on C4 and play only the successive white keys above that note until we reach C5, the result is a **major scale**. Because our scale begins and ends on C, we call this scale a C major scale (Example 1.10). The notes also represent a **diatonic pitch collection** of C major. Notes that belong to the C major scale are **diatonic** pitches; a note that is foreign to the scale—such as F♯—is a **chromatic** pitch.

Example 1.10. The C major scale.

The C major scale has no sharps or flats. Notice that as you played each step up from C to C, usually you *skipped* a **whole step** past a black key. There are two places, however—between E and F and between B and C—where the keys were *adjacent*—**half steps**. All ascending major scales—regardless of on which pitch you start—have the following arrangement of whole and half steps:

$$W–W–H–W–W–W–H$$

Each step (or **scale degree**) of the scale has a label describing its function or placement within the scale. The C in a C major scale, for example, is called the **tonic**. This label communicates something of the special status enjoyed by the "goal" note in a scale, as the term is also used to describe the home "key" of a piece of music. The next most important scale degree is the fifth note in the scale (G, if we are playing a C major scale). This note is called the **dominant**. If we go five steps *down* from the tonic (to F), we get the **subdominant**. This label comes from treating the note as a kind of "mirror image" of the dominant (five steps down rather than five steps up), but you will also note that going *up* from C this note is the fourth scale degree.

The tonic, dominant and subdominant are the most important pitches in the scale—bass players in countless garage bands have been able to "get by" with just these three pitches. So important are they that the other scale degrees are named according to their placement with regard to one of these three scale degrees. For example, the second scale degree—D, in our scale—is called the **supertonic** because it is found just above the tonic. The third scale degree (E in our scale) is called the **mediant** because it is found "in the middle" between the tonic and dominant. Likewise, the sixth scale degree—A, in our scale—is called the **submediant** because it is found "in the middle" between the tonic and its subdominant below; you can also think of it as the "mirror image" of the mediant. (Hold middle C down on the keyboard and then play the E above, and the A below, to see the relationship.)

The last step in our scale—the seventh scale degree—is called the **leading tone**, because of its strong tendency to be followed by (or **resolve** to) the tonic. At least in a melody or bass line, a leading tone usually "leads" or resolves to the tonic a half step above. In any major scale, the half steps always occur between scale degrees 3 and 4 and between scale degrees 7 and 1. Note that when scale degree numbers are used, they are often depicted with a circumflex symbol above the number, as in "$\hat{3}$" and "$\hat{4}$."

In singing melodies by scale degrees—a tool for improving sight-singing—it is obviously cumbersome to use the scale degree names. Sometimes simple numbers from 1 to 7 are used; melodies are also sometimes taught in the form of **solfège** syllables. These syllables are commonly used in vocal instruction, especially in Europe. The syllables, moving up the scale, are *do, re, mi, fa, sol, la,* and *ti.* (Incidentally, a parallel conception of the scale has developed in the classical *raga* music of India; there the syllables are *Sa, Ra, Ga, Ma, Pa, Dha,* and *Ni.*) The C major scale with its scale degree names and Western solfège syllables is shown in Example 1.11.

Scale degree names:

tonic   supertonic   mediant   subdominant   dominant   submediant   leading tone   tonic

Solfège:

Do   Re   Mi   Fa   Sol   La   Ti   Do

Example 1.11. C major scale with scale degree names and solfège syllables.

Any major scale has seven scale degrees, but, because the leading tone seems somehow "incomplete" or "frustrated" without its resolution to the tonic, we usually include the final tonic an octave above the starting pitch—thus, we are likely to sing the scale as a sequence of eight pitches, "*do–re–mi–fa–sol–la–ti–do.*" This scale can be divided into two four-note segments called **tetrachords**; the lower tetrachord begins on the tonic, while the upper tetrachord begins on the dominant.

Several well-known songs employ major scales. One of the most famous major scales occurs at the beginning of the Christmas carol "Joy to the World!," the music of which was composed by George Frideric Handel (1685–1759) (Example 1.12). Richard Rodgers and Oscar Hammerstein II wrote a very clever song employing solfège syllables for their musical *The Sound of Music* (which was also made into a classic movie). The song, "Do Re Mi" is set in the context of a music lesson, and each phrase of the song begins on a solfège syllable moving up the scale. The last line of the song "brings us back to *do*" on a high note, illustrating the concept of octave equivalence.

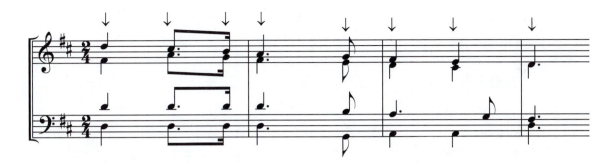

Example 1.12. George Frideric Handel, "Joy to the World!," opening.

LEVEL MASTERY 1.3.

a. Spell the indicated major scales, given the tonic. Use pitch class names.

A♭ _____ _____ _____ _____ _____ _____ _____

C♯ _____ _____ _____ _____ _____ _____ _____

E _____ _____ _____ _____ _____ _____ _____

G♭ _____ _____ _____ _____ _____ _____ _____

A _____ _____ _____ _____ _____ _____ _____

F♯ _____ _____ _____ _____ _____ _____ _____

b. Notate the indicated major scales, in the indicated clefs. Use accidentals as needed.

B major

A♭ major

B♭ major

(Continued)

(Continued)

C♯ major

G♭ major

F♯ major

MAJOR KEY SIGNATURES

Because the major scale always has the W–W–H–W–W–W–H pattern of whole and half steps (half steps always occurring between scale degrees 3 and 4 and between scale degrees 7 and 1), any major key other than C will require the consistent use of certain accidentals to preserve the pattern. For example, a G major scale will require F♯, while an F major scale will require B♭. A **key signature** is a pattern of sharps or flats appearing after the clef at the beginning of a staff, indicating which pitch classes must be *consistently* raised or lowered. The key signatures for major keys are shown in Table 1.1. Notice that in sharp signatures, the accidentals are arranged by fifths, ascending (F♯–C♯–G♯, etc.); in flat signatures, the accidentals are arranged by fifths, descending (B♭–E♭–A♭, etc.). Also notice that flats and sharps are not mixed together in the same key signature.

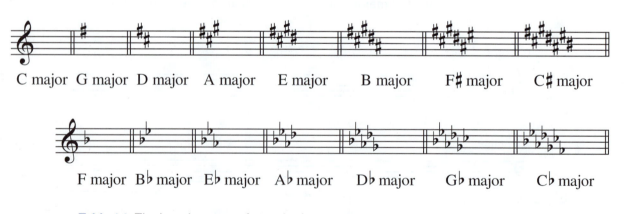

C major G major D major A major E major B major F♯ major C♯ major

F major B♭ major E♭ major A♭ major D♭ major G♭ major C♭ major

Table 1.1. The key signatures for major keys.

Several strategies can be used to help you remember how to construct key signatures. The last accidental in a *sharp* key is the *leading tone* (go up a half step from the last sharp to identify the key); the last accidental in a *flat* key is the *subdominant* (the next-to-last flat is the key). To remember the order of sharps, a convenient expression is "Father Charles Goes Down And Enters Battle." Because the order of flats is the reverse of sharps, a convenient expression for remembering the order of flats is, "Battle Ends And Down Goes Charles's Father."

In which octave do the sharps and flats go? Notice that for flat key signatures, the arrangement of flats is always "by pairs" arranged in ascending fourths, with each pair a step lower than the previous (e.g., B♭–E♭, A♭–D♭, G♭–C♭, etc.). This is true regardless of the clef used. For sharp key signatures, the arrangement is grouped by "2, 3, 2" in descending fourths (F♯–C♯, G♯–D♯–A♯, E♯–B♯) for all clefs *except* tenor clef, where they are arranged in ascending fifths, with each pair a step higher than the previous (something like a mirror image of the way flats are arranged). With practice, the arrangement will look intuitively "correct."

LEVEL MASTERY 1.4

a. Identify the following major key signatures.

b. Write the indicated major key signatures.

Self-Test 1.4 may be done at this time.

Workbook Exercise 1.4 may be done at this time.

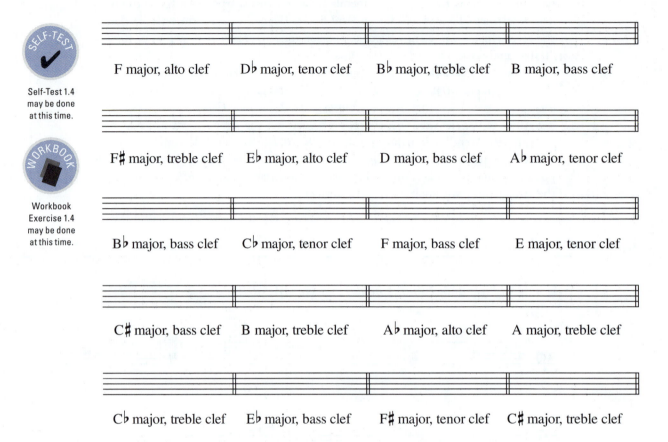

F major, alto clef   Db major, tenor clef   Bb major, treble clef   B major, bass clef

F# major, treble clef   Eb major, alto clef   D major, bass clef   Ab major, tenor clef

Bb major, bass clef   Cb major, tenor clef   F major, bass clef   E major, tenor clef

C# major, bass clef   B major, treble clef   Ab major, alto clef   A major, treble clef

Cb major, treble clef   Eb major, bass clef   F# major, tenor clef   C# major, treble clef

THE MINOR SCALE FORMS AND THEIR SCALE DEGREES

In contrast to the major scale, which has only one form, there are *three* forms of the minor scale. Any piece of music in a "minor key" normally moves among the three different forms very fluidly; the characteristics of each minor scale were shaped by melodic and harmonic considerations. Let's find out what this means.

The Natural Minor Scale

Since we stuck to the white keys in our exploration of the major scale, let's begin there in our study of the minor scales. If you start a scale on A, the sixth scale degree (submediant) of our C major scale, and move up the white keys (A–B–C–D–E–F–G), the result is the **natural minor scale**. A minor is the **relative minor** scale of C major; every major scale has its relative minor scale, which is found by beginning a new scale on the *sixth* scale degree of the major scale. This also means, of course, that any minor scale has its **relative major** scale, found by beginning a new scale on the *third* scale degree of the natural minor scale. The whole/half step pattern for the ascending natural minor scale is:

$$\text{W–H–W–W–H–W–W}$$

The half steps, then, occur between the *second* and *third* scale degrees, and between the *fifth* and *sixth* scale degrees (Example 1.13). Another way of looking at this is that the difference between the major and minor scales is that a minor scale has *lowered third, sixth, and seventh scale degrees*; by lowering the third, sixth, and seventh scale degrees of C major, for example, we get C minor. The relationship between C major and C minor (or any major and minor scale that share the same tonic) is a **parallel** relationship; C minor is the **parallel minor** of C major, and C major is the **parallel major** of C minor.

tonic supertonic mediant subdominant dominant submediant subtonic tonic

Example 1.13. The natural minor scale on A.

All of the scale degree names for natural minor are the same as those for minor, with one crucial exception: Notice that the characteristic half-step motion from the seventh scale degree (leading tone) to the tonic in the major scale is replaced here by a whole step. As a result, the seventh scale degree in the natural minor scale does not have the same unstable, "leading" quality; therefore, the seventh scale degree in the natural minor scale is called the **subtonic**. (Remember the "mirror-image" rationale for the subdominant and submediant in the major scale? Here, the subtonic is the "mirror" of the supertonic.)

The Harmonic Minor Scale

Another type of minor scale is the **harmonic minor scale**, which retains the leading tone. We can think of this as chromatically *raising the subtonic, replacing it with the leading tone* (see Example 1.14 and compare it with Example 1.13). The whole/half step pattern for the ascending harmonic minor scale is:

$$\text{W–H–W–W–H–1½–H}$$

tonic supertonic mediant subdominant dominant submediant leading tone tonic

Example 1.14. The harmonic minor scale on A.

The Melodic Minor Scale

As implied by its name, the harmonic minor scale works well for harmonies. However, it is somewhat awkward for melodies. Try playing the scale shown in Example 1.14. You might notice a rather large "gap" between the submediant (F) and the leading tone (G♯). The scales we have studied to this point have been made up of either half steps (minor seconds) or whole steps (major seconds). The distance between the F and G♯, however, is *three* half steps; this interval is an *augmented second*. Such a "gap" was considered difficult to sing in a melody (try it for yourself); in fact, some writers in the seventeenth and eighteenth centuries advised would-be composers to use the effect of the augmented second sparingly, and then only for communicating extreme emotional anguish. Example 1.15 shows one such effective use of the augmented second, over a text that translates as "my tears."

Example 1.15. Barbara Strozzi (1619–1677), "Lagrime mie," opening phrase.

The **melodic minor scale**, accordingly, has a *raised sixth scale degree* (the **raised submediant**) *along with the leading tone* when the scale is *ascending* (Example 1.16). You might notice that the lower tetrachord sounds "minor" but the upper tetrachord sounds "major."

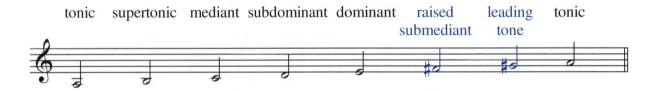

Example 1.16. The ascending melodic minor scale on A.

The *descending* form of the melodic minor scale is the same as natural minor. Thus, the melodic minor scale is the only minor scale that differs in its ascent and descent. The complete melodic minor scale is shown in Example 1.17.

Example 1.17. The melodic minor scale on A, ascending and descending.

One very clear example of how the melodic minor scale is used can be seen in the Bourrée from J. S. Bach's Lute Suite in E minor, BWV 996, shown in Example 1.18. The tonic of this piece is E. Notice how the melodic line rising from the dominant (B) to the tonic (E) does so by means of C♯ (the raised submediant) and D♯ (the leading tone); no sooner does the melody ascend to E, however, than it descends back down to B by means of D natural (the subtonic) and C natural (the submediant).

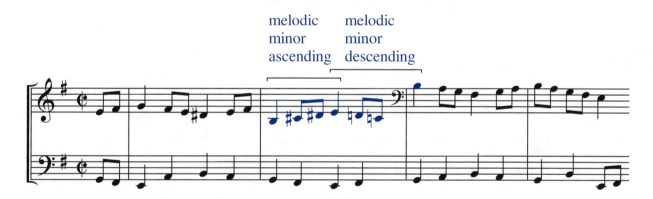

Example 1.18. Bach, Bourrée, Lute Suite in E minor, BWV 996, mm. 1–4.

All three forms of the minor scale have the same lower tetrachord; it is in the treatment of the *sixth and seventh scale degrees* that they show their characteristic differences. Thus, we may summarize their distinguishing marks as follows:

- **Natural minor:** natural (unaltered) sixth and seventh scale degree
- **Harmonic minor:** raised seventh scale degree (leading tone)
- **Melodic minor:** raised sixth and seventh scale degree when ascending, natural ("lowered back down") sixth and seventh degree when descending

a. Spell the indicated minor scales, given the tonic. Use pitch class names.

E♭ HARMONIC MINOR:

E♭ _____ _____ _____ _____ _____ _____ _____

G♯ NATURAL MINOR:

G♯ _____ _____ _____ _____ _____ _____ _____

F MELODIC MINOR, DESCENDING:

F _____ _____ _____ _____ _____ _____ _____

B♭ MELODIC MINOR, ASCENDING:

B♭ _____ _____ _____ _____ _____ _____ _____

D NATURAL MINOR:

D _____ _____ _____ _____ _____ _____ _____

F♯ HARMONIC MINOR:

F♯ _____ _____ _____ _____ _____ _____ _____

b. Notate the indicated minor scales, in the indicated clefs. Use accidentals rather than key signatures. Write the scale ascending and descending if the descent is different from the ascent.

C♯ melodic minor

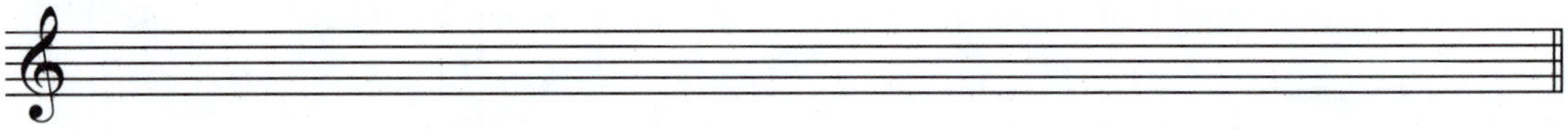

B♭ harmonic minor

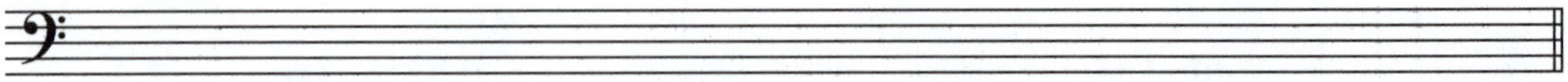

A♭ natural minor

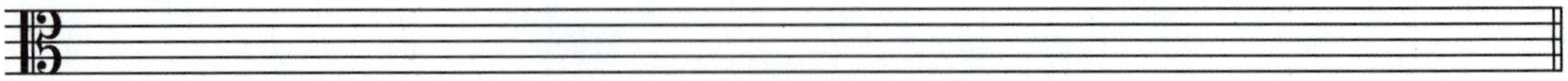

E harmonic minor

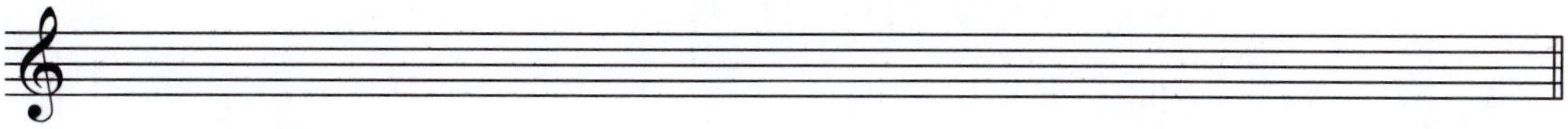

G melodic minor

G♯ natural minor

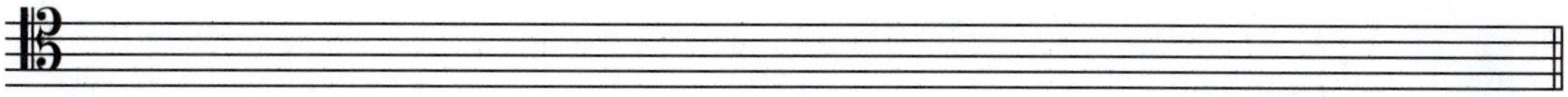

c. Scale degree roundup. Fill in the blanks below.

KEY:	SCALE:	PITCH:	SCALE DEGREE NUMBER:	SCALE DEGREE NAME:
B	major	G♯	$\hat{6}$	_____
F♯	harmonic minor	_____	$\hat{7}$	leading tone
D♯	natural minor	C♯	_____	_____
E♭	melodic minor, ascending	C♮	_____	_____
D	_____	F♯	$\hat{3}$	_____
B♭	major	_____	_____	subdominant
E	natural minor	_____	_____	supertonic
D♭	major	C	$\hat{7}$	_____

d. The following scales are missing accidentals. Add the necessary accidentals to create the specified scales.

Self-Tests 1.5 and 1.6 may be done at this time.

Workbook Exercises 1.5, 1.6, and 1.7 may be done at this time.

G natural minor

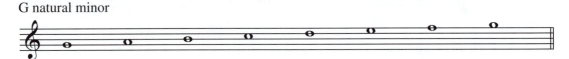

B♭ major

F♯ major

E♭ melodic minor

G♯ melodic minor

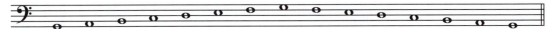

F natural minor

MINOR KEY SIGNATURES

Minor key signatures refer to the natural minor scale; the use of any other form of the minor scale is shown through accidentals in the music. Looking at Example 1.18, we see that the key signature for E minor is one sharp, the same as the key signature for G major. Two keys that share the *same key signature*, such as E minor and G major, are said to have a **relative** key relationship (for example, E minor is the relative minor of G major). Two keys that share the *same tonic*, such as G major and G minor, have a **parallel** key relationship (for example, G major is the parallel major of G minor).

The order and arrangement of flats and sharps are exactly the same for minor key signatures as for major ones.

Because the difference between a major key and its *parallel* minor is the lowering of three scale degrees, there are simple ways to quickly find parallel-related key signatures:

- *To find the key signature for the parallel minor of a flat key, simply add three flats.* These will always indicate the lowering of scale degrees 7, 3, and 6 in the key, in that order (reading left to right).
- *To find the key signature for the parallel minor of a sharp key, simply remove the last three sharps.* These will always correspond to scale degrees 6, 3, and 7, in that order (reading left to right).
- D major and G major, which have less than three sharps in their key signatures, can be changed to their parallel minors by removing the sharps and then *adding* the flat that would make the difference. For example, to go from D major to D minor one would remove both sharps and then add one flat—B♭—to the key signature.

LEVEL MASTERY 1.6.

Write the following key signatures:

Self-Tests 1.7, 1.8 and 1.9 may be done at this time.

E♭ Major   B Major   B♭ minor   C♯ minor

C♯ Major   A♭ Major   The relative major of G minor   The parallel minor of F Major

(Name the key: ____) (Name the key: ____)

Workbook Exercises 1.8 and 1.9 may be done at this time.

The relative minor of F♯ Major   The parallel major of E♭ minor   E major   D♭ Major

(Name the key: _____)

F♯ minor   G major   The parallel major of F♯ minor   The relative minor of C♯ Major

(Name the key: ____)

THE CIRCLE OF FIFTHS AND CLOSELY RELATED KEYS

All of the major keys and their relative minor partners can be arranged in a clock-like circle, with C major and A minor occupying the "12 o'clock" position, as shown in Example 1.19. Moving clockwise along the circle from this point provides the sharp keys, adding a sharp for each position, the tonic *ascending* by perfect fifths; moving counterclockwise from this point provides the flat keys, adding a flat, the tonic *descending* by perfect fifths. The sharp and flat keys meet enharmonically at the "6 o'clock position," with F♯/G♭ major and their relative minor partners, D♯/E♭ minor. Two additional enharmonic key pairs (C♯ major/A♯ minor [seven sharps], C♭ major/A♭ minor [seven flats]) are not shown in this diagram, though they are sometimes found in the music literature.

The circle of fifths provides a convenient diagram for measuring the relative distance between keys in the tonal system. A piece of music usually does not remain in the same key for its entire duration; **modulation**, or changing key within a composition,

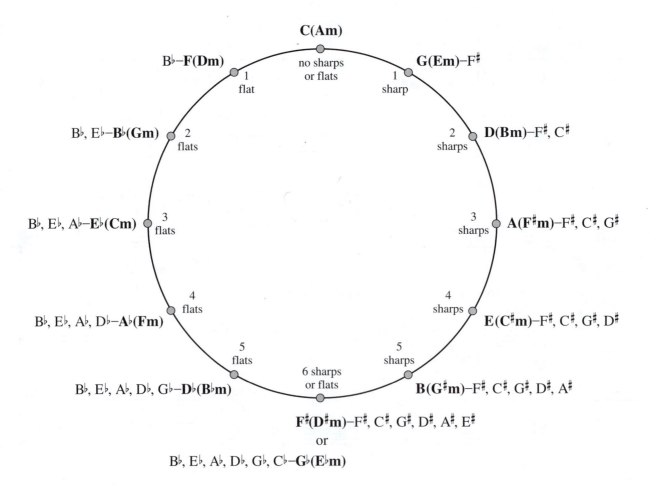

Example 1.19. The Circle of Fifths.

For more
on key
relationships
and their
connection
to changes in
musical style,
see Web
Feature 1.1.

is very common (we will examine how this is done in Chapter 17). However, certain keys are perceived to be "closer" to the tonic than others. The **closely related keys** for any major or minor tonic key are those that are adjacent in either direction on the circle, along with their relative major or minor partners. For example, to find the closely related keys of E major, find E major on the circle of fifths and include its relative minor and the key pairs on either side of it. Thus, the closely related keys of E major are: C♯ minor (the relative minor), B major and G♯ minor (the keys one step "clockwise"), and A major and F♯ minor (the keys one step "counterclockwise").

CONCLUSION

Several of our "listening studies" in the Prelude chapter illustrated the pre-eminence of pitch in our conceptions of music. We heard, for example, how Scott Johnson's treatment of recorded speech fragments enabled us to hear "melodies" in the spoken materials. We also discussed how Xenakis's *Concrèt PH* was somewhat problematic as a piece of music, in part because of its absence of pitched material. In this chapter, we examined pitch more closely—in how pitch is notated, in the structure of a pitch itself (in the harmonic series), and in the way that scales help us to measure spatial relationships between and among pitches. In Chapter 2 we will expand what we have learned about scales into other kinds of scales besides major and minor; we will also consider more closely how relations among pitches can be measured as intervals.

Terms to Know

accidental	leading tone	relative major/minor
bass clef	major scale	sharp
C clef	mediant	staff
chromatic	melodic minor scale	subdominant
diatonic	natural	submediant
enharmonic	natural minor scale	subtonic
flat	octave	supertonic
fundamental	octave equivalence	tetrachord
grand staff	overtone (or harmonic)	timbre
half step	parallel major/minor	treble clef
harmonic minor scale	pitch	whole step
harmonics	pitch class	

Self-Test

1.1. Provide ASA pitch labels for the following pitches:

1.2. Notate the indicated pitches.

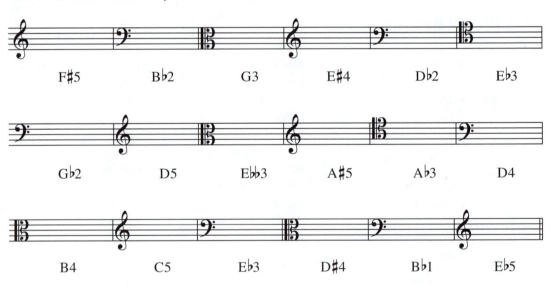

F♯5   B♭2   G3   E♯4   D♭2   E♭3

G♭2   D5   E♭♭3   A♯5   A♭3   D4

B4   C5   E♭3   D♯4   B♭1   E♭5

1.3. For each of the notes below, provide an enharmonic equivalent. (For some notes, there may be more than one equivalent.) The first is done for you.

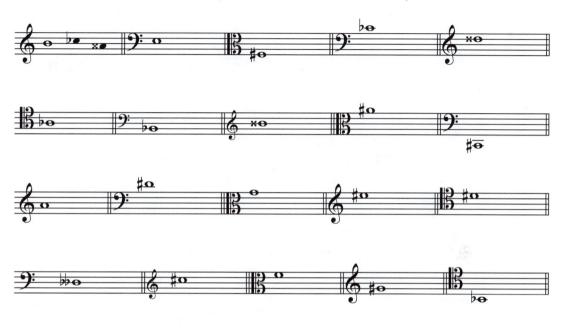

1.4. Write the key signatures for the following major keys in the specified clefs:

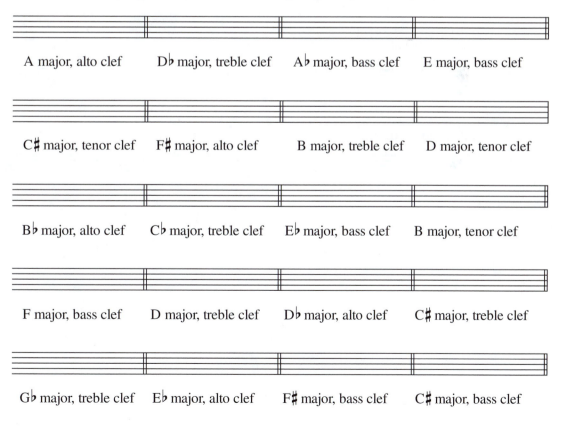

A major, alto clef	D♭ major, treble clef	A♭ major, bass clef	E major, bass clef

C♯ major, tenor clef	F♯ major, alto clef	B major, treble clef	D major, tenor clef

B♭ major, alto clef	C♭ major, treble clef	E♭ major, bass clef	B major, tenor clef

F major, bass clef	D major, treble clef	D♭ major, alto clef	C♯ major, treble clef

G♭ major, treble clef	E♭ major, alto clef	F♯ major, bass clef	C♯ major, bass clef

1.5. Write the indicated scales, using accidentals (do not use key signatures). Be sure to notate the ascending and descending form of melodic minor.

G major

F natural minor

G♯ harmonic minor

A♭ major

C♯ major

D harmonic minor

D♭ major

E♭ natural minor

C♯ melodic minor

B♭ melodic minor

1.6. Fill in the blanks below. Be sure to specify the type of minor scale if the pitch fits only one scale form.

PITCH	SCALE DEGREE NAME	SCALE
_____	submediant	E♭ Major
G	mediant	_____ minor (all forms)
F♯	raised submediant	_____
D♭	_____	E♭ natural minor
_____	leading tone	C♯ harmonic minor
E	_____	B minor (all forms)
F	dominant	_____ major
_____	supertonic	A major
B	_____	D melodic minor, {ascending/descending}
G	_____	F minor (all forms)

1.7. Write the key signatures for the following minor keys in the specified clefs:

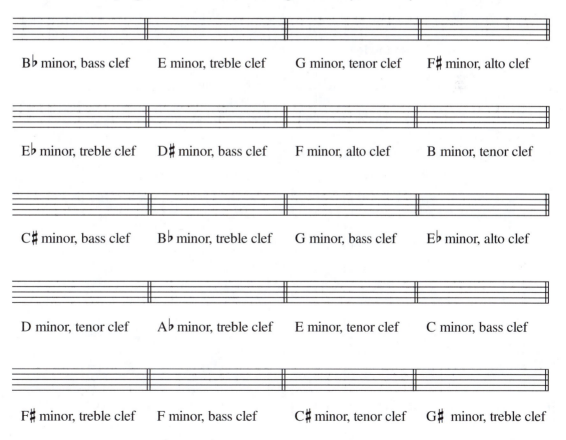

B♭ minor, bass clef   E minor, treble clef   G minor, tenor clef   F♯ minor, alto clef

E♭ minor, treble clef   D♯ minor, bass clef   F minor, alto clef   B minor, tenor clef

C♯ minor, bass clef   B♭ minor, treble clef   G minor, bass clef   E♭ minor, alto clef

D minor, tenor clef   A♭ minor, treble clef   E minor, tenor clef   C minor, bass clef

F♯ minor, treble clef   F minor, bass clef   C♯ minor, tenor clef   G♯ minor, treble clef

1.8. Write the key signatures for the following keys in the specified clefs, and identify the key:

The relative minor of B major, treble clef	The parallel major of F♯ minor, tenor clef	The relative major of B♭ minor, bass clef	The parallel minor of A♭ major, alto clef

Key: _____   Key: _____   Key: _____   Key: _____

The relative minor of G major, tenor clef	The parallel major of D minor, bass clef	The relative major of C minor, bass clef	The parallel minor of C♯ major, alto clef

Key: _____   Key: _____   Key: _____   Key: _____

The relative minor of E major, treble clef	The parallel major of B♭ minor, tenor clef	The relative major of A♭ minor, bass clef	The parallel minor of F major, alto clef

Key: _____   Key: _____   Key: _____   Key: _____

1.9. Provide the following pitch names:

- the supertonic of the relative minor of E major: _____

- the submediant of the parallel major of B minor: _____

- the raised submediant of the melodic minor form of the relative minor of B♭ major:

  _____

- the leading tone of the relative minor of the major key that has five flats in its key signature:

  _____

Apply This!

1.1. Analysis. Friedrich Kuhlau (1786–1832), *Allegro agitato* from Fantasie for solo flute, op. 18, no. 1 (1821), mm. 1–8. Study the melodic line—play it on a piano if you can. Consider the key signature. Then, on a sheet of music paper, arrange all of the notes you encounter into a scale (do not count any octave duplications, or the notes that are marked with parentheses in measures 3 and 7). You should be able to arrange the notes into a major or minor scale; if the scale you arrange is not major or minor, start on a different note until you find it. What scale is the basis for this excerpt?

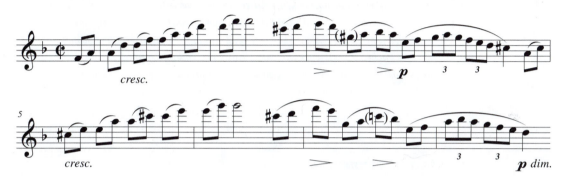

1.2. Improvisation. Choose a pitch that you can sing or play comfortably. Create an improvisation (or, if you wish to write it down, a composition) based exclusively on that one pitch. Make that pitch as interesting as you can by varying its rhythm, its dynamics (loud, soft, or shades in between), its articulations and timbre. How many ways can you vary the sound without changing the pitch?

CHAPTER 2

DIMENSIONS OF PITCH 2
Modes, Intervals, Consonance and Dissonance

OVERVIEW

In this chapter we look at additional relationships *between pitches. We begin with the diatonic modes and how they can be regarded as altered versions of the major and minor scales. Then, we will examine intervals—the distance between pitches. Finally, we consider dissonance and consonance, the qualities of tension and repose that coexist in music and provide it with much of its dramatic and expressive qualities.*

CHAPTER OUTLINE

AUDIO LIST

Bernard Herrmann, "The Murder," from *Psycho: A Suite for Strings* (Los Angeles Philharmonic Orchestra, cond. Esa-Pekka Salonen)

Richard Strauss, Introduction from *Also Sprach Zarathustra*

DIATONIC MODES

Although most Western concert music from about 1600 to the end of the nineteenth century has employed the major and minor scales, folk and popular music can also use other scales called **diatonic modes**.

There are two ways to conceive of modes. One way is to think of them as beginning on any of the white keys. Thus, playing a scale on the white keys from C to C gives us the **Ionian mode**; from D to D gives us the **Dorian mode**; from E to E, **Phrygian mode**; from F to F, **Lydian mode**; from G to G, **Mixolydian mode**; from A to A, **Aeolian mode**; and from B to B, **Locrian mode**. This is illustrated in Example 2.1.

C Ionian

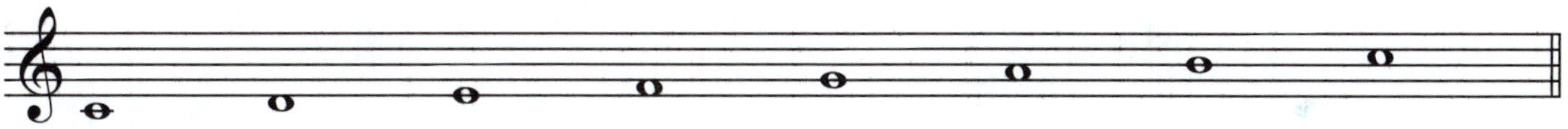

D Dorian

E Phrygian

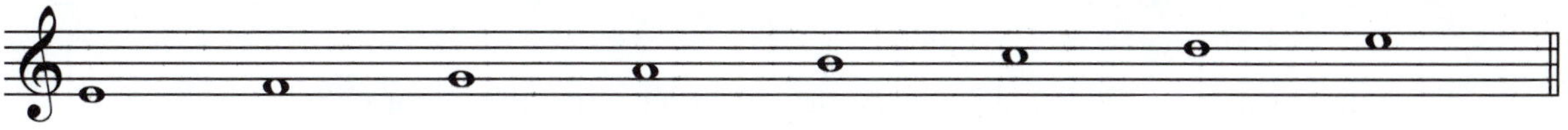

F Lydian

G Mixolydian

(Continued)

A Aeolian

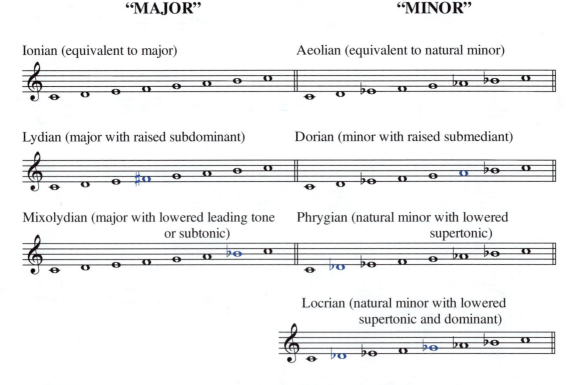

B Locrian

Example 2.1. The "white key" approach to classifying modes.

Another way to classify modes is by their "major" or "minor" qualities—that is, whether they more closely resemble a major or a natural minor scale. In fact, you may have noticed that Ionian mode is the same as the major scale, and Aeolian mode is the same as the natural minor scale. The other modes can be thought of as "major" or "minor" scales in which certain characteristic scale degrees have been raised or lowered, much the same way as we have seen in the melodic minor scale. Example 2.2 summarizes these differences, with each mode beginning on the same pitch: C.

"MAJOR"   ### "MINOR"

Ionian (equivalent to major)   Aeolian (equivalent to natural minor)

Lydian (major with raised subdominant)   Dorian (minor with raised submediant)

Mixolydian (major with lowered leading tone   Phrygian (natural minor with lowered
or subtonic)   supertonic)

Locrian (natural minor with lowered
supertonic and dominant)

Example 2.2. The "major"/"minor" approach to classifying modes.

The diatonic modes are common in Anglo-American folk songs; the sea shanty "What Shall We Do with the Drunken Sailor" and the British ballad "Scarborough Fair," for example, are both in Dorian mode, and the American fiddle tune "Old Joe Clark" uses Mixolydian mode. Contemporary composers often use the diatonic modes when they want to evoke something "old," folk-like, or exotic. For example, both the opening melody of Led Zeppelin's "Stairway to Heaven" and the theme to the TV show *Gilligan's Island* use the Aeolian mode, with its characteristic subtonic scale degree. Modes are also commonplace in much rock music—the Mixolydian mode, for example, is found in rock songs as diverse as Coldplay's "Clocks" and the Kingsmen's "Louie Louie."

LEVEL MASTERY 2.1.

a. Spell the indicated modal scales, given the tonic. Use pitch class names.

B♭ AEOLIAN:

B♭ _____ _____ _____ _____ _____ _____ _____

G♯ PHRYGIAN:

G♯ _____ _____ _____ _____ _____ _____ _____

G LYDIAN:

G _____ _____ _____ _____ _____ _____ _____

E♭ MIXOLYDIAN:

E♭ _____ _____ _____ _____ _____ _____ _____

D LOCRIAN:

D _____ _____ _____ _____ _____ _____ _____

F♯ DORIAN:

F♯ _____ _____ _____ _____ _____ _____ _____

b. Notate the indicated modal scales, in the indicated clefs. Use accidentals.

F Mixolydian

(Continued)

A♭ Ionian

B♭ Phrygian

E Lydian

A Locrian

F Aeolian

Apply This! 2.1 may be done at this time.

c. The following scales are missing accidentals. Add the necessary accidentals to create the specified scales.

Apply This! 2.2 may be done at this time.

D Phrygian

B♭ Lydian

Workbook Exercise 2.1 may be done at this time.

B Dorian

To experiment with other kinds of scales, see Web Feature 2.1.

For a study in non-Western scale construction, see Web Feature 2.2.

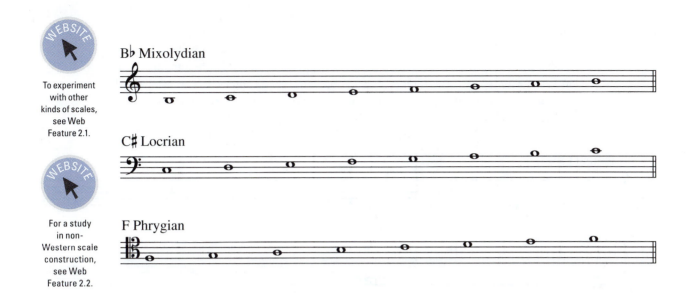

B♭ Mixolydian

C♯ Locrian

F Phrygian

THE SPACE BETWEEN THE TONES: INTERVALS

Any combination of two pitches is called a **dyad**. The distance between the two pitches is called an **interval**. An interval may be **melodic**, involving pitches that appear successively, or it may be **harmonic**, involving pitches that occur simultaneously. Regardless of whether an interval is melodic or harmonic, it is classified according to two criteria: *size* and *quality*.

Example 2.3 shows the intervals that occur above C, using—for now—only the white keys of the piano. Any interval that is an octave or less in size is called a **simple interval**. Above each interval is its **generic interval** label, from the **unison** (two of the same pitch) to the octave. The numbering for generic intervals always includes both **boundary tones**, the tones that represent the lower and upper boundary of the pitch space (or the "floor" and "ceiling," to use an analogy from physical space). Thus, C to A is a sixth, for example, because in ascending from C to A, *counting* C and A, we have six diatonic steps: *C–D–E–F–G–A*.

Unison (1)   Second (2)   Third (3)   Fourth (4)   Fifth (5)   Sixth (6)   Seventh (7)

Example 2.3. White-key intervals above C (treble, alto, and bass clefs).

Example 2.4 shows the other diatonic intervals that occur within the white-key collection, arranged by their generic interval size. Notice that if both notes are found on lines or on spaces, the interval is an "odd numbered" interval (a unison, third, fifth, or seventh); if one note is on a line and the other on a space, the interval is "even numbered" (a second, fourth, or sixth).

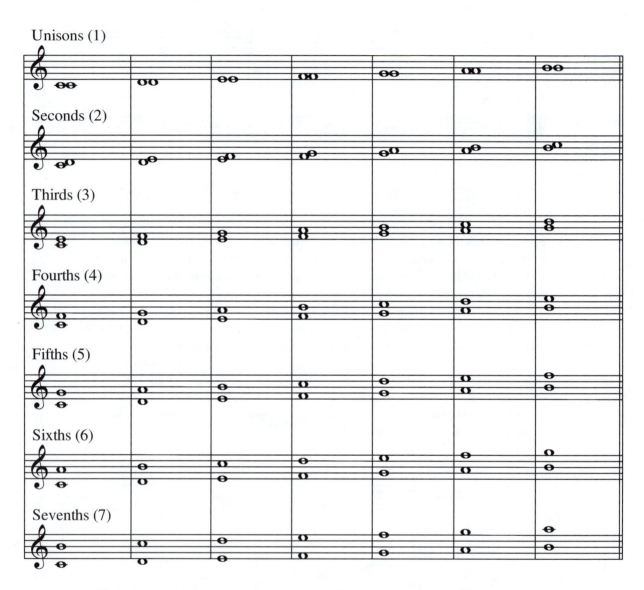

Example 2.4. Intervals found within the white-key pitch-class collection, arranged by generic interval size.

Provide the generic interval number (1, 2, 3, etc.) for the intervals below. The first one is done for you as an example.

Workbook
Exercise 2.2
may be done
at this time.

INTERVAL QUALITY

Although generic interval labels are helpful as a first step in describing an interval, we can be more precise in our descriptions. For example, the distances between C–D and E–F on the piano keyboard would, generically, both be characterized as "seconds." However, one clearly has a greater distance between the tones than the other (there is a black key between C and D, whereas E and F have no black key in between). An interval is further described by its **quality**: perfect (P), major (M), minor (m), augmented ($^+$), or diminished ($^{\circ}$). Thus, for example, a minor third is written as m3; a perfect fifth, P5. Example 2.5 shows the intervallic quality of the diatonic intervals that had been listed in Example 2.4.

P1	P1	P1	P1	P1	P1	P1
M2	M2	m2	M2	M2	M2	m2
M3	m3	m3	M3	M3	m3	m3

(Continued)

Example 2.5. Intervals found within the white-key pitch-class collection, with specific interval quality labels.

Perfect Intervals

Review the harmonic series shown in Example 1.9. The first interval, C2 to C3, is an octave. C3 to G3 is a fifth, and G3 to C4 is a fourth. Unisons, fourths, fifths and octaves are **perfect intervals**. A perfect interval, by itself, carries no connotations of being "major" or "minor"; thus, there is no such thing as a "major fifth" or "minor fourth." Increasing the size of a perfect interval by raising the upper note a half step or lowering the lower note a half step—a **chromatic** alteration—makes it **augmented**; the reverse of this, decreasing a perfect interval by lowering the upper note a half step or raising the lower note, makes it **diminished**.

It can be useful to think of the analogy of a movable funhouse "floor" and "ceiling" when conceptualizing intervallic space—especially when spelling intervals. Begin by spelling the generic (diatonic) interval first, and then add accidentals as needed; notes are raised or lowered, thus increasing or decreasing the overall intervallic space, in the same way that the floor or ceiling is raised or lowered, thus increasing or decreasing the overall physical space. See Example 2.6.

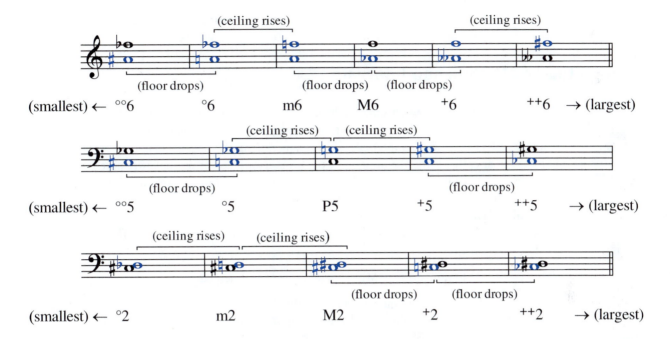

Example 2.6. Expansion/contraction of intervals, using the floor/ceiling metaphor.

For some historical background about the tritone, see Web Feature 2.3.

Note that special care must be taken with the pitches F and B. Example 2.5 shows the irregularities involving F and B; examining the fourths and fifths row, for example, note that all of the fourths and fifths are perfect except for those involving F and B. The interval from F to B is an *augmented* fourth, and the interval from B to F is a *diminished* fifth. The augmented fourth and diminished fifth are enharmonic intervals; for example, C to G♭ (a diminished fifth) sounds the same as C to F♯ (an augmented fourth). Both intervals are sometimes also called a **tritone** (TT), because the interval is equivalent to three consecutive whole steps (C–D, D–E, E–F♯).

In conclusion, then, when altering all perfect intervals, the order of interval quality, from smallest to largest, is:

Diminished ← Perfect → Augmented

Major and Minor Intervals

Seconds, thirds, sixths, and sevenths are all examples of **major/minor intervals**. That is, they can appear in a larger (major) or smaller (minor) form. We already encountered this in our perusal of the piano keyboard; the distance from C to D is a **major** second, whereas the distance from E to F is a **minor** second. In the same way, the interval from C to E is a major third, whereas C to E♭ is a minor third. Increasing the size of a minor third by one half step, either by chromatically raising the upper tone or lowering the lower tone, results in a major third. In the same way, a major third can be "shrunk" to a minor third by chromatically lowering the upper tone or raising the lower tone (again, recall the "floor" and "ceiling" analogies).

Augmented and Diminished Intervals

Self-Tests
2.1 and 2.2
may be done
at this time.

Workbook
Exercises 2.3
and 2.4 may
be done at
this time.

We have already seen how chromatically increasing a perfect interval by a half step results in an *augmented* interval, and decreasing a perfect interval in the same manner results in a *diminished* interval. Likewise, increasing the size of a major interval by chromatically raising the upper note or chromatically lowering the lower note will result in an augmented interval. Decreasing the size of a minor interval, either by chromatically lowering the upper note or chromatically raising the lower note, will result in a *diminished* interval.

When altering any major or minor intervals, the order of interval quality, from smallest to largest, is:

$$\text{Diminished} \leftarrow \text{Minor} \leftrightarrow \text{Major} \rightarrow \text{Augmented}$$

Occasionally one will encounter intervals that are chromatically expanded or contracted still one more half step. These are called *doubly augmented* or *doubly diminished* intervals, and their abbreviations are similarly $^{++}$ or $^{\circ\circ}$.

Compound Intervals

Self-Test 2.3
may be done
at this time.

Intervals larger than an octave are called **compound intervals**. Their numeric labeling continues beyond the eight of the octave: for example, the interval from C4 to D5 is a major ninth; C♯4 to E5 is a minor tenth, and so on. For larger intervals it is helpful to invoke octave equivalence and use the generic label for the interval within an octave, modified by the descriptor "compound." For example, C4 to A5 is a major thirteenth, but it can also be called a compound major sixth, since it is equivalent to an octave plus a major sixth. Compound intervals are most commonly invoked in discussing more complex extensions of harmony, as, for example, in jazz.

SPELLING INTERVALS

Two principles help simplify the spelling of intervals. First, if the interval in question is found between the pitches in the C major diatonic collection, begin with those unmodified pitches; then, after restoring the modifying accidental to the starting note, make sure that both tones have the same accidental to create the desired interval. For example, if we are given an F♯ and the instruction to write the note that is a major third above, we could start with F and then write an A above it, since F–A is a diatonic major third interval in the C major collection. Next, we restore the sharp that was taken away from the F♯, and add a sharp (the same accidental) to the A that we wrote to complete the interval, thus resulting in the major third F♯–A♯.

The second principle is an outgrowth of the first: if the interval in question is not found between the pitches in the C major diatonic collection (that is to say, *chromatic*), we would proceed as above and then further modify either the upper or lower note, keeping in mind the "floor" and "ceiling" analogies. For example, suppose we are asked to provide the pitch an augmented second below B. The pitch below B in the C major diatonic collection, A, is a major second away; to make that interval an augmented second, we must either "raise the ceiling" or "lower the floor" to increase the distance between the pitches. Since the upper note is provided, we cannot change it; we must instead "lower the floor" by making the A an A♭.

Always start with the pitch-class *letter names*, and then apply the above principles; in this way you can avoid errors that result from enharmonic spellings. For example, even though B♯ and C are enharmonically equivalent pitches, a minor third below D♯ would be B♯, not C (since the letter names "B" and "D" indicate some interval of a third, whereas the letter names "C" and "D" indicate some sort of second).

Finally, remember these simple hints to keep in mind (you might want to look at Example 2.5 as you consider these). **In the major scale:**

- Seconds are always major seconds (M2s) except between scale degrees 3 and 4 (*mi–fa*), and between scale degrees 7 and 1 (*ti–do*).
- Thirds are always major thirds (M3s) between scale degrees 1 and 3 (*do–mi*), 4 and 6 (*fa–la*), and 5 and 7 (*sol–ti*). The others are minor thirds (m3s).
- Fourths are always perfect (P4s) except between scale degrees 4 and 7 (*fa–ti*).

What about larger intervals? We can simplify identifying those as well, by *inverting* larger intervals.

INVERSION OF INTERVALS

All simple intervals may be **inverted** by raising the lower tone or lowering the upper tone by an octave, leaving the other tone intact (Example 2.7). (The same principle applies to compound intervals, with the slight modification that the changed note must be raised or lowered more than one octave.)

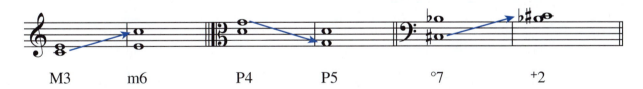

M3   m6   P4   P5   °7   +2

Example 2.7. Examples of interval inversion.

Two easy principles apply to inverting intervals. The first is that the generic interval number pairs involved always add up to 9; thus, seconds invert to sevenths, thirds invert to sixths, and fourths invert to fifths (and, of course, vice versa). The second principle pertains to interval qualities, as follows:

Diminished   ← (inverts to) →   Augmented
Minor   ← (inverts to) →   Major
Perfect   ← (inverts to) →   Perfect

Thus, the inversion of a m3 is a M6; the inversion of a $^+$2 is a °7; the inversion of a P4 is a P5, and so on.

LEVEL MASTERY 2.3.

a. Add one or more accidentals to each interval to make it the indicated quality. Find at least two solutions for each of these. The first example is done for you.

1. (two solutions)   2.   3.   4.

M3   P5   m6   ++4

5.   6.   7.   8.

+6   m2   °4   m7

9.   10.   11.   12.

°5   ++3   +4   +2

13.   14.   15.   16.

M3   +6   M6   °6

17.   18.   19.   20.

M7   +5   °7   ++2

21.   22.   23.   24.

+4   °4   ++4   °7

b. Identify the intervals below, both by generic number and quality (e.g., m2, M3, ⁺6, etc.)

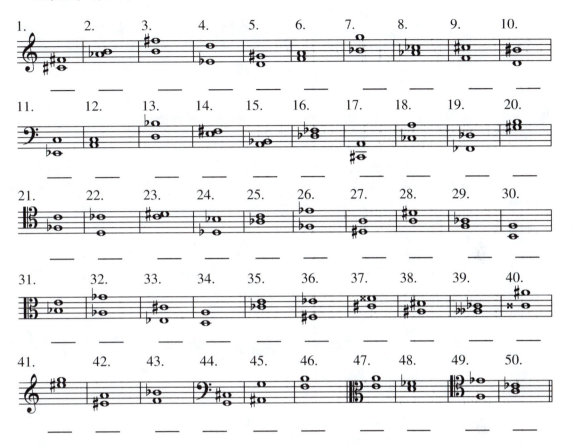

c. Notate the pitch that is the specified interval *above* the note provided.

(Continued)

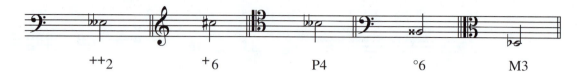

++2   +6   P4   °6   M3

Self-Test Exercises 2.3 and 2.4 may be done at this time.

d. Notate the pitch that is the specified interval *below* the note provided.

m3   +5   M6   P5   +6

Apply This! 2.3 may be done at this time.

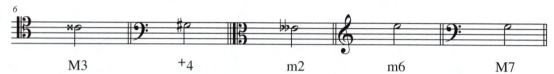

M3   +4   m2   m6   M7

Workbook Exercises 2.5 and 2.6 may be done at this time.

m7   m3   M3   °7   °5

°7   m3   m6   M7   M6

LEVEL MASTERY 2.4.

Self-Test 2.5 may be done at this time.

Notate the inversions of the intervals below. Fill in the quality of the interval and its inversion in the blanks provided.

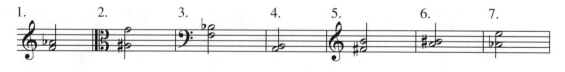

Apply This! 2.4 may be done at this time.

Workbook
Exercise 2.7
may be done
at this time.

CONSONANT AND DISSONANT HARMONIC INTERVALS

One of the reasons why we find music so pleasing is its ebb and flow of tension and release, or action and stability. In musical tones, we describe this psychological quality as **consonance** and **dissonance**. Dissonant intervals seem to have a restless or unstable quality; consonant intervals sound stable or passive. Consonant intervals include the perfect unison, the perfect octave, and the perfect fifth (the **perfect consonances**); major and minor thirds and sixths (the so-called **imperfect consonances**). Dissonant intervals include all seconds and sevenths, and all augmented or diminished intervals. Bernard Herrmann's famous "murder chord" from the shower scene in Alfred Hitchcock's movie *Psycho* uses the strong dissonance of minor seconds and their inversions, major sevenths, to enhance the shock and violence of the murder; each note is gradually added, highest to lowest, finishing with the chord shown in Example 2.8.

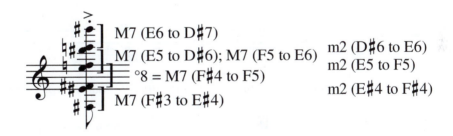

Example 2.8. Intervallic composition of Bernard Herrmann's "murder chord."

Dissonance is not necessarily the same as "ugliness." When we hear dissonant intervals, we rather expect some kind of *resolution*; we expect the unstable impulse to reach a point of stability. An artful composer, however, may think of innumerable ways to *delay* the resolution; this prolonged and sometimes multilayered process of dissonance resolution, like twists in the plot of a novel or film, can enhance our enjoyment.

The most consonant intervals are those that happen to belong to the first five overtones in the harmonic series (Example 2.9). Collectively, these tones constitute a **major triad**.

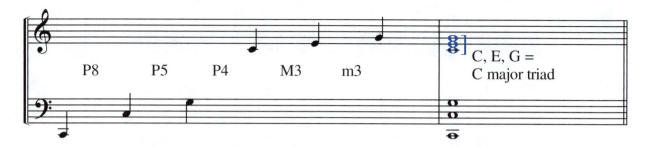

Example 2.9. Derivation of the major triad from the harmonic series.

For more on the contextual quality of dissonance, see Web Feature 2.4.

The perfect fourth has an unusual role, sometimes consonant and sometimes dissonant. Because of its perfect quality, medieval theorists often classified it as a consonance along with the unison, fifth, and octave; the earliest written evidence of harmony in Western music, from a ninth-century treatise entitled *Musica Enchiriadis*, actually contains an example of harmony in perfect fourths (Example 2.10). As the third came into its own as an acceptable consonance during the Renaissance and in the following centuries, however, the triad came to be heard as the frame of tonal reference, and the fourth, when appearing above the bass, came to be heard as a dissonance that would resolve to a third (Example 2.11). On the other hand, in a twentieth- or twenty-first-century musical idiom characterized by "harsher" dissonances, the fourth might well be heard as having a more tonal character, and thus consonant (Example 2.12).

Nos qui vivimus benedicimus Dominum   et hoc nunc et   usque   in   sae- cu-lum.

Example 2.10. A chant from the *Musica Enchiriadis*, showing a succession of perfect fourths.

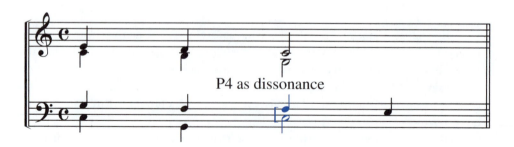

Example 2.11. The fourth as a contextual dissonance, when appearing above the bass.

(P4 as consonance)

Example 2.12. The fourth as a contextual consonance, as it might be found in certain examples of Western "contemporary" (twentieth- and twenty-first-century) music.

CONCLUSION

In this chapter we expanded our study of scales to include diatonic modes; we also learned about intervals and how they enable us to measure spatial relationships between pitches. Finally, we learned about dissonance and consonance, and how patterns of tension and relaxation can be used to enhance musical expression.

A solid understanding of intervals is essential to understanding other concepts to come, such as key relationships, combining melodic lines in counterpoint, and building triads and seventh chords. Early in your musical training is the best time to master these concepts. The musician who does not will soon be at a disadvantage.

The good news is that although at this point the learning curve of mastering theory fundamentals appears to be steep indeed, the curve will level off soon enough, as you find that many "new" concepts to come have an underlying logic supported by the basic concepts you are learning right now.

Terms to Know

augmented	imperfect consonance
boundary tone	inverted/inversion (applied to intervals)
compound interval	major (applied to intervals)
consonance	melodic interval
diatonic mode	minor (applied to intervals)
diminished	perfect
dissonance	quality (applied to intervals)
dyad	simple interval
generic interval	tritone
harmonic interval	

Self-Test

2.1. Using the first interval in each row as a starting point, alter the interval quality chromatically using the "floor and ceiling" analogy discussed in this chapter, following the instructions for each interval. Then, identify the interval that results from the change, making sure to include quality labels (M, m, °, +). In each example do not change the generic size of the interval. The first change in the first row is done for you as an example, but the interval identification is left for you to solve.

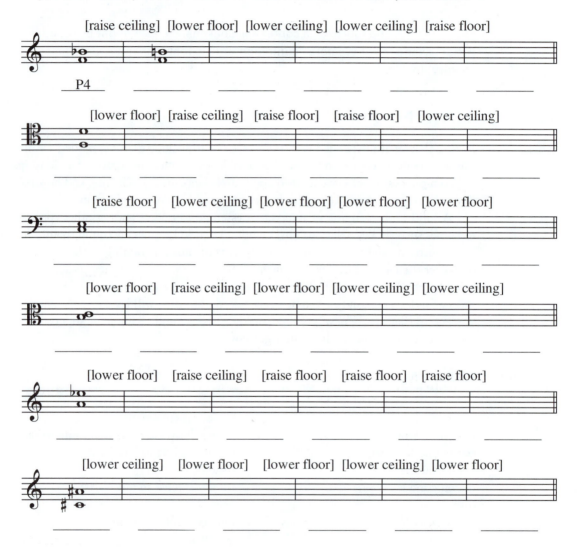

2.2. Identify the following intervals. Be sure to use quality labels.

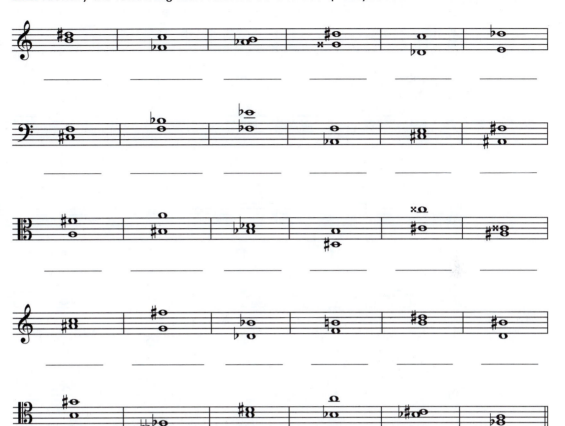

2.3. Provide the octave-equivalent simple-interval label for the following compound intervals. The first is done for you as an example.

+4

2.4. Notate the specified intervals *above* the note provided.

M3   °5   m6   m3   +4   m7

m2   +4   P4   °7   M6   +2

m3   M6   M7   +5   +6   P5

+6   M3   +4   P5   °7   °8

+5   °3   M6   m6   °4   +4

2.5. Notate the specified intervals *below* the note provided.

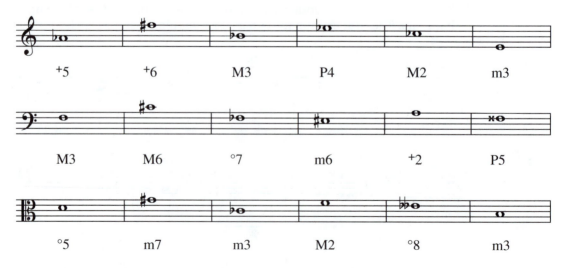

+5   +6   M3   P4   M2   m3

M3   M6   °7   m6   +2   P5

°5   m7   m3   M2   °8   m3

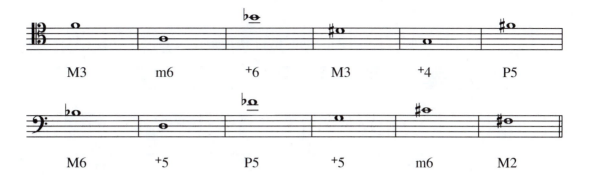

| M3 | m6 | +6 | M3 | +4 | P5 |

| M6 | +5 | P5 | +5 | m6 | M2 |

2.6. Identify the inversions of the following intervals:

P4 _____   +5 _____   °5 _____   m2 _____

+6 _____   +3 _____   +2 _____   °8 _____

m3 _____   M3 _____

Apply This!

2.1 Analysis. Identify the mode of the following melodies. Assume each melody ends on the tonic. Some melodies may not contain all scale degrees, but all contain their modally distinctive scale degrees.

a.

"She Moved Through the Fair" [Traditional English folk song]

b.

"The Three Ravens" [Anonymous, from *Melismata*, 1611]

c. The melody below contains two modes, changing mode with the change of meter to $\frac{4}{4}$. Identify both modes.

"O Mistress Mine" [Traditional English melody]

2.2. Improvisation. Improvise a melody in Phrygian mode, paying particular attention to the scale degrees that give the mode its distinctive character. Try additional improvisations in the Aeolian, Dorian, and Locrian modes. Do any of these modes seem easier to improvise in than others? If so, why do you suppose that is?

2.3. Identify the melodic intervals spanned by the numbered brackets, and harmonic intervals enclosed by the numbered boxes, filling in the appropriate blanks below. Reduce any compound interval numbers to their simple equivalents.

Arnold Schoenberg, "Geübtes Herz" ("Experienced Heart"), op. 3 no. 5.

TEXT: Do not turn away my simple heart because it has loved so much!

1. _____   2. _____   3. _____   4. _____

5. _____   6. _____   7. _____   8. _____

9. _____   10. _____   11. _____   12. _____ .

2.4. Johann Sebastian Bach, Two Part Invention no. 6 in E major, BWV 777. The examples below depict the beginning of Bach's invention in E major (featured as the example of polyphony in the Prelude chapter), altered so that the parts are synchronized. Identify the harmonic intervals in both lines by size and quality; reduce the compound interval numbers to their simple equivalents. Are the two examples exact intervallic inversions of each other?

CHAPTER 3

DURATION, RHYTHM, AND METER

OVERVIEW

After considering how music is represented in pitch in the last two chapters, we move in this chapter to how music is represented in time. *Music must unfold in time to exist. Western music customarily segments time in regular durations; the organization of durations in a hierarchical structure is called meter. We will study the different types of meter: Duple or triple, simple or compound. We will also learn how meter is organized from the "top down" by successive symmetrical divisions—divisive meter—or from the "bottom up" by combining small units into larger groups of unequal size—additive meter. Rhythm describes how a series of durations are notated in reference to the prevailing meter.*

AUDIO LIST

Johann Sebastian Bach, Brandenburg Concerto no. 3 (iii) (21st Century Symphony Orchestra)

Johann Sebastian Bach, Two-Part Invention no. 4 in D minor (Glenn Gould, piano)

"Minuet" from the *Notebook for Anna Magdalena Bach*, BWV Anh. 114, attributed to J. S. Bach

Cosmic Voices from Bulgaria, "Dilmano, Dilbero"

Hoobastank, "The Reason"

Scott Joplin, "The Entertainer"

Led Zeppelin, "Kashmir"

Richard Wagner, Prelude to Act I, *Tristan und Isolde*

TIME: THE WELLSPRING OF MUSIC

In Chapter 2 we noted how for many people it would be difficult to conceive of music that did not have a melody. It would be even more difficult to conceive of music without rhythm, for music is a time-based or **temporal** art form. The visual arts—painting, sculpture, architecture, and so forth—operate in the domain of space; a performance of music unfolds in time.

Rhythm is the parameter of music that deals with its temporal organization—our experience of how time passes and the degree to which time is measured. Rhythm results from the interaction of two aspects of temporal organization: the **duration**, or length, of a musical event and the **pulse or beat**, a regular subdivision of time. When you tap your foot, clap, or nod your head to a piece of music, you are physically responding to the beat of the music. The speed of these pulses is called **tempo**. Musicians may use general descriptive terms, often in Italian, to convey a sense of tempo, such as *Presto* (very fast), *Allegro* (fast), *Andante* ("walking" or medium tempo), *Adagio* (slow), or *Largo* (very slow). Metronome markings offer a precise measurement of tempo by instructing the performer of how many beats per minute a particular durational value should represent. In some styles of music a performer may introduce subtle variations of tempo—a practice called **rubato**—to enhance the expressive effect of a passage.

The way that pulses are combined in music into larger groupings of strong (stressed) and weak (unstressed) beats is called **meter**. Let's look at a couple of examples of how pulses are organized into a meter.

METRIC STRUCTURE

SOUND EXAMPLE 3.1: HOOBASTANK, "THE REASON"

Listen to the introduction to this song, the first twelve seconds (just until the bass guitar enters). First we hear a regularly repeated E3 on the piano—our first **pulse stream**. We can represent this pulse stream graphically with regularly spaced dots as follows:

(piano)   •   •   •   •   •   •   •   •

The drum kit is next to enter; high-hat cymbals double the piano pulse, and the bass or kick drum, alternating with the snare, provide pulses that synchronize with every other piano note (two piano pulses equal one drum beat). We show the pulse stream articulated by the drum kit at a level above the piano pulse stream on our diagram.

(drum kit)   •   •   •   •
(piano)   •   •   •   •   •   •   •   •

Focusing again on the drum beat, you will notice that the drum pattern alternates between the kick drum and the snare, with the kick drum always coming first. The kick drum beats, then, give us yet another, higher-level pulse stream:

(kick drum only) •   •
(drum kit)   •   •   •   •
(piano)   •   •   •   •   •   •   •   •

Finally, an electric guitar comes in with notes that occur exactly *in between* the piano pulses. This means that there is an implied 2:1 subdivision to the piano pulse (otherwise, how would we precisely measure the points where the guitar notes enter?). Now our pulse stream diagram looks like this:

(kick drum only) •   •
(drum kit)   •   •   •   •
(piano)   •   •   •   •   •   •   •   •
(guitar)   • • • • • • • • • • • • • • • •

We now have a diagram of the **metric structure** of the song. A metric structure is a set of hierarchically layered pulse streams in a piece of music. There are usually three or four tappable pulse streams in a piece of music, although there can be more. As the music unfolds you are likely to hear one of these pulse streams as the "main beat," the beat you would tap your foot to. This is the **primary pulse stream**. Which of the instruments in "The Reason" do you find articulating the primary pulse stream? Notice how the second half of the diagram—reading left to right—is an exact duplicate of the first. It is this alternating, regular pattern of beats that gives us meter. Melodically or harmonically, beat patterns can also be reinforced by the use of an **ostinato**—a repeating pattern in the accompaniment (such as the electric guitar line in "The Reason"). In popular music, the term **riff** is sometimes used to describe a distinctive melodic or rhythmic figure that is repeated like an ostinato.

We can organize this metric structure into still higher levels. Consider, for example, that once the bass guitar enters it repeats the same note in sync with the piano pulse sixteen times and then changes pitch, repeating the next note again for sixteen piano pulses. Even though the *rhythm* of the bass guitar is the same as the piano, those attacks can be combined into larger groupings based on the changes of pitch. The regularity of the bass guitar's changes of pitch thus gives us another pulse stream; in tonal music, **harmonic rhythm** (the rate at which harmonies change in a piece) also has a role in establishing a pulse stream. "Zooming out" our picture to include the bass, then, our diagram now looks like this:

```
(bass guitar)  .                             .
(kick drum)    .        .        .        .        .        .        .
(drum kit)     .    .    .    .    .    .    .    .    .    .    .    .
(piano)        . . . . . . . . . . . . . . . . . . . . . . . . . . . .
(guitar)       ..................................................
```

Notice that all of our successive pulse streams, reading bottom to up, are in a 2:1 ratio, with the exception of the bass guitar, which is in a 4:1 ratio with the kick drum. We can therefore add another implied pulse stream, between the kick drum and bass guitar levels:

```
(bass guitar)  .                             .
               .              .              .              .
(kick drum)    .        .        .        .        .        .        .
(drum kit)     .    .    .    .    .    .    .    .    .    .    .    .
(piano)        . . . . . . . . . . . . . . . . . . . . . . . . . . . .
(guitar)       ..................................................
```

If you heard the pattern of the drum kit (kick and snare) as representing the primary pulse stream (or "P.P.S."), you might find yourself counting the pattern in groups of four beats, with the first beat receiving a little extra emphasis ("*one*–two–three–four"). If so, we can vertically "slice" our diagram to look like this (notice that the bass guitar is omitted here, since you would need to count "one–two–three–four" *twice* before the note changes):

```
                        .
(kick drum)             .              .
(drum kit) P.P.S. →     .        .        .        .
(piano)                 .    .    .    .    .    .    .    .
(guitar)                . . . . . . . . . . . . . . . .
```

Our previous diagram, which included the bass guitar, had four of these groupings. A regularly recurring grouping of stressed and unstressed beats is called a measure or **bar**. In music, measures are marked off with vertical lines through the staff, called **bar lines**. The first beat of the measure, usually receiving the most emphasis, is called the **downbeat**. Musical phrases may begin on one or more weak beats before the first downbeat—this is called an **anacrusis**, or "pickup beat."

Other varieties of bar lines are shown in Example 3.1. A **double bar line** is used to indicate large sectional divisions or places where there is a change of meter. A double bar line in which the second line is thickened indicates the end of a movement or piece. Two dots flanking the center line of the staff indicate that a section of the music is to be repeated, and the resulting double bar line is sometimes called a **repeat sign**; if the beginning of the section being repeated is a point later than the beginning of the music, the beginning of the repeated section is shown by another double bar line with dots, a mirror reflection of the concluding repeat sign. **First and second endings** are shown with numbered brackets above if the end of a repeated section differs from its first playing.

Apply This! 3.1 may be done at this time.

See Web Feature 3.1 for an interesting example of the effect of changing tempo on perception of the primary pulse stream.

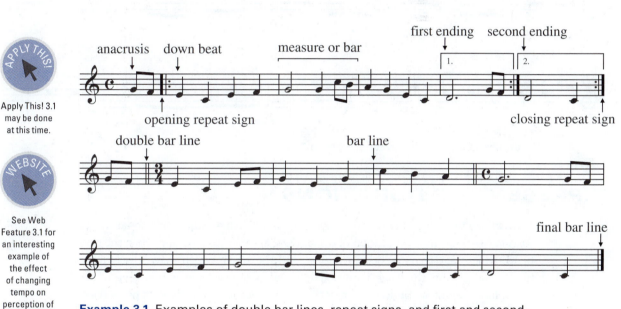

Example 3.1. Examples of double bar lines, repeat signs, and first and second endings.

TYPES OF METER

Metric structure is further classified by whether a measure is perceived to have two, three, or four beats. **Duple meter** refers to a metric structure with two beats per measure. **Triple meter** refers to a metric structure with three beats per measure. **Quadruple meter**, with four beats per measure, is closely related to duple meter; however, the third beat is not emphasized as strongly as the downbeat—something like "ONE–two–*three*–four." "The Reason" is an example of quadruple meter.

Meter is also categorized by how the beat *itself* is divided. In "The Reason," the primary pulse stream is further subdivided into a 2:1 ratio. When the beats in a measure are divided by 2, the meter has a **simple** subdivision. Thus, "The Reason" is an example of **simple quadruple** meter.

When the primary pulse stream in the measure is subdivided into a 3:1 ratio, the meter has a **compound** subdivision. The traditional jig "The Irish Washerwoman" (Example 3.2) is in **compound duple** meter, because it has two beats in the primary pulse stream for each measure (making it an example of duple meter), but the beats themselves are subdivided into 3, not 2 (making the subdivision compound). See the metric structure diagram below.

Example 3.2. "The Irish Washerwoman."

REPRESENTING DURATIONS

Now we can use musical notation to represent what we have uncovered so far in "The Reason." In notating the duration of a note there are two basic components: the **note-head**, which may or may not be filled in, and the **stem**, which may or may not be further modified with a **flag**. Durational notation does not convey how long in time (as in, how many specific seconds) a note will last, but it rather gives its proportional relationship with other durations in the same texture. Western rhythmic notation tends to be organized in successive 2:1 ratios (though there are, of course, exceptions).

Table 3.1 shows the commonly used durational symbols. The foundational unit of duration in modern music is the **whole note**, an unfilled notehead with no stem (in scores from the Baroque period and earlier one may also encounter the **breve**, which is equivalent in duration to two whole notes). A whole note can be divided into two **half notes** (an unfilled notehead with a stem), four **quarter notes** (a filled notehead with a stem), or eight **eighth notes** (a filled notehead with a stem that has a flag attached). Finer subdivisions are possible (sixteenth notes, thirty-second notes, and so on). Durations shorter than a quarter note have a **flag** extending off to the right of the stem; more than one of these notes are connected with a bar called a **beam**. Adding a flag or a beam to a note halves its durational value; thus, an eighth note has one flag or beam, a sixteenth note has two, a thirty-second note has three, and so on. This is shown in Table 3.1.

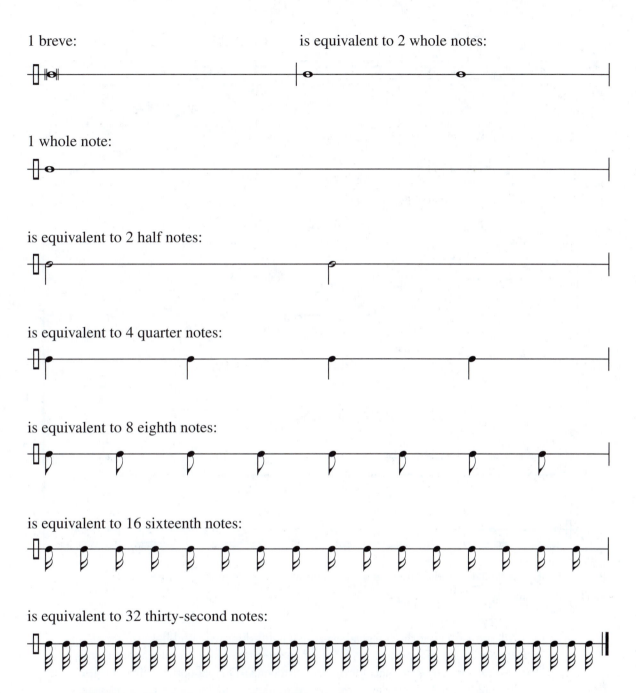

1 breve: is equivalent to 2 whole notes:

1 whole note:

is equivalent to 2 half notes:

is equivalent to 4 quarter notes:

is equivalent to 8 eighth notes:

is equivalent to 16 sixteenth notes:

is equivalent to 32 thirty-second notes:

Table 3.1. Chart of common durational values.

Any duration can be added to another duration by connecting the two notes with a curved line called a **tie**. (Note that the two notes must be of the same pitch; when two notes of different pitches are connected, the curved line is called a **slur**, and it indicates to smoothly connect the two notes.) The tie is drawn to connect the noteheads, not the tops of the stems (Example 3.3).

Example 3.3. Correct and incorrect ways of drawing a tie.

Our metric structure chart for "The Reason" can be represented in musical notation as shown in Example 3.4.

Example 3.4. Metric structure of Hoobastank, "The Reason," in durational notation.

Adding a dot after the notehead expands a note's duration by adding *half the value* of the note or dot that *precedes* it. A dotted quarter note, for example, is equal to a quarter note plus an eighth note (or three eighth notes). Double-dotted values are also possible, adding half the value of the preceding dot. A double-dotted quarter note, for example, equals a quarter note plus an eighth note (represented by the first dot) *plus* a sixteenth note (represented by the second dot).

Less commonly, a dotted note may be divided in two rather than three, resulting in two other dotted notes—for example, a dotted quarter note could be divided into two dotted eighth notes. Table 3.2 shows some of the subdivisions for dotted note values, in twofold and threefold subdivisions.

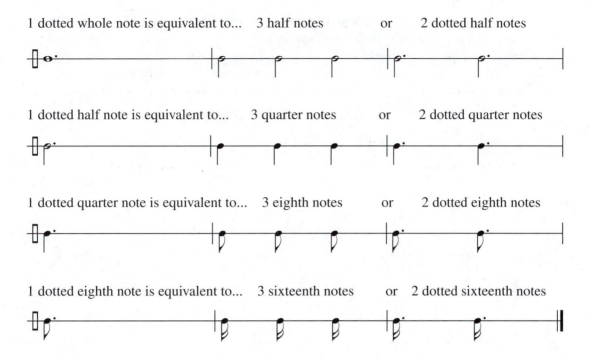

Table 3.2. Chart of common dotted durational values.

Other divisions of the beat sometimes occur as exceptions to the prevailing metric structure—these are generically called **tuplets**. The most common of these is a **triplet**—three notes occupying the time of two. Other tuplets include quintuplets (five notes in the time of four, or in the time of three if in compound meter), sextuplets (six notes in the time of four), and so on. Tuplets are usually notated by grouping the notes together with a number above or below the notes. For example, a triplet occupying the time of a quarter note would be notated as three eighth notes, grouped together with a "3" above or below the grouping. Example 3.5 shows several examples.

Self-Tests 3.1 and 3.4 may be done at this time.

Workbook Exercises 3.1 and 3.7 may be done at this time.

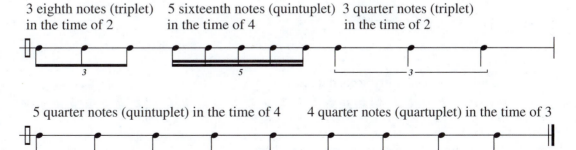

Example 3.5. Examples of tuplet durational values.

The measured *absence* of sound is notated by **rests**, which are organized in the same way as note values. These are shown in Table 3.3. The principles of dotting and double-dotting are the same for rests as they are for notes. Ties, however, are not used to connect rests of different durations as they are used for notes. In notating rests, remember that a half rest sits *above* the center line whereas a whole rest hangs *under* the next-to-highest line.

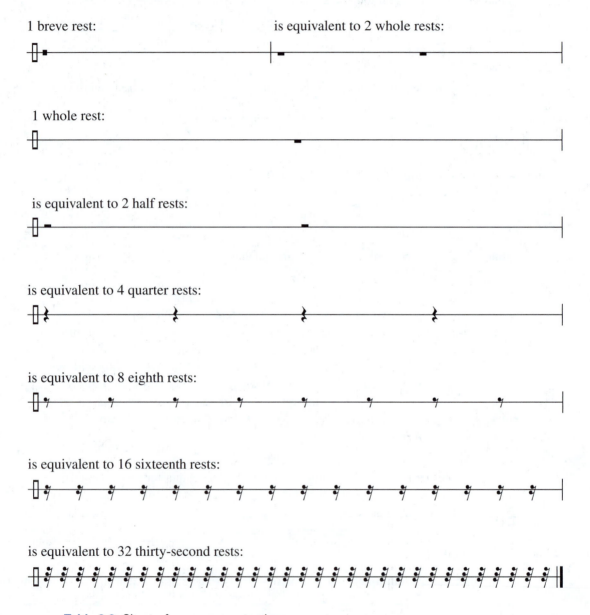

1 breve rest: is equivalent to 2 whole rests:

1 whole rest:

is equivalent to 2 half rests:

is equivalent to 4 quarter rests:

is equivalent to 8 eighth rests:

is equivalent to 16 sixteenth rests:

is equivalent to 32 thirty-second rests:

Table 3.3. Chart of common rest values.

Rests are usually broken up, if necessary, to show the prevailing metric structure even in the absence of sound. In Example 3.6 below, a half rest's worth of silence is broken up into two quarter rests in simple triple meter, and into an eighth rest and a dotted quarter rest in compound duple meter.

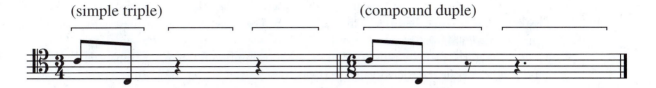

Example 3.6. Breaking up a rest to show the prevailing metric structure.

How fine can a rhythmic subdivision get? Theoretically, the potential for finer and finer subdivision is infinite, limited only by human perception. The more rapid durations get, the more notes tend to blur together in a "cluster" of noise or a buzz. This effect is actually quite popular in "drum-and-bass" styles of electronic music; the electronica artist Brian Transeau (BT) has programmed durations as small as 2048th notes in his music.

LEVEL MASTERY 3.1.

a. Fill in the blanks to show how many of the shorter notes or rests are equivalent to the longer note or rest.

1. ♩ × _____ = 𝅗𝅥.

2. 𝄾 × _____ = ▬

3. ♪ × _____ = 𝅗𝅥..

4. ♪. × _____ = 𝅗𝅥.

5. 𝄾. × _____ = ▬.

6. 𝄾 × _____ = 𝄾.

7. ♪ × _____ = 𝅝·

8. ▬ × _____ = ▪

9. ♩ × _____ = |O|

10. 𝄾· × _____ = 𝄽.

11. ♪ × _____ = 𝅗𝅥

12. 𝄾 × _____ = ▬..

Self-Test 3.2 may be done at this time.

Workbook Exercise 3.2 may be done at this time.

METER SIGNATURES

The meter of a musical composition is shown at the beginning of the first measure, and at the beginning of a measure any time the meter changes, by the **meter signature** (sometimes also called the "time signature"). The upper number of the meter signature *usually* shows the number of beats in the measure, usually corresponding to the beats in the primary pulse stream. The lower number in the meter signature *usually* indicates the durational value of the note perceived as the "beat" in the primary pulse stream. Thus, "The Reason" has a meter signature of $\frac{4}{4}$; following the primary pulse stream, there are four beats in a measure (the top "4"), and the value of a beat is a quarter note (the bottom "4"). $\frac{4}{4}$ is sometimes also shown as **C**, a historical designation meaning "**common time**."

Exceptions to this rule generally involve compound meter. In "The Irish Washerwoman" (see Example 3.2), the primary pulse stream consists of two beats per measure, with the durational value of the beat a dotted quarter note (equivalent to three eighth notes). In these instances, the *first subdivision* of the prevailing pulse is normally indicated as the bottom number in the meter signature, and as a result the top number is a *multiple of 3*, usually 6, 9, or 12. "The Irish Washerwoman" has six eighth notes per measure (eighth notes being the first subdivision of the dotted-quarter pulse stream), and so the meter signature is $\frac{6}{8}$.

Occasionally, meter signatures with less common **beat values** are encountered. These usually are chosen by the composer to communicate something of the desired style to the performer. For example, a $\frac{2}{2}$ meter would have the same number of quarter notes as $\frac{4}{4}$, but it is often used to signify a meter of two beats per measure in a march-like tempo, referred to as "**cut time**" (the symbol **¢** is sometimes also used to designate this meter). Similarly, $\frac{3}{8}$ is the same type of meter as $\frac{3}{4}$, but the choice of eighth notes to have the beat would indicate a livelier tempo. Finally, a meter of $\frac{3}{2}$ or $\frac{4}{2}$ is sometimes chosen, rather than $\frac{3}{4}$ or $\frac{4}{4}$, to indicate a more serious, solemn character. This style of notation is sometimes called *stile antico* ("old style").

LEVEL MASTERY 3.2.

a. Circle the appropriate metric category labels (simple/compound, duple/ triple/ quadruple) for the meters below.

$\frac{4}{4}$	simple	compound	duple	triple	quadruple
$\frac{3}{8}$	simple	compound	duple	triple	quadruple
$\frac{6}{16}$	simple	compound	duple	triple	quadruple
¢	simple	compound	duple	triple	quadruple

<table>
<tr><td>$\frac{9}{4}$</td><td>simple</td><td>compound</td><td>duple</td><td>triple</td><td>quadruple</td></tr>
<tr><td>$\frac{3}{4}$</td><td>simple</td><td>compound</td><td>duple</td><td>triple</td><td>quadruple</td></tr>
<tr><td>$\frac{12}{8}$</td><td>simple</td><td>compound</td><td>duple</td><td>triple</td><td>quadruple</td></tr>
</table>

b. Add one or more rests to the end of each measure to complete it. Be sure to break up rests as needed to properly convey placement of groupings in the metric structure. Do not change the order of any notes in the measure.

SELF-TEST

Self-Test 3.3 may be done at this time.

WORKBOOK

Workbook Exercise 3.3 may be done at this time.

ACCENT

When faced with a steady stream of stimuli, your brain attempts to organize the data into manageable "chunks." Psychologists call this "chunking," and it accounts for how you are able to remember things like phone numbers (a "chunk" of three numbers, followed by another "chunk" of four numbers). We may search for identifiable patterns, or an event in the stream that is different in some way from the others.

When a musical event is emphasized in some way that sets it apart from its immediate neighbors in a musical texture, we say that particular event is **accented**. Listening to "The Reason," it was probably easy to locate the downbeat. Because this pulse receives more emphasis at the beginning of the metric grouping, it is an example of **metrical accent**.

Other types of accent include:

- **dynamic accent**—a note played more loudly (often marked with a >), or more softly, than its neighbors.
- **contour accent**—a note that is significantly higher or lower than its neighbors. If the pattern of registral deviation is regular, the deviation will usually be heard as the beginning of the grouping (Example 3.7).

perceived metric grouping, in the absence of other distinguishing features (such as dynamics)

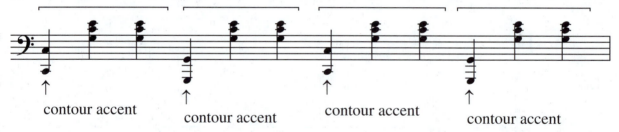

Example 3.7. An example of metric grouping created by differences in register.

- **agogic accent**—a note receiving emphasis by simply being longer in duration than its neighbors, either notated as such or sometimes interpreted by the performer with a **fermata** (hold) that extends the value (Example 3.8).

* = agogic accent

Example 3.8. Johann Sebastian Bach, Chaconne from Partita no. 2 for violin solo, BWV 1004, mm. 1–5a, showing agogic accents.

Obviously, it is possible for more than one type of accent to occur simultaneously. A note, for example, may occur on the downbeat, be significantly lower or higher in register, be louder, and be held for a longer duration all at once.

LEVEL MASTERY 3.3.

In each of the musical excerpts below, label the types of accent (metric, dynamic, agogic, or contour) marked by the arrows. Some musical events may be accented in more than one way.

a. Mozart, Piano Sonata no. 15 in F major, K. 533 (ii), mm. 1–4.

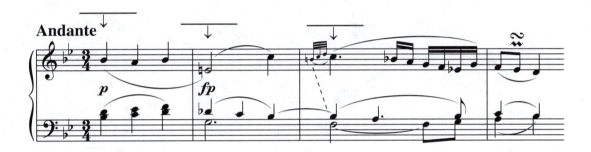

b. Chopin, Nocturne in E♭ major, op. 9, no. 2, mm. 1–8.

(Continued)

c. Ludwig van Beethoven (1770–1827), "Écossaise," WoO 23, mm. 1–8.

ORGANIZING METER: BEAMING AND SYNCOPATION

Another aspect of chunking is shown in the way that subdivisions are grouped to show the meter. Notes that are an eighth note or less in duration occurring *within* a beat are usually connected with beams. Example 3.9 shows two versions of the same rhythmic pattern—the second, with beams, clarifies where these notes fall within the metric grouping.

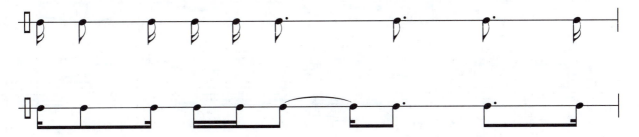

Example 3.9. Use of beams and ties to clarify metric organization.

When an accent occurs on a weak beat or a weaker part of a beat, the resulting metrical disruption is called **syncopation**. Syncopations usually involve agogic or dynamic accents, though it is possible for a syncopation to be a contour accent as well (by definition a syncopation does *not* involve a metrical accent). In Scott Joplin's rag "The Entertainer" (Example 3.10), lower-register octaves alternate with chords on the weak part of the beat in the accompaniment. The "oom-pah" pattern allows us to hear the single notes and octaves in the bass register as defining the strong part of the beat, through contour accents. Against this, however, the agogically accented notes (which, incidentally, are also contour accents) in the right hand melody continually fall on the weaker part of the beat.

When syncopation occurs outside the boundaries of a beat, a tie is used to connect the end of one beat with the beginning of another; in that way, the *visual* boundaries of the beat are maintained. Ties may be used to connect any two or more durations if the pitch of the note is not changed; they are usually used in connection with syncopations within the measure or notes that extend past the bar line.

(Continued)

Example 3.10. Scott Joplin (1868–1917), "The Entertainer," mm. 1–16.

Sometimes a new metric grouping is superimposed within the confines of a prevailing meter. **Hemiola** is a temporary metric disruption with a 2:3 ratio; two beats are accented against a meter of three pulses, or vice versa. Hemiola may occur within a measure (as, for example, in the interplay between $\frac{6}{8}$ and $\frac{3}{4}$, both of which consist of six eighth notes), or it may extend across the bar line to involve several measures. A very well known example of hemiola within a measure is "America" from the Leonard Bernstein and Stephen Sondheim musical *West Side Story* ("I-like-to-be-in-A—me–ri–ca"). The third movement of Beethoven's Piano Sonata in G Major, op. 14 no. 2, shown in Example 3.11, contains a hemiola extending across the bar line for its first two full measures (an implied $\frac{3}{4}$ metric pattern), followed by the "correct" meter of $\frac{3}{8}$ for the next two measures. The alternation of these two metric patterns in the

PART 1: Fundamentals and Diatonic Harmony

first eight measures thus helps to establish the humorous character of this movement, which Beethoven labeled a *scherzo* (an Italian word that means "joke").

For a close study of hemiola and other conflicting metric groupings, see Web Feature 3.2.

For an examination of performative issues in tempo, meter, and notation, see Web Feature 3.3.

See Web Feature 3.4 at this time for an interesting study in changing metric groupings.

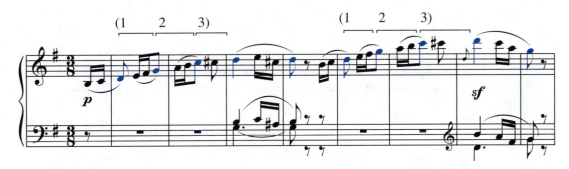

Example 3.11. Beethoven, Piano Sonata in G Major, op. 14 no. 2 (iii), mm. 1–8.

Polymeter occurs when two or more meters are combined simultaneously. This is similar to hemiola that extends past the bar line, except it often involves more complex ratios. Example 3.12 shows superimposed groupings of 5 and 7.

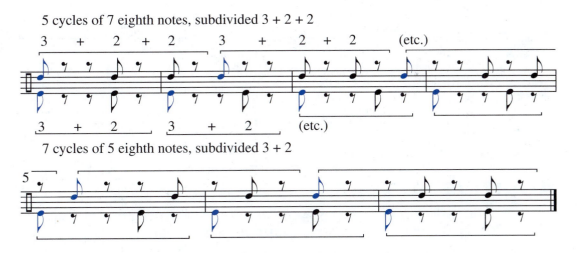

Example 3.12. An example of polymeter, found in King Crimson's "Thrak."

LEVEL MASTERY 3.4.

Using beams and ties, group the following series of durations into the specified meters. Do not change the order of the notes in each series, and do not insert any rests between notes. You may need to insert one or more rests at the end of the final measure of each line; if so, be sure to break up rests as needed to reflect the metric structure. The first line is done for you as an example.

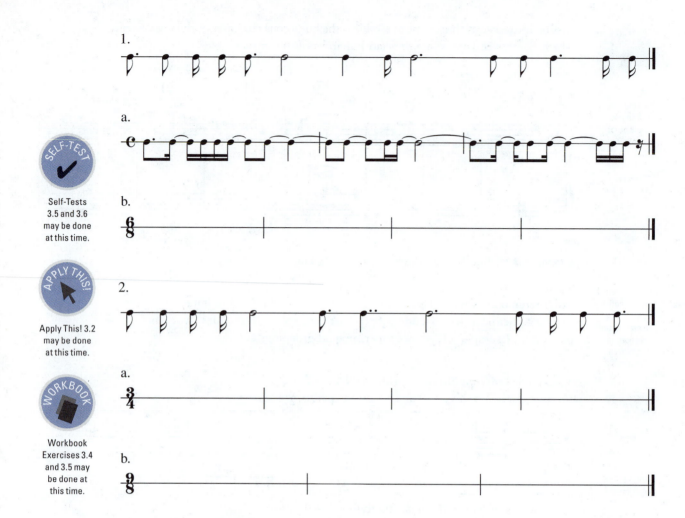

Self-Tests 3.5 and 3.6 may be done at this time.

Apply This! 3.2 may be done at this time.

Workbook Exercises 3.4 and 3.5 may be done at this time.

ADDITIVE METERS

SOUND EXAMPLE 3.2: COSMIC VOICES FROM BULGARIA, "DILMANO, DILBERO" (*BULGARIAN CHORAL FOLK SONGS, VOL. 2*)

"Beautiful Dilmana,
Can you teach me to push the peppers so that they flower,
and bear much fruit,
and I can have as much as I wish?"
"Well, you push the peppers deep into the ground,
and they will flower and bear much fruit,
and you will have as much as you wish."

Thus far, we have focused on *top-down*, or *divisive*, metric structures. In "The Reason," for example, we can see from the uppermost level down that each layer is consistently subdivided into 2. In "The Irish Washerwoman," some layers are divided into 2, others 3, but again the divisions are consistent for each beat grouping.

To our ears, the first line of "Dilmano, Dilbero," which is sung twice, might sound as if it were a syncopated rhythm in $\frac{4}{4}$:

Any semblance of a consistent beat grouping quickly dissipates in the second line of the song, however, which is also sung twice. Instead, the beat groupings seem to alternate between those that are subdivided into 2 and those that are subdivided into 3, with the result that the beat groupings appear to be unequal. The pulses at the *lowest* level, however, are consistent across both beat groupings. Therefore, it makes sense to think of this metric structure as **additive** in conception—built from the "bottom up" by assembling small, even units of rhythmic subdivision like so many building blocks into groupings of either 2 or 3. Because the "uneven" beat groupings of additive meter mix simple (2) and compound (3) subdivisions, additive meter is sometimes also called **mixed meter**. The rhythmic groupings of "Dilmano, Dilbero" can be read as follows:

$$
\begin{array}{lll}
(2)^* & 3 + 3 + 2, & 3 + 3 + 2 \\
& 3 + 3 + 2, & 3 + 3 + 2 \\
& 3 + 3 + 3 + 2, & 3 + 3 + 2 \\
& 3 + 3 + 3 + 2, & 3 + 3 + 2 \\
\end{array}
$$

* = anacrusis

Additive meter signatures often involve prime numbers such as 5, 7, or 11; occasionally a number such as 8 is grouped unevenly as, for example, 3 + 3 + 2 (as we saw in the opening of "Dilmano, Dilbero") or 3 + 2 + 3.

Additive metric structures are very common in the folk music of Eastern Europe. They crossed over into Western concert music in the early twentieth century, particularly through the music of Bela Bartók (1881–1945) and Igor Stravinsky (1882–1971).

Additive meters are generally capable of more than one possible grouping. For example, $\frac{5}{8}$ can be grouped as 3 + 2 (which is more common) or 2 + 3. Dave Brubeck's "Take Five" is a famous example of a jazz composition in $\frac{5}{4}$, subdivided consistently as 3 + 2; the same meter and subdivision are found in "Everything's Alright," from Andrew Lloyd Webber and Tim Rice's *Jesus Christ Superstar*, and Jethro Tull's "Living in the Past."

Web Feature 3.5 examines a famous example of additive and mixed (changing) meter.

a. In the manner of Level Mastery 3.4, group the following duration series into the indicated meters. Be sure to subdivide the measures as indicated above each meter signature.

a. (4+3)

b. (3+2)

c. (3+2+3)

d. (4+2+3+4)

b. The following measures need to have tuplets inserted into them. First, determine the missing durational value; then, write the proper tuplet to complete the measures, as indicated by the instructions above each measure.

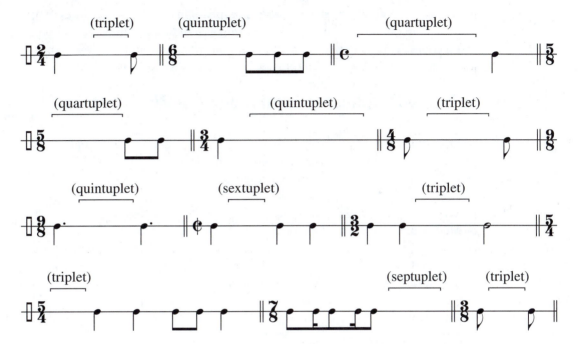

CONCLUSION

Music is a performing art. A musical score is not in itself "music" until it is performed; the score only contains *instructions* for performance. Moreover, countless pieces of music—from improvisations to folk songs learned "by ear"—can be played without a score. What the performing arts—music, theater, and dance—all have in common is that their performances all unfold in time. A musical experience is a temporal experience.

Rhythm and meter describe ways in which musical time is "carved up" for our consumption. Meter results from the grouping of equal portions of time (beats per minute, for example) into patterns of greater and lesser emphasis ("strong" and "weak" beats). At the musical surface, notes of greater and lesser duration result in what we called rhythm.

In music we may interact with time in other ways. The session drummer is prized for his or her metronomic sense of timing; the concert pianist learns to play the music of Chopin and other Romantic-era composers with rubato, "borrowing from" and "adding to" the duration of certain beats to give the music a breathing ebb and flow. In certain extremely minimalistic types of music (such as Erik Satie's piano piece *Vexations*, which consists of a short passage of music played slowly 840 times, lasting some 17 hours), we may momentarily lose our sense of the passing of time and instead experience time as a constant "now."

Your experience of time in music—especially with a piece of music that you know well—will likely change over the years as you develop your musical skills. Through practicing and listening, you will learn to hear larger groupings of musical time—spans of coherence that occur over greater intervals. You will also learn to recognize and even anticipate those moments of rubato in others' performances, sensing where rubato can be applied to enhance our understanding of longer musical phrases and sections. Time is indeed the wellspring from which musical expression emerges; a piece of music that occurs "out of time" is a nonexistent piece of music.

Terms to Know (* indicates terms found in Web Features)

additive (mixed) meter
agogic accent
anacrusis
bar line
breve
common time
compound (applied
   to meter)
contour accent
cut time
double bar line
downbeat
duple (applied to meter)
dynamic accent

fermata
first and second ending
harmonic rhythm
hemiola
measure
meter
meter signature
   (time signature)
metric modulation*
metrical accent
ostinato
polymeter
polyrhythm*
pulse stream

quadruple (applied
   to meter)
repeat sign
rhythm
riff
rubato
simple (applied to meter)
slur
stile antico
syncopation
tempo
tie
triple (applied to meter)
triplet

Self-Test

3.1. Match the durational values of the notes in each numbered measure with their equivalents in the lettered measures.

3.2. Match the durational values of the rests in each numbered measure with their equivalents in the lettered measures.

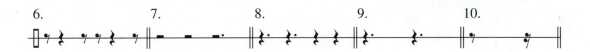

3.3. Provide the appropriate metric categorization for the meters below.

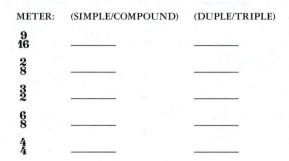

METER:	(SIMPLE/COMPOUND)	(DUPLE/TRIPLE)
9/16	_____	_____
2/8	_____	_____
3/2	_____	_____
6/8	_____	_____
4/4	_____	_____

3.4. Notate the specified tuplets in each of the empty measures, and complete each measure with one or more rests that fill the appropriate duration. The first measure is done for you as an example.

EXAMPLE

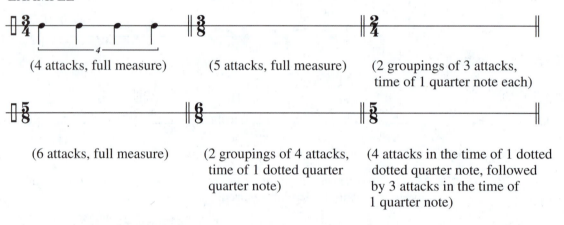

(4 attacks, full measure)   (5 attacks, full measure)   (2 groupings of 3 attacks,
                                                                    time of 1 quarter note each)

(6 attacks, full measure)   (2 groupings of 4 attacks,   (4 attacks in the time of 1 dotted
                                  time of 1 dotted quarter   dotted quarter note, followed
                                  quarter note)   by 3 attacks in the time of
                                                                    1 quarter note)

3.5. Organize the durational series below into the specified meters. Fill in any space at the end of your last measure with the appropriate rests; use ties to preserve any durational values that fall across beats in a syncopation. Do not insert rests anywhere into the series itself, and do not change the order or value of any notes in the series.

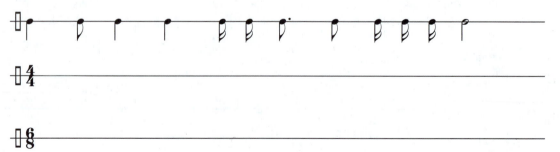

3.6. The following durational series have bar lines, but no beaming. First, identify a likely meter for each series. Then, beam the notes according to the proper meter. Do not insert any rests or change any durations. There may be more than one answer; if so, identify each possible meter and beam the durations accordingly for each one.

a.

b.

c.

d.

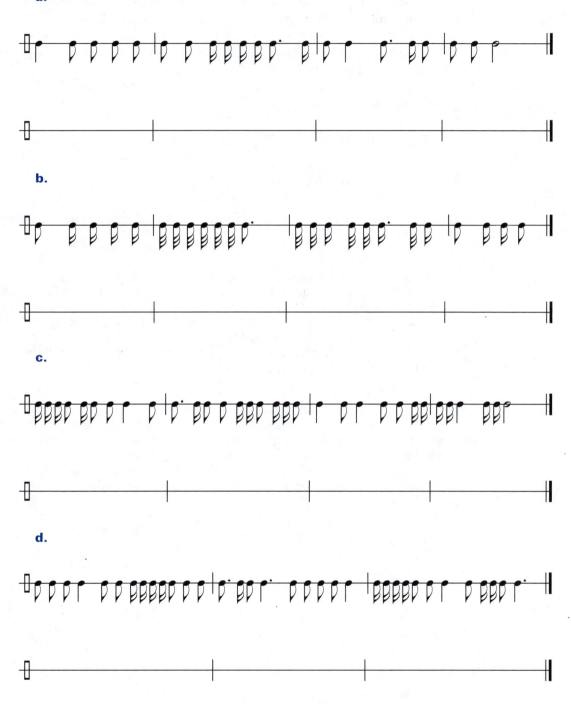

Apply This!

3.1. Construct a metric structure diagram for the following pieces, disregarding any ornaments in the melodic line. Label the primary pulse stream and identify the metric classification for each example. Do not consult scores, if available, except to check your work afterward. Your instructor may choose to substitute other pieces.

    a. "Minuet" from the *Notebook for Anna Magdalena Bach*, BWV Anh. 114, attributed to J. S. Bach

    b. Fleetwood Mac, "Dreams"

    c. Robert Schumann, *Arabeske* in C major, op. 18, opening theme only

3.2. Analysis: Led Zeppelin, "Kashmir"

    a. Construct a metric structure diagram for the piece, based on the first [1:12] of the song.

    b. Focus your attention on the rhythmic interaction between the guitar riff and the drum kit. Would this rhythmic interaction be best described as syncopation, hemiola, or polymeter? Based on what you have established to be the primary pulse stream, assign a meter signature for the drum kit. Then, provide a rhythmic notation for the guitar riff (assign a meter signature that would be appropriate for the guitar riff alone, and write the rhythm with appropriate durational symbols and bar lines, but do not attempt to notate pitches).

    c. The chords at [0:53–1:05] contain syncopations. Using the meter signature you have given the drum kit based on your interpretation of the metric structure diagram, write down the durational values of the chord sequence, using appropriate beams and ties to show the groupings against which the syncopations occur. The duration values of the first four chords in each measure can also be written as a tuplet—rewrite the rhythm of the chord sequence accordingly, using the appropriate tuplet.

CHAPTER 4

TRIADS AND SEVENTH CHORDS

OVERVIEW

This chapter examines the basic elements of harmony: triads and seventh chords. Both are examples of tertian harmony, which uses major or minor thirds as its building blocks. After considering these chords and how they appear in inversions—arrangements of notes in a chord—we see how composers in the Baroque era represented these harmonies by means of figured bass, allowing performers to improvise suitable harmonic accompaniments over a bass line.

CHAPTER OUTLINE

TRIADS AND CHORD QUALITY

Although the earliest surviving notated Western music dates from approximately the ninth century, most of the music we think of as "classical" dates from between approximately the late seventeenth century to the early twentieth century, a period sometimes called the **common practice** period. Although the music of the common practice period differs vastly in performance medium and surface stylistic details, it shares two key features:

- *Common-practice pieces use a particular pitch class as a goal or "home base"—the* **tonic***—to which other pitches are hierarchically related.* Music organized in this hierarchical, syntactical fashion is called **tonal music**, and this organization is **tonality**.
- *Common-practice pieces tend to use the major or minor third as the basic "building block" for harmonic structures*—a feature known as **tertian** harmony. Even very complex, towering chords—such as the chord shown in Example 4.1—can be built from the basic unit of the third.

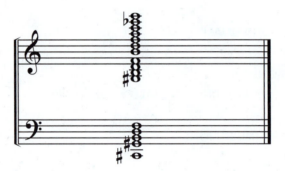

Example 4.1. A very large tertian chord, from Gustav Mahler's unfinished Tenth Symphony (1911).

Each note in a triad is called a **chord member**. When the triad is stacked in major or minor thirds as closely together as possible, the lowest note of that triad is called its **root**. The note a third above the root is called the **third** of the chord, and the note a fifth above the root is called the **fifth**. When arranged in this way, the triad is said to be in **root position**. The type of thirds used and their arrangement determines the triad's **quality**. We can conceptualize the stacking of thirds in this way (four possibilities):

| m3 | M3 | m3 | M3 |
| M3 | m3 | m3 | M3 |

For example, the triad C–E–G would be an example of the first possibility: C–E, a major third, is below E–G, a minor third. The triad A–C–E illustrates the second possibility: A–C, a minor third, is below C–E, a major third. Both the first and second possibilities are named after the *quality of their lower third*. Thus, the first possibility (M3 below m3) is called a **major triad** (the quality abbreviation is **M**); the second possibility (m3 below M3) is called a **minor triad** (the quality abbreviation is **m**). The boundary tones (highest and lowest pitches—see Chapter 2) of both the major and minor triads make a perfect fifth when the pitches are stacked as closely together as possible in root position (Example 4.2).

Example 4.2. Major and minor triads, with boundary tones spanning a P5.

The third and fourth possibilities are named after the *quality of the fifth* that they span. For example, the third possibility, two stacked *minor* thirds, results in the boundary tones being a *diminished* fifth. This is called a **diminished triad** (abbreviated with the diminished symbol we encountered in Chapter 2, °). The fourth possibility, two stacked *major* thirds, results in the boundary tones being an *augmented* fifth. This is called an **augmented triad** (abbreviated with the augmented symbol from Chapter 2, ⁺).

Every triad is named from its *root* and *quality*. For example, G–B–D is a G major (or GM) triad; G–B♭–D is a G minor (or Gm) triad. Example 4.3 shows the various triad qualities over a root of G.

M   m   °   +

Example 4.3. The four triad qualities.

LEVEL MASTERY 4.1.

a. Identify, by quality, the root-position triads below. Use the symbols M, m, ⁺, or °.

b. For each of the roots provided, add a third and fifth to spell a root-position triad of the quality indicated.

1.	2.	3.	4.	5.	6.	7.	8.	9.	10.
M	o	o	+	+	m	+	M	+	+

11.	12.	13.	14.	15.	16.	17.	18.	19.	20.
m	m	o	+	M	M	+	o	M	m

c. Given the pitch and the chord member of the triad, complete the triad in the indicated quality. An example is provided for you.

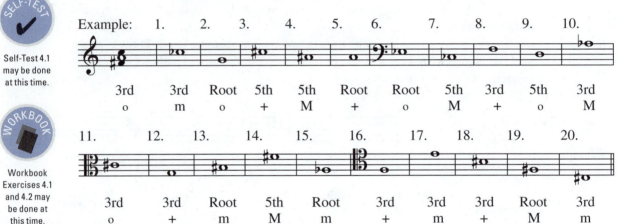

Example:	1.	2.	3.	4.	5.	6.	7.	8.	9.	10.
3rd	3rd	Root	5th	5th	Root	Root	5th	3rd	5th	3rd
o	m	o	+	M	+	o	M	+	o	M

11.	12.	13.	14.	15.	16.	17.	18.	19.	20.
3rd	3rd	Root	5th	Root	3rd	3rd	3rd	Root	3rd
o	+	m	M	m	+	m	+	M	m

Self-Test 4.1 may be done at this time.

Workbook Exercises 4.1 and 4.2 may be done at this time.

TRIAD INVERSIONS

Triads with chord members other than the root occupying the bass are called **inversions**. Once the tones are arranged as closely together as possible within the octave, a triad has three possible permutations.

- If the *root* of the triad is in the bass, it is said to be in **root position**.
- In **first inversion**, the *third* of the triad is in the bass.
- In **second inversion**, the *fifth* of the chord is in the bass. Because of the dissonant fourth occurring above the bass, the second inversion is considered to be the least stable position.

Inversions of chords are specified using **inversion symbols**, which are based on generic intervals above the bass (Example 4.4). A first-inversion triad is designated with a 6, to show that the root is a sixth above the bass. A second-inversion triad is designated with the numbers $^6_4$ to show that, with the fifth in the bass, the third and the root are found a sixth and a fourth above the bass, respectively.

Apply This! 4.1 may be done at this time.

Self-Test 4.2 may be done at this time.

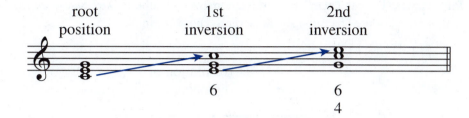

Example 4.4. Inversions of a C major triad.

SEVENTH CHORDS AND CHORD QUALITY

We have seen that triads in root position are made up of two stacked thirds. When we add yet another third atop the triad, the result is a **seventh chord**. The new chord member added above the root, third, and fifth is called the **chord seventh**. Most seventh chords have a two-part quality label: the first part indicates the *quality of the triad* created by the root, third and fifth of the chord, and the second part indicates the *quality of the interval* from the root to the chord seventh. Thus, the chord (lowest to highest) C–E–G–B is made up of a major triad and a major seventh interval from C to B, so it is labeled a **major-major seventh** (abbreviated MM[7]). The chord A–C–E–G is made up of a minor triad and a minor seventh interval from A to G, so it is labeled a **minor-minor seventh** (abbreviated mm[7]).[1] A seventh chord comprising a major triad and a minor seventh (e.g., G–B–D–F) is called a **major-minor seventh** or **dominant seventh**. All of these seventh chord qualities, using C as a common root, are shown in Example 4.5.

$$MM^7 \qquad mm^7 \qquad Mm^7 \text{ or dom.}^7$$

Example 4.5. Major-major, minor-minor, and major-minor seventh chords built upon a C root.

---

[1] The major-major seventh and minor-minor seventh are sometimes referred to as a "major seventh" and "minor seventh," respectively, especially in conversation.

Are there such things as minor-major sevenths? Theoretically, yes, but most of the time a so-called "minor-major seventh" is not a functional seventh chord, but a minor triad with a *melodic dissonance* at the interval of a major seventh. This dissonance behaves like a leading tone to resolve up by half step (Example 4.6). However, Pink Floyd's "Us and Them" (from the landmark rock album *Dark Side of the Moon*) makes poignant use of a minor-major seventh chord (Example 4.7).

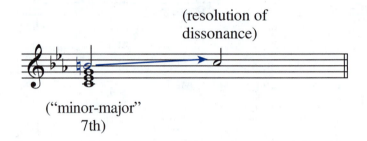

(resolution of dissonance)

("minor-major" 7th)

Example 4.6. A "minor-major seventh chord" resulting from melodic dissonance.

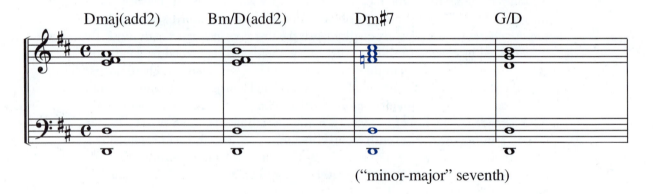

Dmaj(add2)   Bm/D(add2)   Dm♯7   G/D

("minor-major" seventh)

Example 4.7. Pink Floyd, "Us and Them," harmonic reduction including minor-major seventh chord.

Other seventh chords involve the diminished triad. There are two such chords: one has its chord seventh at the interval of a minor seventh above the root (e.g., G♯–B–D–F♯), and is called a **half-diminished seventh**—the triad is diminished but the interval of the seventh is not. The other type has its chord seventh at the interval of a diminished seventh above the root (e.g., G♯–B–D–F), and is called a **fully diminished seventh** because both the triad and the seventh interval above the root are diminished. The half- and fully diminished seventh chords, using C as their common root, are shown in Example 4.8. Notice in spelling a fully diminished seventh on C, we must ensure that the chord seventh is a true generic seventh above the root; we cannot respell the pitch enharmonically. Thus, the chord seventh above C must be a B♭♭, not an A, for C–A is a sixth, not a seventh.

Half-diminished seventh chord
(C–B♭ is a minor seventh)

Fully diminished seventh chord
(C–B♭♭ is a diminished seventh)

Example 4.8. Half-diminished and fully diminished seventh chords built on C.

LEVEL MASTERY 4.2.

SELF-TEST ✓

Self-Test 4.3
may be done
at this time.

WORKBOOK

Workbook
Exercise 4.3
may be done
at this time.

Given the root, spell a root-position seventh chord of the quality indicated.

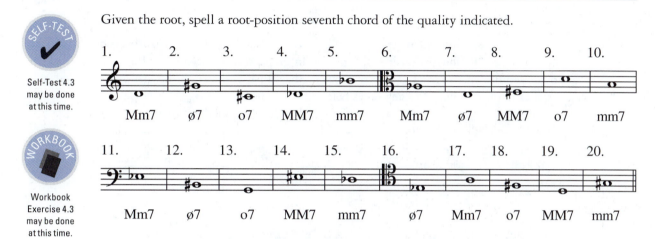

1.	2.	3.	4.	5.	6.	7.	8.	9.	10.
Mm7	ø7	o7	MM7	mm7	Mm7	ø7	MM7	o7	mm7

11.	12.	13.	14.	15.	16.	17.	18.	19.	20.
Mm7	ø7	o7	MM7	mm7	ø7	Mm7	o7	MM7	mm7

SEVENTH CHORD INVERSIONS

Like triads, seventh chords frequently appear in inversions.

- *The inversion symbol for a first-inversion seventh chord is* $^6_5$. Recall that a first-inversion triad has the inversion symbol ^{6}; for a first-inversion seventh chord, we also add a "5" to signify the addition of the chord seventh (occupying a generic fifth, or its compound equivalent, above the bass note). The strong dissonance between the root and the chord seventh is accounted for with the stacked numbers (a sixth and a fifth above the bass respectively).
- *The inversion symbol for a second-inversion seventh chord is* $^4_3$. Again, the stacked numbers (4 and 3) point out the dissonance of a second between the root (a fourth above the bass) and the chord seventh (a third above the bass).
- In **third inversion**, the *chord seventh* is the bass note. The inversion symbol for a third inversion is $^4_2$. As we learned in Chapter 2, the "4" (fourth) above the bass is a dissonant interval; the "2" shows the dissonance created by the root located a second (or its compound equivalent) above the chord seventh in the bass.

Example 4.9 shows the different inversions of an A major-minor seventh chord.

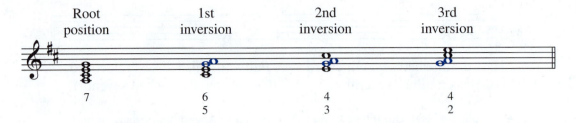

Example 4.9. A major-minor seventh chord in its different inversions.

LEVEL MASTERY 4.3.

Identify the quality and inversion of the following seventh chords. Use inversion symbols (use "R" for root position). Some are in grand-staff notation—for these, use octave equivalence to stack the notes above the bass line, as shown in the first grand-staff example. Do not place any notes below the bass note.

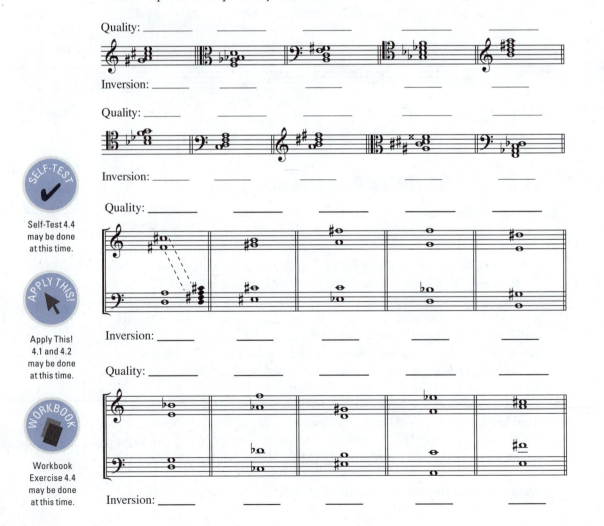

INTRODUCTION TO FIGURED BASS

Figured bass, or *thoroughbass*, is a kind of harmonic shorthand consisting of a bass line with Arabic numerals below the notes, indicating the intervals that provide the missing notes of the chord. Figured bass was a fixture of Baroque music and persisted well into the Classical period (where it can be found in some of Mozart's scores, for example). The figured bass information was part of a line that was labeled the **continuo**; the bass line would be played by cello or viola da gamba (sometimes reinforced with bassoon), and a harpsichord player or organist would double the bass part and improvise a suitable accompaniment using the information provided by the figured bass numbers. Such accompaniments were usually not written down in full, and in this respect the practice of figured bass rather resembles the use of lead sheets in jazz and popular music, the distinction being that a continuo player would be provided with the bass line and would fill in "from the bottom up," rather than be given the melody and chord symbols and fill in "from the top down."

Figured bass symbols communicated two important things: They alerted the performer to intervals above the bass note other than the diatonic third and fifth, and they provided information about chromatic alterations applied to notes above the bass. The introduction of figured bass predates the root-based theory of triads and seventh chords and their inversions by some 120 years. Thus, figured bass does not describe "chords" per se—rather, it provides information about *intervals above the bass*, which in turn *result* in chords.

Let's examine some passages from Bach's Cantata no. 140, "Wachet auf, ruft uns die Stimme" ("Sleepers awake! The voice calls us"), beginning with the opening measures of the first chorale, shown in Example 4.10. In this passage, you will notice that some of the bass notes in the continuo part do not have figured bass numbers. Where there are no numbers, it was assumed that the performer would play the notes a diatonic third and fifth above the bass note. In the first two beats of measure 1, we see that above the E♭ in the bass is a G played by the viola and a B♭ played by the second violin, the generic (diatonic) third and fifth above E♭ in the key of E♭ major. On the third beat, however, the bass line moves down by step while the upper voices remain stationary. The numbers 6, 4, and 2 now appear, referring to the pitches at those generic (diatonic) intervals above the bass note *instead of* the third and fifth. Thus, in the key of E♭ major the diatonic sixth above D would be B♭; a fourth above would be G; and a second would be E♭. These three pitches are all found in the strings. Figured bass numbers are always arranged, top to bottom, from highest to lowest generic interval number, 9 being the highest number possible and 2 the lowest; however, the actual *registral* placement of those intervals will not necessarily match the *visual* arrangement of the numbers. Compound intervals and octave equivalence may also play a role.

Figured bass more often than not indicated *deviations* from the norm; thus, thirds and fifths usually were not indicated in the figured bass unless they were chromatically altered in some way or, occasionally, to indicate a change back to "normalcy" after a significantly different chord. For example, the downbeat of measure 2 offers a cautionary "5" to indicate a pitch located a diatonic fifth above the bass note, after the stacked figured bass numbers below the previous bass note. In the absence of further numeric information, it may be assumed that a third above the bass is to be played as well, thus avoiding an open-fifth sonority. Likewise, a 7 below a bass note, as in measures 3 and 4, signifies a note located a diatonic seventh above the bass note; again in the absence of information that would indicate otherwise, the presence of a third or fifth (or both) above the bass is also assumed.

Observe how smoothly the voices above each bass note are arranged, even accounting for the differences in timbre between the strings and double reed instruments (a *taille* is a forerunner of the modern English horn). The keyboard player would likewise ensure smooth voice leading in his or her realization of the continuo part.

See Web Feature 4.1 for a discussion of how figured bass specifies chromaticism before attempting Level Mastery 4.4 or subsequent exercises.

Example 4.10. Bach, Cantata no. 140 [i] mm. 1–4.

Spell the chords indicated by the figured bass, in three- or four-part keyboard texture (as indicated by the figured bass) above the bass note provided in each measure below. Assume the key is C major throughout. Each example is an isolated chord—no progression is implied.

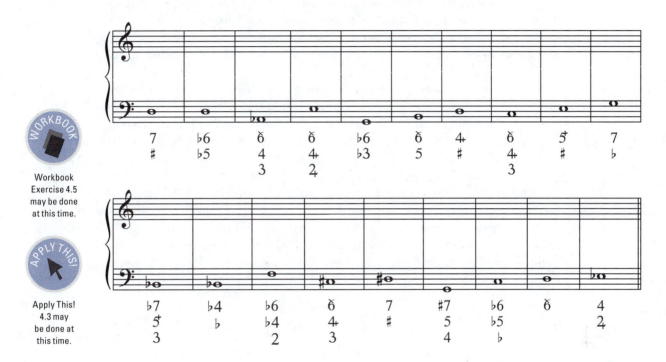

Workbook Exercise 4.5 may be done at this time.

Apply This! 4.3 may be done at this time.

POP CHORD SYMBOLS

In popular music, one usually finds chord symbols above the staff, showing the root and quality of the chord and occasionally the bass note as well. These symbols function somewhat like figured bass in that they enable musicians to improvise their specific parts within the framework provided by the chord symbols.

- If a chord symbol consists of a pitch-class name only (e.g., A), the implication is that the chord is a major triad, and the indicated pitch class is the root of the chord. Sometimes a capital M or the abbreviation "maj" is found to indicate major as well (as in AM or Amaj); a small triangle after the root (Δ) also indicates major quality, especially in jazz styles.
- A minor triad is indicated by a lowercase m, the abbreviation "min," or a minus sign following the root (as in Am, Amin, or A−). Sometimes the root of the chord is given in lower case, as it is for keys; thus, "f" would represent an F minor triad.

- A diminished triad is usually indicated with the abbreviation "dim" or the degree sign (°) after the root (as in Cdim or C°).
- Augmented triads are indicated with the abbreviation "aug" or a plus sign (as in Caug or C⁺); sometimes other indications, such as "⁺5" or "♯5," are used to denote an augmented triad.

A plain or superscript 7 following the root with no uppercase M (e.g., A7) indicates a *major-minor* seventh chord. A plain or superscript 7 following a minor chord symbol (e.g. Am7) indicates a *minor-minor* seventh; a *major-major* seventh is written with either an uppercase M (e.g., AM7) or a small triangle (∆) after the root (usually in jazz notation).

Fully and half-diminished seventh chords are also found in popular music notation. A plain or superscript 7 afterward (as in Cdim7) always indicates a fully diminished seventh chord. A half-diminished seventh chord, however, is usually notated as a minor seventh chord with a flatted fifth, a plain or superscript "♭5" or "−5" appearing after the plain or superscript 7 (in this respect the Arabic numerals have a function somewhat similar to those in figured bass).

Chords that appear in inversion are not indicated with "classical" inversion symbols; rather, a second pitch-class name, located below or after the first and separated by either a horizontal line or a diagonal slash, is used to indicate the bass note. These are sometimes called **"slash" chords**. Example 4.11 shows some sample pop notations for inversions of an A major triad and A major-minor (or "dominant") seventh. Compare these with the symbols in Examples 4.4 and 4.9.

Example 4.11. A major triad and A major-minor seventh chord inversions, with pop chord symbols.

Apply This! 4.4 may be done at this time.

Workbook Exercise 4.6 may be done at this time.

These so-called "slash" chord symbols are also used to indicate chords in which the bass note is not a chord member, as in the introduction to Todd Rundgren's "Love is the Answer," a reduction of which is shown in Example 4.12. Note that the first three chords can also be labeled as seventh chords; both interpretations are provided.

Keep in mind that there is considerable variation in both pop chord symbols and in figured bass practice, so in some scores the symbols may not be exactly as they are indicated here. Still, the principles are the same.

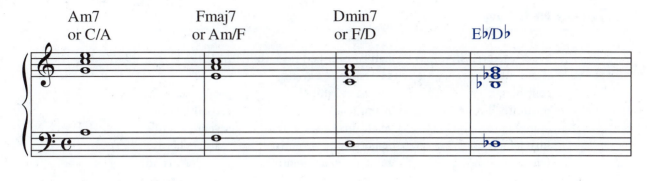

Example 4.12. Todd Rundgren, "Love is the Answer," introduction (harmonic and rhythmic reduction), showing "slash" pop chord symbols.

CONCLUSION

Triads and seventh chords are the foundation of the vast majority of pieces in Western music, and it is a fundamental of effective musicianship to know how such chords are spelled and used. You should know how the same chord might be labeled in different keys, as well as different styles of music. A versatile musician will be fluent in reading figured bass, Roman numerals and inversion symbols (covered in the next chapter), and pop chord symbols—whatever the style calls for.

At the same time, mastery of chords as discrete individual sounds is not enough. When learning a foreign language you may have found that it was easy enough to learn individual words ("shoe," "sister," "table," "book"), but that it was much more difficult to put those newly-learned words together into intelligible sentences and pronounce them properly in conversation (to say nothing of using them in conversation at the usual fast pace and flow of a native speaker!). So it is with chords. Chords are put together into logical sequences called **progressions** that follow a harmonic syntax normative for the musical style. We will begin to explore harmonic syntax in the next chapter, when we examine how harmonic function affects chord labeling in common-practice Western music.

Terms to Know

augmented triad	half-diminished seventh	quality
chord member	inversion (of a triad)	root
continuo	inversion symbols	root position
diminished triad	major triad	second inversion
dominant seventh	major-major seventh	seventh chord
fifth (of a triad)	major-minor seventh	"slash" chord
figured bass	minor-minor seventh	third (of a triad)
first inversion	minor triad	third inversion
fully diminished seventh	progression	triad

Self-Test

4.1. Write the specified triads below, in root position.

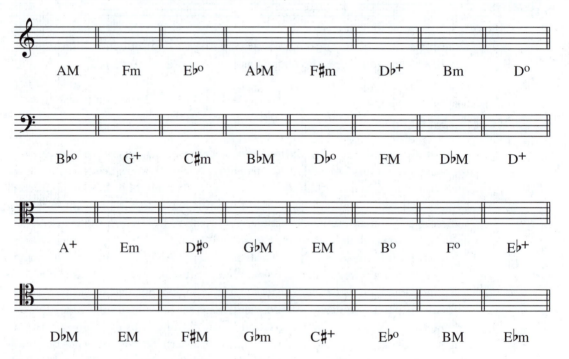

AM	Fm	E♭°	A♭M	F♯m	D♭+	Bm	D°

B♭°	G+	C♯m	B♭M	D♭°	FM	D♭M	D+

A+	Em	D♯°	G♭M	EM	B°	F°	E♭+

D♭M	EM	F♯M	G♭m	C♯+	E♭°	BM	E♭m

4.2. Using pitch names, fill in the blanks below to complete the triads indicated. Then, identify the triad by naming the root and providing the appropriate quality symbol (M, m, $^+$, °). (The first of the triad names is done for you as an example.)

TRIAD:

major:		C♯		AM
minor:			F	
augmented:	G♯			
diminished:	D♭			
major:	B♭			
major:		G♭		
diminished:			B	
minor:		F♯		
augmented:		D		
minor:			C	

4.3. Write the specified seventh chords below, in root position.

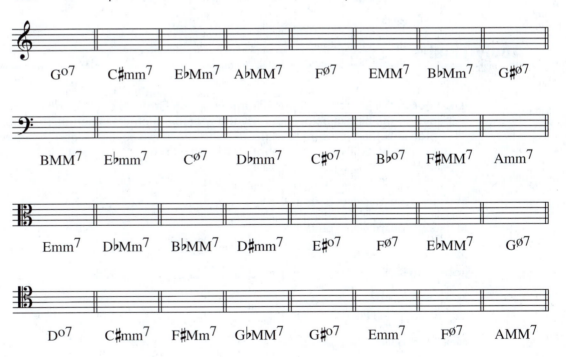

G°7   C♯mm7   E♭Mm7   A♭MM7   Fø7   EMM7   B♭Mm7   G♯ø7

BMM7   E♭mm7   Cø7   D♭mm7   C♯°7   B♭°7   F♯MM7   Amm7

Emm7   D♭Mm7   B♭MM7   D♯mm7   E♯°7   Fø7   E♭MM7   Gø7

D°7   C♯mm7   F♯Mm7   G♭MM7   G♯°7   Emm7   Fø7   AMM7

4.4. Write the specified seventh chords below, in the inversions indicated by the figured bass, using the indicated notes as the bass.

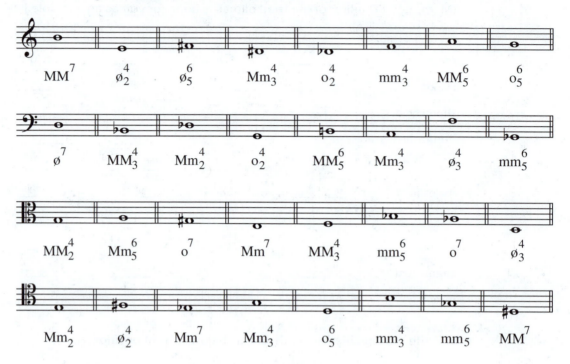

Apply This!

4.1. Look at the score to Robert Schumann's "Ich Grolle Nicht," found on the following pages. In the blanks below, identify the *root* (by pitch-class name), the *quality* of the chords specified (be sure to indicate if the chord is a seventh), and the *inversion* (using the appropriate inversion symbol). If the chord is a root-position triad, write "R."

	ROOT:	QUALITY:	INVERSION:
Measure 2, quarter-note beats 1 & 2:	_____	_____	_____
Measure 3, quarter-note beats 1 & 2:	_____	_____	_____
Measure 3, quarter-note beats 3 & 4 (piano only):	_____	_____	_____
Measure 4, quarter-note beat 3 (right-hand piano only):	_____	_____	_____
Measure 5, quarter-note beats 3 & 4 (piano only):	_____	_____	_____
Measure 6, quarter-note beats 1 & 2:	_____	_____	_____

Measure 6, quarter-note beats 3 & 4:   _____   _____   _____

Measure 7, quarter-note beats 1 & 2:   _____   _____   _____

Measure 7, quarter-note beats 3 & 4
(piano only):   _____   _____   _____

Measure 8, quarter-note beats 1 & 2:   _____   _____   _____

Measure 8, quarter-note beats 3 & 4:   _____   _____   _____

Measure 9, quarter-note beats 1 & 2:   _____   _____   _____

Measure 10, quarter-note beats 3 & 4
(piano only):   _____   _____   _____

Measure 11, quarter-note beats 1 & 2:   _____   _____   _____

Measure 11, quarter-note beats 3 & 4:   _____   _____   _____

Measure 12, quarter-note beats 3 & 4:   _____   _____   _____

Measure 13, quarter-note beats 1 & 2:   _____   _____   _____

Measure 14, quarter-note beats 3 & 4:   _____   _____   _____

Measure 15, quarter-note beats 1 & 2:   _____   _____   _____

Measure 28, quarter-note beats 1 & 2:   _____   _____   _____

Measure 28, quarter-note beats 3 & 4:   _____   _____   _____

Measure 29, quarter-note beats 1 & 2:   _____   _____   _____

Measure 30, quarter-note beats 3 & 4:   _____   _____   _____

Measure 31, quarter-note beats 3 & 4:   _____   _____   _____

Measure 35, quarter-note beat 3:   _____   _____   _____

4.2. Look at Example 4.7 ("Us and Them") again. What are the roots, qualities, and inversions (if applicable) of the first, second, and fourth chords?

	1.	2.	4.
Root:	_____	_____	_____
Quality:	_____	_____	_____
Inversion:	_____	_____	_____

Using Example 4.7 as a model, add the necessary figured bass.

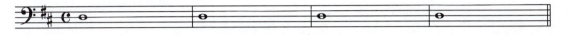

4.3. Improvisation: Figured bass realization. If you have some fluency at the keyboard you might want to try this exercise. Below is a passage from a sonata for violin and continuo by Elisabeth Jacquet de la Guerre (1665–1729). The violin line is provided, along with the bass line and figured bass. Using this information, improvise a keyboard accompaniment (two or three parts in the right hand, above the bass line) using the harmonies indicated by the figures. Try to make your connections from chord to chord as smooth as possible. Experiment with different chord voicings.

4.4. For the harmonic reduction below (from Bach's Prelude in C major from Book 1 of *The Well-Tempered Clavier*), provide pop chord symbols.

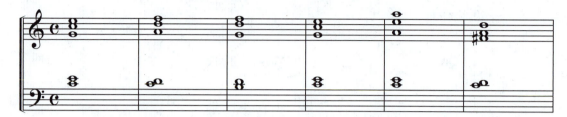

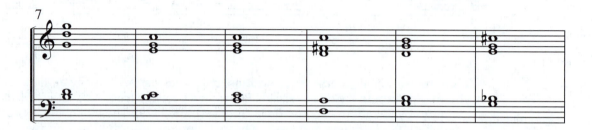

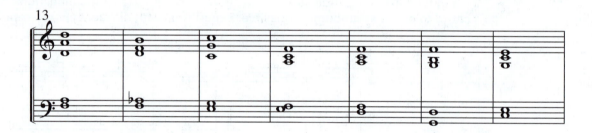

CHAPTER 5

DIATONIC CHORD LABELS

OVERVIEW

This chapter builds upon the previous one by showing how chords may be labeled with Roman numerals that show a chord's hierarchical function in the key as well as its quality and inversion. The chapter concludes with a brief introduction to the harmonic functions: Tonic, Predominant, and Dominant.

CHAPTER OUTLINE

In Chapter 4 you learned that tonality is based on tertian harmony (sonorities built on thirds), and that three pitches stacked in major or minor thirds (e.g., C–E–G) make up a triad, whereas four pitches stacked in major or minor thirds make up a seventh chord. In this chapter you will learn the basic nomenclature used to label chords in harmonic progressions.

DIATONIC TRIADS IN MAJOR KEYS

When we build triads over the scale degrees of the C major scale, the resulting triads are as shown in Example 5.1.

Example 5.1. Diatonic triads of C major, showing qualities.

Notice that there is only one diminished triad, and there are no augmented triads. The order of the qualities as the scale ascends—M, m, m, M, M, m, °—is the same for any major key. Example 5.2, for example, shows the diatonic triads for A♭ major.

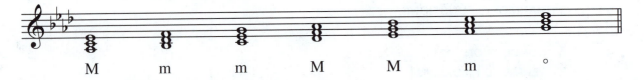

Example 5.2. Diatonic triads of A♭ major, showing qualities.

ROMAN NUMERALS

In 1722 the French composer and theorist Jean-Philippe Rameau published an important monograph, *Traité de l'harmonie* (Treatise of Harmony). The most influential aspects of Rameau's theory had to do with chord inversions, but Rameau also provided labels for chords that derived from the root's scale degree function in the key. Rather than the Arabic numbers used in figured bass or the naming of scale degrees, triads in a key are labeled with **Roman numerals**. The size of the Roman numeral indicates the triad's quality—uppercase symbols are used for major and augmented triads, while lowercase is used for minor and diminished triads. Augmented and diminished triads are further distinguished with their symbols after the Roman numeral. Example 5.3 shows the diatonic triads of C major with their Roman numeral labels.

| I | ii | iii | IV | V | vi | vii° |

Example 5.3. The diatonic triads of C major, with Roman numeral labels.

DIATONIC TRIADS IN MINOR KEYS

For minor keys, more diatonic triads are possible, depending on the form of the minor scale used. Example 5.4a illustrates the diatonic triads for each form of the C minor scale.

Natural Minor:

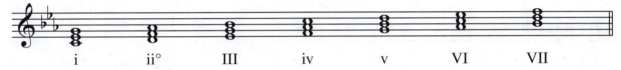

| i | ii° | III | iv | v | VI | VII |

Harmonic Minor:

| i | ii° | III+ | iv | V | VI | vii° |

Melodic Minor (ascending):

| i | ii | III+ | IV | V | ♯vi° | vii° |

Example 5.4a. Diatonic triads of C minor, different scale forms.

The most common minor-key triads are based on the *harmonic* minor scale (see Example 5.4b)—an obvious name for this scale type, as this scale is used to generate *harmonies*.[1] The one chord not taken from harmonic minor, III, is taken from the natural minor scale; this is because the major III (which includes the subtonic) is much more stable than the augmented III+ (which includes the leading tone).

---

[1] In particular, the harmonic minor scale allows for the half-step melodic resolution of scale degrees 6 to 5 and 7 to 1. These melodic resolutions are examples of **tendency tones**, which will be covered in more detail in Chapter 7.

Most commonly used triads in minor:

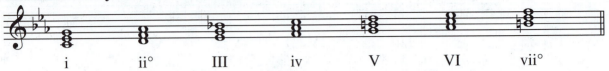

Example 5.4b. The most common triad varieties for each scale degree in minor keys.

Among the other chords found in Example 5.4a, the minor dominant chord (from natural minor) is common in folk and popular music (when the "minor" scale used is actually Aeolian or Dorian mode). Notice also that in ascending melodic minor, the *raised-submediant triad* requires a raised root, resulting in a diminished triad. Because the root is itself raised, a large sharp is placed before the Roman numeral label.

LEVEL MASTERY 5.1.

a. Provide Roman numeral labels for the root-position triads below, given the key (note: key signatures are not provided). Be sure to show the triad quality with the Roman numeral label (uppercase for major, lowercase for minor, addition of ⁺ or ° symbols for augmented and diminished respectively).

b. Notate the root-position triads indicated. Begin by finding the root as the correct scale degree for the key. Then spell the triad in the correct quality. Do not use key signatures.

1.   2.   3.   4.   5.   6.   7.   8.   9.   10.

F: vi   A♭: vii°   e♭: III⁺   g: VI   D: iii   A: IV   B♭: V   b♭: III   g: #vi°   E: vii°

11.   12.   13.   14.   15.   16.   17.   18.   19.   20.

a: #vi°   E♭: IV   a♭: VI   A: vi   b: ii°   B: V   A♭: iii   f#: iv   g#: vii°   e♭: #vi°

c. Identify the following triads, providing both the Roman numeral and the inversion symbol for each triad, given the key provided.

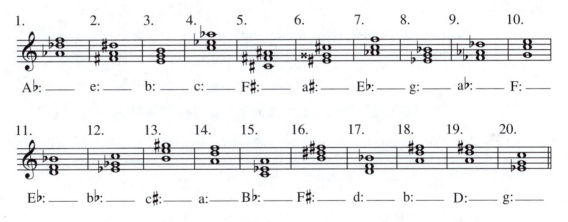

1.   2.   3.   4.   5.   6.   7.   8.   9.   10.

A♭: ____   e: ____   b: ____   c: ____   F#: ____   a#: ____   E♭: ____   g: ____   a♭: ____   F: ____

11.   12.   13.   14.   15.   16.   17.   18.   19.   20.

E♭: ____   b♭: ____   c#: ____   a: ____   B♭: ____   F#: ____   d: ____   b: ____   D: ____   g: ____

Self-Test 5.1 may be done at this time.

d. Notate the indicated inverted triads in the keys specified. Do not use key signatures.

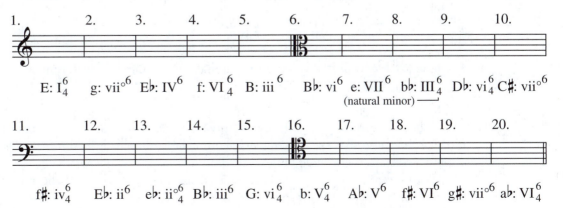

1.   2.   3.   4.   5.   6.   7.   8.   9.   10.

E: I⁶₄   g: vii°⁶   E♭: IV⁶   f: VI⁶₄   B: iii⁶   B♭: vi⁶   e: VII⁶   b♭: III⁶₄   D♭: vi⁶₄   C#: vii°⁶
(natural minor) ——

11.   12.   13.   14.   15.   16.   17.   18.   19.   20.

f#: iv⁶₄   E♭: ii⁶   e♭: ii°⁶₄   B♭: iii⁶   G: vi⁶₄   b: V⁶₄   A♭: V⁶   f#: VI⁶   g#: vii°⁶   a♭: VI⁶₄

Workbook Exercises 5.1 and 5.2 may be done at this time.

DIATONIC SEVENTH CHORDS IN MAJOR KEYS

Example 5.5 shows the diatonic seventh chords for C major. A superscript 7 is added to the Roman numerals to distinguish them from triads (in figured bass terms, remember, this would alert the performer that there was an added tone at the interval of a seventh above the bass). One new quality symbol is introduced as well; for the seventh chord built on the leading tone a degree sign with a slash through it ($^\emptyset$) is used to indicate the half-diminished seventh, replacing the diminished degree sign. (The degree sign found with diminished triads is used for fully diminished seventh chords.)

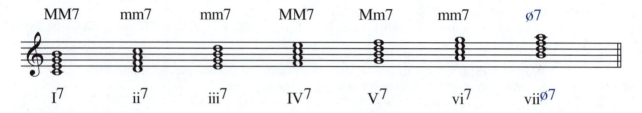

Example 5.5. Diatonic seventh chords of C major, with Roman numerals and quality symbols.

DIATONIC SEVENTH CHORDS IN MINOR KEYS

As with diatonic triads, there are more diatonic seventh possibilities available in minor keys. Once again, most of the commonly used diatonic sevenths, which are shown in Example 5.6, are derived from harmonic minor.

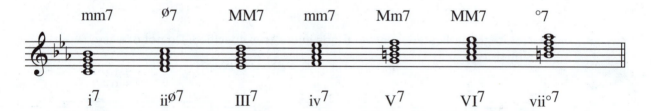

Example 5.6. Most common diatonic seventh chords of C minor, with Roman numerals and quality symbols.

The i^7 and III^7 chords are significant exceptions, using the subtonic from natural minor. Notice also that the supertonic seventh chord in minor is a *half-diminished* seventh, and the seventh chord built on the leading tone is *fully diminished*.

Other seventh chords may be generated using the ascending melodic minor scale (raised sixth and seventh scale degrees). Of these, the *raised-submediant seventh chord* requires special mention: the chord is half-diminished in quality. As with the raised-submediant triad, the raised root is signified by a large sharp placed before the Roman numeral label (♯vi°⁷).

LEVEL MASTERY 5.2.

a. Given the root and the key, spell a root-position seventh chord diatonic to the key and label it with a Roman numeral (and additional quality symbol if necessary). Be sure to include the superscript "7" to indicate a root-position seventh chord. Do not use key signatures.

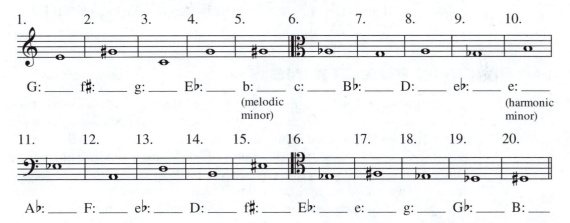

G: _____ f♯: _____ g: _____ E♭: _____ b: _____ c: _____ B♭: _____ D: _____ e♭: _____ e: _____
                                                  (melodic   (harmonic
                                                   minor)   minor)

11.   12.   13.   14.   15.   16.   17.   18.   19.   20.

A♭: _____ F: _____ e♭: _____ D: _____ f♯: _____ E♭: _____ e: _____ g: _____ G♭: _____ B: _____

b. Identify the following seventh chords, providing both the Roman numeral and the inversion symbol for each triad, given the key provided.

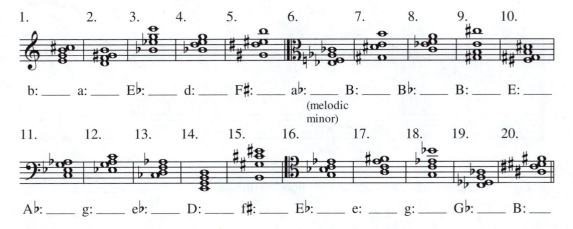

b: _____ a: _____ E♭: _____ d: _____ F♯: _____ a♭: _____ B: _____ B♭: _____ B: _____ E: _____
                                                     (melodic
                                                      minor)

11.   12.   13.   14.   15.   16.   17.   18.   19.   20.

A♭: _____ g: _____ e♭: _____ D: _____ f♯: _____ E♭: _____ e: _____ g: _____ G♭: _____ B: _____

Apply This! 5.1
may be done
at this time.

Workbook
Exercises 5.3,
5.4, and 5.5
may be done
at this time.

c. Notate the indicated root-position and inverted seventh chords in the keys specified. Do not use key signatures.

1. C: iii$_5^6$　2. d: VI$_3^4$　3. g#: vii°^{7}　4. D: ii$_2^4$　5. E♭: vi$_5^6$　6. b♭: V^7　7. f#: ii$^{ø4}_3$　8. F: IV$_2^4$　9. A: vii$^{ø6}_5$　10. A♭: IV$_3^4$

11. A: vi^7　12. B: iii$_2^4$　13. D♭: IV$_5^6$　14. c#: V$_5^6$　15. f: III^7　16. E: vii$^{ø4}_3$　17. G: vi$_5^6$　18. b: VII$_3^4$　19. b: vii°^{7}　20. F#: iii$_5^6$

HARMONIC FUNCTIONS

You may have heard it said that music is a "universal language." While this common expression is not exactly correct, it is true that Western music has its own *syntax*, and we can illustrate this using an example from language. If we consider the sentence "Susie threw the ball," we see that the meaning of the sentence is shaped by the order and the function of the words (subject–verb–object). If we change the word order to "the ball threw Susie," we have something that is grammatically correct but that, given the words' connotations, does not make sense; similarly, a sentence such as "the Susie ball threw" seems to be randomly constructed. Something like this happens in music too. Try playing through the chord progression in Example 5.7, if you can. Do the chords seem to follow each other logically?

Example 5.7. A randomly arranged harmonic progression.

It doesn't appear to have a goal or logical flow. Try playing through the progression in Example 5.8, however, which consists of the same chords in a different order. Does this progression seem to be more "singable" and purposeful?

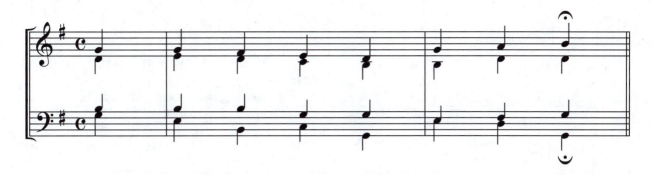

Example 5.8. "Old Hundredth," opening phrase—the harmonic progression of Example 5.7 in correct order.

The orderly directional "flow" of a musical phrase is determined by the **harmonic function** of its chords. There are three main categories of harmonic function: Tonic (T), Dominant (D), and Predominant (PD).

- As its label indicates, the tonic chord (I) has a **tonic function**.
- V and vii° are **dominant function** chords.
- The most common **predominant** chords are ii and IV. The remaining chords, vi and iii, have a predominant function *if they occur before ii or IV*. (Other contexts for these chords will be addressed in Chapter 13.)

Tonic and dominant chords alone can certainly suffice to make a coherent musical statement: the first movement of Mozart's "Eine Kleine Nachtmusik" contains nothing but I and V for the first ten measures (Example 5.9).

Example 5.9. Mozart, "Eine Kleine Nachtmusik," K. 525 (i), mm. 1–10. *(Continued)*

(Continued)

Adding a *predominant* chord, however, *intensifies* the drive to the V. Because the predominant function precedes the dominant function in a phrase, and the dominant function usually demands a (sometimes thwarted or delayed) resolution to the tonic—the point of greatest stability—we can generalize that goal-directed phrases in common-practice-period music follow a fundamental pattern of T → PD → D (→ T). (The last T is in parentheses because, as will be seen in the next chapter, some phrases end on V rather than I.) Examples 5.10 through 5.13 provide several instances of the T→PD→D (→T) pattern, with Roman numeral labels and harmonic functions provided.

Example 5.10. Bach, Prelude in C major, BWV 846 from *The Well-Tempered Clavier* (Book 1), mm. 1–4. *(Continued)*

(Continued)

$$\text{D} \qquad\qquad\qquad\qquad\qquad \text{T}$$

$$\text{V}^6_5 \qquad\qquad\qquad\qquad\qquad \text{I}$$

$$\text{T} \qquad\qquad\qquad\qquad\qquad\qquad\qquad\qquad\qquad \text{PD}$$

g: i $\qquad\qquad\qquad\qquad\qquad\qquad\qquad\qquad$ ii$^{\varnothing4}_{\ \ 2}$

Example 5.11. Mozart, Symphony no. 40 in G minor, K. 550 (i), mm. 1–9.
(Continued)

(Continued)

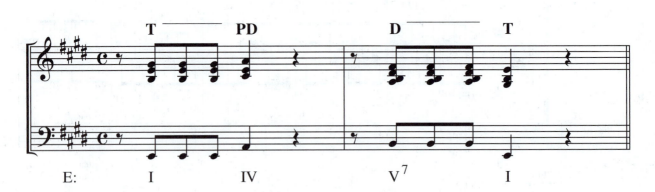

Example 5.12. Eddie Cochran, "Summertime Blues."

Example 5.13. Marvin Gaye, "What's Going On," verse 1 [0:17–0:45], melody and harmonic reduction.

Each of these examples has a goal-directed quality because of the arrangement of the T→PD→D (→T) pattern, but compare them to the progression of the verse in Maroon 5's "This Love" (V_5^6, i, iv^7, vii^{o6}_5 in C minor). By beginning and ending the progression with dominant-function chords, Maroon 5 ensure that the phrase is "open-ended," lacking in resolution until the arrival of the chorus on an emphatic tonic chord (Example 5.14a). The chorus, however, can be analyzed in the relative major of C minor, E♭ major; each of its phrases ends emphatically with a perfect authentic cadence in E♭ (Example 5.14b).

Example 5.14a. Maroon 5, "This Love," verse progression, with Roman numeral and harmonic function analysis.

Example 5.14b. Maroon 5, "This Love," chorus progression, with Roman numeral and harmonic function analysis.

LEVEL MASTERY 5.3.

For each of the excerpts below, provide the harmonic analysis (Roman numerals and inversion symbols) below the staff. (Tones marked with parentheses should not be counted as part of your analysis; disregard those chords marked with an asterisk.) Then, above the staff, identify the harmonic functions—T, PD, or D—of the chords you have analyzed.

a. George Frideric Handel (1685–1759), "Since By Man Came Death," no. 46 from Part III, *Messiah*, mm. 1–6.

b. Beethoven, Piano Concerto no. 5 ("Emperor"), op. 73 (ii), mm. 9–13a (strings only). The "D" function assigned to the I$_4^6$ chord will be explained in Chapter 10.

c. Robert Schumann (1810–1856), "Die Rose, die Lilie," no. 3 from *Dichterliebe*, op. 48, mm. 1–4.

CONCLUSION

Roman numerals are useful tools for labeling tonal harmonies; they tell us the chord's root (by scale degree in the key) and quality. By itself, however, a Roman numeral does not tell us about a chord's harmonic function, which can change depending on the context. A C major triad, for example, has a different function in the key of F major or A♭ major than it does in C major. Having an understanding of harmonic function—and the proper order or "flow" of harmonic syntax—will allow us to determine if a chord progression is normative (if it "makes sense") or not. Understanding harmonic function early on will help you with analyzing phrases, providing a proper harmonization for a melody, and other musical activities.

Terms to Know

dominant (harmonic function)
harmonic function
predominant (harmonic function)

Roman numeral
tonic (harmonic function)

Self-Test

5.1. Provide the necessary key signature and chords, given the keys, Roman numerals, and inversion symbols provided.

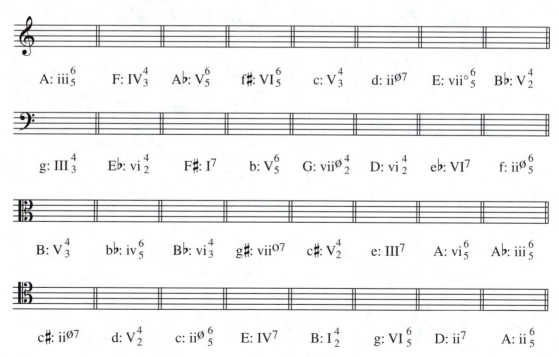

Apply This!

5.1. For each of the excerpts below, provide the harmonic analysis (Roman numerals and inversion symbols) in the blanks below the staff (blanks are provided to show the harmonic rhythm of each excerpt). Tones marked with parentheses should not be counted as part of your analysis; disregard those chords marked with an asterisk. Then, above the staff, identify the harmonic functions—T, PD, or D—of the chords you have analyzed.

a. J. S. Bach, "Wo soll ich fliehen hin," BWV 5, mm. 1–4 and 10b–12.

b. Franz Schubert (1797–1828), *36 Originaltänze*, D. 365 no. 3, mm. 1–8.

A♭:

CHAPTER 6

INTRODUCTION TO COUNTERPOINT AND VOICE LEADING

OVERVIEW

This chapter begins with a consideration of the common characteristics of a well-formed melodic line and how melodies may be combined in note-against-note counterpoint. After learning the different types of part-against-part voice-leading motions, you will be introduced to the basic elements of first, second, and third species counterpoint.

Up to this point, we have focused on basic concepts involving pitch organization in music: melodic and harmonic intervals, and harmony (triads and seventh chords). We have also examined how music is organized in time through rhythm and meter. Now we will begin to integrate the horizontal (melodic) and vertical (harmonic) dimensions of music in time, through **counterpoint** (from the Latin *punctus contra punctum*, meaning "point against point" or note against note, as a *punctum* was a type of musical note in the middle ages)—the controlled coordination of independent melodic lines.

Music was composed according to contrapuntal principles for centuries before composers began to consider how chords themselves might be hierarchically related; in other words, prior to the common practice period, chords were thought of as merely sonorities that were the result of multiple *independent* melodic lines. Even after composers began to think of music in "chordal" as well as linear terms—well into the common practice period—so-called *species counterpoint* continued to be the foundation of many composers' musical training. The theorist and composer Johann Joseph Fux (1660–1741) attempted to systematize the principles of counterpoint in an influential treatise entitled *Gradus ad Parnassum* ("Steps to Parnasssus"), first published in 1725. Fux organized the principles of counterpoint into graduated steps or types of counterpoint that he called **species**. Each species involved counterpoint against a given melody, called the **cantus firmus** (from the Latin for "fixed song"—plural *cantus firmi*), or *cantus* for short. In the Renaissance, the cantus often came from a fragment of a Gregorian chant.

- **First species** counterpoint involves the setting of a second voice—the counterpoint—above or below the cantus in a 1:1 or "note against note" ratio.
- **Second species** counterpoint sets two notes of counterpoint against each note of the cantus, thus in a 2:1 rhythmic ratio; in some respects second species counterpoint may be regarded as a more embellished version of first species counterpoint.
- In **third species** counterpoint, the contrapuntal part is further elaborated, allowing for either a 4:1 rhythmic ratio in simple meters or a 3:1 rhythmic ratio in compound meters.
- **Fourth species** counterpoint introduces ties to produce syncopations involving carefully prepared and resolved dissonances.
- Finally, **fifth species** counterpoint, so-called "free counterpoint," allows for all of the melodic and rhythmic principles in the first four species.

Fux's text was highly regarded by Bach and was studied by Mozart, Haydn, and Beethoven, among others, and—as we shall see in this chapter—contrapuntal principles fundamentally shaped their musical thinking. The principles of counterpoint are thus inseparable from music of the common practice period. Understanding how music works in its linear dimension—even when the texture of the music seems to consist of a series of block chords—will help provide you with a better sense of shape and direction as a performer.

This chapter provides only an introduction to counterpoint, enough to provide you with a foundation for our study of harmony and voice leading in subsequent chapters. We shall confine our discussion of contrapuntal principles in this chapter to those covered in the first three species of Fux's method; the major innovation of fourth species—a special type of dissonance called the suspension—will be addressed in detail in Chapter 11.

CONSTRUCTING A MELODIC LINE

While it is difficult to list "ingredients" for a good melody, there are some general principles we can consider. First, always consider whether your melodic line is singable, and try singing it yourself. From earliest times, the voice has remained the model for instrumental music.

- Melodies are primarily stepwise from note to note, since steps are easier to sing than frequent leaps; this is called **conjunct** motion. Where **skips** of a third or **leaps** larger than a third (**disjunct** motion) are involved, they are used sparingly. Sixths are much less common; where they occur they tend to be ascending (again, this is because ascending leaps are easier to sing). Try singing each of the melodic fragments in Example 6.1a. Which is more singable?

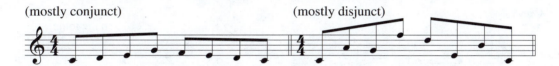

Example 6.1a. Conjunct versus disjunct motion.

- In general, any melodic skip or leap is often followed by stepwise movement in the opposite direction, helping to fill in the gap. If there are two consecutive leaps and/or skips in the same direction, they usually outline a triad (Example 6.1b).

Example 6.1b. Treatment of skips and leaps in Beethoven, Piano Sonata no. 8 in C minor, op. 13 ("Pathétique") (ii), mm. 1–8.

- Augmented and diminished intervals, whether melodic or harmonic, tend to be avoided in strict counterpoint. This prohibition, Leonard Bernstein's memorable

"Maria" from *West Side Story* notwithstanding, includes the tritone (augmented fourth or diminished fifth). In fact, even a succession of three whole steps, outlining a tritone (e.g., C–D–E–F♯), was also avoided.

A well-formed melodic line usually also has a clearly defined direction toward a "goal," rather than meandering seemingly aimlessly:

- The melody ideally begins on a member of the tonic triad (scale degrees 1, 3, or 5) and the overall melodic contour should resemble an arch; there should be a clear **focal point**, or highest pitch, that ideally would appear only once in the melodic line (often about two-thirds of the way through). The melody should conclude with a stepwise motion to the tonic, either as scale degrees 7–1 or 2–1 (Example 6.1c).

Example 6.1c. Focal point and conjunct motion to tonic in Beethoven, Piano Sonata no. 8 in C minor, op. 13 ("Pathétique") (ii), mm. 1–8.

- Finally, melodic **sequences** (the immediate repetition of a melodic figure at a higher or lower pitch level) are acceptable but should not be overdone at the risk of becoming overly predictable. A good rule of thumb is that a melodic figure being sequenced should not be repeated more than twice (Example 6.1d).

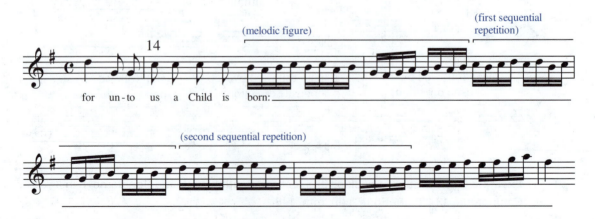

Example 6.1d. Melodic sequencing in Handel, "For Unto Us a Child Is Born" from *Messiah*, mm. 13b–18a.

Compose a melody to go above each of the following bass lines, observing the characteristics of a good melodic line. Your melody should consist of one note for each bass
pitch provided, and each tone in the melody should be consonant with the bass. Do
not merely duplicate the bass tones in another octave—instead, strive for a variety of
consonant harmonic intervals in your melodic line, while simultaneously aiming for
a melody that is mostly conjunct. The first is done for you as an example.

Bb:

f#:

d:

E:

(Continued)

A♭:

VOICE LEADING AND TYPES OF MOTION

The directed motion of parts from tone to tone is called **voice leading**. Voice leading favors *conjunct motion*, which in turn leads to smooth connections between chords. Consider the opening of the second movement of Beethoven's "Pathétique" piano sonata, op. 13 (Example 6.2a). The accompaniment is broken into arpeggiated figurations. Because the figurations are more or less constant, our attention focuses instead on the outer voices—the melody and bass line, which are also set apart by their placement at registral extremes. By isolating these outer voices, the result is a **reduction** of the music, stripping away the surface figuration to show the underlying structure. A two-voice reduction of the Beethoven passage (Example 6.2b) reveals how much of the motion from note to note, by part, is stepwise, as well as the variety of harmonic intervals found between the two parts.

Example 6.2a. Beethoven, Piano Sonata no. 8 in C minor, op. 13 ("Pathétique") (ii), mm. 1–8.

——— = step (conjunct motion)

- - - - = leap (disjunct motion)

Example 6.2b. A two-voice reduction of Example 6.2a, showing conjunct and disjunct motion in outer voices (numbers indicate consonant generic intervals).

There are five types of motion accounted for between pairs of voices: *contrary*, *parallel*, *oblique*, *similar*, and *stationary*.

- In **contrary motion**, two voices move in opposite directions. Parts that move in contrary motion are perceived to be equally active and independent—ideal for polyphony (Example 6.3).

Example 6.3. The Beach Boys, "Good Vibrations" [3:13–3:19].

- In **oblique motion**, one voice moves, in either direction, while the other remains stationary (either repeated or simply sustained).
- In **parallel motion**, two lines move in the same direction by the same generic interval. Example 6.4 shows both parallel motion (in the upper parts) and oblique motion (in the relation of those parts to the bass).

Example 6.4. Handel, "Pastoral Symphony," no. 13 from *Messiah*, Part 1, mm. 1–3.

Parallel motion between perfect consonances (**parallel fifths** or **parallel octaves**) *is to be avoided altogether* (Example 6.5). This "rule" is sometimes difficult to understand from our present perspective, since we are accustomed to hearing parallel perfect fifths and perfect octaves in the "power chords" associated with guitar-based rock music, such as "Smoke on the Water" or "Smells Like Teen Spirit." However, the perfect octave and perfect fifth, as harmonic intervals, are most likely to fuse into a single, thicker sonority. This is, of course, why such a sonority is aesthetically well suited to hard rock power chords! (In fact, so-called "octave doublings" are frequently found in Romantic-era piano and orchestral music, precisely for the purpose of thickening and reinforcing the line—an idea close in conception to "power chords." See Example 6.6.)

Example 6.5. Examples of parallel perfect fifths and parallel perfect octaves in a two-part texture.

Example 6.6. Chopin, Prelude in G minor, op. 28, no. 22, mm. 1–4, showing octave-doubled bass voice.

- In **similar motion**, two parts move in the same direction, but by *different* generic intervals (Example 6.7).

Trumpets (at sounding pitch)

Horns (at sounding pitch)

Example 6.7. Handel, "Alla Hornpipe" from Suite in D major, HWV 349, mm. 11–18 (trumpets and horns only, at sounding pitch).

One kind of similar motion to avoid, between soprano and bass in a four-part texture, is **direct fifths (octaves)**, also called **hidden fifths (octaves)**. This refers to similar motion *into* a perfect fifth, octave or unison, with a leap in the soprano (Example 6.8). The sudden appearance of a perfect fifth or octave in the texture appears, in its inconsistency, to call undue attention to itself; in the case of a direct movement to the unison, the aural effect is that one voice has even "disappeared" (Example 6.9).

Example 6.8. Examples of direct fifth and direct octave in a two-part (soprano and bass) texture.

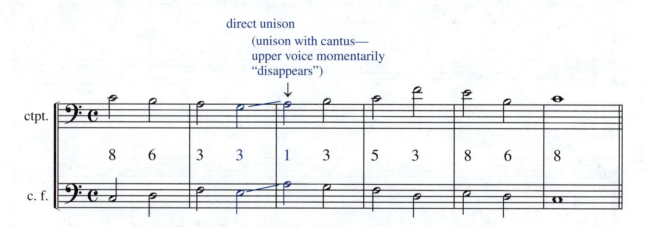

Example 6.9. Example of direct unison in a two-part texture.

- Finally, **stationary motion**, paradoxically, does not involve motion at all, but instead describes repeated notes in both parts. Stationary motion is not to be confused with parallel motion.

Identify the type of voice leading motion (contrary, oblique, similar, parallel, stationary) denoted by the voices connected with lines in each of the excerpts below.

a. Beethoven, Piano Sonata no. 21 in C major ("Waldstein"), op. 53 (i), mm. 1–3.

1. _____   2. _____   3. _____

b. Haydn, String Quartet in G minor, op. 74, no. 3 (ii), mm. 5–9a.

1. _____   2. _____   3. _____   4. _____   5. _____

c. Palestrina, Ricercare in G minor, mm. 1–6.

Self-Test 6.1
may be done
at this time.

Workbook
Exercise 6.1
may be done
at this time.

1. _____   2. _____   3. _____

4. _____   5. _____   6. _____

The stylistic norms for which types of voice-leading motion were preferred, and under what circumstances, vary with the historical period. We have already seen how parallel octaves, for example, were acceptable in the nineteenth century when viewed as a "doubled" bass line (Example 6.6), and that parallel octaves are also fixtures of contemporary rock music. Fux's guidelines for species counterpoint are most applicable for the construction of Renaissance counterpoint, and so they may seem to a modern reader to be unnecessarily restrictive, especially given that some of these rules seem to have been relaxed in later musical eras (for example, can you spot Beethoven's direct octave in Example 6.2b?). Nevertheless, strict instruction always provides a solid foundation for learning how and where to relax the restrictions later. As Pablo Picasso reportedly said, "Learn the rules like a pro, so you can break them like an artist."

INTRODUCTION TO THE FIRST THREE SPECIES OF COUNTERPOINT

First Species

First species counterpoint involves note-to-note matching of a cantus with another part in a 1:1 rhythmic ratio. The following rules pertain to the *harmonic* intervals created by the two parts:

- *Only consonant intervals* are allowed in the first species: perfect octaves, unisons, and fifths; major and minor thirds; and major and minor sixths, plus compound versions of these intervals. (Note that in this context the perfect fourth is treated as a dissonance.) Of these intervals, a perfect octave, unison, or fifth should be used to begin the phrase. Within the phrase there should be more imperfect consonances (thirds and sixths) than perfect ones; the perfect unison or octave should be used only for the beginning and/or ending.
- There should be *variety of motion* in order to ensure independence of the parts. Avoid the overuse of any one type of motion—for example, depending on the length of the cantus, one will generally find no more than three to five parallel thirds or sixths in a row. Of these three types of motion, contrary motion is best, as it best preserves the independence of parts.
- Avoid **crossing voices** (when the lower voice moves higher than the upper voice, or when the upper voice moves below the lower voice) or **overlapping voices** (when the *higher* voice moves to a lower pitch than the *immediately previous* note in the *lower* voice, or the *lower* voice moves to a higher pitch than the *immediately previous* note in the *higher* voice) (Example 6.10).

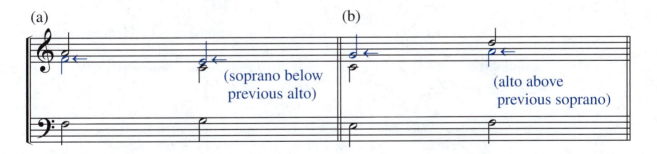

(a)   (b)

(soprano below previous alto)

(alto above previous soprano)

Example 6.10. Two examples of overlapping voices, soprano and alto parts.

There are rare moments in eighteenth-century counterpoint when crossing voices occur; in Example 6.11, for example, the tenor crosses above the alto part in the penultimate measure in order to avoid parallel octaves with the soprano. Nevertheless, crossing voices can make it difficult for the ear to distinguish between the two parts. Be especially mindful of this when writing parts in different clefs.

Example 6.11. J. S. Bach, "Ach Gott und Herr," BWV 255, showing crossing voices in measure 7.

Ah, God, my Lord, a heavy horde,
the sins by me committed!
Thy Son alone can all atone
that I may be acquitted.

(text translation by Henry S. Drinker)

- *Perfect consonances* ideally should be approached by *contrary* motion, particularly at the end of a phrase. Such a harmonic or melodic formula, used to signify a pause or completion of a musical phrase, is called a **cadence** (see the conclusion of Example 6.12).

Example 6.12 illustrates the principles thus far covered.

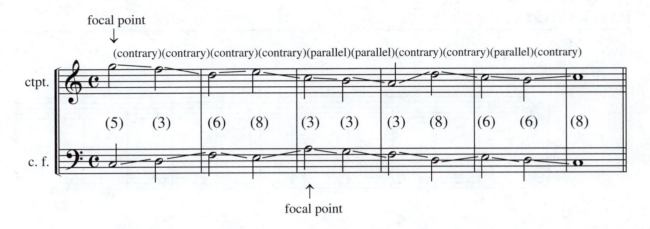

Example 6.12. Illustration of first-species counterpoint, illustrating proper contrapuntal procedures.

- *Two perfect consonances in a row*—e.g., an octave followed by a fifth—should be avoided, as the resulting sound is considered too empty and austere (Example 6.13).

Example 6.13. Example of two consecutive perfect consonances in a two-part texture.

- Finally, it is uncommon to find both voices approaching a third or sixth by disjunct similar or parallel motion, but otherwise treatment of these intervals is more flexible, keeping in mind that they should occur within the phrase.

Compose a first-species counterpoint for each cantus below.

(Jeppesen)

Exercise 6.2
may be done
at this time.

Second Species

In second species counterpoint, the counterpoint voice moves in a 2:1 rhythmic ratio with the cantus. The rules of the first species also apply to second species, with one important change: whereas dissonances were prohibited in the first species counterpoint, in second species counterpoint carefully controlled *unaccented* (occurring "off the beat" or on an unstressed pulse) *dissonances* are introduced.

- The most common dissonance in second species counterpoint is the **unaccented passing tone** (Example 6.14a). A dissonant passing tone moves by step (either up or down) from a previous consonance and then resolves in the *same direction* to a new consonance, which must be a third away from the previous consonance. **Accented** passing tones (occurring "on the beat" or on a stressed pulse) are not permitted in second species counterpoint.

- Unaccented **passing figures** (*consonant* passing tones) may also be used to produce unaccented consonances (rather than dissonances, hence the distinction from passing tones) with the cantus, as shown in Example 6.14b.

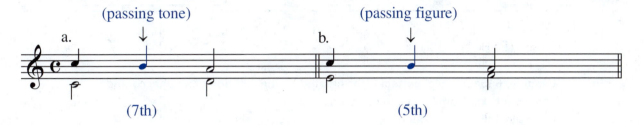

Example 6.14a and b. Passing tones and passing figures in a two-part texture.

- In order to maintain a 2:1 ratio against each note of the cantus, except for the final octave or unison in the last measure, *consonant skips or leaps* to other tones that imply a completed triad with the other two tones *are also acceptable* (Example 6.14c). The only type of unaccented consonance that involves a *step* is the motion from a fifth to a sixth or vice versa (referred to as 5–6 or 6–5 motion), examples of which are shown in Example 6.14d.

Example 6.14c. Consonant skips outlining an implied triad with the cantus note.
Example 6.14d. Stepwise unaccented consonances in 5–6 and 6–5 harmonic intervals with the cantus note.

- *Repeated notes* are to be avoided in second species counterpoint, because it thwarts the desired goal-directed motion.
- The counterpoint part may begin with a rest equal to half the duration of the first cantus note (thus begin with a half rest if your cantus is in whole notes); this actually helps to enhance the perception of independent parts.
- The penultimate note of the counterpoint part may relax the 2:1 rule, being the same duration as the cantus note, in order to signal the arrival of the cadence. The cadence concludes on the downbeat of the last measure.
- Finally, *check your work* to ensure that the added unaccented tones have not created any parallel perfect fifths or octaves with the cantus, as shown in Example 6.15a. Unaccented notes may also not be "inserted" between successive accented perfect fifths or octaves, as in Example 6.15b.

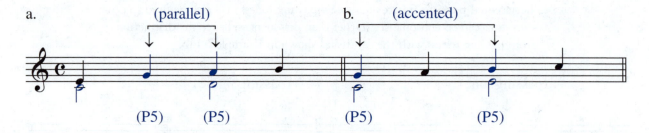

Example 6.15a. Parallel perfect fifths created by the addition of an unaccented consonant skip from E to G, then a step to A.

Example 6.15b. Unaccented passing tones inadequately "disguising" accented perfect fifths.

LEVEL MASTERY 6.4.

Compose a second-species counterpoint for each cantus below. As you do so, be especially alert for any parallel or direct perfect intervals that could be created by unaccented notes.

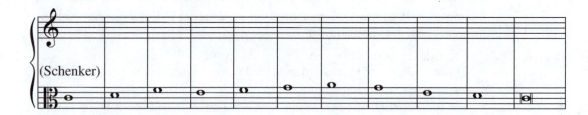

Workbook
Exercise 6.3
may be done
at this time.

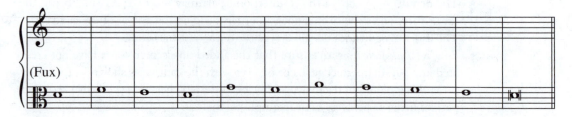

Third Species

In third species counterpoint, the ratio of subdivision (of the cantus) moves to 4:1 in simple meters or 3:1 in compound meters. The principles of melodic writing and the second species of counterpoint apply here, with the following significant additions.

- Example 6.16a illustrates a **neighbor tone**, an unaccented dissonance that is approached by step and then resolves in the *opposite direction* to the original consonance. Neighbor tones and passing tones will appear on the unaccented (second and fourth) eighth notes within the beat.
- Third species counterpoint also allows for the *accented* passing tone, which only occurs in the third eighth note of the beat in a 4:1 texture, as part of a descending line (Example 6.16b).

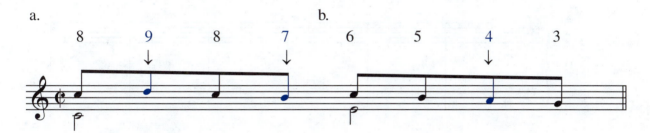

Example 6.16a. Neighbor tones above and below the structural pitch in third-species counterpoint.
Example 6.16b. An accented passing tone in third-species counterpoint.

- Occasionally in compound meter one may also encounter an *unaccented imperfect consonance* as in Example 6.17. This is an example of a **neighbor figure**.

Example 6.17. A neighbor figure in third-species counterpoint.

- Finally, third species counterpoint can also use the **changing tone**, sometimes called a *neighbor group* or *double incomplete neighbor* (Example 6.18). The changing tone is actually a group of four notes; note that the elaborations involve the upper and lower neighbors of the beginning and ending pitch that they modify, and that they occur on the second and third subdivision of the beat in a 4:1 texture. The neighboring tones may occur in either order (upper-lower or lower-upper).

Example 6.18. The changing tone or neighbor group in third-species counterpoint.

LEVEL MASTERY 6.5.

Compose a third-species counterpoint for each cantus below.

a.

b.

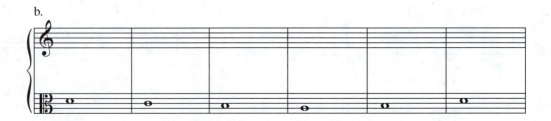

Apply This! 6.1 may be done at this time.

CONCLUSION

With this chapter, we begin our study of part writing, the craft of combining melodic lines into cohesive, goal-directed harmonic progressions. Remember that the earliest Western art music was vocal music; accordingly, your lines should be singable. Our examination of melodic construction kept this in mind, aiming for conjunct motion, avoiding wide leaps or augmented intervals, and a single focal point for a pleasing shape.

We also considered the different classifications of voice-leading motion where two parts are concerned: oblique, parallel, similar, contrary, and of course stationary (where there is no motion at all). Of these, contrary motion is preferred, because it provides independent motion to the parts. Parallel motion should be used sparingly, and only with imperfect consonances; parallel fifths or octaves causes the parts to appear to "fuse" together, temporarily disrupting the independent texture. Ideally there should be a variety of voice leading motions in your part writing.

Terms to Know

conjunct	focal point	reduction
contrary motion	leap	sequence
counterpoint	oblique motion	similar motion
crossing voices	overlapping voices	skip
direct (or hidden) fifths (or octaves)	parallel fifths (or octaves)	stationary motion
disjunct	parallel motion	voice leading

Self-Test

6.1. Label the type(s) of motion that occur(s) in the reduction of the Postal Service song "Such Great Heights" below.

6.2. Critique the following cantus firmi according to the principles for melodic writing discussed in this chapter.

a.

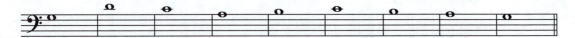

b.

c.

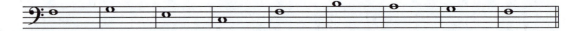

Apply This!

6.1. **Analysis.** Provide harmonic analysis (Roman numerals and inversion symbols) for the passage below. Disregard the chord marked with an *. Identify the types of voice leading, chord by chord, between the highest and lowest parts. Which type(s) of voice leading predominate(s)? Which species of counterpoint best describes the type of soprano-bass activity in this passage?

Camille Saint-Saëns (1835–1921), Symphony no. 3 ("Organ") (iv) (strings only)

CHAPTER 7

FORCES OF RESOLUTION
Tendency Tones, Cadences, and Closure

OVERVIEW

This chapter shows how melodic and harmonic dissonances are harnessed by means of tendency tones, notes that show a strong tendency to resolve in a particular direction, especially in harmonic contexts. From there we examine cadences—harmonic goal-points in a piece of music that function rather like musical punctuation.

CHAPTER OUTLINE

AUDIO LIST

Johann Sebastian Bach, Prelude no. 1 in C major from *The Well-Tempered Clavier,* Book 1, BWV 846

Chicago, "If You Leave Me Now"

Billy Joel, "She's Always a Woman"

Scott Joplin, "The Entertainer"

Wolfgang Amadeus Mozart, Piano Sonata in A major, K.331 (i)

Richard Rodgers and Oscar Hammerstein II, "Do Re Mi" from *The Sound of Music* (motion picture soundtrack)

Clara Schumann, Trio in G minor op. 17 (i)

Robert Schumann, *Arabeske* in C major, op. 18

Stephen Schwartz, "Defying Gravity" (from *Wicked*)

U2, "Where the Streets Have No Name"

TENDENCY TONES

The first, third, and fifth scale degrees are the most stable tones in a key, since they are also the members of the tonic triad. Thus, tones that are not part of the tonic triad are less stable to varying degrees; for example, we know that the seventh scale degree in the major and harmonic minor scales is called the "leading tone" because of its strong tendency to resolve upward. Scale degrees 2 (supertonic), 4 (subdominant), and 6 (submediant) are similarly unstable tones. All of these tones are called **tendency tones** because they display a *strong tendency to resolve in particular directions*, especially in harmonic contexts. Each tendency tone is paired with its tone of resolution to form **tendency tone pairs**. See Example 7.1, which shows the closing chords of the quartet "Bella Figlia" from Verdi's 1851 opera *Rigoletto*.

Example 7.1. Giuseppe Verdi (1813–1901), "Bella Figlia" (Act IV, *Rigoletto*), closing measures. *(Continued)*

(Continued)

"Bella Figlia" closes with a series of V^7 to I progressions in the key of D♭ major. Notice how each voice in the quartet either resolves by step to scale degree 1 or 3 or remains on scale degree 5 (since the dominant scale degree is a common tone of both chords). The resolutions involve scale degrees 4 to 3 (a 4–3 tendency tone pair), 2 to 1 (a 2–1 tendency tone pair), or 7 to 1 (a 7–1 tendency tone pair).

Example 7.2 illustrates how tendency tones are played out in the first four measures of Bach's Prelude no. 1 in C major (BWV 846) from *The Well-Tempered Clavier*, Book 1. The top system shows the musical surface; the bottom system shows its harmonic/textural reduction to a five-voice texture.

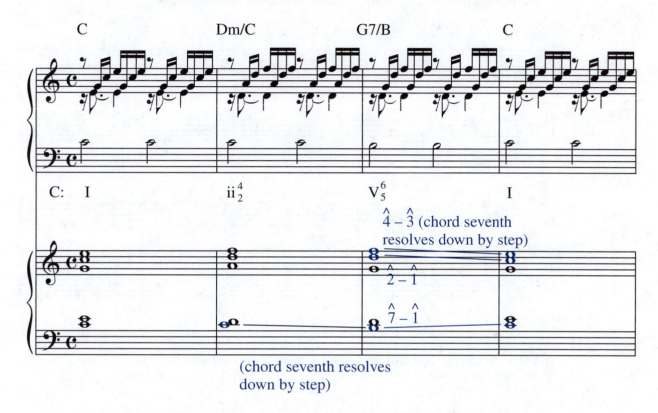

Example 7.2. Bach, Prelude no. 1 in C major, from *The Well-Tempered Clavier*, Book 1, BWV 846, mm. 1–4 with textural reduction.

As the bottom system of Example 7.2 shows, the tendency tone pairs for each voice in the third and fourth measures include scale degrees 4–3 and 2–1 in the top two voices and 7–1 in the bass. The G in the alto voice is the common tone in both chords; the 2–3 motion in the tenor is a keyboard-related expedient that prevents the rapid repetition of the tonic that would happen if scale degree 2 were to go to 1.

Continuing our examination of Example 7.2, notice the resolution of the ii$^4_2$ in measure 2; the bass voice has the chord seventh, and it resolves down by step. In a seventh chord, *chord sevenths tend to resolve downward by step*, and this applies even when the chord is not a V^7.

a. Using Example 7.1 as a model, label, by scale degree, the tendency tone pairs in each of the dominant seventh chord resolutions below.

b. Using tendency tone patterns, resolve each dominant seventh chord appropriately.

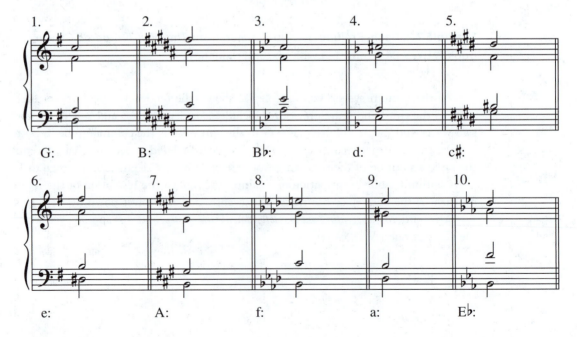

MORE RESOLUTION PRINCIPLES

Let's see how other chord sevenths resolve in Bach's piece. Example 7.3 shows measures 12 through 15. First, prepare a textural reduction modeled after the one in the bottom system of Example 7.2. Then, without attempting Roman numeral labels at this point, find the root, quality, and inversion symbol for each of these chords. Which measures have seventh chords, and in those measures, which voice has the chord seventh? How does the chord seventh resolve in each case?

Example 7.3. Bach, Prelude no. 1 in C major from *The Well-Tempered Clavier*, Book 1, BWV 846, mm. 12–15.

Example 7.3 illustrates another important principle: *chromatically inflected tones tend to resolve in the direction that they have been altered.* A chromatically raised tone—such as the C♯ in measure 12—will tend to resolve upward by step (usually half step). A chromatically lowered tone—such as the B♭ in measure 12—will tend to resolve downward by step (again, usually a half step).

To better understand why the chromatically altered tones resolve the way they do in measures 12 and 13, examine the chord in measure 12 more closely, asking the following questions:

1. What is the quality of the chord in measure 12?
2. Given its quality, what is this chord likely to be? (a _____ of some key)

3. Taking the chords in measures 12 and 13 *out of* the context of C major, in what key would these chords diatonically occur? (Hint: Given your answer for question 2, what scale degree is represented by the root? What key would normally have both B♭ and C♯ in a harmonic minor scale?)

4. Given your answer about which scale degree is represented by the root in question 3, to which tendency tone pair does it belong? What tendency tone pairs are represented by the G–F in the bass line? The E–D in the alto line? (These scale degrees would be of the key you found in response to the third question.)

Having determined from these steps the key to which the chord in measure 12 would normally "belong," we encounter another tendency tone pair not found in the resolution of a dominant seventh chord: 6–5. The chord seventh of a fully-diminished seventh chord in a minor key normally resolves downward; if a fully diminished seventh chord occurs in a major key, the chord seventh is chromatically lowered, and thus it will resolve downward. Measures 14 and 15 illustrate this principle. The A♭ in the tenor in measure 14 is chromatically lowered (from A natural), and so it is a lowered sixth scale degree in C major; it thus resolves downward, as a 6–5 tendency tone pair that is also chromatically inflected.

Of course, this is not always how these tendency tone scale degrees function in a melodic line. Not *all* fourth scale degrees, for example, must resolve to the third scale degree in a melodic line; there are plenty of examples of melodic lines that, on the surface, move upward from a "tendency tone" rather than downward. Often, however, the tendency tone resolution still operates at a background, structural level. In the opening of Bach's Fugue no. 11 in F major (BWV 856) from the *Well-Tempered Clavier*, Book 1 (Example 7.4, upper staff), the B♭ (scale degree 4) on the downbeat of the third measure appears to "resolve" on the surface to C. At a deeper level, however, the pitches that receive metrical accents outline a descending line made up of the tendency tone pairs 6–5 and 4–3 (Example 7.4, lower staff).

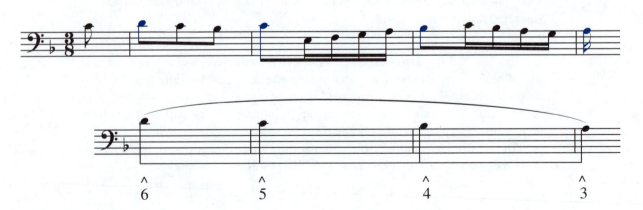

Example 7.4. Bach, Fugue no. 11 in F major from *The Well-Tempered Clavier*, Book 1, BWV 856, fugue subject and melodic reduction.

a. Using Example 7.3 as a model, label, by scale degree, the tendency tone pairs in each of the diminished seventh chord resolutions below. Note which voice moves upward or downward as the result of a chromatic alteration.

Self-Test 7.1 may be done at this time.

Workbook Exercises 7.1 and 7.3 may be done at this time.

b. Using tendency tone patterns in each voice, resolve each diminished seventh chord appropriately. Label the scale degrees involved in each tendency tone resolution.

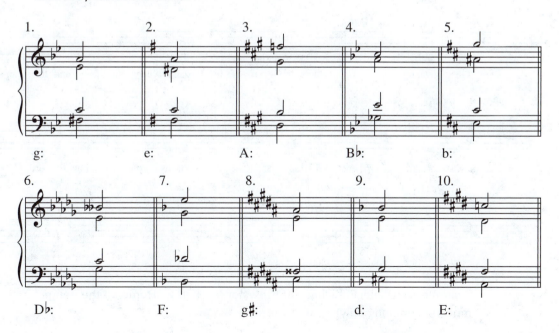

c. Label the tendency tone pairs in the melodic line below (from Brahms's Symphony no. 1, 4th movement).

CADENCES

We have already seen that harmony in Western music has syntactical qualities that resemble the structure of language. Music also resembles language in its way of marking *pauses* in the flow of information. In language, punctuation marks the ends of sentences or clauses, isolates individual elements in lists, or sets aside parts of a sentence for an aside or for greater emphasis. Similarly, **cadences** in music are melodic or harmonic formulas that mark conclusions of phrases, sections, or entire compositions. Just as punctuation carries various degrees of finality—a period conveys a definite end to a sentence, whereas a semicolon does not—cadences are also characterized by whether they are **open** (or inconclusive) or **closed** (conclusive or final).

Consider the folk song "Home on the Range." When one hears only the first phrase (measures 1–8 of Example 7.5), the ending sounds inconclusive. Examining the melody reveals why—the last note is not a member of the tonic chord. An ending on the second scale degree—the first part of a 2–1 tendency tone pair—calls for some sort of closure. This closure is provided by the second phrase of the song (measures 9–16 of Example 7.5), which ends on the tonic; in this way, the 2–1 tendency tone pairing is manifested not only at the surface level ("all day") but also in the final note of each phrase ("play," "day").

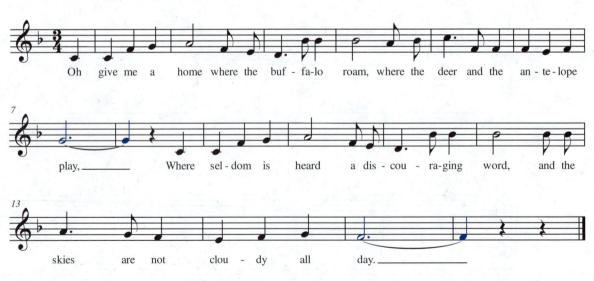

Example 7.5. Daniel E. Kelley and Brewster M. Higley, "Home on the Range," mm. 1–16 (melody only).

Closure is relative—a melodic line need not end on the tonic to signify closure. For example, the first section of Thelonious Monk's 1944 composition "Well You Needn't" (Example 7.6) has phrase endings on scale degrees 4, ♭2, and 4 (in measures 2, 4, and 6 respectively) before finally concluding on a tonic triad member—in this case scale degree 5 rather than the tonic. Closure is still achieved, although not with the emphatic finality of "Home on the Range."

Example 7.6. Thelonious Monk (1917–1982), "Well You Needn't," mm. 1–8 (melody only).

In common-practice music, the term *cadence* usually refers to *harmonic patterns* that mark the end of phrases. **Authentic** cadences involve the *dominant triad or seventh chord resolving to the tonic triad ($V^{(7)} \rightarrow I$)*, and are thus suitable for ending compositions (as well as sections within compositions).

- A **perfect authentic cadence** (abbreviated PAC) must consist of a *root-position* V or V^7 chord resolving to a *root-position* I (or i in minor) *and* must conclude on the *tonic in the soprano.*

Example 7.7 shows perfect authentic cadences in three different genres.

Example 7.7a. Mozart, Menuetto from String Quartet K.458 ("Hunt" Quartet), mm. 1–8.

Example 7.7b. Scott Joplin, "The Entertainer," mm. 17–20.

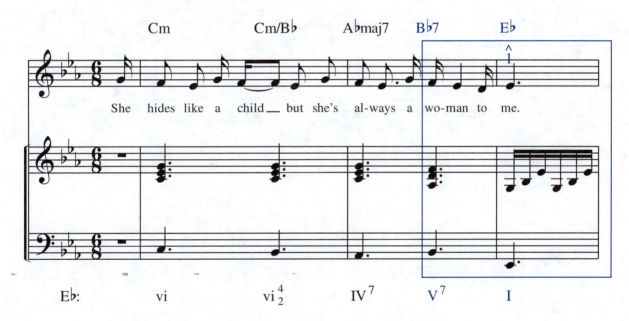

Example 7.7c. Billy Joel, "She's Always a Woman," [0:24–0:29].

- An **imperfect authentic cadence** (abbreviated IAC) is a V (or V^7) to I (or i) cadence in which either chord appears in inversion *or* the soprano line concludes on scale degrees 3 or 5. Thus, a V^6–I cadence is an imperfect authentic cadence, even if the soprano ends on the tonic.

Example 7.8 illustrates imperfect authentic cadences in three different genres; in Example 7.8a, the melody's resolution in measure 4 to scale degree 3 is delayed.

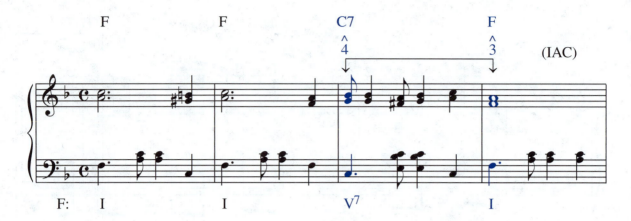

Example 7.8a. "Choucoune" ("Yellow Bird"—traditional Haitian melody).

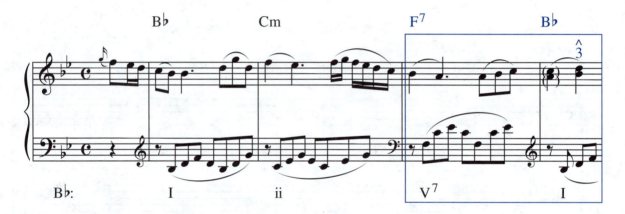

Example 7.8b. Mozart, Piano Sonata in B♭ major K.333 (i), mm. 1–4.

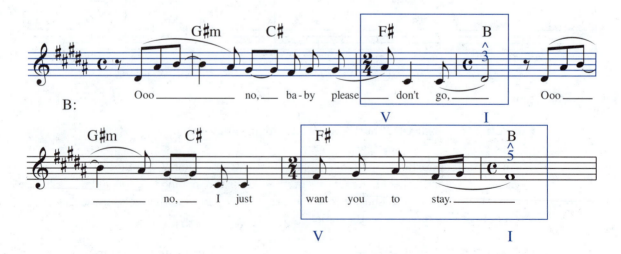

Example 7.8c. Chicago, "If You Leave Me Now," [0:35–0:47].

- A **half cadence** (abbreviated HC) *ends* on V; the penultimate chord is usually a tonic, supertonic, or subdominant chord.

Thus, we can represent a half cadence as $x \rightarrow$ V, since the V may be approached in more than one way. A half cadence functions like a comma in a sentence; it implies an *incomplete* musical statement. A phrase that ends on a half cadence is often immediately followed by a phrase ending on an authentic cadence (Example 7.9).

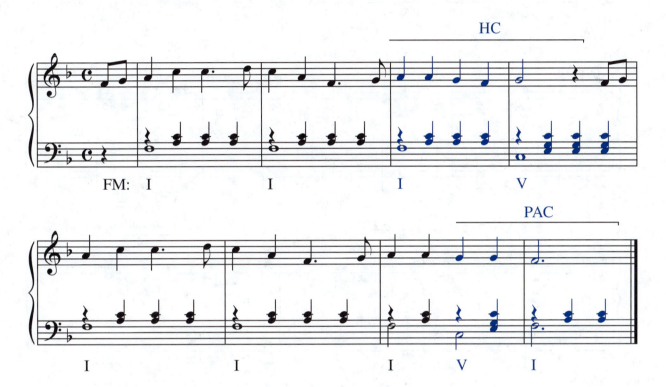

Example 7.9. Stephen Foster (1826–1864), "Oh! Susanna," mm. 1–8, melody and harmonic/textural reduction.

A special type of half cadence that occurs in minor keys, called the **Phrygian cadence**, involves the approach of a V chord from a iv[6] chord; the sixth created in the iv[6] by the bass and the chord root move out by contrary motion to the doubled root in the V chord (Example 7.10). This was a popular closing cadence for slow movements in multi-movement Baroque works; the second movement of Bach's Brandenburg Concerto no. 3, in fact, consists of nothing but the two chords of a Phrygian cadence, leaving conductors and performers to determine what material—if any—will make up the slow movement in approaching the final cadence (Example 7.11).

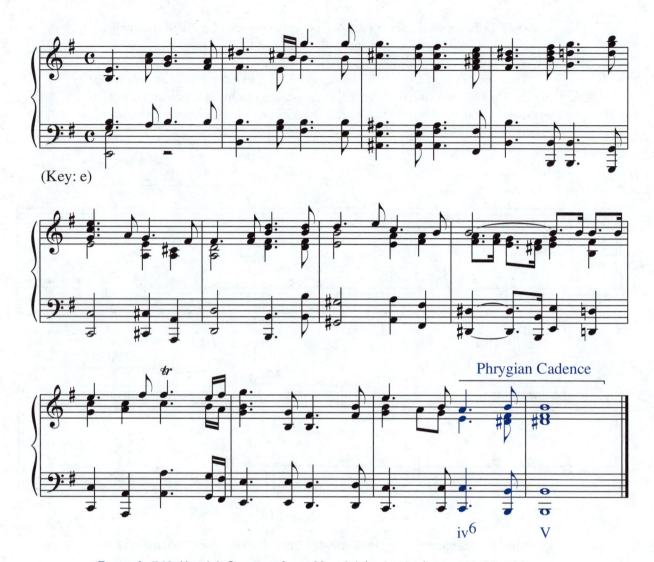

(Key: e)

Phrygian Cadence

iv⁶   V

Example 7.10. Handel, Overture from *Messiah* (reduction), mm. 13–24, with Phrygian cadence marked.

Adagio.

(strings)

Example 7.11. Bach, Brandenburg Concerto no. 3, second movement.

- In a **deceptive cadence** (abbreviated DC), $V^{(7)}$ resolves to something other than a tonic chord ($V^{(7)} \rightarrow x$, where x is not I).

A deceptive cadence results because we expect the tendency tones in a V or V^7 to resolve to tones in a tonic chord. The most common deceptive cadence progression is $V \rightarrow vi$ (Example 7.12); the tendency tone pairs of 7–1, 2–1, and 4–3 (if V^7 is used) are all followed, but the bass moves 5–6 rather than 5–1.

Example 7.12. A deceptive cadence of V–vi, in major and minor.

See Web Feature 7.1 for other examples of deceptive cadences.

Usually the effect of a deceptive cadence is to extend the musical phrase briefly to allow for the "correct" (expected) conclusion on an authentic cadence. "Defying Gravity," from Stephen Schwartz's musical *Wicked* (Example 7.13), concludes with a considerable build-up—complete with a ritard (slowing of tempo)—to the expected I chord. Although we do briefly hear the tonic *pitch*, unaccompanied [5:27], the expected tonic *harmony* is replaced with the unexpected vi chord almost immediately thereafter, prolonging the coda that follows (the tonic chord soon arrives at [5:44]).

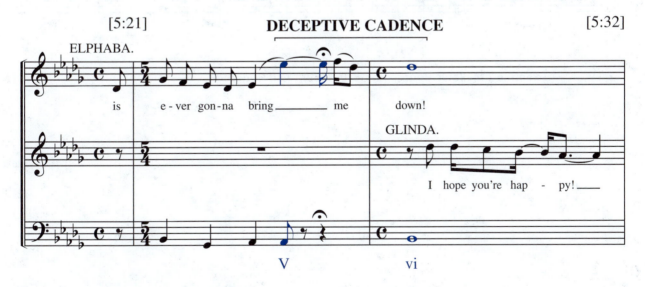

Example 7.13. Stephen Schwartz (b. 1948), "Defying Gravity," from *Wicked*, 2003 [5:21–5:32].

- The **plagal cadence** (abbreviated PC) uses the progression IV → I (or iv → i in minor).

The plagal cadence is often found in the "Amen" conclusion of many church hymns, where it functions to reaffirm the tonic after an authentic cadence at the end of the hymn (Example 7.14). Rarely is it used alone to conclude a movement or an entire composition; one notable exception, from the first movement of Clara Schumann's Trio in G minor (1846), is shown in Example 7.15.

PLAGAL CADENCE

IV   I

Example 7.14. Louis Bourgeois (1510–1559), "Old Hundred."

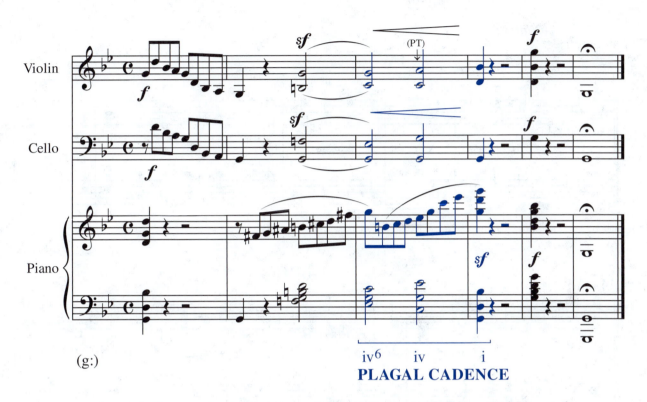

iv^6 iv   i

PLAGAL CADENCE

(g:)

Example 7.15. Clara Schumann (1819–1896), Trio in G minor (i), mm. 282–287.

Sometimes a phrase ends on a chord that appears to function briefly in another key (which may not be confirmed by the music that follows). In Example 7.16, from Jean Sibelius's *Finlandia* (1899), the cadence at measures 146–147 would appear to be vii$^{ø6}_5$–III. A more elegant interpretation, however, would be to read this as a half cadence in F minor (ii$^{ø6}_5$–V), even though the phrase that follows is not in F minor but A♭ major. In this situation we would label the cadence vi:HC, where the "vi" represents the implied key's relationship to the tonic (F minor being the vi of A♭ major).

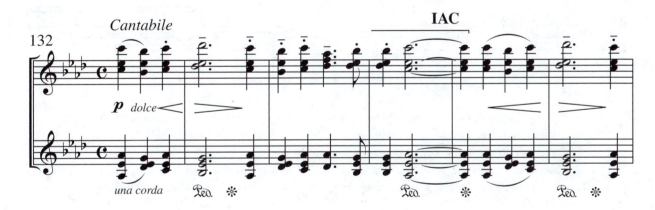

Example 7.16. Jean Sibelius (1865–1957), *Finlandia*, mm. 132–155. *(Continued)*

(Continued)

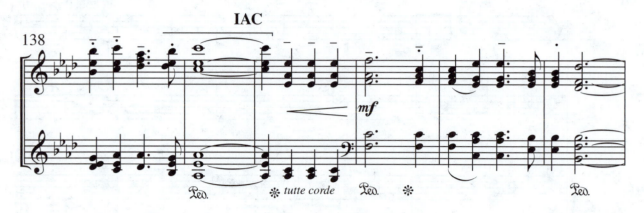

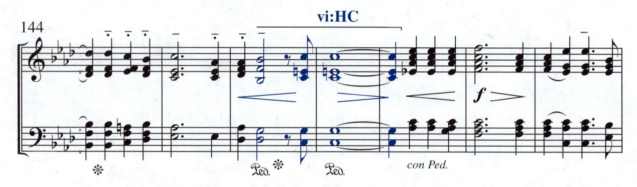

Robert Schumann's *Arabeske* (Example 7.17), one of our listening examples from Chapter 1, has a ii:IAC at measure 4, a V:IAC at measure 8 (acting globally as a half cadence in the tonic key of C major), an IAC at measure 12, and a PAC at measure 16. Thus, with the work beginning on a I and looking at the chords that conclude each of the cadences, a large-scale progression of I–ii–V–I unfolds over the first twelve measures, with measures 13–16 providing a more conclusive repetition of measures 9–12.

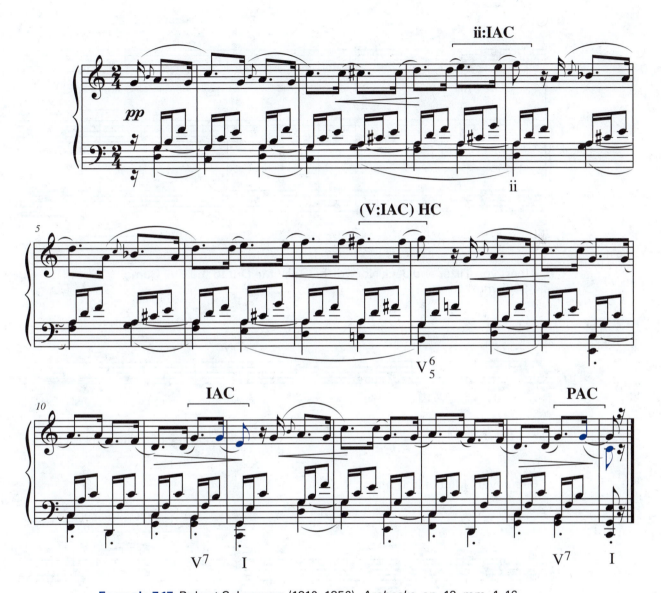

Example 7.17. Robert Schumann (1810–1856), *Arabeske*, op. 18, mm. 1–16.

LEVEL MASTERY 7.3.

Label the cadences, marked in brackets in each score excerpt on the following pages, by type (PAC, IAC, HC, DC, PC). If the cadence does not fit one of these main categories, consider whether it might function in another key (as, for example, a vi:HC).

a. Franz Schubert (1797–1828), "Der Lindenbaum" from *Winterreise*, no. 5, mm. 9–12.

Cadence: _____

Am Brun - nen vor dem To - re   da steht   ein Lin den - baum;

b. Albert von Tilzer and Jack Norworth, "Take Me Out to the Ball Game" (1908), mm. 49–56.

Cadence: _____

root,   root root for the   home   team;   If   they   don't win it's a   shame. ___

(Note: the key of this excerpt is C major)

c. Beethoven, Minuet in G major, WoO 10, no. 2, mm. 1–4.

Cadence: _____

d. Edvard Grieg (1843–1907), "Death of Åse," no. 2 from *Peer Gynt Suite no. 1*, op. 46, mm. 1–8.

e. George Frideric Handel (1685–1759), "Hallelujah!" from *Messiah*, Part 2, mm. 92–95.

Cadence: _____

f. Queen, "Don't Stop Me Now" (1978), [1:18–1:29].

(key: F)

g. Beethoven, Piano Sonata no. 12 in A♭ major, op. 26 (i), mm. 9–16.

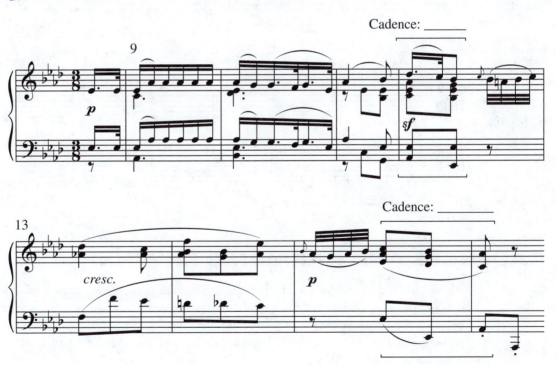

h. Jonathan E. Spilman (1812–1896), "Flow Gently, Sweet Afton."

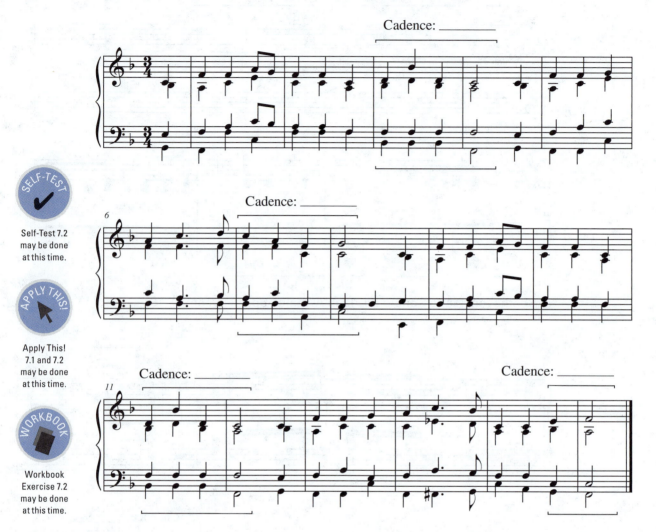

CADENCES AND HARMONIC RHYTHM

Although cadences are classified by particular harmonic progressions (such as V–I or iv⁶–V), not every example of these distinctive progressions is a cadence. A cadence by definition occurs at the *end* of a musical phrase, acting as a harmonic *goal* for the passage. The final chord of a cadence usually occurs on the strong beat in a metric structure (Example 7.18).

Mozart, Piano Sonata no. 11 in A major, K.331 (i), mm. 5–8.
(strong beats)

A: V⁷ I

Maroon 5, "This Love."
(strong beats)

She's said   good-bye too | ma-ny times be-fore

E♭:   V⁷   I
                                   (implied)

Example 7.18. Metric placement of typical cadences.

One way to recognize the location of cadences is to observe changes in the harmonic rhythm. A cadence is often heralded by acceleration in the harmonic rhythm beforehand, or (less frequently) deceleration. Accelerating the harmonic rhythm gives the impression of being propelled toward the cadence; deceleration, on the other hand, can be used as a dramatic device to increase harmonic tension, which is then released with the closure provided by the cadence (Example 7.19a and b). It is often easier to recognize cadences in music when they are heard; with practice, you will find it easier to recognize cadences in a musical score by sight.

G: I ———————————————————————— ii⁴₂ ———
(harmonic rhythm)

Example 7.19a. Acceleration of harmonic rhythm before a cadence: Beethoven, Piano Sonata op. 14, no. 2 (i), mm. 1–8. *(Continued)*

(Continued)

(increase in harmonic rhythm) - - - - - - - - - - - - - - -

(prevailing harmonic rhythm has been two chords per measure)

(harmonic rhythm slows down) - - - - - - - - - - -

Example 7.19b. Deceleration of harmonic rhythm before a cadence: Stephen Schwartz, "March of the Witch-Hunters" from *Wicked*, mm. 46–52. *(Continued)*

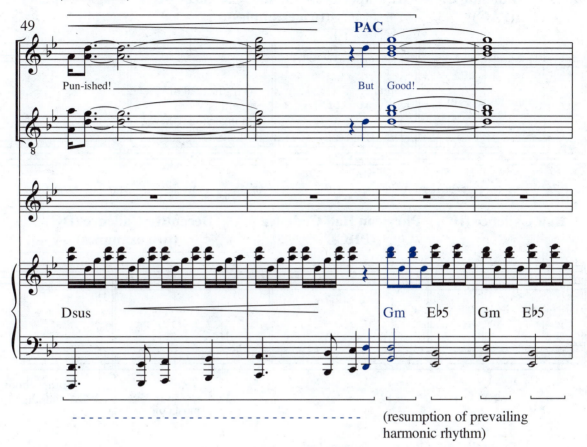

(resumption of prevailing harmonic rhythm)

CONCLUSION

In this chapter, we began the process of building up units of musical structure "from the bottom up." By examining how certain tones are connected to others in tendency tone pairs, we provide a tonal context for the discussion of dissonance that was introduced in Chapter 2. Combinations of tendency-tone pairs give us the proper resolution of dominant chords to their corresponding tonic, leading us to the consideration of how cadences serve to punctuate the musical flow. Example 7.20 provides a concise summary of these cadences, with examples. In the next chapter we will move into successively larger units of grouping musical flow.

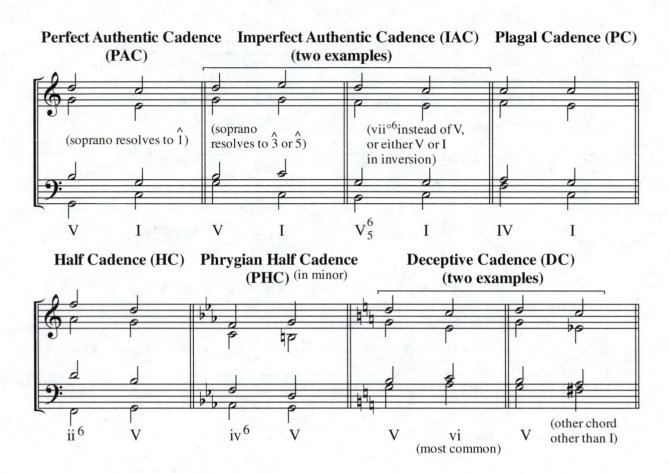

Example 7.20. Table of cadences.

Terms to Know

cadence

closed (applied to
  cadences)

deceptive cadence (DC)

half cadence (HC)

imperfect authentic
  cadence (IAC)

open (applied to cadences)

perfect authentic cadence
  (PAC)

Phrygian cadence (PHC)

plagal cadence (PC)

tendency tones

Self-Test

7.1. Resolve the following dominant and diminished seventh chords, in the keys indicated, using the tendency tone patterns discussed in this chapter. Identify the key and label each chord with Roman numeral and inversion symbol (all chords will be a V^7 or vii^{o7}, in root position or in some inversion). Then label your tendency-tone pairs voice by voice, using scale degrees.

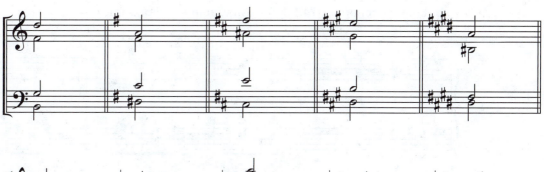

7.2. Identify the cadences marked with brackets in the following musical examples. Provide Roman numeral/inversion symbol analysis, and circle any tones that do not belong to the prevailing harmony.

a. Fréderic Chopin (1810–1849), Nocturne in E-flat major, op. 9 no. 2, mm. 1–4.

b. Luigi Boccherini (1743–1805), Minuet in A major, mm. 1–4.

c. Wolfgang Amadeus Mozart (1756–1791), "Ave Verum Corpus," mm. 34–37.

d. Modest Mussorgsky (1839–1881), "Gopak" from *The Fair at Sorochintsy*, mm. 26–33.

e. Harry Dacre (1860–1922), "Daisy Bell (Bicycle Built for Two)," mm. 1–8.

Apply This!

7.1. Analysis.

Consider the example below, a stereotypical cadence from the traditional carol "The Twelve Days of Christmas." Based on your harmonic analysis of the passage, would you say that this is an example of a deceptive cadence? Why or why not?

7.2. Improvisation.

Using only the Roman numerals and inversion symbols provided below, play the following progressions at the keyboard. (Lowercase letters indicate minor keys.) Work with a partner and see if you can spot any tendency tone resolution errors in one another's playing (leading tones not resolving upward by step, chord sevenths not resolving downward by step, etc.).

A: iii_5^6–vi–ii_5^6–V–I

f: i^6–$\text{ii}^{\circ 6}$–i_4^6–V–i

G: I–vi–ii^6–V^7–I

e♭: i–i_2^4–$\text{ii}^{\circ 4}_3$–V

CHAPTER 8

PART WRITING WITH ROOT-POSITION TRIADS

OVERVIEW

This chapter begins a study of part writing—the realization of harmonic progressions through controlled voice leading. After beginning with a consideration of chord spacing and doubling, the basic principles of part writing are examined before moving to specifics of how one root-position chord is connected to another through "the law of the shortest way."

In the last chapter we examined the role that tendency tones play in resolving the V (or vii°⁷) chord to I. In this chapter we will begin to more generally explore how chords are put together in progressions, through **part writing**—the governing procedures by which individual voices move from one chord to the next. Although music is sometimes in more or less than four parts, in this chapter we will work in four-part textures, corresponding to the vocal parts of soprano, alto, tenor and bass.

There are three common **scores**, or visual layouts, for four-part textures. Example 8.1 shows a C major chord written in **keyboard score**. Example 8.2 shows the same C major chord written in **choral score**, with the soprano and alto parts in treble clef and the tenor and bass parts in bass clef; Example 8.3 shows the chord in **open score**, one part per staff. The specific clefs used in open score will vary according to the medium. Example 8.3 shows the chord scored for the string quartet medium (reading top to bottom: treble, treble, alto, and bass clefs).

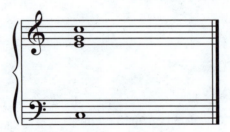

Example 8.1. C major chord in keyboard score.

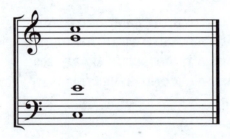

Example 8.2. C major chord in choral score.

Example 8.3. C major chord in open score.

CHORD SPACING

The arrangement of chord members in a four-part texture, whether the chord is a triad or a seventh chord, is called **spacing**.

- When there is *less than an octave* between the *tenor and soprano*, the chord is in **close spacing**.
- When there is *an octave or more* between the *tenor and soprano*, the chord is in **open spacing**.

See Example 8.4.

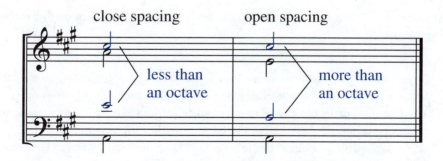

Example 8.4. Examples of close and open spacing.

In arranging a chord, do not allow more than an octave between *soprano and alto*, or between *alto and tenor* (Example 8.5). More than an octave between *tenor and bass* is acceptable.

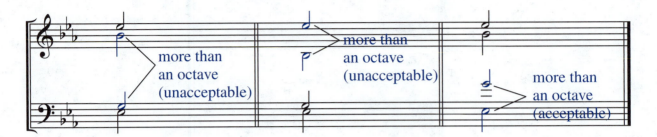

Example 8.5. Examples of unacceptable and acceptable chord spacing between adjacent voices.

DOUBLING

When setting a triad in a four-voice texture, one of the tones must be doubled.

- *In a root-position triad, the root of the chord (the bass) is doubled* (Example 8.6).

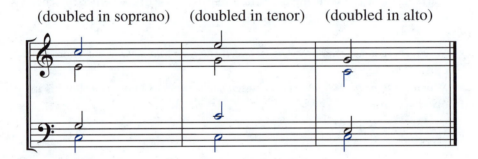

Example 8.6. Three root-position triads, each with the root doubled in a different voice.

- *In a first-inversion triad, the soprano note is usually doubled. Depending on the context in which a first-inversion triad appears, other parts may be doubled*, in order to avoid parallel fifths or octaves or other voice leading errors. If the soprano note cannot be doubled, then double the bass; if neither soprano nor bass doubling works satisfactorily, double the inner voices (alto doubled by tenor) (Example 8.7). Avoid doubling the bass in a first-inversion V chord; this results in doubling the leading tone (an active tendency tone). This topic is addressed in more detail in Chapter 9.

(doubled in bass)   (doubled in tenor)   (doubled in alto)

Example 8.7. Three first-inversion triads each with the soprano note doubled in a different voice.

- *In a second-inversion triad, double the bass note* (the fifth of the triad). The most common context of a $^6_4$ chord is in the progression I$^6_4$ (or i$^6_4$)–V (a so-called "cadential six-four chord"); in this progression, the bass and its doubling part *do not move* from the first chord to the next. Example 8.8 shows the second-inversion triad, grouped together with its chord of resolution, with the bass doubled three different ways. This topic is addressed in more detail in Chapter 10.

Example 8.8. Second-inversion triads, with resolutions to V, the bass doubled in three different voices.

LEVEL MASTERY 8.1.

Spell the following triads in the indicated spacings and inversions, in four-part texture with proper doubling. Do not use key signatures.

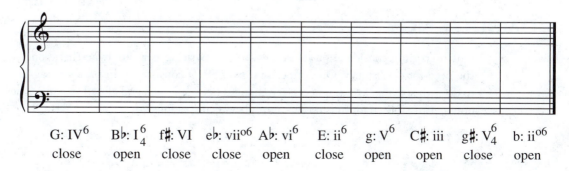

| G: IV^6 | B♭: I$^6_4$ | f♯: VI | e♭: vii^{o6} | A♭: vi^6 | E: ii^6 | g: V^6 | C♯: iii | g♯: V$^6_4$ | b: ii^{o6} |
| close | open | close | close | open | close | open | open | close | open |

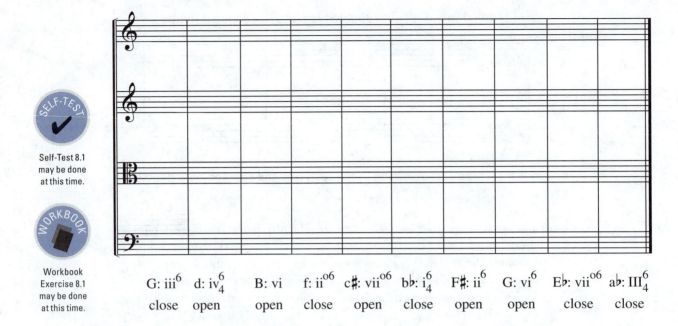

Self-Test 8.1
may be done
at this time.

Workbook
Exercise 8.1
may be done
at this time.

G: iii^6 d: iv$^6_4$ B: vi   f: ii^{o6} c#: vii^{o6} bb: i$^6_4$ F#: ii^6 G: vi^6 Eb: vii^{o6} ab: III$^6_4$

close   open   open   close   open   close   open   open   close   close

FROM DOUBLING TO VOICE LEADING

Voice leading considerations are shaped by the contrapuntal aesthetic that guided polyphony from the Renaissance until the twentieth century (and, for some composers, beyond). *Independence* between parts was valued. Perhaps, if you have had experience performing in a vocal or instrumental ensemble, you can understand why—it is somehow more satisfying for all involved if everyone has a singable, melodic part instead of a single repeated note all the time. Of the different relationships between parts, parallel motion is least desirable because it locks two parts together, preventing independent movement; contrary motion is most preferable because it tends to emphasize the independence of parts. It is best to use a mixture of different part-against-part motions for variety, using parallel motion with extreme care (and not at all in the case of perfect intervals). At the same time, too much independence—as for example parts that frequently cross and obscure each other's lines—make it difficult for the listener to keep track of each part in the texture, so another goal is to strive for *clarity* of parts.

CONSISTENCY

Our overriding consideration for successful part writing is a purely aesthetic one—the need for consistency. One important example of consistency in part writing has to do with spacing: avoid unnecessary changes between open and closed spacing. The only permissible conditions for changing between spacings are:

- Repetitions of the *same harmony* (Example 8.9a);
- *Connection by thirds*, in which the third of the first chord moves to the third of the second chord in the same voice (Example 8.9b);
- A spacing change *facilitated by an inverted chord* so the movement from one spacing to another is not direct (Example 8.9c).

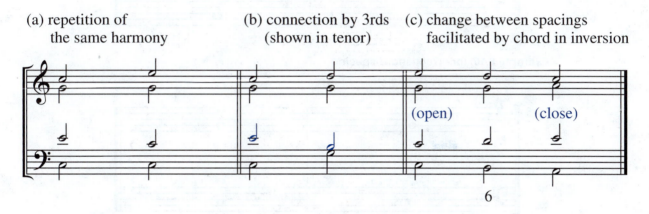

(a) repetition of
    the same harmony

(b) connection by 3rds
    (shown in tenor)

(c) change between spacings
    facilitated by chord in inversion

Example 8.9. Acceptable methods of changing between open and close spacing.

GENERAL PART WRITING PRINCIPLES

Although the music of the common-practice period is quite diverse in style, genre, and texture, nevertheless we can find that a few stylistic generalizations apply.

- *Stepwise motion* in parts is preferred, following what composer Anton Bruckner called *the law of the shortest way*.
- The intervals found in melodic writing tend to be diatonic; diminished and augmented intervals are rare.

The "Golden Rule" of part writing is this: *Treat each voice respectfully*. This means to give each voice a good line to sing, by observing the following guiding principles:

PRINCIPLE 1. *Keep voices a reasonable distance apart, allowing each voice to be heard clearly and independently.* If the voices are too close (overlapping, or too close together in the lower parts), they are confusing; if they are too distant, they do not mesh well. In general, *place no more than an octave between adjacent voices* (with this exception: the bass may separate a little more from the tenor). Example 8.10 shows chords with unacceptable spacing errors; Example 8.10 shows the same chords arranged with acceptable spacing.

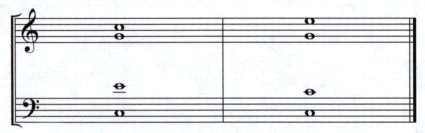

(more than an
octave between
tenor and alto)

(more than an octave
between alto and soprano)

Example 8.10. Incorrect chord spacing.

(more than an octave
between bass and tenor
is acceptable)

Example 8.11. Acceptable chord spacing.

PRINCIPLE 2. *Let each voice follow its natural inclination, respecting tendency tones.* That means that when a voice has a strong tendency to move to a specific note, generally allow it to do so. We learned in Chapter 7 how certain scale degrees—7, 4, 2, and sometimes 6—are associated with tendency tone pairs that determine their resolution to more stable tones associated with the tonic triad: 7–1, 4–3, 2–1, 6–5. Those tendencies should be honored in part writing.

Example 8.12 shows how tendency tones may be used to properly resolve a dominant seventh chord in its different inversions to the tonic chord. The most important tendency tone resolution—especially if it is in an outer voice—is to resolve the leading tone to the tonic (7–1). Next most important is the resolution of the chord seventh, which in this chord is scale degree 4 (4–3).

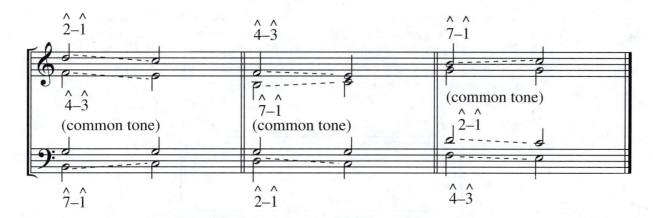

Example 8.12. Resolutions of dominant seventh chords in different inversions, showing disposition of tendency tones.

Resolving a root-position dominant seventh chord presents a different problem. If we strictly follow all of the tendency tone resolutions, we find that the dominant seventh will resolve to an *incomplete* tonic triad in which the fifth is missing (Example 8.13a). This is perfectly acceptable. (However, *always* include the third—"open fifth" sonorities are not acceptable in common-practice style.) If a complete tonic chord is desired, it is permissible in this circumstance for the leading tone *in an inner voice* (tenor or alto) to resolve down to the fifth of the tonic chord, as shown in Example 8.13b. This is called a **free resolution**. A dominant seventh chord may also be spelled *incompletely*, again usually lacking the fifth because of the importance of the leading tone; this will also resolve to a *complete* triad, as shown in Example 8.13c.

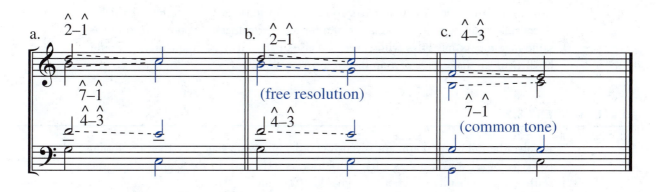

Example 8.13. (a) Complete-to-incomplete V⁷–I resolution; (b) Free resolution of leading tone to create a complete-to-complete resolution; (c) Incomplete-to-complete V⁷–I resolution.

Melodic augmented seconds and augmented fourths are to be avoided when changes of harmony are involved. Occasionally, however, a descending melodic movement of a diminished fifth or diminished seventh may be used in the bass. A diminished fourth is also sometimes permitted, if the context is one of a connection by thirds, as shown in Example 8.14 (see "Consistency" above).

Example 8.14. Connection-by-thirds spacing change in minor, example of a permissible diminished-fourth leap (in tenor).

Another aspect of the principle of letting each voice follow its natural course is to *resolve chromatic tones in the direction of their alteration*: raised notes up, lowered notes down, as discussed in Chapter 7. Such resolutions are almost always stepwise.

PRINCIPLE 3. *Let each voice do something independent and interesting.* This means that situations that cause voices to "fuse" together (as in parallel perfect fifths or octaves) or be hard to hear should be avoided. Sometimes, students will place a common tone in an inner voice, such as an alto line, and make it stick there for as long as possible. Unfortunately, the sameness of the part causes it to recede into the background if other parts are moving, and consequently it becomes harder to pick out in the texture. Make sure that individual parts do not remain stationary for too long. (It helps to consider your exercises as being written for real performers; if you had to sing the same note for six measures while everyone else's parts changed frequently, it would be difficult to make your part an inspired performance!)

LEVEL MASTERY 8.2.

Resolve the following dominant seventh chords, following tendency tone resolution patterns for all voices, unless a free resolution is indicated. In the blanks above the staff, indicate whether the chord is complete (C) or incomplete (I).

(free res.)

c#: V^7 F: V$^6_5$ A: V$^4_2$ bb: V^7 Eb: V$^4_3$

(free res.)

D: V$^4_2$ f: V^7 B: V^7 Ab: V$^6_5$ f#: V$^4_3$

Self-Test 8.2 may be done at this time.

Workbook Exercise 8.2 may be done at this time.

CONNECTING TRIADS WITH THE SAME ROOT

When a root-position triad is repeated, a spacing change is permissible. In both chords, the root is usually doubled. Under certain circumstances, the fifth may be omitted; this is especially common in three-part writing. The bass note may change octave if necessary. Example 8.15 shows examples for both four-part (SATB) and three-part (SAB) textures.

four parts   three parts

Example 8.15. Connecting two triads with the same root in four-part and three-part writing.

CONNECTING TRIADS A FOURTH (FIFTH) APART

We have already seen in our study of tendency tones how V resolves to I. The most economical part writing solution calls for the common tone shared by both chords to be held in the same voice; the remaining two parts (other than the bass) proceed by the "law of the shortest way," in parallel thirds or sixths (Example 8.16).

Example 8.16. Connecting two triads with roots a fourth (fifth) apart, using common tone connection.

A second method, especially when the soprano and bass are moving in contrary motion, is to have all three upper parts move in similar motion, again following the "law of the shortest way." If the leading tone is in an inner voice, it may move downward to scale degree 5 by free resolution. See Example 8.17.

Example 8.17. Connecting two triads with the root a fourth (fifth) apart, using similar motion in upper voices.

For three-part writing, triads should always have at least a root and a third (never omit the third), and aim for smooth voice leading (Example 8.18).

Eb: I   IV   iii   vi   ii   V   V   I

Example 8.18. Connecting two triads with the root a fourth (fifth) apart in three-part (SAB) writing.

CONNECTING TRIADS A THIRD (SIXTH) APART

Connecting triads a third or sixth apart in a four-part texture is usually simple, because the chords will always have two common tones. The remaining upper voice will move stepwise. In three-part textures, be especially careful to avoid parallel fifths. See Example 8.19.

four parts   three parts

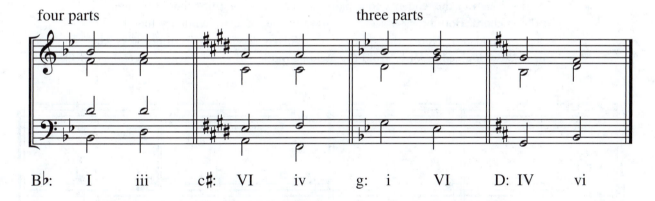

Bb: I   iii   c#: VI   iv   g: i   VI   D: IV   vi

Example 8.19. Connecting two triads with the root a third (sixth) apart.

CONNECTING TRIADS A SECOND (SEVENTH) APART

When connecting triads a second (or, less commonly, a seventh) apart, all of the parts will move—there are no common tones. How the parts move will depend on whether the outer voices are moving in contrary or parallel motion.

- If the soprano and bass move in contrary motion, the alto and tenor simply move in the same direction as the soprano to the nearest chord tone (Example 8.20).

four parts   three parts

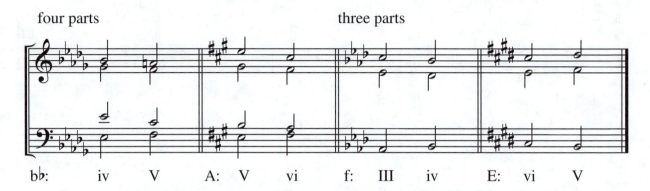

b♭: iv V A: V vi f: III iv E: vi V

Example 8.20. Connecting two triads with roots a second apart, when outer voices move in contrary motion.

- If the soprano and bass move in parallel motion, the usual solution is to double the third of the second chord in the progression, as shown in the first of the major and minor progressions in Example 8.21.

A quick review of the tendency tone pairs explains why the third should be doubled in the vi chord: Both of the voices that move to the tonic are tendency tone resolutions, 7–1 and 2–1. Notice that when V^7 is resolved deceptively in minor keys, the third is also doubled in VI to avoid the melodic motion of an augmented second.

Example 8.21. $V^{(7)}$–VI progressions in major and minor, showing doubling of the third at resolution.

Finally, *the vii° triad almost never appears in root position*; to do so would call for doubling the root, which is the leading tone. Instead, it is best to use the vii° triad in first inversion and double the bass (alternatively, the soprano may be doubled if it is not the leading tone). This will be demonstrated in the next chapter.

a. Add alto and tenor voices to the four-part progressions below, using common tones as much as possible and following "the law of the shortest way" otherwise. Use proper doubling and spacing.

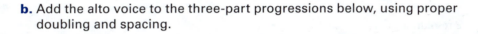

eb: i   VI   iv   i   F: I   iii   vi   V   B: vi   IV   ii   V   Eb: I   ii   V   vi

b. Add the alto voice to the three-part progressions below, using proper doubling and spacing.

Db: I   vi   IV   V   e: VI   iv   i   V   c: i   III   VI   iv   E: I   IV   V   vi

CONCLUSION

Part writing can be difficult at first, because it seems as if there are so many "rules" to remember. You might find that parallel fifths and octaves, like weeds, are especially difficult to eradicate. To learn part writing is to master the common grammar of a historical style; it can be difficult, but with repeated exposure and practice comes familiarity, and it begins to make much more sense and become much more enjoyable. You will also come to recognize how common-practice part writing principles are found in other styles of music: pop and rock, film music, and jazz. Finally, familiarity with common-practice style will also make it easier for you to predict the likely direction of musical progressions, making you a more skillful sight-reader and improviser.

It helps to remember the few principles that are introduced at the beginning of this chapter: *Let each voice be heard clearly and independently; let each voice follow its natural inclination; let each voice do something independent and interesting.* These principles provide the rationale for all of the specific procedures involved in writing four-part harmony. For example, incorrect chord spacing results in tones in the low register being indistinct from each other, thus not allowing each voice to be heard clearly and independently; Doubling a leading tone creates a conflict between allowing each voice to follow its natural inclination (resolving to the tonic) and having its independence.

If you keep these principles in mind, along with the tendency tone pairs introduced in Chapter 7, you will find that your part writing will be free of the most common errors.

Terms to Know

choral score	keyboard score	open spacing
close spacing	open score	part writing
free resolution		

Self-Test

8.1. Spell the following triads in the indicated spacings and inversions, in four-part texture with proper doubling. Do not use key signatures.

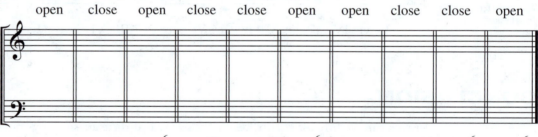

G: IV   b: ii^{o6} eb: VI$^6_4$ A: iii   F#: IV^6 c#: V$^6_4$ bb: iv   B: vii^{o6} Eb: I$^6_4$ c: vii$^{o6}_4$

8.2. Spell the indicated dominant seventh chords, in the proper inversion and spacing. Then, resolve the chords to I as indicated, following tendency tone resolution patterns for all voices, unless a free resolution is indicated. In the blanks above the staff, indicate whether the chords are complete (C) or incomplete (I). Use key signatures. The first one is done for you.

8.3. Given the first chord, add a soprano part to the bass lines below, following the chord progressions given. Then, add alto and tenor voices, using common tones as much as possible and following "the law of the shortest way" otherwise. Use proper doubling and spacing.

E: I   V   vi   IV   d: i   VI   iv   V   B♭: vi   IV   V   I   b: i   III   VI   V

8.4. Add the alto voice to the three-part progressions below, using proper doubling and spacing.

f: i   VI   iv   V   d: III   VI   iv   V   G♭:   ii   V   iii   vi   D: vi   IV   V   I

Apply This!

8.1. On the next page is an example of a "Sacred Harp" song, a type of American hymn that dates from the eighteenth century. Composers of these hymns often lacked formal "classical" training and composed instead by instinct—how parts sounded together—following the words of colonial composer William Billings, "Nature must lay the foundation, Nature must inspire the thought."[1] As a result, this example contains a number of "improper" doublings, crossed voices, and parallel perfect intervals. Find and label them all.

---

[1] William Billings, "To All Musical Practitioners." In Gilbert Chase, ed., *The American Composer Speaks: A Historical Anthology, 1770-1965* (Louisiana State University Press, 1965), 30.

TENNESSEE Unknown composer, first published in *Baptist Harmony* (1834)

Afflictions, though they seem severe,
Are oft in mercy sent;
They stopp'd the prodigal's career,
And caused him to repent.

Although he no relenting felt
Till he had spent his store,
His stubborn heart began to melt
When famine pinch'd him sore.

CHAPTER 9

PART WRITING WITH FIRST-INVERSION TRIADS AND SEVENTH CHORDS

OVERVIEW

This chapter considers the application of part-writing principles involving first-inversion triads and seventh chords.

CHAPTER OUTLINE

Although part writing with root-position chords is certainly serviceable, it is usually not entirely adequate for smooth progressions. Looking at the progressions in Chapter 8, the bass lines have a tendency to "leap" excessively, and when all the chords are in root position, there is little distinction between chords that act as the goal of a passage and chords that may serve a transitory or embellishing function. Using first-inversion triads—triads with the third in the bass—can improve your part writing in the following ways:

- Bass lines will be more naturally melodic (remember that melodies favor conjunct motion) and interesting;
- The relative "weight" or function of chords (structural versus embellishing) will be clarified.

DOUBLING IN FIRST-INVERSION TRIADS

As we learned in the previous chapter, arranging triads in a four-part texture requires the doubling of a chord member. We saw that in root-position triads the root is normally doubled. Doubling in first-inversion triads is more contextual, depending on the voice leading from the chord preceding the first-inversion triad and the voice leading to the chord that follows it. Example 9.1 shows the three doubling scenarios:

- The bass (third of the triad) is doubled in the tenor or alto;
- The soprano is doubled in the tenor or alto;
- The tenor and alto are doubled.
- *Note: Doubling the bass note of a V⁶ triad should be avoided.* This note is the leading tone and, as an active tendency tone, should not be doubled to avoid the situation of either parallel octaves or one voice not following its proper tendency tone resolution pattern.

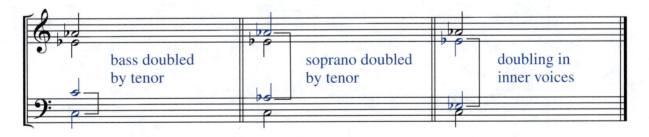

Example 9.1. Doubling in a first-inversion triad.

Often the specific doubling solution will be determined by the structure of the chords on either side of it. Given the task of assigning parts over the bass line in Example 9.2a, the solution in Example 9.2b is incorrect because of parallel fifths between the soprano and alto; Example 9.2c contains parallel octaves between the bass and alto.

Example 9.2d, which uses the I⁶ doubling from Example 9.2b and the voicing of the ii chord in Example 9.2c, offers the smoothest voice leading solution.

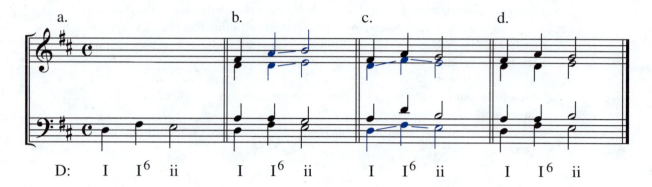

Example 9.2. Incorrect and correct doubling solutions for a first-inversion triad.

LEVEL MASTERY 9.1.

Provide alto and tenor for the following progressions. Begin each progression in the spacing indicated (you may change spacing by the end). Make sure that your doubling in the first-inversion triad does not create parallel fifths or octaves with the chords before or after it.

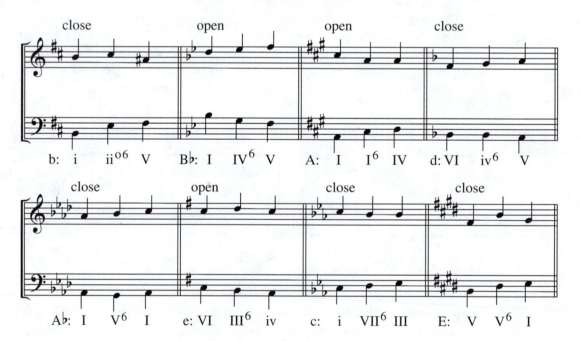

PARALLEL FIRST-INVERSION TRIADS

In progressions where first-inversion triads occur consecutively, one will usually find the root of at least one chord in the soprano to avoid parallel fifths; the doubling in the two chords will usually also be different, to avoid parallel fifths or octaves (Example 9.3). Note the use of the minor v chord in Example 9.3b.

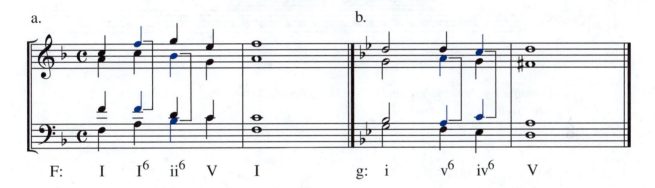

Example 9.3. Part writing of progressions with consecutive first-inversion triads, doublings shown with brackets.

Sometimes chains of consecutive first-inversion triads appear in the literature, often as part of a sequence. Such passages do not function in the same way as a single first-inversion triad, usually serving a passing function between chords or keys. Example 9.4 shows a progression of parallel first-inversion triads from Vivaldi's *Four Seasons*.

Example 9.4. Antonio Vivaldi (1678–1741), "Spring," from *The Four Seasons*, mm. 51–55. *(Continued)*

(Continued)

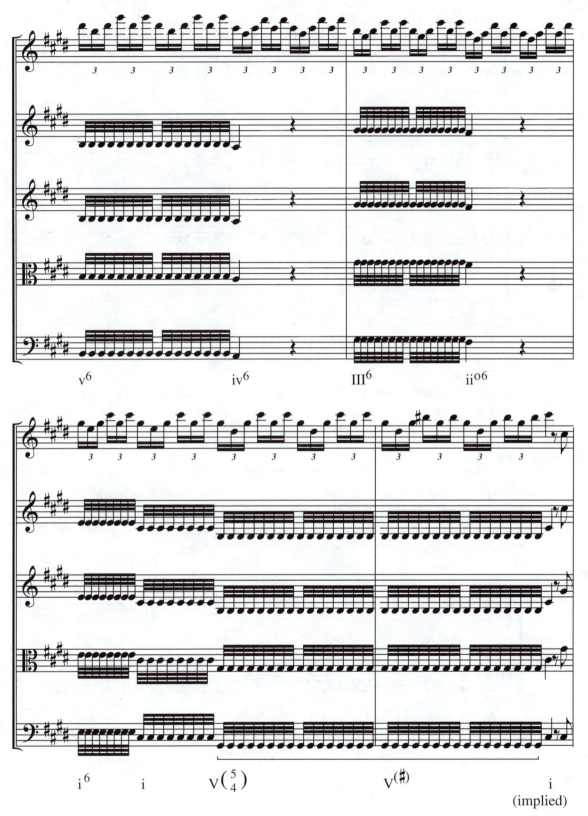

In the late Middle Ages and early Renaissance, some composers, such as Guillaume Dufay (c. 1400–1474) and Gilles Binchois (c. 1400–1460), employed a compositional technique called **fauxbourdon** ("false bass"), which involved three voices moving in primarily parallel motion in the intervals corresponding to the first inversion of the triad (Example 9.5).

Example 9.5. Guillaume Dufay, "Ave Regina Coelorum," excerpt, parallel passages in brackets.

LEVEL MASTERY 9.2.

Provide alto and tenor for the following progressions. These contain consecutive first-inversion triads, sometimes with the outer voices in parallel motion. Begin each progression in the spacing indicated (you may change spacing by the end). Make sure that your doublings do not create parallel fifths or octaves.

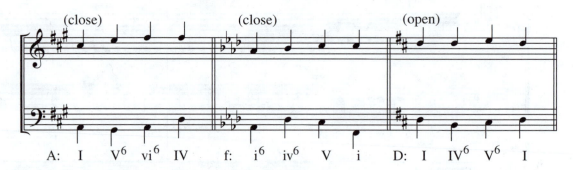

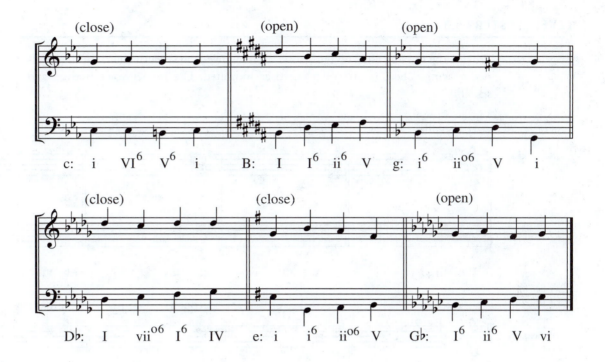

RESOLVING DIATONIC SEVENTH CHORDS IN FIRST INVERSION

Diatonic seventh chords normally resolve with the root motion from chord to chord going up a fourth or down a fifth (except for the vii°7 chord, where root motion is stepwise up to the tonic). Recall from Chapter 7 that voice leading in dominant seventh chords usually follows tendency tone patterns, and that in all diatonic seventh chords the chord seventh normally resolves downward stepwise. Example 9.6 demonstrates these principles as applied to first-inversion seventh chord resolutions.

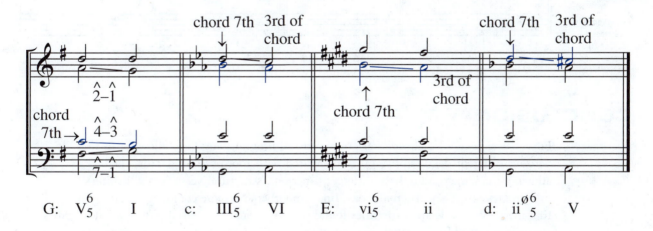

Example 9.6. First-inversion seventh chord resolutions.

Provide the missing alto and tenor for each first-inversion seventh chord, in the specified spacing. Then, resolve each chord as indicated. Use proper voice leading and spacing.

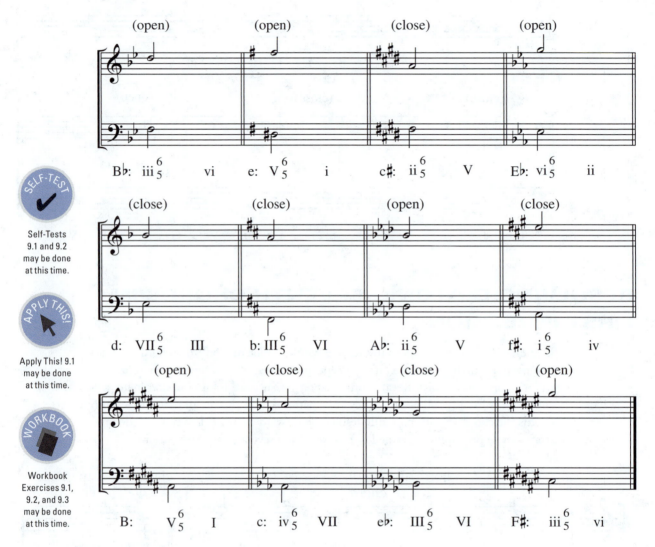

Self-Tests 9.1 and 9.2 may be done at this time.

Apply This! 9.1 may be done at this time.

Workbook Exercises 9.1, 9.2, and 9.3 may be done at this time.

CONCLUSION

First-inversion chords help add variety to musical progressions. They allow for us to perceive different degrees of stability compared with root-position chords, thereby allowing the same triad to have different functions (structural versus embellishing) in a progression. They also make bass lines smoother and more conjunct. Chains of first-inversion chords are sometimes found in transitional sequential passages, and something resembling parallel first-inversion chords (though not conceived as such) is found in the late-medieval and early-Renaissance practice of *fauxbourdon*. First-inversion seventh chords commonly resolve to a triad with its root a perfect fourth higher or perfect fifth lower; the chord seventh resolves down by step to the third of the triad that follows, just as it does for dominant seventh chords. In the next chapter we will examine the functions and voice leading for second-inversion triads and seventh chords.

Terms to Know

fauxbourdon

Self-Test

9.1. Provide alto and tenor for the following progressions. Begin each progression in the spacing indicated (you may change spacing by the end). Make sure that your doubling in the first-inversion triad does not create parallel fifths or octaves with the chords before or after it.

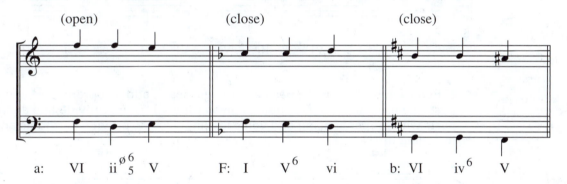

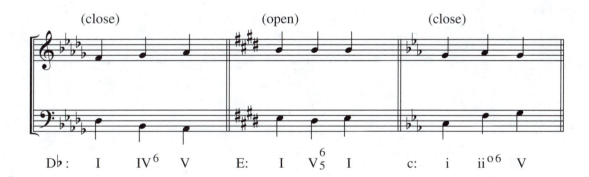

(Continued)

e: VI III⁶ iv   f♯: VI iv⁶ V   A♭: vi V⁶ I

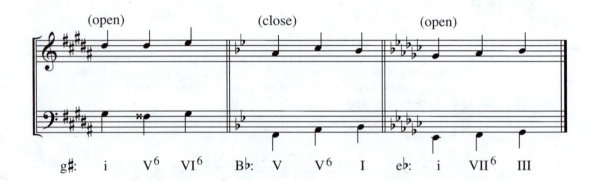

g♯: i V⁶ VI⁶   B♭: V V⁶ I   e♭: i VII⁶ III

9.2. Referring to the figured bass where necessary, add a soprano part above the bass line provided (the first note is given for you). Then, provide alto and tenor parts with proper spacing and voice leading. Finally, provide harmonic analysis, including the key.

Apply This!

9.1. Analysis. Locate and label the first-inversion triads or seventh chords in the following musical excerpts.

a. Haydn, Piano Sonata in C major, Hob.XVI:35 (i), mm. 126–131.

b. Aerosmith, "I Don't Want to Miss a Thing" [0:47–1:12] (chord progression only).

D:

c. Vivaldi, Violin Concerto in F minor, op. 8, no. 4 ("Winter") (i), mm. 56–63 (piano reduction). (The harmonic rhythm is two chords per measure.)

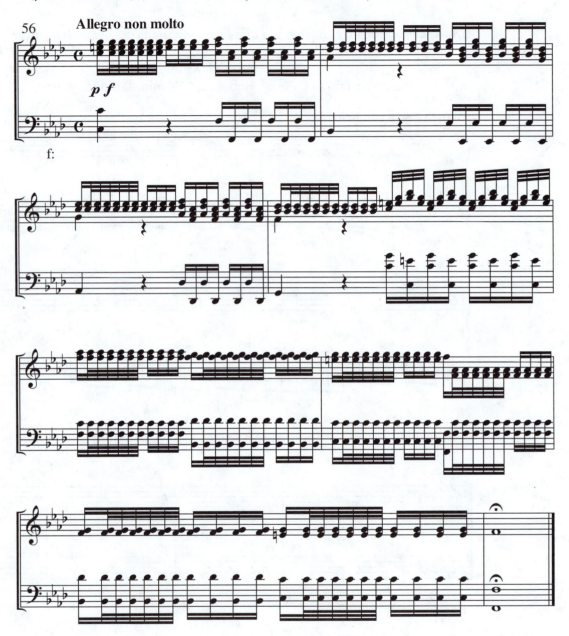

CHAPTER 10

PART WRITING WITH SECOND-INVERSION TRIADS AND SEVENTH CHORDS

OVERVIEW

This chapter considers the application of part writing principles involving second-inversion triads and seventh chords. In addition, the specific functional contexts of second-inversion chords—cadential, passing, neighboring, arpeggiating, and pedal—are introduced.

INTRODUCTION

We learned in the last chapter that first-inversion triads may be used as a substitute for root-position triads in a progression to create smoother bass lines. Second-inversion triads, however, are not used so freely. Unlike first-inversion triads, second-inversion triads always have a *fourth* (or its compound equivalent) above the bass; remember from Chapter 2 that although a fourth between upper voices is a consonance, a fourth above the bass was historically considered a dissonance (Example 10.1). As a result, the second-inversion triad is perceived to be the least stable of the triad positions, and it is only used in certain contexts for certain purposes.

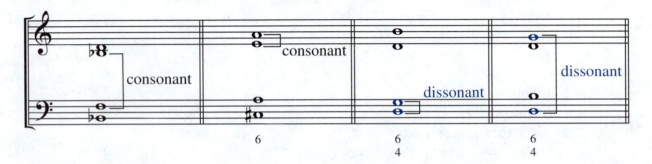

Example 10.1. Contextual consonance/dissonance of the fourth.

DOUBLING

When writing a second-inversion triad in a four-part texture, always double the bass (fifth of the chord). See Example 10.2.

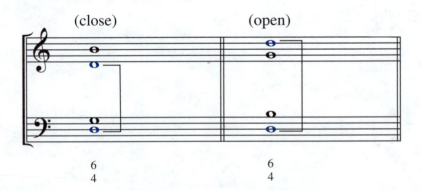

Example 10.2. Doubling in a second-inversion triad.

Compared with root-position and first-inversion triads, second-inversion chords are generally found less frequently, and where they are used they tend to be found in very specific contexts. The cadential $^6_4$ is the most common of these.

THE CADENTIAL $^6_4$ CHORD

A cadential $^6_4$ chord is a *tonic triad in second inversion immediately preceding a dominant function chord at a cadence.* In resolving, the bass note remains the same while the sixth and the fourth above the bass move by step to the fifth and third respectively. See Example 10.3.

Example 10.3. Cadential $^6_4$ chords in Mozart Piano Sonata in A major, K.331 (i), mm. 1–8.

The cadential $^6_4$ chord is often found immediately preceding a soloist's cadenza in a classical concerto; the cadenza interrupts the expected motion toward V, which is finally satisfied when the V chord signals the end of the cadenza (Example 10.4).

The cadential $^6_4$ chord also occurs in popular music, especially ballads, such as Elton John's "Don't Let the Sun Go Down on Me" (at the end of both the verse and the chorus—see [1:55] and [2:35]); Chicago's "You're the Inspiration" (in the chorus's title line at [0:56] and elsewhere, and at the end of the chorus at [1:10]); and Celine Dion's "My Heart Will Go On" (at the end of the chorus, at [1:35]). Although in each of these examples each $^6_4$ chord resolves to V, they do not all do so directly—at the end of the chorus to "You're the Inspiration," for example, the resolution to V finally comes some six seconds later in the song, after other elaborative movement in the inner voices.

Example 10.4. Mozart, Piano Concerto no. 20 in D minor, K.466 (i), mm. 361–366.

OTHER CONTEXTS FOR THE $^6_4$ CHORD

Second-inversion triads and seventh chords are found in four other contexts that serve to *elaborate* and *expand* the progression of which they are a part; this contrapuntal expansion is called **prolongation**. Note that although the *cadential* $^6_4$ chord is always a second-inversion *tonic* triad (in spelling, at least), the $^6_4$ chord types below are often chords *other than* the tonic. Where second-inversion V's are used in any of the contexts below, they may also include the chord seventh (and thus be $^4_3$ chords). All of these are named for the *behavior of the bass line*.

The Passing $^6_4$ and $^4_3$ Chord

In a progression using the passing $^6_4$ chord, the bass line approaches the $^6_4$ chord by step and then proceeds to the next chord by step in the same direction. The chord is often used to connect a root-position and first-inversion chord (Example 10.5).

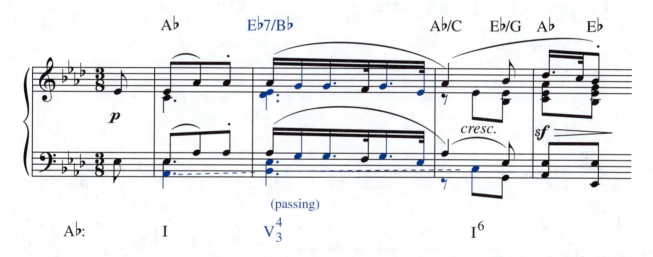

Example 10.5. Beethoven, Piano Sonata no. 12 in A♭ major, op. 26 (i), mm. 1–4.

The Neighboring $^6_4$ and $^4_3$ Chord

A neighboring $^6_4$ chord occurs between two chords of the *same* harmony and inversion. For example, a V$^6_4$ or $^4_3$ can occur between two root-position tonic chords (see Example 10.6).

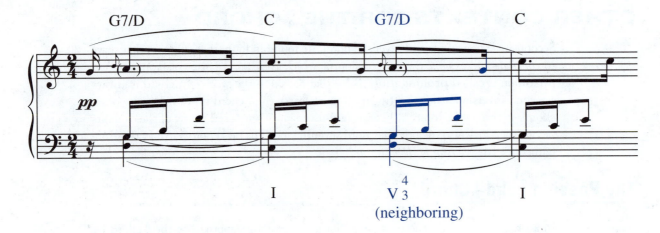

Example 10.6. Neighboring $\frac{4}{3}$ chord in Schumann, "Arabeske," mm. 1–2.

The Arpeggiating $\frac{6}{4}$ and $\frac{4}{3}$ Chord

Occasionally a second-inversion chord occurs along with the same chord in root position and first inversion, allowing for the bass line to move in an arpeggio. This is an example of an arpeggiating $\frac{6}{4}$ chord. Unlike the passing and neighboring $\frac{6}{4}$ chords, the arpeggiating $\frac{6}{4}$ is the *same harmony as the chords around it* (Example 10.7).

Example 10.7. Arpeggiating $\frac{6}{4}$ and $\frac{4}{3}$ chords in "America."

The Pedal $\frac{6}{4}$ Chord

The pedal $\frac{6}{4}$ chord occurs over a *stationary bass*, while the upper voices usually move by neighboring stepwise motion (intervals of 5–6–5 and 3–4–3 above the bass, respectively). There are two common varieties: I–IV$\frac{6}{4}$–I and V–I$\frac{6}{4}$–V. See Example 10.8.

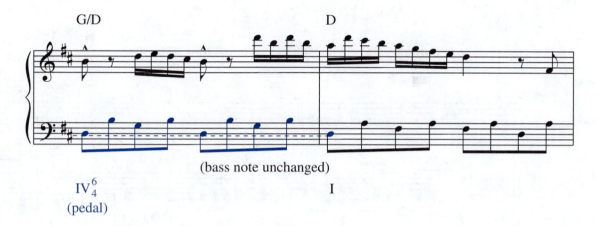

(bass note unchanged)

IV$^6_4$ I
(pedal)

Example 10.8. Muzio Clementi (1752–1832), Sonatina in D major, op. 36, no. 6 (i), mm. 1–4.

LEVEL MASTERY 10.1.

Locate the $^6_4$ or $^4_3$ chords in the excerpts below; identify them with the appropriate Roman numeral below the staff, and label them by type (cadential, passing, neighboring, arpeggiating, pedal).

a. Johannes Brahms (1833–1897), *Variations on a Theme by Haydn*, op. 56 (var. 1) mm. 1–5.

b. Beethoven, Piano Sonata no. 15 in D major, op. 28 ("Pastorale") (i),
mm. 1–10.

D:

c. Giuseppe Giordani (1751–1798), "Caro mio ben," mm. 25b–30a.

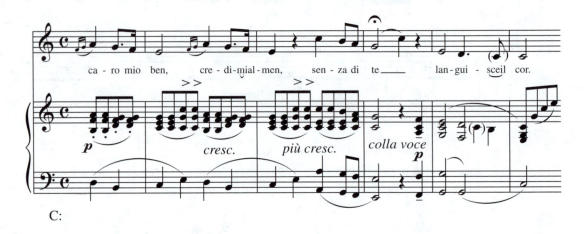

ca - ro mio ben, cre - di-mi al-men, sen - za di te____ lan-gui - sce il cor.

C:

d. Christoph Willibald Gluck (1714–1787), "O del mio dolce ardor" from
Paride ed Elena, mm. 1–6.

O del mio dol - ce ar -

d:

SELF-TEST ✔

Self-Test 10.1 may be done at this time.

APPLY THIS!

Apply This! 10.1 may be done at this time.

WORKBOOK

Workbook Exercises 10.1, 10.2, and 10.3 may be done at this time.

CONCLUSION

Because of the characteristic dissonant fourth above the bass, second-inversion triads and seventh chords are generally confined to one of the following patterns: cadential, passing, neighboring, arpeggiating, and pedal. The cadential $^6_4$ chord is found preceding the V at a cadence, where it thus serves to embellish the V chord. Each of the other $^6_4$ chord types are classified according to how the bass moves before and after the chord.

Second-inversion triads and seventh chords are a common source of errors in part writing. There is a tendency to overuse them, in an effort to "add more variety" to one's part writing. In fact, second-inversion chords are less common than those in root position or first inversion.

Terms to Know

arpeggiating $^6_4$ neighboring $^6_4$ pedal $^6_4$

cadential $^6_4$ passing $^6_4$

Self-Test

10.1. Given the key, bass line, and figured bass in the progressions below, provide upper voices and harmonic analysis. Label the type of $^6_4$ or $^4_3$ chord being used (cadential, passing, neighboring, arpeggiating, pedal).

PART 1: Fundamentals and Diatonic Harmony

Apply This!

10.1. Analysis. Locate the $^6_4$ or $^4_3$ chords in the excerpts below; identify them with the appropriate Roman numeral below the staff, and label them by type (cadential, passing, neighboring, arpeggiating, pedal). Some excerpts contain more than one $^6_4$ or $^4_3$ chord.

a. Beethoven, Piano Sonata in F minor, op. 2 no. 1 (ii), mm. 1–8.

b. Josephine Lang (1815–1880), "Frühlingsglaube," no. 1 from *Lieder*, op. 25 (1838–1860), mm. 55–69. Disregard notes in parentheses in determining your analysis. Measures with brackets indicate a single chord for that measure.

(Continued)

60
— les wen — — — — den, nun muss sich

65
Al — les, Al — les wen — — — — — den!

c. Ozzy Osbourne, "Crazy Train" (1981).

A   E/A   D/A   A5

A:

d. Clara Schumann (1819–1896), Prelude in D minor, op. 16, no. 3 (1845), mm. 1–5a.

PART 2

FORM AND CHROMATIC HARMONY 1

CHAPTER 11

MELODIC FIGURATION
Non-Chord Tones

OVERVIEW

Music is embellished and enlivened through non-chord tones. Non-chord tones are pitches outside of a given harmony that occur as melodic dissonances. They are classified according to their function—how they are approached and resolved. In this chapter we examine each type of non-chord tone and cumulatively add them to a chorale setting of a well-known melody.

CHAPTER OUTLINE

AUDIO LIST

Johann Sebastian Bach, Brandenburg Concerto no. 3 (iii)

Ludwig van Beethoven, "Für Elise"

Chicago, "If You Leave Me Now"

Phil Collins, "In the Air Tonight"

Electric Light Orchestra, "Mr. Blue Sky"

The Postal Service, "Such Great Heights"

Richard Wagner, Prelude to Act I, *Tristan und Isolde*

INTRODUCTION TO MELODIC AND TEXTURAL REDUCTION

We have already seen from the discussion of accents in Chapter 3 that not every pitch is perceptually "created equal." Certain tones are perceived as more important than others—longer in duration, louder, higher or lower in register, and so on. Certain tones are also used to embellish a structural melodic line.

As an analogy of sorts, consider the following two sentences:

- Susie threw the ball.
- Susie angrily threw the hard rubber super-ball down with such great force that it shattered the neighbor's window, after her brother tattled on her.

Both sentences express the same structural idea: *Susie threw the ball.* The second sentence, however, contains a great deal of embellishment, giving us much more information—about the ball, about Susie's emotional state, about the reason for her action, and about its consequences (and also about her treacherous brother).

So it is with music: a melody is usually made up of **structural tones** that are elaborated by **decorative tones** at successive layers of ornamentation. When a decorative tone is not a member of the harmony that supports it, it is an example of a **non-chord tone** (or *non-harmonic tone*). To see how non-chord tones add variety and interest to a melodic line, consider Example 11.1a, which comes from the Postal Service song "Such Great Heights." The bass line is also provided as a point of reference for the discussion that follows.

Example 11.1a. The Postal Service, "Such Great Heights" (2003), first phrase.

This melodic line tends to alternate between long tones (or tones that are repeated) and short, single tones. The longer tones are agogic accents; these same pitches also are metric accents, occurring on metrically strong beats (or sometimes just before them, as a syncopation). Another factor seems to group these pitches together when the bass line is considered—each structural pitch forms a perfect consonance, either a fifth or an octave, with the bass. The shorter G in measure 1 and the F in measure 2 are examples of **incomplete neighbors**, a decorative tone that is either approached by a leap from a consonance and resolved by a step to another consonance, *or* approached by a step from a consonance and resolved by a leap to another consonance (in other words, a stepwise motion is involved in the approach or the resolution, but not both). When these decorative tones are omitted, the melodic reduction reveals an essentially stepwise descent from the tonic to the subdominant, lingering there before completing its descent to the tonic (Example 11.1b). In moving from the D to the B♭ over the G in measure 3, however, the melodic line passes downward through the C (note that G–B♭–D, being stacked thirds, makes a triad); this C is an example of a **passing tone**, a decorative tone that is approached by step from a consonance and continues in the same direction, resolving by step to another consonance.

Example 11.1b. "Such Great Heights," reduction of melodic line.

The opening of the well-known piano piece "Für Elise" by Beethoven (Example 11.2a) offers a more complex example for melodic and textural reduction:

Example 11.2a. Beethoven, "Für Elise" WoO 59, mm. 1–8.

Even though the music proceeds in time as single sixteenth-note attack-points, it is difficult to think of all of the sixteenth notes in measures 2 through 4, for example, as a single melodic line sweeping up from the bass to the treble clef. In fact, those sixteenth notes spell out broken-up triads, called **arpeggios**; by realigning the arpeggios as chords, we can see in Example 11.2b that what appeared to be a (mostly) single line is actually made up of six voices. Because they shape the registral boundaries of the passage, our ears are drawn to the **outer voices** in the texture—the melodic line (which first calls attention to itself by being unaccompanied) and the bass.

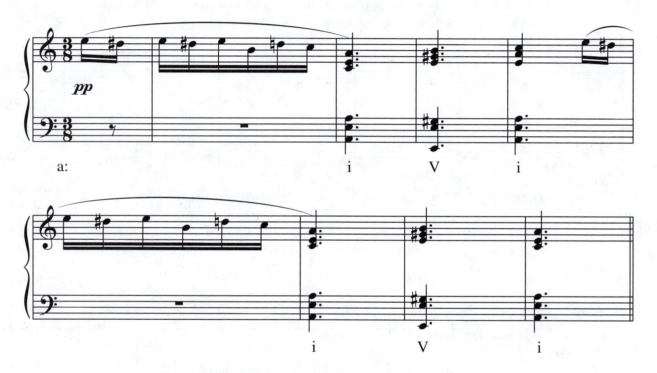

Example 11.2b. "Für Elise," with textural reduction of measures 2–4 and 6–8 to show hidden voice leading.

Now, let's consider the melodic line itself. Notice how the melody begins by alternating between E and D♯. The E occurs on the strong part of the beat, and is diatonic to the key; the D♯ is an embellishing chromatic pitch, occurring as it does on the weak part of the beat. The D♯ is a **neighbor tone**, approached from the structural E *by step* and then resolved *by step* in the *opposite direction*, returning to the E. The little turn at the end of measure 1 is also made up of decorative tones, but exactly which tones are decorative depends on how we hear the E that dominates the beginning of the measure—is the E part of a tonic harmony (A–C–E) or part of a dominant harmony (E–G♯–B)? This issue is examined in Web Feature 11.1; for now, though, we will elaborate individual lines in a simple harmonic progression, progressively adding non-chord tones.

AN EXERCISE IN EMBELLISHMENT: "MY COUNTRY, 'TIS OF THEE"

We can observe how different types of non-chord tones function by progressively elaborating a well-known tune. Example 11.3 shows a four-part setting of "America (My Country, 'Tis of Thee)."

Example 11.3. An unadorned four-part setting of "My Country, 'Tis of Thee."

It's not bad, but it's rather bland and stodgy. Adding non-chord tones, and varying their distribution among the parts, can give the surface an overall sense of momentum and direction.

Neighbor Tones

Repeated tones (in the melody, for example) can be elaborated by *neighbor tones*. There are two types of neighbor tones: **upper neighbors** (abbreviated UN, involving the step above the chord tone) and **lower neighbors** (abbreviated LN, involving the step below the chord tone). A neighbor tone usually happens on the unstressed (or **unaccented**) part of the beat; if it happens on the beat, we can describe it as an **accented** upper or lower neighbor (abbreviated AUN or ALN respectively). The changing tone or **neighbor group** (NG)—a kind of "double neighbor" tone complex involving one upper and one lower neighbor, in either order—can also be used to elaborate a repeated tone. Example 11.4 shows the previous four-part setting with various neighbor tones added and labeled. Note especially the two different neighbor groups in measures 1 and 3.

Example 11.4. "My Country, 'Tis of Thee," embellished with neighbor tones.

Passing Tones

Melodic skips of a third can be filled in by *passing tones*, either accented (APT) or unaccented (UPT or simply PT, since passing tones are usually unaccented). A whole step can also be filled in by a **chromatic passing tone** (CPT). Example 11.5 further elaborates the texture of Example 11.4 with various passing tones.

Example 11.5. "My Country, 'Tis of Thee," embellished with neighbor and passing tones.

Incomplete Neighbors: Appoggiaturas and Escape Tones

There are two types of incomplete neighbors, depending on whether the tone is approached by leap and resolved by step ("leap-step") or approached by step and resolved by leap ("step-leap").

- An incomplete neighbor that is approached by leap and resolved by step is called an **appoggiatura** (APP). Appoggiaturas are *usually accented*.

- An incomplete neighbor approached by step and resolved by leap is called an **escape tone** (ET); escape tones are *usually unaccented*.

In both cases the resolution is usually (but not always) in the opposite direction from the approach. Appoggiaturas and escape tones are added in Example 11.6.

Example 11.6. "My Country, 'Tis of Thee," with appoggiaturas and escape tones.

a. Locate and label the passing and neighbor tones in the following excerpt. A pop-chord harmonic analysis is provided to assist you (chords in parentheses indicate that the harmony is implied).

Mozart, Piano Sonata in D major, K.284 (iii), var. II, mm. 1–8.

b. Add passing tones, neighbor tones, appoggiaturas and escape tones to the following progression. Aim for one to two non-chord tones per beat to embellish the texture. Be sure to include at least one of each of the following: PT, APT, CPT, LN, UN.

Suspensions, Retardations, and Anticipations

A **suspension** is a type of *accented* dissonance (occurring on a stressed beat) that is created when a consonance is held over into the next harmonic change, becoming a dissonance as a result of movement by another voice, and resolving downward by step. The aural effect is that one voice moves to its place in the new chord after the other voices. Suspensions usually occur in an upper voice; they may be tied or **rearticulated** (sounded again with the movement in the other voices).

There are three parts to a suspension:

- The **preparation** (the consonant tone as part of the first chord);
- The **suspension** itself (the holding over of the tone with the chord change to become an accented dissonance);
- The **resolution** (the movement of the now-dissonant tone downward by step to a new consonance with the new chord), which usually occurs on an unstressed beat or offbeat.

TYPES OF SUSPENSIONS. Suspensions are labeled using the figured bass symbols for the intervals formed by the *suspension* and *resolution* above the bass. Fortunately, there are only five common varieties, shown in Example 11.7.

Example 11.7. Common varieties of suspensions, with their figured bass labels.

- A 9–8 suspension involves an interval of a ninth resolving to an octave (or their compound equivalents). The "2–1" label for such a suspension is rarely used, as it implies an interval of a second resolving to a unison (creating the aural impression that the dissonant voice has "disappeared" in the texture). Its most common context is for the resolution to be part of a root-position chord, as shown in Example 11.7a.
- A 7–6 suspension involves an interval of a seventh resolving to a sixth, or their compound equivalents. Note that because the interval of resolution is a sixth, the resolution of a 7–6 suspension occurs as part of a first inversion or (less commonly) a second or third inversion chord, as shown in Example 11.7b.

- A 4–3 suspension involves an interval of a (usually perfect) fourth resolving to a third; the resolution almost always occurs as part of a root-position chord, as shown in Example 11.7c. In pop music, the symbol "sus" indicates a triad with the third replaced by a fourth above the bass, functioning much like the suspended fourth within a triad but often without the proper preparation or resolution.

Note that all of the suspension numbers so far involve a *decrease* of the interval above the bass, since the resolution of a suspension is always downward by step (a "lowering of the ceiling"). The one exception to this rule is the 2–3 suspension, also called a **bass suspension**. In this suspension, the suspension is in the *bass part itself.* The resolution is still downward by step (a "lowering of the floor"). Example 11.7d shows an example of this suspension.

Finally, in a **suspension with change of bass** (SCB), *the bass moves simultaneously with the resolution,* often to another chord member; this radically changes the numerical label, as shown in Example 11.7e.

Example 11.8 shows several rearticulated suspensions in a keyboard piece by Bach, with the appropriate suspension labels added in the figured bass. Note that when more than one suspension occurs simultaneously, the higher pair of numbers goes above the lower pair, even if that does not match the actual arrangement of the voices; thus, the second suspension labels show the 9–8 above the 4–3, even though in the music the 4–3 suspension is found in the soprano, above the 9–8 suspension in the alto.

Example 11.8. Bach, Prelude no. 12 in F minor from *The Well-Tempered Clavier,* Book 2, BWV 881, mm. 1–4.

Sometimes the resolution of a suspension is itself ornamented with one or more non-chord tones. This is a **suspension with ornamented resolution** (SOR). Example 11.9 shows a suspension with ornamented resolution involving the addition of an appoggiatura.

(SOR)

6   7   4 – 3
4

Example 11.9. An example of a suspension with ornamented resolution (SOR).

Suspensions are also occasionally found in chains or sequences. The most common type of **suspension chain** involves a series of 7–6 suspensions. For example, consider the series of parallel sixths found in Example 11.10a. If the movement of the upper voice is displaced to the offbeats (syncopated), the result is a chain of 7–6 suspensions, as shown in Example 11.10b. (Can you figure out how this chain of suspensions is further ornamented by additional non-chord tones?)

Example 11.10a. A series of parallel sixths.

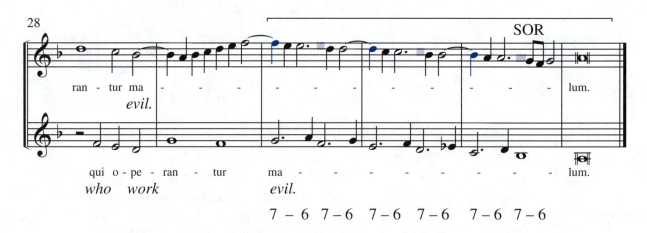

SOR

ran - tur ma - - - - - - - - lum.
evil.

qui o - pe - ran - tur ma - - - - - - - lum.
who   work   evil.

7 – 6 7 – 6 7 – 6 7 – 6   7 – 6 7 – 6

Example 11.10b. The same series of parallel sixths, used as the foundation for a chain of 7–6 suspensions (from Roland de Lassus (1532–1594), "Expectatio Justorum," mm. 30–32).

An interesting example of a chain of suspensions with ornamented resolutions is found in a pseudo-Baroque choral passage from the Electric Light Orchestra song "Mr. Blue Sky" (1977), starting at [3:17] into the song. Example 11.11a shows the descending parallel-tenths motion in reduction (minus the suspensions); Example 11.11b shows the choral parts with their 4–3 suspensions and the lower neighbors that ornament the resolutions.

Example 11.11a. Electric Light Orchestra, "Mr. Blue Sky" (1977), [3:17–3:24], textural reduction showing descending parallel tenths.

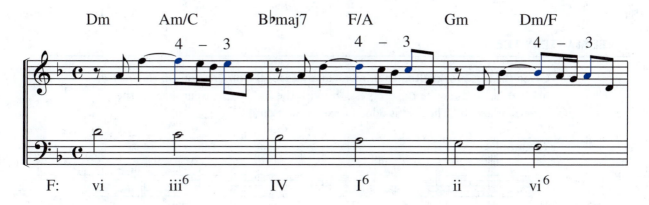

Example 11.11b. "Mr. Blue Sky," choral interlude at [3:17–3:24], showing elaborated 4–3 suspensions.

RETARDATIONS. Retardations function in the same manner as suspensions, except that they resolve *upward* by step. The second statement of the theme in Bach's Prelude in F minor (Example 11.8) concludes with retardations (Example 11.12).

Example 11.12. Bach, Prelude no. 12 in F minor from *The Well-Tempered Clavier*, Book 2, BWV 881, mm. 9–12.

ANTICIPATIONS. Anticipations (ANT) function as the opposite of suspensions. Instead of "holding over" after the harmony around it has changed, an anticipation will move to a chord tone of the harmony to come, *anticipating* the change of harmony. Anticipations are frequently found at cadences; see measure 13 of Example 11.16 for an example.

LEVEL MASTERY 11.2.

Given the key, provide Roman numeral analyses for the progressions in the measures marked "a," and rewrite the progressions with the indicated suspensions in the measures marked "b." The first is done for you as an example.

Self-Tests 11.1,
11.2, and 11.3
may be done
at this time.

Workbook
Exercises 11.1,
11.2, and 11.3
may be done
at this time.

Pedal Point

The pedal point, or pedal tone (PED), is different from all of our previous dissonances—it is not defined by its movement (approach and resolution) but rather its *lack* of movement in relation to the other voices. Its name comes from its context in organ music, where such long sustained bass tones are often played using the foot pedals. See Example 11.13 below.

Example 11.13. A pedal point below the V chord in a I–V–I harmonic progression.

The second bass note in Example 11.13 is clearly dissonant with the chord above it. One way of interpreting this chord is to treat the *soprano and alto* voices as neighbor tones, and thus the underlying harmony as a single tonic chord; this would be especially appropriate if the progression were to be played at a fast tempo. At a slow tempo, however, we are more likely to hear this progression as being made up of three distinct chords, the second chord a dominant harmony between two tonic harmonies. If we interpret this second chord as a V chord, the *bass* becomes a dissonance, labeled as a pedal point or PED.

Pedal tones are commonly used in rock and pop music. The Phil Collins song "In the Air Tonight" has a tonic pedal point that is sustained for nearly the entire song over a natural-minor harmonic progression of i–VII–VI–VII, shown in Example 11.14. The steadily droning pedal tone enhances the song's foreboding mood. The introduction to Chicago's "If You Leave Me Now," shown in Example 11.15, also has a tonic pedal point, but the voice leading is more "classical" than the parallel-triad motion of the Phil Collins example.

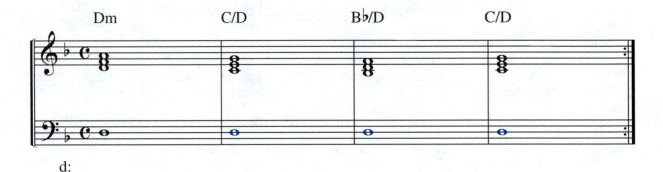

Example 11.14. Phil Collins, "In the Air Tonight," prevalent harmonic progression.

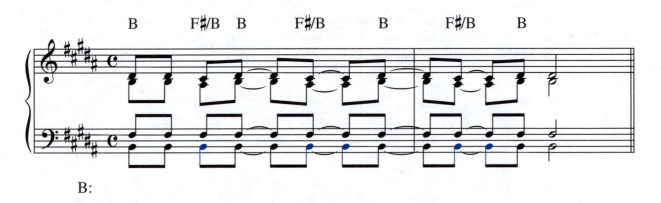

Example 11.15. Chicago, "If You Leave Me Now," introduction.

Example 11.16 at last shows our fully elaborated "My Country, 'Tis of Thee" in all its melodically embellished glory, with suspensions, retardations and anticipations added to the other non-harmonic tones; the final cadence has also been extended in order to allow for the use of a pedal tone. As this final version shows, however, there is something to be said about tasteful restraint when employing non-harmonic tones!

Example 11.16. "My Country, 'Tis of Thee," fully elaborated.

See Web Feature 11.1 at this time for an examination of how non-chord tones were used differently in different historical periods.

LEVEL MASTERY 11.3.

Label the non-chord tones shown in parentheses in each of the following musical excerpts. The blanks below the staff indicate the harmonic rhythm of the passage. If you are unable to provide a Roman numeral analysis, try using chord symbols.

a. Beethoven, "Écossaise," WoO 23, mm. 1–8.

b. Bach, Invention no. 15 in B minor, BWV 786, mm. 1–5. (Disregard non-chord tones that are part of ornaments such as trills.)

c. Philip Glass, "The Hours," mm. 89–95. (The non-chord tones in this excerpt are all in the melodic line. Parentheses have not been provided in this example, but a harmonic analysis has been provided with pop-chord symbols.)

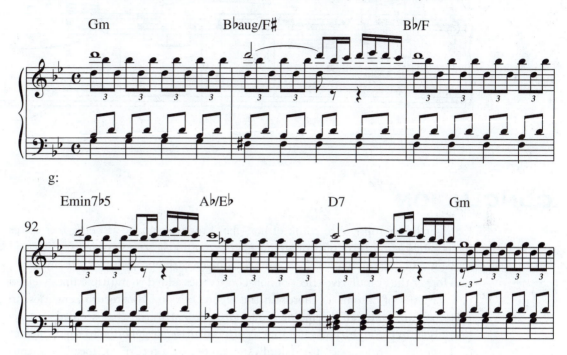

g:

d. Beethoven, Piano Sonata no. 12 in A♭ major, op. 26, mm. 1–16.

Andante con Variazioni.

Apply This!
11.1, 11.2,
and 11.3 may
be done at
this time.

Workbook
Exercise 11.4
may be done
at this time.

(Continued)

CONCLUSION

It might be appropriate to think of non-chord tones in music as being like spices in cooking. Just a little bit can enhance a piece of music's expressive qualities and make it truly distinctive. Melodic embellishment is the procedure for many variation forms; the cumulative effect of non-chord tones added to multiple lines yielded new varieties of chromatic chords in the eighteenth and nineteenth centuries. In this way, the "vertical" harmonic paradigm of tonal music that seemed to have taken hold in the eighteenth and nineteenth centuries, largely due to the influence of Rameau's theories, was increasingly supplanted by a return to linear, "horizontal" principles by the end of the nineteenth and early twentieth centuries. (The "Tristan chord," discussed in Web Feature 11.1, can be regarded as the intersection of the middle of the single melodic line that begins the work with the entry points of three new lines.)

Considering both the vertical and horizontal dimensions of music, in balance, will result in your having a more holistic and nuanced understanding of musical structure. There is no doubt that a single well-chosen chord can have great communicative power—consider the authority of the chord that opens Beethoven's "Eroica" symphony, the shock of the opening chord of the last movement of Beethoven's ninth symphony, or the mystery implied by Wagner's "Tristan" chord. But, of course, chords do not exist in a vacuum; a vertical "slice" of music usually does not tell us much about that chord's context. If you are a singer or a player of a monophonic instrument such as a trumpet or clarinet, you know that music is also the product of the interaction of individual lines in counterpoint. These lines generally move from points of tension to relaxation and repose; the appearance of moments where this movement is interrupted or thwarted adds to music's dramatic interest and expressive power.

Terms to Know

Alberti bass (in Web
    Feature 11.1)
anticipation
appoggiatura
arpeggio
chromatic passing tone
    (CPT)
decorative tones
escape tone
incomplete neighbor (IN)
metrical dissonance (in
    Web Feature 11.1)

neighbor group (UN vs.
    LN, or upper vs. lower
    neighbor)
neighbor tone
non-chord tone
    (non-harmonic tone)
outer voices
passing tone (PT)
pedal point (PED)
preparation
rearticulated suspension
resolution

retardation
structural tones
submetrical dissonance
    (in Web Feature 11.1)
supermetrical dissonance
    (in Web Feature 11.1)
suspension (SUS)
suspension chain
suspension with change
    of bass (SCB)
suspension with orna-
    mented resolution (SOR)

Self-Test

11.1. Add the indicated unaccented non-chord tones to the harmonic fragments below. Use the empty measures to copy the fragments and then add the specified non-chord tones.

1. neighbor tone
2. passing tone
3. neighbor group

4. escape tone
5. anticipation
6. two neighbor tones

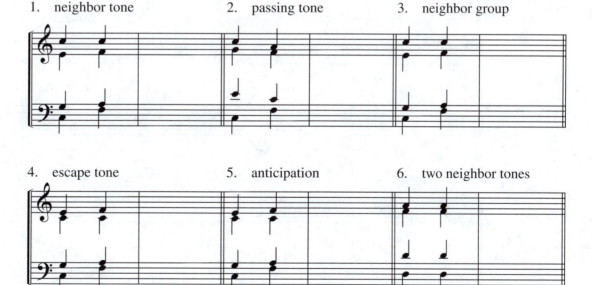

(Continued)

7. two passing tones   8. chromatic passing tone   9. escape tone

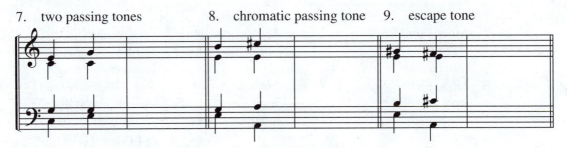

11.2. Add the indicated accented non-chord tones to the harmonic fragments below. Use the empty measures to copy the fragments and then add the specified non-chord tones.

1. appoggiatura   2. accented passing tone   3. accented neighbor tone

4. two accented passing tones   5. appoggiatura   6. two accented neighbor tones

7. two appoggiaturas   8. accented passing tone   9. accented neighbor tone

11.3. Add the indicated suspensions or retardations to the harmonic fragments below. Use the empty measures to copy the fragments and then add the specified non-chord tones. Provide the proper numerical labels (7–6, 4–3, etc.) for each suspension.

1. suspension in tenor 2. retardation in soprano 3. suspension in alto

4. two suspensions 5. suspension in bass 6. suspension with change of bass

7. suspension with ornamented resolution 8. suspension in tenor 9. suspension in soprano

Apply This!

11.1. Analysis. Circle and label (by type) the non-chord tones in each of the following excerpts.

a. Elfrida Andrée (1841–1929), Piano Sonata in A major, op. 3 (1870) (i), mm. 1–8. Begin with the "pop-chord" analysis above the staff; use that to determine Roman numerals. (Note: Do not assign Roman numerals to chromatic harmonies in the passage for which no blank is given.)

b. Bach, Toccata and Fugue in D minor, BWV 565, mm. 1–3. (Assume a tonic harmony is intended for the first one and a half measures.)

c. Brahms, "In Stiller Nacht," *Deutsche Volkslieder*, WoO 33, no. 8.

11.2. Composition. Provide non-chord tones for the setting of the hymn tune "Old Hundredth" below, in the manner of the "My Country, 'Tis of Thee" setting in this chapter. Label all non-chord tones. You should aim for at least one non-chord tone per beat; vary your distribution of non-chord tones among parts so that they are not all in the same voice. Check your work carefully for any parallel perfect fifths or octaves.

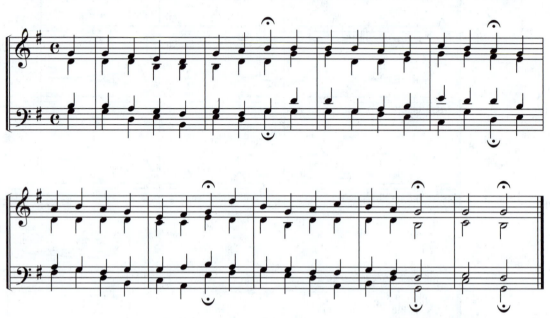

11.3. Improvisation. Many jazz improvisations take the form of elaborating a "standard" with non-chord tone embellishments. Choose a simple jazz standard such as Rodgers and Hart's "My Funny Valentine," and try embellishing the melody as the basis of an improvisation. Keep the structure of the original melody in mind as you perform the improvisation, and be mindful of the "changes"—that is, the harmonic progression underlying the melody and the goal-directed nature of phrases as they head toward cadences.

CHAPTER 12

MOTIVES, PHRASES, AND PERIODS

OVERVIEW

With this chapter we begin a study of music's formal structures. Starting with the motive—a short, characteristic melodic and rhythmic idea—we move to successively larger levels of structure, including the sentence, the phrase, and how phrases can be combined into different types of periods. We also learn how to represent even larger hierarchical levels of musical structure at a glance by means of arch mapping.

AUDIO LIST

Johann Sebastian Bach, Prelude no. 1 in C major from *The Well-Tempered Clavier*, Book 1 (BWV 846)

Ludwig van Beethoven, Piano Sonata no. 2 in A major, op. 2 no. 2 (iii)

Miles Davis, "Well You Needn't"

Franz Joseph Haydn, Symphony no. 101 ("Clock") (iii)

Elton John, "Goodbye Yellow Brick Road"

Queen, "We Are the Champions"

Wolfgang Amadeus Mozart, Piano Sonata in A major, K.331 (i)

In Chapter 7, we learned that cadences in music put brief pauses in the musical flow, like pauses in speech or punctuation marks in writing. Music is also organized into larger units to maintain a cohesive flow of information. In the same way that sentences are combined into paragraphs, and—depending on the length of the writing—these paragraphs are combined into sections (often marked with headings) and then potentially into chapters, music is experienced as *phrases* that are then organized into successively higher levels of structure. It is these higher levels that we will explore in this chapter.

MOTIVES

Beethoven's Fifth Symphony (Example 12.1), one of the most famous opening moments in musical history, is an excellent example of the power of a **motive**— a short, distinctive musical idea that recurs throughout a work. A motive may be *melodic*, *rhythmic*, or *both*. For example, we can split Beethoven's opening motive into two components: A durational pattern of "short-short-short-long" (Example 12.2a) and a melodic interval of a descending third (Example 12.2b).

Example 12.1. Beethoven, Symphony no. 5 (i), mm. 1–5.

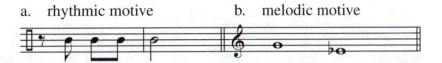

Example 12.2. Beethoven's Fifth Symphony motive: rhythmic and melodic components.

Beethoven built upon this motive to create larger units of material throughout this symphony (some 256 times in the first movement alone!). For example, immediately after the opening five bars comes this phrase (presented in Example 12.3 in Liszt's transcription for piano):

= short-short-short-long motive

Example 12.3. Beethoven, Symphony no. 5 (i) (Liszt transcription), mm. 6–21.

Notice in Example 12.3 that although the *rhythmic* short-short-short-long motive is unchanged, the *melodic* motive has already undergone alteration (though the contour of high-high-high-low is mostly retained).

In the second movement, we see the rhythmic motive expanded in duration and repeated, as shown in Example 12.4. Here, the contour is also reversed (ascending rather than descending), and the third is bridged with a passing tone.

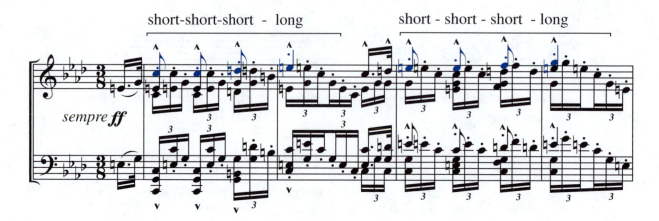

Example 12.4. Beethoven, Symphony no. 5 (ii) (Liszt transcription), mm. 32–35.

A motive, then, is something like a musical building block—it is not usually further divisible in itself without losing its distinctive character, but it can be combined and developed into more extensive musical phrases. Example 12.5 shows one way of generating a longer line from a motive—simple repetition of a rhythmic figure. What rhythmic motive is found in Example 12.5? What melodic motive? Are the repetitions identical?

Example 12.5. Bach, Fugue no. 2 in C minor from *The Well-Tempered Clavier*, Book 1, fugue subject.

Besides repetition, a motive can be developed through melodic **sequence** (repeating the melodic motive at a higher or lower pitch level in the *same voice*), or by **imitation** (restating the material in a *different voice* in the texture, sometimes at the same pitch, sometimes at a higher or lower pitch level).

"Bossa Na Praia (Beach Samba)," by Geraldo Cunha and Pery Ribeiro, is an excellent example of melodic sequence (Example 12.6). In addition, measures 7–9 are a *harmonic* sequence of measures 3–5 (the chord progression is transposed down a third). Notice also how the root motion is predominantly up a fourth or down a fifth, along the circle of fifths.

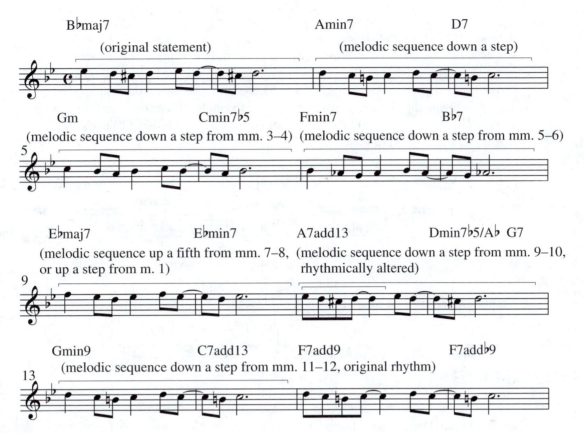

Example 12.6. Cunha and Ribeiro, "Bossa Na Praia" (1967), mm. 1–16.

For a more detailed consideration of how motives are used in a Bach composition, see Web Feature 12.1.

For an interesting case study of motives in a Thelonious Monk jazz standard, see Web Feature 12.2.

Sequence is a useful teaching tool—it offers variety while at the same time reinforcing learning through repetition (of a contour and rhythmic pattern). Singers often sing a short scale or other melodic fragment and then sequence up by half steps in their warm-up activities. Perhaps to underscore the role of sequence in teaching, Rodgers and Hammerstein's "Do Re Mi" from *The Sound of Music*—a song with which the governess Maria teaches the von Trapp children the rudiments of solfège and the major scale—employs sequences. In the first and second subphrases (*do* . . . and *re* . . .), the second phrase is a modified sequence of the first, differing in its second half (but, like the first, using only three adjacent pitches for its material). The third and fourth subphrases (*mi* . . . and *fa* . . .) collectively make up a sequence of the first two. Once *sol* (or "sew—a needle pulling thread") is reached, a new melodic pattern is heard—a descending leap of a perfect fifth, followed by an ascending scale of six notes. This too is subjected to sequence, heard three times in all before the closing line "bring us back to *do*."

A motive can also be varied by contrapuntal devices such as **augmentation** (replicating the motive with proportional expansion of durations—a motive of quarter notes might be augmented to appear in half notes, for example), **diminution** (the opposite of augmentation—notes in proportionally shorter durations), **retrograde** (pitches, and less commonly rhythms, of the motive appearing in reverse order), and **inversion** (the contour of the motive is reversed so that it appears "upside-down").

Motivic inversion can be classified as real or tonal. In **real inversion**, a motive is inverted *exactly*—so that the *qualities* of the intervals are matched, usually requiring chromatic pitches (Example 12.7a). In **tonal inversion**, the intervallic qualities are altered to fit the diatonic constraints of the key (Example 12.7b). Tonal inversion is more common in tonal music than real inversion, unless the original material was highly chromatic to begin with.

To see how a motive can be "played out" across a broad span of music in Queen's "We Are the Champions," see Web Feature 12.3.

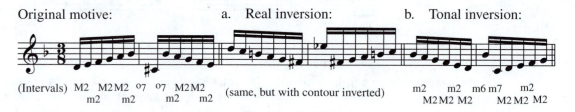

Example 12.7. Real and tonal inversion, compared.

PUTTING IDEAS TOGETHER: SENTENCE STRUCTURE

Musical material is often organized in **sentence structure**—two shorter iterations of an idea followed by a longer, more elaborated statement that is usually twice as long. The melodies in Example 12.8 show how the sentence structure principle is found in a variety of contexts; brackets are used to show the "short-short long" proportions in each excerpt.

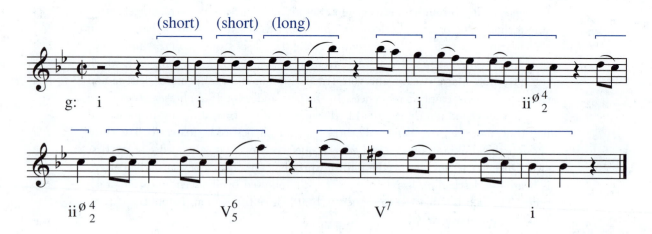

Example 12.8a. Mozart, Symphony no. 40 (i), primary theme, mm. 1–9.

Example 12.8b. French folk song, "Sur le Pont d'Avignon."

Example 12.8c. Gioacchino Rossini (1792–1868), Overture from *The Barber of Seville*, mm. 26–30, piano reduction.

Example 12.8d. Charlie Parker, "Now's The Time," mm. 1–4.

Sentence structure can be found in a detail as small as the arrangement of rhythmic motives (the opening phrase of Mozart's Symphony no. 40, Example 12.8a) or in the proportion of phrases themselves (John Williams's "Imperial March"). Sentence structures can sometimes be found at more than one level simultaneously, as the end of Example 12.8c shows.

PHRASE STRUCTURE

Musicians often use the word "phrase" instinctively—often associated with the "phrasing" they practice to enhance the musicality of their performances. In this context, "phrasing" usually refers to the slur markings or other grouping details a composer or editor might add to a score. These markings, however, are not necessarily the same as a musical phrase, and in fact they may contradict it. A **phrase** is *a musical* *statement that progresses in a goal-directed fashion to conclude with a cadence.* Look at and listen to Example 12.9, the opening of the first movement of Mozart's Piano Sonata in A major, K.331. How many phrases are there? Where do the cadences occur, and how do you know they are cadences?

Example 12.9. Mozart, Sonata in A major, K.331 (i), mm. 1–8.

You probably noticed the rhythmic motive in measure 1, which is repeated in measures 2, 5, and 6. The motive elaborates a steady quarter note–eighth note pattern that we see in the repeated E4s in the middle voice. The only places this quarter note–eighth note pattern momentarily ceases are at the ends of measures 4 and 8. We have already seen that a cadence functions as a kind of musical punctuation, a brief kind of repose often signaled by a change of harmonic rhythm. In measures 1 and 2, for example, if we consider the sixteenth notes to be upper neighbor non-chord tones, we have one chord (appearing in two inversional positions) in each measure: I, I⁶ | V⁶, V⁴₃. In measures 3 and 7, however, the harmonic rhythm speeds up—each measure has more than one chord, not merely a change of inversion. In addition, measures 1–2 and 5–6 are identical, so that strongly suggests that measure 5 is the beginning of a phrase, like measure 1 (and that also explains why hearing an imperfect authentic cadence from measure 4 to measure 5 would be incorrect).

Thus, Example 12.9 consists of two phrases. Phrases are often combined in pairs in this fashion: The first phrase ends inconclusively (often on a V chord), and the second phrase ends conclusively, usually on a perfect authentic cadence, providing closure to the opening left by the first phrase (see also Example 9.6, "Home on the Range"). When two phrases follow this pattern, the first, inconclusive phrase is an antecedent phrase, and the second, conclusive phrase is a consequent phrase. *The unit comprising an antecedent phrase followed by a consequent phrase is called a* period. A period in which the antecedent and consequent phrases begin identically, as in Example 12.9, is called a **parallel period**. A period in which both phrases are identical in length, is additionally called a **symmetrical period**.

Now look at (and listen to) how Mozart continues his theme, as shown in Example 12.10. How is it similar to Example 12.9? How is it different?

Example 12.10. Mozart, Sonata in A major, K.331 (i), mm. 9–18.

Measures 13 and 14 look very much like our opening material. This "opening" material again comes after a half cadence (in measure 12), and the very end of the example is again a perfect authentic cadence. Comparing the beginning of the example (measure 9) with the beginning of the second phrase (measure 13), however, we see that—although they share the rhythmic motive—the two phrases are *different* melodically. Mozart also emphasizes this melodic difference with a change of texture, to an arpeggiated accompaniment in measures 9 and 10. Thus, Example 12.10 is a **contrasting period**.

Another difference is that the second phrase of Example 12.10 is longer than the first. Having returned to the opening material in measure 13, one might expect Mozart to stick to a four-measure phrase concluding with a perfect authentic cadence, as the consequent phrase in Example 12.9 was. But instead, Mozart comes to rest briefly on an *imperfect* authentic cadence, in measure 16. This is conclusive, but not conclusive enough—so the phrase continues in a **phrase extension** to finish on the expected perfect authentic cadence two measures later.

A third type of period is the **similar period**, in which each phrase begins with material that is related by sequence. One very simple—and terse—example is the "Mexican Hat Dance" (Example 12.11) shown below.

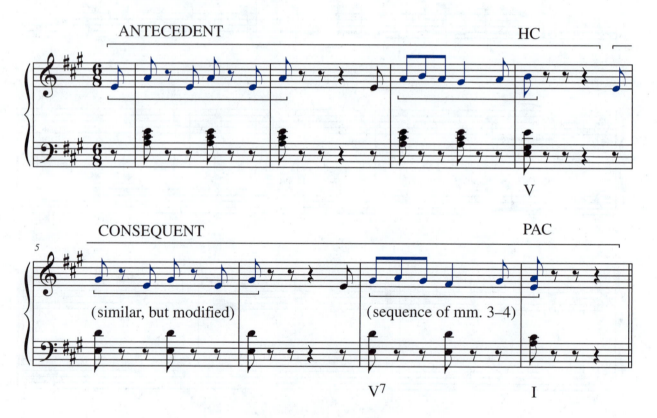

Example 12.11. Traditional, "Mexican Hat Dance."

LEVEL MASTERY 12.1.

Analyze the phrase structure of each of the musical excerpts below. Begin by locating and identifying the cadences. Based on the cadences you find, determine whether or not the excerpt is a period, or simply two phrases. If the excerpt is a period, determine whether the period is parallel, similar, or contrasting.

a. Giles Farnaby (c. 1563–1640), "The New Sa-Hoo," from *The Fitzwilliam Virginal Book*, early seventeenth century, mm. 1–8.

b. Mozart, Piano Sonata in D major, K.284 (iii) (theme, mm. 1–8a)

c. Traditional reel, "Speed the Plough," mm. 1–8.

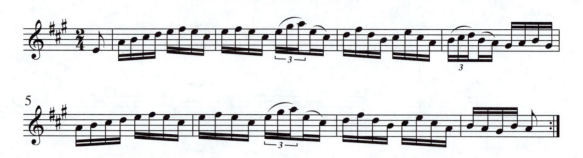

d. Mozart, Minuet in F major, K.4 (1762), mm. 1–8.

LARGER PHRASE GROUPINGS

Two phrases must be in an antecedent-consequent relationship in order to make a period. If they are not—for example, if two consecutive phrases end with perfect authentic cadences—they are simply two phrases. Occasionally, however, antecedent and consequent phrases may be found in a larger asymmetrical combination called a **three-phrase period**. In a three-phrase period, the last phrase *must* end with a perfect authentic cadence, while the first two usually end on a weaker cadence (half cadence or imperfect authentic cadence). Melodically, three-phrase periods may be in aba, aa′b, or abb′ form, or each phrase may present new melodic material, as shown in Example 12.12.

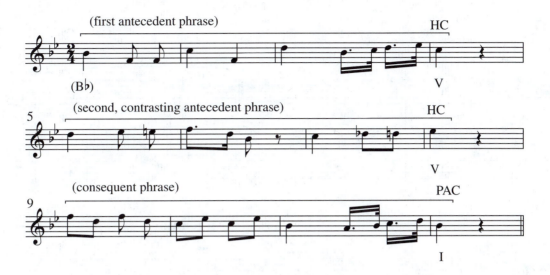

Example 12.12. Mozart, "Voi, che sapete" from *The Marriage of Figaro*, K.492.

Sometimes, four phrases are combined into a **double period**. The second phrase often ends with a half cadence or an authentic cadence in the dominant key, and the last phrase concludes with a perfect authentic cadence, thus doubling the proportions of the usual antecedent–consequent period. The first two phrases make up the antecedent half of a double period, while the second two make up the consequent half. See the cadential pattern in Example 12.13.

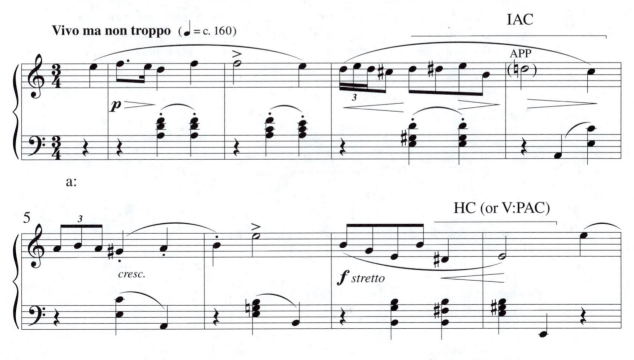

Example 12.13. Chopin, Mazurka in A minor, op. 7, no. 2, mm. 1–16. *(Continued)*

(Continued)

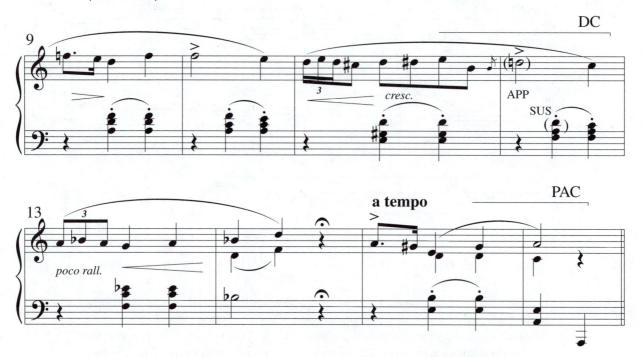

Phrases may also be grouped together in non-periodic ways—they may be connected melodically, for example, but not show the cadential patterns associated with periods. The result is a **phrase group**. In Example 12.14, for example, measures 1–8 suggest a periodic structure (perhaps the first half of a double period), but this is not at all confirmed by what follows in measures 9–24, which has three phrases, one of which is six measures long.

Example 12.14. Joseph Haydn (1732–1809), Piano Sonata in E major, Hob.XVI/13 (1767), (ii). *(Continued)*

(Continued)

We can now consider how the proportions created by these larger units may be seen as higher-level durations, that is, ways of carving out time.

HYPERMETER

So far we have considered phrase structure from the finer details of motives within phrases and how they may be combined (including sentence structure) to how phrases are combined by antecedent-consequent pairs into periods, and beyond that into larger structures such as phrase groups or double periods. At this point review the Mozart theme shown in Example 12.9. The first part of the theme, you might recall, is a symmetrical parallel period. The second cadence—a perfect authentic cadence— is stronger than the first, a half cadence in measure 4, thereby providing closure and making this little excerpt a more-or-less self-contained unit for further study.

Now, reviewing what you learned about metric structure diagramming in Chapter 3, prepare a diagram of the pulse streams in this excerpt. Which durational value is the finest (thereby belonging at the bottom of your diagram)? Which level of the metric structure do you think represents the primary pulse stream? Now—at what metric level should the *uppermost* part of the diagram be?

Since meter is hierarchical, it occurs on a number of levels simultaneously. The smallest level is the smallest duration in, or implied by, the piece; the largest is the entire piece. There may be any number of intermediate levels in between, depending on length and complexity. We already know that meter is organized by regular alternations of stressed (strong) and unstressed (weak) pulses; this principle applies to *groups* of measures as well. The grouping of measures within a phrase, or phrases within a still larger structure, into successively larger groupings is called **hypermeter**. Since Example 12.9 is divided into two four-measure phrases, there is a **periodicity**, or regularity, to the proportions represented by the phrases; each four-measure phrase similarly may be grouped into two segments of two measures each, which alternate between stressed and unstressed measures with the regularity of inhaling and exhaling. Thus, we can add higher-level grouping to our metric structure diagram so that we have something like Example 12.15. Groupings above the solid line represent hypermetric groupings.

Example 12.15. Metric structure diagram for Mozart K.331 (i), mm. 1–8.

Unfortunately, all levels of metric structure are not necessarily equally perceptible in real time. It is fairly easy for us to hear the hierarchical structure of a bar of music in clear $\frac{6}{8}$ time; there are two primary pulses, the first of which is stronger than the second, and each primary pulse is subdivided by three: "*one*–two–three, two–two–three . . ." It is also not too difficult to hear the structure on the phrase level; we are usually able to recognize two, three, or four bar phrases without much trouble (especially when, as in our Mozart example, there is recurring material to signify the beginning of new phrases).

At the same time, this diagram represents only the first eight measures of Mozart's eighteen-measure theme, which is followed by six variations and a short coda, totaling 134 measures. Other pieces of music are less periodic, having a greater variety of phrase lengths, section lengths, and sublevels of structure. As phrase groupings become more complex or as we attempt to keep track of longer time spans in our memory, it becomes more difficult to make precise statements about how long the levels last and how they are subdivided into smaller groups. When this happens it is useful to go into some kind of graphing approach to aid us in recalling the hierarchical structure. The metric structure diagram technique introduced in Chapter 3 is useful for "fine-level" analysis or global observations about a particular metric organization, but when an entire piece is concerned, or when there are different phrase lengths or sections, plotting out layers of aligned pulse stream dots can be time consuming; also, showing the internal metric structure of measures is redundant and has no bearing on diagramming phrase structure. For more complex or large-scale musical forms, **arch maps** are useful for showing how phrases combine into larger structural units.

ARCH MAPS: A TOOL FOR ANALYSIS OF PHRASE STRUCTURE

In the process of filling out an arch map, we work in between the note-to-note level and the conception of the piece as a whole. We learn the work by understanding how the distinguishing parts of it form the whole. The arch map is really a way of getting into the piece, to begin to see the real issues that might form a good discussion and a deeper understanding of the work. Arch maps can also make us appreciate details of a piece that might otherwise go unnoticed if we only focus on the measure-by-measure details.

An arch map uses a **time line** as its foundation. The line is divided into whatever units are most useful for what one intends to demonstrate. For example, if one is analyzing a piece with a steady meter and tempo, one measure is a useful unit of measurement (or, if the piece is lengthy, consistent groups of five or ten measures, in the manner of a ruler). If one is working with recorded music for which a score is not available, the time line can be literally time-based, using minutes (subdivided into six groups representing 10 seconds of time) as the basic unit of measurement. For our arch map of Mozart's K.331 theme in its entirety (Examples 12.9 and 12.10 together), since it lasts only eighteen measures, we will choose a measure as our basic unit (Example 12.16). Since a piece of music normally begins on measure 1 (rather than "measure 0"), our time line accordingly begins at 1. The arch map can extend for as long as needed, but it will end on the downbeat of a hypothetical "next measure." In our Mozart example, the theme lasts for eighteen *full* measures, ending only at the unheard downbeat of the nineteenth measure. For the purposes of our arch map, then, the diagram will end at the unheard measure nineteen, and that last number is shown in parentheses. See Example 12.16 below.

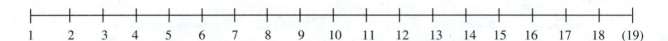

1 2 3 4 5 6 7 8 9 10 11 12 13 14 15 16 17 18 (19)

Example 12.16. Arch map time line marked off in one-measure increments, 1 through 19.

In Example 12.17, we turn our attention to measures 1 through 8 of Mozart's theme, using arches to represent the phrases. Since the second (consequent) phrase begins on measure 5, the second arch begins at the beginning of the fifth bar, representing the exact location of the division in the music. The place where the two arches meet is called a **seam**; *there is never a "gap" between arches.*

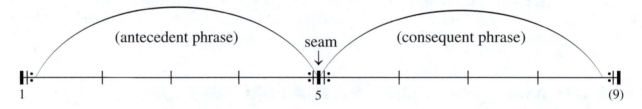

Example 12.17. Arch map of Mozart K.331, mm. 1–8, showing antecedent and consequent phrase arches.

Returning to our melody (see Example 12.9), we may want to show smaller divisions of the phrase, especially if our intent is to show something of the form of the melody. For example, each four-bar phrase divides easily into two two-bar subphrases, a division enhanced by the presence of contrasting rhythmic figures in measures three and seven. In the first two-bar subphrase of each phrase, the repeated rhythmic motive encourages a further twofold subdivision; the second two-bar subphrases do not divide so easily. Example 12.18 shows the first eight measures of Mozart's theme in more detail, adding these subdivisions. Notice that each phrase subdivides into a sentence structure. Also, a final arch over the entire eight-bar span has been added, making it clear that this is the highest hierarchical level in this excerpt (Mozart's theme up until the double bar). Notice also that if an area is going to be subdivided into arches (such as measures 1–2) it is *completely* subdivided. In this way one avoids situations such as the incorrect subdivision shown in Example 12.19.

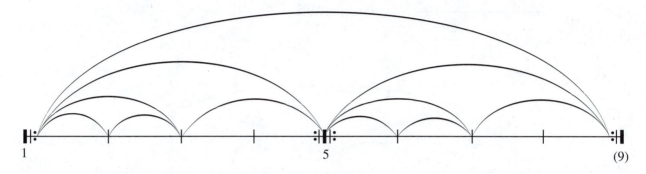

1   5   (9)

Example 12.18. Arch map of Mozart K.331 (i), mm. 1–8, showing phrase subdivisions and arch spanning a period.

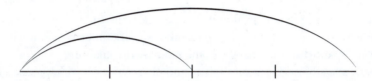

Example 12.19. Incorrect (incomplete) subdivision of an arch.

What if a melody has a pickup beat? *A seam will always coincide with the downbeat of a measure, even if an anacrusis is involved.* In the same way that musicians usually refer to an anacrusis by its relation to the following measure ("the pickup to measure 1"), in an arch map, any anacrusis is "rounded off" to the following measure. We can show the presence of an anacrusis by adding a small Greek letter *alpha*, or α, to the seam where the pickup occurs.[1] Example 12.20 shows the arch map for the first sixteen measures of "Home on the Range." Compare it with the music in Example 9.6 and see if you can connect the musical details in Example 9.6 with the points in the arch map below. Note the use of α to show pickups to phrases and subphrases. Aside from the number of measures in each phrase, what similarities do you see between the phrase structure of Example 12.20 and that of Example 12.18?

---

[1] The Greek *alpha* is used, rather than A or a, to denote an anacrusis because *A* usually denotes formal sections within a piece while *a* denotes subsections, such as the melodic material associated with subphrases in a melody.

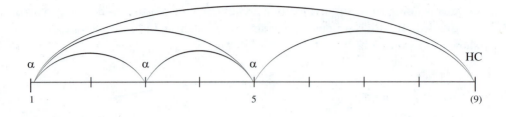

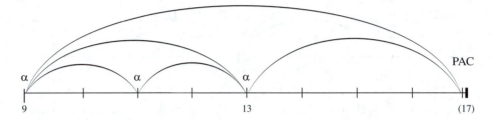

Example 12.20. Arch map for "Home on the Range," mm. 1–16.

Constructing an arch map allows us to see the structure of the melody in a glance and it can also be used as an aid to remember specific information about it. It is in longer time spans that arch maps become most useful, enabling us to take in lengthy time spans at a single glance through a kind of "aerial view" of a piece and allowing us to quickly compare two sections that may be quite far apart when experienced in real time. In the next section, we will apply arch mapping to higher levels of musical structure; in so doing we lose some of the fine details that we might notice from measure to measure, but we will gain awareness of other formal processes at work that are only visible from the "wide view."

LEVEL MASTERY 12.2.

Using Example 12.20 as a model, prepare an arch map for each of the musical excerpts in Level Mastery 12.1.

WHEN PHRASES COLLIDE: ELISION

In writing, run-on sentences—when a period or other punctuation mark is missing from a clause or sentence, causing it to "run on" to the next—are to be avoided. In music, however, phrases often "run onto" each other, usually dovetailing upon a *single chord that acts as the closing chord of a cadence in the first phrase and the first chord of the next phrase.* The effect is something like the sentence: "Everything's coming up roses are red, violets are blue," in which two complete sentences dovetail on the word "roses." When two phrases "run together" in this way, it is called a phrase **elision**.

Consider Elton John's "Goodbye Yellow Brick Road," which begins simply enough, metrically speaking—the opening piano chords are quarter notes in $\frac{4}{4}$ time. The first verse is also musically balanced, with a four-bar phrase in sentence structure ending with an authentic cadence on the line "listened to my old man." The second phrase is similar, but the text is left open as the verse concludes ("too young to be singin' . . .").

With the completion of the line of text that the cadence left unfinished (". . . the blues"), we head into an unusually long chorus beginning at [0:39] into the song. In contrast to the short eight-bar verse, the chorus is nearly twice as long: sixteen bars, two of which—at [1:11] and [1:21] are in $\frac{2}{4}$ rather than $\frac{4}{4}$. The first section of this chorus ([0:39–0:51]), three measures long, is related to the verse, based on the same three-chord harmonic sequence transposed. When the dominant seventh chord at the end of this section ([0:50]) resolves as expected to the tonic, we encounter an elision, as the tonic resolution is also the beginning of a new thematic idea ("So goodbye yellow brick road").[2] Another, more dramatic elision—on a deceptive cadence, no less—occurs coming out of this section at [1:23], at which point a reprise of the chorus's first section ensues. The entire pattern of symmetrical verse and lengthy, asymmetrical chorus is then repeated to complete the song.

In retrospect, the differences in phrase structure of the verse and chorus are striking, as seen in the arch map in Example 12.21. The verse is symmetrical, laid out in a regular $\frac{4}{4}$ meter over two eight-measure phrases. The chorus, however, is asymmetrical in its phrase structure and more complex overall. This interplay between symmetry and asymmetry is one of the features that give music its dynamic formal shape, and awareness of these details can make a performance smoother, more coherent, and more exciting.

Self-Test 12.1
may be done
at this time.

Apply This!
12.1 and 12.2
may be done
at this time.

Workbook
Exercise 12.1
may be done
at this time.

For a more
complex
example
of elision
in a Haydn
symphony,
see Web
Feature 12.4.

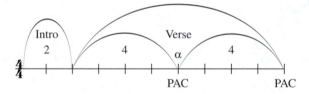

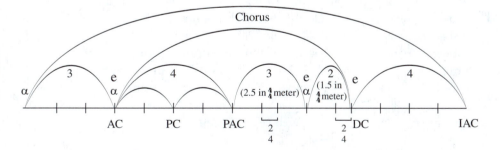

Example 12.21. Arch map of Elton John, "Goodbye Yellow Brick Road," first verse and chorus [0:00–1:38].

---

[2] This is labeled as "AC" on the diagram because while the background vocals cadence on the mediant scale degree, implying an IAC, the lead vocal begins the next section with the tonic scale degree in the melodic line on the downbeat, implying a PAC.

CONCLUSION

In this chapter we began to explore how phrases are built from the "bottom up"—from motives into phrases, then into periods or even larger units. We have also seen how sections of different lengths can be combined into forms of some complexity. Often, as in our examples from composers as diverse as Elton John and Joseph Haydn (see Web Feature 12.3), phrases are "run into" one another through elision.

We have also considered how a piece of music may be analyzed from the "top down," by means of arch map diagramming. In your own work with arch maps you may find it easiest to begin at the highest level—the entire movement, or entire piece—and then work inward to the lowest hierarchical levels. For example, in creating an arch map of the third movement of Haydn's Symphony no. 101, one might find it easiest to begin with the explicitly articulated "main sections" of the movement—the *Menuetto* and *Trio* sections, and within each of those sections the portions that are marked off from each other by the repeat signs. Then, one can look for significant **recapitulations**, or returns of previous material, such as measure 49 in the *Menuetto* and measure 150 in the *Trio*. From there, one would usually look for important cadences as markers of the ends of phrases or periods.

Ultimately, analysis of music must proceed in both directions—"top down" and "bottom up." Often you will find yourself shifting perspective, back and forth between the two. In the same way that a film usually does not consist solely of close-ups or of wide shots, but varies perspective for variety and completeness, the process of analysis involves both attention to detail and an eye (and ear) for long-term connections between seemingly unrelated events.

Terms to Know

antecedent phrase
arch map
augmentation (applied to motives)
consequent phrase
contrasting period
diminution
double period
elision
hypermeter

imitation (real vs. tonal)
inversion (applied to motives)
lead-in (see Web Feature 12.4)
minuet (see Web Feature 12.4)
motive
motivic parallelism (see Web Feature 12.3)

parallel period
period
periodicity
phrase
phrase group
recapitulation
retrograde
seam
sentence structure
sequence

Self-Test

12.1. For each of the musical excerpts that follow, label the cadences. Label any instances of antecedent phrases, consequent phrases, and periods. Finally, identify the overall form of each excerpt: period (label by type—parallel, similar, or contrasting), double period, or three-phrase period or phrase group (identify the thematic form with letters, such as abb').

a. Giovanni Paisello (1740–1816), "Nel cor più non mi sento" from *La Molinara*, mm. 9–16.

b. Attributed to Bach, Minuet in G from the *Notebook for Anna Magdalena Bach*, mm. 1–16.

(Continued)

c. Beethoven, Piano Sonata no. 8 in C minor ("Pathétique") (iii), mm. 1–17.

d. Traditional American tune, "Arkansas Traveler."

e. Mozart, "Mi tradì quell' alma ingrata" from *Don Giovanni*.

Mi tra - di __ quell' al - ma in - gra - ta, quell' al - ma'in - gra - ta,

(Continued)

in - fe - li - ce, o Di - o! mi fa, in - fe - li - ce, o

Di - o! mi fa, in - fe - li - ce, o Di - o! o _ Dio! mi fa.

Apply This!

12.1. Analysis. For the musical composition beginning on the next page, prepare an analysis that incorporates as much as possible of what you have learned in the last two chapters. Begin by locating and identifying cadences on the score (some are located, at least, for you, as they are in keys other than the tonic). Based on the types of cadences, determine whether phrases are antecedent or consequent, and if there is an antecedent-consequent phrase pattern, label on the score the type of period that results. If there are motives that serve to unify the composition, label them on the score.

Next, prepare an arch map for the piece, using Example 12.21 as your model. Your arch map should include the location and type of cadences, and show how phrases combine into larger units. If phrases begin with an anacrusis, indicate this with α; if phrases elide together, show this with μ. You do not need to show subphrase divisions unless a phrase is found to be in sentence structure.

Beethoven, Piano Sonata no. 2 in A major, op. 2 no. 2 (iii).

SCHERZO.
Allegretto.

PART 2: Form and Chromatic Harmony 1

12.2. Composition. Many composers begin the work of composing a piece by sketching out the form of the work beforehand. If they are fulfilling a commission for a work of a certain length, for example, they plan how many measures will be needed to fill the time span; from this they can determine a suitable place for the climax, return of the opening theme, and so forth. In the same way, you can use an arch map to provide a template for a musical composition.

Imagine that you have been commissioned to compose a short waltz lasting two minutes in length. Using a tempo of ♩ = 90, determine how many measures you will need to compose a two-minute work. Next, make an arch map comprising that number of measures. Your composition should be in three sections: the first section a symmetrical parallel period, the second section a symmetrical contrasting period with different thematic material, and the final section a return (either exactly, or slightly modified or abbreviated) of the first section. The second section does not have to comprise the same number of measures as the first. Mark the appropriate cadences at the ends of your phrases within each period. Be sure the final cadence of your arch map is a perfect authentic cadence.

Once your arch map is completed, use it as a guide to compose a simple melody following its form. Mark out a sheet of manuscript paper or create a notation file with the required number of measures. Choose a key for your composition and add the key signature. At the appropriate measures, transfer the cadence information from your arch map—these will be your goal points as you compose your melody. You might want to sketch in the ending scale degrees for your melody at these cadences—the tonic for a perfect authentic cadence, for example, or the leading tone for a half cadence. The concluding note of the cadence should occur on the downbeat of the measure.

Once you have added the necessary goal points for your melodic lines, begin writing your tune. You do not need to work out a harmonic analysis, but it might be helpful to sketch in chord symbols that would go with your melodic line. Keep the harmony simple, and the harmonic rhythm mostly regular; it is perfectly acceptable for two or more melodic notes to have the same harmony if the harmony fits with the notes. Remember that the harmonic rhythm often changes in advance of a cadence.

Once you have finished, try out your melody at a keyboard or other instrument. If you have worked out chord symbols, try having a classmate accompany your melody at the keyboard or on guitar. How does your melody sound? Do any parts need to be changed? It is perfectly fine to revise your melody to improve its shape or playability, as long as the number of measures and phrase/period structure are not changed. Share your compositional efforts with your classmates.

CHAPTER 13

HARMONIC FUNCTION APPLIED
Prolongation and the Phrase Model

OVERVIEW

Harmonic function is revisited in this chapter, to show how it is manifest in an archetypal phrase model. Periods may be classified harmonically—how harmonic function is played out across two or more phrases—as well as thematically. This chapter also introduces prolongation, different means of expanding a harmonic function through contrapuntal embellishment, allowing for perception of structural and embellishing levels of harmony.

INTRODUCTION: HARMONIC FUNCTION REVISITED

In Chapter 5 you were introduced to the three main categories of harmonic function: tonic (T), dominant (D), and predominant (PD). The same chord may have different functions depending on the key in which it is found: A C major chord, for example, would have a tonic function in C major (as a I), a dominant function in F major or F minor (as a V), and a predominant function in G major (as a IV), A minor (as a III), or E minor (as a VI). However, this tells only part of the story regarding harmonic function.

For example, while vi or iii would normally have a PD function at the *beginning* or *middle* of a phrase, there are other times when these chords might be used at the *end* of a phrase *deceptively*. When V moves to vi in a deceptive cadence, for example, the vi substitutes for the I as a kind of "false tonic." Here vi functions as a **tonic substitute**, labeled with a T within square brackets, [T]. Similarly, iii can be used deceptively (albeit rarely) as a **dominant substitute**, or [D]. In both instances the deceptive chord in question shares two common tones with the triad for which it is substituting.

The cadential $\frac{6}{4}$ chord presents another special case. Because the cadential $\frac{6}{4}$ chord is a second-inversion tonic chord, one would expect it to have a tonic harmonic function. However, as can be seen from both of the cadences in Example 13.1 (Mozart K.331 [i]), the cadential $\frac{6}{4}$ chord comes after a chord with a predominant function: ii^6. This would be a **retrogression** (backward harmonic movement).

Example 13.1. Mozart, Piano Sonata K.331 (i), mm. 1–8, with harmonic function analysis at beginning and end of phrases.

Examining the cadential $^6_4$ chord from a linear perspective, however, we can see that it is a *product of dissonances embellishing the dominant-function V chord that follows it*. In other words, the cadential $^6_4$ chord is *spelled* like a tonic chord in second inversion, but it does not have a tonic *function*. Instead, it *embellishes* and thus is part of the dominant chord to which the predominant chord resolves, and so it has a *dominant* (D) function.

LEVEL MASTERY 13.1.

Label the harmonic function above each of the chords in the progressions below. If labeling a iii or vi chord, consider whether it appears at the beginning or the end of the progression.

1. Bb: I   IV   V

2. G: ii^6 V   vi

3. c#: i   VI   iv

4. Ab: iii   vi   ii

5. d: i^6 ii$^{ø6}_5$ V

6. b: i   iv$^6_4$ i

7. D: I   IV   ii

8. Eb: I   V   vi

9. B: vi   V   I

PERIODS AND THE PHRASE MODEL

In Chapter 12 we learned how periods are classified according to their thematic structure—whether the phrases began with identical (parallel), similar, or different (contrasting) material. We can also classify periods according to how they employ *harmonic functions* in the phrase model.

Remember that a period is made up of two phrases—an antecedent phrase (usually ending on a half cadence) and a consequent phrase (usually ending on a perfect authentic cadence). We can summarize the structure in a diagram like this:

ANTECEDENT   CONSEQUENT

‖ T   PD–D ‖ *x*   D–T ‖
                             HC   PAC

Consider *the beginning of the consequent phrase*, the part marked with an *x* above. The antecedent phrase introduces an incomplete phrase model: T–PD–D. The lack of resolution to a final T explains why the opening phrase, by itself, does not give us a feeling of satisfactory closure. How then is this lack of resolution rectified?

- One solution is to *start over again*, and complete the phrase model the second time around, as shown below:

ANTECEDENT   CONSEQUENT

‖ T   PD–D ‖ T   PD–D–T ‖
                             HC   PAC

This is an **interrupted period**. The progression of T–PD–D–T is *interrupted* by the half cadence at the end of the antecedent phrase; in the consequent phrase the phrase model is *repeated from the beginning* and completed. Often this "starting over" quality of the interrupted period is reinforced melodically as well, so that an interrupted period is also a parallel period. The first half of the theme from the first movement of Mozart's Sonata in A major, K.331 (Example 13.1) is an interrupted period.

- The other solution is to *continue* from where you left off:

ANTECEDENT   CONSEQUENT

‖ T   PD–D ‖ D   –T ‖
                             HC   PAC

This is a **continuous period**, in which the phrase model actually *continues across the antecedent phrase's cadence* to be completed by the consequent phrase. Two diverse examples are shown in Example 13.2; the verse from Jimmy Buffett's "Margaritaville" (Example 13.2b) is presented in a reduction to show the sentence structure of the melodic line in each phrase and to clarify the application of the phrase model. Both of our examples also make use of melodic sequence, so they are also similar periods.

Example 13.2a. Mozart, Symphony no. 41 in C major ("Jupiter"), K. 551 (i), mm. 1–8 (reduction).

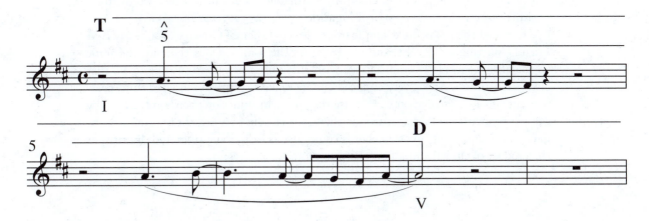

Example 13.2b. Jimmy Buffett, "Margaritaville," verse (melodic reduction).
(Continued)

(Continued)

These categories (interrupted versus continuous) are based on *harmonic* criteria; thus, they are independent from the *thematic* categories of parallel, similar, and contrasting periods. A period may be parallel and interrupted, for example, or it may be similar and continuous.

Workbook Exercise 13.1 may be done at this time.

CONTRAPUNTAL EXPANSION OF THE PHRASE MODEL: PROLONGATION

In Chapter 10 we examined the different functional contexts for $^6_4$ or $^4_3$ chords: cadential, passing, neighboring, arpeggiating, and pedal. With the exception of the cadential $^6_4$, all of these contexts have one thing in common: In each case, the $^6_4$ or $^4_3$ chord is surrounded by chords of the *same* harmony, sometimes in the same position and sometimes (as in the passing $^6_4$ chord) in a different inversion. In other words, the $^6_4$ chord is *part of an expansion, or* **prolongation**, *of the harmony that frames it.*

Consider the following example from the conclusion of Queen's "You're My Best Friend," starting at [2:37] (Example 13.3). As the song reaches the end, the tonic (B major) is continually emphasized, with three brief neighboring dips to V[6] that always return to I. At the very end, the guitars make a surprising upward shift, passing through a vii[o6] to end on I[6]. Because the dominant-function chords are so brief by comparison with the I's that surround them, the closing bars present a **tonic prolongation**; the dominant-function chords could just as easily be interpreted, linearly, as the product of embellishing non-chord tones.

Example 13.3. Queen, "You're My Best Friend" [2:37–2:51].

Because the first, repeated, prolongation in Example 13.3 involves a neighbor-tone-like movement in the bass, it is a **neighboring prolongation**, indicated by an upper case N spanning the chord progression, below the harmonic analysis. The last three chords in the song, with a passing-tone-like movement in the bass, provide a **passing prolongation**, indicated by an upper case P spanning the chord progression, below the harmonic analysis. Example 13.4 shows the Queen excerpt with a **layer analysis**, detailing the prolongations and the harmonic function.

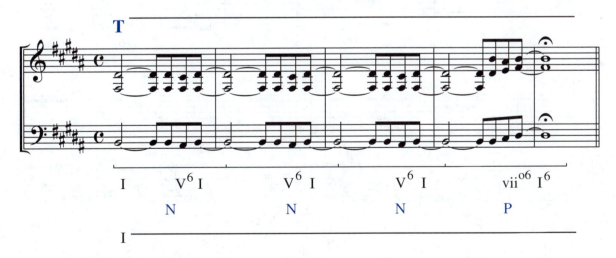

Example 13.4. Queen, "You're My Best Friend" [2:37–2:51], with layer analysis (prolongations and harmonic function) added.

Prolongation reveals the structural essence of a chord progression, showing what underlies the more elaborative surface. Example 13.5 shows an extended half cadence from the first movement of Beethoven's Piano Sonata in D minor, op. 31 no. 2, "The Tempest." It would be cumbersome to analyze each and every alternation of V and i as we approach the end of the phrase. The V chord receives metrical emphasis, however, occurring on the downbeats; thus, this passage is a **dominant prolongation**, a prolongation of V. Prolongations usually extend a tonic or dominant function. When a prolongation occurs without any movement in the bass, in a progression such as I–IV$^6_4$–I or V–I$^6_4$–V (such as we see here), the result is a **pedal (PED) prolongation**. Often such prolongations can also be accounted for as the product of non-chord (especially neighboring) tone activity in the upper voices.

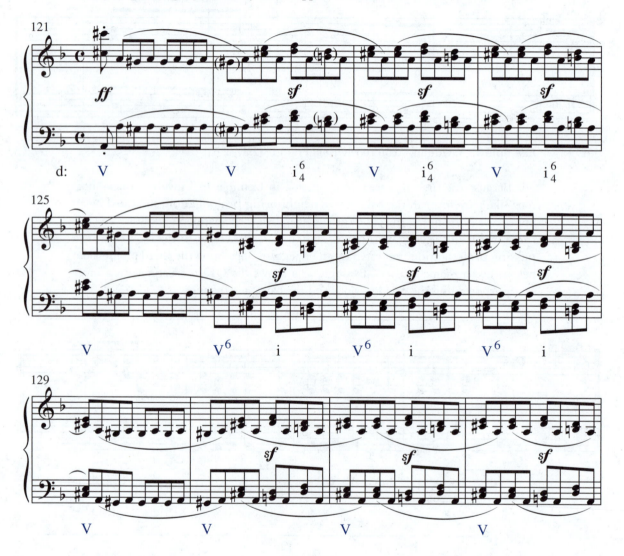

Example 13.5. Beethoven, Piano Sonata in D minor, op. 31 no. 2 ("The Tempest") (i) mm. 121–138. *(Continued)*

(Continued)

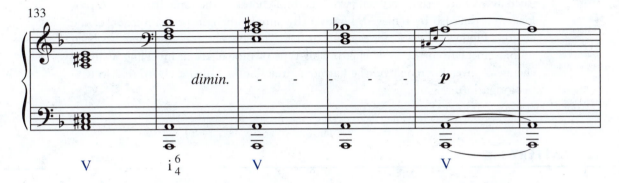

Sometimes a prolongation involves a skip in the bass line. In those progressions where the bass note of the embellishing chord acts as an incomplete neighbor (the generic label for the appoggiatura and escape tone), the prolongation involved is an **incomplete neighbor (IN) prolongation**. Example 13.6 shows how Beethoven makes use of two incomplete neighbor prolongations of the tonic in the first two measures of the second movement of his "Pathétique" sonata. (Note that measure 3, incidentally, is not a passing prolongation; even though the bass line is moving by step, the chords on beats 1 and 2 are of two different harmonies.)

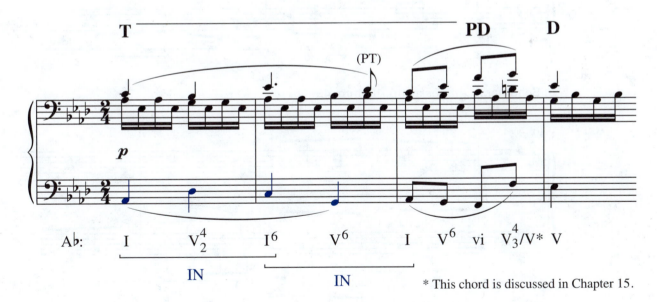

* This chord is discussed in Chapter 15.

Example 13.6. Beethoven, Piano Sonata no. 8 in A♭ major, op. 13 ("Pathétique") (ii), mm. 1–4, with layer analysis (prolongations and harmonic function) added.

Each of the prolongations we have examined so far involve an *embellishing chord* (such as a V) occurring between two structural chords of the same harmony. A prolongation can also be achieved, however, by simply changing the inversion of the chord; a I followed by a I⁶, for example, is not a "progression" because there has been no movement from the tonic chord. This type of prolongation, involving a simple change of inversion to extend the harmonic function, is called a **chordal skip (CS) prolongation**.

LEVEL MASTERY 13.2.

Label the prolongation bracket(s) found in each of the excerpts below. Use the labels N, P, IN, CS, or PED.

a. Joseph Haydn, Piano Sonata in D major, Hob. XVI/37 (i), mm. 9–11a.

b. Schumann, *Arabeske*, op. 18, mm. 49–56.

c. Heinrich Isaac, "Innsbruck, Ich muss dich lassen," mm. 10–19a.

d. Karl Jenkins, *Palladio: Concerto Grosso for String Orchestra* (i), mm. 3–6.

Apply This!
13.1, 13.2
and 13.3 may
be done at
this time.

Workbook
Exercise 13.2
may be done
at this time.

CONCLUSION

Understanding how harmonic function and prolongation work can be a tremendous asset to your musicianship. As you familiarize yourself with prolongations you will understand how a V chord at a cadence, for example, is functionally different than the same chord as it might appear in a prolongation. Such awareness can lead to more nuanced and understanding performances.

Music is made up of *patterns*, and understanding or being able to predict how patterns unfold in music will aid you in your sight-reading and improvising. The different kinds of prolongations, the different progressions associated with the T–PD–D phrase model—these are all musical patterns, and you will soon discover how certain patterns predominate in different musical styles.

Arthur Rubinstein tells a story in his autobiography about a time when he appeared with the Berlin Philharmonic. His performance of a Brahms piano concerto went very well, but when he went onstage to play an encore, he found the piece he had ready had vanished from his memory. So, thinking quickly, he improvised an encore in the style of the piece he intended to play. The ability to pull that off requires a thoroughgoing familiarity with musical style, and how to use the patterns that are commonly encountered in the music you play.

Terms to Know

chordal skip prolongation (CS)
continuous period
dominant prolongation
dominant substitute [D]
incomplete neighbor prolongation (IN)

interrupted period
neighboring prolongation (N)
passing prolongation (P)
pedal prolongation (PED)

prolongation
retrogression
tonic prolongation
tonic substitute [T]

Apply This!

13.1. Analysis. Provide the harmonic analysis (Roman numerals and inversion symbols) for each excerpt. (Some chords have been provided for you—you will learn about these in later chapters.) Then, prepare a layer analysis—locate and label any prolongation patterns you may find. Mark prolongations by function (T, PD, or D) and by type (passing, neighboring, pedal, or chordal skip).

a. Beethoven, Piano Sonata in F minor, op. 2 no. 1 (i), mm. 1–8.

b. Chopin, Nocturne in E minor, op. 72 no. 1, mm. 1–5.

c. Verdi, "Bella Figlia" from *Rigoletto*, Act IV, mm. 1–8.

d. Sly and the Family Stone, "Everyday People."

13.2. Composition. Using what you have learned to this point, you are now equipped to write a short 16-measure composition, made up of two periods, each consisting of two four-bar phrases. Begin by outlining the cadences:

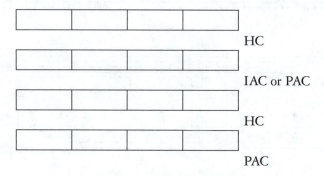

HC

IAC or PAC

HC

PAC

    Given the cadential plan above, the first and third phrases (antecedent phrases of your periods) will follow the phrase model T–PD–D; the second and fourth phrases (consequent phrases) will follow the phrase model T–PD–D–T. Fill in the boxes above with the functions, approximately where they should come in the phrase.

    Now that you have the functional phrase models in place, you can move to staff paper. Choose a key, a meter, and structural chords that will fit the functions within the phrase model. Remember, the I chord is a T function; V and vii° have a D function, and PD chords include ii (often in first inversion), IV, iii and vi. Following the circle of fifths backward from V–I, we see that ii usually precedes V (IV can be used as a substitute), whereas vi usually precedes ii (in a pattern of descending-third motion, vi will also often go to IV). The iii chord is farther back in the circle of fifths and usually precedes vi in a circle-of-fifths harmonic sequence (iii–vi–ii–V–I). Think of ways to include harmonic variety in your phrase models, but also remember that simplicity is important; there is no need to include one of every chord in each phrase! At this point, remember, your chords should be thought of as *structural* pillars in each phrase.

    The next step is where you can elaborate your structural chords through prolongation. If, for example, you have a T–PD–D–T pattern in one phrase realized as I–ii^6–V–I, one way to introduce prolongations might be as follows:

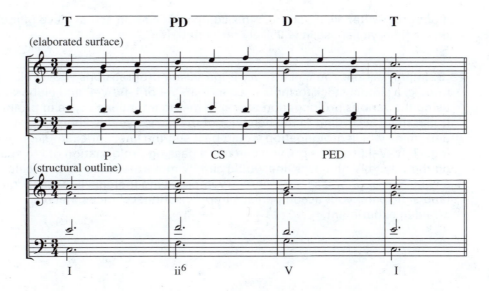

When you have provided an elaborated surface for all four phrases, you may retain the chorale-like texture of our example and simply add a few non-chord tones for color and interest, or you may recast your piece in a different stylistic texture. For example, we could transfer our previous example to a Classical-era texture by means of Alberti bass figurations in the accompaniment:

Or, if a Romantic-era waltz is desired:

Your final step should be to add appropriate expression markings (slurs, dynamics and so forth) as desired. Give your piece a title if you choose, and hear it performed if possible—after all, if you treat this composition as an actual piece of music, rather than a theory exercise, it will likely turn out better!

13.3. Improvisation. You can also try improvising progressions with prolongations. Choose a simple stock formula such as I–ii^6–V–I or I–IV–V–I, and elaborate upon it using the various prolongation types. Remember that each type of prolongation is classified according to the behavior of the bass; use this knowledge to help you determine which prolongation would best suit the line. For example, if you are playing a I–IV–V–I progression, you can use a passing prolongation of I to span I and I^6 on the way to IV; the bass line would simply move stepwise up the scale. If you play a wind, string or brass instrument, try improvising melodic lines that complement (and anticipate) your accompanist's improvisational choices. Relax and don't be afraid to experiment.

CHAPTER 14

HARMONIC PROGRESSION AND SEQUENCE

OVERVIEW

Harmonic function governs the order of chord progressions according to the PD–D–T pattern of the phrase model. The phrase model is also often embellished by patterns of harmonic sequence. In this chapter we examine the most common chord progressions, working backward through the circle of fifths. This chapter also considers common varieties of ascending and descending harmonic sequences characterized by linear intervallic patterns.

AUDIO LIST

Johann Sebastian Bach, Brandenburg Concerto   Nat "King" Cole, "Autumn Leaves"
no. 2 in F major, i

In Chapter 5 you learned how harmonic function governs the order of chord progressions, and how harmonic functions often follow a PD–D–T pattern. In this chapter we will examine the most common chord-to-chord progressions, beginning with the viiº and its similarities with the V chord. From there, we will work backward through the circle of fifths to understand how the short progressions we have studied so far can be combined into larger units. Finally, we will look at other common varieties of harmonic sequence.

THE viiº

Like the V or V⁷, the viiº triad is resolved using tendency tone patterns. The viiº triad is sometimes used as a substitute for V, since it shares its three tones with V⁷; more commonly the viiº is "fleshed out" by adding a chord seventh.

The viiº *triad* almost never appears in root position or second inversion, because of the dissonant tritone found above the bass in both of those positions. Instead, *the viiº chord is most often used in first inversion, with the bass doubled*, often in a passing prolongation (Example 14.1). Notice that the tenor line's E–D–C neatly mirrors the bass line's C–D–E. The viiº⁶ occurs in the midst of a **voice exchange** between the bass and tenor; the pitches C and E appear to be switched between the parts, inverting the interval.

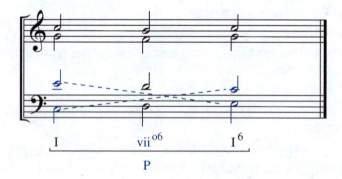

Example 14.1. Passing prolongation involving viiº⁶, showing voice exchange.

Because of its dominant function status, the vii°⁶ chord resolves most commonly directly to I, less often to some form of V. In resolving to I, the leading tone should resolve up by step to the tonic; the bass (scale degree 2) should resolve to the tonic as part of a 2–1 tendency tone pair or should resolve to the mediant if the chord of resolution is I⁶. Since the bass note is the doubled note, the other scale degree 2 should resolve in contrary motion with the bass to avoid parallel octaves. See the examples of passing prolongation in Example 14.2.

a. Mozart, Piano Sonata in F major, K. 533 (ii), mm. 1–4

b. Beethoven, Piano Sonata in F minor, op. 2 no. 1 (i), mm. 1–8

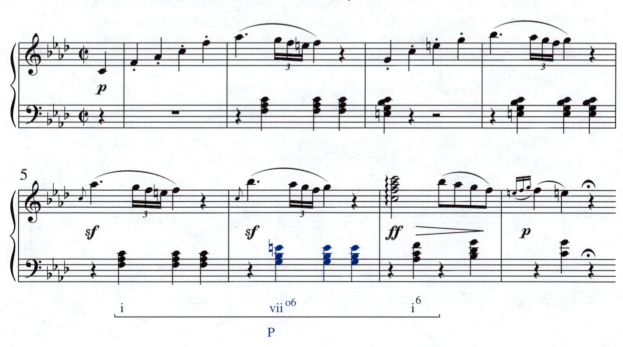

c. Schumann, "Soldier's March" from *Album for the Young*, mm. 1–4.

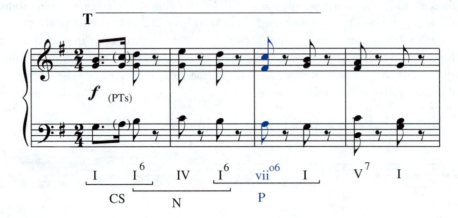

I	I^6	IV	I^6	vii^{o6}	I	V^7	I

CS N P

Example 14.2. Examples of vii^{o6} in passing prolongations.

In minor keys, the root of the chord is the *leading tone* drawn from the *harmonic minor* scale. In minor the root of the vii^o triad must be raised to produce the leading tone. The vii^o triad is thus identical in major or minor; when the chord seventh is added to the triad, however, two different seventh chord qualities are possible.

- A seventh chord built on the leading tone can be either fully diminished (vii^{o7}) or half diminished (vii^{ø7}, in major keys). In major keys, the chord frequently appears in its fully diminished form, its seventh (the sixth scale degree) chromatically lowered.

A vii^{o7} or vii^{ø7} will most commonly resolve either directly to I or to V^7 in some inversion. Resolving to V^7 is easily achieved by motion of the chord seventh (which should resolve down by step anyway), down by step to the root of the V. (In terms of scale degrees, this is a 6–5 tendency tone pair.) Example 14.3 shows how the vii^{o7}, in each of its inversions, resolves to various inversions of V^7.

a: vii^{o7} V$^6_5$ vii$^{o6}_5$ V$^4_3$ vii$^{o4}_3$ V$^4_2$ vii$^{o4}_2$ V^7

Example 14.3. Resolutions of vii^{o7} to V, in each of their inversions.

In the nineteenth century the V^7 and vii^{o7} appear so frequently together that the chord seventh of the vii^{o7} might be better interpreted as a dissonant ninth added to the V^7, resulting in a kind of "superdominant." Notice the voice exchange between the seventh and ninth in Example 14.4.

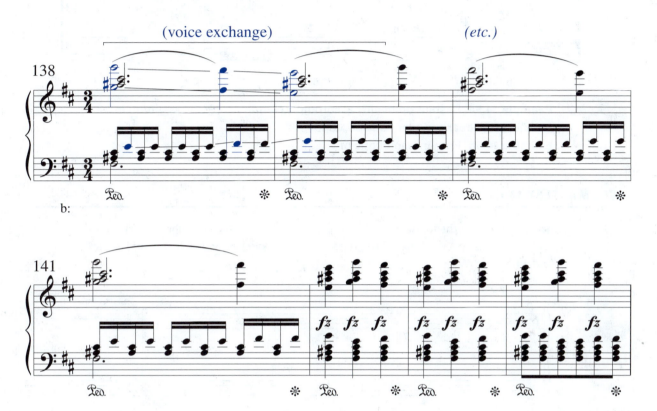

Example 14.4. Schubert, Symphony no. 8 in B minor, D759 ("Unfinished") (i), mm. 138–144 (piano reduction by Richard Kleinmichel).

The $vii^{ø7}$ requires extra caution in resolution, because of the perfect fifth interval found between the third and the chord seventh when the chord is spelled in its most compact arrangement (Example 14.5a). To avoid parallel fifths, either *revoice the chord* so that the interval between these two chord tones is *inverted to a perfect fourth*, or *resolve the $vii^{ø7}$ to a V^6_5 first*, treating the chord seventh of the $vii^{ø7}$ as a non-chord tone of the V^6_5. Example 14.5b shows both of these approaches.

Example 14.5a. Resolution of vii^{ø7} according to tendency tones, resulting in parallel fifths between tenor and soprano.
Example 14.5b. Proper resolutions of vii^{ø7}.

LEVEL MASTERY 14.1.

Spell and resolve the following half and fully diminished seventh chords, in the keys and inversions specified, using the tendency tone model provided in Examples 14.3 and 14.5.

Self-Test 14.1 may be done at this time, as a review of harmonic functions.

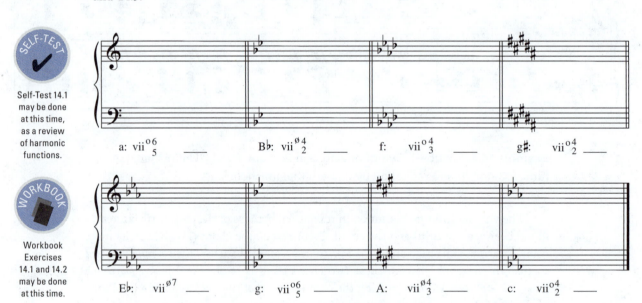

a: vii^{o6}₅ ____   B♭: vii^{ø4}₂ ____   f: vii^{o4}₃ ____   g♯: vii^{o4}₂ ____

E♭: vii^{ø7} ____   g: vii^{o6}₅ ____   A: vii^{ø4}₃ ____   c: vii^{o4}₂ ____

Workbook Exercises 14.1 and 14.2 may be done at this time.

THE ii⁽⁷⁾ AND IV⁽⁷⁾ IN MAJOR AND MINOR

The ii and IV chords are the most common predominant chords to be found immediately before V or vii°. The ii chord is particularly common in first inversion, and so—having the same bass note and one other common tone with the root position IV–ii⁶ is virtually interchangeable with IV in preceding the V.

When the chord seventh is added, ii⁷ is more common than IV⁷. This is because the structure of the IV⁷ chord contains *two interlocking perfect fifths* when spelled in its most compact close spacing (see Example 14.6a). If resolving a root position IV⁷ directly to V is absolutely essential, the spacing of the IV⁷ should be arranged such that the chord seventh is in a lower register than the third (see Example 14.6b). Another solution is to interpose one or more connecting chords, such as a cadential $^6_4$ or a vii°⁷, between the IV⁷ and the V.

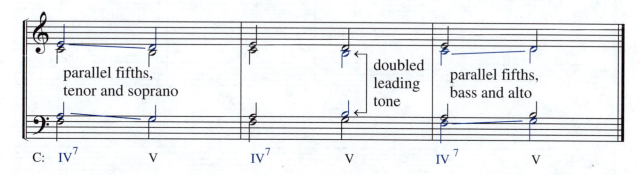

Example 14.6a. Part writing difficulties in resolving a root position IV⁷ to V.

For a detailed study of how Bach treated these resolutions in his Prelude in C major from Book 1 of *The Well-Tempered Clavier*, see Web Feature 14.1.

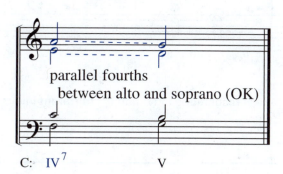

Example 14.6b. A satisfactory voicing of IV⁷, resolving to V.

The minor-key IV⁷ and ii⁷ chords differ in quality from their major-key counterparts.

- *The most common form of the subdominant seventh in minor is a minor-minor seventh* (iv⁷), derived from the harmonic (or natural) minor form of the scale.
- *The most common form of the supertonic seventh in minor is a half-diminished seventh chord* (ii°⁷).

In both of these chords the usual tendency tone patterns apply—*chord sevenths resolve downward by step* and scale degree six (the third of iv⁷ and the fifth of ii°⁷) will usually resolve down a half step to scale degree five. *The sixth scale degree in minor almost never resolves upward*, because the result would be an augmented second from the submediant to the leading tone. See the examples in Example 14.7. Note that the progression of iv$_5^6$–V is exceedingly rare because it would be impossible to allow the chord seventh to resolve downward and avoid parallel fifths, and so it is not included below (ii$^{\varnothing4}_3$ would be used instead of iv$_5^6$ in such instances).

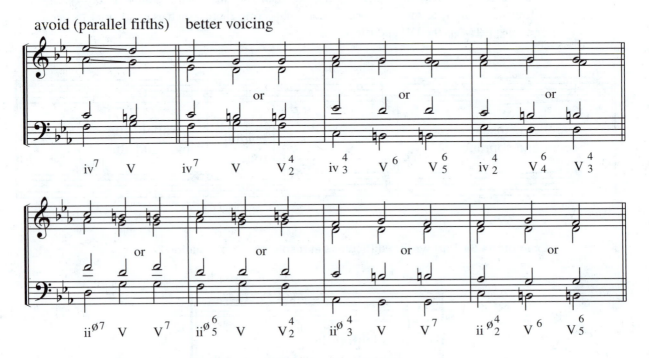

Example 14.7. Typical resolutions of iv^7 and ii$^{\varnothing7}$ (different inversions) in minor.

LEVEL MASTERY 14.2.

Spell the following ii$^{(7)}$ and IV$^{(7)}$ chords, in the keys and inversions specified, and resolve them to V (in root position or inversion, as required).

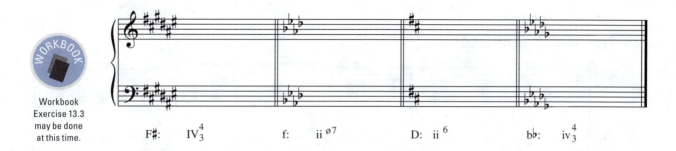

Workbook Exercise 13.3 may be done at this time.

F♯: IV$_3^4$ f: ii^{ø7} D: ii^6 b♭: iv$_3^4$

THE vi$^{(7)}$ IN MAJOR AND MINOR

The vi chord is a weaker predominant chord than ii or IV, and consequently it usually precedes either of those chords en route to the V chord (Examples 14.8 and 14.9). The progression I–vi–IV–V, in which the root proceeds by thirds on its way down to the submediant, is familiar from countless 1950s doo-wop songs and Hoagy Carmichael's "Heart and Soul." If the vi chord has a chord seventh, the presence of the seventh—as with other diatonic seventh chords—will serve to intensify the need for resolution to the next chord, and the chord seventh will resolve downward by step.

("America")

My coun-try, T'is of thee,

I   vi   ii^6 V   i   VI   ii^{o6} V   I   vi   ii^6 V

Example 14.8. The I–vi–ii–V progression, in major and minor.

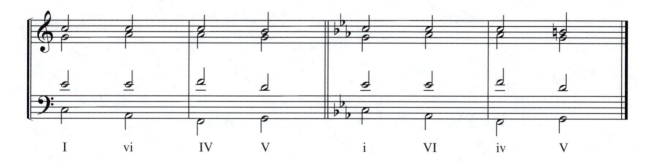

I   vi   IV   V   i   VI   iv   V

Example 14.9. The I–vi–IV–V progression, in major and minor. *(Continued)*

(Continued)

("Doo-Wop" progression)

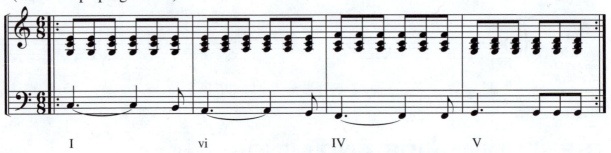

    I   vi   IV   V

The vi chord rarely resolves directly to V itself, because of voice-leading issues involving parallel fifths or octaves, or the melodic augmented second in minor. The outer voices must be moving in contrary motion for proper resolution to occur (Example 14.10).

Example 14.10. Richard Strauss, *Also Sprach Zarathustra*, mm. 13–21 (piano reduction).

In minor, the submediant chord is usually derived from the natural minor form of the scale, taking the form of a major triad or a major-major seventh chord.

Occasionally one finds a "vi°" or "vi°⁷" in minor, the raised-submediant scale degree root of which is arguably derived from the ascending melodic minor scale. Often, however, such chords are better accounted for as little more than decorative chords that are the product of surface voice leading.

THE iii⁽⁷⁾ IN MAJOR AND MINOR

The iii chord is the weakest of the predominant function chords, and consequently it is also the rarest. It almost always precedes a vi chord as part of a circle-of-fifths harmonic progression (iii–vi–ii–V–I). The only other resolution involves movement up by second; iii → IV is part of the descending third "Pachelbel" progression, for example (in such a progression, however, one must be careful to avoid parallel fifths—see Pachelbel's solution in Example 14.23). As with the other diatonic triads, a chord seventh may be added to intensify the need for resolution to the next chord.

LEVEL MASTERY 14.3.

Spell the following iii⁽⁷⁾ and vi⁽⁷⁾ chords, in the keys and inversions specified, and resolve them as indicated.

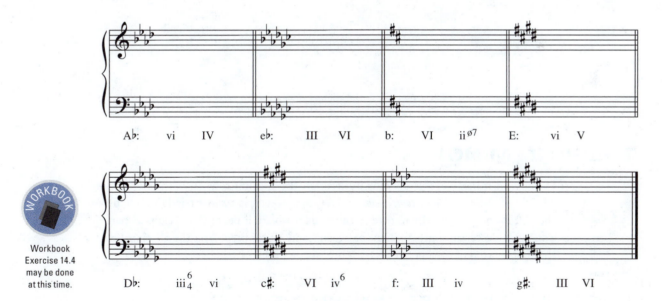

Workbook Exercise 14.4 may be done at this time.

SUMMARY OF HARMONIC MOTION

- The chord progressions we have examined in this chapter can be summarized according to three basic root motions (movement of the root from chord to chord): *Up a second*, *Down a third*, and *Up a fourth/Down a fifth*.

Table 14.1 provides the applicable progressions for each root motion. The only exceptions involve the iii chord; V and vii° do not normally resolve to iii or III, and—as we have seen—iii will almost always move up by fourth or down by fifth to vi.

TABLE 14.1. Summary of harmonic progressions, classified by root movement.

MAJOR KEYS			
Up a 2nd:	**Down a 2nd:**	**Down a 3rd:**	**Up a 4th (Down a 5th):**
I → ii	vi → V (rare)	I → vi	I → IV
iii → IV (rare)		vi → IV	ii → V
IV → V		IV → ii	iii → vi
V → vi			V → I
vi → vii°			vi → ii
vii° → I			

MINOR KEYS			
Up a 2nd:	**Down a 2nd:**	**Down a 3rd:**	**Up a 4th (Down a 5th):**
i → ii°	VI → V (rare)	i → VI	i → iv
iv → V		VI → iv	ii° → V
V → VI		iv → ii°	III → V
VI → vii°			V → i
vii° → i			VI → ii°
			VII → III

THE VII IN MINOR

Self-Test 14.2 may be done at this time.

Usually, in minor keys, the vii° is built upon the leading tone in harmonic minor. The chord built on the *subtonic in natural minor*, however, is a *major* triad (VII). Unlike the vii°, it does not usually resolve to the tonic. Instead, it usually functions as part of a stepwise descending progression (between I and VI) or preceding the III chord with the root motion of up a perfect fourth or down a perfect fifth.

THE DIATONIC (DESCENDING FIFTH) CIRCLE-OF-FIFTHS HARMONIC SEQUENCE

Looking at Table 14.1, it is evident that the category with the most examples is that involving root motion of up a fourth or down a fifth. We have already seen that ii–V–I is a very common progression, involving two consecutive root motions of this type. We can extend this basic pattern back from the concluding ii–V–I to create a **diatonic circle-of-fifths sequence**. This type of sequence earns its name from the fact that the roots proceed *counter-clockwise* along the circle of fifths. A diatonic circle-of-fifths sequence need not be complete, but to be considered a sequence it must consist of at least four chords (such as vi–ii–V–I), in which the root motion of the first pair of chords is repeated a step lower in the second pair of chords.

A complete diatonic circle-of-fifths sequence is shown in Example 14.11. At one point in a complete progression the root motion must proceed by tritone (augmented fourth or diminished fifth) in order to stay within the confines of the key. In major keys this tritone root motion happens between IV and vii°; in minor keys it occurs between VI and ii°. Normally, remember, the diminished chord appears in first inversion to prevent the tritone interval above the bass note; this also results in a smoother bass line.

Example 14.11. Complete diatonic circle-of-fifths sequences, in major and minor.

The minor-key diatonic circle-of-fifths sequence offers an interesting ambiguity to the listener, at least at first. Since it involves the VII, if the sequence begins on the tonic then the opening chords of the sequence (i–iv–VII–III) can just as easily be heard as vi–ii–V–I in the key of the relative major. As the sequence continues, however, the major "mood" of the passage quickly fades as its minor context becomes clearer.

In the first movement of Bach's Brandenburg Concerto no. 2 in F major, the sequence shown in Example 14.12 takes place between two different thematic statements in D minor (found in the first and last two measures of the example). (Note: the trumpet part on the top line is a piccolo trumpet in F; transpose its part a perfect fourth higher to get the sounding pitch.)

Example 14.13 shows a textural reduction of the diatonic sequence in Example 14.12. Notice that every chord in the sequence is a seventh chord; chord sevenths are commonly used in these sequences to add to the momentum and transitional nature of the passage. The chord sequence to "Autumn Leaves" is also made up entirely of diatonic seventh chords (Example 14.14). Notice that in both Examples 14.13 and 14.14 the location of the chord seventh alternates between voices in each chord; the chord seventh is held over, suspension-like, from a consonance in the previous chord.

Example 14.12. Bach, Brandenburg Concerto no. 2 in F major, BWV 1047 (i), mm. 31–41. *(Continued)*

(Continued)

(Continued)

PAC

(Continued)

(thematic statement, D minor)

Example 14.13. Three-part voice-leading reduction of circle-of-fifths sequence in Example 14.12 (mm. 33–36).

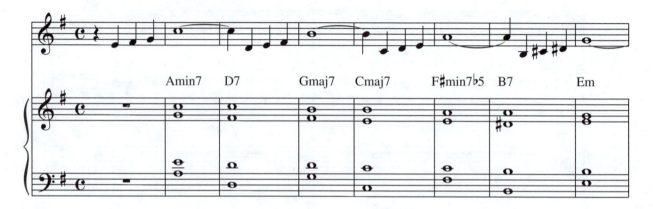

Example 14.14. Kosma, "Autumn Leaves," chord progression.

The diatonic circle-of-fifths sequence is a common transitional device in Baroque music. Example 14.15 shows how the sequence facilitates a key change from C minor to the relative major, E♭ major.

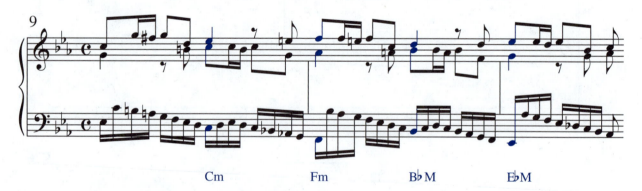

Example 14.15. Bach, Fugue in C minor from *The Well-Tempered Clavier*, Book 1, mm. 9–11a.

A more elaborate example (harmonically as well as texturally) is shown in Example 14.16. After defining the tonic by stating the opening motive over a series of I–Vs in G major, a diatonic circle-of-fifths sequence begins in measure 3, stopping on D major on the third dotted-quarter beat of measure 4 (note the change in texture, especially in the bass, at this point).

In some ways the diatonic circle-of-fifths sequence can be considered to act as a kind of harmonic "elevator," allowing the composer to move to different keys at will simply by "getting off the elevator" at the appropriate point in the sequence. By staying on the sequence for only four chords, as he does in Example 14.15 (Cm, Fm, B♭, E♭), Bach is able to smoothly move from the minor tonic to its relative major. By staying on the sequence for seven chords, as he does in Example 14.16 (G, C, F♯, Bm7, Em, A7, D), Bach is able to smoothly move from the major tonic to its dominant.

Example 14.16. Bach, Brandenburg Concerto no. 3 in G major, BWV 1048 (iii), mm. 3–5a.

The chord provided in each example below is the beginning of a partial or complete circle-of-fifths sequence, the extent of which is indicated by the number of blanks on each line. Using proper voice leading, complete the indicated sequences, and complete the blanks with a Roman numeral harmonic analysis. Finally, add pop chord symbols.

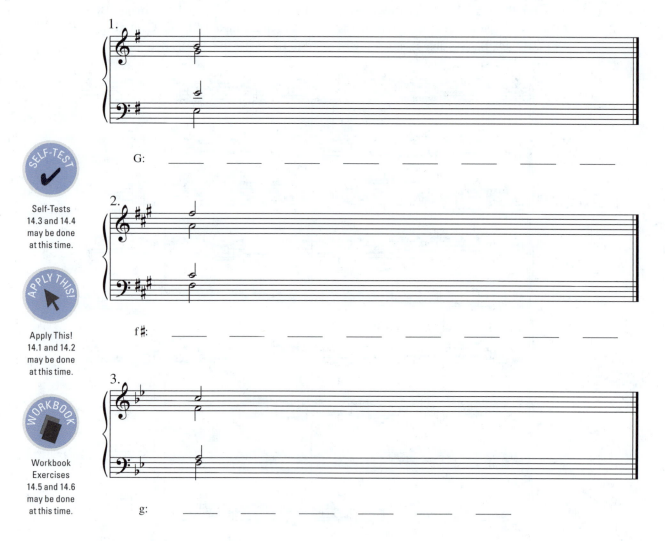

Self-Tests 14.3 and 14.4 may be done at this time.

Apply This! 14.1 and 14.2 may be done at this time.

Workbook Exercises 14.5 and 14.6 may be done at this time.

THE REVERSE (ASCENDING FIFTH) CIRCLE-OF-FIFTHS HARMONIC SEQUENCE

Although circle-of-fifths sequences in common-practice music commonly travel counter-clockwise along the circle of fifths, these sequences are sometimes found in reverse, with each chord in the chain acting as a *subdominant* of the one that follows it

(Example 14.17). As a result, the root motion *ascends* (rather than descends) by perfect fifth or *descends* (rather than ascends) by perfect fourth. Because the root motions travel *clockwise* along the circle of fifths rather than *counterclockwise*, this is called a **reverse circle-of-fifths harmonic sequence**.

Example 14.17. Schumann, *Arabeske*, mm. 152–159.

The reverse circle-of-fifths sequence is almost never complete; often it involves no more than three chords, terminating on the tonic. Thus, if the last two chords are IV→I (a plagal cadence), then the IV is preceded by a *VII chord with a lowered root* (a so-called ♭VII), which can also be regarded as a "IV of IV" (Example 14.18). "Hey Joe," famously covered by Jimi Hendrix, is made up of a five-chord reverse circle-of-fifths pattern: C–G–D–A–E (Example 14.19). Sometimes the elements of the pattern are rotated so that the pattern begins, rather than ends, on the tonic: AC/DC's "Back in Black," for example, uses the pattern E–D–A.

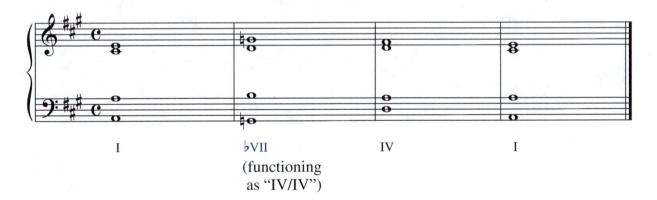

Example 14.18. A reverse circle-of-fifths progression in A major.

Example 14.19. The reverse circle-of-fifths progression in Jimi Hendrix's version of "Hey Joe" (1966).

Sometimes a progression will toggle back and forth among three chords along the circle of fifths, for example E–A–D–A. This progression is found in songs such as the Romantics' "What I Like About You" (1980) and John Cougar Mellencamp's "R.O.C.K. in the U.S.A." (1985).

THE DESCENDING THIRD HARMONIC SEQUENCE

Another familiar harmonic sequence is the chord progression associated with Johann Pachelbel's Canon in D major. In this sequence, the basic root motion of a descending fourth (seen in Example 14.20 as the opening I–V) is then repeated at successive levels descending by thirds. This harmonic sequence is also found in several pop and rock songs of the 1970s through 1990s, such as the Pet Shop Boys' "Go West," Blues Traveler's "Hook," and Green Day's "Basket Case," and its frequency in music is humorously demonstrated by comedian Rob Paravonian in his famous YouTube video "Pachelbel Rant."[1]

---

[1]As of November 2015, this video has been viewed over 13 million times. http://www.youtube.com/watch?v=JdxkVQy7QLM

Example 14.20. Johann Pachelbel (1653–1706), Canon in D major, mm. 5–8.

Notice the pattern of alternating thirds and fifths between the soprano and bass voices in Example 14.20. This is an example of a **linear intervallic pattern**, which is a repeated interval pattern between two voices.

Related to the descending third harmonic sequence is the descending 5–6 sequence, so named because of the linear intervallic pattern of alternating fifths and sixths. If we were to take Pachelbel's progression and make every other chord (starting with the second chord) a first-inversion chord, the result would be a descending 5–6 sequence. Two examples are shown in Example 14.21; Beethoven's progression in the op. 109 piano sonata is almost exactly replicated in Coven's 1971 song "One Tin Soldier." Note the linear intervallic pattern common to both excerpts, shown in Example 14.21c.

a. Beethoven, Piano Sonata No. 30 in E Major, Op. 109 (1st mvt.), mm. 1–4.

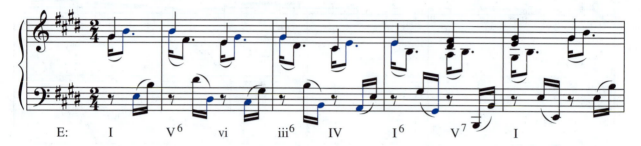

E: I   V⁶   vi   iii⁶   IV   I⁶   V⁷   I

b. Dennis Lambert & Brian Potter, "One Tin Soldier" (as performed by Coven, 1971) (original key: C major)

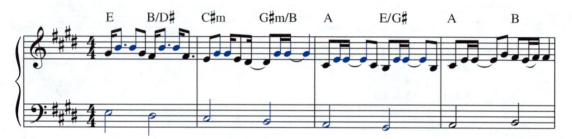

c. Voice-leading reduction

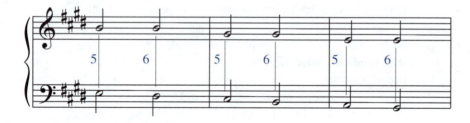

Example 14.21. Two examples of the descending 5–6 sequence.

THE ASCENDING SECOND 5–6 HARMONIC SEQUENCE

An ascending second 5–6 harmonic sequence also uses the linear intervallic pattern 5–6, but this time the initial movement is in the *upper* voice (Example 14.22). Since the ascending-second pattern is distributed in an alternating fashion between the moving upper voice and the bass, this can be regarded as an attempt to offset the parallel fifths that would result if both voices moved at the same time.

Example 14.22. Ascending second 5–6 harmonic sequence, voice-leading reduction.

Example 14.23 shows a typical instance of this sequence:

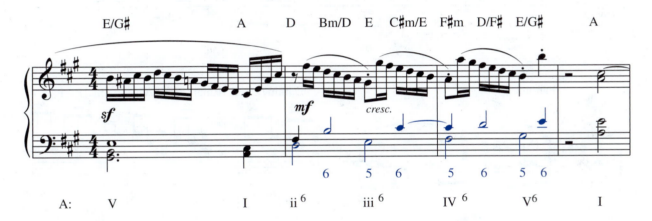

Example 14.23. Mozart, Piano Concerto no. 23 in A major, K.488 (i) (piano reduction by Carl Reinecke), mm. 258–261.

Example 14.24 shows this same sequence played out over a broader span of time in a passage from Grieg's *Peer Gynt* suite:

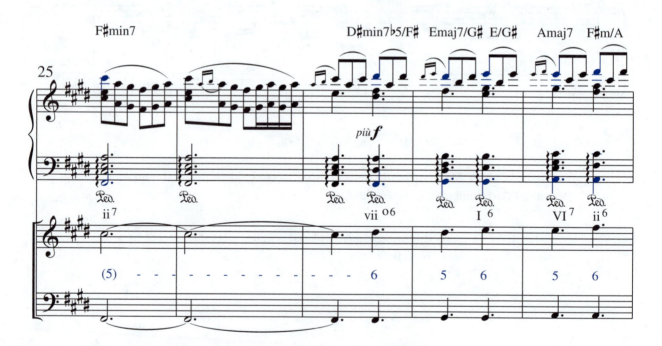

Example 14.24. Edvard Grieg (1843–1907), "Morning Mood," no. 1 from *Peer Gynt* (piano reduction by the composer), mm. 21–29.

THE DESCENDING SECOND 7–6 HARMONIC SEQUENCE

The descending second 7–6 harmonic sequence is often associated with chains of suspensions. Example 14.25 shows its use in a Bach violin partita. Compare the score excerpt with the voice-leading reduction below it.

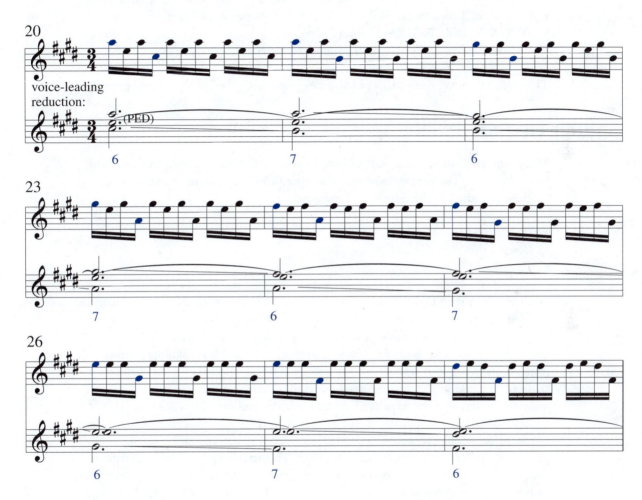

Example 14.25. Bach, Prelude from Violin Partita no. 3 in E major, BWV 1006, mm. 20–28.

HARMONIC PROGRESSION IN POPULAR MUSIC

Popular music, as a whole, does not follow as strict a harmonic-function-determined syntax as "classical" music. Most of the aforementioned harmonic sequences in this chapter, for example, with the exception of the descending third "Pachelbel" sequence, are not all that common in pop and rock music. Instead, much popular music relies on cyclical or "loop"-driven progressions, often involving permutations or rotations of I, IV, V, and vi (in major keys). Consider the following examples:[2]

- I–V–vi–IV: Journey, "Don't Stop Believin'"; Rod Stewart, "Forever Young"; U2, "With or Without You"
- V–vi–IV–I: Marvin Gaye, "Sexual Healing"; Spice Girls, "Wannabe"
- vi–IV–I–V: Toto, "Africa"; John Legend, "All of Me"; Joan Osborne, "One of Us"
- IV–I–V–vi: Taylor Swift, "We Are Never Ever Getting Back Together"
- IV–I–vi–V: Pink Floyd, "Learning to Fly"
- I–vi–V–IV: Prince, "Purple Rain"; Alanis Morissette, "You Learn"

There are, of course, many other possibilities from this rather limited chord palette.

CONCLUSION

Many aspects of music theory can be described as *applications or generalizations of basic principles*. In this chapter, we have seen that chord-to-chord progressions can be summarized according to three basic root motions:

- Up a second
- Down a third
- Up a fourth/Down a fifth.

Similarly, from the PD–D–T order of a ii–V–I progression we are able to build longer harmonic sequences based on the same principle of root motion (ascending a fourth, descending a fifth). Harmonic sequences can be a powerful means of generating momentum toward the goal of a harmonic progression, as well as enabling transitions from one key to another. Harmonic sequences can be categorized by their characteristic linear intervallic patterns (repeated interval patterns between two voices), as well as by the direction of the sequence (ascending or descending).

Popular music, in general, is not as bound to the same principles of harmonic syntax as common-practice era "classical" music. Its syntax instead is often "loop"-driven or cyclical rather than goal-directed. The *reverse* circle-of-fifths harmonic sequence, however, is one example of a goal-directed circle-of-fifths harmonic pattern in pop music; it frequently includes the ♭VII chord, a chord that is often borrowed from Mixolydian mode (in popular music) or from the parallel minor key (in "classical" music). Noting the differences between the diatonic circle-of-fifths sequence and the reverse circle-of-fifths sequence offers one illustration of how harmonic patterns contribute to differences in musical style.

---

[2] I am indebted to my colleague, Michael Baker (University of Kentucky) for most of these examples as well as this rotational concept. Other examples—and progressions—may be found on the website "Cliché Progressions," http://vjmanzo.com/clicheprogressions/index.php?title=Main_Page.

Terms to Know

ascending second 5–6 harmonic sequence

descending third harmonic sequence

descending second 7–6 harmonic sequence

diatonic circle-of-fifths harmonic sequence

linear intervallic pattern

reverse circle-of-fifths harmonic sequence

voice exchange

Self-Test

14.1. For each of the chords below, provide its Roman numeral and inversion symbol in the left blank for the keys indicated, along with its harmonic function (T, PD, or D) in the right blank. One option in the first example is provided for you as a model.

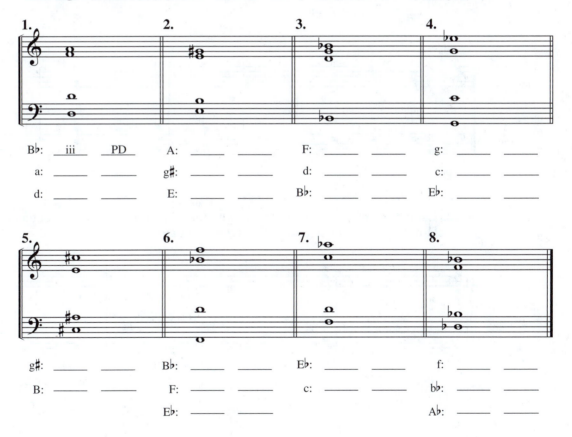

1.
B♭:   iii   PD
a: _____   _____
d: _____   _____

2.
A: _____   _____
g♯:   _____   _____
E: _____   _____

3.
F: _____   _____
d: _____   _____
B♭:   _____   _____

4.
g: _____   _____
c: _____   _____
E♭:   _____   _____

5.
g♯:   _____   _____
B: _____   _____

6.
B♭:   _____   _____
F: _____   _____
E♭:   _____   _____

7.
E♭:   _____   _____
c: _____   _____

8.
f: _____   _____
b♭:   _____   _____
A♭:   _____   _____

14.2. Each of the progressions below includes one or more doubling, chord spelling, or voice-leading errors. Find and correct them. In some cases you might need to rewrite the progression with different spacing or chord voicing.

C:

a:

F:

14.3. Using the first two chords as a model for your sequence, construct a diatonic circle-of-fifths sequence ending with a perfect authentic cadence in G minor.

B♭:   I   IV   ___ ___ ___ ___ ___ ___ ___

Apply This!

14.1. Locate and identify the type of harmonic sequence in each excerpt. Mark the linear intervallic patterns at work in the sequence.

a. Bach, Allemande from Partita no. 4 in D major, BWV 828, mm. 18–21.

b. Clara Schumann (1819–1896), Trio in G minor for Violin, Cello and Piano, op. 17 (i), mm. 30–41a.

(Continued)

14.2. Composition. A **chaconne** is a kind of set of variations over a recurring harmonic progression (a related type of piece, the **passacaglia**, usually involved variations over a recurring bass line; some pieces, such as Pachelbel's celebrated canon, fit into both categories). The diatonic circle-of-fifths progression was a common model for chaconnes, as was the Pachelbel progression and the "lament" progression (in minor) of i–i$^4_2$–iv^6–V.

For this composition exercise, plan out a piece in which the fixed harmonic progression (and fixed bass line) is repeated for eight cycles in all. If your piece is in a minor key, use a diatonic circle-of-fifths progression or the "lament" progression; for a major-key piece, use the Pachelbel progression. For the first appearance of your progression, provide a harmonic analysis (Roman numerals and inversion symbols) with prolongation analysis if applicable below the staff. Above the staff, provide a functional PD–D–T analysis for your progression.

Over this progression write a melodic line for voice (a "vocalise," a melody sung on textless syllables) or solo instrument. Try to write a different melodic line for each repetition of the harmonic progression; you may choose to return to a reprise of the first melody on the eighth and final repetition in order to give your piece a formal closure. Give each melodic line a satisfactory shape, with a clear focal point. If your repeated harmonic progression originally ended on V, be sure to resolve the final V with an authentic cadence at the end of the piece. Have your composition performed in class if possible.

14.3. Improvisation. An excellent way to learn how to improvise, and become more comfortable trying it out for yourself, is to study and compare the recordings of great improvisers. Certain "standards" such as "Autumn Leaves," which we discussed in this chapter, have been recorded hundreds of times. You might want to investigate different performances of "Autumn Leaves" in your university or local public library. Some performances are fairly straightforward; in others, so-called "harmonic substitutions" and "extensions" that add ninths, elevenths, and thirteenths to the harmony transform the basic circle-of-fifths progression to a point where following the progression can be a challenge. Embrace this challenge. Listening and keeping track of where the musicians are in the course of their chart will enhance your appreciation of their craft and improve your own skills as an improvising musician.

CHAPTER 15

SECONDARY CHORDS AND TONICIZATION

OVERVIEW

We saw in Chapters 4 and 5 that major-minor and fully-diminished seventh chords occur only once diatonically in a key, and that they were associated with $V^{(7)}$ and $vii^{o(7)}$ respectively. Chords of these qualities are used for tonicization—the process of setting up a diatonic chord within a key as a fleeting but unconfirmed "tonic," using a secondary dominant or leading-tone (diminished) triad or seventh chord preceding it. For example, C7 is the dominant chord of F major, but in the key of C, C7 would be a V^7 of IV, since F major is IV in the key of C. In the same way that diatonic chords may be linked in a diatonic circle-of-fifths harmonic sequence, chains of secondary dominants can be used to create chromatic circle-of-fifths harmonic sequences.

AUDIO LIST

Johann Sebastian Bach, Prelude no. 1 in C major from *The Well-Tempered Clavier*, Book 1, BWV 846

Queen, "You're My Best Friend"

Richard Rodgers and Oscar Hammerstein II, "Do Re Mi" from *The Sound of Music* (motion picture soundtrack)

The system of diatonic harmonic function gives progressions structure, but with only seven triads and seventh chords one can go only so far. By the addition of chromatically inflected chords—still governed by the principles of tendency tones and voice leading—our harmonic palette is vastly increased.

SECONDARY DOMINANT (AND DOMINANT SEVENTH) CHORDS

Let's begin by reviewing the diagram of diatonic seventh chord qualities below, for major and minor keys (discussed in Chapter 4):

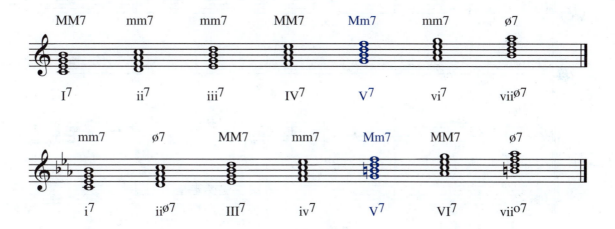

Notice that in both major and minor keys, the major-minor seventh (Mm7) chord is found only once, built over the dominant scale degree. Because of the tendency tones contained within this chord, there is a strong tendency for the V^7 to resolve to I, with the root motion from chord to chord proceeding up a perfect fourth or down a perfect fifth. Similarly, when a major-minor seventh chord is built on some other tone by chromatic alterations, there is a strong tendency for that chord to resolve to a chord with its root up a perfect fourth or down a perfect fifth. In this way, the major-minor seventh chord may be understood to function as a "V of" the chord that follows it.

For example, consider the opening of Beethoven's first symphony (Example 15.1); pop-chord symbols have been added to facilitate your reading.

Example 15.1. Beethoven, Symphony no. 1 in C major, op. 21 (i), mm. 1–4.

The symphony is in the key of C major, but that is hardly implied from its opening two chords. Given that a major-minor seventh chord is a "V of something," the opening C7 chord functions as a "V of" the F major chord to which it resolves. The C7 chord is a **secondary dominant** chord, built on the dominant *of* the chord that follows. Taken out of context, the progression appears to be a $V^7 \rightarrow I$ in F major; because of this, we would say that F major (the IV of C) is being set up as a fleeting pseudo-tonic, a process called **tonicization** (the major-minor seventh chord preceding the IV chord **tonicizes** F major). In the same way, looking at measures 3–4, the D7 chord is a secondary dominant of G, tonicizing G major (the V of C). Each of the three phrase segments in this passage, in fact, begins with a major-minor seventh chord; the major-minor seventh in measure 2 is a true V^7 of C major, resolving deceptively to vi.

Tonicization is like a hint of a *possible* key change, *without* going so far as to confirm the key change by a cadence in the new key. The key of the passage in Example 15.1 is still C major. Thus, the "$V^7 \rightarrow I$ in F major" of the first phrase segment would actually be analyzed as V^7/IV (meaning "V^7 of IV") $\rightarrow$ IV in the key of C; the "$V^7 \rightarrow I$ in G major" of the phrase segment beginning in measure 5 would similarly be analyzed as $V^7/V \rightarrow V$ in C.

- The first part of the dual Roman numeral label describes the *type* of dominant relationship—in this case, V^7 (as we will learn later, secondary vii^{o7}'s are also possible).
- The second part of the label—in this case, IV—tells us *which chord* the V^7 tonicizes.

Secondary dominant chords are always labeled by their relation to the chord they tonicize—as a V or V^7 of the chord that follows them—never by the root of the secondary dominant chord itself. In other words, a secondary dominant built on the tonic (as for example the first chord of Example 15.1) would never be labeled a "I^7," because that label describes a *diatonic* I^7 chord, which would be a *major-major* seventh in a major key.

The harmonic function of secondary dominants is indicated with a D in *parentheses*—(D)—to indicate their *localized* dominant function in relation to the chords that they tonicize. A harmonic function diagram of the Beethoven passage would thus look something like this:

m.	1			2			3		4
	V^7/IV	$\rightarrow$	IV	V^7	$\rightarrow$	vi	V^7/V	$\rightarrow$	V
	(D)	$\rightarrow$	PD	D	$\rightarrow$	[T]	(D)	$\rightarrow$	D

Example 15.2 shows a rather humorous moment from the second movement of Beethoven's Piano Sonata op. 14 no. 2. Notice that following the initial $V^7 \rightarrow I$, Beethoven sequences this gesture twice, with a $V^7/ii \rightarrow ii$ followed by a $V^7/iii \rightarrow iii$. Each dominant seventh chord is resolved properly according to the tendency tone patterns for each tonicization. Part of the humor of this passage, however, has to do with what the secondary dominant seventh chords are concealing—for without

them, the progression is a lumbering I–ii–iii progression, complete with parallel fifths and octaves (Example 15.3). This stepwise progression seems to be highlighted by Beethoven's accent markings, which emphasize the resolution rather than the dissonance and which occur on the metrically weak beats. In contrast to the clumsiness of this antecedent phrase, Beethoven follows this with a harmonically orderly consequent phrase (mm. 19–20), as if the preceding moment of harmonic awkwardness never happened.

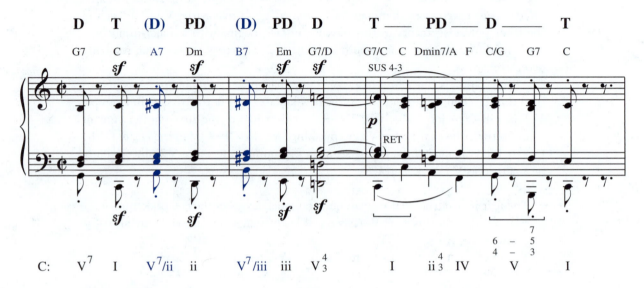

Example 15.2. Beethoven, Piano Sonata no. 10 in G major, op. 14 no. 2 (ii), mm. 17–20.

Example 15.3. Harmonic reduction of Example 15.2, mm. 17–18 (secondary dominant chords removed).

Any consonant (major or minor) triad can be tonicized. Example 15.4 shows the available *secondary dominant triads* for C major and C minor, all major triads. Secondary dominant chords do not necessarily need to be seventh chords; there must, however, be a *change of quality in the chord.* For example, in a major key, changing the quality of the iii chord from minor to major results in a V/vi. Note that there is no such thing as V/IV in a major key, because that would be the same as a I chord; to tonicize IV, add a lowered chord seventh to the tonicizing triad, creating a major-minor seventh (V^7/IV).[1] (A V/iv triad *is* possible in a minor key, however, because the quality of the tonic chord is changed from minor to major.)

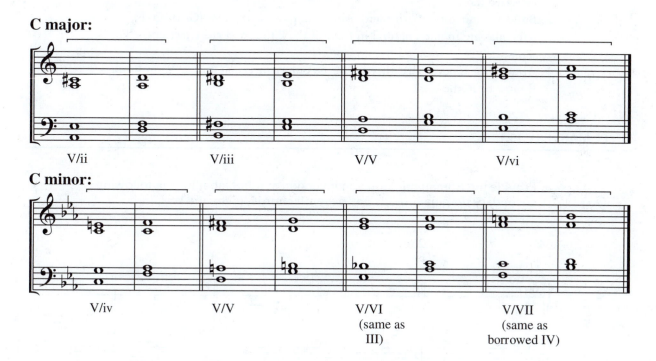

C major:

V/ii   V/iii   V/V   V/vi

C minor:

V/iv   V/V   V/VI   V/VII
                         (same as   (same as
                           III)   borrowed IV)

Example 15.4. Secondary dominant triads of C major and C minor.

Diminished and augmented triads cannot be tonicized; thus, there is no such thing as a V/vii° in major, for example, or minor or a V/ii° in minor. This is because since tonicization may be thought of as a fleeting but unconfirmed "key change," diminished triads cannot stand as the tonic for a key (there is no such key as "C diminished").

To spell a secondary dominant chord:

• Start with the chord to be *tonicized.*
• Find the note a *perfect fifth above, or a perfect fourth below, the root of that chord* and build a major triad (or a major-minor seventh) above that note. Remember that accidentals will be necessary, ensuring that the chord is a major triad or major-minor seventh chord.

---

[1]Similarly, the V/III and V/VI in minor are the same as the diatonic VII and III chords, respectively, built from the natural minor scale; the tonicizing function of these chords is made explicit by adding a seventh to create major-minor seventh chords (V^7/III and V^7/VI).

- Finally, arrange the tones in the order indicated by the desired inversion.

Thus, to spell a V^6_5/VI in e minor:

1. Locate the chord that would be VI—in this case, C major;
2. Find the note a perfect fifth above or a perfect fourth below the chord being tonicized (G).
3. Build a dominant seventh chord using that pitch as the root (G–B–D–F), remembering to put a natural in front of the F to cancel the effect of the key signature's F♯.
4. Arrange the tones so that they are in the proper inversion (for V^6_5/VI in E minor, B must be in the bass).

LEVEL MASTERY 15.1

a. Provide the Roman numeral and inversion symbol label for the following secondary dominant triads and seventh chords, given the key.

b. Spell the indicated secondary dominant triads and seventh chords.

SELF-TEST ✔

Self-Tests 15.1 and 15.2 may be done at this time.

WORKBOOK

Workbook Exercises 15.1 and 15.2 may be done at this time.

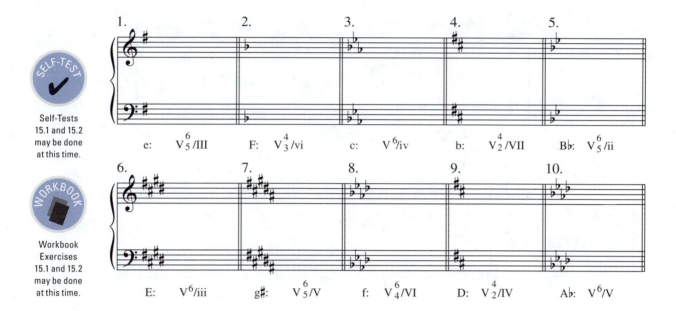

1. e: V^6_5/III
2. F: V^4_3/vi
3. c: V^6/iv
4. b: V^4_2/VII
5. B♭: V^6_5/ii

6. E: V^6/iii
7. g♯: V^6_5/V
8. f: V^6_4/VI
9. D: V^4_2/IV
10. A♭: V^6/V

RESOLVING SECONDARY DOMINANT CHORDS

Secondary dominant seventh chords resolve like any dominant seventh chord, according to the tendency tone patterns *of the key being tonicized:*

- The *chord seventh* should *resolve downward* by step to the third of the chord being tonicized.
- The **tonicizing leading tone** (the leading tone of the key being tonicized) should *resolve up by minor second* to the root of the chord being tonicized, or down to the fifth of the chord being tonicized through free resolution if it is occurring in an inner voice.
- The other tones similarly resolve according to the tendency tone patterns *of the key being tonicized.*

Example 15.5 shows these voice-leading patterns in a tonicization of B minor (the iii of G).

Tendency tones in B minor (key being tonicized)

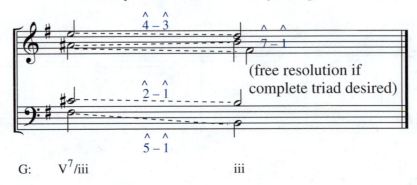

$\hat{4} - \hat{3}$

$\hat{7} - \hat{1}$

(free resolution if complete triad desired)

$\hat{2} - \hat{1}$

$\hat{5} - \hat{1}$

G: V^7/iii   iii

Example 15.5. Typical secondary dominant voice-leading resolution patterns.

LEVEL MASTERY 15.2.

Using Example 15.5 as your model, spell and resolve the following secondary dominant seventh chords. As with Example 15.5, label the tendency tones involved (applied
to the key being tonicized).

1.   2.   3.   4.

a: V^6_5/V   V   E♭: V^4_3/vi   vi   d: V^4_2/iv   iv   e: V^7/III   III

5.   6.   7.   8.

B: V^6_5/ii   ii   F: V^7/iii   iii   b: V^4_2/VII   VII   c♯: V^4_3/VI   VI

9.   10.   11.   12.

WORKBOOK

Workbook
Exercise 15.3
may be done
at this time.

f: V^6_5/iv   iv   g♯: V^4_2/V   V   D♭: V^7/vi   vi   D: V^6_5/iii   iii

RECOGNIZING AND IDENTIFYING SECONDARY DOMINANT CHORDS

To identify a potential secondary dominant chord, begin with the chord's quality:

- *If a triad, is the chord a chromatically inflected major version of a diatonically minor triad?* If so, check to see if the chord to which it resolves has its root a perfect fourth higher or a perfect fifth lower. If it does, the chord is probably a secondary dominant triad.
- *Is the chord in question a major-minor seventh?* If so, if the chord to which it resolves has its root a perfect fourth higher or a perfect fifth lower, and if the chord to which it resolves is diatonic to the home key, it is most certainly a secondary dominant seventh chord.

Be aware that sometimes a secondary dominant chord may resolve deceptively, just as a diatonic dominant or dominant seventh chord can. Example 15.6 shows one such scenario. The second chord, a V^7/vi, would usually resolve to vi, (D minor). A deceptive cadence in D minor, however, would have the A^7 resolving to B♭; B♭ is a diatonic chord (IV) in the home key of F. Thus, in Example 15.6 the V^7/vi is able to resolve deceptively to IV.

F: I V^7/vi   IV   V   I

Example 15.6. Deceptive resolution of a secondary dominant seventh chord.

THE CHROMATIC CIRCLE-OF-FIFTHS SEQUENCE

Secondary dominant chords are often used to add intensity to a circle-of-fifths sequence. For example, V/V or V^7/V may substitute for ii in preceding V; V/ii or V^7/ii can substitute for vi, and V/vi or V^7/vi can substitute for iii. Chains of major triads or major-minor seventh chords can also be used in harmonic sequences to travel counterclockwise around the circle of fifths, each chord having a dominant function to the chord that follows in a **chromatic circle-of-fifths sequence** (Example 15.7).

Example 15.8 shows the voice leading for a passage involving major-minor seventh chords exclusively. In progressing from chord to chord, the chord seventh resolves down by step as expected; the leading tone (third of the chord), however, does *not* resolve up by step but instead slides down a half-step, becoming the chord seventh of the next dominant seventh chord. In this way, the two tendency tone voices move in parallel tritones. Because all of the chords are the same quality, it is impossible to determine exactly when we will stop. Only when a dominant seventh chord resolves to a stable major or minor triad do we finally know that we have reached our destination. If the diatonic circle-of-fifths sequence resembles a harmonic "elevator," the chromatic circle-of-fifths sequence might be likened to a treadmill or a hamster's exercise wheel.

Example 15.7. Secondary dominants replacing diatonic seventh chords in a circle-of-fifths harmonic sequence; example from Mozart, Symphony no. 40 in G minor, K.550 (i), mm. 44–51. *(Continued)*

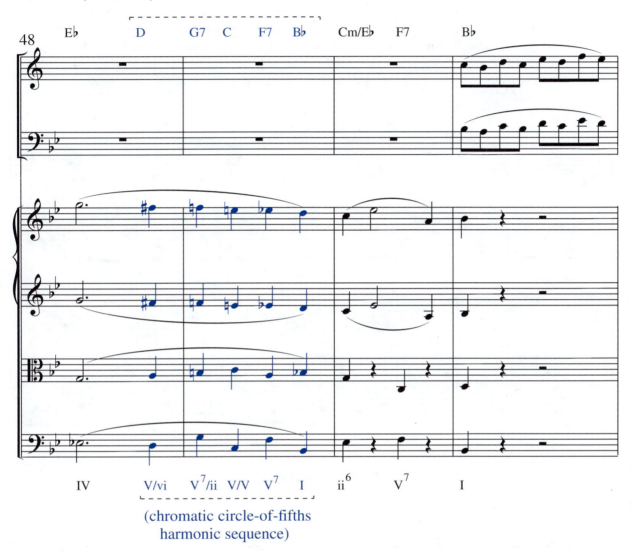

(chromatic circle-of-fifths
harmonic sequence)

Example 15.8. A complete chromatic circle-of-fifths sequence.

Examples 15.9 and 15.10 show two examples of chromatic circle-of-fifths harmonic sequences from popular music of two different eras. "Sweet Georgia Brown" (made famous as a theme song for the Harlem Globetrotters) is based on a sequence that includes three major-minor seventh chords (E^7, A^7, and D^7) before arriving at the goal harmony of G major. The central section of "Awaken," by the British progressive rock group Yes, cycles completely through all twelve chords of the circle of fifths [5:12–6:34].

Example 15.9. Bernie-Pinkard, "Sweet Georgia Brown."

Example 15.10. Yes, "Awaken," chromatic circle-of-fifths progression.
(Continued)

(Continued)

Chromatic circle-of-fifths sequences are more likely to be incomplete than diatonic circle of fifths sequences. This is because, with twelve chords of the same quality, a chromatic circle-of-fifths sequence can easily pall if overdone. Diatonic circle-of-fifths sequences (see Chapter 14), on the other hand, are often found encompassing a complete cycle, likely because they are shorter (up to only seven chords) and made up of chords of varying qualities.

PASSING SECONDARY DOMINANT CHORDS

Sometimes secondary dominant chords are used to connect chords that are part of a third progression (roots descending by third) by means of passing $^6_4$ or $^4_3$ chords. Example 15.11 shows two versions of a I–vi–IV progression in D major. The second version smooths the motion from chord to chord with passing secondary dominants—a progression featured in the Beatles song "Maxwell's Silver Hammer" [2:04–2:08].

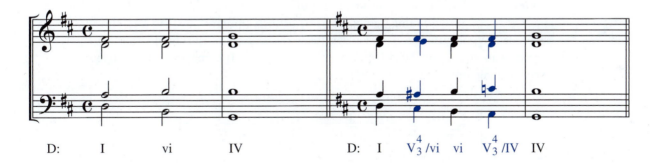

Example 15.11. The descending-third I–vi–IV progression expanded with passing secondary dominants, as in the Beatles' "Maxwell's Silver Hammer" [2:04–2:08]

Example 15.12, a backing-vocal progression from Queen's "You're My Best Friend" [0:56–1:14], also uses secondary dominants to connect between I, vi, and IV.

The voice leading is less traditional, but the functions and syntax of these secondary dominants remain the same.

0:56

Example 15.12. Queen, "You're My Best Friend," backing vocal harmonies [0:56–1:14].

Example 15.13 shows another common progression in popular music, an apparent V/V resolving to IV rather than V; this resolution is famously found in The Beatles' "Yesterday," but it can also be heard in the Rolling Stones' "As Tears Go By" and REM's "Nightswimming," among others. In such a progression, this would not be a true V/V, because the apparent dominant connotation of the chord is not confirmed. A more accurate label for such a chord would be II (a major-quality version of the diatonic minor ii).

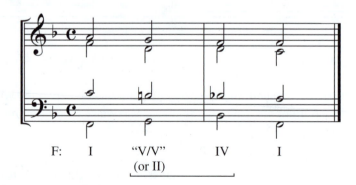

Example 15.13. Apparent V/V (or II) resolving to IV.

Locate and label (providing Roman numeral and inversion symbol) the secondary dominant chords in the following musical excerpts.

a. Schubert, "Ave Maria," op. 52 no. 6, mm. 1–2.

b. Claude-Michel Schönberg and Herbert Kretzmer, "I Dreamed a Dream" (from *Les Miserables*), mm. 12–21. The key is F major. (Note: How would you label the F minor chord?)

c. Brahms, Rhapsodie, op. 119 no. 4, mm. 1–13.

d. Beethoven, Piano Sonata in E major, op. 90 (ii), mm. 1–25a.

(Continued)

SECONDARY LEADING-TONE (DIMINISHED) CHORDS

Secondary leading-tone chords are diminished triads or fully diminished seventh chords (less commonly, half-diminished seventh chords) that have the *leading tone of the key being tonicized* as their root. Example 15.14 shows the available secondary leading-tone fully diminished seventh chords for C major and C minor.

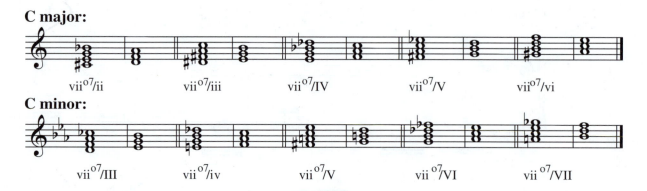

C major:

vii°⁷/ii   vii°⁷/iii   vii°⁷/IV   vii°⁷/V   vii°⁷/vi

C minor:

vii°⁷/III   vii°⁷/iv   vii°⁷/V   vii°⁷/VI   vii°⁷/VII

Example 15.14. Secondary leading-tone fully diminished seventh chords in C major and C minor.

Harmonic functions of secondary leading-tone chords are indicated by a D in parentheses—(D)—just like secondary dominant chords.

To spell a secondary leading-tone chord, find the pitch a *minor second* lower than the root of the chord being tonicized; then build a diminished triad (or a fully diminished seventh chord) above that tone, being careful to make any necessary chromatic alterations necessary to ensure the proper quality. Finally, properly arrange the pitches in the inversion needed.

Thus, to spell a vii°⁴₂/iii in G major:

1. Locate the chord that would be iii—in this case, B minor;
2. Find the root a *minor second* below the chord being tonicized. In this case, the root would be A♯. (Be careful not to resort to enharmonics; A♯, not B♭, is a true minor second away from B.)
3. Build a fully diminished seventh chord from that root pitch. The easiest way to do this is to stack consecutive minor thirds above the root: A♯–C♯–E–G. Be careful not to write any enharmonic intervals, and remember to chromatically alter any pitches needed to ensure a fully diminished seventh chord quality.
4. Arrange the tones so that they are in the proper inversion (for vii°⁴₂/iii in G, G must be in the bass).

a. Provide the Roman numeral, quality (° or ⌀), and inversion symbol label for the following secondary leading-tone (diminished) triads and seventh chords, given the key.

b. Spell the indicated secondary leading-tone (diminished) triads and seventh chords.

Self-Tests 15.3 and 15.4 may be done at this time.

Workbook Exercises 15.4 and 15.5 may be done at this time.

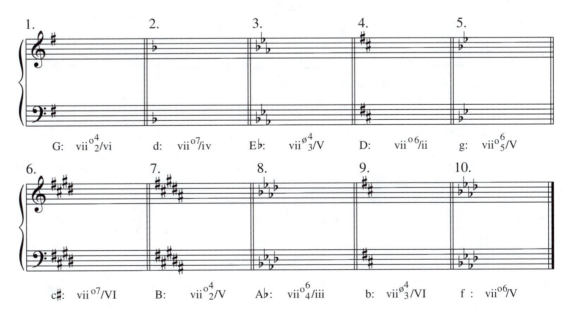

G: vii°4/2/vi   d: vii°7/iv   E♭: vii⌀4/3/V   D: vii°6/ii   g: vii°6/5/V

c#: vii°7/VI   B: vii°4/2/V   A♭: vii°6/4/iii   b: vii⌀4/3/VI   f: vii°6/V

RESOLVING SECONDARY LEADING-TONE CHORDS

Secondary leading-tone chords are resolved like any diminished triad or fully diminished seventh chord built on the leading tone, using the tendency tone patterns for the *key being tonicized.*

- If the chord is a triad, it will usually be in first inversion.
- The root of the secondary leading-tone chord should resolve up by half step (minor second) to the root of the chord being tonicized.
- If the chord is a seventh chord, the chord seventh should resolve downward by step to the fifth of the chord being tonicized.
- The other tones similarly resolve according to the tendency tone patterns *of the key being tonicized.*

Example 15.15 illustrates these tendency tone patterns.

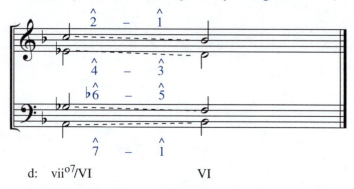

Example 15.15. Typical secondary leading-tone (fully diminished) seventh chord voice-leading resolution patterns.

LEVEL MASTERY 15.5.

Using Example 15.15 as your model, spell and resolve the following secondary leading-tone (diminished) seventh chords. As with Example 15.12, label the tendency tones involved (as applied to the key being tonicized).

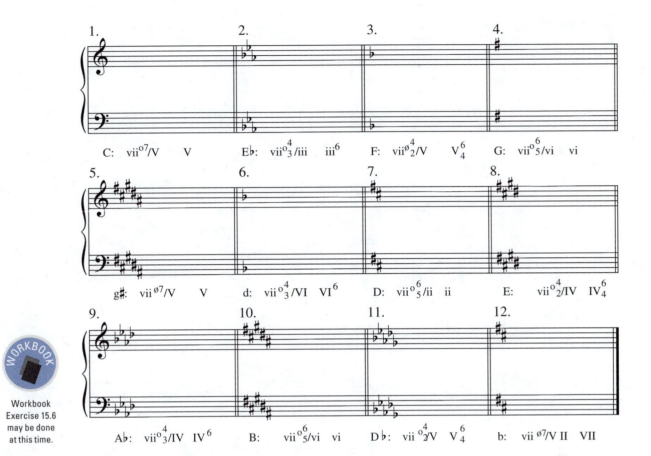

1. C: vii°⁷/V   V

2. E♭: vii°$_3^4$/iii   iii⁶

3. F: vii∅$_2^4$/V   V$_4^6$

4. G: vii°$_5^6$/vi   vi

5. g♯: vii∅⁷/V   V

6. d: vii°$_3^4$/VI   VI⁶

7. D: vii°$_5^6$/ii   ii

8. E: vii°$_2^4$/IV   IV$_4^6$

9. A♭: vii°$_3^4$/IV   IV⁶

10. B: vii°$_5^6$/vi   vi

11. D♭: vii°$_2^4$/V   V$_4^6$

12. b: vii∅⁷/V   II   VII

Workbook
Exercise 15.6
may be done
at this time.

RECOGNIZING AND IDENTIFYING SECONDARY LEADING-TONE CHORDS

For more on secondary chords in musical context, see Web Feature 15.1.

To identify a secondary leading-tone chord, first confirm that the chord's quality is either a diminished triad or a fully diminished seventh chord (half-diminished secondary leading-tone chords are also possible, though they are much less common).[2] The root of the secondary leading-tone chord should resolve upward by minor second to the root of the next chord. If it does, the chord in question is a secondary leading-tone chord.

---

[2]If the chord is a fully diminished seventh chord, be mindful of inversions. After stacking the notes of the chord in close spacing, look to see if the distance between any of the adjacent tones is an augmented second rather than a minor third—if there is an augmented second, the higher tone is the root and the lower tone is the chord seventh. If there is no augmented second, the chord is in root position.

Locate and label (providing Roman numeral and inversion symbol) the secondary leading-tone (diminished) chords in the following musical excerpts.

a. Beethoven, Piano Sonata no. 8 in C minor, "Pathetique," op. 13 (i), mm. 1–2. (As part of your analysis, identify the non-chord tones in measure 2.)

b. Schubert, Zwölf Ländler, op. 171 no. 3, mm. 1–8.

c. Paul Simon, "American Tune," [1:55–2:15], chord progression only.

For more about secondary dominant and leading-tone chords in score context, see Web Feature 15.1.

d. Mozart, Piano Sonata in D major, K.311 (ii), mm. 63–74. (This excerpt contains both secondary dominant and diminished chords.)

Self-Test 15.5
may be done
at this time.

Apply This!
15.1, 15.2,
and 15.3 may
be done at
this time.

Workbook
Exercises
15.7 and 15.8
may be done
at this time.

CONCLUSION

Taken out of context, what would be the most likely label and key for the chord shown in Example 15.16?

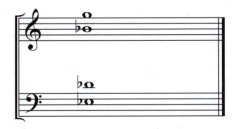

Example 15.16. An E♭ major-minor seventh chord.

Given the quality—a major-minor seventh—and knowing that a chord of this quality is most likely a "V^7 of something," we would first conclude that this chord is a V^7 of A♭ major (or A♭ minor). But it could also be a V^7/V in D♭ major, a V^7/IV in E♭ major (or minor), a V^7/VI in C minor, a V^7/III in F minor, or a V^7/ii in G♭ major, to name several. In each of these keys, A♭ major or minor can be tonicized. Regardless of how the A♭ is labeled, however, the *E♭ dominant seventh remains the same* and behaves in the same fashion. It is really a matter of labeling . . . but the labeling is important. The multiple identities available to the same chord will take on added importance as we negotiate ways of modulating, or changing keys.

Terms to Know

chromatic circle-of-fifths harmonic sequence
secondary dominant (or dominant seventh) chord

secondary leading-tone (secondary diminished) chord
tonicization
tonicizing leading tone

Self-Test

15.1. Identify the following secondary dominant triads and seventh chords.

d: ____   B♭: ____   c: ____   A♭: ____   f: ____   D♭: ____   b♭: ____   e♭: ____

a: ____   C: ____   G: ____   b: ____   A: ____   c♯: ____   B: ____   F♯: ____

15.2. Spell the indicated secondary dominant triads and seventh chords. Use the appropriate key signatures.

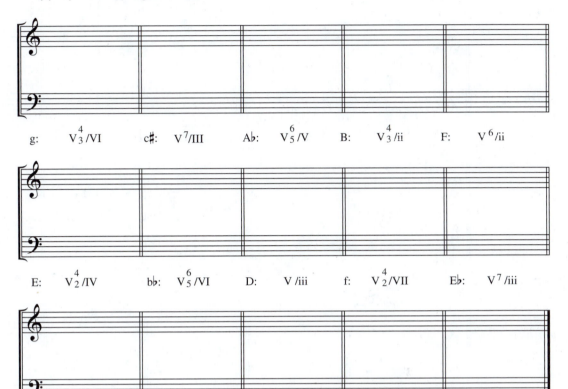

g: V_3^4/VI   c♯: V^7/III   A♭: V_5^6/V   B: V_3^4/ii   F: V^6/ii

E: V_2^4/IV   b♭: V_5^6/VI   D: V/iii   f: V_2^4/VII   E♭: V^7/iii

f♯: V/V   a♭: V_3^4/III   B♭: V_5^6/vi   e: V_2^4/VI   A: V^6/ii

15.3. Identify the following secondary leading-tone triads and seventh chords.

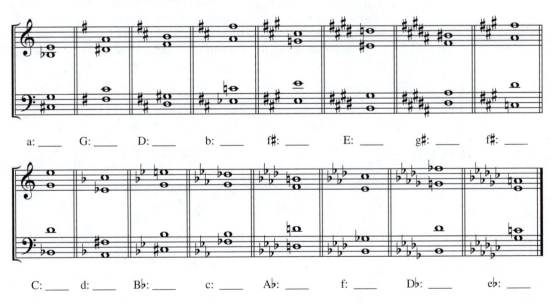

a: ____   G: ____   D: ____   b: ____   f♯: ____   E: ____   g♯: ____   f♯: ____

C: ____   d: ____   B♭: ____   c: ____   A♭: ____   f: ____   D♭: ____   e♭: ____

15.4. Spell the indicated secondary leading-tone triads and seventh chords. Use the appropriate key signatures.

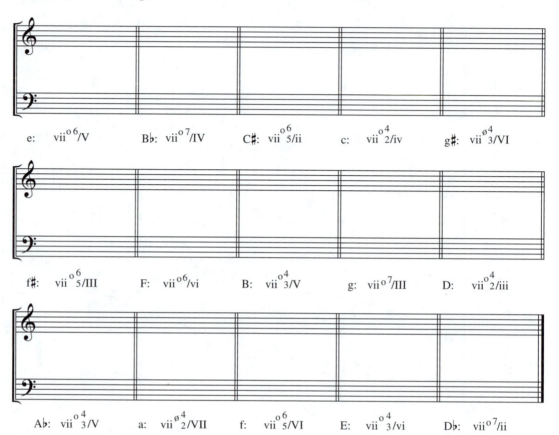

e: $\text{vii}^{\circ 6}/\text{V}$ Bb: $\text{vii}^{\circ 7}/\text{IV}$ C#: $\text{vii}^{\circ 6}_{5}/\text{ii}$ c: $\text{vii}^{\circ 4}_{2}/\text{iv}$ g#: $\text{vii}^{\varnothing 4}_{3}/\text{VI}$

f#: $\text{vii}^{\circ 6}_{5}/\text{III}$ F: $\text{vii}^{\circ 6}/\text{vi}$ B: $\text{vii}^{\circ 4}_{3}/\text{V}$ g: $\text{vii}^{\circ 7}/\text{III}$ D: $\text{vii}^{\circ 4}_{2}/\text{iii}$

Ab: $\text{vii}^{\circ 4}_{3}/\text{V}$ a: $\text{vii}^{\varnothing 4}_{2}/\text{VII}$ f: $\text{vii}^{\circ 6}_{5}/\text{VI}$ E: $\text{vii}^{\circ 4}_{3}/\text{vi}$ Db: $\text{vii}^{\circ 7}/\text{ii}$

15.5. Using the bass, soprano, and figured bass symbols as your guide, provide the missing alto and tenor parts for the hymn "Melita" (also known as the "Naval Hymn" or "Eternal Father, Strong to Save") below. Then, add the harmonic analysis (Roman numerals and inversion symbols) below the staff, mark harmonic functions above the staff, and label any instances of prolongation below your harmonic analysis.

(Continued)

Apply This!

15.1. **Analysis.** On the following page is the opening section of Robert Schumann's "Grillen" (no. 4 from *Fantasiestücke*, op. 12). Provide a harmonic analysis (Roman numerals and inversion symbols), and label harmonic functions above the staff. Note the key provided for you at the beginning of the piece. Given the key, how does this piece's opening differ from the opening of a typical Classic-era composition? (Hint: Think in terms of harmonic function.) How does this work's opening, at least initially, obscure the actual tonic?

15.2. Analysis. The following passage from Mozart's Fantasy in C minor, K.475, contains a chromatic circle-of-fifths harmonic sequence that is elaborated (and to some extent concealed) by non-chord tones. Assuming that the harmonic rhythm is one chord per measure, identify the chords by root and quality (do not use Roman numerals), indicating also whether the chord is a seventh chord. Also, identify the non-chord tones; if the non-chord tone is a suspension, identify by type (9–8, 4–3, and so on). Remember that the passage may also employ an arpeggiated texture, and that therefore what appears to be a single rapid line might be better analyzed as the product of more than one voice.

a. Mozart, Fantasy in C minor, K.475, mm. 130–136a.

(Continued)

b. Study the excerpt from the first movement of Beethoven's Sonata in C major, op. 53 ("Waldstein") below, analyzing the root, quality, and inversion of the arpeggios in the left hand. Which circle-of-fifths harmonic sequence (diatonic or chromatic) does its harmonic progression more closely resemble? Bracket the longest part of the passage that follows the sequence. Which chord progressions do *not* conform to the root motion pattern of a circle-of-fifths chord sequence? Circle those progressions.

Beethoven Sonata no. 21 in C major, op. 53 "Waldstein" (i), mm. 104–109.

(Continued)

15.3. Composition. Try adding secondary dominant or leading-tone chords to your composition project from Chapter 12's "Apply This" section. Places where the root progression moves up by perfect fourth or down by perfect fifth are ideal for a secondary dominant seventh chord: C–F could become C7–F, Am–D could become A7–D, and so on. Secondary leading-tone (fully diminished) seventh chords might need to actually be inserted *between* existing chords. If you have a progression of G–Em, for example (I–vi in G), for example, you could try adding a fully diminished seventh chord built on a root a minor second below the second chord: I–vii°7/vi–vi or G–D♯°7–Em. Or, try using inversions for smoother voice leading, e.g., I–vii°$^6_5$/vi–vi or G–D♯°$^6_5$–Em.

15.4. Improvisation. Secondary dominant chords add chromatic zest to diatonic circle-of-fifths progressions. For example, play a vi⁷–ii⁷–V⁷–I progression in the key of G. Turning the first two diatonic sevenths into secondary dominant seventh chords results in the progression V⁷/ii–V⁷/V–V⁷–I, the first half of "Sweet Georgia Brown." Try an improvisation using these four chords as a groove. Or, in any improvisation you are playing, try adding a "flat-seventh" to the leading chord in any root progression that moves up by perfect fourth or down by perfect fifth (see "Composition" above).

CHAPTER 16

MODE MIXTURE

OVERVIEW

Borrowed chords, so named because they "borrow" distinctive elements from the parallel major or minor key, are often used by composers to express ambivalent or bittersweet emotions. The process of incorporating chords from the parallel minor in the context of a major key, or vice versa, is called mode mixture. Like the interplay of light and shadow in art, expression in Western music is enhanced by the interplay of major and minor.

CHAPTER OUTLINE

AUDIO LIST

Enya, "Once You Had Gold"

INTRODUCTION

Occasionally we find triads or seventh chords with *roots* that are diatonic to the key, but that are of a different *quality*. For example, Robert Schumann's song "Ich Grolle Nicht" (Example 16.1) is in C major, but the seventh chord over the supertonic in measure 3 is not a minor seventh (as a diatonic ii⁷ would be) but instead is half-diminished, as the iiᵒ⁷ would be in C minor. The effect of the change is to give the passage a more poignant or melancholy tone. (To verify this, try playing the opening phrase of Schumann's song with a diatonic ii⁷ instead of a iiᵒ⁷, and maybe even sing the opening melodic line, substituting an A♮ for the notated A♭. Does the diatonic version sound "brighter" or "happier"?)

Example 16.1. Schumann, "Ich Grolle Nicht," mm. 1–4a.

Chords like the iiᵒ⁷ in major are called **borrowed chords**, because they are *"borrowed" from the parallel key*; the process of incorporating chords from the parallel minor in a major key, or vice versa, is called **mode mixture**.

- The scale degrees usually affected by mode mixture in major keys are those that differ between the parallel major and minor scales: scale degrees 3, 6, and 7.

MODE MIXTURE IN MAJOR

Example 16.2 shows the most common borrowed chords in major with their Roman numeral labels. Notice that the case of the Roman numeral is changed, and other symbols (such as ᵒ) added, to reflect their change of quality. Notice also the special flat sign added before the Roman numerals of chords that have the lowered third, sixth, or seventh scale degree as their root. This is because in those chords the root *itself* is lowered.

(in C major)

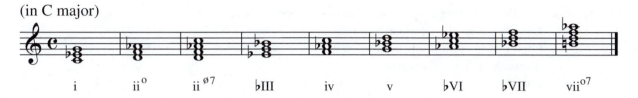

i	ii°	ii°⁷	♭III	iv	v	♭VI	♭VII	vii°⁷

Example 16.2. Borrowed chords in C major.

The most commonly used borrowed chords in Example 16.2 have the lowered sixth scale degree (ii°⁷, iv, and ♭VI). The borrowed supertonic chord is more common as a triad in first inversion (ii°⁶) or as a seventh chord (ii°⁷) than as a root-position triad. Because the flatted submediant scale degree is chromatically lowered, it should resolve downward by step.

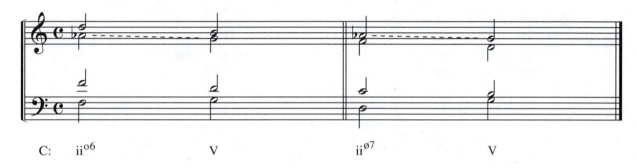

C: ii°⁶   V   ii°⁷   V

Example 16.3. Resolutions of ii°⁶ to V, and of ii°⁷ to V.

The borrowed ♭VII and vii°⁷ chords have different roots. The ♭VII is borrowed from the natural minor scale and is thus built upon the subtonic; the vii°⁷ is borrowed from the harmonic minor and is built upon the leading tone. The vii°⁷ is actually more commonplace in major keys than the diatonic vii°⁷ (Example 16.4).

Legato assai

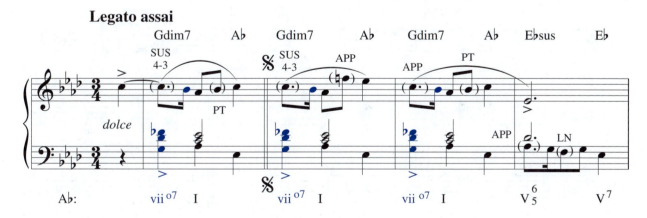

Example 16.4. Chopin, Mazurka in A♭ major, op. 17 no. 3, mm. 1–4.

The ♭VII is less frequently found in common-practice art music (at least in major keys), but it is very common in popular music, where it often functions as a substitute for V (preceding the tonic) or as a kind of "pre-predominant," preceding the IV (Example 16.5; see the discussion of the reverse circle-of-fifths harmonic sequence in Chapter 14).

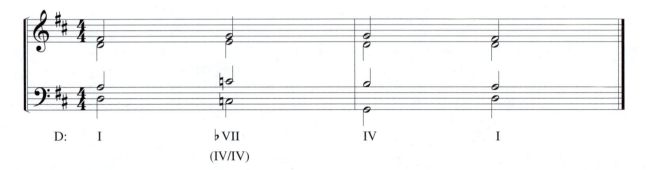

D: I   ♭VII   IV   I
                      (IV/IV)

Example 16.5. The ♭VII functioning as a IV/IV in a reverse circle-of-fifths progression.

Generally, borrowed chords substitute for their diatonic counterparts in similar harmonic contexts and with the same harmonic function. For example, ii$^{\varnothing7}$ and iv often appear in place of ii^7 and IV, and precede V in the same way that the diatonic ii^7 and IV would. ♭VI may be found in a deceptive cadence, substituting for the diatonic vi.

Mode mixture is very common in popular music, especially when a bittersweet or melancholy emotional affect is intended. Cole Porter's classic song "Every Time We Say Goodbye," composed in 1944, makes use of a shift from the diatonic IV to the borrowed iv accompanying the lyric "how strange the change from major to minor," a beautiful example of tone painting (Example 16.6). The same IV → iv movement can be heard repeatedly in the background "oohs" in the Beatles' "In My Life."

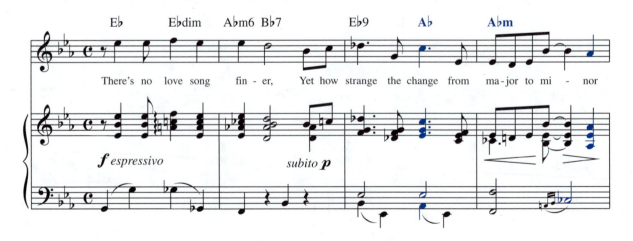

Example 16.6. Cole Porter (1891–1964), "Every Time We Say Goodbye," mode mixture as tone painting.

In Enya's "Once You Had Gold," a deceptive cadence occurs where the vi is immediately followed by ♭VI [1:17–1:23] (Example 16.7).

Example 16.7. Enya (b. 1961), "Once You Had Gold" (1995), mode mixture in deceptive cadence.

Example 16.8 shows a particularly interesting "doubly deceptive" passage from the Electric Light Orchestra's "Mr. Blue Sky." The V⁷/vi on "never mind" resolves deceptively to IV, and the stepwise build-up past ♭VI and ♭VII suggests an arrival on the tonic, which is instead replaced by vi.

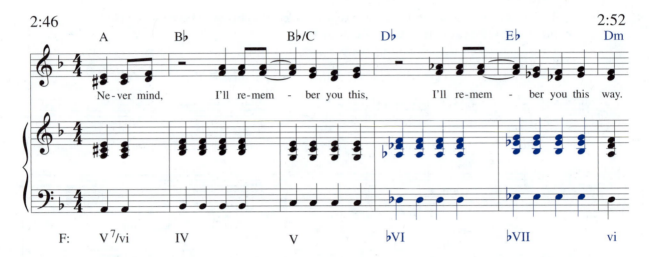

Example 16.8. Electric Light Orchestra, "Mr. Blue Sky" [2:46–2:52].

Sometimes borrowed chords in popular music are not the result of mixing major and minor modes per se, but of the consistent use of modes other than major or minor. Simon and Garfunkel's version of the traditional British ballad "Scarborough Fair," for example, derives its major IV in an otherwise "minor" context from the Dorian mode. Coldplay's "Clocks" is based on the Mixolydian mode, which allows this "major" song to have a minor v chord in the progression that dominates much of the song: I–v–ii (Example 16.9).

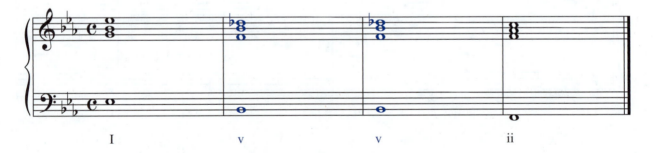

Example 16.9. I–v–ii progression in E♭ (Mixolydian) major.

MODE MIXTURE IN MINOR

Although in major keys mode mixture involves chords that contain $\hat{3}$, $\hat{6}$, and $\hat{7}$, in minor keys scale degrees $\hat{6}$ and $\hat{7}$ are already variable because of the different forms of minor scale (for example, any chord with a "major" 6th or 7th scale degree might just as easily be explained as deriving from the melodic minor scale). Thus the only true borrowed chords in minor involve $\hat{3}$. The Baroque practice of ending a minor-key composition with a major tonic triad (the so-called **Picardy third**) is an example of this kind of mode mixture.[1]

Less commonly, the submediant chord in minor may have a raised root, using the raised submediant scale degree from ascending melodic minor. When applied to a triad, the resulting chord is diminished, the raised root signified by a generic sharp sign before the Roman numeral (♯vi°); when applied to a seventh chord, the resulting chord is half-diminished (♯vi⌀7). Technically, this is a kind of mode mixture as well. The progression in Example 16.10 is found in the Beatles' "While My Guitar Gently Weeps" as well as Chicago's "25 or 6 to 4."

Example 16.10. The raised-submediant ♯vi⌀7 in a descending linear progression.

RECOGNIZING AND SPELLING BORROWED CHORDS

Because the scale degrees involved in mode mixture are usually $\hat{3}$, $\hat{6}$, and $\hat{7}$ in major keys or $\hat{3}$ in minor, borrowed chords are usually easy to recognize:

- The chord has a *diatonic root*, but its *third or fifth* is altered, changing the quality of the chord (ii° or iv in major, I in minor)
- The chord has an *altered root* (usually lowered in a major key; less commonly raised in a minor key). The root alteration is signified by a generic accidental (sharp or flat) before the Roman numeral (e.g., ♭III, ♭VI or ♭VII in major; ♯vi° in minor). The Roman numeral case is also changed to reflect the change in chord quality.

In spelling borrowed chords, generally lowering $\hat{3}$, $\hat{6}$, or $\hat{7}$ will be sufficient to create a borrowed chord. Remember that scale degrees $\hat{3}$, $\hat{6}$, and $\hat{7}$ are altered *together*

---

[1]The practice dates back to the sixteenth century and is often thought to have been named for the Picardie region of France, though the name more likely derives from the Old French *picart* (or *picarde*), meaning "sharp" or "pointed."

when two of them appear in the same chord. For a ♭III chord, for example, remember to lower the fifth of the chord ($\hat{7}$) as well to preserve the triad's major quality; similarly, in a ♭VI chord the fifth of the chord ($\hat{3}$) will be lowered as well.

LEVEL MASTERY 16.1.

a. Spell the indicated borrowed chords in four-part texture, using correct doubling.

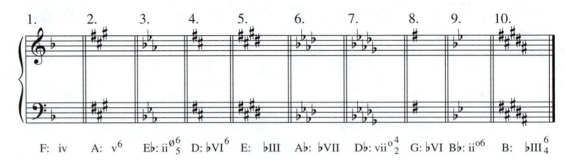

F: iv   A: v⁶   E♭: ii^{ø6}₅   D: ♭VI⁶   E: ♭III   A♭: ♭VII   D♭: vii^{o4}₂   G: ♭VI   B♭: ii^{o6}   B: ♭III⁶₄

b. Each of the progressions below contains one or more chords that could be replaced by borrowed chords. First, provide a harmonic analysis. Then, in the blank staff below, rewrite the progression with the substitution of the appropriate borrowed chords.

(Continued)

Apply This!
16.1 may
be done at
this time.

Workbook
Exercises 16.1,
16.2, and 16.3
may be done
at this time.

CONCLUSION

Mode mixture refers to the use of tones or chords from the parallel minor key (if the mode is predominantly major—more common) or parallel major key (if the mode is predominantly minor—less common). The tones involved in mode mixture are those tones that differ between parallel major and minor keys: $\hat{3}$, $\hat{6}$, and $\hat{7}$. In minor keys, $\hat{6}$ and $\hat{7}$ are already variable (because of the different forms of minor scales), so only the third scale degree is generally involved in minor.

Normally mode mixture involves **borrowed chords**—chords "borrowed" from the parallel minor or major key. In most cases this involves changing the quality of the chord, with the size of the Roman numeral changing accordingly (in borrowing a subdominant chord from the parallel minor, for example, IV becomes iv). The harmonic function of the chord does not change, nor does its customary place in a harmonic progression.

When the root of the chord is the 3rd, 6th, or 7th scale degree, a borrowed chord in a major key shows that the root itself has been changed (lowered) by adding a flat before the Roman numeral, and changing the case of the Roman numeral to indicate the change in quality. For example, in borrowing a submediant chord from the parallel minor, vi becomes ♭VI.

Mode mixture became a popular expressive device in the Romantic era, and even today it is commonly used by pop songwriters to impart a bittersweet or nostalgic quality to their music.

Terms to Know

borrowed chord   mode mixture   Picardy third

Self-Test

16.1. Spell the following borrowed chords, as indicated by the key and Roman numeral quality. Use key signatures and any necessary accidentals.

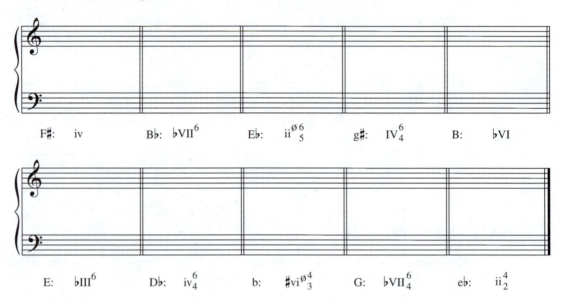

F#: iv   Bb: bVII⁶   Eb: ii°⁶₅   g#: IV⁶₄   B: bVI

E: bIII⁶   Db: iv⁶₄   b: #vi°⁴₃   G: bVII⁶₄   eb: ii⁴₂

Apply This!

16.1. Analysis. Locate and label the borrowed chords in each of the following excerpts. You do not need to provide a full harmonic analysis. Where necessary to clarify the identity of chords, certain non-chord tones are indicated with parentheses.

a. Fanny Mendelssohn Hansel (1805–1847), "Bergeslust," op. 10 no. 4 (1850), mm. 9–18a.

hoch ü - ber sich — den blau - en, den kal - ren Him - mels - dom, hoch

A:

(Continued)

b. Pauline Viardot (1821–1910), "Le Rêve de Jésus" (1890), mm. 8–18a.

(Continued)

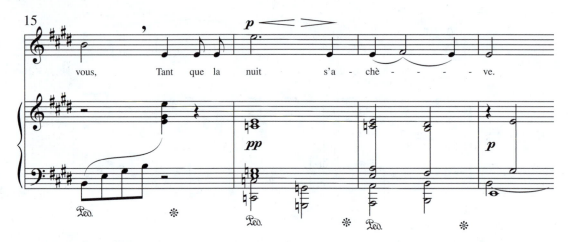

15

vous,   Tant que la nuit   s'a - chè - - - ve.

c. U2, "Magnificent" (2009). **Aural analysis.** The key and bass line is provided. Determine the quality of each chord and provide Roman numerals. Mark an asterisk by each chord that is an example of mode mixture. The upper staff is left blank for your use if needed.

VERSE (1:15–1:52)   (3x)

f♯:

CHORUS, excerpt (3:28–3:49)

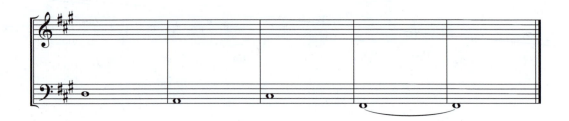

PART 3

FORM AND CHROMATIC HARMONY 2

CHAPTER 17

MODULATION 1

OVERVIEW

This chapter introduces modulation—how to change from one key to another. Tonal relationships in a piece of music may be likened to cities or towns, and the process of modulation like the highways one takes on a road trip. Some roads offer a quick "express" way to reach one's destination, while other roads may take a more leisurely "scenic route." In this chapter, we examine two types of modulation: common chord and chromatic.

AUDIO LIST
The Flaming Lips, "Do You Realize?"

THE HARMONIC JOURNEY: THERE AND BACK AGAIN

Perhaps you have already experienced the pleasure of a "road trip"—a weekend trip with friends, sometimes to the beach or the city, or perhaps with no destination in mind but just a drive for the sake of the freedom of it. Let's imagine that we are planning such a road trip. You can pull out a road map, find your location, and ask yourself, "Where do I want to go?"

Now that you have decided your destination, you have other decisions to make. Do you want to take the most direct route possible, such as an interstate highway, or do you want to try the "scenic route," such as a series of state or county roads? Taking the interstate will be fastest, but it has a certain generic quality—you'll miss some of the roadside attractions and most of the restaurants at the exits will be fast-food chains. Taking the "scenic route" may have more beautiful scenery, and the food might be better—you might find fresher local cuisine and get to talk with some of the "locals"—but it will also take much longer and there is no guarantee that the food will always be a terrific experience. There is also the decision of how many rest stops you might need to take along the way, and how long you might stop at each one.

Web Feature 17.1 provides some historical context for how modulation was considered as a "journey" narrative.

In some ways, a musical composition is like a road trip. We best experience a piece of music in real time; looking at an analytical diagram is no more a substitute for the actual experience of listening to music than studying a road map replaces driving to and experiencing your destination. Part of the road trip's allure is not only the destination but how you get there; in the same way, many pieces of music involve a "trip" to and from the tonic, traversing any number of other keys (some close, some distant), and every piece of music has its own "route" for doing so. We can listen to a piece of music from the common-practice era in terms of a "journey" narrative.

COMMON CHORD MODULATION

In Chapter 2 you learned about closely related keys and their placement in adjacent positions along the circle of fifths. Each of the closely related keys may also be found quickly by remembering the major or minor diatonic triads found in relation to the tonic; given the tonic of G major, for example, its closely related keys are A minor (ii), B minor (iii), C major (IV), D major (V), and E minor (vi). In Chapter 14 we learned that each of these diatonic triads (closely related keys) may be tonicized by means of secondary dominant or secondary leading-tone chords. If tonicization involves a fleeting "set up" of a diatonic triad as a "temporary tonic," then we can also change key, or **modulate**, by setting up *new predominant and dominant functions* in relation to the newly established tonic and confirming the new key with a cadence. For example, consider the opening eight measures of the first movement of Clementi's Sonatina in G major, op. 36, no. 2 (Example 17.1):

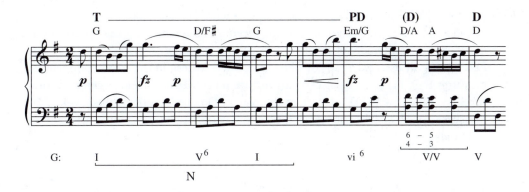

Example 17.1. Clementi, Sonatina in G Major, op. 36 no. 2 (i), mm. 1–8.

As the example shows, measures 1–4 can be analyzed as a neighboring tonic prolongation; a predominant chord does not appear until measure 6. Based on the evidence of this excerpt, we can interpret the entire passage as being in G major, ending on a half cadence. This would be the case if the music that followed remained in G major, as in the "pseudo-Clementi" passage in Example 17.2.

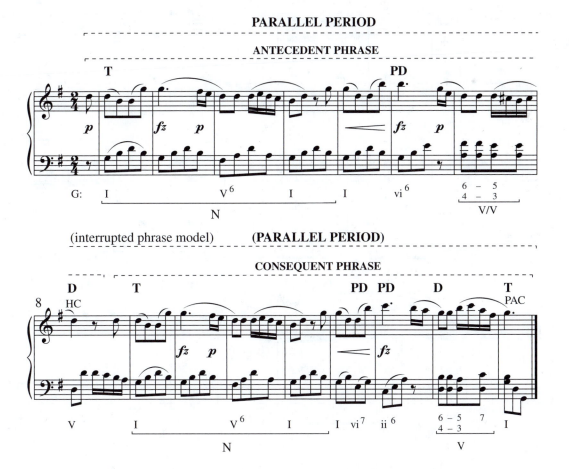

Example 17.2. Pseudo-Clementi, Example 17.1 as the beginning of a parallel double period.

Example 17.3, however, shows how Clementi actually continues. Measure 7 introduces C♯, a pitch foreign to G major, serving as the tonicizing leading tone of D major. For the remainder of Example 17.3, C♯ has *consistently* replaced C natural, and D is repeatedly asserted as an **ostinato** (a repeated pattern in the accompaniment) in measures 8–9, 11, and 14–17. D seems to have replaced G as the key center; in measures 13–14, a new PD–D–T pattern (ii^6–V–I in D major) confirms the new key. By measures 19–22 we hear the repeated cadential pattern as a perfect authentic cadence in D major.

Example 17.3. Clementi, Sonatina in G major, op. 36 no. 2 (i), measures 1–22.

How did we get to this point? Measures 1–5 are resolutely in the key of G major, containing either the I or the V; measure 6 contains the first chord (vi[6]) with a pre-dominant function, and measures 7–8 tonicize D major, introducing the new key that is asserted in the following measures. Measures 9–12 steadily assert a D major harmony, followed by the PD–D–T pattern in D major at measures 13–14; this harmonic pattern (4 measures of a D major harmony, followed by a 2-measure PD–D–T pattern) is repeated in measures 15–20.

So, if measures 1–5 assert the key of G major, and measures 7–22 fit into the key of D major, we need to look again at measure 6. It so happens that E minor functions as ii in D major as well as vi in G major; so E minor is a **common chord**, *functioning in both keys* (Example 17.4). This key change is an example of a **common chord modulation**; a harmony or group of harmonies acts as a pivot between the two keys, enabling a smooth transition between them.[1]

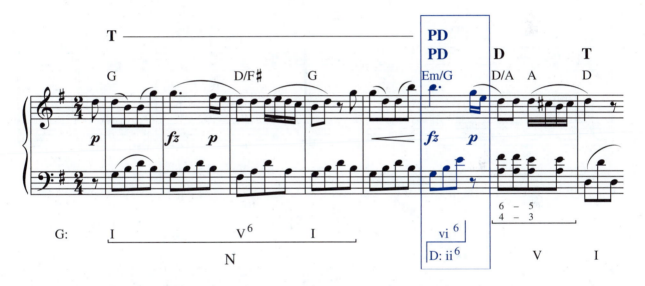

Example 17.4. Clementi, Sonatina in G major, op. 36 no. 2 (i), mm. 1–8, showing common chord modulation.

The smoothness of the transition in Example 17.4 illustrates two important points about modulation:

- *The actual key change usually occurs immediately before we become aware of it.* At the point of the pivot, we are still interpreting the harmony as belonging to the key

---

[1] The common chord modulation is sometimes also called a **pivot chord modulation**, and the connection between the keys a **pivot chord**. This term is not sufficiently precise, however—as we will soon see, other chords that are not diatonic may also function as "pivots" between keys. Thus, in this text the term "pivot" will be used generically, to refer to any chord that has this connecting function.

to which we are accustomed. A kind of subterfuge, or double identity, establishes a new key before it is made obvious by consistently adding accidentals and new harmonic-function patterns.

- The smoothness of the change is also *affected by the strength of the common chord's harmonic function in each key*; if the common chord has a tonic or dominant function in either of the keys, the effect of the key change will seem more abrupt or dramatic.

Example 17.5 shows common chord modulations involving differing harmonic functions for comparative effect; if you have the opportunity, play through each one. As you play through them, which seem to be the smoothest or least perceptible? Which are more surprising?

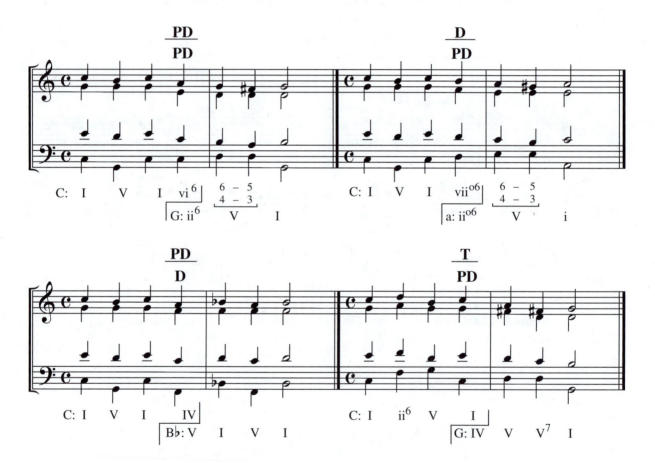

Example 17.5. Comparative common chord modulations. *(Continued)*

(Continued)

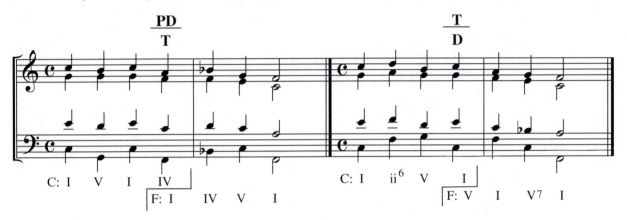

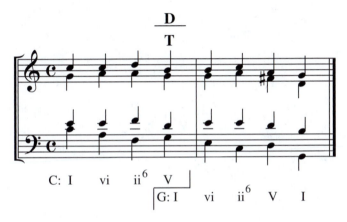

In our harmonic "road trip," a common chord modulation is something like a temporary merger of two interstate highways that then split again, enabling the traveler to smoothly transition from one highway to another. As Example 17.5 shows, however, the brief "merge" may lead the traveler in different directions. Most of the pathways in Example 17.5 involve motion to closely related keys: the dominant, the relative minor, or the subdominant. Note, however, what happens when the common chord is a predominant in the old key and a dominant in the new key; since a dominant chord must be a major triad, and the only major predominant is IV, this forces the key change to a foreign key a whole step below the tonic. On our harmonic "road trip," we might think of closely related keys as towns within the state borders, and foreign keys as towns that are out of state. As the various pathways of Example 17.5 demonstrate, most common chord modulations result in transitions to closely related keys; the C-to-B♭ pathway is an exception to the rule.

1. Each of the common chords below is missing one of its Roman numeral labels, in either the opening or closing key. Fill in the blanks to show the chord's dual labeling.

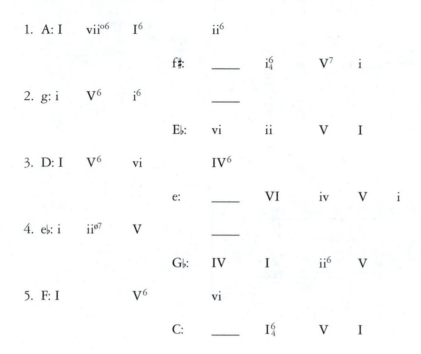

1. A: I   vii^{o6} I^6 ii^6

         f♯:   ____   i$^6_4$ V^7 i

2. g: i   V^6 i^6 ____

         E♭:   vi   ii   V   I

3. D: I   V^6 vi   IV^6

         e: ____   VI   iv   V   i

4. e♭: i   ii^{ø7} V   ____

         G♭:   IV   I   ii^6 V

5. F: I   V^6 vi

         C: ____   I$^6_4$ V   I

2. Given the key provided at the opening of each of the following musical excerpts, determine the key to which the music has modulated at the conclusion of the excerpt. Then, analyze the boxed common chord within each excerpt, providing its labeling in each key in the manner of number 1 above.

a. Benny Anderson, Bjorn Ulvaeus and Stig Anderson, "S.O.S.," [0:36–0:44].

b. Schubert, Waltz, op. 27 no. 9, mm. 1–16.

c. Mendelssohn, Song Without Words in G minor, op. 19 no. 6 ("Venetian Gondola Song"), mm. 7–17. Parentheses have been placed around the non-chord tones in measures 14–17 to facilitate your analysis.

d. Schumann, *Dichterliebe*, "Wenn ich in deine Augen seh,'" op. 48, no. 4, mm. 1–8.

Self-Test 17.1 may be done at this time.

(Continued)

Apply This!
17.2a may
be done at
this time.

Workbook
Exercise 17.1
may be done
at this time.

wenn ich küs - se dei____ nen Mund, so werd' ich ganz und gar ge - sund.

CHROMATIC MODULATION

A chord does not have to be diatonic to both keys in order to be used as a *pivot* from one key to another. A **chromatic modulation** occurs when the pivot chord is *chromatically altered in either key*. The most common chromatic alterations involve changing the pivot chord's quality through mode mixture or turning it into a secondary dominant chord.

Example 17.6a shows a passage from Franz Schubert's Impromptu no. 1 in C minor, op. 90, D.899. This section begins in A♭ major, a closely related key (VI) of C minor, but by the end of the excerpt we have reached a perfect authentic cadence in C♭ major, which is not a closely related key of C minor *or* A♭ major. How does Schubert so seemingly effortlessly reach this distant key?

Example 17.6a. Schubert, Impromptu in C minor, op. 90 no. 1, D.899, mm. 41–51a. *(Continued)*

(Continued)

Example 17.6b is a textural reduction of the Schubert excerpt, stripping away the non-chord tones (which you should nevertheless identify for practice). The harmonic analysis for the example easily fits A♭ major up through measure 47, but the F♭s and the G♭ dominant-seventh chords after that point make an analysis of C♭ major much more logical. The two keys meet at the D♭ minor chord on the downbeat of measure 48. This chord is diatonic to C♭ major (ii), but it is chromatically altered in the old key of A♭ major—borrowed from the parallel minor, it would be analyzed as iv. The modulation works in the same way as a common chord modulation, but because the pivot chord is *not diatonic to both keys*, it is a chromatic modulation. Because the harmonic function of the chord is still weak (PD in both keys), the transition is very smooth.

Example 17.6b. Textural reduction and harmonic analysis of Example 17.5a.

(Continued)

(Continued)

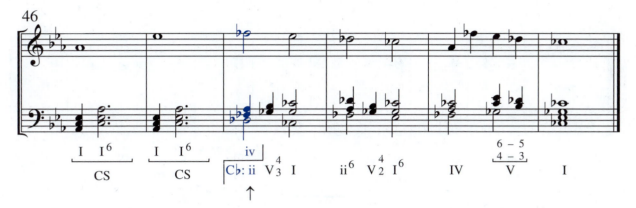

A more contemporary example of a chromatic modulation, made to work with great dramatic effect, is found in the song "Do You Realize?" by the Flaming Lips. Most of this song is made up of chords diatonic to C major, as Example 17.7 (the harmonic progression of the first verse) shows.[2] Notice the use of the minor-inflected IV–iv–I progression—the same progression the Beatles used in "In My Life"—to accompany the poignant line "everyone you know someday will die" [1:15–1:21]. The borrowed iv is also heard in the guitars at 0:33, dissonant against the major IV implied by the vocal line's A and C. These appearances of the borrowed iv (F minor) prepare us for the use of that chord in effecting the chromatic modulation at 1:54, a brief dramatic flourish into E♭ major (Example 17.8).

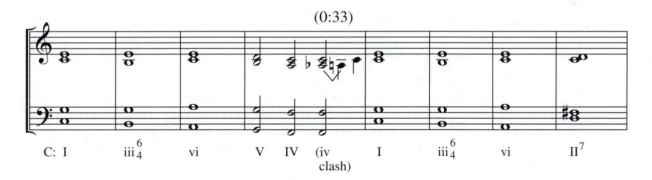

Example 17.7. The Flaming Lips, "Do You Realize?," harmonic progression of verse 1. *(Continued)*

---

[2] The prevalence of parallel perfect fifths and octaves in this illustration demonstrates, perhaps, the contrast between voice-leading practices in the "classical" and popular-music genres. Altering the texture to "correct" the voice leading would result in changing the relationship between the melodic line and bass throughout.

(Continued)

(0:50)

IV⁷   iii   vi   V   IV   V   I   iii⁶₄   vi   IV   iv   I

(1:54)   (2:09)

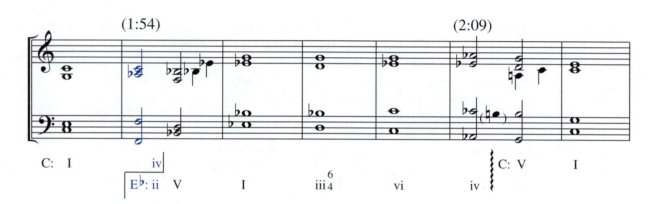

C: I   iv   C: V   I

       E♭: ii   V   I   iii⁶₄   vi   iv

Example 17.8. The Flaming Lips, "Do You Realize?," chromatic modulation in bridge at 1:54.

As both of these examples show, chromatic modulation works the same way that common chord modulation does—using a chord that is functional in both keys as a pivot between the first key and the next. The outcome in chromatic modulation, however, can be dramatically different. Because the pivot chord is, by definition, chromatic in at least one of the keys, modulations to foreign keys are quite possible. The Schubert excerpt in Example 17.6a has a modulation from A♭ major to C♭ major. The Flaming Lips song in Example 17.8 modulates from C major to E♭ major. In each of these two examples, the keys are in a **chromatic mediant relationship** to each other, meaning:

• Two keys (or two chords) are a *major or minor third apart* from one another;
• Both keys (or chords) have the *same quality*.

Thus, for example, C major and E major are in a chromatic mediant relationship; C major and E minor are not.

Beethoven made chromatic mediant relationships a major component of his harmonic style; Example 17.9 comes from the middle of a piano sonata movement in the key of G major. At this point, however, Beethoven has briefly touched on E major (a key related by chromatic mediant to the tonic) before repeating the pattern in C major (a key closely related to the tonic, but related by chromatic mediant to E major). (Which chord in the passage acts as the pivot in the chromatic modulation that occurs?)

Example 17.9. Beethoven, Piano Sonata in G major, op. 79 (i), mm. 59–74.

Self-Test 17.2 may be done at this time.

Workbook Exercise 17.2 may be done at this time.

Each of the chromatic pivot chords in the progressions below is missing one of its Roman numeral labels, in either the opening or closing key. Fill in the blanks to show the chord's dual labeling.

1. D: $\quad$ I $\quad$ ii$^6_5$ $\quad$ V $\quad$ ♭VI

   E♭: $\quad$ ____ $\quad$ vi $\quad$ ii$^6_5$ $\quad$ V $\quad$ I

2. A♭: $\quad$ I $\quad$ IV^6 $\quad$ ____

   F: $\quad$ iv $\quad$ I$^6_4$ $\quad$ V $\quad$ I

3. A: $\quad$ I $\quad$ vii$^{\circ6}$ $\quad$ I^6 $\quad$ IV $\quad$ iv

   B♭: $\quad$ ____ $\quad$ vi $\quad$ ii^6 $\quad$ V $\quad$ I

CONCLUSION

In generations past, people did not travel as frequently or as far as they do today. Many people lived in one town, or one state, their entire lives. The widespread availability of the automobile, and later air travel, led to a much more mobile society; people today are able to travel not only to other states, but to other countries, with an ease that our great-grandparents could scarcely have dreamed of.

Similarly, the period of music history from 1700 to 1900 saw an unparalleled expansion in the area of harmonic travel. Like geographic travel, the rapid harmonic expansion of the late eighteenth and nineteenth centuries was made possible by the invention of new technologies—the tuning system of equal temperament and the modern-day piano. Equal temperament was introduced during J. S. Bach's lifetime, but it only gradually gained acceptance; most of Bach's compositions modulate only to those keys that are closely related to the tonic. Still, C. P. E. Bach's discussion of available keys in the *Essay on the True Art of Playing Keyboard Instruments* implies that a greater variety of available modulation destinations were available than would have been to his father a generation earlier. The modern piano was introduced in the early nineteenth century, bringing with it an almost orchestral capacity for dynamic and textural contrast; this inspired composers to try new and daring techniques. In Chapters 18 and 28 we will see more of these modulation techniques.

Terms to Know

chromatic mediant relationship
chromatic modulation

common chord (pivot chord) modulation

Self-Test

17.1. Which of the keys below would *not* be accessible from D major by means of a diatonic common-chord modulation?

a) f♯ minor
b) C major
c) B♭ major
d) E major
e) B minor

17.2. Which of the keys below would *not* be accessible from F major by means of a chromatic modulation, using a borrowed iv in F major as the pivot chord?

a) A♭ major
b) D♭ major
c) G♭ major
d) A major
e) B♭ minor

Apply This!

17.1. Analysis. Choose the label that best describes the type of modulation (diatonic common-chord or chromatic) that occurs in each of these excerpts. In some excerpts there may be more than one analyzable modulation. (Note: The opening key of the excerpt may not always be that implied by the given key signature.)

a. Beethoven, Piano Sonata no. 31 in A♭ major, op. 110 (iii), mm. 9–16.

(Continued)

(Continued)

b. Bach, Two-Part Invention no. 13 in A minor, BWV 784, mm. 1–7.

(Continued)

(Continued)

c. Haydn, String Quartet in D major, op. 50 no. 6 (i), mm. 26–43.

(Continued)

(Continued)

(Continued)

17.2. Composition. Complete the phrase below, using a common chord modulation to a closely related key. End the phrase with a perfect authentic cadence in the new key.

17.3. Improvisation.

a. Using Roman numerals and inversion symbols, write progressions that link the keys indicated below, using the specified types of modulation. Be sure that the old and new keys are sufficiently prepared and established, using different T–D–T or T–PD–D–T progressions before and after the key change.

After writing your progressions (remember—use Roman numerals and inversion symbols, not musical notation!), play them at the keyboard, striving for correct voice leading (minimal movement within parts, or "the law of the shortest way") as much as possible. (Lower case letters indicate minor keys.)

G	{common chord modulation}	e
E	{common chord modulation}	B
F	{chromatic modulation}	A
c	{common chord modulation}	E♭

As a variant of this exercise, trade progressions with a classmate and play one another's progressions. Discuss the smoothness or abruptness of your choices together.

CHAPTER 18

MODULATION 2

OVERVIEW

In this chapter, we continue our study of modulation by looking at some less common modulation techniques that you might encounter in the music you study: Common-tone, sequential, monophonic, and direct modulation.

CHAPTER OUTLINE

AUDIO LIST

The Eagles, "New Kid in Town"

Robert Schumann, "Im Wunderschönen Monat Mai" (from *Dichterliebe*, op. 45)

INTRODUCTION

In the previous chapter we examined two of the most common varieties of modulation: common chord and chromatic modulation. This chapter introduces other modulation types that are somewhat less common, but that you may nevertheless encounter.

COMMON-TONE MODULATION

In the same way that we can connect between two keys by means of a common chord, we can also connect two keys by a single common *tone*. Two chords with a chromatic mediant relationship share just one common tone (Example 18.1); often this tone is emphasized in the melodic line, as shown in Example 18.2. Note the chromatic mediant relationship between the F♯ major chord in measure 25 (V of B minor) and the first chord of the D major section (D major in measure 26). Common-tone modulations often involve chromatic mediant relationships between keys or chords.

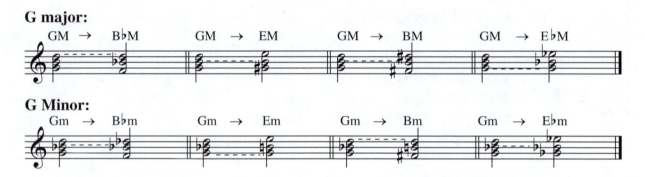

Example 18.1. Examples of chromatic mediant relationships from G major and minor, with common tones shown.

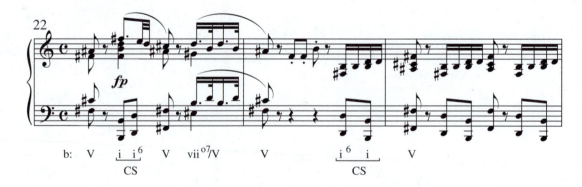

Example 18.2. Mozart, Fantasy no. 4 in C minor, K.475, mm. 22–26. *(Continued)*

(Continued)

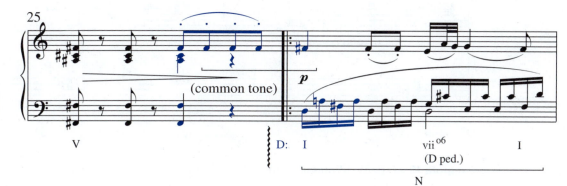

V   D: I   vii°⁶   I
     (D ped.)
           N

Self-Tests
18.1 and 18.2
may be done
at this time.

SEQUENTIAL MODULATION

Sometimes the continuity we perceive in a key change is due to sequence. In **sequential modulation**, a passage is repeated, literally transposed, in the new key, which may or may not be closely related. Take another look at Example 17.8. Although the C major chord in measure 67 could be interpreted as a ♭VI in E major (a chord borrowed from the parallel minor), one could also interpret this passage as a I–V⁷ progression in E major (measures 59–65) followed by a literal transposition of that same progression in C major (measures 67–73). In a sequential modulation, there must be both a harmonic *and* a melodic sequence involved.

MONOPHONIC MODULATION

Modulations are possible even in a monophonic texture—that is, when the line is unaccompanied (you can find monophonic modulations in Bach's Cello Suites or Violin Partitas, or in the midst of extended cadenzas in a concerto for a solo monophonic instrument such as the clarinet or flute). How can a modulation occur when there is no accompaniment to provide a harmonic backdrop? The answer lies in the selective use of certain "cue" pitches, especially accidentals that would imply the leading tone of the new key or the third or sixth scale degree of the new key (to indicate whether the new key is major or minor). Arpeggios can help to confirm the tonality after the modulation has occurred. Composers will often use **compound melody**—the use of registral extremes to imply two or more lines in a single line part—to project harmonic content in a monophonic texture. See the excerpts in Example 18.3. In Example 18.3a, Bach uses differences in register to imply a mostly three-part texture outlining the progression i–v⁶–iv⁶₅–V. In Example 18.3b, arpeggiations are used in a circle-of-fifths harmonic sequence that facilitates a modulation to the relative major.

Example 18.3a. Bach, Minuet II from Cello Suite no. 1, BWV 1007, mm. 1–4.

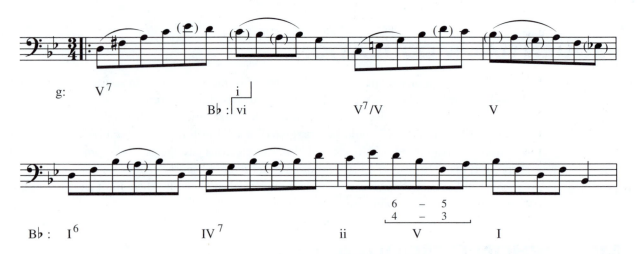

Example 18.3b. Monophonic modulation in Bach, Minuet II from Cello Suite no. 1, BWV 1007, mm. 9–16.

In Example 18.4, a single line "meanders" into several keys. The line begins in C minor, as indicated by the C minor arpeggio and the B♮ leading tone. A c♯°⁷ chord, with the cue accidentals C♯ and B♭, indicates a modulation into D minor has occurred (a fully-diminished seventh chord occurs diatonically only over the leading tone in minor); the E major-minor $^6_5$ at the end of the third measure, with the cue accidental G♯, likewise confirms that we have modulated to A minor (a major-minor seventh chord occurs diatonically only over the dominant scale degree).

(Dm: i = Am: iv)

Example 18.4. An example of monophonic modulation.

DIRECT MODULATION

Each of the preceding categories of modulation, including those in the previous chapter, deals with the ways that two keys can be *connected*:

- A chord found (diatonically or chromatically) in both keys (common-chord modulation or chromatic modulation)
- A tone found in both chords where a modulation takes place (common-tone modulation)
- An identical melodic and harmonic passage that is transposed sequentially in the new key (sequential modulation).

Sometimes, however, the music simply seems to "begin anew" in the new key with *no connection* to the old key, especially at the beginning of a new phrase. This is called a **direct modulation** or **phrase modulation**. Direct modulation should be thought of as the "none of the above" category in analyzing modulations; usually a connecting factor is present.

Study Example 18.5. The opening 17 measures establish the key of D major through a fanfare-like repetition of motives that seldom strays from I and V. Measures 13–17 extend the V through a pedal prolongation—a drawn-out half cadence. After the dramatic pause of measure 18 the music re-enters, surprisingly, on a C major chord, the beginning of a circle-of-fifths harmonic progression that ultimately cadences in A minor at measure 22. Although the C major chord could be analyzed as a ♭VII in D major (borrowed from D minor), which would imply a chromatic modulation, and even though both the A major and C major chords share a common tone, implying a common-tone modulation, this is better analyzed as a direct modulation because there is a clear break between the phrases; the C major chord really sounds like a new beginning.

Example 18.5. Domenico Scarlatti (1685–1757), Sonata in D major, K.491, mm. 1–22.

Self-Test 18.3
may be done
at this time.

Apply This! 18.1
may be done
at this time.

As this excerpt shows, a modulating passage may display more than one category of modulation. There may be a surprising "directness" to a common-tone modulation, for example, or a sequential modulation may also involve a chromatic pivot chord. It is best to consider all options and weigh how perceptible each one is—test your ear as well as your eye. Stylistic considerations can also help: for example, Baroque and Classic-era music usually makes use of common chord modulations; in late Classic and early Romantic-era music one finds more chromatic modulations (often in conjunction with mode mixture, which began to increase at about the same time). The Romantic era is the period when we start to see widespread use of common-tone and sequential modulations. All of these are generalizations, of course; exceptions can always be found in the literature.

PROGRESSIVE TONALITY

If tonality can be likened to a road map, modulations act like cloverleaf intersections; they assist in transitions from one route to another along the harmonic road trip we began in the previous chapter. Ultimately, though, the trip ends with a return to home, and so the vast majority of pieces in common-practice period art music finish in the piece's tonic. When a piece ends in a *different* key than the one in which it began, this is called **progressive tonality**; the psychological effect of ending in a key other than where we began is that we have somehow arrived at a "different place," and so in common-practice art music progressive tonality usually serves some sort of transitional purpose. In operas and oratorios, for example, progressive tonality is often found in **recitatives**, short pieces that advance the plot or narrative as they act as transitions between the larger arias or choruses. Because the arias or choruses that bookend the recitative are usually in different keys, the recitative's musical function is to smooth the transition from the previous piece's key to the key of the piece that follows. In a recitative, especially if the text is particularly dramatic, one may find several modulations before the music settles on the new key of the aria or chorus that is to come.

Progressive tonality is common in popular music. Modulations often occur toward the end of songs in pop and rock music; usually the song ends (fades out) in the new key, usually a half or whole step higher than the opening tonic.

The modulation at the end of a pop song is such an established convention that the Eagles song "New Kid in Town" actually draws upon this convention and does something surprising with it. Most of the song is resolutely in E major, although the chorus hints at a move to C♯ minor (the relative minor) through the tonicizing chord at [0:53], for example. Still, despite the chorus's repetition of a modally inflected i–IV progression in C♯ minor ("Johnny come lately"), the F♯ major chord is eventually followed by an F♯ minor seventh chord at [1:08], a ii[7] of E major that brings us back, through a ii–V–I, to the tonic.

The pattern established by the verse and chorus is broken at [2:24], with the arrival of the transitional "bridge" section. A deceptive cadence at [2:35–2:39] ("you're willing to hold her") soon leads us to an A minor seventh chord at [2:42] ("Tears").

This chord becomes the pivot in a chromatic modulation to G major, functioning as a borrowed iv^7 in E major and as a ii^7 in the new key of G. The next verse begins in the new tonic of G major at [2:46].

Thus far, "New Kid in Town" behaves much like a great number of other pop songs—a modulation to a higher key occurs toward the end of the song, usually on the last verse (which it is at this point) or the last chorus. We would then expect the song to fade out in the new, higher key. That does not happen, however: after the verse and an additional chorus in the new key, the song modulates *back* to the tonic at [3:35], again by a chromatic modulation and again involving an A minor seventh chord (the ii^7 in G becomes the borrowed iv^7 in E). With the chorus's concluding iv^7–V–I progression [3:35–3:39] ("he's holding her, and you're still around"), the song unexpectedly returns to the tonic. Perhaps the intrusion of the relative minor (C♯ minor) in the choruses represents the intrusion of the "new kid {or new key} in town." Perhaps the return to the tonic at the end even portrays the idea that the character who has lost his love to the "new kid in town" is "still around." We will return to a closer examination of music's narrative aspects in Chapter 31.

CONCLUSION

The types of modulation featured in this chapter expanded the harmonic tools available to a composer in the eighteenth and nineteenth centuries, especially since they opened up pathways to more distant keys than were possible using diatonic common-chord modulation. With the exception of direct modulation, each of these types still manages to "connect" the new key with the old, although the connections—a harmonic sequence, a single common tone—become more tenuous. At the same time, these modulations can seem more abrupt, allowing modulations to serve a dramatic or even narrative function. We will conclude our exploration of modulation techniques in Chapter 28.

Terms to Know

common-tone modulation	progressive tonality
compound melody	recitative
direct (or phrase) modulation	sequential modulation
monophonic modulation	

Self-Test

18.1. Given the triad provided, list the triads that are in a chromatic mediant relationship with it. Then, identify the common tone between the given triad and each chromatically related triad. One blank in the first question is provided as an example.

a. E♭ major   *C major*   _____   _____   _____

    common tone: *G*   _____   _____   _____

b. C♯ minor   _____   _____   _____   _____

    common tone: _____   _____   _____   _____

c. A♭ minor   _____   _____   _____   _____

    common tone: _____   _____   _____   _____

18.2. Write the chromatic-mediant-related major-minor seventh chords for each major-minor seventh chord provided, arranging them in inversions that will provide the smoothest voice leading from the chord provided. Next, provide the major key for which the new chord has a *dominant* function, label the inversion, and fill in the common tone(s). You may write an enharmonic equivalent if it is more logical (for instance, if the key in which the chord serves as a dominant seventh does not exist). One example is provided for you.

A: V$^6_5$ ___F___: V$^4_3$ ____: V__   ____: V__   ____: V__

E♭: V$^4_3$ ____: V__   ____: V__   ____: V__   ____: V__

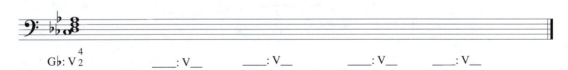

G♭: V$^4_2$ ____: V__   ____: V__   ____: V__   ____: V__

18.3. At 2:09 into the Flaming Lips song "Do You Realize?," another modulation occurs from E♭ major back to C major, returning to the tonic (see Example 16.7). Which of the types of modulation discussed in this chapter best explain the key change that occurs here?

Apply This!

18.1. Analysis. Choose the label that best describes the type of modulation that occurs in the following excerpts. Your choices are: common-tone, sequential, and direct. In some excerpts there may be more than one analyzable modulation.

a. Beethoven, Bagatelle in G minor, op. 119 no. 1, mm. 9–24.

b. Wagner, Prelude to *Parsifal*, mm. 45–50a. (Be mindful of the transposing instruments in this passage. Some empty staves have been omitted to save space.)

18.2. Composition. Complete the passage below by adding a second phrase, related to the first by means of a sequential modulation to a foreign key. You may choose the key, but make sure the second phrase is a literal transposition of the first. Do not change the key signature, but instead modify with necessary accidentals.

18.3. Improvisation. Using Roman numerals and inversion symbols, write progressions that link the keys indicated below, using the specified types of modulation. Be sure that the old and new keys are sufficiently prepared and established, using different T–D–T or T–PD–D–T progressions before and after the key change.

After writing your progressions (remember—use Roman numerals and inversion symbols, not musical notation!), play them at the keyboard, striving for correct voice leading (minimal movement within parts, or "the law of the shortest way") as much as possible. (Lowercase letters indicate minor keys.)

a. A♭ [common tone modulation] f

b. g [sequential modulation] a

As a variant of this exercise, trade progressions with a classmate and play one another's progressions. Discuss the smoothness or abruptness of your choices together.

CHAPTER 19

CANON AND FUGUE

OVERVIEW

We return to the examination of counterpoint and polyphony we began in Chapter 6 by looking at two common contrapuntal genres: canon and fugue. Canons involve strict imitation, somewhat like a round such as "Row, Row, Row Your Boat." Fugues are less strict, however, and they can vary much more from piece to piece. In the nineteenth and twentieth centuries, composers experimented with fugal style even as they adhered to its time-honored contrapuntal techniques.

CHAPTER OUTLINE

AUDIO LIST

J. S. Bach, Fugue in G minor from *The Well-Tempered Clavier*, Book 1, BWV 861

Gentle Giant, "On Reflection"

INTRODUCTION

Most of the examples we have seen in preceding chapters have been homophonic in texture (recalling the texture categories introduced in Chapter 1). Yet, as we have learned from our study of part writing and its application in various musical styles, independence of parts—particularly between soprano and bass—remains paramount. The controlled coordination of independent melodic lines is called **counterpoint** (from the Latin *punctus contra punctum*, meaning "point against point" or note against note, as a *punctum* was a type of musical note in the middle ages). Two polyphonic genres—canon and fugue—came about around the use of contrapuntal techniques. They reached their zenith in the Baroque period (roughly 1600 to 1750), and were a staple of musical training for many composers thereafter.

CANON: LASSUS, "QUI SEQUITUR ME" ("HE THAT FOLLOWETH ME")

This motet for two voices by Roland de Lassus (1532–1594), part of a set of twelve *Cantiones Duarum Vocum* (motets for two voices) composed in 1577, begins with a setting of the words "He that followeth me" in which the lower voice follows the upper voice exactly, a perfect fifth lower (Example 19.1). This type of strict imitation is also called **canonic** imitation; an entire piece composed in this way is called a **canon** (from the Greek *kanon*, meaning "rule" or "law"). The leading voice is called the *dux*, and the voice that follows is called the *comes*. The familiar rounds "Row, Row, Row Your Boat" and "Three Blind Mice" are examples of canons in which the **pitch interval**—the intervallic distance between the two parts—is the unison (or octave).[1] Although these are simple examples, canons can be more complex. A **mirror canon** is a canon in which the *comes* is the inversion of the *dux*. In a so-called **crab canon**, the *comes* is the *dux* in retrograde (backward). Bach's "Musical Offering" contains examples of both mirror and crab canons.

The pitch interval of imitation in Example 19.1 is a perfect fifth below; there is also a **time interval** of imitation, which is defined as the distance between the two parts in time. In this excerpt, the time interval is, after the first note, a whole note.

The temporal displacement of a whole note between the parts prevents this from being parallel fifths, but all the same the lower part follows the upper part very closely (a fitting musical portrayal of the text).

---

[1]One compelling contemporary example of a canon, involving eight parts at the pitch interval of (mostly) a diatonic fifth, is the first movement of Symphony no. 3 ("Symphony of Sorrowful Songs") by the Polish composer Henryk Górecki.

Apply This!
19.1a may
be done at
this time.

Workbook
Exercise 19.1
may be done
at this time.

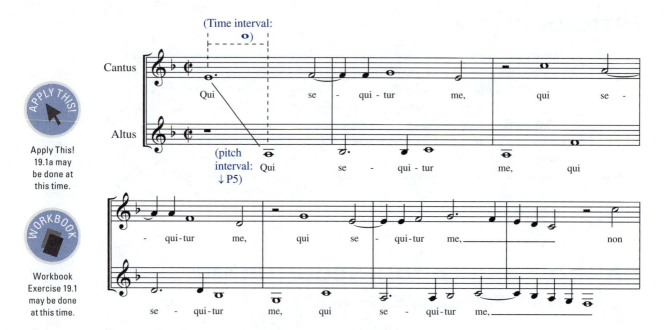

Example 19.1. Roland de Lassus, "Qui Sequitur Me," mm. 1–7.

FUGUE: THE EXPOSITION

A **fugue** is a kind of contrapuntal piece in a polyphonic texture, based on a short theme called a **subject**, which is initially stated by one voice and then imitated by the other voices that enter in succession. It differs from a canon in that the imitation is not consistently strict; sections including the subject often alternate with sections of free counterpoint.

A fugue begins with a section called the **exposition**, in which the subject is introduced by one voice in the texture at a time, each voice entering with the subject and cumulatively adding to the texture. The subject is first stated by a single voice in the tonic. Afterward, another voice usually enters with an imitation of the subject at the fifth (up a perfect fifth or down a perfect fourth); an entry with this kind of tonal relationship to the previous subject is called an **answer**.

Answers are either *real* or *tonal*. In a **real answer**, the subject is transposed to the dominant with no alterations (Example 19.2).

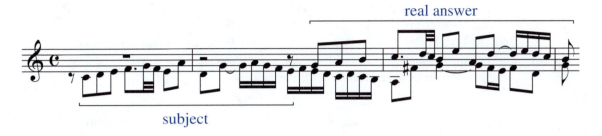

Example 19.2. A real answer, as found in J. S. Bach, Fugue in C major from *The Well-Tempered Clavier*, Book 1, BWV 846, mm. 1–4a.

A **tonal answer** will have one or more notes transposed to fit the key (Example 19.3). This is usually because a real version of the subject would have the effect of "rushing" to the dominant key before the tonic has been adequately established at the beginning of the piece. A subject would require a tonal answer given any of the following conditions:

• If the subject *contains the fifth scale degree in a position of prominence toward the beginning*, that note (which would be the supertonic if transposed up a perfect fifth or down a perfect fourth) is often changed to the tonic in the answer. In Example 19.3, the subject begins on the fifth scale degree; this is the note that is changed in the answer.

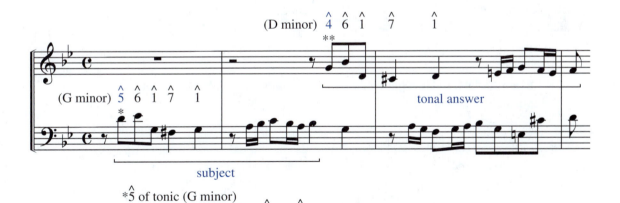

*$\hat{5}$ of tonic (G minor)
**first note tonally altered; $\hat{4}$, not $\hat{5}$, of dominant (D minor)

Example 19.3. A tonal answer, as found in J. S. Bach, Fugue in G minor from *The Well-Tempered Clavier*, Book 1, BWV 861, mm. 1–4a.

• If the subject itself *moves toward the dominant key*, a tonal answer is necessary to rein in the tendency to move out of the range of closely related keys. Here the alteration of the subject may be more extensive. Example 19.4a shows a subject from a fugal passage in Bach's *Magnificat* BWV 243, ending with a tonicization of the dominant. Example 19.4b shows a real answer for this subject, which ends in a tonicization of E major (the "dominant of the dominant," not a closely related key). Bach's solution is shown in Example 19.4c, a tonal answer in which all but the first note is changed—or rather, the first melodic interval is changed and the remainder of the subject is altered as a result.

Example 19.4. Bach, "Sicut locutus" from Magnificat, BWV 243—subject and possible answers.

- Subjects containing *scale degree 7* may also have tonal answers; a fifth up from $\hat{7}$ would be $\hat{4}$, but in practice $\hat{4}$ is often replaced by $\hat{3}$ (Example 19.5).

Example 19.5. Bach, Fugue no. 23 in B major from *The Well-Tempered Clavier*, Book 1, BWV 868, mm. 1–5a. *(Continued)*

(Continued)

Sometimes a subject that has one of the above conditions for allowing a tonal answer will nonetheless have a real answer, in order to *maintain its distinctive contour*. Bach's Little Fugue in G minor, for example, opens with a G minor arpeggio that would be destroyed if the second note were tonally altered (Example 19.6)

Example 19.6. Little Fugue in G minor, BWV 578: Fugue subject and answer, mm. 1–10.

The fugue subject from Bach's famous Toccata and Fugue in D minor presents a more extreme case of preserving the original contour. The first pitch is scale degree 5, and it is emphasized as a pedal tone throughout. In the answer, not only is scale degree 5 answered with scale degree 1 (rather than 2), but the *entire subject* is transposed to the subominant, rather than the dominant, in order to maintain the original contour (Example 19.7).

Example 19.7. Toccata and Fugue in D minor, BWV 565: Fugue subject and answer, mm. 30b–34.

As the last three examples show, after a voice has stated the subject, it usually does not drop out; it continues either with free counterpoint or with a recurring idea called a **countersubject**. You can recognize a countersubject by its consistent appearance alongside entries of the subject.

Subsequent voices in the exposition usually enter in the same tonic–dominant tonal pattern. Thus, if a fugue has three parts, the exposition's tonal pattern is tonic–dominant–tonic; if there are four parts, the tonal pattern is tonic–dominant–tonic–dominant. Often, there is a short passage of transitional counterpoint between two entries; this is called a **link**. Once all of the parts have stated the subject or answer, the exposition ends.

The G minor fugue from Book 1 of Bach's *Well-Tempered Clavier* (BWV 861) provides a clear example of what we have covered so far. The exposition of this fugue is shown in Example 19.8, with the various parts labeled.

Example 19.8. Bach, Fugue in G minor, BWV 861, mm. 1–8.

AFTER THE EXPOSITION

After the end of the exposition, every fugue reveals its own individuality. There is no single "cookie-cutter" form to a fugue. Generally speaking, you can expect to find further entries of the subject (and countersubject, if one is used) in other keys. Sometimes more than one entry appears consecutively in close proximity; this is called an **entry group**. An entry group that involves *all* of the voices in the texture is called a **counterexposition**; functioning something like a second exposition, the order of voice entries is often different from what they were in the exposition. Sometimes entries in an entry group overlap; this is called **stretto**. Subject entries may also be developed by **inversion** (reversing the contour of the subject so that it appears "upside down"), **retrograde** (reversing the order of pitches in the subject so that the melodic line is "backward"), **augmentation** (proportionally increasing the durational value of notes in the subject, usually twofold or fourfold), or **diminution** (the reverse of augmentation, proportionally *decreasing* the notes' durational values); these still "count" as subject or answer entries.

Subject entries, then, function as landmarks in the course of the fugue. In between them are transitional passages, usually ending in a different key from where they began. We have already noted the link in the exposition; this describes a transitional passage that is shorter than the length of the subject. A transitional passage that is longer than the subject is called an **episode**. Episodes often contain melodic or harmonic sequences, and they also often contain **false** or **partial entries** of the subject. Episodes, then, are defined by their *absence* of a complete subject entry. Finally, there may be a short concluding coda that brings the piece to a close, reasserting the tonic. Example 19.9 begins where Example 19.8 left off, illustrating many of these terms.

Example 19.9. Bach, Fugue in G minor, BWV 861, mm. 8–34, with annotations. *(Continued)*

(Continued)

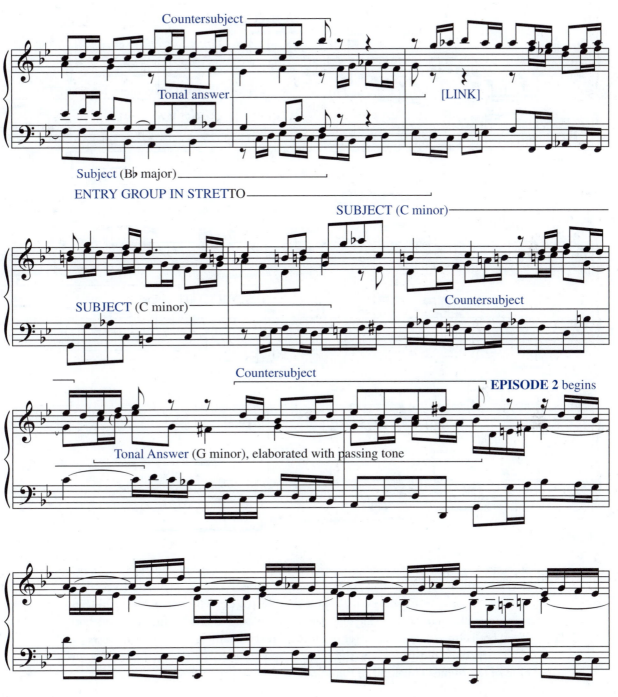

(Continued)

Sometimes a fugue has two subjects, each of which unfolds in the course of an exposition with the tonic–dominant tonal pattern of subject and answer. The Kyrie from Mozart's *Requiem* is a good example of a **double fugue**. The two subjects are contrasting in character, one strong and declamatory and the other a flurry of sixteenth notes; both also are consistently set to different texts. Example 19.10, which shows the voice parts only, illustrates how the subjects and answers are arranged in the beginning of the fugue. This kind of fugue can be distinguished from a fugue that has a countersubject in that the second subject's first appearance is found accompanying the *first subject*, not the answer.

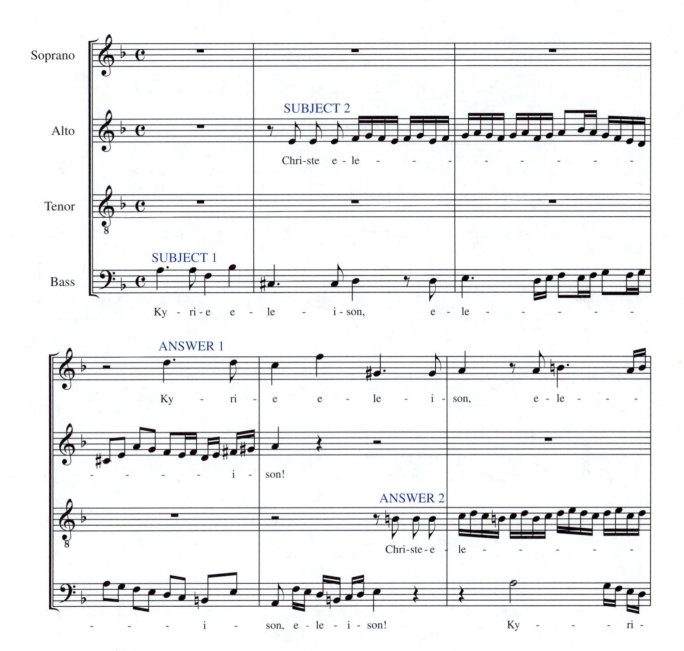

Example 19.10. Mozart, Kyrie from *Requiem*, mm. 1–15 (voice parts only). *(Continued)*

(Continued)

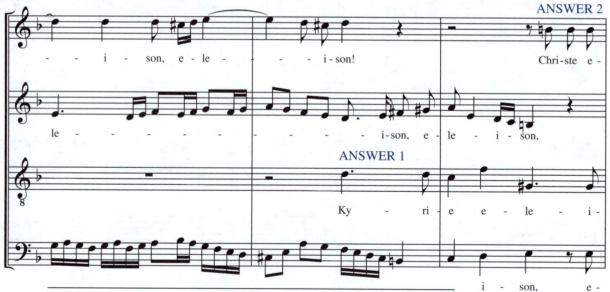

PART 3: Form and Chromatic Harmony 2

(Continued)

le - - - - - - - - - - - i

e - le - - i - son, e - le - i - son, e

son, e - le

le - - - i - son, -e - le - i-son, e - le - i - son,

Two terms related to *fugue* need to be mentioned here. A **fughetta** is simply a small fugue, one that may be less elaborate in its use of episodes and development of the subject. A **fugato** is a passage in fugal style that occurs within a larger work. One example of a fugato can be found in the third (scherzo) movement of Beethoven's Fifth Symphony (see the "Trio" section, measures 141–160).

LEVEL MASTERY 19.1.

For each of the fugue subjects below, determine whether the appropriate answer would be real or tonal (if tonal, which of the conditions for a tonal answer best applies?). Then, in the blank staff below, write a suitable answer for the subject, at the dominant level either above (P5 above) or below (P4 below) the subject, as indicated. The first few notes of the first two examples are provided for you to get you started. (Note: The two lines are not intended to be voices sounding simultaneously.)

a. Bach, Fugue in C major, BWV 946.

Subject:

Answer (above):

b. Max Reger, Fugue in G♯ minor.

Self-Test 19.1
may be done
at this time.

c. Mozart, Fugue in G minor, K.401.

Apply This!
19.1, 19.2,
and 19.3 may
be done at
this time.

d. Bach, Fugue in E♭ major from *The Well-Tempered Clavier*, Book 2, BWV 876.

Workbook
Exercise 19.2
may be done
at this time.

CONTEMPORARY APPLICATIONS:
BARTÓK, HINDEMITH, SHOSTAKOVITCH

Although fugue is commonly associated with Baroque music, there are examples of the genre well into the nineteenth and twentieth centuries (for a nineteenth-century example, see Apply This! 19.1b). Twentieth-century composers such as Bela Bartók (1881–1945), Paul Hindemith (1895–1963), and Dmitri Shostakovitch (1906–1975) developed their own contemporary versions of the practice. Examine each of the fugue openings below. What elements have been preserved from Baroque practice? What elements have been changed to make these more contemporary applications of fugal technique? Which appears to be the most "traditional" and which the most "radical"?

Example 19.11. Bartók, *Music for String Instruments, Percussion, and Celesta* (1936) (i), mm. 1–12.

Example 19.12. Hindemith, Fuga secunda in G from *Ludus Tonalis* (1942), mm. 1–17.

Example 19.13. Shostakovitch, Fugue in C minor, op. 87 no. 20 (1950–51), mm. 1–20.
(Continued)

(Continued)

CONTEMPORARY APPLICATIONS:
GENTLE GIANT, "ON REFLECTION" (1975)

Gentle Giant was a British band that was active in the 1970s. Their keyboard player Kerry Minnear was classically trained at the Royal Academy of Music in London, where he earned a degree in composition; his classical training is especially evident on this song. "On Reflection" is a characteristic example of "progressive rock," a style that freely mixed elements of classical and jazz into the rock idiom.

The first verse, for unaccompanied voices, employs four-part imitative counterpoint with a tonic–dominant–tonic–dominant tonal plan that suggests a fugal exposition [0:00–0:30]. A more homophonic, chordal texture characterizes the song's chorus [0:30–0:57]. The second verse adds piano and tuned percussion (vibraphones and marimba), each instrument doubling one of the voice parts. After a contrasting ballad section [1:57–4:04], the instrumentation becomes more electric, and from 4:27 to the end, the imitative counterpoint returns, but this time instrumentally and using the standard instrumentation of a rock band. The counterpoint also repeats, so that the concluding section might be thought of as a canon with imitation at the fifth.

On the surface, then, "On Reflection" contains several elements of Renaissance and Baroque musical style: the imitative counterpoint, modal scales, and madrigal-like singing in the choruses. Formally, though, "On Reflection" is very much a rock song, with an opening section with an alternating verse-and-chorus structure, a contrasting middle section or "bridge," and a repeating fade-out at the end.

CONCLUSION

Canon and fugue were common assignments in the eighteenth and nineteenth centuries for aspiring composers. If canonic writing involved setting a pattern and following it strictly, fugue allowed for some creative elaboration of a basic idea; in fact, the outline of a typical fugue corresponds well to the pattern of classical rhetoric: *inventio* (the choice or discovery of a subject), *dispositio* or *elaboratio* (the development and embellishment of the subject), and *elocutio* (the artful summary to achieve closure). Perhaps it is because of this grounding in rhetoric that every fugue is different; it may be considered a *process* rather than a form. Fugues are also found in some composers' last works; we have already seen Mozart's use of a double fugue in the "Kyrie" from his *Requiem* (Bach's *Art of Fugue*, Beethoven's "Grosse Fuge" for string quartet, and the finale of Verdi's *Falstaff* are other examples). When writing a fugue for the battle scene in *Macbeth*, Verdi wrote a friend: "You will laugh when you see that I have written a fugue for the battle! I, who detest everything that smacks of theory. But I assure you that in this case, the fugue form is permissible. The mad chase of subjects and counter-subjects, and the clash of dissonances, and the general uproar can suggest a battle quite well."

Terms to Know

answer (real vs. tonal)	*dux*	link
augmentation	entry group	mirror canon
canon	episode	pitch interval
comes	exposition	retrograde
counterexposition	false entry	sequence
countersubject	fugato	stretto
crab canon	fughetta	subject
diminution	fugue	time interval
double fugue	inversion (of a subject)	

Self-Test

19.1. For each of the answers accompanying the fugue subjects on the following page, indicate whether the answer is real or tonal. If tonal, circle the altered note(s) and be able to discuss which condition for requiring a tonal answer (prominent fifth scale degree toward the beginning of the subject, or modulation to the dominant) applies.

a. Bach, Fugue in B major from *The Well-Tempered Clavier*, Book 2, BWV 892.

b. Brahms, from Motet "Schaffe in Mir, Gott, ein Rein Herz," op. 29 no. 2.

c. Pachelbel, Fugue in A major, T.287.

Apply This!

19.1. Fugue analysis. Using the analysis of the Bach G minor fugue (BWV 861) in this chapter as a model, prepare an analysis of the fugues found on the following pages. Include in your analysis the end of the exposition, the beginnings and endings of all subjects and answers as well as the keys in which each entry appears, countersubject (if there is one), and beginnings and endings of all episodes and links. In addition, if you spot any unusual devices such as inversion, augmentation, or stretto, indicate that on your analysis as well.

a. Bach, Fugue in C minor from *The Well-Tempered Clavier*, Book 1, BWV 847.

(Continued)

(Continued)

b. Clara Schumann (1819–1896), Fugue in D minor, op. 16 no. 3 (1845).

Andante con moto.

(Continued)

(Continued)

(Continued)

19.2. Review the conditions for a real or tonal fugue answer in this chapter. Then, determine whether the appropriate answer for the given subjects below would be real or tonal, and write your answer transposed to the dominant key of the given subject.

(Continued)

19.3. Improvisation.

Spontaneous Canon. This exercise is for two people, one taking the role of *dux* (leader) and one the role of *comes* (follower). Together, improvise a spontaneous canon, using the rhythm motives below. Start by trying a canon at the time interval of one measure. The *dux* will clap, tap, or intone (on "ta" or another neutral syllable) the first motive; then the *comes* will imitate that same motive *while* the *dux* continues with the next motive. Use different timbres so that the parts are more easily distinguishable. Aim for no interruptions in the flow. You may repeat motives, but do not use the same motive two measures in a row. The *comes* must simultaneously listen to the motive being clapped as they replicate the motive they just heard the *dux* play in the previous measure.

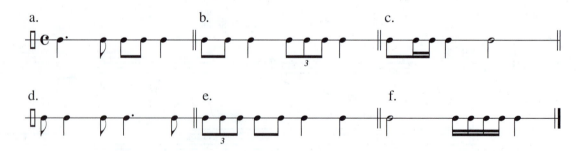

Next, experiment with the time interval—try it with the *comes* entrance coming in after two measures, or after two beats. You will probably find this exercise to be more difficult if the entries are too close together (or, conversely, too far apart).

Finally, try this exercise in "free form," the *dux* spontaneously inventing his or her own motives rather than confining them to the ones provided above. Keep all motives within the time of a measure, so that there is no "overlap" between the *dux* and the imitation in the *comes*.

For further challenge, try singing or playing short melodic motives instead of rhythmic motives. In this case the *dux* will need to make sure that the motives all fit a fixed repeating harmonic progression (such as I–V).

CHAPTER 20

BINARY AND TERNARY FORMS

OVERVIEW

This chapter, the first of several devoted to examining common classical formal structures in music, considers two formal archetypes: binary, or two-part (balance, dialectic), and ternary, or three-part (departure and return).

CHAPTER OUTLINE

AUDIO LIST

Johann Sebastian Bach, Bourrée from Lute Suite in E minor, BWV 996

The Pennywhistlers, "Dilmano, Dilbero"

Javanese Gamelan, "Hudan [iTunes sic: "Nudan"] Mas"

Wolfgang Amadeus Mozart, Piano Sonata in A major K.331 (i)

The Orb, "Little Fluffy Clouds"

Dwight Yoakam, "Guitars, Cadillacs"

INTRODUCTION: THE TWO-PART PRINCIPLE

Have you ever considered how much of our world seems to be organized into two parts? When we walk, we tend to do so in regular left, right, left, right patterns. We have two ears, two hands, two eyes, even two nostrils. We inhale and exhale. Time passes in a regular alternation of day and night. The ocean, under the influence of phases of the moon, moves in an alternation of high and low tides.

Music is often organized into two parts as well. For example, a period is made up of two phrases, an antecedent and a consequent phrase; two periods are sometimes combined into double period structures. Some songs are made up wholesale of the simple alternation of two melodic ideas, each of which is sometimes repeated as well. The Bulgarian song "Dilmano, Dilbero" (see Chapter 3) has an AABB structure: The *A* lines follow a 3+3+2, 3+3+2 rhythmic pattern while the more elaborate *B* lines follow the rhythmic pattern 3+3+3+2, 3+3+2. The Javanese *bubaran* "Hudan Mas" (Web Feature 2.3) is made up of two 16-beat thematic ideas, each of which is repeated (AABB) an indefinite number of times, allowing all members of the ceremonial party to process in or out of the court (a social function similar to the playing of Edward Elgar's "Pomp and Circumstance" march at graduations). Many American square dance tunes, such as "The Arkansas Traveler" (Example 20.1), follow the same pattern—two alternating, repeated sections. Like "Hudan Mas," the AABB pattern in such square dance tunes is repeated an indefinite number of times, according to the fancy of the dancers or the musicians.

Example 20.1. Traditional American folk tune, "The Arkansas Traveler."

One can still find this age-old two-part pattern in modern popular music. Dwight Yoakam's "Guitars, Cadillacs" follows a regular alternation of verse and chorus (Example 20.2); the verse and chorus are both parallel periods. "Little Fluffy Clouds," by the British techno group the Orb, is in a two-part form as well (Example 20.3); the underlying harmonic progression is the same in both sections, but the "themes" consist of spoken-word samples. The two sections are also distinguished by changes of texture (presence or absence of the sampled electric guitar arpeggios that are heard in the choruses) and by differences in treatment of the spoken-word samples (complete sentences in the verses, repetition of the phrase "little fluffy clouds" and "stuttered" sample fragments in the choruses).[1]

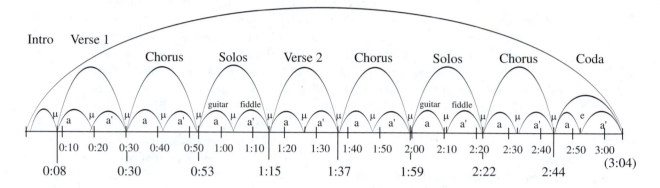

Example 20.2. Dwight Yoakam, "Guitars, Cadillacs," formal diagram with CD timings.

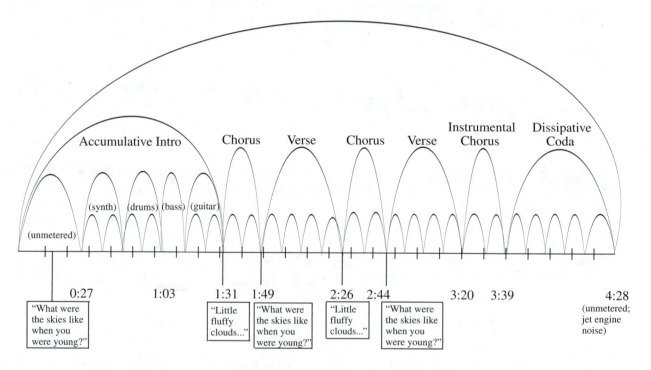

Example 20.3. The Orb, "Little Fluffy Clouds," formal diagram with CD timings.

---

[1] These pop-music examples may not necessarily correspond to classically understood "binary form," but they are contemporary manifestations of the two-part principle of organization that gave rise to binary form in the Baroque and Classic eras.

In music of the common-practice period, the AABB two-part form is known as **binary form**. The stylized dance movements (Allemande, Courante, Sarabande, and so forth) that comprise the dance suites of the Baroque era (such as Bach's French or English Suites for keyboard) tend to be in binary form. In some larger Classical-era compositions, binary forms make up a section *within* the overall piece.

TYPES OF BINARY FORMS

Classical binary forms are classified according to their *harmonic structure* and their *thematic structure*.

- Harmonically, binary forms come in two types: **sectional** and **continuous**.
  - If the first half of a binary form ends on an *authentic cadence in the tonic* (Example 20.4), the form is described as **sectional binary**.
  - If the first half ends on a *half cadence or modulates*, the form is called **continuous binary** (Example 20.5).

Example 20.4. Mozart, Piano Sonata in A major, K.331 (i), mm. 1–8.

Example 20.5. Bach, Bourrée, Lute Suite in E Minor, BWV 996, mm. 1–8).

Thematically, binary forms are also classified by whether or not there is a *substantial (not necessarily complete) return of the opening theme, in the tonic, in the second half*. Example 20.6 shows the second half of Mozart's K.331 theme. At measure 13 the opening material returns, heralded by the half cadence in the previous measure. This is not a literal return, however—it appears instead to be an altered version of the second phrase of the first half (mm. 5–8 in Example 20.4).

Example 20.6. Mozart, Piano Sonata in A major, K.331 (i), mm. 9–18. *(Continued)*

(Continued)

When there is a return of opening material (or **recapitulation**) in the tonic, in the second section, we call this **rounded binary form**. The return of the opening material is often immediately preceded by a half cadence in the tonic; before this half cadence, there can be considerable variety. Some binary-form pieces begin their second section in the tonic, others in another key; in some pieces the beginning of the second section modulates frequently, in others, the key area remains fairly stable. If the piece is in rounded binary form, however, one will almost always eventually encounter a half cadence to set up the return of the opening material.

For contrast, let us see how the second half of Bach's Bourrée proceeds (Example 20.7). Is there a "substantial return" of the opening material (from the beginning of Example 20.5) here? Not really. The *rhythmic motive* of the opening theme is constant throughout the second half, but the *melody* does not return. Consider also that in rounded binary form the opening material returns in the *tonic*, usually after a *half cadence* in the tonic key. When the second half of the piece consists of new thematic material, as in Example 20.7, this is called **simple binary form**.

Example 20.7. Bach, Bourrée, Lute Suite in E minor, BWV 996, mm. 9–24.

(Continued)

(Continued)

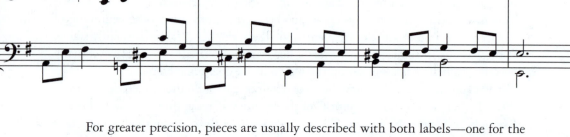

For greater precision, pieces are usually described with both labels—one for the harmonic structure and one for the thematic structure. Thus, Mozart's K.331 theme is in **sectional rounded binary form**; Bach's Bourrée is in **continuous simple binary form**. Occasionally one may also use the labels *symmetrical* or *asymmetrical*, just as we did for periods, to indicate whether the two parts are of equal or unequal length; if the form is asymmetrical, it is usually the second part that is longer. Both Mozart's K.331 theme and Bach's Bourrée are asymmetrical.

Sometimes a piece of music in binary form does not have a repeat sign, because of a change of texture or dynamics (louder the second time, for instance), or, in orchestral music, a change of orchestration; instead, there is a **written-out repeat**. Robert Schumann's "Soldier's March" from the collection of piano pieces *Album for the Young* has a written-out repeat for its first sixteen measures, measures 9–16 being identical to measures 1–8 (Example 20.8). The movement to the dominant at the end of the first half (measures 15–16) and the return of opening material in the second half (measures 25–28) makes this an example of asymmetrical, continuous rounded binary form.

Munter und straff.

Example 20.8. Schumann, "Soldier's March," from *Album for the Young*, op. 68.

Binary forms are found in European and American folk music as well. Turlough O'Carolan (1670–1738), a blind Irish itinerant musician and composer, composed several hundred tunes for the Celtic folk harp; one such example is "Morgan Magan," shown in Example 20.9. O'Carolan usually improvised his accompaniment, so he did not specify any harmonic progression or accompaniment—the bass line and harmonic analysis shown is one possible setting among many. (Obviously, the harmonic analysis provided implies that some tones in the melody are non-chord tones—it is left for you to determine which tones are non-chord tones and what type of non-chord tone they would be.) Even without the accompaniment and harmonic analysis, you should be able to tell from the melodic material that there is no change of key in the first section—the melody implies an authentic cadence at measures 15–16. Likewise, from scanning the second section of the piece we can see that, although the first and second sections *end* similarly, there is no substantial return of the opening material as such in the second section. Thus, "Morgan Magan" is an example of sectional simple binary form.

Example 20.9. O'Carolan, "Morgan Magan," with bass line and harmonic analysis added. *(Continued)*

(Continued)

IV 6/I IV 6   V 6/V⁶/V V   I IV ii V   I⁶ V   I

Apply This!
20.1 may
be done at
this time.

Self-Tests
20.1 and 20.2
may be done
at this time.

Some binary forms do not contain a return of the opening phrase from the first section, as in rounded binary form, nor are they made up of entirely new material in the second section, as in simple binary form. Instead, there is a return of *closing* material from the first section at the end of the second section, so that the two binary sections "rhyme" or close with similar material; this is called **balanced binary form**. Example 20.1 ("Arkansas Traveler") at the beginning of this chapter is in balanced binary form—the final two measures of the first section are the same as the final two measures from the second section.

The "balance" in this case has nothing to do with the proportion of sections, but rather with *similar endings* for each section. If a piece of music is in continuous, balanced binary form, the closing material of the first section will return in the second section in the tonic, rather than the dominant or relative major key. In some balanced binary forms, the entire consequent phrase from the first section will return in the second (for an example of this, see the "Menuet" section of the third movement of Mozart's "Eine Kleine Nachtmusik," shown in Example 20.11).

LEVEL MASTERY 20.1.

For each of the binary-form pieces that follow, determine the tonal structure (sectional or continuous), the thematic structure (simple or rounded), and whether the ends of the sections are balanced. In addition, locate cadences within the piece to determine the work's overall tonal plan.

a. Bach, "Courante" from Partita no. 5 in G major, BWV 829.

(Continued)

(Continued)

PART 3: Form and Chromatic Harmony 2

b. Brahms, Waltz, op. 39 no. 5.

Apply This!
20.3 may
be done at
this time.

Workbook
Exercises
20.1 and 20.2
may be done
at this time.

TERNARY FORM

Another basic principle that we see manifested in musical structure is that of departure and return. We have already seen how the principle of departure and return is manifested in modulation and key relationships within a piece—this same principle is often found on a formal or thematic level as well. A piece that has three main parts—a first *A* section, a contrasting *B* section, and a reprise of *A*—is in **ternary form**. Ternary form is one of the simplest formal principles in music.

SIMPLE TERNARY FORM

Look at the Chopin piece in Example 20.10. The first 16 measures of the piece are in C major, in a quiet dynamic, a rather light and simple homophonic texture, and a higher register with a rather limited range. This section has four phrases (what type of period structure best describes this section?), and the fourth phrase ends on a perfect authentic cadence in C major in measures 15–16, giving this section closure and apparent self-containment.

Now look at measures 17–32. This section is in a different key altogether (A♭ major), is louder and thicker in its texture, and has a much wider range, with the accompaniment extending to a much lower register. Like the first section, this second section also ends on a perfect authentic cadence, this time in A♭ major. Overall, this section appears to have little similarity with the first 16 measures; it may as well be another piece altogether.

The final printed measure of the piece presents a direct transition back to C major and the opening section. The instruction "D. S. al fine" (or "dal segno al fine,") instructs the performer to return to the symbol at the beginning of the second measure of the piece and play the opening section again, until the "Fine" (or end) at measure 16.[2]

Example 20.10. Chopin, Mazurka in C major, op. 33 no. 3. *(Continued)*

---

[2]A similar instruction sometimes found in music, "D.C. al fine" (or "da capo al fine," which literally means "from the head to the finish"), instructs the performer to go back to the very beginning of the piece. These instructions were a common convention of ternary form pieces, allowing the publisher to save on engraving and printing costs by not reprinting a whole section of music; in performance, however, it was not uncommon for the performer to add melodic embellishments to the return of the opening section, especially in vocal pieces. Because the "da capo" instruction is found so often in simple ternary form pieces, simple ternary form is sometimes also called **da capo form**.

(Continued)

Simple ternary form (*ABA*) is commonly found in the **arias** (solo vocal movements) of Baroque and Classic operas and oratorios. An aria commonly occurs after a recitative (see Chapter 18); if the function of the recitative was to advance the plot through sung narration (as is often the case of an oratorio) or through sung dialogue (as in an opera), the aria would present a pause in the narrative, allowing a character to more fully express his or her feelings or reaction to what has happened. The ternary form of a so-called **da capo aria** allows the text to similarly fall into three parts; the *A* section could, for example, express the character's emotion or reaction to plot developments, whereas the *B* section could perhaps go into more detail, explaining for example *why* the character felt that way. The return of *A* then comes as a kind of summary of the character's emotions.[3]

---

[3]An example of a da capo aria can be found in the workbook.

Simple ternary form is often confused with rounded binary form. There are two important differences, however:

- Although rounded binary form does feature a return of opening material, remember that rounded binary form also has *two repeated sections*, and the recapitulated material is usually not literal but is usually shortened or otherwise substantially changed. Thus, on a diagram rounded binary form appears to be "ABA′ with repeats," but in performance the form is played out as "A, A, BA′, BA′."
- The first *A* section and the *B* section in rounded binary form usually have *inconclusive endings*, such as a modulation to another key at the end of the first *A* section or a half cadence of the tonic at the end of the *B* section. By contrast, since the sections of a simple binary form are usually not repeated, each section of a simple ternary form normally ends in an *authentic cadence* in the key of that section—usually a perfect authentic cadence, as we saw in Example 20.10.

COMPOUND TERNARY FORM

A three-part form in which *each section is itself in binary form* is called **compound ternary form** (sometimes also called **minuet and trio** form or **menuetto and trio** form). This type of ternary form is most often found in the "Minuet" or "Menuetto" movements of a Classic-era multi-movement work such as a symphony, sonata, or string quartet. (Beethoven eventually replaced the so-called "Menuetto" movements with a faster-paced "Scherzo" movement, but the form usually remained the same.)

Compound ternary form derives from the Baroque dance suite. The movements in those suites were usually in some kind of binary form, and some suites had two Minuet movements (Minuet I, Minuet II) which were performed in such a way that Minuet I would be reprised following Minuet II. Eventually those two movements, and the way they were played, were consolidated into a single movement. The "Minuet II" movement was thus absorbed into the form as a contrasting section, often called the "Trio"; thus, compound ternary form is sometimes also called **minuet and trio form**. Like the contrasting middle section in simple ternary form, the Trio section of a compound ternary form is usually in a different key, most commonly the dominant (if the movement is in a major key) or the parallel major (if the movement is in a minor key).

The third movement of Mozart's "Eine Kleine Nachtmusik" Serenade in G major, K.525, shown in Example 20.11, offers a good example of Classic-era compound ternary form. The *A* part of the ABA form is the Menuetto section, measures 1–16; the *B* part is the Trio section, measures 17–36. Each of these sections is itself a binary form:

- The Menuetto section is in sectional rounded binary form, with a partial return of opening material seen at measure 13.
- The Trio section moves to the dominant, D major, and offers a change of texture as well as a contrast of dynamics (in fact, the Trio's pattern of soft-loud-soft inverts the Menuetto's loud-soft-loud dynamic pattern). It is in sectional rounded

binary form, with the opening material returning at measure 29. Unlike the Menuetto, the Trio has a *complete* return of opening material; nevertheless, because of the *two-part* structure of measures 17–36 this is not ternary form, but rounded binary form.

MENUETTO

Example 20.11. Mozart, Serenade in G major from *Eine Kleine Nachtmusik* (iii), K.525. *(Continued)*

(Continued)

(Continued)

Menuetto da capo

LEVEL MASTERY 20.2.

The following piece is an example of compound ternary form. Prepare an arch map for the movement, detailing not only its three main sections and binary components of each section but down to the phrase level. Identify cadences, and determine whether the binary sections have a simple, rounded, or balanced thematic structure, and a sectional or continuous tonal structure.

a. Haydn, Piano Sonata no. 5 in A major, Hob.XVI/5 (ii).

(Continued)

(Continued)

Menuetto da capo

SONG FORM (AABA)

Related to ternary form is **song form**, which—as its name suggests—is most often found in popular songs of the "Tin Pan Alley" era in the first half of the twentieth century, the work of composers such as Irving Berlin, Jerome Kern, and George Gershwin. The opening theme (A) is repeated, usually ending with an authentic cadence in the tonic each time. This is followed by a contrasting and often more transitory *B* section, often hinting at moving to another key. (Songwriters often call this *B* section the **bridge** or **middle eight**, because very often these songs are made up of thirty-two measures in all, with eight measures for each section.) The *B* section usually ends openly, with a half cadence in the tonic that facilitates the return to *A*. The overall form, then, is AABA. Songs such as Harold Arlen's "Over the Rainbow" (immortalized by Judy Garland in *The Wizard of Oz*) or George Gershwin's "I Got Rhythm" have a *repeated A* section ending on an *authentic cadence* each time. Note that the phrases need not be both perfect authentic cadences; the first *A* may end with an imperfect authentic cadence, with the second *A* ending more conclusively on a perfect authentic cadence. (One example of this is the theme from the TV cartoon series *The Flintstones*—compare the phrase ending "modern stone-age family" with the phrase ending "right out of history.")

Song form is found in many jazz standards as well, which is not surprising because many "Tin Pan Alley" popular songs were used as the source material for jazz improvisation. In Chapter 12 we examined Miles Davis's performance of Thelonious Monk's composition "Well You Needn't." The theme on which the total performance is based [0:00–1:01] is in AABA form:

- The *A* section [0:00–0:15] is distinguished by the major-triad arpeggio that opens each phrase, over a repeated two-chord progression, ending with a truncated version of the ascending arpeggio, heard twice [0:11–0:15]. The *A* section is repeated from 0:15 to 0:30.
- At 0:30, the contrasting *B* section begins; here, the truncated-arpeggio motive that concluded the *A* section is isolated and developed. Harmonically, the *B* section breaks free of the two-chord repetition of the *A* section, gradually ascending upward to *B* major (a tritone away from the tonic) before descending back to the tonic and the return of the *A* section at 0:46.
- The final *A* section in the song form lasts from 0:46 to 1:01.

Some rock and country songs are also in song form. The Beatles frequently relied on the form in their earlier songs. "Eight Days a Week" is particularly notable in that the overall AABA form of the song is also replicated in miniature (*aaba*), at the phrase level, in the *A* section itself (Example 20.12). After a brief introduction [0:00–0:07], the *A* section is heard as the first verse, lasting from 0:07 to 0:35. The second verse repeats the *A* section [0:35–1:02]. The bridge (*B* section) follows, lasting from 1:02 to 1:16. The final verse heralds the return of *A* [1:16–1:44].

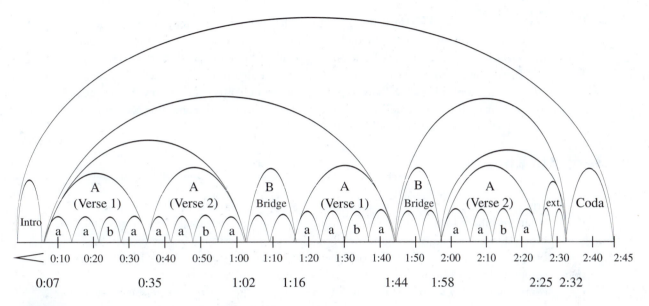

Example 20.12. The Beatles, "Eight Days a Week."

Apply This!
20.2, 20.4,
and 20.5 may
be done at
this time.

Workbook
Exercise 20.3
may be done
at this time.

Now let's look at the structure of the A section a little more closely. The a subsection of A begins with a repeated phrase, ending on a plagal cadence. The contrasting b subsection ("hold me, love me") begins at 0:21. The A section comes to a close with the return of the a subsection at 0:28. Another interesting feature of this song is that both the b subsection of A and the B section as a whole are distinguished by moves to B minor.

"Eight Days a Week" also extends the song form, somewhat, by its repetition of the bridge and last verse. This is a common device of song form; one could arguably describe the overall form of "Eight Days a Week," as recorded, as AABABA. As it might appear in a printed score, though, the musical material (three verses, with a contrasting section separating the second and third verses) itself comprises AABA form.

CONCLUSION

Binary and ternary forms are two of the most basic formal structures in Western concert music—and in other styles as well. The fact that binary form can be found in both "classical" and popular music, for example, can perhaps be seen as evidence of how the two repertoires have influenced each other over the centuries. Certainly the music of O'Carolan, an ostensibly "folk" composer, represents a kind of meeting point—not usually associated in the same rarified category as J. S. Bach or Vivaldi, his music seems to bear some of their influences.

Our survey of ternary form, meanwhile, shows that the basic principle of departure and return has many manifestations. Simple (or "da capo") ternary form consists of three essentially independent self-contained sections (the third of which is a repeat of the first), ending with authentic cadences. The three sections may be made more elaborate by being further subdivided into rounded binary form; when this happens, the result is compound ternary form. In song form, the opening *A* section is repeated.

Binary and ternary formal structures are often also found *within* larger forms. We will find a number of such examples in the form chapters that follow. Be on the lookout for such sections, not only in the musical examples to come but also in the music you may be studying with your studio teacher.

Terms to Know

aria	da capo form	rounded binary form
balanced binary form	head	sectional binary form
binary form	middle eight	simple binary form
bridge	minuet (menuetto) and	simple ternary form
compound ternary form	trio	song form
continuous binary form	recapitulation	written-out repeat
da capo aria		

Self-Test

20.1. What are some of the musical features that determine if a piece, or part of a piece, is in sectional binary form? Continuous binary form?

20.2. What are some of the musical features that determine if a piece, or part of a piece, is in simple binary form? Rounded binary form? Balanced binary form?

Apply This!

20.1. Analysis. Identify the type of binary form for each of the scores below. Prepare an arch map formal diagram using Examples 20.2 and 20.3 as your models.

a. Mozart, Piano Sonata no. 6 in D major, K.284 (iii), mm. 1–17.

(Continued)

(Continued)

b. Traditional American tune, "Soldier's Joy."

c. Bach, Double from Partita no. 1 in B minor for solo violin, BWV 1002

d. Haydn, String Quartet in G minor, op. 74 no. 3 (ii), mm. 1–22.

(Continued)

(Continued)

e. Scott Joplin, "Solace," mm. 53–84.

(Continued)

(Continued)

(Continued)

(Continued)

20.2. Analysis. Prepare a formal analysis of each of the following compositions, using Example 20.3 as a model. Be prepared to discuss which elements (theme, key, harmony, texture, dynamics, etc.) provide contrast for the *B* section and which retain some continuity from section to section. The examples may be in simple ternary, compound ternary, or song form.

   a. Schumann, "Humming Song," no. 3 from *Album for the Young*, op. 68.

(Continued)

(Continued)

b. Traditional Welsh lullaby, "All Through the Night"

Sleep my love and peace at-tend thee, all through the night. Guar - dian an - gels

God will lend thee, all through the night. Soft the drow - sy hours are creep - ing,

Hill and vale in slum-ber sleep-ing, He his lov-ing vi - gil keep-ing all through the night.

c. Grieg, Waltz, no. 2 from *Lyrical Pieces*, op. 12

Allegro moderato.

(Continued)

PART 3: Form and Chromatic Harmony 2

(Continued)

(Continued)

d. Mozart, String Quintet no. 4 in G minor, K.516 (ii)

(Continued)

(Continued)

(Continued)

(Continued)

(Continued)

(Continued)

(Continued)

(Continued)

(Continued)

(Continued)

Minuetto da capo

20.3. Composition. Applying what you have learned to this point, you are now ready to write a short composition for piano in rounded binary form, containing six phrases total (details are found below). To integrate the phrases and to make the piece sound more like music and less like a part-writing exercise, decide on a pattern of durations that will become a rhythmic motive in the melodic line. You may wish to link the rhythmic motive with a particular melodic contour, such as a neighbor-group figure or a passing-tone figure. Use a classical piano texture with melody and Alberti bass accompaniment, rather than the four-voice "choral" style sound in part-writing exercises.

In your composition, you are free to use all of the diatonic harmonies (in the proper syntactical order), including $^6_4$ chords (in the proper context). You may also use longer progressions such as the circle-of-fifths sequence or the Pachelbel progression. You should also feel free to use secondary dominant and/or secondary diminished chords. (Do not use any vii° chords in root position.)

Formal aspects: Your composition should be in two broad sections, with repeat signs at the beginning and end of both sections. The first section should consist of one period (two phrases in an antecedent-consequent pattern), with the second phrase containing a modulation to the appropriate closely related key (dominant if the piece is in a major key, relative major if the piece is in a minor key). Make your modulation as smooth and convincing as possible; as we have seen, using a suitable diatonic common chord is generally the simplest and smoothest way. Label the type of period.

The second section should consist of two independent phrases, followed by a period (two phrases in an antecedent-consequent pattern). The second section may begin in the key in which you finished the first section, or it may begin in a different closely related key. By the end of the second independent phrase, however, you should arrive at a half cadence in the tonic key, setting up the return of your opening material (remember that the return of opening material in rounded binary form is also back in the tonic). Label the type of period used.

Harmonic aspects: Before you write any of the actual music, begin with a compositional plan, one in which you envision the overall form and large-scale harmonic progression. Consider where and how each phrase will close and how it will relate to succeeding phrases. (Remember to review the formal instructions above as you do this, to ensure that your phrases end with the correct cadences, in the proper keys.)

Then decide on the length of each phrase; four measures is most common. Think about the general harmonies that will lead to each cadence, using the phrase model (T–PD–D–T) as your guide. You may wish to lay out controlling harmonies at this point by writing in Roman numerals and inversion symbols. Next, lay out the specific harmonies *within* each measure (the exact rhythmic placement will have much to do with your choice of meter and melodic motives).

Finally, sketch out and refine your melodies for each phrase, aiming to give each phrase a smooth arch shape with the high point about two-thirds through. Remember that after you have tended to all the formal and harmonic structural details, the melody itself should not sound like an afterthought! Aim for a tune that is singable. Remember also that whatever you write at the beginning of the piece should return at the beginning of the final period, in order for the piece to be in rounded binary form.

Prepare a neat copy of your piece, using notation software or written out neatly on staff paper (if writing by hand, make sure that your beats in both staves are vertically aligned—it will be much easier to read), and have it performed in class if time permits.

20.4. Composition. The AABA "song form" has shown itself to be remarkably versatile, found in a wide range of musical contexts. Try composing a piece in song form. The model often followed by songwriters in the first half of the twentieth century consisted of the following:

The *A* section was usually an eight-bar phrase ending on an authentic cadence, most often a perfect authentic cadence. This phrase would then be repeated exactly, so the result is two eight-bar phrases rather than a period (because of the identical cadences).

The *B* section must be in contrast to the *A* section—usually the contrast is harmonic as well as thematic. To balance the length of the *A* sections, the *B* section is also usually eight measures long (which is why this section is sometimes referred to as the "middle eight"). The *B* section usually ends with a half cadence, or a tonicization of the dominant, facilitating the return of the *A* section.

Following are some tunes you might study as models. All are in AABA form. Analyze the songs first to determine where the sections fall and how the songwriter fosters continuity between the *A* and *B* sections, and back.

- George Gershwin, "I Got Rhythm"
- Harold Arlen, "Over the Rainbow"
- Hank Williams, "Hey Good Lookin'" (the *A* section employs sentence structure)
- Johnny Marks, "Rudolph the Red Nosed Reindeer"
- The Beatles, "I Want to Hold Your Hand" (Like "Eight Days a Week," a number of Beatles songs are in AABA form with the final BA repeated. Other examples—among many—include "A Hard Day's Night," "I Should Have Known Better," "If I Fell," "Ticket to Ride," "Yesterday," "When I'm 64," "Honey Pie," "Lady Madonna," and "Hey Jude" minus the extended coda.)
- Paul Simon, "Tenderness" (unusual bridge)
- Green Day, "Wake Me Up When September Ends"
- Bob Dylan, "Spirit in the Water" (each verse is in AABA form)

20.5. Improvisation.

a. The specifics of binary form may be difficult to execute in true improvisation, because if an improvised passage is too difficult to remember a true repetition might not be possible. Still, you can practice improvisation using a basic harmonic framework in binary form. The progression below is based on the theme from the third movement of Mozart's Piano Sonata no. 6 in D major, K.284 (see "Apply This!" Example 20.1a above). Learn to read and interpret the progression by itself first, at the keyboard (without musical notation). Then try improvising your own melodic line over the progression. Working with a partner, trade off solos and improvise your own variations.

$\|{:}\ \mathrm{I} \qquad \mathrm{vi} \qquad\| \mathrm{ii}^6 \qquad \mathrm{V} \qquad\| \mathrm{I} \qquad \mathrm{ii}^6 \qquad\qquad\| \mathrm{V}^{6-5}_{4-3} \qquad\|$

$\| \mathrm{I}^6 \qquad \mathrm{vi}^6 \qquad\| \mathrm{V/V} \quad \mathrm{V}^6/\mathrm{V} \qquad\| \mathrm{V} \quad \mathrm{vi}^6 \ \mathrm{V}^{6-5}_{4-3}/\mathrm{V} \qquad\| \mathrm{V} \qquad {:}\|$

$\|{:}\ \mathrm{V}^7/\mathrm{ii}\ \mathrm{V}^7/\mathrm{V}\ \mathrm{V}^7\ \mathrm{I} \qquad\| \mathrm{vi} \qquad \mathrm{IV} \qquad\| \mathrm{V}^6_5 \quad \mathrm{I} \qquad \mathrm{V}^6\ \mathrm{V}^4_3/\mathrm{V} \qquad\| \mathrm{V}^{6-5}_{4-3} \qquad\|$

$\| \mathrm{I} \qquad \mathrm{vi} \qquad\| \mathrm{ii}^6 \qquad \mathrm{V} \qquad\| \mathrm{I}^6 \qquad \mathrm{ii}^6\ \mathrm{V}^{6-5}_{4-3} \qquad\| \mathrm{I} \qquad {:}\|$

b. Many jazz improvisations can be seen as a fusion of ternary form with theme-and-variations form (which is addressed in Chapter 23). Usually the "theme and variations" aspect unfolds over multiple "choruses" where performers improvise repeatedly over a set of "changes." The ternary aspect occurs where the **head**, or opening theme of the piece, is repeated to close the performance. Thus, improvisation can be incorporated into ternary form by improvising over *one* chorus and then return to the head. By jazz standards, this would be admittedly truncated, but sometimes it is best to start small! You will have a chance to develop this exercise, with extended improvisation that takes the "long line" of a trajectory involving multiple choruses, in the improvisation exercise for Chapter 23.

CHAPTER 21

SONATA FORM

OVERVIEW

Sonata form is one of the most prominent formal innovations of the late eighteenth and early nineteenth centuries, found in nearly all instrumental genres of the common-practice period. This chapter provides an introduction to the basic elements of the form, through a close reading of a Beethoven sonata movement.

AUDIO LIST

Domenico Scarlatti, Sonata in E major, K.380 (Longo 23)

Wolfgang Amadeus Mozart, Symphony no. 40 in G minor, K.550 (i)

Ludwig van Beethoven, Piano Sonata in G major, op. 14 no. 2 (i)

Radiohead, "Paranoid Android"

INTRODUCTION: THE EVOLUTION OF SONATA FORM

The term **sonata** literally means "sound piece," and it has referred to various forms and genres in its long history. Very generally, it has come to refer to multimovement works for a solo instrument or one or two instruments with accompaniment. At least in the Classic era, the most common pattern for these movements would be:

1. An *allegro* or fast first movement (usually in *sonata form*, covered in this chapter);
2. A slower or *andante* second movement that might be in ternary form or rondo form (discussed in Chapter 22);
3. An *allegro* third movement, usually in compound ternary form;
4. An *allegro* or *presto* (very fast) movement that might be in rondo form or sonata form.

Tonally, the outer movements would be in the tonic whereas the inner movements would most likely be in a closely related key. Other multimovement instrumental works from the eighteenth and nineteenth centuries (such as a symphony or string quartet) also follow this plan.

Because of its commonplace occurrence in the first *allegro* movement, **sonata form** is also sometimes called **sonata-allegro form** or **first-movement form**. These synonyms are not entirely accurate, however, because sometimes slow movements are in sonata form (three of the four movements of Mozart's Symphony no. 40 in G minor, for example, are in sonata form.)

Sonata form in the late eighteenth century usually consisted of three sections:

- the **exposition** (in which thematic material in two contrasting tonal areas—usually the tonic and the dominant or relative major key—is introduced),
- the **development section** (in which the material introduced in the exposition is "developed" through frequent key changes, sequencing, and fragmentation of material); and
- the **recapitulation** (in which the thematic material from the exposition returns, in the tonic).

A related genre, the **sonatina** ("little sonata"), is much smaller in dimension than a sonata form; it may have, for example, a very short developmental section or even no development section at all.

Because a sonata has three main sections, the last of which is a return of earlier material, one might assume that sonata form is a kind of ternary form; in fact, it actually evolved out of *continuous rounded binary form*, marked by an increase in overall length, along with an earlier transition to the dominant (if in a major key) or relative major (if in a minor key). In addition, early sonata forms incorporated a greater separation between the two key areas in the first section (characterized by the use of the **caesura**—a brief pause in the rhythmic and textural flow, usually marked by a half cadence in the second key area). As each section grew in length, composers also began to incorporate previously heard material, rather than new material, early on in the second section.

Incipient sonata form can be found in some of the harpsichord sonatas of Domenico Scarlatti (1685–1757), a contemporary of Bach's whose sonatas are nearly all in binary form. His Sonata in E major K.380 (Longo 23), composed around 1754, is interesting for how material from the first section is treated in the second. The full score is shown as Example 21.1. Although this sonata is really an example of balanced binary form, the *proportion* of closing material returning at the end to qualify this as balanced binary form is unusually substantial. The annotations on the example show other ways in which this piece *foreshadows* the essential features of late-eighteenth-century sonata form.

Example 21.1. Domenico Scarlatti, Sonata in E major, K.380 (L. 23), complete score. *(Continued)*

(Continued)

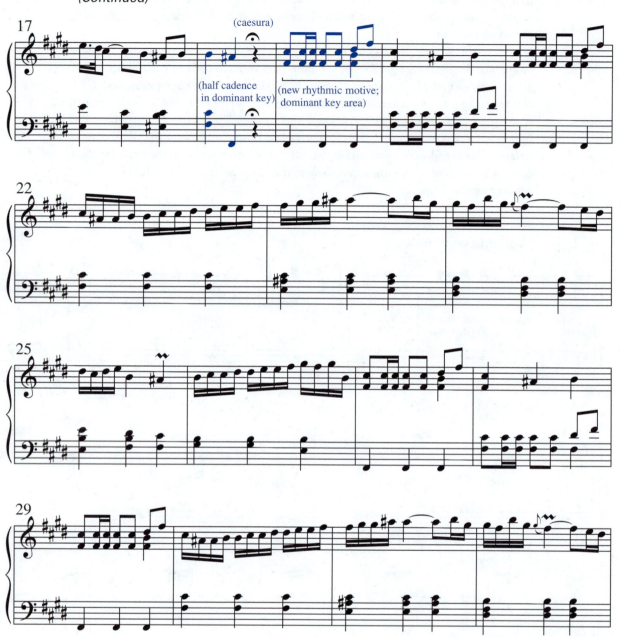

(Continued)

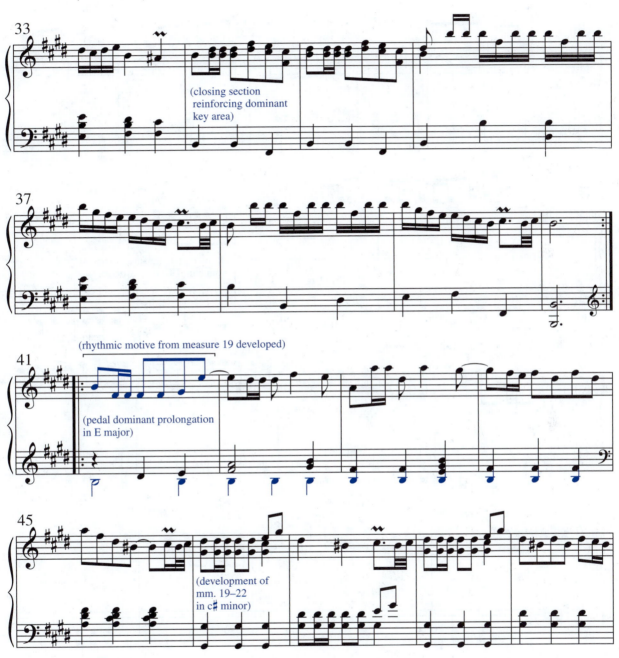

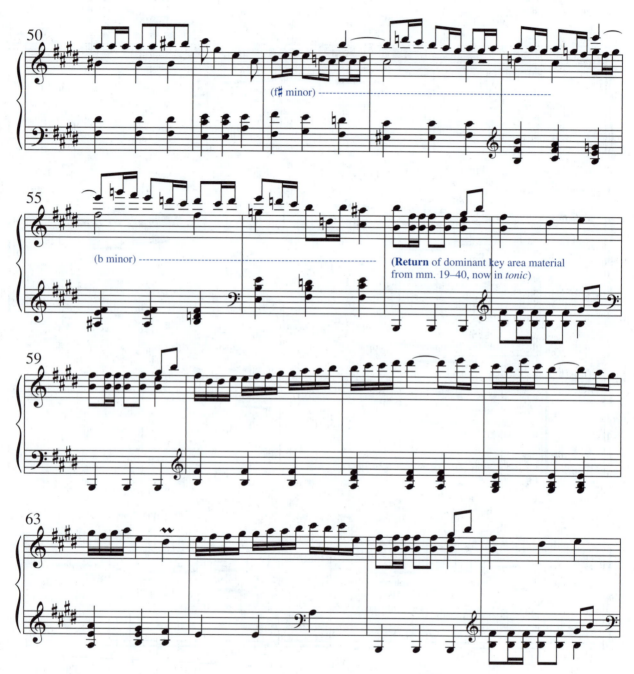

(Continued)

(Continued)

Now that we have seen how Classic-era sonata form began to emerge, we can examine how a typical sonata form movement works. The first movement of Ludwig van Beethoven's Piano Sonata no. 10 in G major, op. 14 no. 2, believed to have been composed in 1798, offers a particularly clear example for our study.

THE EXPOSITION

The **exposition** introduces the major thematic material to the listener. Its conclusion is usually marked by a repeat sign, indicating that the exposition is to be played twice (a vestige of sonata form's origins in rounded binary form).

The tonal structure of the exposition involves two tonal areas: The tonic, with its own **primary theme**, followed by the dominant (if the piece is in a major key) or the relative major (if the piece is in a minor key), with a contrasting **secondary theme**. Within each tonal area, there may be more than one theme. Sometimes—especially in the sonatas of Franz Joseph Haydn—the same theme appears in each tonal area; such sonatas are **monothematic**. The exposition thus presents a kind of struggle between the two tonal areas (and their associated themes), setting up the escalating conflict among keys in the development section and the "triumph" of the tonic in the recapitulation.[1]

In Beethoven's piece the exposition comprises the first 63 measures of the piece. The first tonal area, with its own distinctive theme, is established in measures 1–8 (Example 21.2); the phrase pattern of T–PD–D unfolds twice before ending on a perfect authentic cadence. As the phrase reaches its cadence, the accompaniment texture changes to an Alberti bass pattern, evoking motion as we move into the transition.

Example 21.2. Beethoven, Sonata in G major, op. 14 no. 2 (i), mm. 1–8.

The **transition** is a modulatory passage that facilitates movement from the first tonal area to the second tonal area; it is found in Beethoven's sonata beginning at the pickup to measure 9, lasting until measure 25. As you examine Example 21.3,

---

[1] A sonata form movement may begin with an introduction, usually in a slower tempo; the introduction is not, however, usually repeated with the rest of the exposition.

notice that the excerpt begins in G major, but a modulation to D major takes place in measure 14 (what type of modulation is it?). At measure 19 the phrase comes to rest on a V of D major, lasting until measure 25. The ascending melodic line in measures 24–25 fills in the caesura and provides a lead-in to the confirmation of the second tonal area, with its own associated theme.

Another aspect of the transition that should be mentioned here is its phrase structure. The first and second tonal areas are both characterized by fairly straightforward, self-contained phrase structures; the transition, on the other hand, seems to spin off, avoiding a clear cadence until just before the arrival of the second tonal area.

Example 21.3. Beethoven, Sonata in G major, op. 14 no. 2 (i), mm. 9–25.
(Continued)

(Continued)

The theme of the second tonal area (measures 26–47a, Example 21.4) is distinctively different in length, contour, and register from the theme in the first tonal area. Here, there are actually three different ideas, annotated in the score. With the arrival of the perfect authentic cadence in measure 47, we move by elision into the **closing section**.

Example 21.4. Beethoven, Sonata in G major, op. 14 no. 2 (i), mm. 26–47a.

(Continued)

36

I and V of the second tonal area

cresc.

41

cresc.

Section 3, mm. 41–47: a rapid scalar passage leading to the perfect authentic cadence in measures 46–47

43

f

sf

45

sf

p

The closing section (mm. 47–63a, Example 21.5) affirms the second tonal area and serves to firmly establish the new key, confirming the arrival on the perfect authentic cadence that had occurred just before. With the conclusion of the closing section in the dominant key, a return to the original tonic is as easy as repeating the exposition, since I in the new key is equivalent to V in the original key. In a minor-key sonata form, returning to the tonic from the relative major usually requires a few transitional measures, since III does not usually go directly to i.

Example 21.5. Beethoven, Sonata in G major, op. 14 no. 2 (i), mm. 47–63a.

The exposition is usually repeated in performance, a practice that has the added attraction of helping the listener become familiar with the important themes before they are developed. In later sonata form pieces, the repeat sign is often omitted from the second part of the original rounded binary form—the development and recapitulation—and so the development and recapitulation are not repeated here.

THE DEVELOPMENT SECTION

The development section is the dramatic heart of sonata form. If sonata form can be said to have a narrative or "plot," then the characters are introduced in the exposition. In the development section, conflict ensues and the narrative reaches its climax.

Beethoven's development section begins in the second half of measure 63 (after the exposition's repeat sign), ending at the C♯5 with the fermata in measure 124 (Example 21.6). Key changes are more frequent and new keys are explored; note that the keys are not always closely related keys. Part of a sonata form's narrative quality is the tonal "struggle"—the more distant the key, the more drama. The development section often reaches an extended V or V⁷ of the tonic toward the end; this is called the **retransition**, and it alerts the listener to the imminent return of the first tonal area.

Example 21.6. Beethoven Sonata in G major, op. 14 no. 2 (i), mm. 63b–125a.
(Continued)

(Continued)

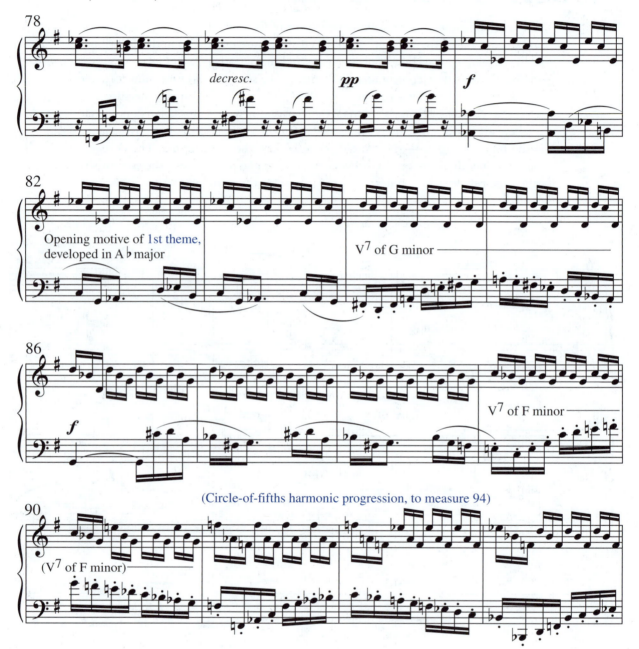

PART 3: Form and Chromatic Harmony 2

(Continued)

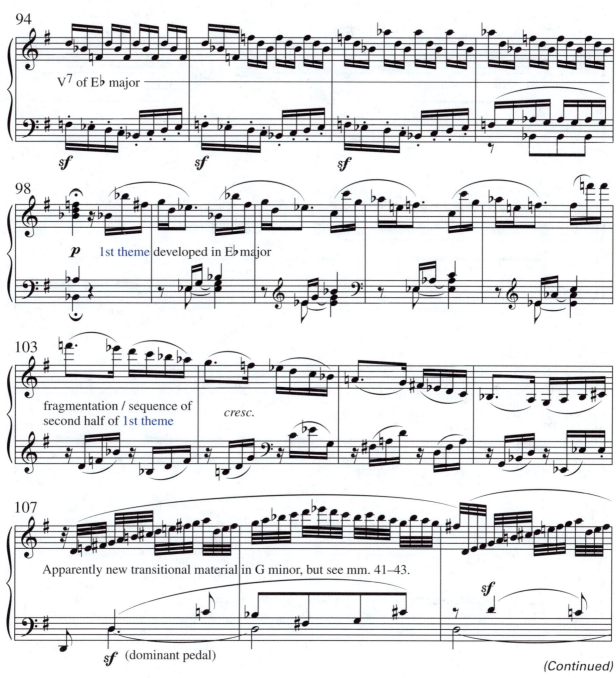

(Continued)

(Continued)

THE RECAPITULATION

The recapitulation is heralded by the return of first tonal area (the tonic), with a reprise of the exposition's thematic material; this is analogous to the "substantial return" of opening material in the second section of rounded binary form. The primary theme and secondary theme are both featured, but this time the secondary theme appears in the tonic (in the case of a minor-key sonata, a secondary theme that appeared in the relative major in the exposition may return in the parallel major in the recapitulation). Some sonatas boldly emphasize this return of the opening material; others rather sneak into it. Here, Beethoven brings it in following a moment of dramatic uncertainty, the chromatic lead-in to the phrase ending precipitously on C♯5 (measure 124). The primary theme leads off the exposition from measure 124b to measure 132.

The transition section in a recapitulation, or **second transition**, would appear to be unnecessary; since the "second tonal area" (with its secondary theme if there is one) will be in the tonic this time, there is no necessary key change. In some sonatas, then, the transition will be markedly shorter; in other sonatas, especially those of Beethoven, this transitional passage may be extended with additional modulations, suggesting a second developmental section. Beethoven's approach here is fairly conservative; the second transition begins with the same material heard in the exposition's transition (mm. 133–136), but then he sequences this material up a perfect fourth, momentarily touching on C major (mm. 137–140) (Example 21.7). The reason for this key change is quite economical; having used the first transition to move up a fifth from G major to D major, in the second transition Beethoven moves up a fifth from the subdominant (C major) to bring us back to the tonic.

When looking at an unfamiliar Classic-era piece in sonata form, the two transitions (exposition and recapitulation) can be useful for determining exactly where the first tonal area ends. The first tonal area will usually be the same in both the exposition and the recapitulation; the second tonal area material will also be the same but for the key (dominant or relative major in the exposition, tonic or parallel major in the recapitulation). The transition may begin with material from the first tonal area (this is often the case with Mozart, for example), but will end differently owing to the differing tonal destinations. The cadence immediately before the transition will usually be the end of the first tonal area material.

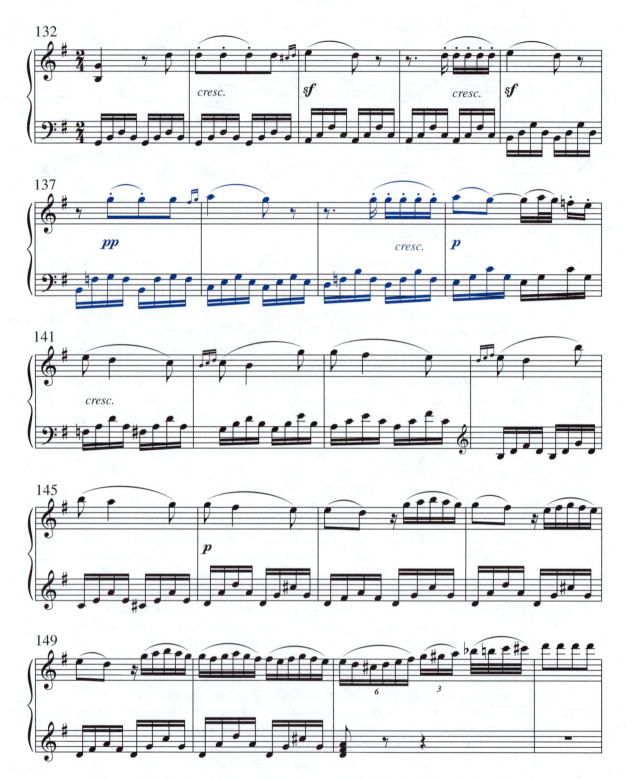

Example 21.7. Beethoven, Sonata in G major, op. 14 no. 2 (i), mm. 132–152.

After the second transition, the second tonal area's thematic material follows, this time in the tonic, from measure 153 to 174a. The closing section, again in the tonic, lasts from measure 174 to the downbeat of measure 187. It is at this point that Beethoven adds an optional section to the sonata form—a coda, providing a general relaxation of mood and a gentle summary of the preceding music, with references to the primary theme over a tonic pedal tone (mm. 187b–200) (Example 21.8). As in the primary theme, the unfolding of the T–PD–D–T pattern helps to reaffirm the tonic.

For another sonata-form analysis, this time of an orchestral work in a minor key, see Web Feature 21.1.

For a consideration of the "sonata principle" of development in a Radiohead song, see Web Feature 21.2.

Self-Tests 21.1 and 21.2 may be done at this time.

Apply This! 21.1 may be done at this time.

Example 21.8. Beethoven, Sonata in G major, op. 14 no. 2 (i), mm. 187b–200.

LEVEL MASTERY 21.1.

1. In the sonata movement on the following pages, locate the following:
   a. The end of the exposition;
   b. The beginning of the recapitulation;
   c. The beginning of the second tonal area's thematic material (confirm this by looking for the corresponding points in both the exposition and recapitulation). Is this movement monothematic?

d. The beginning and ending of the transition between the first and second tonal areas, in both the exposition and recapitulation (how does the composer handle the problem of "transitioning" in the recapitulation when there is no need to modulate?).

   e. The caesura, if there is one.

2. Determine the key areas visited in the development section (you can do this, to start, by searching for cadences and noting in which keys they occur). Are any of these keys distantly related to the tonic? What thematic or motivic material is employed in the development section? Are there any passages that employ new thematic material? If the development uses previously heard material, how is the material altered or developed? Is there a retransition, and if so, where does it occur?

3. Is there a coda? Is there an introduction?

4. When you have found all of these things, prepare an arch map outlining the proportions of the exposition, development, and recapitulation, the location of themes or tonal areas within each section, and the tonal plan of the movement.

Mozart, Piano Sonata in A minor, K.310 (i).

(Continued)

(Continued)

(Continued)

(Continued)

(Continued)

(Continued)

(Continued)

(Continued)

(Continued)

(Continued)

(Continued)

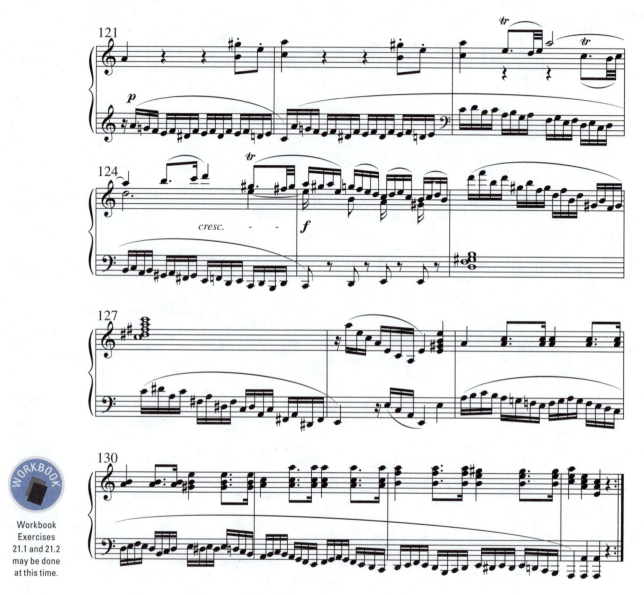

Workbook
Exercises
21.1 and 21.2
may be done
at this time.

CONCLUSION

Sonata form grew out of rounded binary form in the following ways:

- First, whereas the first half of a piece in rounded binary form often merely ended on the dominant (V) or briefly modulated to the dominant key (if in a major key) or relative major (if in a minor key), in sonata form the first half of the binary form (which became the exposition) *modulated to the dominant or relative major earlier*, so that the two tonal areas were more or less equally proportional.

- Second, the "contrasting material" that began the second half of rounded binary form was also greatly *expanded in length*, drawing upon the thematic material from the first half and developing it through fragmentation, sequence, and frequent modulation. As sonata form evolved, the development section became the dramatic highlight of the form—perceived distances of various keys from the tonic aided in creating a kind of dramatic curve to the piece.
- Third, the "substantial return" at the end of the second part in rounded binary form became expanded to a *full return*, in which both of the main thematic elements of the exposition were reprised in the tonic.

Eventually sonata form became the major formal design of the Classic era. Its shadow extended long into the nineteenth and twentieth centuries. For example, Franz Liszt's *Sonata in B Minor* expands each of the sections of sonata form into movements all their own, connected with segues. Later composers have composed sonatas that may not be "tonal" in a classically functional sense but that use contrasts of texture and style to denote the two major thematic areas in an exposition. Progressive rock bands of the 1970s such as Yes and later art-rock-inspired bands such as Radiohead have also drawn upon aspects of the sonata principle (see Web Feature 21.2) to build more complex, if often intuitive, musical structures.

One reason that sonata form became such a popular template for larger musical structures has to do with its dramatic or narrative connotations. The development of the classical sonata form in the late eighteenth and early nineteenth centuries shares some parallels with the development of the novel in literature during the same period; themes in music could function much as characters in a novel, with thematic transformation functioning as a musical analogue for character development. The principle of departure and return, so important to an epic narrative, had its musical equivalent in sonata form as well, in its tonal structure. We will explore the concept of narrativity in music in more detail, across a variety of musical styles and genres, in Chapter 31.

Terms to Know

caesura	monothematic sonata	secondary theme
closing section (closing theme)	primary theme	sonata form
	recapitulation	sonata principle
development section	retransition	sonatina
exposition	second transition	transition (in sonata form)

Self-Test

21.1. What is the difference between sonata form and the form of a sonata? (Remember, a "sonata" in the Classic era usually consisted of several movements.)

21.2. Based on the descriptions of the various formal components of sonata form provided in this chapter, identify the section from which each of the unidentified musical excerpts likely comes (from among the choices given below). In arriving at your decision, consider the relation of each excerpt's tonality to its given key signature; also consider whether the excerpt ends in the key in which it begins, the overall tonal stability of the passage, and so on. Your choices are:

Exposition—First tonal area
Exposition—Transition
Exposition—Second tonal area
Closing section
Development section

Example a.

legato

Example b.

Example c.

(Continued)

(Continued)

Example d.

Example e.

Apply This!

21.1. Analysis. Answer the following questions about the sonata-form movement at the end of this chapter.

EXPOSITION

1. The first tonal area/primary theme is in the key of _____.
2. Does the transition to the second tonal / secondary theme begin at measure 9 or 19? Explain the reasoning behind your answer. (Hint: Find the corresponding passage in the recapitulation and compare them.)

3. Does the secondary theme begin at measure 23 or 36? (Hint: Look for the corresponding passages in the recapitulation and compare them.)

4. The second tonal area is in the key of _____. What is this key's relation to the tonic? _____ Is this relationship expected for a classical sonata exposition?   Yes   No

5. Does the closing section begin at measure 59 or measure 67? Explain the reasoning behind your answer.

6. Is this a monothematic exposition?   Yes   No

DEVELOPMENT

7. The opening of the development (mm. 75–78) most closely corresponds to which measures in the exposition? _____. What is the function of this passage?

8. Measures 79–82 are in the key of _____. Which theme appears in this passage?

9. Provide a harmonic analysis for measures 83–99 below. Assuming that by the end of this passage we have returned to the tonic, where would be the most likely point that a modulation has occurred, and by what means was the modulation achieved? (The passage can be analyzed with only one key change.)

83–84:   85–86:

87–88:   89–90:

91–92:   93–94:

95:               96–97:   98–99:

RECAPITULATION

10. Compare measures 118–130 in this section with measures 19–35 in the exposition. Which measures are similar to one another? Which measures have been changed? Compare the treatment of thematic material in the portions that have been changed.

11. How do measures 168–185 function, formally, in this piece?

Mozart, Piano Sonata no. 14, K.457 (i).

(Continued)

(Continued)

(Continued)

(Continued)

(Continued)

(Continued)

(Continued)

(Continued)

(Continued)

(Continued)

(Continued)

(Continued)

182

CHAPTER 22

RONDO

OVERVIEW

Having seen how the principle of departure and return manifests itself in ternary form in Chapter 20, in this chapter we extend that principle with additional departures and returns to create rondo form. Rondos most commonly consist of five or seven sections; some rondos also employ thematic development in the manner of a sonata form, resulting in sonata-rondo form. In this chapter we will examine each of these common types and also look at deviations from the typical pattern.

AUDIO LIST

François Couperin: "Les Baricades Mistérieuses"

Beethoven, Piano Sonata no. 8 in C minor, op. 13 ("Pathétique") (ii and iii)

Wolfgang Amadeus Mozart, Rondo K.494 (iii of Piano Sonata in F major, K.533/494)

Wolfgang Amadeus Mozart, Piano Sonata in B♭ major, K.333 (iii)

Dave Brubeck Quartet, "Blue Rondo à la Turk"

INTRODUCTION: EXTENDING THE PRINCIPLE OF DEPARTURE AND RETURN

Suppose you need to take care of a few errands, but you are somewhat pressed for time. In order to make the best use of your time, you plan your outing by making a to-do list:

- Buy milk, eggs, and bread at the supermarket
- Pick up laundry at dry cleaner
- Return books to the library

Unfortunately, you leave the list at home and need to rely on your memory. You remember the milk, eggs, and bread easily enough—you need them for breakfast in the morning—and the dry cleaner is on your way home. Coming home, though, you find the library books on the kitchen table. Mildly bothered that you need to make another trip, you head back out to the library, frustrated that what was intended to become a single trip has instead become two.

This simple illustration symbolizes the structure of another popular Classic-era form, the **rondo**. In Chapter 19 we learned how the basic principle of departure and return is manifested in ternary form. Rondo form extends this idea, with one or more additional departures and returns. In this chapter we will consider five-part and seven-part rondo forms, as well as other pieces that use the rondo principle.

For a look at a Baroque predecessor of the Classic-era rondo, see Web Feature 22.1.

CHARACTERISTICS OF CLASSIC-ERA RONDOS

The Classic-era rondo begins with, and returns to, a regularly recurring theme (usually in the tonic) called the **refrain** (designated as *A* in the formal discussions that follow). The refrain is usually a tonally self-contained unit, often ending on an authentic cadence in the tonic and serving as a point of departure for contrasting sections called **episodes**. Episodes usually feature different themes and often are in contrasting keys as well.

Classic-era rondos are usually of the five-part (ABACA) or seven-part (ABACAB'A) variety. Within these standard "templates," though, there can be considerable variety; for example, there may be **transitions** and/or **retransitions**. Transitions occur *after* the refrain, *before* an episode. Like the transition in a sonata form, such a passage assists in modulating to the key of the episode and usually ends on a *half cadence in the new key* to set up the episode's arrival. A **retransition** leads back to the refrain *from the episode*, usually by means of an extended passage on the *V of the tonic* to facilitate the return of the refrain.

Self-Tests 22.1, 22.2, and 22.3 may be done at this time.

THE FIVE-PART RONDO: BEETHOVEN, PIANO SONATA NO. 8 IN C MINOR, OP. 13 ("PATHÉTIQUE"), SECOND MOVEMENT

The famous "Adagio cantabile" second movement from Beethoven's Piano Sonata no. 8 in C minor, op. 13 ("Pathétique") is a five-part rondo. The refrain in A♭ major, measures 1–16 (Example 22.1), is a self-contained unit: a contrasting period (antecedent phrase, measures 1–4; consequent phrase, measures 5–8), repeated an octave higher with an extra layer of accompanying figuration (measures 9–16) and closing with a perfect authentic cadence.

Example 22.1. Beethoven, Piano Sonata no. 8 in C minor, op. 13 ("Pathétique") (ii), mm. 1–16. *(Continued)*

(Continued)

The passage after the refrain (Example 22.2) resembles a transition; it begins with a reference to F minor (measures 17–19) before modulating to E♭ major (measures 22–23). The cadence in E♭ major is extended (measures 24–28), ultimately becoming the V of the tonic and preparing us for the refrain. It is at this point that, if we have been deceived, we realize that this "transition" was in fact the first episode. Thus, measures 17–24 constitute the first episode (the *B* section in the overall form), rather than a transition. The repeated cadence on E♭ major and the lingering pause that follows (measures 25–28) represents a brief retransition back to the refrain.

Example 22.2. Beethoven, Piano Sonata no. 8 in C minor, op. 13 ("Pathétique") (ii), mm. 17–28. *(Continued)*

(Continued)

The refrain's return in measures 29–36 is abbreviated, the contrasting period occurring only once (it is not shown here as it is virtually identical with the first eight measures of the piece). It is not uncommon, in the Classic era, for a varied refrain to occur—a shortened version of the refrain as we have here, or perhaps some elaboration or variation of the melodic line. Nevertheless, the refrain will still be in the tonic.

The second episode (*C* in the overall form) begins on the anacrusis (pickup beat) to measure 37 (Example 22.3). It is noticeably different from what has come before: Note the change of mode to the parallel minor (A♭ minor), and the new rhythmic element—triplet sixteenth notes—in the accompaniment. Again, there is no transition to this new section. This second episode is longer and more harmonically adventurous than the first; by measures 42–44 we have changed key to E major (enharmonically a chromatic mediant relationship with the tonic), with the perfect authentic cadence in the new key closing on the downbeat of measure 44 (by what means of modulation was the key change achieved?). Beethoven now has a rather significant compositional challenge—smoothly returning back to the tonic to present the refrain one last time. He does this in measures 48–50, a weak retransition. Looking at the chord arpeggiated in the bass in measures 48–49, how would this chord be analyzed in A♭ major? Can it be analyzed in E major? (How could it be analyzed in E major if it were respelled enharmonically?)

Example 22.3. Beethoven, Piano Sonata no. 8 in C minor, op. 13 ("Pathétique") (ii), mm. 37–50. *(Continued)*

The final refrain (measures 51–66) is again complete, but this time Beethoven retains the triplet sixteenth note rhythmic element from the second episode. The movement concludes with a brief coda (measures 67–73), repeating the concluding V^7–I cadential formula to bring this movement to a peaceful close.

A formal diagram of the second movement of Beethoven's "Pathétique" is shown in Table 22.1; "rt" indicates a retransition.

TABLE 22.1. Formal structure of Beethoven, Piano Sonata no. 8 in C minor, op. 13 ("Pathétique") (ii).

section	A	B	[rt]	A	C	[rt]	A	Coda
mm.	1–16	17–28	25–28	29–36	37–50	48–50	51–66	67–73
key	A♭	fm → E♭	V/A♭	A♭	a♭ → E →	V/A♭	A♭	A♭

THE SEVEN-PART RONDO: BEETHOVEN, PIANO SONATA NO. 8 IN C MINOR, OP. 13 ("PATHÉTIQUE"), THIRD MOVEMENT

The third movement of Beethoven's "Pathétique" sonata is also a rondo, but this time the form has seven parts: ABACAB'A. The section designated B' is a return of the first episode (B) material in the *tonic* rather than in the key of its first appearance. Let's look at how this form plays itself out in Beethoven's piece.

The tonic of this movement is the key of the piece, C minor. The refrain (measures 1–17, Example 22.4) begins the piece; again, the concluding perfect authentic cadence makes it a formally self-contained unit. The form of the refrain is interesting in its lack of symmetry; unlike the perfectly balanced symmetry we saw in the refrain of Beethoven's second movement, it is a three-phrase period in ABB form or **bar form**, with one antecedent phrase (measures 1–4) and two consequent phrases (measures 5–8 and 9–12). A brief extension of the second consequent phrase (measures 12–17) concludes the refrain.

Example 22.4. Beethoven, Piano Sonata no. 8 in C minor, op. 13 ("Pathétique") (iii), mm. 1–17. *(Continued)*

(Continued)

Measures 18–24 function as a transition to E♭ major, the key of the first episode (Example 22.5). This episode is unusually long (measures 25–61) and thematically rich, with three ideas, annotated on the score. Beginning at measure 51, there is a series of V⁷–I cadential patterns; this begins the retransition to the refrain (note the extended V of C minor at measures 58–61).

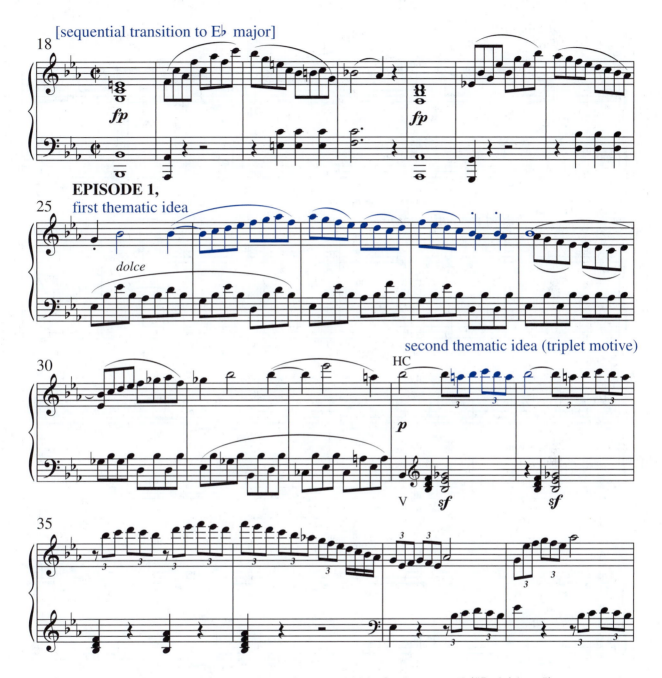

Example 22.5. Beethoven, Piano Sonata no. 8 in C minor, op. 13 ("Pathétique") (iii), mm. 18–61. *(Continued)*

(Continued)

(Continued)

(Continued)

The refrain follows from measure 62 to 78, exactly as its first appearance. With the pickup to measure 79 we find ourselves in the second episode (the *C* section in the form), this time with no transition (Example 22.6). The form of this episode resembles AABA song form, the contrasting material found in measures 95–98. The retransition begins at measure 107; notice how long the retransition is, with 14 measures of a dominant prolongation. Extending the V and elaborating it with pedal i$^6_4$ chords creates considerable dramatic tension with the expectation that we will soon arrive on the tonic and the return of the refrain. (This is one crucial way that Beethoven's music differs from, say, Mozart's—whereas Mozart frequently accelerates the harmonic rhythm of a passage before the cadence, Beethoven frequently *decelerates*, increasing the tension as chords take longer to resolve.)

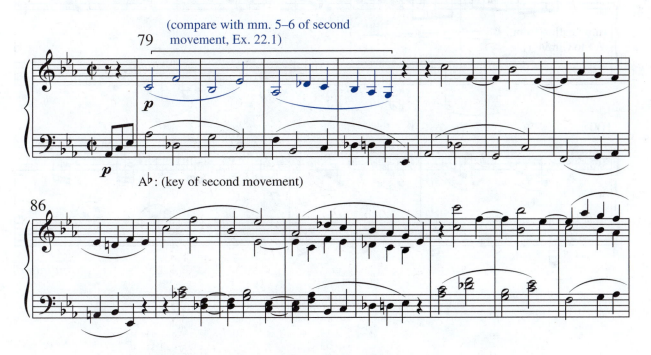

Example 22.6. Beethoven, Piano Sonata no. 8 in C minor, op. 13 ("Pathétique") (iii), mm. 79–120. *(Continued)*

(Continued)

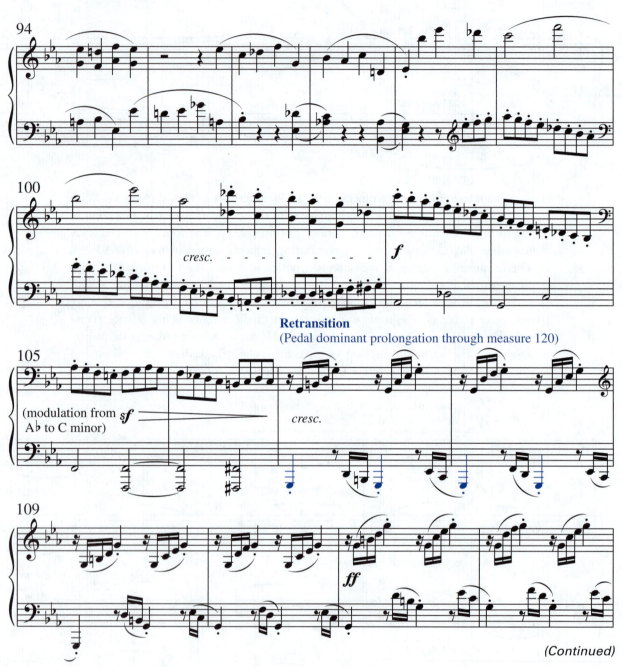

Retransition
(Pedal dominant prolongation through measure 120)

(Continued)

(Continued)

The next refrain is abbreviated, lasting only from measure 121 to 128 and omitting the second consequent phrase. What appears to be the second consequent phrase (the left hand melody in measures 129–130) turns out to be the beginning of a transition to *B'* as the material is sequenced and used to lead into the key of the return of *B*, this time in C major (the parallel major of the tonic) rather than E♭ major (Example 22.7).

sequence, tonicizing F minor (iv of C minor)

Example 22.7. Beethoven, Piano Sonata no. 8 in C minor, op. 13 ("Pathétique") (iii), mm. 129–134.

The material from the first episode then returns in the tonic (though in major), and again we hear all three ideas. The last chordal idea then leads us toward the retransition, again by means of harmonic sequence (see measures 158–163 in Example 22.8).

Example 22.8. Beethoven, Piano Sonata no. 8 in C minor, op. 13 ("Pathétique") (iii), mm. 154–170.

The last refrain (measures 171–182) is again abbreviated, lacking the second consequent phrase; the first consequent phrase is also melodically varied (Example 22.9).

Example 22.9. Beethoven, Piano Sonata no. 8 in C minor, op. 13 ("Pathétique") (iii), mm. 179–182a.

An extended coda follows, incorporating the triplet-eighth-note motive from the *B* section before surprisingly visiting the key of A♭ major one last time before the close (measures 203–210, Example 22.10).

Example 22.10. Beethoven, Piano Sonata no. 8 in C minor, op. 13 ("Pathétique") (iii), mm. 203–210.

A formal diagram of the third movement of the "Pathétique" is shown in Table 22.2. Transitions and retransitions are indicated by "t" and "rt" respectively. By comparison with the second movement, the third movement of the "Pathétique" is more elaborate—not only because of the return of *B* in the parallel-major tonic, but also the presence of transitions and retransitions (and the lengths of those retransitions). We have also seen that the refrain is varied more in its appearances to include not only abbreviation of the theme but also melodic variation. In the remainder of this chapter we shall closely examine other rondo pieces and see other variations of the form.

TABLE 22.2. **Formal structure of Beethoven, Piano Sonata no. 8 in C minor, op. 13 ("Pathétique") (iii).**

section	A	[t]	B	[rt]	A	C	[rt]
mm.	1–17	18–24	25–61	51–61	62–78	79–120	107–120
key	c	c → f →	E♭	E♭ → V/c	c	A♭	V/c
(continued)							
section	A	[t]	B′	[rt]	A	Coda	
mm.	121–128	129–134	134–170	158–170	171–182	182–210	
key	c	c → V/C	C	C → V/c	c	c (A♭) c	

LEVEL MASTERY 22.1.

Prepare a formal analysis of the rondo movement found on the following pages.

- Begin by determining the extent of the refrain—what is its form? With what type of cadence does it conclude? Where does the refrain return in the movement, and are subsequent appearances ever altered from the original appearance?
- In between, how are the episodes distinguished from the refrains, thematically and/or tonally? What key areas does Haydn employ as part of the movement's tonal plan? Would it be accurate to call this a monothematic rondo? Are there transitions or retransitions, and if so, where (and what distinguishes them within the episodic material)?
- Finally, based on the number of sections you find overall, does this movement more closely resemble a five-part or a seven-part rondo?

Summarize your findings in diagram form. Your diagram may be modeled after one of the tables found in this chapter, or you might wish to prepare an arch map.

Haydn, String Quartet, op. 33 no. 3 ("The Bird"), Hob.III:39, (iii).

(Continued)

(Continued)

(Continued)

(Continued)

(Continued)

(Continued)

(Continued)

(Continued)

(Continued)

(Continued)

(Continued)

(Continued)

(Continued)

(Continued)

(Continued)

(Continued)

(Continued)

(Continued)

PART 3: Form and Chromatic Harmony 2

(Continued)

(Continued)

Apply This!
22.1 may
be done at
this time.

THE SONATA-RONDO: MOZART, PIANO SONATA NO. 13 IN B♭ MAJOR, K.333, THIRD MOVEMENT

You may have noticed that the way the first episode in the seven-part rondo appears first in a closely related key (usually the dominant key in a major-key work, or the relative major key in a minor-key work) and then later returns in the tonic key (the *B′* section) resembles the secondary theme in sonata form. Some seven-part rondos exploit the second episode as a kind of "development section" within the rondo, using previously heard material and modulating frequently within the section, furthering the similarity to sonata form. A seven-part rondo with a developmental *C* section is called a **sonata-rondo**.

A sonata-rondo differs from a true sonata form in two important respects:

- First, *a sonata-rondo does not have a repeating exposition.* The "development" *C* section is preceded by sections that collectively have the form *ABA*, rather than *ABAB* (as in the case of an exposition with repeats).
- Second, the sonata-rondo will usually have an additional, final statement of the refrain (*A*) before its conclusion, whereas the end of the recapitulation—if there is no coda—will have the secondary theme (and closing section) in the tonic.

The third and final movement of Mozart's Piano Sonata no. 13 in B♭ major, K.333, composed in 1788, is an excellent example of a sonata-rondo; as we will see, it also shows Mozart's gift for "tweaking" the conventions of the sonata-rondo form. The entire score, with analytical annotations, is found on the following pages.

Allegretto grazioso

A: **Refrain.** (What is this refrain's phrase structure? Does it resemble the refrain of the second movement of Beethoven's "Pathétique"?)

End of Refrain (P.A.C.)   **TRANSITION** (to m. 24) (Unusually tuneful material for a

transition)   (modulation to the dominant, F major)

To discover the effect of this transitional passage (measures 17–24) in approaching the B section, try this: Play the refrain and omit the transition, jumping directly from the second beat of measure 16 to the third beat of measure 24. Does it sound as though you have truly left the key, or does it sound rather like a tonicization of V?

(Continued)

(Continued)

B: EPISODE I, in dominant. Whereas the transition was more thematic, Episode I is more motivic, concluding with a flourish of figuration.

(Continued)

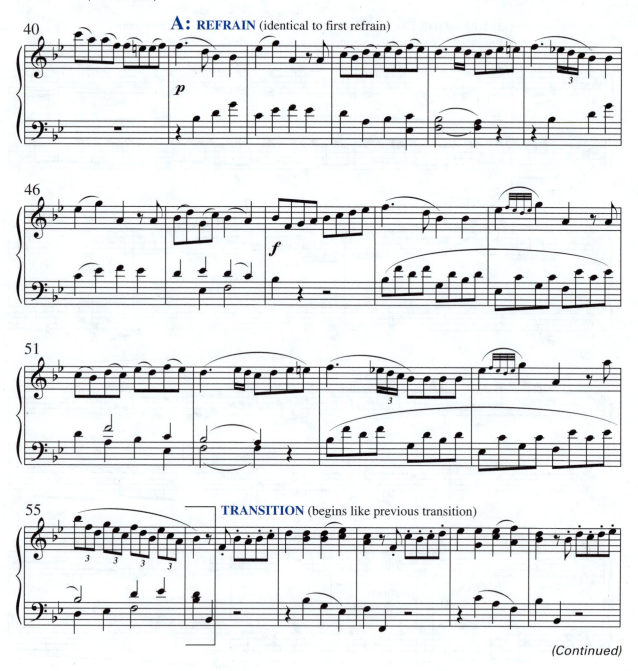

(Continued)

(Continued)

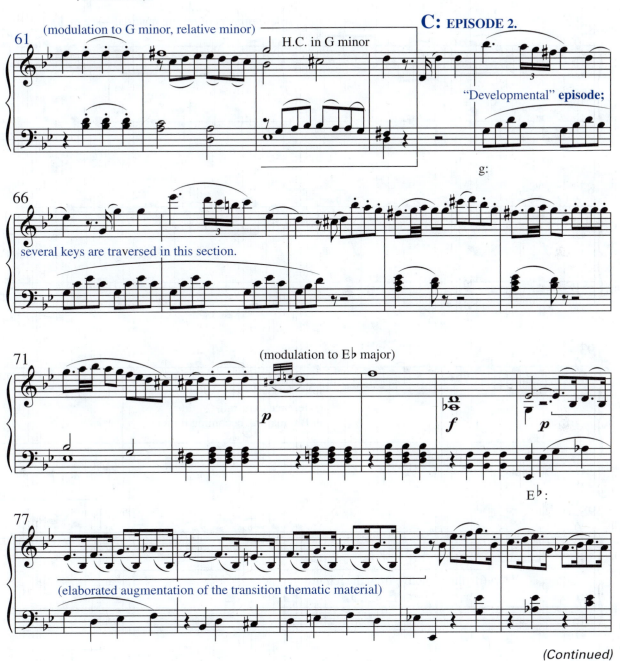

(Continued)

(Continued)

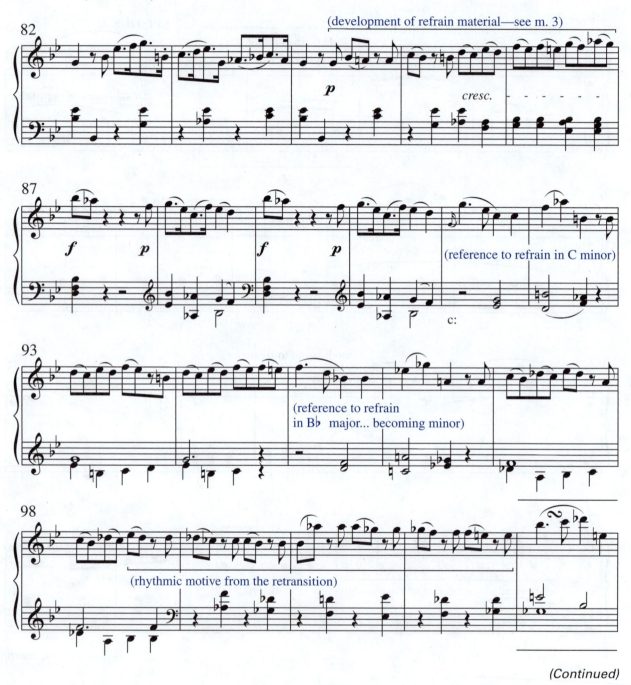

(Continued)

RETRANSITION

V

A: REFRAIN

(Continued)

(Continued)

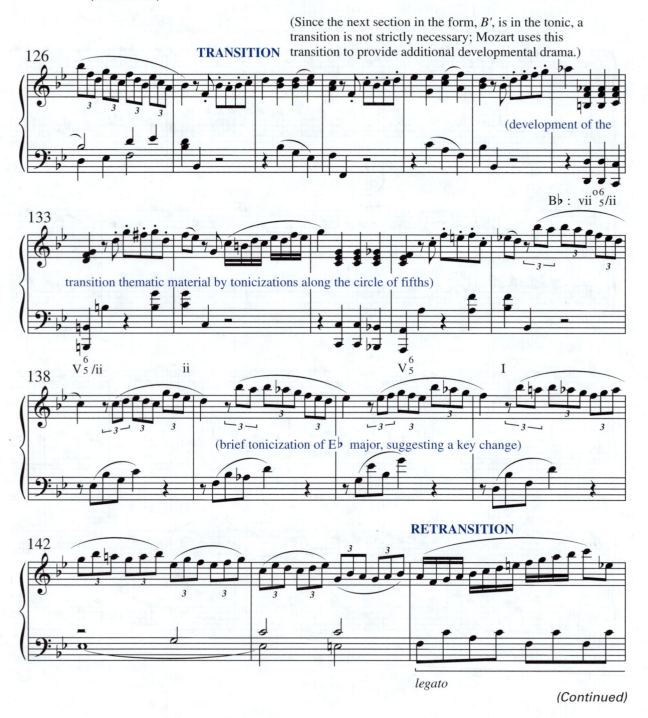

(Since the next section in the form, *B'*, is in the tonic, a transition is not strictly necessary; Mozart uses this transition to provide additional developmental drama.)

TRANSITION

(development of the

B♭ : vii°⁶₅/ii

transition thematic material by tonicizations along the circle of fifths)

V⁶₅/ii   ii   V⁶₅   I

(brief tonicization of E♭ major, suggesting a key change)

RETRANSITION

legato

(Continued)

(Continued)

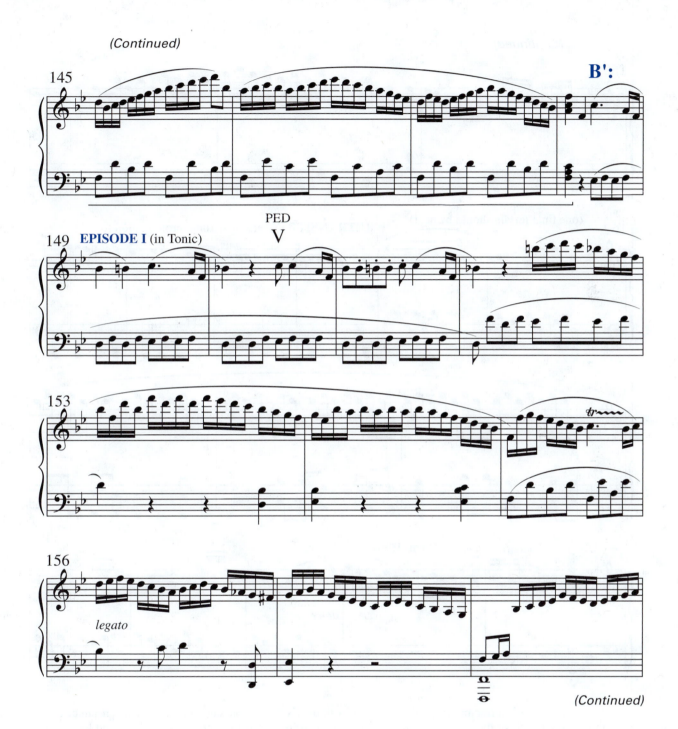

(Continued)

(Continued)

(one final refrain should be next)

RETRANSITION serving a Tonic prolongation function

Cadenza in tempo* (to m. 199)

dolce

legato

* Why is a cadenza—a free improvisational (or quasi-improvisational) passage found in a concerto in order to highlight the skills of the soloist—even necessary in this solo work? It might help to go back and look at the structure of the refrains thus far; in each refrain, the theme is heard twice, with the second time louder (and with a more active accompaniment) than the first. This is actually the common practice in Classical concerti for a soloist and orchestra—the soloist plays the theme first, and then the orchestra (sometimes with the soloist) plays the theme as well. In this piece for solo piano, Mozart is actually paying tribute to the sound and texture of a different genre and medium (in measures 168–170, for example, leading up to the cadenza, one can easily imagine hearing this passage played vigorously by a string section).

(Continued)

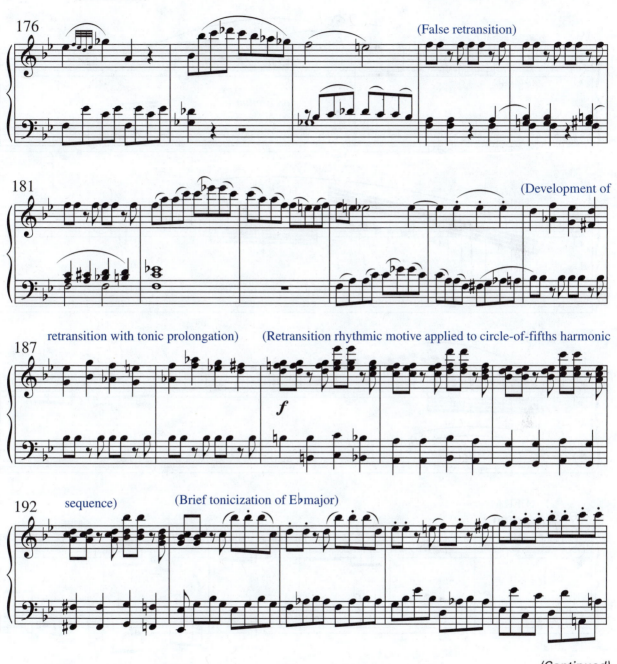

(Continued)

ad libitum

(V)

A: REFRAIN
a tempo

p

f

(Continued)

(Continued)

(Continued)

For a more elaborate variant of the Classic rondo, see Web Feature 22.2.

Self-Test 22.4 may be done at this time.

The overall form of the third movement of Mozart's Piano Sonata K.333 is shown in Table 22.3.

TABLE 22.3. Formal structure of Mozart, Piano Sonata no. 13 in B♭ major, K.333 (iii).

section	A	[t]	B	[rt]	A	[t]	C
mm.	1–16	17–24	24–40	36–40	41–56	56–64	65–104
key	B♭	B♭ → F	F	V/B♭	B♭	B♭ → V/g	g → E♭ → Cm → B♭m → V/B♭

(continued)

section	[rt]	A	[t]	B′	[rt]	Cadenza	A	Coda
mm.	105–111	112–127	128–148	148–171	164–171	171–199	200–207	207–225
key	V/B♭	B♭	B♭	B♭	B♭	B♭: I$_4^6$ → V	B♭	B♭

THE RONDO IN POPULAR MUSIC?

With its sectionalized structure of self-contained refrains alternating with contrasting episodes, one would expect that rondo form is well represented in popular music genres. Surprisingly, this would not seem to be the case. The closest that a pop song comes to rondo form might be in certain expanded AABA song forms, where *A* refers to a verse and chorus that always appear together. Separating the verse and chorus, with the bridge section given the letter *C*, we would have the form ABABCAB. This form reveals, however, that it still differs from rondo form in a number of respects.

Rondo forms can be found in popular music in contexts where the composer has had some classical training and/or has emulated classical rondo form. One such well known example is Dave Brubeck's "Blue Rondo à la Turk." The refrain, based on a Turkish folk rhythm, is in $\frac{9}{8}$ meter, divided as three measures of 2+2+2+3 followed by a measure of 3+3+3. Harmonically the refrain sequences back and forth between F major and A minor. A brief transition (t1) developing the refrain material [1:19–1:39] leads us into the key of A major and the *B* section, now consistently in $\frac{9}{8}$ meter subdivided as 3+3+3. The theme of the *B* section is clearly derived from the refrain. The arrival of the *C* section is foreshadowed by a new transition (t2, found at

1:52–2:13) that alternates, jump-cut style, between two measures of the 2+2+2+3 refrain motive and two measures of a shuffling blues. The three eighth notes of the $\frac{9}{8}$ meter are reinterpreted as triplets in the blues groove; this reinterpretation of durational values is an example of metric modulation (see Web Feature 3.4 and the discussion of Peter Gabriel's "The Rhythm of the Heat"). Once we arrive at *C*, we find we are in the tonic of F major again; this section is a 12-bar blues with a more relaxed feel, lasting from 2:13 to 5:35.

The retransition out of *C* back to the refrain is here a return of t2, again alternating between the additive-meter style of the refrain and the relaxed blues shuffle of *C*. The return of *A* is quite abbreviated compared to its first appearance (it lasts only twelve seconds, 5:53–6:05), and again it is followed, after a return of t1, by *B* [6:05–6:25], concluding the piece.

An examination of the formal structure of Brubeck's "Blue Rondo à la Turk," as shown in Table 22.4, shows that this piece differs from a "classical" rondo in several respects. First, even though the transition between *B* and *C* makes references to the *A* theme, there is no refrain between *B* and *C* as one would find in both the five- and seven-part rondo. There is also no concluding refrain. Also, note that although *B* appears twice, as one would have in a seven-part rondo, the second *B* section does not appear in the tonic. Because of this, the rondo ends in a different key than that in which it began.

Apply This!
22.2 and 22.3
may be done
at this time.

Workbook
Exercises
22.1, 22.2,
22.3, and 22.4
may be done
at this time.

TABLE 22.4. **Formal structure of Brubeck, "Blue Rondo à la Turk."**

A	[t1]	B	[t2] (refs. to A)	C (12-bar blues)	[t2]	A	[t1]	B
0:00–1:19	1:19–1:39	1:39–1:52	1:52–2:13	2:13–5:35	5:35–5:53	5:53–6:05	6:05–6:25	6:25–6:47
F, a	a → A	A	F	F	F	F	a → A	A

Because of the omission of the refrain between *B* and *C*, and the arrangement of the two transitions, one could in fact count *A*, transition 1, and *B* as one formal unit since those sections return in the exact same order. In that case, "Blue Rondo à la Turk" could also be analyzed as ternary form: *A* (0:00–1:52), *B* (2:13–5:35), *A* (5:53–6:47) with transitions between the sections.

CONCLUSION

Rondo form is potentially one of the simplest musical forms: A recurring refrain and two contrasting ideas are all that are needed to string a rondo together. Even the transitions between sections, we have seen, are optional. Perhaps the simplicity of this form provides composers with a challenge—how to make such a simple form creatively rewarding in other ways.

Our experience in analyzing the rondos in this chapter points out an interesting aspect of musical form. Depending on the piece of music, we may find that the different parameters of form—formal order, tonal areas, phrase structure, thematic development, and so on—are often treated with varying degrees of experimentation, so that something "traditional" in one parameter is balanced by something more "radical" in another. For example, Mozart's K.333 rondo is quite conservative in its key areas (all of which are closely related to the tonic) and its phrase structure (there are elisions between phrases, but most of the phrases are four or eight measures in length). On the other hand, it is more "radical" in its overall form, with its insertion of a lengthy and dramatic cadenza in an unexpected place. In contrast, the second movement of Beethoven's "Pathétique" sonata is completely traditional in its treatment of five-part rondo form; its choice of tonal areas in the episodes, however, is more experimental, as the first episode is more transitory and the second episode heads to the quite distant key of E major. Sometimes the "radical" elements of a musical form are subtler than matters of key relationships. For example, Brubeck's "Blue Rondo à la Turk"—which we have seen is rather formally impoverished as a rondo (and may in fact not be a rondo at all, but ternary form)—is more interesting in its use of metric subdivisions and metric modulation.

Analyzing a piece of music in this way—considering the different **parameters** of music (harmony, key relationships, form, phrase structure, texture, rhythm and meter, register, and so forth) and how they work together as complementary and sometimes competing forces—is called **parametric analysis**. When analyzing a piece of music, we may first do a harmonic analysis of the piece, given that harmony is often a central aspect of our music theory study. Harmonic analysis, however, only scratches the surface of a piece's structure in many instances. When you study a piece of music, be sure to examine it from as many perspectives as possible.

Terms to Know

bar form	parameter	rondeau
couplet (Web Feature 22.1)	parametric analysis	seven-part rondo
episode	refrain	sonata-rondo
five-part rondo	retransition	transition

Self-Test

22.1. How does the French Baroque *rondeau* (see Web Feature 22.1) prefigure the Classical rondo form? In what ways is it different?

22.2. Briefly summarize the harmonic and structural characteristics of a refrain. What does it mean when the refrain is described as a "self-contained" unit within the overall structure?

22.3. What is the difference between a transition and a retransition?

22.4. In what ways does a sonata-rondo resemble sonata form? How does it differ from sonata form?

Apply This!

22.1. Analysis. Using the formal diagrams in this chapter (Tables 22.1, 22.2, 22.3 and 22.4) as your model, prepare a similar diagram of the formal structure of each of the pieces on the following pages. In addition, answer the following questions about each example:

- Which of the main Classical rondo types discussed (five-part rondo, seven-part rondo, or seven-part sonata-rondo) does this example most closely resemble?
- Analyze the phrase/period structure of the refrain of each example.
- Comment on the presence/absence of transitions, retransitions, or a coda.

a. Haydn, Piano Sonata no. 50 in D major, Hob. XVI/37 (iii).

Note: Each of the main sections of this rondo is in binary form. Identify the type of binary form (sectional/continuous, simple/rounded) used in each section.

(Continued)

(Continued)

(Continued)

(Continued)

(Continued)

(Continued)

(Continued)

(Continued)

129

b. Mozart, Horn Quintet in E♭ major, K.407 (iii).
What is the form of measures 74–105?

(Continued)

(Continued)

(Continued)

(Continued)

(Continued)

(Continued)

(Continued)

(Continued)

(Continued)

(Continued)

(Continued)

(Continued)

(Continued)

(Continued)

(Continued)

112

118

(Continued)

(Continued)

(Continued)

(Continued)

(Continued)

(Continued)

(Continued)

(Continued)

(Continued)

PART 3: Form and Chromatic Harmony 2

c. Schumann, "Grillen" from *Phantasiestücke*. One of the sections of this rondo has a self-contained form. Begin by determining the form of measures 17–44; then determine how that section fits within the overall form of the piece.

(Continued)

(Continued)

(Continued)

(Continued)

(Continued)

(Continued)

(Continued)

(Continued)

22.2. Composition. Composing a rondo is similar to composing a piece in ternary form. The process is merely more extensive. Begin by composing a suitable refrain. As we have seen, the refrain should be a self-contained unit, beginning and ending in the tonic and ideally ending on a perfect authentic cadence. It might be easiest to construct the refrain as a parallel period.

Each appearance of the refrain can be a literal repetition, so once that is composed you can plan out the form of the piece as a whole. For example, if your refrain is 16 measures long, you could plan to fit episodes of a similar size in between. An outline of a five-part rondo (without transitions, retransitions, or coda) would thus look something like this:

A: Measures 1–16
B: Measures 17–32
A: Measures 33–48
C: Measures 49–64
A: Measures 65–80

Using notation software such as Finale or Sibelius, you can even "cut and paste" your refrains into the appropriate measures to save time.

Composing the episodes can be more of a challenge. They should be sufficiently different from the refrain to be recognized as contrasting material. As with the refrains, you should ideally plan the phrase structure in advance, so that the episodes have a logical shape and flow. The episodes should be in keys other than the tonic, and they should end in such a way that they lead smoothly into the refrains. You may want to facilitate this by adding suitable retransitions (note, however, that this may result in your needing to "shift" later refrain appearances in your score in order to make room for the extra measures).

Try to have your composition performed if possible.

22.3. Improvisation. A rondo can be fun to improvise. As a group, compose a simple melody to function as a refrain; as in the composition exercise above, this can be a parallel period, ending on a perfect authentic cadence. Sing or play this refrain as an ensemble—if singing, unison would be fine, or the group could be split so that some sing the melody and some sing a simple accompanying bass line.

The episodes can be improvised by soloists. One could start with an open-ended *rondeau*; the refrain and episodes could all be in the tonic, and episodes could be parallel periods like the refrain. The *rondeau* would then be performed as an alternating call-and-response between the ensemble refrain and solo episodes. Once this is mastered, you can make your improvised episodes more challenging with a little pre-planning: for example, vary the keys and determine a tonal structure. If your rondo is in a major key, the first episode could be in the dominant key, and the second episode in the relative minor.

Those who feel more comfortable with improvising can even improvise transitions and retransitions to and from their episodes, making sure that the transition would end on a half cadence in the key of the episode and the retransition would end on a half cadence in the tonic.

With two volunteers from the ensemble to improvise brief episodes, one can easily create a five-part (ABACA) rondo. If one desires more input from individuals, others could be asked to improvise the transitions and retransitions. (This would require those in charge of the episodes to actively listen for the half cadence in their key!) Above all, have fun.

CHAPTER 23

VARIATION FORMS

OVERVIEW

The principle of variation in music is found across cultures, genres, and historical eras, from the "Theme and Variations" form of Western art music to the process of improvising over a set of chord "changes" in jazz and the "composed improvisations" inherent in the performance of North Indian raga.

AUDIO LIST

Handel: Chaconne in G Major, HWV 435

Glass, "The Kuru Field of Justice," Act I, Scene 1 from *Satyagraha* (*Songs from the Trilogy* edit)

U2, "With or Without You"

Miles Davis, "Well You Needn't"

Beethoven, "Seven Variations on 'God Save the King,'" WoO 78

Charles Ives, "Variations on 'America'" (Hans-Ola Ericsson, organ)

King Oliver's Creole Jazz Band, "Dippermouth Blues" (*Louis Armstrong and King Oliver*)

John Mayall and Bluesbreakers with Eric Clapton, "Hideaway"

Fatboy Slim, "Right Here, Right Now" (single version, from *Why Try Harder: Greatest Hits*)

Hariprasad Chaurasia, "Raga Darbari Kanada"

INTRODUCTION

Perhaps when you were younger you enjoyed sitting down with a friend and playing melodies over the repeating progression shown in Example 23.1. This progression is sometimes called the "Heart and Soul" progression, after the song of the same name by Hoagy Carmichael, although it is found in countless other songs (including 1950s "doo-wop" songs). Improvising a variation over a fixed musical structure is one of the most universal forms of music making.

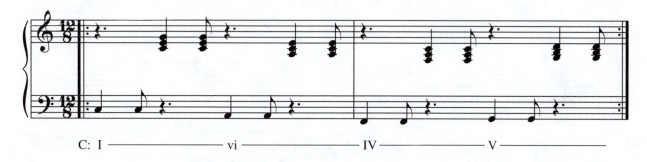

C: I —————————— vi —————————— IV ——————— V ———————

Example 23.1. A repeating descending-third root progression in C major.

CONTINUOUS VARIATIONS

In the performance of the accompaniment progression shown in Example 23.1, most likely whoever was playing the melodic line probably began with a fragment of Hoagy Carmichael's song "Heart and Soul" but went on to make up new melodic ideas that fit over the progression. This is an example of **continuous variations**; the melodic line does not ornament a fixed theme but continues with new ideas. The harmonic progression repeats, each phrase usually ending on V to propel the performance onward into another phrase (and another melodic variation).

Continuous variations are commonly associated with two Baroque genres—the **chaconne** and the **passacaglia**. Both of these terms are closely related and to some extent are interchangeable, sometimes merely evidence of the nationality or training of the composer (*chaconne* is a French word and *passacaglia* is Italian; adding to the confusion, both words have a Spanish origin). Generally, a *chaconne* refers to a set of continuous variations over a fixed (or slightly varied) *harmonic progression*, whereas the *passacaglia* is a set of variations over a fixed **basso ostinato** or repeating *bass line* (sometimes also called a **ground bass** or simply **ground**).

Example 23.2 shows the opening progression and three variations (out of twenty-one) from Handel's Chaconne in G major, HWV 435, published in 1733. This set of variations is based on a harmonic progression that was commonplace for Baroque variation forms (J. S. Bach used an almost identical progression for his celebrated *Goldberg Variations*).

Example 23.2. Handel, Chaconne in G major, HWV 435 (G 239), theme and variations 1, 5, and 14. *(Continued)*

(Continued)

Var. 5.

I   CS   I⁶   IV   V

PAC

Var. 14.

g: i   v   iv   V

i i   iv P iv⁶ i ii°⁶₅ V i

Comparing the theme and variations in Example 23.2, the progression is not identical for each variation; very closely related chord substitutions (for example, vii^{o6}/V instead of V_3^4/V or ii^6 instead of IV) are occasionally used. Each progression ends with an authentic cadence, which suggests, harmonically, that this piece at least has more of a "sectional" than "continuous" character. Melodically these three Handel variations do not seem to share much in common beyond the underlying harmonic framework; in other words, even though the piece begins with a designated "theme," the actual "theme" is the *harmonic progression* rather than the opening melodic line.

Variation 14 is in the parallel minor, G minor, one of eight (variations 9 through 16) in that key. It was common for Baroque and Classical variation forms to have at least one variation that would change mode to the parallel major or minor key.

Since Handel's "Chaconne" is based on a fixed harmonic progression, it is—superficially, at least—not all that different from our two kids jamming on the "Heart and Soul" progression. Why is it that some improvisations have a towering, inevitable quality about them, bringing the listener along to an inexorable climactic point in the performance, while others meander aimlessly, seemingly marking time? Granted, Example 23.2 shows only three of Handel's twenty-one variations, but they vary considerably in texture, range, and rhythmic density. Let's look at two contemporary approaches to the problem of generating interest when there is no variety in the harmonic progression, phrase lengths, and/or the bass line.

Contemporary Chaconne no. 1: Philip Glass, "Kuru Field of Justice"

Philip Glass's "Kuru Field of Justice" (from the opera *Satyagraha*) is based on an arpeggiated harmonic progression of i–VII–VI–V in F minor.[1] In the passages scored for low strings (such as at the beginning) the progression is found in root position, but interestingly in the passages scored for winds Glass writes the arpeggios in two-part contrary motion, with the progression as i–VII^6–VI_4^6–V_2^4 (2:00–2:09) or as i^6–VII^6–VI^6–V [2:19–2:28]. There are four related melodic "skeletons," shown in Example 23.3; the second (labeled *b*) is developed from the first two notes of the first (labeled *a*), while the third (labeled *c*) uses the first three notes of *b*. The fourth melody is based more closely on the bass line of the harmonic progression, first in parallel thirds with the progression's root motion and then doubling it.

---

[1]A full-length version of "Kuru Field of Justice" appears on the recording of Glass's opera *Satyagraha* (CBS M3K 39672, 1985), where it is Act I, Scene 1. An edited version appears on the compilation *Songs from the Trilogy* (CBS MK 45580, 1989). Because this edited version is available as an online download, the timings in this section refer to the *Songs from the Trilogy* version.

Example 23.3. Melodic structure of Glass, "Kuru Field of Justice."

In contrast to the static harmonic progression, the meter constantly changes in Glass's piece. Table 23.1 summarizes the metric variation in the first 3:18 of the song. Overall, the meter expands from $\frac{5}{8}$ to $\frac{9}{8}$. (In the full-length version, there is a climactic choral entry with a meter of $\frac{17}{8}$, subdivided as 4+3+3+3+2+2!).

TABLE 23.1. **Metric variation in Philip Glass, "The Kuru Fields of Justice" (*Songs from the Trilogy* edit) [0:00–3:18].**

Section (timing)	Meter (number of measures)
0:00–0:13	$\frac{5}{8}$ (3), $\frac{3}{4}$ (1)—repeated 2 times
0:13–0:26	$\frac{3}{4}$ (8)
0:26–0:37	$\frac{5}{8}$ (3), $\frac{3}{4}$ (1)—repeated 2 times
0:37–0:50	$\frac{3}{4}$ (8)
0:50–1:06	$\frac{7}{8}$ (8)
1:06–1:25	$\frac{9}{8}$ (subdivided 4+3+2) (8)
1:25–1:59	$\frac{4}{4}$ (16)
1:59–2:26	$\frac{9}{8}$ (subdivided 4+3+2) (12)
2:26–2:50	$\frac{4}{4}$—(12)
2:51–3:18	$\frac{9}{8}$ (subdivided 3+3+3) (12)

Contemporary Chaconne no. 2: U2, "With or Without You"

Entire pop songs may be built on the repetition of a simple chord progression. This is the case with U2's "With or Without You," which uses register and dynamics quite effectively even as the harmonic parameter remains largely static.

After a nine-second introduction prolonging the tonic chord, the progression of I–V–vi–IV in D major begins, heard twice before the entrance of U2's lead singer Bono's vocals. The melodic contours throughout "With or Without You" are shown in Example 23.4.

Example 23.4. U2, "With or Without You" melodic contours. *(Continued)*

(Continued)

Chorus A' (1:26)

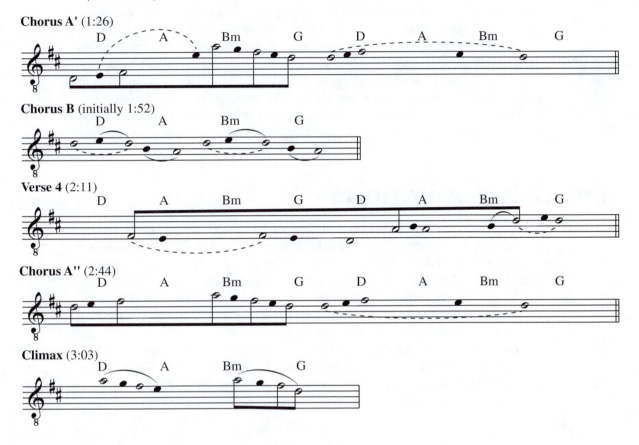

Chorus B (initially 1:52)

Verse 4 (2:11)

Chorus A'' (2:44)

Climax (3:03)

Apply This!
23.1 and 23.2
may be done
at this time.

The first three verses are low in register and fairly limited in range, centered around the notes D3, E3, and F#3. The first appearance of the title phrase [1:00], which we will call Chorus A, consists exclusively of the same three pitches, but on its second appearance [Chorus A′, 1:26] Bono jumps up an octave into his falsetto range and finishes the chorus an octave higher.

The brief instrumental interlude that follows is distinguished by the strong appearance of drums and a chiming guitar riff, introducing Chorus B ("and you give yourself away") at 1:52. This chorus is higher in register (the range is A3 to D4). Verse 4 [2:11–2:28] begins in the same range as the previous verses but doesn't stay there for long; at 2:20–2:27, the melodic line climbs back up to D4.

When Chorus A returns [Chorus A′, 2:44], it is now an octave higher. All the while, the texture has grown more assertive and the dynamic has grown louder, until the climax, a full-voice "oh" from A4 down to D4 [3:03–3:21]. Unlike the other vocal phrases, which lead into the beginning of the repeated chord progression (adding to the "continuing" effect of this continuous variation), the climax vocal begins *on* the first chord of the progression, adding to its impact.

Following the climax, the progression momentarily pauses on the tonic chord from 3:39 to 4:04, as haunting wordless falsetto vocals reach as high as D5. Following this, the four-chord progression returns for an instrumental coda until the fade-out.

Aside from the opening nine seconds and the post-climax "pause" from 3:39 to 4:04, the harmonic progression of I–V–vi–IV never changes; the bass guitar plays the root of each chord in steady eighth notes throughout. Unlike Glass's "Kuru Field of Justice," the meter never changes. Interest over the course of the song is sustained by gradually increasing dynamics, an increase in syncopation within the texture (heard in the snare drum and guitar), and—especially—a steady rise in register and increase in range.

Workbook Exercise 23.2 may be done at this time.

SECTIONAL VARIATIONS

Another common variation form is **sectional variations**, variations clearly divided into self-contained structural units that build upon one another. The most common sectional variation form in common-practice art music is the **theme and variations** form, in which a theme (usually ending with a perfect authentic cadence) is the basis for any number of variations based on the theme's melodic and harmonic structure. Unlike the chaconne or passacaglia, which are based on a *harmonic* progression or bass line, each variation is *melodic*, based on the original theme.

Beethoven's "Seven Variations on 'God Save the King'" was composed in 1802–1803 (the melody is also known to Americans as "America" or "My Country, T'is of Thee"). Beethoven's setting of the theme, cast in sectional simple binary form, is shown in Example 23.5a. We shall consider three of the seven variations that follow.

Example 23.5a. Beethoven, "Seven Variations on 'God Save the King,'" WoO 78, theme.

Variation 2 (Example 23.5b) is an **ornamental variation** of the theme, in which the melody is elaborated with non-chord tones (see if you can find where the original theme is "hiding" in the texture). The harmonization of the melody is quite similar to the theme, although there are some differences (compare the eighth measure of each, for example).

Example 23.5b. Beethoven, "Seven Variations on 'God Save the King,'" WoO 78, Variation 2.

Variation 4 (Example 23.5c) is the midpoint in the seven variations, and so Beethoven has arranged for this variation to be the most "distant" from the opening theme. (Can you find the opening theme's melody in the texture?)

Example 23.5c. Beethoven, "Seven Variations on 'God Save the King,'" WoO 78, Variation 4.

Variation 6 (Example 23.5d) bears the tempo marking "Alla Marcia" (in march style). Here the theme is substantially unchanged and easy to find in the texture—what is changed, however, is its *presentation*. Sometimes Classic-era variations refer to other genres, such as a military march or an operatic aria. By changing the *style* in which the theme appears, the result is a **character variation**—the theme takes on a different "character."[2]

Example 23.5d. Beethoven, "Seven Variations on 'God Save the King,'" WoO 78, Variation 6. *(Continued)*

---

[2] The Beatles' "You Know My Name (Look up the Number)," found on *Anthology 2* (Apple/EMI CDP 7243 8 34448 2 3, 1996) is an excellent example of character variation in rock. After a brief introduction (0:00–0:17), the theme is presented in a driving, "heavy" rock style (0:17–1:06). The first variation (1:06–2:16), with its offbeat saxophones and loping beat, might be described as '60s-era ska (a more uptempo forerunner of reggae). The second variation (2:16–3:49) is characterized by a mambo rhythm and a "lounge-singer" vocal. A "soft-shoe" variation follows with a stride piano accompaniment and ocarinas (3:49–4:28), and then there is a "jazz" variation with a swung rhythm, open-to-closed hi hat hits, a sparse "comping" piano reminiscent of Count Basie, and gruff nonsensical scat singing (4:29–5:18). The ensemble is joined by a saxophone solo and vibraphone for the jazz-styled coda (5:18–5:43). All this, even though the lyrics to the song are no more than the title of the song.

(Continued)

This set of variations ends with a lengthy coda (thirty-seven measures) that in fact contains an eighth variation of the theme before it concludes.

The *Variations on "America"* by Charles Ives (1874–1954), written when the composer was still a teenager, presents a very different approach to variation using the same tune. With the CD timings in this discussion[3] you should be able to follow along.

The piece begins with a fanfare-like introduction in ternary form [0:00–1:11], the outer *A* sections developing the first phrase of the theme and the *B* section developing the second. The theme that follows [1:11–2:00] is given a quiet, simple chorale-like treatment. Unlike Beethoven's setting of the theme, there are no repeats of phrases.

The first variation [2:00–3:04] is ornamental, with the theme in the left hand and the right hand given over to a florid countermelody of mostly chromatic sixteenth and thirty-second notes. This time Ives repeats the second phrase, so this variation is in bar form (ABB). This is followed by an altogether darker, more dissonant five-part setting [3:04–4:05] characterized by descending chromatic lines in an imitative texture.

---

[3] Timings refer to the recording by Hans-Ola Ericsson found on *Organ Music from the USA* (BIS 510, 1993).

A bitonal interlude comes next, with the right hand playing the theme in F major and the left hand in imitation in D♭ major, the ♭VI of F [4:05–4:36]. The interlude has the function of setting apart the section that follows (Variations 3 and 4) from those that came before. In the third and fourth variations, Ives changes his approach; these are in more of a character variation style. The third variation [4:37–5:30] is in the key of D♭ major, a key foreshadowed by the bitonal interlude; its prevailing style might be described as a carnival waltz in $\frac{6}{8}$; the accompaniment features a distinctive motive of $\hat{5}$ modified with a chromatic lower neighbor (A♭–G–A♭). The theme is played twice in this variation, a left-hand countermelody added to the second time. The fourth variation [5:31–6:27] is in F minor, iii of D♭ major and the parallel minor of the tonic; this one is marked by Ives as a "Polonaise" (a rather stately dance in triple time with the distinctive repeated rhythmic motive of an eighth note, two sixteenth notes, and four eighth notes). Like the first variation, Ives repeats the second phrase, so once again it is in bar form.

Before the fifth and final variation there is another bitonal interlude [6:27–6:45], which in its tonal organization is something of a mirror image of the first—this time the left hand is in F major and the right hand is in A♭ major, the ♭III of F.

The final variation [6:45–7:48] is marked "Allegro—as fast as the pedals can go"; Ives famously remarked that playing the pedal variation was "almost as much fun as playing baseball." This is a return to the ornamental variation style; although the theme is presented fairly straightforwardly, the bass line is obviously ornamented a great deal. The theme is heard twice; the ending of the second playing is extended with chromatic development, bringing the listener to the coda [7:49–8:57] and the return of the fanfare motive.

Though not a perfect mirror form, Ives's *Variations on "America"* does have a quasi-symmetrical structure; the first pair of ornamental variations balances a second pair in character variation style. Between these is a bitonal interlude in F major over D♭ major (a tonal relationship of I over ♭VI); this interlude is balanced by a second bitonal interlude in A♭ major over F major (a tonal relationship of ♭III over I), separating the two character variations from the return of the ornamental style. The piece is also framed by an introduction and a coda.

LEVEL MASTERY 23.1.

On the following pages you will find Mozart's Twelve Variations on "Ah, vous dirais-je, Maman" (the same tune as "Twinkle, Twinkle, Little Star"). Is this an example of continuous variation or sectional variation? Briefly comment on the relation of each variation to the theme—do some variations appear to be more closely related to the theme than others? Which ones? Also, consider the relation of one variation to the next. What elements are retained from one variation to the next? What elements are changed?

(Continued)

PART 3: Form and Chromatic Harmony 2

(Continued)

(Continued)

(Continued)

PART 3: Form and Chromatic Harmony 2

(Continued)

(Continued)

(Continued)

(Continued)

(Continued)

(Continued)

(Continued)

(Continued)

(Continued)

PART 3: Form and Chromatic Harmony 2

(Continued)

(Continued)

(Continued)

(Continued)

(Continued)

(Continued)

(Continued)

Self-Tests 23.1 and 23.2 may be done at this time.

JAZZ IMPROVISATION AS VARIATION

The process of melodic transformation that occurs in a theme and variations is similar to improvising on a "standard" in jazz. For our example we will use Thelonious Monk's composition "Well You Needn't," since we studied it as an example of song form in Chapter 20. At this time we can consider what Davis does in the remainder of his performance.

The opening presentation of Monk's theme [0:00–1:01] is referred to as the **head** of the composition, corresponding to the "theme" in a theme and variations. Each of the solos that follow—by Davis and by pianist Horace Silver—are variations using the **changes**, or underlying harmonic structure, of Monk's composition, as well as certain motives found in the head. Each complete set of changes is a discrete structural unit, referred to as a **chorus**. After the head, Davis solos for two choruses. The first chorus [1:01–2:03] is shown in Example 23.6.[4]

―――――――――

[4] Web Feature 12.2 uses this passage to examine Davis's use of motives derived from Monk's theme in his improvisation.

Example 23.6. Transcription of first solo (Davis) in Miles Davis's recording of Thelonious Monk's "Well You Needn't."

Davis's second chorus [2:04–3:06] is shown in Example 23.7. It is useful to compare the two. Are there any similarities or do they appear to be completely different?

Example 23.7. Transcription of second solo (Davis) in Miles Davis's recording of Thelonious Monk's "Well You Needn't."

The third chorus [3:07–4:09, shown in Example 23.8] is a piano solo by Silver; note the playful quote from "Pop! Goes the Weasel" at measures 13–16 [3:31–3:38].

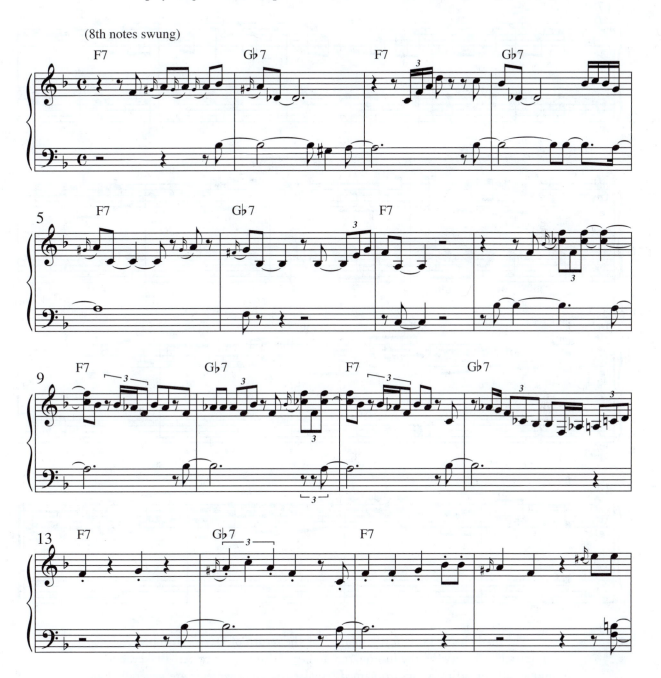

Example 23.8. Transcription of third solo (Silver) in Miles Davis's recording of Thelonious Monk's "Well You Needn't." *(Continued)*

Workbook
Exercise 23.3
may be done
at this time.

The final chorus [4:10–5:10], marked by the return of Davis's trumpet, features an interchange between the full quartet and brief drum solos by Art Blakey, a technique called **trading fours** (so named because the solo segments are generally four measures in length). Passages of trading fours are common in the final variation, or chorus, of a jazz performance. The performance ends with a brief coda [5:11–5:24], repeating the last motivic fragment of Monk's tune.

TWELVE-BAR BLUES

The twelve-bar blues form is also a common template for variation. The standard form is twelve measures divided into three four-bar phrases; if there is a text, the words often follow an AAB form (the first line is repeated, followed by a rhyming concluding line). The most basic harmonic progression for the twelve-bar blues is as follows:

(measure)	1	2	3	4
	I	—	—	—
	5	6	7	8
	IV	—	I	—
	9	10	11	12
	V	—	I	—

WEBSITE

Other variants of the blues progression are found even in some of the earliest recorded blues. See Web Feature 23.1.

This pattern is so associated with the blues that it is often referred to as the **blues progression**. Several variants of this pattern exist. The most common variation involves a movement to IV on measure 10, resulting in a V–IV retrogression. Other variants include moving to IV on measure 2 and back to I in measure 3, or a so-called "turnaround" that moves quickly through a circle-of-fifths progression in the last two measures. The progression below incorporates all of these variants.

(measure)	1	2	3	4		
	I	IV	—	—		
	5	6	7	8		
	IV	—	I	—		
	9	10	11	12		
	V	IV	I	vi	ii	V

Melodically, the blues may involve either the major or minor form of the **pentatonic** scale or the so-called **blues scale**. The term *pentatonic* is used to describe any scale with five pitches per octave; the **major pentatonic scale** is built on scale degrees 1, 2, 3, 5, and 6. Rotating these pitches to start on scale degree 6 (and thus in the relative minor) gives us the **minor pentatonic scale**, which uses scale degrees 1, 3, 4, 5, and 7 of the natural minor scale. Adding a chromatic passing tone to the minor pentatonic scale, between scale degrees 4 and 5, gives us the most common variety of the blues scale. All of these scales are shown in Example 23.9. In performance, the differences between these scales may blur, especially since blues playing often relies on "bent" notes as an expressive device.

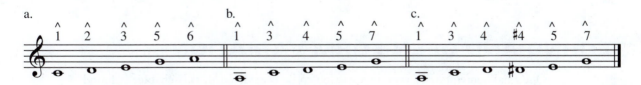

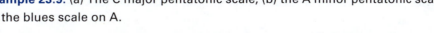

Example 23.9. (a) The C major pentatonic scale; (b) the A minor pentatonic scale; (c) the blues scale on A.

A performance of the blues usually involves the repetition of the blues progression over several choruses, often in a mixture of fixed material (such as sung verses or the head of a jazz composition in twelve-bar-blues form) and improvised passages (solos over the blues progression). The process resembles continuous variation in that the improvised passages usually are not ornamental variations of an opening theme. Freddie King's "Hideaway," as performed by John Mayall and the Bluesbreakers (featuring a young Eric Clapton on guitar), provides an excellent example of how "composed" (if not notated) and improvised passages coexist within the same blues-based variation form. It can be broken down as follows:

Chorus 1 [0:00–0:21]: "Theme," distinguished by five-note lead-in motive

Chorus 2 [0:21–0:42]: Improvised solo by Clapton

Chorus 3 [0:42–1:01]: An eight-note riff played by the full band, and repeated in sequence with each chord change

Chorus 4 [1:02–1:22]: Improvised solo by Clapton

Chorus 5 [1:22–1:43]: Improvised solo, begun with dramatic "stop time" hits on I, IV and I in the first four measures (Clapton's melodic material in this portion is likely worked out beforehand)

Chorus 6 [1:43–2:05] A new riff played by the full band in straight (rather than shuffled) eighth notes, sequenced similarly to the riff in Chorus 3

Chorus 7 [2:05–2:26] Improvised solo by Clapton

Chorus 8 [2:26–2:48] Improvised solo by Clapton continues

Chorus 9 [2:48–3:12] Return of the opening "theme" with its five-note lead-in motive, an octave higher than its first appearance; closing cadence

Apply This!
23.3 may
be done at
this time.

Workbook
Exercise 23.4
may be done
at this time.

The blues progression is found in innumerable rock and jazz songs, as well as some country songs (such as Hank Williams's "Move It On Over" and Johnny Cash's "Folsom Prison Blues"). Altered or expanded versions of twelve-bar blues form are also found in a number of rock songs. For example, the Doors' "Riders on the Storm" is a minor-key twelve-bar blues that substitutes VII and VI for the V and IV in measures 9 and 10. U2's "I Still Haven't Found What I'm Looking For" is made up of a twenty-four-bar expanded blues progression; the verses (sixteen measures) repeat the first eight bars of the blues progression, retaining and repeating the final four bars for the refrain. That the song does not stylistically resemble a blues only confirms how thoroughly the blues progression and blues forms have permeated much rock music.

TECHNO AND OPEN-FORM VARIATION

One final contemporary type of variation to be considered in this chapter is found in techno and other forms of electronic dance music. This genre has many different styles, but here we might make note of some of its common features.

First, the instrumentation is largely electronic, making use of drum machines, synthesizers, and samples of previous recordings, arranged or **sequenced** into repeating grooves called **loops**. In its purest or most "minimal" form techno may be based on only one such loop, one repeating harmonic progression (or even one chord). Variation, in this case, is achieved by changes of *texture*—adding or subtracting various **tracks** or individual layers of sound. In live performance, a DJ (abbreviated for "disc jockey," a now-archaic reference to broadcasters who would artfully sequence phonograph records on their radio programs) will add or subtract these layers by mixing in a rather improvised fashion, creating lengthy **sets** of multiple songs by matching tempos of different recordings and segueing one song into the next. Thus, a **remix** (the term for a newly created mix) is a fluid musical form, and DJs frequently create new mixes of others' work.

"Right Here, Right Now" (1999) by British DJ Fatboy Slim (a.k.a. Norman Cook) illustrates several formal and stylistic aspects of techno. The bulk of the song makes use of three different string orchestra samples from The James Gang song "Ashes, the Rain, and I" (1970). Harmonically the entire song is based on a progression of | i | VII$_{(A \text{ ped.})}$ IV$^6_4$|, a pedal prolongation of the tonic; texturally, however, there is constant variation. The formal summary below is based on the edited version of "Right Here, Right Now" found on the 2006 compilation *Why Try Harder*.

CD TIMING	BRIEF TEXTURAL DESCRIPTION	PHRASE LENGTH[5]
0:00–0:14	progressive filter opening, string loop 1, crescendo	8 bars
0:14	string loop 1 addition of acoustic guitar and sitar sounds	4 bars
0:24	string loop 2, addition of acoustic guitars and sitars	8 bars
0:38	vocal sample ("Right here, right now") crescendo	8 bars
0:54	string loop 2, drum machine loop	16 bars
1:24	cut-up vocal sample, drum machine loop (strings out)	4
1:32	string loop 2, drum machine loop	8
1:48	string loop 3	8
2:03	cut-up vocal	4
2:12	added turntable scratches, drum machine loop	4
2:18	string loop 1	8
2:34	string loop 2	8
2:49	string loop 3, "Right here, right now" vocal sample	8
3:04	"here" echo, pedal C	4
3:12	string loop 2, drum machine loop	4
3:20	add cut-up vocal sample	4
3:28	string sample 3, "Right here, right now" vocal sample	8
3:43	"here" echo, bass pedal C, fade out	6

---

[5] The phrase length is based on a primary pulse stream of 160 beats per minute in $\frac{4}{4}$ meter.

Although many techno songs are based on a single loop or harmonic progression, it would be somewhat inaccurate to label them as modern-day chaconnes or passacaglias. More popular, "crossover" variants of the style can involve alternation of two different loops in formal sections, analogous to the verse and chorus in a pop song (Fatboy Slim's "Praise You" and the Orb's "Little Fluffy Clouds," discussed in Chapter 20, are examples of this approach). Because certain instruments, vocals, or even entire sections of a song can be omitted, extended, or rearranged in a remix, it would be appropriate to call techno a kind of **open-form variation**. Arguably there is no "original version" of such a work—the version of "Right Here, Right Now" that appears on Fatboy Slim's 1999 album *You've Come a Long Way, Baby* may itself be a later version of some unreleased form of the song, and even after its edited single release a number of official and "bootleg" (unauthorized) remixes of the song have also been made, not counting Cook's own live performances (and live remixes) of the song. There are also numerous remixes of "Little Fluffy Clouds," made by the Orb and by others. In a sense, this is no longer a variation "form" but rather a *process* of variation that is itself potentially endlessly variable.

VARIATION AS A PROCESS: NORTH INDIAN RAGA

Another expression of variation as a process, rather than as a fixed form, is found in the performance of ragas in Indian music. In Chapter 2 you were introduced to some South Indian (or Carnatic) ragas, which were presented as examples of scales. A raga in performance is much more than a scale, however. Each raga also consists of characteristic melodic turns and motives, so that two ragas can share the same scalar pitch material but be entirely different from each other in performance. Moreover, each performance of a particular raga is also likely to be different, as those distinctive melodic turns are developed in different ways during performance through improvisation. Ragas embody variation in perhaps its purest form—a musician can spend years of study (and many do) mastering all the nuances of a single raga.

Example 23.10 shows the scalar source material for *Raga Darbari Kanada,* an older North Indian (Hindustani) raga dating back to at least the seventeenth century. Note that the ascending form of the scale resembles the Western natural minor scale; the third and sixth scale degrees (*Ga* and *Dha*, respectively), however, are not only flatter than Western tuning but are also characteristically treated with a slow, subtle vibrato. Notice also that the skeletal structure of the descent is not a direct descending scale; this type of raga is called a *vakra* ("crooked") raga. The specifics of the descent—where to change direction, and on which pitches—are part of the nuances of this particular raga, usually passed on from teacher to student by ear. Listening to and comparing a number of recordings of this raga will give you a better understanding of just how variable it is.

~ indicates wide, ornamental vibrato

Example 23.10. An overview of *Raga Darbari Kanada*.

A typical performance of a raga begins with an unmetered improvisation called an *alap*; every *alap* is different, and some *alap* performances may last for several minutes. It is in this opening section that the content and distinctive features of the raga are revealed only gradually to the audience. *Raga Darbari Kanada* has several distinctive features, such as the wide ornamental vibrato on certain notes (shown in Example 23.10) and the winding contour of its descent; because the actual pitch content of *Raga Darbari Kanada* is shared with several other ragas, ornamentation and melodic arrangement are very important. Thus, a savvy listener may be able to identify the raga from hearing it even before the complete scale is revealed.

This raga is associated with music of a slow, solemn nature, and it is characteristically performed at midnight. The rules and traditions of performing a raga, handed down from master to student over many generations, can be regarded as a kind of living variation—each performance is a variation on the raga.

An approximate and simplified comparative transcription of the first two minutes of three different performances in *Raga Darbari Kanada* is shown in Example 23.11. The top staff is a vocal performance by the Dagar Brothers; the middle staff is a performance on the *bansuri* (a bamboo flute) by Hariprasad Chaurasia; the bottom staff is a performance on the *sarod* (a lute-like instrument) by Vilayat Khan.[6] Each "measure" corresponds to five seconds of music, and two of the performances have been transposed to a D tonic for easier comparison. For space reasons much of the intricate ornaments and glides between pitches have been omitted; also omitted is the *tamboura* drone instrument and (in Vilayat Khan's performance) the striking of drone strings. Collectively the three performances show an overall descending trajectory, with considerable variation in the rate at which new notes of the raga are introduced (these are marked with arrows and Indian scale degree names). It is also evident that Vilayat Khan's performance is the "busiest" in terms of ornamentation and contour, whereas Hariprasad Chaurasia's performance is the "simplest" with minimal ornamentation.

---

[6] Dagar Brothers, *Music of India Volume 5*, EMI His Master's Voice EALP 1921 (1965); Hariprasad Chaurasia, *Raga Darbari Kanada and Dhun in Mishra Pilu*, Nimbus NIM 5365 (2006); Vilayat Khan, *The Supreme Genius of Ustad Vilayat Khan*, EMI EASD 1332 (1968).

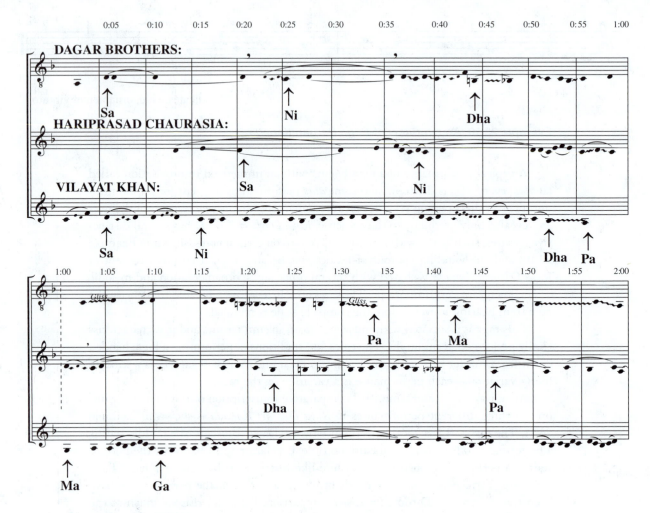

Example 23.11. A comparative transcription of three different performances of *Raga Darbari Kanada*.

Self-Test 23.3 may be done at this time.

The variability of these performances might imply that they are "improvised" in the way a blues guitarist might improvise a solo (as in Eric Clapton's performance of "Hideaway"). However, Indian musicians consider the *alap* to be an individual *composition* that is realized in a specific performance.

CONCLUSION

In our survey of variation we have covered a broad swath of terrain. We have seen that North Indian raga performance is an ongoing process of variation of a particular collection and ordering of pitches (sometimes arranged in a scale, sometimes not). In common-practice Western art music, variation sometimes occurs over a recurring bass line or harmonic progression, sometimes as progressively ornamented versions of a theme, and sometimes by setting a theme in various stylistic contexts. In contemporary popular genres such as techno, which are heavily dependent on studio recording technology, variation by adding or subtracting layers of texture is commonplace, a compositional technique shared by certain varieties of minimalism (to be examined in Chapter 30).

Once again as we consider each of these possibilities we are drawn to parametric analysis. In analyzing a variation form, it can be useful to determine which parameters remain unchanged from variation to variation and which parameters are changed (and how they are changed). You will get better at this with practice, because to a certain extent such analysis depends on **stylistic competency**—the degree of familiarity with the norms of a given genre. For example, an audience member during the Classic era would more likely recognize a reference to a military march or a vocal aria during a set of variations performed on piano than a modern-day listener; a fan of techno would be more likely to recognize subtle changes in the percussive texture than a jazz aficionado who might notice only that the harmonic progression (if there is one) is extremely repetitive. The versatile musician will develop a set of working stylistic competencies for a variety of musical genres.

Terms to Know

basso ostinato	ground bass (ground)	remix (in techno)
blues progression	head (in jazz)	sectional variations
blues scale	loop (in techno)	sequence (in techno)
chaconne	major pentatonic scale	stylistic competency
changes (in jazz)	minor pentatonic scale	theme and variations
character variations	open-form variation	track (in techno)
chorus (in jazz)	ornamental variations	trading fours (in jazz)
continuous variations	passacaglia	twelve-bar blues

Self-Test

23.1. Below is the melodic line for Harry Dacre's song "Daisy Bell" (also known as "A Bicycle Built for Two"). Using this melody as your point of departure, compose three *ornamental variations* on this theme. You should begin by determining a rudimentary harmonization for the tune. In the first variation, elaborate the melodic line primarily with passing tones. In the second variation, use appoggiaturas and escape tones. Finally, in the third variation, use suspensions. For the sake of simplicity, try to use the same harmonization for each variation.

(Continued)

(Continued)

23.2. Briefly describe the difference(s) between a chaconne and a passacaglia. Then consider the four variations (out of a total of thirty-two) by Beethoven below. Even though this piece would be an example of sectional variations—because the variations are clearly demarcated—the variations do not appear to have much melodic resemblance to the theme. Instead, based on the variations you see below, do these variations appear to be closer in style to a chaconne or a passacaglia? What features in the music lead you to your conclusion?

Beethoven, Thirty-Two Variations on an Original Theme, WoO 80, theme and variations 1, 4, 7, and 25.

(Continued)

(Continued)

(Continued)

(Continued)

23.3. In the same manner as the analysis of Fatboy Slim's "Right Here, Right Now" found in this chapter, examine how changes of texture help to define form and create interest in Daft Punk's "Around the World" (original version on *Homework*, released in 2001; a "radio edit" is available through digital download services such as iTunes). Try to isolate different layers, or tracks, in the mix and label them (as many of these sounds are electronic in origin, you need not be specific as to "instrumentation"—a label descriptive of the sound would suffice). You may prepare an analysis in table format with CD timings, as was done in this chapter, or you might find it instructive to show your findings in bar graph style (let the *x* axis represent time, measured in CD timings or perceived measures; the *y* axis will represent sound layers, arranged from lowest to highest).

Apply This!

23.1. Analysis: Bach, Cantata no. 78, *Jesu, der du meine Seele*, BWV 78 (i). You will find the score to the complete movement (in piano-vocal reduction) at the end of this chapter. It is an example of continuous variation, due to the presence of a ground bass theme, the open (half) cadences at the end of each phrase, and the "lead-in" rhythmic activity frequently found at the ends of phrases. Isolate and label the ground bass theme, and locate its appearances throughout the piece. Is it always in the bass? Is it always in the tonic? (If not, in what other keys does it appear, and are those keys closely related to the tonic?) Is the ground bass varied in any way during the course of the composition, and if so, how is it varied?

23.2. Composition. In this chapter we learned that the harmonic progression in Handel's Chaconne in G Major was a common "stock progression" used for many compositions in the Baroque era. Using a variant of the same progression—

$$\|: I \mid V^6 \mid vi \mid V^4_3/V \mid V \mid I^6 \mid ii^6 \mid V \mid I :\|$$

—compose several variations of your own.

23.3. Improvisation. Two ideas for improvisation follow.

a. Using the same progression found in the composition exercise above, try *improvising* several melodic lines of your own, either accompanying yourself at the keyboard or with the assistance of a friend or classmate who can accompany you. If you are a singer, sing on a neutral syllable such as "la" or "ah" rather than using words. (Note to the accompanist: Do not play the same chord voicings over and over, but experiment with various voicings, registers, and textures.) Listen to and respond to each other.

b. The twelve-bar blues progression is one of the most common harmonic templates for improvisation. With a partner, improvise to a blues progression. If you are a singer, sing on a neutral syllable such as "la" or "ah"—or try improvising your own rhyming couplets in an AAB form. If you are an instrumental soloist, take turns soloing on each chorus with your partner. Experiment with the major or minor pentatonic scale, or the blues scale. Try to give your improvised lines a sense of goal direction, anticipating the chord changes and ensuring that your melodic line leads to those new chords.

Bach, Chorus I from Cantata no. 78, *Jesu, der du meine Seele*, BWV 78.

(Continued)

(Continued)

(Continued)

(Continued)

PART 3: Form and Chromatic Harmony 2

(Continued)

(Continued)

(Continued)

(Continued)

(Continued)

(Continued)

(Continued)

(Continued)

(Continued)

(Continued)

(Continued)

(Continued)

(Continued)

(Continued)

(Continued)

(Continued)

(Continued)

(Continued)

(Continued)

CHAPTER 24

CHROMATICISM 1
The Neapolitan Chord and Augmented Sixth Chords

OVERVIEW

Building on our previous consideration of mode mixture and non-chord tones, this chapter address some common chromatic alterations that occur in common-practice music: the Neapolitan (♭II) sixth chord and augmented sixth chords.

We have seen that music exists in two dimensions: the "vertical" dimension resulting from the structure of simultaneous tones into harmony, and the "horizontal" or linear dimension, allowing each part of a chord to also function as a note in a melodic strand. We have also seen how chords may be chromatically altered through mode mixture (borrowing from the parallel minor or major), a process that changes the quality of a chord without changing its function. Chords may be chromatically altered in other ways, however. For example, consider what can be done to the following simple I–ii⁶–V–I progression in F major:

Through mode mixture, we can make the ii⁶ a diminished ii°⁶, as shown below:

We can also alter the second chord still further by lowering the *root* of the chord. This chord, a major triad built on the chromatically lowered second scale degree, is called a ♭**II** or **Neapolitan** chord. Play the progression below and compare it to the previous two.

Like the ii chords from which it is derived, this chord has a predominant (PD) function; it is usually found in first inversion, as the whole-step melodic motion from the fourth to fifth scale degree in the bass is much smoother than an augmented fourth up or diminished fifth down (the 4–5–1 bass motion is, of course, also found in the common ii⁶–V–I and IV–V–I progressions). The first-inversion variety of this chord is often referred to as the **Neapolitan sixth chord** (abbreviated **N⁶**). The "Neapolitan" label is derived from the harmony's association with eighteenth-century Italian Neapolitan opera; the chord's origins are in fact uncertain, but by the end of the eighteenth century its use was well established.

Example 24.1 shows a prominent N⁶ in Mozart's famous "Queen of the Night" Aria ("Der Hölle Rache kocht in meinem Herzen") from *The Magic Flute*. The first phrase quickly establishes the D minor tonality with a passing prolongation of the tonic (measures 1–6); the N⁶ arrives dramatically at measure 9, resolving to V in the following measure. Compare this chord with the other first-inversion E♭ major chord found in measure 7. Remember, a Neapolitan chord resolves with a root motion of a tritone to the V (although, of course, a cadential ⁶₄ chord can be used to soften the change); in contrast, the chord in measure 7 is part of an extended tonicization of G minor, for which the first-inversion E♭ major chord acts as VI⁶ (the progression can be read as VI⁶–vii°⁶–i⁶ in G minor).

Example 24.1. Mozart, "Der Hölle Rache kocht in meinem Herzen" from *The Magic Flute*, mm. 1–10. *(Continued)*

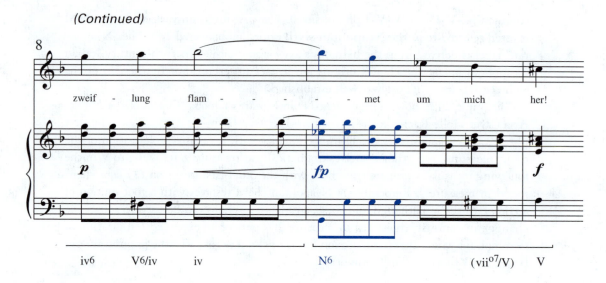

(Continued)

iv6   V6/iv   iv   N6   (vii°7/V)   V

TRANSLATION: The revenge of Hell cooks in my heart,
                Death and despair flame about me!

SPELLING THE NEAPOLITAN SIXTH CHORD, AND SPECIAL ISSUES IN DOUBLING

The Neapolitan chord is more common in minor keys (and arguably more expressively effective, as Example 24.1 shows). In minor keys the chord requires only the lowered root (second scale degree). In major keys, however, remember to lower both the root (second scale degree) *and* fifth (sixth scale degree) in order to retain the chord's major quality (Example 24.2).

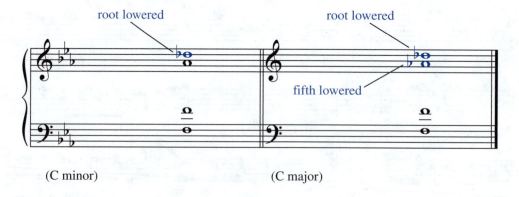

root lowered   root lowered

                      fifth lowered

(C minor)   (C major)

Example 24.2. Neapolitan sixth chords in both C minor and C major.

Resolution of the Neapolitan chord in a four-part texture normally follows a distinctive voice-leading pattern. Because the root of the Neapolitan chord is chromatically lowered, it must resolve downward; this means the lowered second scale degree will resolve to the leading tone in the V chord—an interval of a diminished third. The fifth of the chord is chromatically lowered as well in the major key, compelling it to resolve downward by half step; even in the minor key this would still resolve downward, as a 6–5 tendency tone pair. Thus, in the Neapolitan chord's more conventional appearance in first inversion, the bass is normally doubled (Example 24.3).

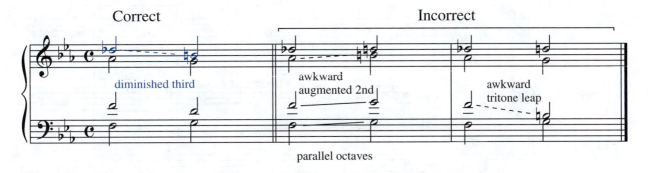

Example 24.3. Correct and incorrect resolutions of the Neapolitan sixth chord.

Example 24.4 shows this resolution in score context. Note that the distinctive resolution of the lowered second scale degree is given over to the solo violin, giving it added prominence.

Example 24.4. Camille Saint-Saëns (1835–1921), *Introduction and Rondo Capriccioso*, op. 28, mm. 15–18.

In Example 24.5, Mozart's resolution from the N6 to V is "softened" by a passing tone in the tenor voice (this chord might also be analyzed as iv in D minor, the key of the movement). Compare the N^6 in measure 143 with the ii^{o6} in measure 141.

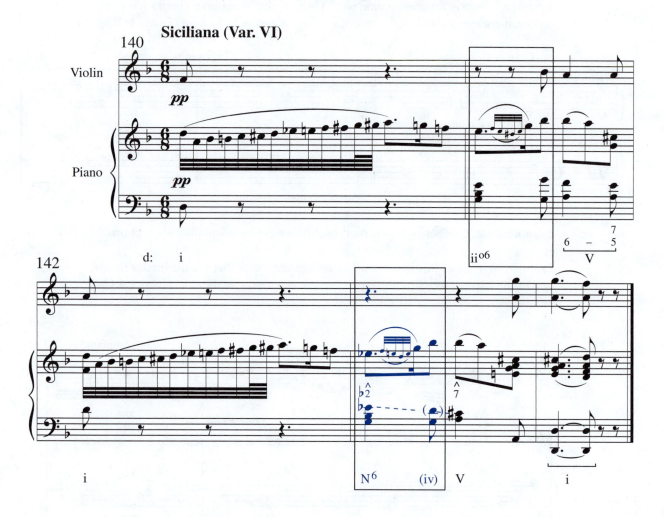

Example 24.5. Mozart, Violin Sonata in F major, K.377 (ii), mm. 140–144.

Occasionally, a Neapolitan chord appears in the literature with the altered second scale degree, rather than the bass, doubled (Example 24.6). This forces one of the lowered tones to resolve upward to avoid parallel octaves. (Note that because of the texture used here, Beethoven would have created parallel octaves in the tenor voice from the previous chord if he had doubled the bass in the Neapolitan chord.)

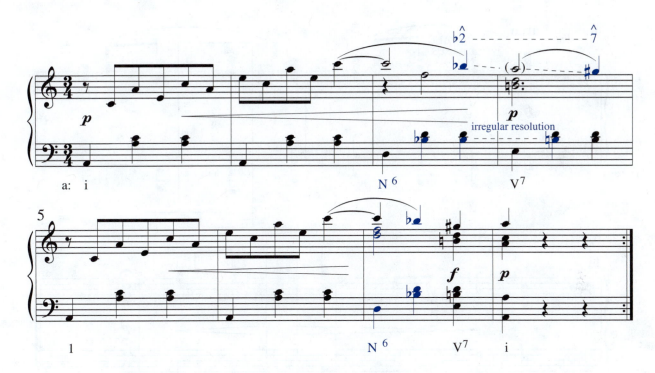

Example 24.6. Beethoven, Bagatelle in A minor, op. 119 no. 9, mm. 1–8.

When the Neapolitan chord appears in root position, it is permissible to double the root. In this context the root in the bass would resolve by augmented fourth up or diminished fifth down to the dominant; the voice doubling the bass would resolve to the leading tone in the V chord as described above. Example 24.7b shows Chopin's use of the root-position Neapolitan chord in his Prelude in C minor; this chord had appeared at the beginning of the piece in the context of an extended tonicization of VI (Ab major), shown in Example 24.7a. In Example 24.7b, the lowered second scale degree in the alto voice (doubling the bass) resolves downward to the leading tone as it should, as the chord itself resolves to V⁷. (The octaves in the bass line are octave doublings to thicken the texture, common in Romantic-era piano music, and should not be mistaken for parallel octaves.)

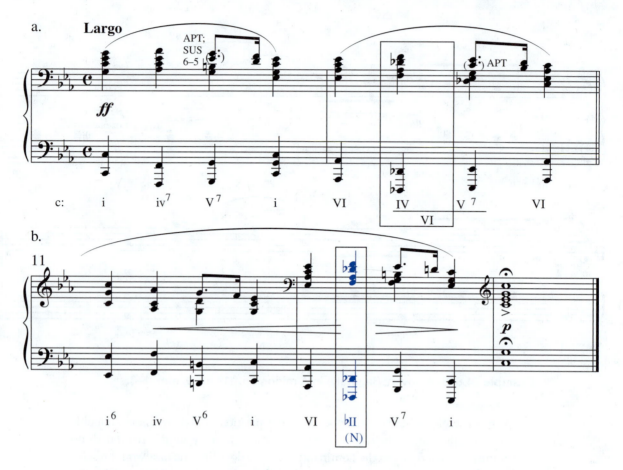

Example 24.7. Chopin, Prelude in C minor, op. 28 no. 20, (a.) mm. 1–2 and (b.) mm. 11–13.

LEVEL MASTERY 24.1

1. Given the ii (ii°) or ii^6 (ii^{o6}) chord in each example, add the necessary chromatic alterations to make each chord a Neapolitan (Neapolitan sixth) chord. You may write your completed chord in the blank measures provided if desired.

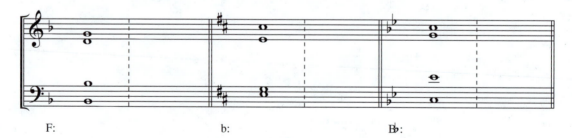

(Continued)

(Continued)

c#:   E♮:   A♭:

2. Complete the indicated Neapolitan sixth chords and resolve each to V, mindful of the voice-leading procedures outlined in the section above (and studying the correct model in Example 15.20). (Stem direction indicates voice part.)

c#:   g: B:

f#:   e♭:   b♭:

AUGMENTED SIXTH CHORDS

Before Jean-Philippe Rameau developed his theory of chord inversion in the early eighteenth century, musicians tended to conceptualize "first-inversion" and "second-inversion" chords as combinations of intervals stacked above the bass, indicated for the performer by figured bass numbers. Thus, first-inversion triads would be referred to as a "chord of the sixth"; a second-inversion triad was a "chord of the sixth and fourth." By chromatic alteration, some "chords of the sixth" could be created that would not be triads when stacked in root position. The most prominent of these are the **augmented sixth chords,** so named because of the distinctive harmonic interval of an *augmented sixth above the bass.*

There are three types of augmented sixth chords, each with a geographical name that admittedly has little to do with its origin—Italian, French, and German. All augmented sixth chords have the following characteristics:

- All are *predominant* function chords resolving to V, either directly or indirectly by means of the cadential $^6_4$ chord.
- All are characterized by the augmented sixth harmonic interval formed by the sixth scale degree in minor (chromatically lowered in major) in the bass and the chromatically raised fourth scale degree in one of the other voices, often the soprano.
- In all augmented sixth chords, the two voices that form the augmented sixth interval characteristically resolve *outward by chromatic contrary motion* to the dominant scale degrees, *forming an octave* (Example 24.8).

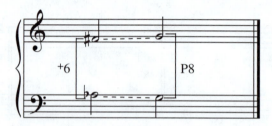

Example 24.8. The augmented sixth interval and its resolution outward to the octave.

THE ITALIAN AUGMENTED SIXTH (It⁺⁶). The Italian augmented sixth chord has the scale degree construction (♭)6–1–1–♯4. It is the only augmented sixth chord with a doubled tone. It often appears between IV⁶ (iv⁶) and V, with one or both tones of the augmented sixth interval functioning as chromatic passing tones. Two typical voicings and their resolutions are shown in Example 24.9. *In the Italian augmented sixth chord, always double the tonic* in four-part writing. In the resolution, the augmented sixth interval always expands outward chromatically to the octave; the two voices doubling the tonic resolve stepwise in contrary motion (either inward or outward).

Example 24.9. The Italian augmented sixth chord in major and minor, two voicings.

Example 24.10 shows the Italian augmented sixth chord in score context.

Example 24.10. Mozart, Piano Sonata no. 14 in F major, K.533 (i), mm. 37–41.

THE FRENCH AUGMENTED SIXTH (Fr⁺⁶). The French augmented sixth chord has the scale degree construction (♭)6–1–2–♯4. *The presence of the second-scale degree is unique to the French augmented sixth.* Its construction and resolution are shown in Example 24.11.

Example 24.11. The French augmented sixth chord in major and minor, two voicings.

Example 24.12 shows an example of a French augmented sixth in score context, in a chorus from Handel's *Messiah*. Because of the slow chromatic wedge of the bass and soprano in this phrase, the augmented sixth of F–D♯ between the bass and soprano in measure 5 seems to logically unfold, preceded by IV⁶. On the third beat of measure 5, the chord is initially an It⁺⁶, but the passing tone motion in the tenor on the fourth beat changes this to a Fr⁺⁶.

Example 24.12. Handel, "Since by Man Came Death," from *Messiah*, mm. 1–6.

THE GERMAN AUGMENTED SIXTH (Ger⁺⁶). The German augmented sixth chord has the scale degree construction (♭)6–1–(♭)3–♯4. *Its distinguishing feature is the presence of the third-scale degree (chromatically lowered in major keys, diatonic in minor keys).* The presence of the perfect fifth between (♭)6 in the bass and (♭)3 means that the German augmented sixth normally does not resolve directly to V, because of the parallel fifths that would result in the voice leading. Instead, it normally *resolves to the cadential ⁶₄ chord* to avoid parallel fifths (Example 24.13).

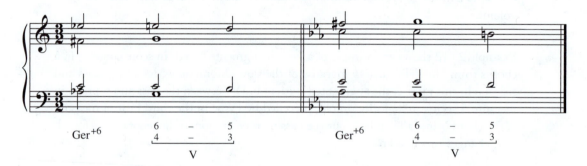

Example 24.13. The German augmented sixth chord in major and minor, two voicings.[1]

---

[1] The bracketed labeling for the cadential ⁶₄ chord here is due to its dominant harmonic function; see the explanation in Chapter 13 and especially Example 13.1.

Example 24.14 shows the German augmented sixth chord in score context.

Example 24.14. Mozart, String Quartet in D minor, K.173 (i), mm. 125–132.

There are times when a composer wishes to use the German augmented sixth chord resolving directly to V, while also avoiding the parallel fifths that would result from such a progression. In the first movement of his Piano Sonata in D major K.284 (Example 24.15), Mozart approaches a half cadence with a dramatic series of predominant chords. Because the harmonic rhythm in measures 13–15 is one chord per measure, we would perceive measure 16 to be one chord—a German augmented sixth chord—as well. Focusing on the last beat of the measure, however, the voice leading directly proceeding to the V chord in measure 17 is that of an Italian augmented sixth.

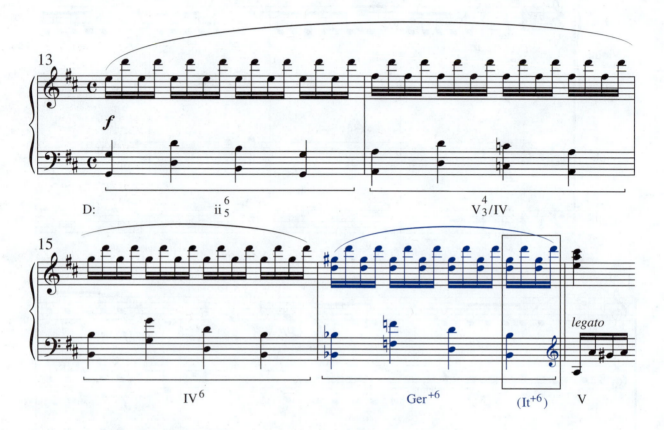

Example 24.15. Mozart, Sonata in D major K.284 (i), mm. 13–17a.

Haydn uses a similar technique in the second movement of his "Drumroll" Symphony no. 103 (Example 24.16). The crucial third scale degree is metrically emphasized in the melodic line; indeed, for much of the first measure in the example, the chord tones all support a German augmented sixth analysis. In the final eighth note, however, the E♭ disappears, and—if we count the D5 on the last eighth note as a chord tone—the remaining tones suggest that the V is approached by means of a French augmented sixth chord (or an Italian augmented sixth if we interpret the D5 as a passing tone). The sound of the German augmented sixth, however, has impressed itself in our memory.

Example 24.16. Haydn, Symphony no. 103 ("Drumroll") (ii), mm. 14–16.

In one of his last string quartets, Haydn avoids parallel fifths still another way—by momentarily crossing voices before doubling E (the tonic) on the last eighth note (Example 24.17).

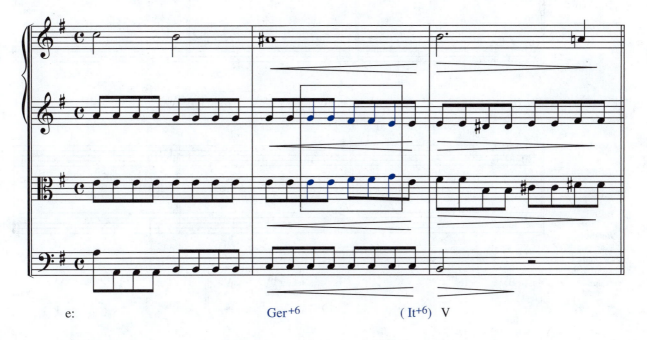

Example 24.17. Haydn, String Quartet, op. 74 no. 3 (ii), mm. 35–37.

Each of these examples suggests that although resolving the German augmented sixth (perhaps the "edgiest" of the augmented sixth chords) directly to V was attractive, the need to avoid parallel fifths was greater.

LEVEL MASTERY 24.2

1. Identify the following augmented sixth chords.

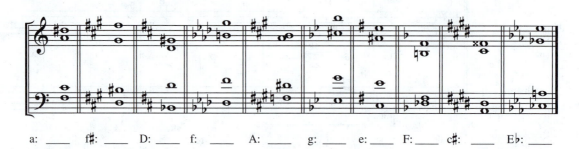

a: _____   f#: _____   D: _____   f: _____   A: _____   g: _____   e: _____   F: _____   c#: _____   Eb: _____

2. Spell the following augmented sixth chords and resolve them as indicated.

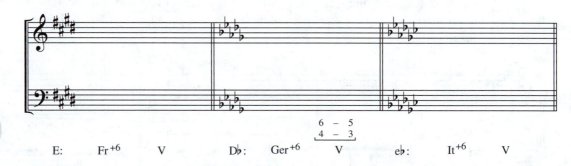

E: Fr⁺⁶   V   Db: Ger⁺⁶ $\frac{6-5}{4-3}$ V   eb: It⁺⁶   V

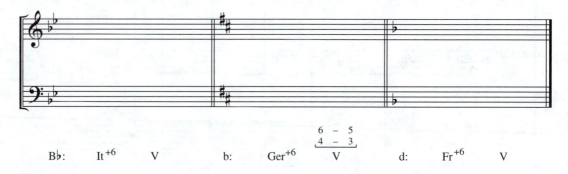

Bb: It⁺⁶   V   b: Ger⁺⁶ $\frac{6-5}{4-3}$ V   d: Fr⁺⁶   V

Self-Test 24.2 may be done at this time.

Workbook Exercises 24.3 and 24.4 may be done at this time.

RELATED CHORDS: THE DOUBLY AUGMENTED $\frac{4}{3}$ CHORD AND THE DIMINISHED THIRD CHORD

THE DOUBLY AUGMENTED $\frac{4}{3}$ CHORD. Related to the augmented sixth chords, though much less common in the literature, is the so-called **doubly augmented $\frac{4}{3}$ chord**. We have already seen that the structure of the German augmented sixth chord prevented direct resolutions to V because of parallel fifths. Another quirk of the German augmented sixth chord is that, *when used in major keys, the voice leading of the chromatically lowered third scale degree must resolve upward to the third of the cadential $\frac{6}{4}$ chord*. Because of this anomaly, in the doubly augmented $\frac{4}{3}$ chord the lowered third scale degree is enharmonically respelled as a *chromatically raised second scale degree*. Thus, a German augmented sixth chord of A♭, C, E♭, and F♯ in the key of C major would be notated as A♭, C, D♯, and F♯. The augmented sixth interval between the lowered sixth scale degree (A♭) in the bass and the raised fourth scale degree (F♯) in an upper voice is retained, but now there is also an interval of a *doubly augmented fourth* formed between the bass note and one of the other upper voices (in this case, A♭ and D♯).

Example 24.18 shows a doubly augmented $\frac{4}{3}$ chord in the overture to Gilbert and Sullivan's operetta *Princess Ida*. The excerpt begins with a passing tonic prolongation in measures 39–42, followed by an extended tonicization of iii (G minor) in measures 48–51 (including a German augmented sixth chord in measure 49). The doubly augmented $\frac{4}{3}$ chord is found at the end of measure 52.

Example 24.18. Arthur Sullivan, Overture to *Princess Ida*, mm. 39–55a.

(Continued)

(Continued)

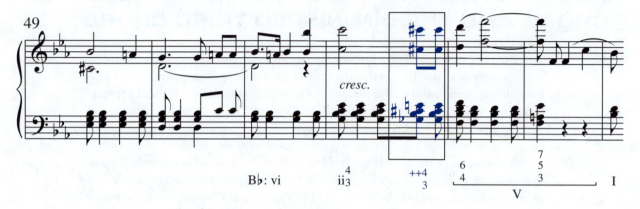

DIMINISHED THIRD (°³) CHORDS. Occasionally augmented sixth chords are found in inversion—the raised fourth scale degree is found in the bass, displacing the sixth scale degree (lowered sixth in major) to another voice. The characteristic augmented sixth interval is thus inverted to a *diminished third*, and the *voice leading resolves inward by chromatic contrary motion to an octave* rather than outward. Such chords are accordingly called **diminished third chords**. They are found in the same varieties as their augmented sixth counterparts (It°³, Fr°³, and Ger°³).

Diminished third chords may have a passing or a neighboring function in a phrase. In the "Crucifixus" from Bach's *Mass in B Minor* (Example 24.19), Bach surprisingly moves to G major by means of a Ger°³ chord in measure 51, concluding a piece that had been based up to that point on a ground bass in E minor. This diminished third chord has a *passing function*, as it is the product of *chromatic passing tones* in the bass and soprano voices.

TRANSLATION: Died and was buried.

Example 24.19. Bach, "Crucifixus," from *Mass in B Minor*, BWV 232, mm. 49–53.

Apply This!
24.2 may
be done at
this time.

A diminished third chord with a *neighboring function* resulting from two *neighboring tones* moving in contrary motion can be seen in Piotr Il'yich Tchaikovsky's "Waltz of the Snowflakes" from *The Nutcracker* (Example 24.20). Much of the excerpt is a tonic prolongation (note the long pedal tone), but as the bass finally descends from the tonic another line moves in contrary motion to it. By measure 42, as the bass has reached C♮, the first violin line has reached A♯; these two parts then engage in a voice exchange as both parts push past the dominant scale degree before converging back.

Example 24.20. Tchaikovsky, "Waltz of the Snow Flakes" (*The Nutcracker*), mm. 37–45.

CHROMATIC HARMONY IN CONTEXT OF THE PHRASE MODEL

All of the chords in this chapter serve as colorful harmonic "enhancers," intensifying a chord's need for resolution. We saw at the beginning of this chapter that a simple ii⁶–V–I progression can be given considerably more character by adding chromatic alterations; the ii⁶ chord was changed to a ii°⁶ and then a ♭II⁶ (or N⁶) but its predominant function was not changed. Similarly, augmented sixth chords may be regarded as chromatically altered versions of triads and seventh chords that we have already encountered:

- The **Italian** $^{+6}$ may be regarded as a *chromatically mutated iv⁶ chord* (mode mixture if the key is major, and then the root raised).
- The **French** $^{+6}$ may be regarded as a *chromatically mutated ii°⁴₃ chord* (mode mixture if the key is major, and then the chord fifth in the bass chromatically lowered).
- The **German** $^{+6}$ may be regarded as a *chromatically mutated iv⁶₃ chord* (mode mixture if the key is major, and then the root chromatically raised).

All of these alterations are illustrated in Example 24.21.

Workbook
Exercise 24.5
may be done
at this time.

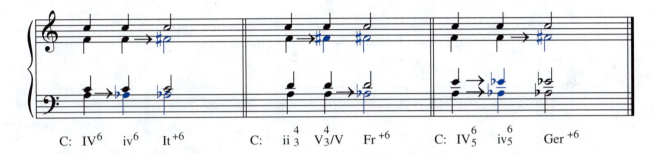

C: IV⁶   iv⁶   It $^{+6}$ C: ii $^4_3$ V$^4_3$/V   Fr $^{+6}$ C: IV$^6_5$ iv$^6_5$ Ger $^{+6}$

Example 24.21. Chromatic mutations of IV⁶, ii⁴₃, and IV⁶₅ to create augmented sixth chords.

CONCLUSION

Being mindful of the interplay—and sometimes the tension—between the "vertical" and "horizontal" dimensions of music will result in a fuller understanding of music's unfolding structure. Sometimes, because of enharmonic ambiguities such as those explored in this chapter, we might find ourselves with the musical equivalent of homonyms—chords that sound alike yet have very different meanings. Thus, in the music of certain nineteenth-century composers such as Wagner, the result is the musical equivalent of a word-association string such as "the world's my oyster soup kitchen floor wax museum" (to borrow the title of a King Crimson song). Parsing the string, we find a chain of "pivot words" (oyster soup, soup kitchen, kitchen floor, floor wax, etc.) that extend phrases to longer lengths and greater complexity. As predominant function chords take on greater levels of elaboration, closure becomes elusive—in Wagner's Prelude to *Tristan and Isolde*, for example, there is only one authentic cadence in 111 measures (some eleven minutes' worth) of music.

Nevertheless, the same structural principles of harmonic syntax that governed our earlier progressions remain underneath all of these innovations. We have seen how all of these chords retain the predominant function associated with the ii⁶ or IV chord (or some variant of those). Even a sentence like "the world's my oyster soup kitchen floor wax museum" makes grammatical, if perhaps not predictable, sense.

Terms to Know

augmented sixth chords (Italian, French, German)

diminished third chords (Italian, French, German)

doubly augmented $\frac{4}{3}$ chord

Neapolitan sixth (N^6) chord

Self-Test

24.1. Complete the indicated Neapolitan sixth chords in the spacing indicated, and resolve them. Use key signatures.

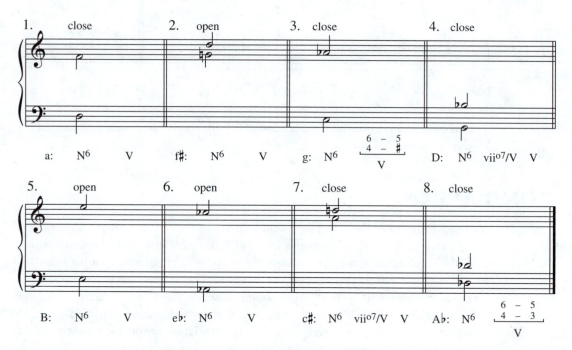

24.2. Spell and resolve the indicated augmented sixth chords, in the keys indicated. You may use key signatures.

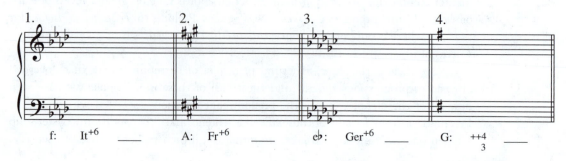

(Continued)

(Continued)

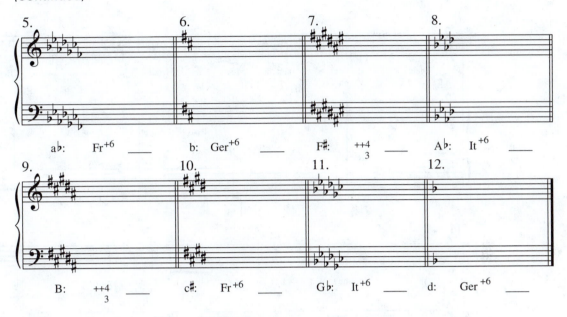

5. ab: Fr⁺⁶ ___ 6. b: Ger⁺⁶ ___ 7. F♯: ⁺⁺⁴/₃ ___ 8. Ab: It⁺⁶ ___

9. B: ⁺⁺⁴/₃ ___ 10. c♯: Fr⁺⁶ ___ 11. Gb: It⁺⁶ ___ 12. d: Ger⁺⁶ ___

Apply This!

24.1. Analysis. Provide harmonic analysis (Roman numerals and inversion symbols) for each excerpt.

a. Schubert, "Der Müller und der Bach," no. 19 from *Die Schöne Müllerin*, op. 25, mm. 1–19. Consider the relation of the text to the harmonic setting.

Wo ein treu-es Her - ze in Lie - be ver -

(Continued)

(Continued)

TRANSLATION: Where a true heart
in love withers,
There the lilies wilt
in every bed;

Then must the full moon
go into the clouds,
So that men do not see her teardrops.

b. Niccolò Paganini (1782–1840), Caprice, op. 1 no. 4, mm. 12–16.

c. Beethoven, Piano Sonata, op. 27 no. 2 ("Moonlight") (i), mm. 1–23. This excerpt contains three modulations (locations of pivot chords are provided). Measures 16 and 18 could be analyzed two different ways, depending on which tones are regarded as non-chord tones. Determine both analyses. Which is more convincing to you, and why?

Adagio sostenuto.
Si deve suonare tutto questo pezzo delicatissimamente e senza sordino.
[The entire piece must be played very delicately and without muting.]

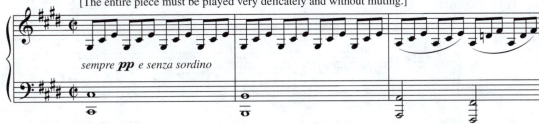

sempre **pp** e senza sordino

E:

(Continued)

(Continued)

PART 3: Form and Chromatic Harmony 2

24.2. Analysis. Find and label the augmented sixth or doubly augmented $\frac{4}{3}$ chord in each of the excerpts below. Complete your harmonic analysis with Roman numerals and inversion symbols for the remaining chords.

a. Beethoven, Symphony no. 5 in C minor, as transcribed by Franz Liszt (i), mm. 6–21.

b. The Beatles, "I Want You (She's So Heavy)." Non-chord tones are in parentheses.

c. Haydn, Piano Sonata in C♯ minor, Hob. XVI/36 (i), mm. 56–59. Analyze this brief passage—which is part of a transitional section with frequent key changes—in A major.

PART 4

ADVANCED CHROMATIC HARMONY AND CONTEMPORARY TECHNIQUES

CHAPTER 25

ALTERATIONS AND ADDITIONS TO TRIADS AND SEVENTH CHORDS

OVERVIEW

Building on earlier chromatic alterations such as mode mixture and augmented sixth chords, composers began experimenting with other alterations in the nineteenth and twentieth centuries, altering chords by raising or lowering the fifth. Composers also enhanced the effect of seventh chords by adding other tertian chord members: ninths, elevenths, and thirteenths. Eventually these additions led to the use of color tones, added tones that were nonfunctional but allowed for richer sonorities.

CHAPTER OUTLINE

INTRODUCTION

The nineteenth century was a time of rapid growth in harmonic experimentation. Often this can be viewed almost as a process of scientific experiment: If the third of a chord can be altered through mode mixture, why not the fifth? If a chord can have a seventh, why not additional tertian chord members such as a ninth, eleventh, or thirteenth? Many of these changes made earlier appearances in music as non-chord tones; during this time, however, such non-chord tones came to be accepted as *part* of the harmony.

We begin with considering chords that extend the tertian structure of chords past the seventh. **Extended tertian chords** build on existing seventh chords by adding additional chord members beyond the seventh, at successive generic thirds— like extra rungs on a ladder. Thus, the added chord members above the root would be the ninth, eleventh, and thirteenth, before the root is doubled two octaves up (at the fifteenth). Example 25.1 shows these successive upper chord members added above a G major-minor seventh chord.

Example 25.1. Adding the chord ninth, eleventh, and thirteenth.

Like augmented sixth chords, extended tertian chords arguably have contrapuntal origins. For example, in the passage from Beethoven's Piano Sonata, op. 90, shown in Example 25.2, G acts as a suspension in measures 70 and 74, embellishing a simple V⁷; in measure 78, the G could be analyzed as a retardation, but it could also be analyzed as part of a V⁹ chord. Later composers would treat the added ninth not as a melodic dissonance to be resolved but as an active chord member in its own right.

Example 25.2. Beethoven, Piano Sonata in E minor, op. 90 (i), mm. 67–81.
(Continued)

(Continued)

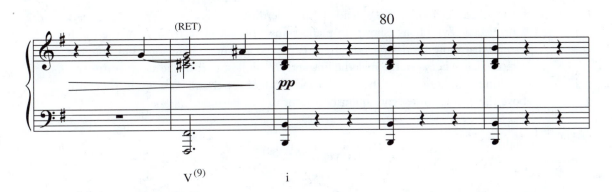

NINTH CHORDS. The first of the extended tertian chords to be widely used in common-practice music, during the Classic era, was the V^9 chord, especially in minor keys (because the added ninth in minor is a minor ninth above the root, this chord's quality is a major-minor-minor ninth chord, abbreviated Mmm^9). This was because the V^7 and the vii^{o7} not only share the same harmonic function but also three common tones, allowing their combination into a kind of "superdominant." Example 25.3 shows the V^9 in the context of Beethoven's famous "Moonlight" Sonata.

Example 25.3. Beethoven, Piano Sonata, op. 27 no. 2 ("Moonlight") (i), mm. 32–37. (Continued)

(Continued)

V^9

Example 25.4 shows an extended "superdominant" passage in Franz Schubert's "Unfinished" Symphony (shown in piano transcription). Here the role of the ninth is somewhat more fluid—melodically it is treated as a non-chord tone, but note the voice exchange between the melodic line and the highest part in the accompaniment, switching the placement of the seventh and ninth of the chord. As a result, the ninth above the bass is almost continuously present in this passage.

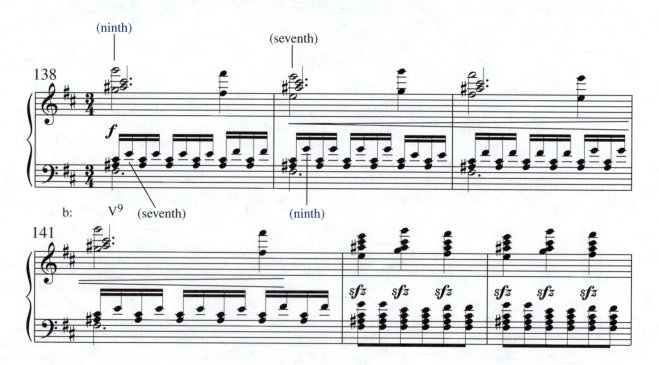

Example 25.4. Schubert, Symphony no. 8 ("Unfinished") (i), mm. 138–143.

In his famous "Liebestraum" (Example 25.5), Liszt begins by harmonizing the C4 of his melody with I, V_3^4/vi, and V^7/ii; in measure 4 he sets the C4 as the ninth in a

V^9/V chord (a major-minor-major ninth, or MmM^9, quality). Notice that C is part of the chord arpeggio, and the "resolution" in the melody is to drop a fifth to F, another chord tone; therefore, C is a chord ninth rather than a non-chord tone.

Example 25.5. Liszt, "Liebestraum," S.541, no. 3, mm. 1–6.

As Example 25.4 shows, ninth chords are often found in five-voice texture, one part for each chord member. *In four-part textures the fifth of the chord is usually omitted,* especially as in a major-mode dominant ninth chord the presence of the 6–5 and 2–1 tendency tone pairs simultaneously would result in parallel fifths (Example 25.6).

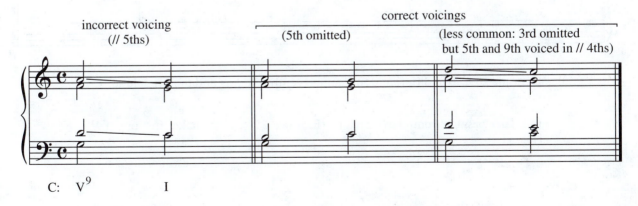

Example 25.6. Correct and incorrect voicing of V^9 chords in a four-part texture.

Predominant chords can also be extended with ninths. Such additions do not change the function or syntax of the chord. Example 25.7 shows how ninth chords function in a major-mode circle-of-fifths harmonic progression. Note that the ninths, like the sevenths, resolve down by step.

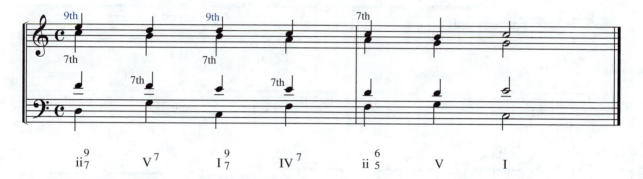

Example 25.7. Resolution of chord ninths in a circle-of-fifths harmonic progression.

ELEVENTH CHORDS. By the late Romantic period composers were using eleventh and thirteenth chords freely. *A V^{11} chord in four-part texture normally omits the third (leading tone) to avoid the M7/m9 dissonance between the third and the eleventh.* In addition, the fifth or the seventh may be omitted, as needed to avoid parallel fifths. Example 25.8 shows two possible four-voice settings of the V^{11} chord, with the eleventh resolving downward by step to the seventh of the next chord.

Example 25.8. Two different dominant eleventh voicings and their resolutions.

In a later passage from "Liebestraum" (Example 25.9), Liszt makes free use of V^{11} chords.

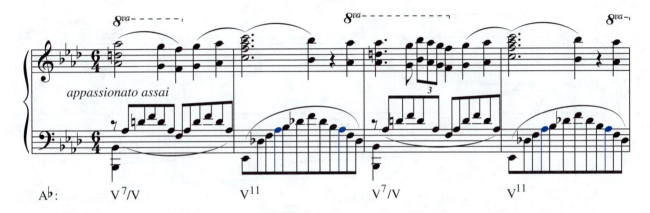

Example 25.9. Liszt, "Liebestraum," mm. 50–53.

In Example 25.10 below, the ninth of the V^{11} chord resolves properly with the harmonic change, but the eleventh does not. By omitting the third of the chord (which would cause a minor-ninth dissonance with the eleventh), the upper part of the chord has a "plagal cadence" quality while the bass suggests an authentic cadence with its 5–1 motion. Impressionist composers such as Claude Debussy and Maurice Ravel often used the V^{11} in this way at cadences; see for example Debussy's "Arabesque no. 1" (measures 41–42, in E major) and "La Fille aux Cheveux de Lin" ("The Girl with the Flaxen Hair") (measures 9–10 in G♭ major, measures 18–19 in E♭ major).

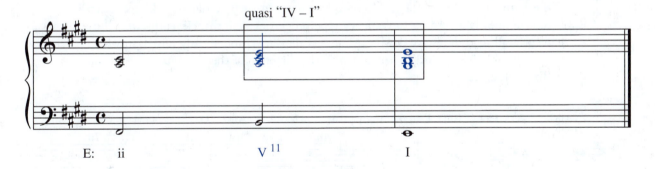

Example 25.10. A Debussyesque V^{11}–I cadence.

THIRTEENTH CHORDS. Adding a third above the chord eleventh yields a thirteenth chord—the last "rung" in our tertian ladder before the double octave (fifteenth) is reached. Examine Chopin's use of thirteenth chords in Example 25.11 below. Chopin's voicing of the V^{13} chord retains its dominant seventh status. Note that *the third (leading tone) and chord seventh are retained, while the fifth, ninth, and eleventh are omitted.* Note also that each dissonance, *except* the thirteenth, resolves according to the tendency tone pair of which it is part (5–1 in the bass, 4–3 and 7–1 in the right hand).

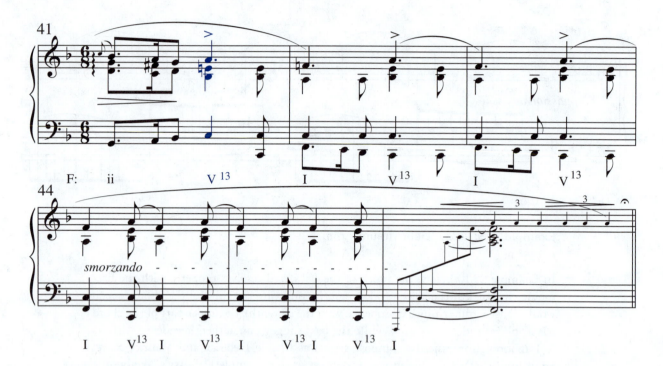

Example 25.11. Chopin, Ballade no. 2 in F major, op. 38, mm. 41–46.

Extended tertian sonorities, often with chromatic modifications, are also a staple of the harmonic language of jazz. The dissonances in such tertian "stackings" often resolve linearly according to tendency-tone properties—ninths, elevenths, and thirteenths all tend to resolve downward, unless they are chromatically raised, in which case they resolve upward in keeping with the direction of their chromatic alteration (Example 25.12).

Example 25.12. Extended tertian sonorities in a jazz harmonic progression, with chord symbols and tendency-tone analysis.

The melodic line of a skilled improvisation will take into account the implied direction of tendency tones, giving the line a goal-directed quality. A sampling of other extended chords, with their jazz chord symbols, is shown in Example 25.13. Like pop chord symbols, jazz chord symbols are not strictly standardized. The first chord assumes, being a dominant ninth chord, that there will be a dominant seventh as well. The third chord, assuming C major, indicates a chromatically lowered seventh. The sixth chord, a C7 to which has been added a raised ninth, assumes a major-minor seventh quality. Nonetheless, each of these chords includes a B♭.

Example 25.13. Extended tertian sonorities in jazz with jazz chord symbols.

Example 25.14 shows a typical instance of extended tertian sonorities in a jazz lead sheet. A block-chord realization (not usually part of a jazz chart) is provided below the melodic line. Play through the progression and locate the added tones.

Example 25.14. Dizzy Gillespie and Frank Paparelli, "A Night in Tunisia," interlude. (Continued)

(Continued)

COLOR TONES. Jazz, as well as late-Romantic and early-twentieth-century classical music, also makes use of **color tones**—added tones that do not change the chord's harmonic function but enrich its sound. The chord eleventh in Example 25.10 is an example of a color tone. In addition to ninths, elevenths, or thirteenths (each of which may be chromatically altered), sometimes triads are "colored" by an added sixth; a "C6" in jazz, for example, would refer not to a C major triad in first inversion but to a C major triad with an added sixth above the root.

1. Identify the following root-position extended tertian sonorities, given the key. The first is done for you as an example.

E♭: V¹¹   b: ____   A: ____   B♭: ____   g♯: ____   f: ____   D: ____   F: ____   D♭: ____   e: ____

2. Spell and resolve the indicated extended tertian sonorities, using proper spacing and voice leading. Be mindful of the indications where certain chord members are to be omitted.

B♭: ii⁹ V⁷   E: V¹¹ I⁷   A♭: ii¹³ V⁷   f♯: i⁹ iv   c: V⁹ i
(omit 5th)   (omit 5th)   (omit 5th)   (omit 5th)

A: vi⁹ ii   F: vi⁹ IV   g: III¹³ VI⁹   B: ii¹¹ V⁷   E♭: vi⁹ ii
(omit 3rd)   (omit 5th)   (omit 5th)   (omit 5th)   (omit 5th)

Self-Test 25.1
may be done
at this time.

Workbook
Exercises
25.1 and 25.2
may be done
at this time.

ALTERED DOMINANT CHORDS

Play the two progressions in Example 25.15 and compare them. The second progression contains an example of an **altered dominant chord**—a triad or major-minor seventh chord in which the fifth has been chromatically raised or lowered. Raising the fifth of the V triad changes its quality from major to augmented and also adds a chromatic tendency tone (remember, such notes have a strong tendency to resolve upward by minor second).

Example 25.15. Two tonic-to-dominant progressions.

Example 25.16 shows a secondary altered dominant, $V_{\sharp5}^7/IV$ (or a C7#5 in jazz chord notation); this progression is found at the beginning of George Gershwin's "Of Thee I Sing." This example also clearly shows how an altered dominant chord might be considered to be the product of non-chord activity; the B♭ can be analyzed as a passing seventh, and the G♯ can be analyzed as a chromatic passing tone.

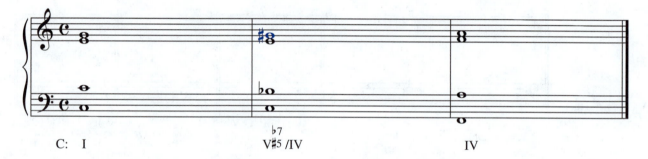

C: I $\qquad\qquad\qquad$ V$\sharp$5 /IV $\qquad\qquad\qquad$ IV

Example 25.16. An altered secondary dominant tonicizing IV.

An altered dominant can also contain a lowered fifth. The lowered fifth (lowered second scale degree) must resolve downward by half step to the tonic. If the leading tone is in an inner voice, it may leap down to the fifth of the tonic chord by free resolution in order to complete the tonic triad (Example 25.17).

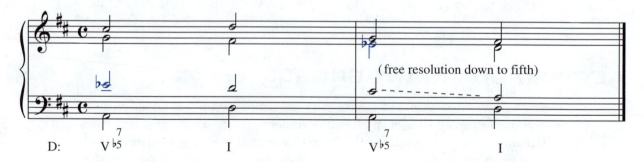

(free resolution down to fifth)

D: V♭5^7 $\qquad\qquad$ I $\qquad\qquad$ V♭5^7 $\qquad\qquad$ I

Example 25.17. Two resolutions of $V_{\flat5}^7$ in D major.

PART 4: Advanced Chromatic Harmony and Contemporary Techniques

Close examination of the dominant seventh with a flatted fifth reveals an interesting property. If we condense the spacing of the $V^7_{\flat 5}$ chord to within an octave (A–C♯–E♭–G), we find that transposing the chord up or down a tritone yields the same pitch classes (allowing for enharmonic substitutions): E♭–G–B♭♭–D♭. Thus, when used as part of a ii–$V^7_{\flat 5}$–I progression, we can write the $V^7_{\flat 5}$ in second inversion (with the flatted fifth in the bass) and get its tritone-transposed equivalent (Example 25.18). This is called a **tritone substitution**, and it is frequently found in jazz voice leading. Example 25.19 shows an example found in Thelonious Monk's "In Walked Bud" (the closing A♭ harmony is approached from A^7 rather than the expected $E♭^7$). Underlying the head's first phrase is a chromatic descent from F down to A♭; approaching the final chord by means of a tritone substitution allows that descent to be uninterrupted.

A♭:   I   ii⁷   V⁺⁶₄*   I

* No satisfactory Roman numeral labeling exists for a second-inversion altered dominant, since the chromatic alteration is in the bass note itself. This labeling accounts for the augmented sixth interval found above the bass note, modeled after figured bass practice.

Example 25.18. A second-inversion flatted-fifth dominant seventh chord used between ii and I.

Example 25.19. The progression of Example 25.16 enharmonically respelled, resulting in a tritone substitution—from Thelonious Monk, "In Walked Bud."

INVERSIONS OF ALTERED DOMINANT CHORDS

As Example 25.18 shows, altered dominant chords may also appear in inversion. When they do, the conventional inversion symbols generally apply, with modifications such as a sharp or flat to show the altered intervals above the bass. However, there is no satisfactory way to provide a functional label to altered dominant chords in second inversion because the altered note is *in* the bass; in such circumstances it is probably best to show the other tones as clearly as possible using figured bass symbols (see Example 25.20). Pop chord symbols are perhaps more effective in conveying the structure of these chords, and those labels are also shown in Example 25.20.

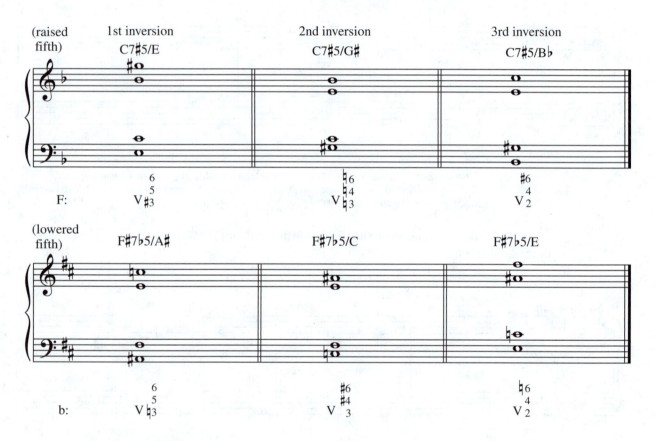

Example 25.20. Altered dominants in inversion.

1. Identify the altered dominants below. Some are altered secondary dominants.

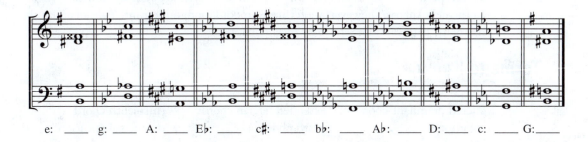

e: ____   g: ____   A: ____   Eb: ____   c#: ____   bb: ____   Ab: ____   D: ____   c: ____   G: ____

2. Given the key, harmonic label, and spacing, spell the indicated root-position altered dominant chords. Use key signatures.

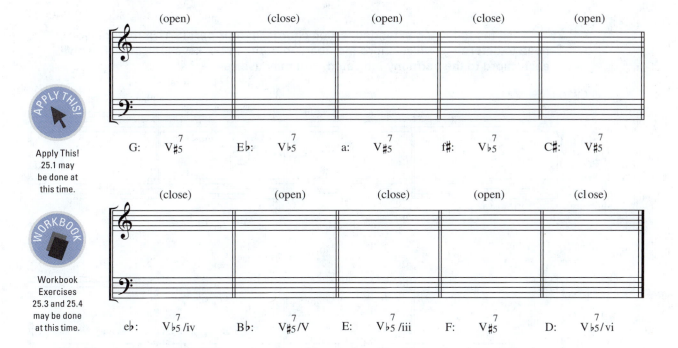

(open)   (close)   (open)   (close)   (open)

G: V$^7_{\sharp5}$ Eb: V$^7_{\flat5}$ a: V$^7_{\sharp5}$ f#:   V$^7_{\flat5}$ C#:   V$^7_{\sharp5}$

(close)   (open)   (close)   (open)   (close)

eb: V$^7_{\flat5}$/iv   Bb: V$^7_{\sharp5}$/V   E: V$^7_{\flat5}$/iii   F: V$^7_{\sharp5}$ D: V$^7_{\flat5}$/vi

*Apply This!
25.1 may
be done at
this time.*

*Workbook
Exercises
25.3 and 25.4
may be done
at this time.*

CONCLUSION

The various "extensions" to common-practice harmony that occurred in the Romantic era can be conceived in two ways: First, a process of *accretion* in the addition of additional thirds above a seventh chord (ninth, eleventh, and thirteenth chords); and second, a process of *mutation* resulting from chromatic alterations (altered dominant chords, as well as the Neapolitan chord and augmented sixth chords examined in Chapter 24). We have also seen from our consideration of color tones that some tones formerly considered to be dissonances are, in some styles, accepted as enriching a particular sonority and, as such, do not require a resolution to a consonance. In some styles of twentieth-century music, extended tertian chords and chords with color tones are accepted as sonorities in their own right. These styles are addressed in Chapter 28. In the next chapter, however, we return to modulation, taking into consideration the harmonic pathways opened up by recent chapters.

Terms to Know

altered dominant chords
color tones
eleventh chord

extended tertian chords
ninth chord

thirteenth chord
tritone substitution

Self-Test

25.1. Spell the following extended tertian chords, in four-part (SATB) texture (you will need to determine which chord members to omit), in the keys indicated. Resolve each chord to the harmony indicated. You may use key signatures.

1. $\text{d: } V^9_7 \quad \text{i}$
2. $\text{E}\flat\text{: } V^{13}_9 \quad I^9$
3. $\text{b: } VII^{11}_7 \quad III^7$
4. $\text{F: } ii^9_7 \quad V^7$

5. $\text{c}\sharp\text{: } V^{11}_9 \quad \text{i}$
6. $\text{G: } ii^{11}_7 \quad V$
7. $\text{g: } V^9_7 \quad VI^7$
8. $\text{e: } V^{11}_{9\,7} \quad \text{i}$

(Continued)

(Continued)

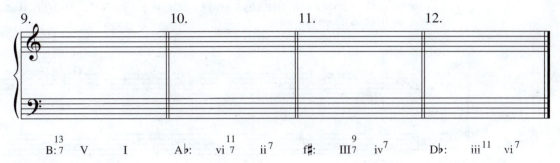

9. $\quad$ 10. $\quad$ 11. $\quad$ 12.

B: 7^{13} $\quad$ V $\quad$ I $\qquad$ A♭: $\quad$ vi 7^{11} $\quad$ ii^7 $\qquad$ f♯: $\quad$ III7^{9} $\quad$ iv^7 $\qquad$ D♭: $\quad$ iii^{11} $\quad$ vi^7

25.2. Spell the following root-position altered dominant chords, in the keys and spacings indicated. You may use key signatures.

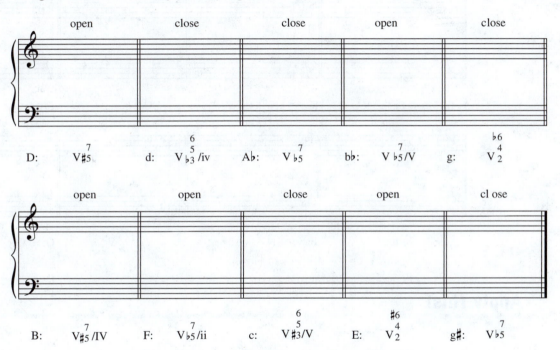

open $\qquad$ close $\qquad$ close $\qquad$ open $\qquad$ close

D: $\quad$ V$^7_{♯5}$ $\qquad$ d: $\quad$ V$^{6}_{♭3}$/iv $\qquad$ A♭: $\quad$ V$^7_{♭5}$ $\qquad$ b♭: $\quad$ V$^7_{♭5}$/V $\qquad$ g: $\quad$ V$^{♭6}_{4}_{2}$

open $\qquad$ open $\qquad$ close $\qquad$ open $\qquad$ cl ose

B: $\quad$ V$^7_{♯5}$/IV $\qquad$ F: $\quad$ V$^7_{♭5}$/ii $\qquad$ c: $\quad$ V$^{6}_{♯3}$/V $\qquad$ E: $\quad$ V$^{♯6}_{4}_{2}$ $\qquad$ g♯: $\quad$ V$^7_{♭5}$

25.3. Chromatic harmony review: Spell and resolve the indicated Neapolitan sixth or augmented sixth chords, in the keys and spacings indicated. You may use key signatures. The first is done for you.

Apply This!

25.1 Analysis. The excerpt on the following page, from Robert Schumann's "Kleine Studie" (Little Étude) from *Album for the Young*, contains two altered dominant chords, one of which is an altered secondary dominant. Find and label them. Label the other chords in the passage as well, along with non-chord tones and tendency tone resolutions (measures 3 and 4 are done for you as an example).

CHAPTER 26

FURTHER CHROMATIC ENHANCEMENTS

OVERVIEW

This chapter brings together additional techniques of chromatic harmony, including extended tonicization, linear chords, and chromatic mediant key relationships.

INTRODUCTION

We have seen in preceding chapters how harmonic language in the nineteenth century was quickly enriched through new explorations of key relationships and modulation and through chromatic inflections of chords. In this chapter we examine additional chromatic expansions of harmony that do not as neatly fit into the categories discussed in previous chapters. Together, these additional harmonic techniques help to fill in some of the gaps in our survey of chromatic harmony so far, as well as to prepare for our study of certain twentieth-century techniques.

EXTENDED TONICIZATION

As the variety of accepted modulation techniques at a composer's disposal grew over the course of the eighteenth and nineteenth centuries, key changes became more frequent (transitory) and tonicizations lasted for longer periods of time, so the distinction between tonicization and modulation became increasingly blurred. In Chapter 15 we learned how tonicizations are accomplished by means of chords that have a *dominant harmonic function* (a V, V^7, vii°, or vii°^{7}) in the key being tonicized. This fleeting moment of tonicization can be extended by preceding the secondary dominant or secondary leading-tone chord with a chord that has a *predominant* function in the key being tonicized. Extended tonicizations are thus somewhat more harmonically elaborate versions of tonicizations, but they usually lack a confirming cadence in the new key.

For example, Robert Schumann's song "Im Wunderschönen Monat Mai" (Example 26.1), the opening song from his cycle *Dichterliebe* ("A Poet's Love"), is an interesting study in tonal ambiguity. Study it carefully from beginning to end. What key do you think is the tonic?

Example 26.1. Robert Schumann, "Im Wunderschönen Monat Mai," no. 1 from *Dichterliebe*, op. 48. *(Continued)*

(Continued)

wun- der-schö-nen Mo-nat Mai, als al - le Knos___ pen spran-gen, da
ist in mei - nen Her - zen die Lie___ be auf - ge-
gan - gen. *ritard.* Im

p

(Continued)

(Continued)

wun - - der-schö-nen Mo-nat Mai, als al - le Vö___ gel san-gen, da

hab' ich ihr ge-stan-den mein Seh - nen und Ver-

lan - gen. *ritard.* - - - - - - -

In the glorious month of May,
When all the buds were bursting,
Love there in my heart bloomed forth.

In the glorious month of May,
When all the birds were singing,
In burning words I told her all
My longing and my yearning.

The beginning and ending of the song seem to imply the tonic as F# minor, even though Schumann never resolves the C#⁷ to an F# minor chord—each time it instead resolves deceptively (and at the very end does not resolve at all!). The opening chord is itself ambiguous, though its function (PD) is not: should we count the G#5 in the melodic line as part of the chord (in which case it would be a ii°⁶₅) or should we analyze it as an appoggiatura (making the chord a iv⁶)?

Assuming that the song is in F# minor, then, the body of the verses presents PD–D–T patterns in a number of keys related to F# minor: A major (III of F# minor), B minor (iv of F# minor), and D major (VI of F# minor); the arrival points of these extended tonicizations all correspond neatly to the ends of phrases in the text. The overall tonal scheme of the verse, then, can be reduced to III–iv–VI–iv⁶–V in the key of F# minor . . . and yet there is still no tonic F# minor chord. Schumann masterfully conveys the exhilarating uncertainty of newly awakening love by withholding the resolution, even as he does provide momentary resolutions in each of the other closely related keys.

Taking such tonal ambiguity to its logical extreme, one can arrive at sections of complete tonal flux such as the passage in Example 26.2. The music of Richard Wagner seldom stays in one key for long. The harmonic analysis provided shows just how fleeting each key area is, and how keys are often determined through harmonic implication rather than by direct confirmation. Keys are signified more by relations between predominant- and dominant-function chords than by explicit dominant-tonic progressions.

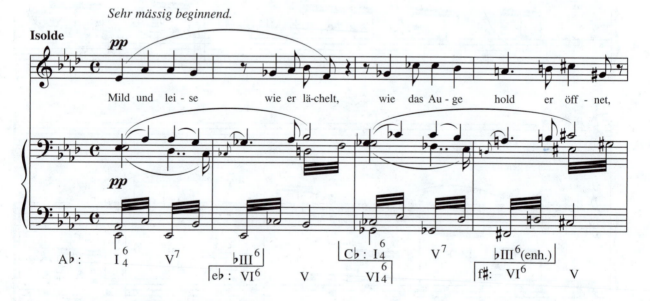

Example 26.2. Richard Wagner, "Liebestod" from *Tristan und Isolde*, mm. 1–8. (*Continued*)

(Continued)

COMMON-TONE (EMBELLISHING) DIMINISHED SEVENTH CHORDS

Sometimes an apparent secondary leading-tone chord's voice leading does not proceed as expected; the chord seventh does not resolve down but rather *stays in place* to become part of the next chord. A diminished seventh chord that functions in this way is called a **common-tone** or **embellishing diminished seventh chord** (labeled "ct°7" rather than with a Roman numeral). This chord is often the product of non-chord tone activity (Example 26.3).

Example 26.3. Schumann, "Kleine Studie," no. 14 from *Album for the Young*, op. 68, mm. 33–39. *(Continued)*

(Continued)

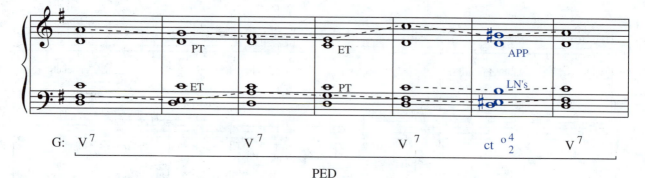

G: V⁷   V⁷   V⁷   ct °⁴₂   V⁷

PED

- Remember that the common-tone diminished seventh can be recognized by having a *common tone* with the *root* of the chord that follows it. (Compare this with the customary resolution of a secondary leading-tone chord, which involves no common tones.)

LEVEL MASTERY 26.1.

Precede the following chords with a common-tone diminished seventh chord, adding your chord to the first part of each measure. Be sure to use the spacing of the chord provided to properly guide your voice leading. The first example is done for you as a model.

Self-Test 26.1 may be done at this time.

Workbook Exercise 26.1 may be done at this time.

LINEAR CHORDS

Some chords may resist an easy functional label; they cannot be explained as any kind of chromatically inflected chord that we have encountered so far. Like augmented sixth chords, they are often the result of the superimposition of musical lines. Such chords are called **linear chords** (LIN). Linear chords tend to have a purely ornamental or coloristic function.

One interesting example occurs in Brahms's Intermezzo, op. 117 no. 2 (Example 26.4a). A "doubly deceptive" cadence occurs at measures 7–9; the V chord resolves not to the major VI (as would normally happen at a deceptive cadence) but to its (enharmomic) parallel minor. Taken on its own, there is no "functional" label for such a chord. A broader context reveals, however, that the chord is the result of a gradual harmonic change, or **chord mutation**, occurring from the end of the first phrase to the beginning of the second (Example 26.4b). Common tones are connected by dotted lines.

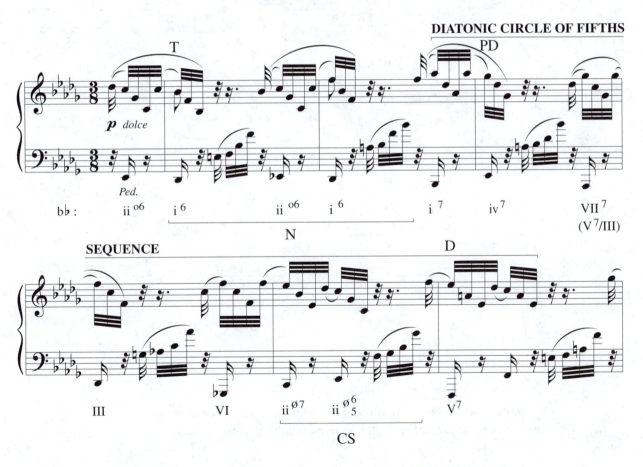

Example 26.4a. Johannes Brahms, Intermezzo in B♭ minor, op. 117 no. 2, mm. 1–11a.

(Continued)

(Continued)

DOUBLY-DECEPTIVE CADENCE

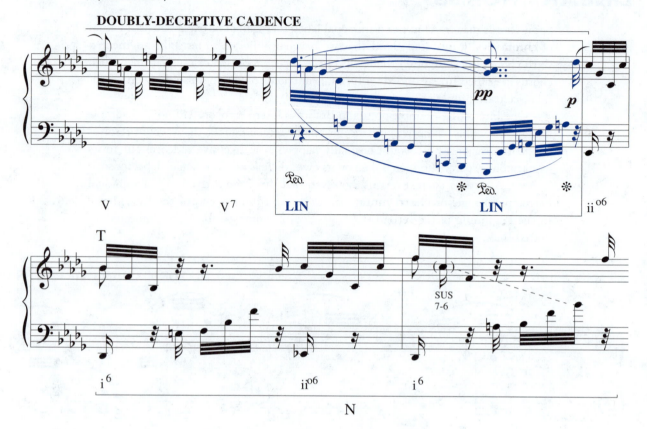

V   V⁷   **LIN**   **LIN**   ii^{o6}

i⁶   ii^{o6}   i⁶

N

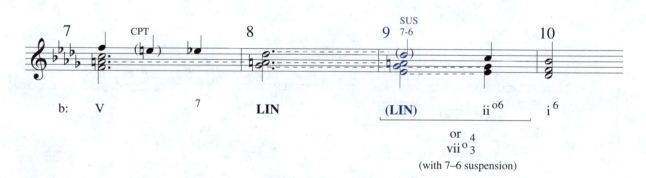

7   CPT   8   9 SUS 7-6   10

b: V   7   **LIN**   **(LIN)**   ii^{o6}   i⁶

or
vii^{o} ⁴₃
(with 7–6 suspension)

Example 26.4b. Voice-leading reduction of Example 26.4a, measures 7–10, showing process of chord mutation (with resulting linear chords).

CHROMATIC MEDIANT RELATIONSHIPS

Other composers in the nineteenth and twentieth centuries explored **chromatic mediant tonal relationships**, in which:

- two chords (or keys) have their roots (or tonics) a major or minor third apart, *and*
- both chords (or keys) are the same modality (both major or both minor).

Example 26.5 shows the chords chromatically related to G major. Note that each pair of chromatic-mediant-related chords shares one common tone.

Example 26.5. Chromatic-mediant-related chords of G major.

One early example of chromatic mediant tonal relationships occurs in the first movement of Beethoven's Piano Sonata no. 21 in C major, op. 53 (the famous "Waldstein" Sonata). The transition from the first tonal area, C major, to the eventual second tonal area, E major, is shown in Example 26.6. (Although the analysis shows measures 20–34 in E minor, this could still be analyzed as E major with plentiful mode mixture.)

Example 26.6. Beethoven, Piano Sonata no. 21 in C major, op. 53 ("Waldstein") (i), mm. 14–42a. *(Continued)*

NEO-RIEMANNIAN THEORY

While chromatic mediant *key* relationships had been used by composers as far back as Haydn and Beethoven, later nineteenth-century compositions often featured chord-to-chord *progressions* employing this relationship. Consider Example 26.7 from the "Gretchen" movement of Liszt's *Ein Faust Symphonie*, composed in 1854. As the chord symbols show, all of the chords are major; the roots move either down a minor third or up a major third (or its enharmonic equivalent). Any kind of Roman numeral analysis is problematic; the music never stays in one key long enough. Nonetheless, there *are* ways that the chords are connected or "flow" from one to another; each pair of chords has one common tone, and the other voices move by the smallest voice-leading increments possible, usually by half or whole step (this is called **parsimonious voice leading**).

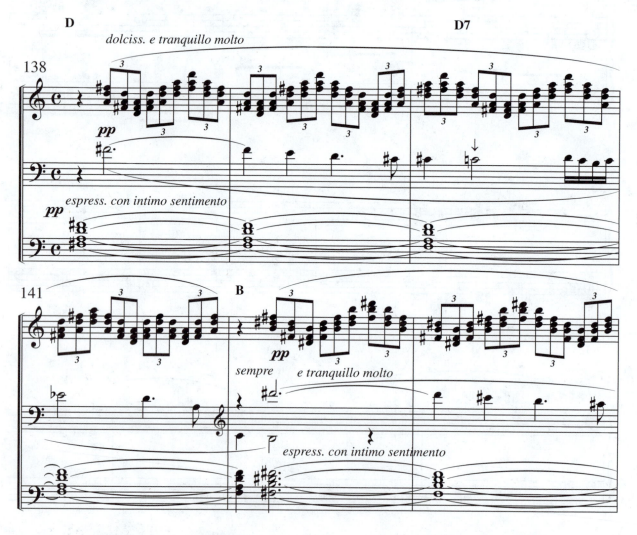

Example 26.7. Liszt, "Gretchen" from *Ein Faust Symphonie*, mm. 138–154 (piano reduction). *(Continued)*

PART 4: Advanced Chromatic Harmony and Contemporary Techniques

(Continued)

(Continued)

(Continued)

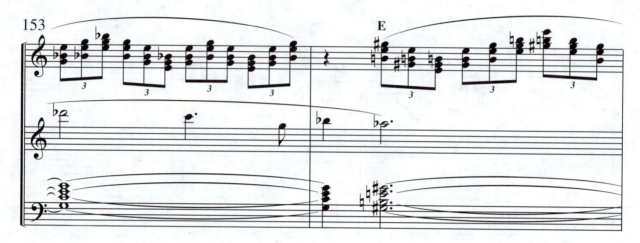

The turn-of-the-twentieth-century theorist and pedagogue Hugo Riemann (1849–1919) considered such progressions as part of a comprehensive system of classifying harmonic progression. Some of his theories were rediscovered and adapted by theorists such as David Lewin, Brian Hyer, and Richard Cohn in the 1990s, and the resulting methodology is called **neo-Riemannian analysis**. Neo-Riemannian analysis simplifies and codifies many of the principles underlying Riemann's various progression types, defining these relations as the results of chord transformations that take place on a *Tonnetz*, or tonal network. In the *Tonnetz* shown in Example 26.8, each triangle represents a triad (or a key, if we are using the *Tonnetz* to measure relationships between keys). Upward pointing triangles represent major triads; downward pointing triangles represent minor triads.[1] The pitches along each horizontal axis are arranged according to the circle of fifths, so that reading triangles that point upward (or downward) from the center of the diagram (C) to the right moves into the sharp keys, and from the center to the left moves into the flat keys. Selected triads are identified in bold for orientation.

In an equal-tempered tuning system (and for our purposes), enharmonic equivalence helps to limit the size of the *Tonnetz* (thus, for example, G♭ major would be the same as F♯ major). In a just-intonation tuning system, however, the *Tonnetz* could extend in all directions along an infinite plane.

---

[1] Incidentally, this symmetrical orientation preserves a concern with symmetry that was an important aspect of much of Riemann's work; since minor triads are the intervallic mirror image of major triads, for example, Riemann believed the fifth of the minor triad to be its "root."

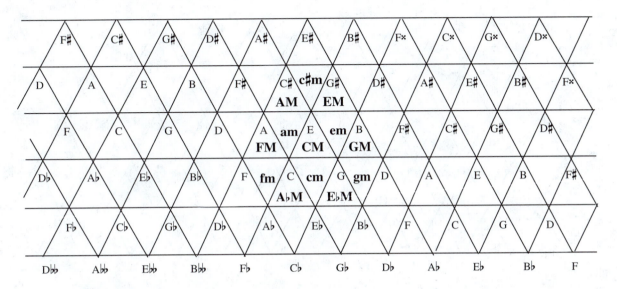

Example 26.8. The neo-Riemannian *Tonnetz*.

From any triangle (triad) on the *Tonnetz*, we can move to any of three adjacent triangles (triads). Each of these triangles shares two common tones with our triangle of origin. Moving from C major to C minor, for example, the triangles share the common P5 C and G; the "leftover" tone moves by half step. This is called a **parallel (P) transformation**, a label already familiar to us from parallel key relationships. Similarly, a move between two triangles that share a common M3 (in this case, C and E, shared by C major and A minor, with the "leftover" tone moving by whole step) is called a **relative (R) transformation**, exactly like relative key relationships. Our final move involves two triangles that share a common m3 (in this case, E and G, shared by C major and E minor, with the "leftover" tone moving by half step); this is called a **Leittonwechsel (L) transformation** (*Leittonwechsel*, a term coined by Riemann, means "leading-tone change"). These three simple transformations, like moves on some triangular-grid gameboard, are shown in Example 26.9.

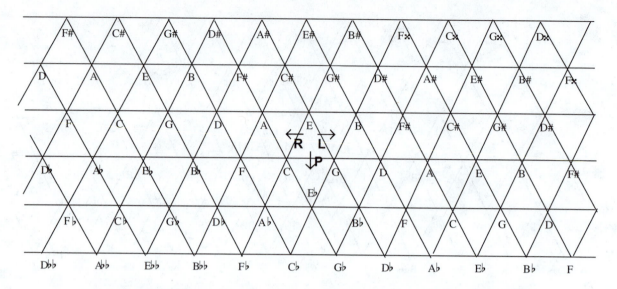

Example 26.9. The three simple neo-Riemannian transformations.

Using the "law of the shortest way," we can determine that, along with the root movement, each of the two common tones in the P, R, and L transformations remain unchanged while the third tone moves by half or whole step (Example 26.10).

——— common tone

- - - - - - movement by half or whole step

Example 26.10. Root-position voice leading for the P, R, and L transformations.

Neo-Riemannian analysis is useful to account for mediant-related progressions for which conventional harmonic syntax would not apply. It is especially powerful when **secondary** and **tertiary transformations** come into play—that is, progressions that are the result of *two* or *three* moves on the *Tonnetz*. (Again using the game analogy, a secondary progression might be likened to the L-shaped move of a knight on a chessboard.) For example, revisiting the Liszt progression in Example 26.7, the first progression of D major to B major could be achieved on the *Tonnetz* by moving first from D major to the intermediate stage of B minor (a relative transformation) and then from B minor to B major (a parallel transformation), resulting in the label **RP**, for relative-parallel (the order of letters in a compound transformation label always follow the order of the actual movements). Similarly, the movement from B major to E♭ major, invoking enharmonic equivalence (E♭ being the enharmonic equivalent of D♯) would be achieved by moving first from B major to D♯/ E♭ minor (enharmonically, a Leittonwechsel transformation), and then from there to E♭ major (a parallel transformation), resulting in an **LP** (Leittonwechsel-parallel) transformation. Note that in secondary transformations *one* common tone is preserved in the move from chord to chord, the other two chord members conventionally moving parsimoniously by half or whole step. The various secondary transformations are illustrated in Example 26.11; the upper row shows transformations from a major triad, while the lower row shows those same transformations from a minor triad.

Example 26.11. The secondary neo-Riemannian transformations.

Along with the simple and secondary neo-Riemannian transformations, one tertiary transformation deserves special mention—the change between two triads that share a common *third*, such as G major and G♯ minor. This progression could be the result of two different transformational paths (LPR or RPL), but the *aural* perception is that the other two voices "slide" chromatically up or down around the stationary third (Example 26.12). Thus, the transformational label **S** (for **Slide transformation**) is often used for such progressions, where two chords or keys of differing mode share a common third. Not only is the S label more streamlined than showing the progression as a tertiary transformation, but it also remedies the imprecision of having two possible transformational paths by focusing instead on the resultant aural impression.

Example 26.12. The S or "Slide" transformation. Solid lines show the actual neo-Riemannian voice leading that results from the tertiary transformational paths; dotted lines show the resultant aural impression.

Neo-Riemannian theory allows us to focus not so much on the specific chord labels in a musical passage as it does the *principles* governing harmonic progression in the passage. Consider the progression in Example 26.13, which is found at the beginning of Act III of Philip Glass's opera *Satyagraha*. As the transformational labels show, there is an impressive degree of symmetry in this passage. The "upper neighbor" and "lower neighbor" motions from chord to chord are revealed to be the same neo-Riemannian transformation (L). Moreover, framing these two L transformations are two S transformations.

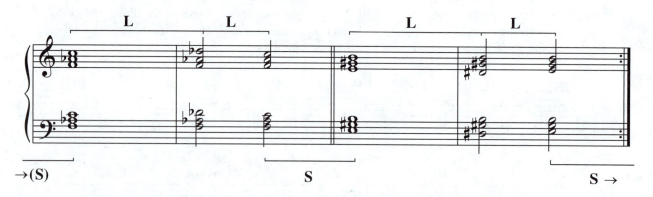

Example 26.13. A harmonic progression from Glass, *Satyagraha*, Act III (New Castle March).

Benjamin Britten's *Hymn to St. Cecilia*, composed in 1942, contains numerous chromatic mediant relationships at the chord-to-chord progression level and also at larger levels such as phrase endings. As Example 26.14 shows, the tonal center E is "prolonged" as the first three chords provide each of the possible major triad harmonizations of E. The first cadence's concluding E major chord ("psalm," measure 5, just before rehearsal number 1) is a PL transformation away from the second cadence's conclusion on C major ("calm," measure 11, just before rehearsal number 2), and the second cadence similarly is a PL transformation away from the third cadence's arrival on A♭ major ("prayer," measure 19, at rehearsal number 3). A♭ major is an LP transformation directly away from E major. The next cadence arrives on E♭ major at measure 25 (four measures before rehearsal number 4), and this introduces a new set of transformations: to C♭ major at measure 31 (a PL transformation), which is followed by a slide (S) transformation to C minor at measure 35. After lingering on an A♭ Lydian sonority for a few measures starting at rehearsal number 5 (measures 38–44), the key dramatically changes back to E major (a PL transformation), framing this first section of the piece with the E major tonic. Notice also that the initial PL–RP chain of transformations found in the first three chords is replicated at a higher structural level at the beginning of the middle section in E♭ major.

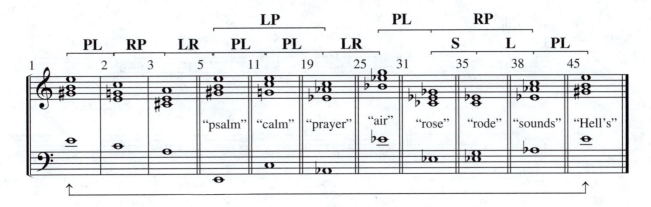

Example 26.14. Britten, *Hymn to St. Cecilia*, tonal overview of first section (mm. 1–67).

Hymn to St. Cecilia also ends with a cycle of neo-Riemannian progressions (measures 235–253, from rehearsal number 26 to the end), an overview of which is shown in Example 26.15.

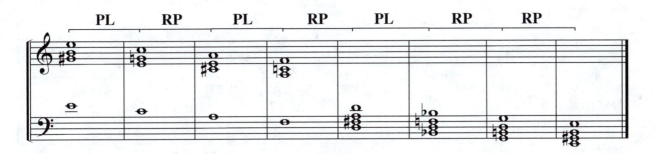

Example 26.15. Britten, *Hymn to St. Cecilia*, tonal overview of conclusion (rehearsal number 26 to end).

LEVEL MASTERY 26.2.

a. In the blanks under each excerpt below, provide the missing neo-Riemannian transformation label. Be sure to consider enharmonic equivalence where it would result in a simpler transformation.

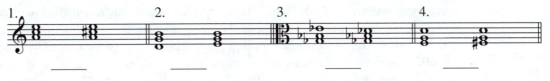

(Continued)

(Continued)

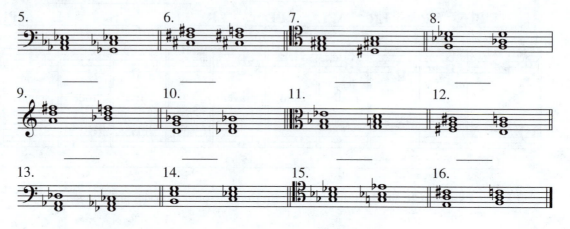

b. Given the first chord and the neo-Riemannian transformation label, provide the missing chord to complete the progression, following parsimonious voice leading.

CONCLUSION

The harmonic innovations considered in this chapter all illustrate the weakening of traditional functional tonality in the nineteenth century. Modulation became more frequent, and dissonances more pervasive, to the extent that in the music of composers such as Richard Wagner tonalities are often only implied by the functional role of certain chords, rather than decisively confirmed. Some harmonies were more elaborative than structural, resolving in ways other than their spelling implied (as in common-tone diminished seventh chords) or even enharmonically spelled in ways that made no sense in the key except as the result of chord mutation or the motion of individual voices (as in linear chords). Finally, chord sequences came to be used not following conventional harmonic syntax but merely by common tone or by parsimonious and chromatic voice leading. For such progressions, Roman numerals no longer make much sense. The labels of neo-Riemannian analysis focus not on labeling specific chords so much as categorizing the type of harmonic progression employed from one chord to the next. As music changed, tools for analyzing that music changed as well.

Terms to Know

chord mutation
chromatic mediant relationship
common-tone (embellishing) diminished
    seventh chord (ct°7)
Leittonwechsel (L) transformation
linear chord (LIN)

neo-Riemannian analysis
parallel (P) transformation
parsimonious voice leading
relative (R) transformation
slide (S) transformation
Tonnetz

Self-Test

26.1. Precede the following chords with the specified common-tone diminished seventh chord, adding your chord to the first part of each measure. Be sure to use the spacing of the chord provided to properly guide your voice leading. The first example is done for you as a model.

26.2. For each key signature provided in the middle of the line, provide the key signatures, and labels, for the chromatic-mediant-related keys below (to the left) and above (to the right). The first one is done for you. For some keys you may need to choose a more practical enharmonic equivalent.

Eb major E major G major Bb major B major

_____ _____ f# minor _____ _____

_____ _____ c minor _____ _____

_____ _____ E Major _____ _____

26.3.

a. In the blanks under each progression below, provide the missing neo-Riemannian transformation label. Be sure to consider enharmonic equivalence where it would result in a simpler transformation.

b. Given the first chord and the neo-Riemannian transformation label, provide the missing chord to complete the progression, following parsimonious voice leading.

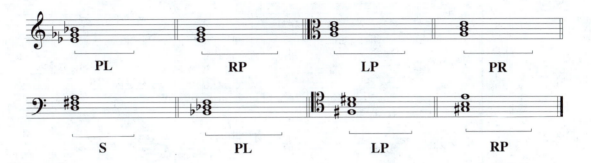

Apply This!

26.1. The following musical excerpt contains common-tone diminished seventh chords and linear chords. Provide harmonic analysis.

1. In stil - ler Nacht, zur er - sten Wacht, ein' Stim be - gunnt zu kla - gen, der

2. Der schö - ne Mond will un - ter gahn, für Leid nicht mehr mag schei - nen, die

(Continued)

(Continued)

(Continued)

(Continued)

Blü - me - lein, mit Thrä - nen rein hab' ich sie all' be - go - ssen.

wil - den Thier traur'n auch mit mir in Stei - nen und in Klüf - ten.

CHAPTER 27

MODULATION 3

OVERVIEW

This chapter revisits the topic of modulation to introduce one last modulation technique—enharmonic modulation, which involves changing the spelling of a chord to change its function and allow it to function a different way in a different key. (Because some of these spellings could include augmented sixth chords or altered dominant chords, we have delayed discussion of this modulation technique until now.)

CHAPTER OUTLINE

INTRODUCTION

In Chapters 17 and 18 we examined several types of modulation. This chapter revisits the topic, introducing one last type of modulation that became very common in the nineteenth century. It might be regarded as more "devious" than the others, because it involves changing the spelling—but not the sound—of a chord. The "deception" of enharmonic modulation—in which a chord is heard and expected to resolve one way but actually resolves in a dramatically different fashion—may be seen to have narrative qualities that were very important to the aesthetic of the Romantic era.

ENHARMONIC MODULATION

Enharmonic modulation was an especially common technique of modulation in music of the Romantic era, though it is also found in music of the Classical era. In this type of modulation, one or more tones of a chord are respelled to an enharmonic equivalent in order to change the chord's function. As an illustration of how this works, play each of the fully diminished seventh chords in Example 27.1.

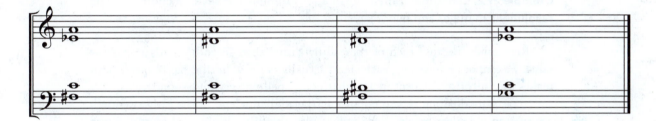

Example 27.1. Enharmonic spellings of a fully diminished seventh chord.

Obviously all of these chords *sound* the same, but each chord would function quite differently in the context of a piece of music, because each chord is spelled differently, with a different root and in a different inversion. Since we know that a diatonic fully diminished seventh chord only occurs built above the leading tone, the root of each chord must be the leading tone of the key in which it functions.

Example 27.2 shows the fully diminished seventh chord and its enharmonic spellings from Example 27.1, now including their resolutions (following tendency tone resolution patterns). Each fully diminished seventh chord can be spelled four different ways; each chord spelling may be resolved in a major or minor key. Thus, for any fully diminished seventh chord there are eight possible outcomes. Play through each one, and notice how drastically different these outcomes are.

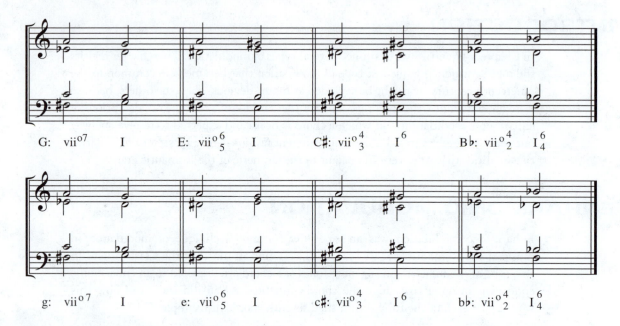

Example 27.2. Enharmonic spellings of a fully diminished seventh chord, with its resolutions in major and minor keys.

Remember, because each of these fully diminished seventh chords *sounds* the same, we cannot perceive how each chord actually *functions* until it has resolved. This makes the "surprise" element in an enharmonic spelling very high—one reason why this type of modulation was so popular in the Romantic era. In the early twentieth century, an old silent-movie cliché was to play the fully diminished seventh chord tremelo style when the villain made his or her first appearance on screen; this may have been because the fully diminished seventh chord contained two tritones (recall the *diabolus in musica* connotations of the tritone), but also it was because the sound of the fully diminished seventh itself was fraught with suspense—upon hearing it, one could not be absolutely certain of how the chord would resolve. Repeating the chord in different inversions (or transpositions sequencing up a minor third) only added to the suspense (Example 27.3).

With great suspense and drama

Example 27.3. A cliché "silent-movie" music cue involving sequential fully diminished seventh chords.

The similarity between the dominant seventh chord and augmented sixth chords is also sometimes used in enharmonic modulations. Example 27.4 shows a passage from Mozart's Piano Sonata in A minor, K.310. The excerpt begins in C major (mm. 50–51). By measure 53–54 the presence of D♭ and B♭ suggests that a modulation to F major or minor is underway; measures 54–56 all suggest a resolution to F is imminent.[1] Notice, however, the spelling of measure 56's harmony in measure 57; the B♭'s have been replaced by A♯'s, signaling to the performer (if not the listener!) that this "dominant seventh" chord will in fact be resolving as a German augmented sixth chord. In measure 58, the C–A♯ augmented sixth interval has resolved outward to octave Bs; while measures 54–57 suggest, to the ear, that the chord will resolve to F major, the resolution turns out instead to be a tritone away from what we were led to expect!

Example 27.4. Mozart, Piano Sonata in A minor, K.310 (i), mm. 50–58.

---

[1] The C♯ in measure 55 is perhaps one of Mozart's enharmonic notational jokes, suggesting that he is about to change key to D minor—the C♯, of course, moves against its tendency back to C♮ in the following measure.

In the second movement of his Fifth Symphony, Beethoven similarly uses the German augmented sixth to suddenly change key from A♭ major to C major (a key related by chromatic mediant to the tonic of the movement). Liszt's piano transcription of this passage is shown in Example 27.5. As we learned earlier in this chapter, when a modulation involves a pivot chord of some sort we recognize the key change only after it has already occurred. Here, the pivot chord is the A♮ fully diminished seventh chord in measures 27–28, which would function as a vii°7/ii in A♭ major but which actually functions as a common-tone diminished seventh chord in C major. By lowering the A♮ (against its expected resolution, since the tone was chromatically raised) back to A♭ in measure 29, Beethoven creates a German augmented sixth chord in the key of C major that resolves to V via the cadential $^6_4$ in the following measure.

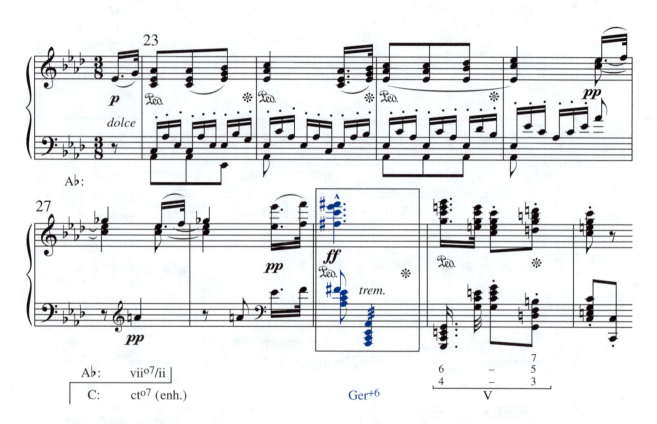

Example 27.5. Beethoven, Symphony no. 5 (ii), Liszt transcription, mm. 23–31.

Given the key provided at the opening of each of the following musical excerpts, determine the key to which the music has modulated at the conclusion of the excerpt. Then, analyze the boxed common chord(s) within each excerpt, providing its labeling in each key. Where only one box is found, you will need to respell the chord to function in one of the two keys.

a. Beethoven, Piano Sonata no. 8 in C minor ("Pathétique"), op. 13 (i), mm. 134–136.

g:

b. Paul Simon, "Tenderness" [0:53–1:14], chord progression only.

C:

c. Schumann, Symphony no. 2, op. 61 (ii), mm. 1–8, strings only.

PART 4: Advanced Chromatic Harmony and Contemporary Techniques

Each of the following figured bass progressions contains an enharmonic modulation involving a reinterpretation of an augmented sixth or diminished third chord. Complete the progression with tenor, alto, and soprano parts (using the opening two chords to help you determine spacing) and provide the harmonic analysis, including the location of the modulation and the new key.

OTHER TYPES OF ENHARMONIC MODULATION

Other chords, such as altered dominant chords, are sometimes used in enharmonic modulations. For example, when a dominant seventh chord is altered to have a lowered fifth, the resulting sonority is enharmonically equivalent to a French augmented sixth chord (and vice versa). One can find examples of this type of enharmonic modulation in some pieces from the second half of the nineteenth and early twentieth centuries.

Example 27.6 shows a particularly inventive example from the first movement of Brahms's Piano Quartet in G minor, op. 25. This passage begins in D major. After several cadential gestures in D major, the V^7 of D is replaced in measure 158 (and again in measure 159) with an altered dominant seventh (in second inversion with the fifth in the bass flatted). This chord is identical to a Fr^{+6} in G minor, and so Brahms subtly changes its function by adding a C natural to the D major chord that follows it in measure 160, making that chord a V^7 of G minor rather than a tonic chord in D major (and thus facilitating the repeat of the sonata-form exposition).

Example 27.6. Brahms, Piano Quartet in G Minor, op. 25 (i), mm. 155–161.
(Continued)

(Continued)

Another type of augmented sixth enharmonic modulation resembles tritone substitution. We have already seen that in jazz a "flatted-fifth" dominant seventh enharmonically maps onto itself when transposed a tritone away, and that this is the basis for so-called tritone substitutions. Similarly, the French augmented sixth chord maps onto itself enharmonically as a French $\frac{4}{3}$ chord (or an altered V_3^4/V with a flatted fifth in the bass) in another key a tritone away (Example 27.7).

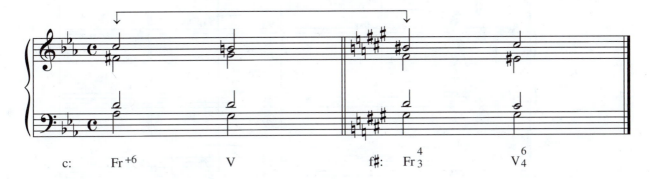

Example 27.7. The Fr^{+6} in C minor and Fr$_3^4$ in F♯ minor, compared.

Example 27.8 provides an illustration of this kind of "double duty" French augmented sixth chord, using a Fr^{+6} as a linear sonority in a modulation from D major to F major. Beginning with a V^9 in measure 68, the chord mutates to an implied Bx$\sharp^{\circ 4}_2$ (the D$\sharp$ is not present) in the following measure, which does not function in D (because it would be a vii$^{\circ 4}_2$ of vii$^{\circ}$). In measure 70 the cellos move by half steps in contrary motion, resulting in a V$^9_{\sharp 5}$ chord. If we interpret the G$\sharp$ in the descending bass line in measure 71 as an accented chromatic passing tone, in the second half of the measure the {G, E$\sharp$, C$\sharp$, B} chord would be a Fr^{+6} in B major or minor (resolving to F$\sharp$, the V of B). Instead of this, however, Mahler treats the chord as a French $^4_3$ chord (or an altered V$^4_3$/V with a flatted fifth in the bass) in F major, bringing us to a cadential $^6_4$ chord (as shown by the harp) in measure 72. (Annotations are not given on the example, in order for you to find these details for yourself.)

Example 27.8. Mahler, Symphony no. 5 (iv, Adagietto), mm. 68–72.

Other enharmonic modulations are possible with altered dominants that have the fifth of the chord raised. A dominant triad that is altered by raising its fifth (as in a V$^{\sharp 5}$) is an augmented triad which, when inverted, is enharmonically equivalent to other root-position augmented triads. For example, in his Prelude in D minor (op. 28 no. 24), Chopin modulates back to the tonic from D♭ major by enharmonically reinterpreting the augmented triad (Example 27.9). The first four measures of the excerpt unfold over an ostinato of the D♭ major triad. That triad is mutated in measure 47 by the appearance of A♮, making it a D♭ augmented triad in root position (compare the melody in measure 47 with two measures before, and notice the accent Chopin gives the changed note). In measure 50 the D♭ in the bass has been enharmonically changed to C♯; now the triad appears to be spelled as a second-inversion F augmented triad, but since C♯ is the leading tone of D minor, we might even interpret this as a V^6 of D minor, altered with the F in the chord as an anticipation of the third in the tonic chord that arrives in measure 51.

Example 27.9. Chopin, Prelude in D minor, op. 28 no. 24, mm. 43–52.

THE OMNIBUS PROGRESSION

In some nineteenth-century compositions, chains of enharmonic Ger^{+6}–V7 reinterpretations lead to a minor-third harmonic sequence called the **omnibus progression**. In Example 24.20 we saw how Tchaikovsky used the Ger^{+6} and Ger^{o3} sonorities to embellish a i_4^6 chord by neighbor motion around the dominant scale degree. If he had continued the chromatic bass descent (and accompanying voice exchange) one step further past the Ger^{o3}, the next chord would have spelled a new dominant seventh chord, {A, C♯, E, G}. This chord could in turn be enharmonically reinterpreted as a new Ger^{+6} chord, {A, C♯, E, F𝄪}, in C♯ major or minor. Example 27.10 takes this opening progression and extends it, showing how the omnibus progression works over the complete traversal of an octave in the bass descent. Note the voice exchange that occurs between the augmented sixth and the diminished third.

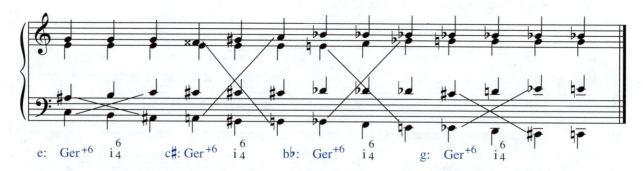

Example 27.10. A full ombinus progression beginning on Ger^{+6} of E minor.

Usually composers did not take full advantage of the sequence as shown in this example; remember, we have already seen that when it comes to sequences, "a little goes a long way," and too much sequential repetition can become predictable and tedious. Example 27.11, a passage from Liszt's "Liebestraum," shows a characteristic use of the omnibus progression.

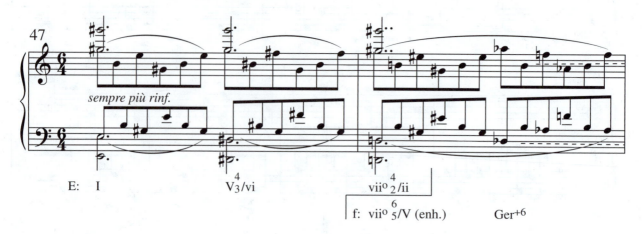

Example 27.11. Liszt, "Liebestraum," mm. 47–50. *(Continued)*

(Continued)

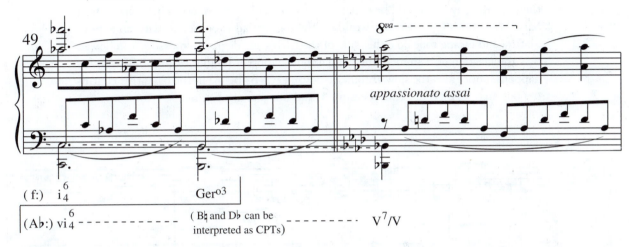

Self-Tests
27.1 and 27.2
may be done
at this time.

Another form of the omnibus progression involves enharmonic reinterpretation of fully diminished seventh chords, as shown in Example 27.12. Note that the first chord of each measure in the example is a respelled fully diminished seventh chord.

Apply This!
27.1, 27.2,
and 27.3 may
be done at
this time.

Example 27.12. An omnibus progression involving fully diminished seventh chords.

Workbook
Exercise 27.1
may be done
at this time.

MODULATION AS NARRATIVE

It is possible to conceive of a work's **tonal plan**—the overall structure of keys touched upon in a piece and their respective relation to the tonic—in narrative terms. Sudden, unexpected modulations, for example, are analogous to twists in the plot of a story. The point where the music reaches the key that is "farthest away" from the tonic may well be interpreted as the climax of the story—how will the characters find their way out of this predicament, or find their way back home? The return to the tonic toward the end, on the other hand, acts as a kind of *denouement* or homecoming.

Mozart's Fantasy in C minor (K.475), composed in 1785, presents an interesting case study of the dramatic and narrative power of modulation. Example 27.13 shows the opening nineteen measures of this piece. Notice that although the key is ostensibly C minor, Mozart uses no key signature. This is not a careless omission on Mozart's part, nor does it refer to C major—it is a *tabula rasa* ("blank slate"), signifying that theoretically any key would be equally accessible within this piece. The opening four bars do establish C minor, but weakly—the tonic triad is decorated with an appoggiatura and escape tone on either side of the fifth scale degree in measure 1, followed by a tonicization of V in measure 2 and a tonicization of IV in measures 3–4. As this happens, notice also the slow chromatic descent (C–B–Bb–A) in the bass; this continues one step further, to Ab, in measure 5, and our journey begins.

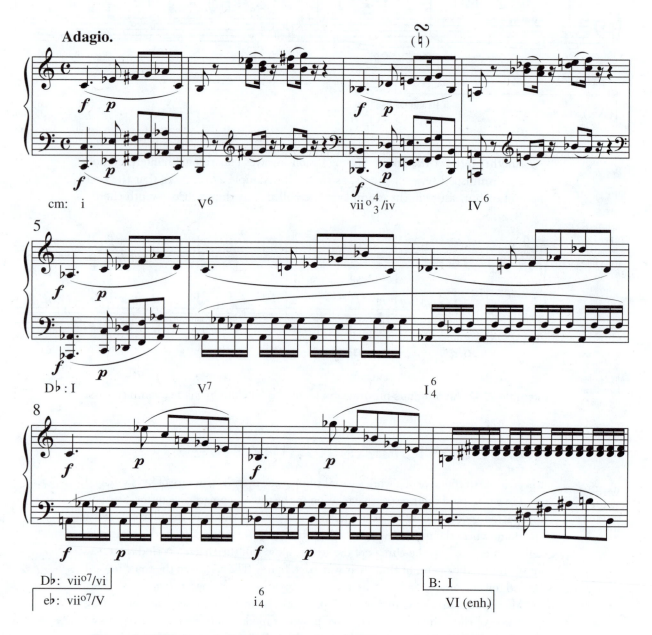

Example 27.13. Mozart, Fantasia in C minor, K.475, mm. 1–19. *(Continued)*

(Continued)

In the remainder of this excerpt, Mozart moves rapidly through a number of key areas, mainly by capitalizing on the strong dominant implications of a major-minor seventh chord (which must be a "V^7 of something") or a second-inversion triad (which most commonly implies a cadential $^6_4$). For example, measures 5–7 briefly establish the key of D♭ major by means of a V^7 of D♭ (measure 6) followed by a I^6_4 in measure 7. Measures 8–9, on the other hand, suggest the key of E♭ minor, due to the i^6_4 in measure 9.

The proliferation of sharps in measure 10 indicates yet another key change; the major-minor seventh chord in measure 11 indicates a movement to B major in measures 10–11 ($I-V^6_5$). Another major-minor seventh chord, in measure 12, indicates a very fleeting reference to D major or minor (A^7 being the V^7 of D), but this is not followed through; instead, the harmony slips chromatically to a first-inversion F minor triad in measure 13. The G major-minor seventh chord in measure 14 tells us that the F minor chord in measure 13 is a iv^6 in C minor (the tonic at last!), followed by a V^7 in the following measure.

Again, however, Mozart does not follow through with the expected tonic chord. In measure 15 we see a first-inversion E♭ minor triad; because of the first-inversion F minor triad just two bars before, and the overall chromatic descent in the bass that began with the B in measure 10, this chord could be interpreted as another iv^6, this time of B♭ minor. Because of the pattern of measures 13–14, we would expect measure 15 to begin a sequence of that pattern a whole step down (iv^6-V^7 in B♭ minor). Once again, however, Mozart does not follow through on these expectations; instead, measures 16–17 present a $V^7-I^6_4$ progression in the key of B major.

Surveying the keys traversed in this passage, then, notice how briefly Mozart stays in the tonic. After measures 1–4 (which arguably weaken the tonic by emphasizing tonicizations rather than a strong statement of the tonic and dominant chords), the only reference to the tonic is through the iv^6-V^7 progression in measures 13–14. Furthermore, almost all of the other keys touched upon in the passage—D♭ major, E♭ minor, B major, and B♭ minor—are not closely related keys of the tonic. This is a highly unusual move so early in a composition of this period, and it is intended to have a disorienting effect—like Hansel and Gretel wandering deeper into the woods.

In literature, the narrative of departure and return goes back to ancient mythology, in epics such as Homer's *The Odyssey*. In music, a tonal version of this narrative can be found in works ranging from the "free fantasias" of C. P. E. Bach through the symphonies of Beethoven and on to Chopin's Ballades and Wagner's operas.

CONCLUSION

Modulation involves a kind of deception. A particular chord changes its function, and sometimes its spelling, without changing its sound.

The ambiguity of the chords involved in enharmonic modulation has to do with symmetry. A fully diminished seventh chord can be spelled four different ways, so that four different roots are possible for the same sonority; these roots are equidistant from one another, and they result from the division of the octave into four equal intervals (the minor third, or its enharmonic equivalent the augmented second). Similarly, the augmented triad can be spelled three different ways, with three different possible roots. These roots are a major third (or its enharmonic equivalent, a diminished fourth) apart, resulting from the division of the octave into three equal intervals. Enharmonic reinterpretation of the augmented sixth as a dominant seventh chord, or vice versa, results in resolutions a tritone apart from one another—the tritone is the interval that results when the octave is divided into two equal parts.

Example 27.14 summarizes how these chords derive from different equal divisions of the octave. Symmetry will become an important compositional consideration in much twentieth-century music.

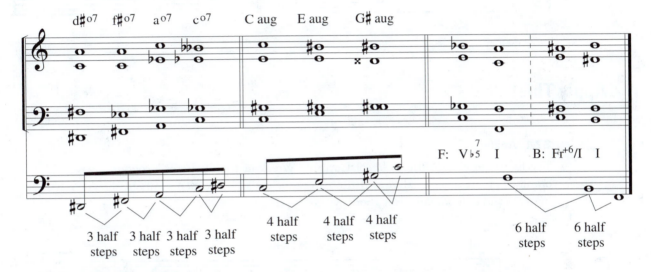

Example 27.14. Enharmonically related chords derived from equal divisions of the octave.

Terms to Know

enharmonic modulation   omnibus progression   tonal plan

Self-Test

27.1. Which of the following chord labels is *not* enharmonically equivalent to the others?

a) G♭: vii°⁷/IV
b) B♭: vii°⁴₂/iii
c) b: vii°⁷
d) D♭: vii°⁶₅/V
e) E: vii°⁴₃/ii

27.2. Given the fully diminished seventh chord below, provide its enharmonic spellings and each chord's harmonic analysis as a diatonic seventh chord in another minor key, using Example 27.4 as your model. Provide resolutions for each chord, using tendency-tone patterns.

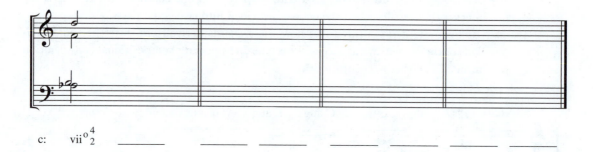

c: vii°$^4_2$ _____   _____   _____

Apply This!

27.1. Analysis.

The following excerpt (from Procol Harum, "Wreck of the Hesperus") contains an omnibus progression. Analyze with Roman numerals and inversion symbols, showing keys and enharmonic pivot chords where applicable.

(Continued)

(Continued)

27.2. Composition.

a. Complete the phrase below, using an enharmonic modulation involving the last chord provided as a pivot. End the phrase with a perfect authentic cadence in the new key.

b. Write a short piece for piano in ternary form. The *A* section should be a double period, ending on a perfect authentic cadence in the tonic key; approach this cadence with an augmented sixth chord, handled with appropriate voice leading. The middle (*B*) section should be in a different key. Use an enharmonic modulation involving one of the chords covered in this chapter to effect your key change back to the tonic at the return of the *A* section.

27.3. Improvisation. At the keyboard, demonstrate how you would effect the following key changes using enharmonic modulations involving the chords indicated:

C minor   →   D♭ major   (augmented sixth chord)

F minor   →   B major   (Neapolitan sixth chord)

C major   →   E♭ minor   (fully diminished seventh chord)

CHAPTER 28

CONTEMPORARY TECHNIQUES 1

OVERVIEW

As the Romantic ethos of personal expression fostered great harmonic and formal development in the nineteenth century, so in the twentieth century one finds almost unimaginable stylistic diversity. At the turn of the twentieth century, composers were faced with the choice of continuing in the trend toward chromatic complexity seen through much of the nineteenth century, or turning away from complexity toward appropriating older styles and models. This dichotomy sowed the seeds for the stylistic variety in music today.

INTRODUCTION: THE PATH TO NEW MUSIC, PATHWAYS BACK TO OLDER MUSICS

As we have seen, the nineteenth century was a time of great harmonic and formal experimentation in music. As composers experimented with the implications of harmony in an equal-tempered system, three trends developed:

1. Tonicizations began to be extended (so that, for example, a chord before a secondary dominant might be a secondary *predominant* of the chord being tonicized), and, from the other end of the continuum, modulations came to be briefer and more frequent.
2. Melodic dissonance came to receive greater metric and durational emphasis. Accented dissonances (such as appoggiaturas and suspensions) became more frequent, and often such dissonances were supermetrical (lasting longer than the beat level of the primary pulse stream).
3. Due in part to the freer use of melodic dissonance, there was a renewed emphasis on the horizontal dimension of music—its linear character. "Harmonies" in this sense would sometimes be merely the result of several overlapping melodic strands—so-called "linear chords."

A TALE OF THREE CHORDS

These three trends can be seen in the three excerpts that follow. All three of them feature different treatments of the sonority that sounds, at least, like a half-diminished seventh chord. Up to this point, we have understood the half-diminished seventh to have two functional contexts: In minor keys, it functions as a $ii^{\varnothing7}$ (resolving to a V with the root moving up a P4 or down a P5), and (less commonly) in major keys, it functions as a $vii^{\varnothing7}$ (resolving to the tonic, with the root moving up a m2). Observe the different (enharmonic) spellings, and resolutions, of the chords that follow.

Our first example comes from the Prelude to Wagner's *Tristan and Isolde* (see also Web Feature 3.3), composed between 1857 and 1859. Wagner is known for his use of **leitmotifs**—symbolic motives woven through the music as a way of advancing and sometimes commenting on the dramatic action. Two of these leitmotifs are shown in Example 28.1a; their appearances in the opening bars of the prelude are shown in Example 28.1b. The first chord of the opera is one of the most famous in Western music—it has come to be called the "Tristan chord" (abbreviated TR). The chord is enharmonically equivalent to a half-diminished seventh chord, and yet it contains two fourths and a third rather than the three thirds that would make up a conventional seventh chord. Its spelling is due to the overlapping of the two leitmotivs. Notice how the chord "resolves"—it appears to change to a French augmented sixth chord, but not for long. Ultimately the phrase comes to end on an unresolved dominant seventh chord. (The Tristan chord makes many appearances throughout the opera, but it is only resolved in the closing bars of the finale as the two lovers are united in death.)

Example 28.1a. Two leitmotifs from Wagner's *Tristan and Isolde*.

Example 28.1b. Wagner, Prelude to *Tristan and Isolde* (piano reduction), mm. 1–11, with leitmotifs and Tristan chord shown.

Other composers followed suit with their own novel resolutions of the "half-diminished" sonority. Richard Strauss, in his *Till Eulenspiegel's Merry Pranks* (1894–95) depicted the mischievous peasant folk hero with the unusual chord and resolution shown in Example 28.2. Like Wagner's Tristan chord, this came to be called the "Till chord." It basically functions in F major as a vii^{o4}_{3} with a raised third, but it resolves as if it were an augmented sixth chord.

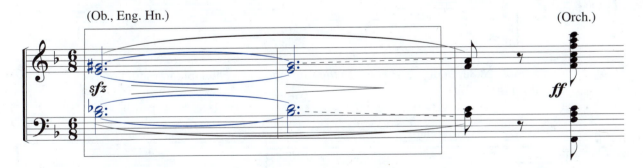

Example 28.2. Strauss, *Till Eulenspiegel's Merry Pranks*, "Till chord" at mm. 47–48.

The opening chord of Achille-Claude Debussy's *Prelude to the Afternoon of a Faun*, composed in 1894, presents another variation on the half-diminished sonority and its resolution (Example 28.3a). Debussy's approach throughout the piece involves chord mutation—gradual chromatic alteration of chords to form other chords. As Example 28.3b shows, two voices move up one semitone (+1), while two others are enharmonically respelled.

Example 28.3a. Debussy, *Prelude to the Afternoon of a Faun* (piano reduction), mm. 1–6.

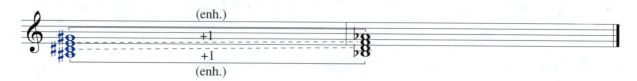

Example 28.3b. Debussy, *Prelude to the Afternoon of a Faun*, mm. 4–5, voice-leading reduction.

The influence of Wagner could not be ignored. Some composers, such as Gustav Mahler (1860–1911), Anton Bruckner (1824–1896), and Max Reger (1873–1916), extended the chromatic path forged by Wagner to the point where tonality no longer seemed to exert its cohesive control. Other composers, such as Achille-Claude Debussy (1862–1918), Maurice Ravel (1875–1937), Erik Satie (1866–1925), Igor Stravinsky (1882–1971), and Bela Bartók (1881–1945), resisted the chromatic pull of Wagner and turned instead to music of the past for new inspirations. This divergence led to an extraordinary variety of styles and compositional techniques that has continued to the present. Rather than attempt an orderly historically grounded stylistic survey, then, in this chapter we will consider some of twentieth-century tonal music's more pervasive harmonic innovations.

IMPRESSIONISM

The term *Impressionism* originated in the art of several late-nineteenth-century French painters, who sought to depict the mood or ambience of subjects through light and color, rather than to clearly depict the object itself. Because the *impression* of the object was more important than depicting the object itself, blurred or even murky outlines were preferred over simple lines and shapes, and muted colors were preferred. The movement's name, originally pejorative, is derived from Claude Monet (1840–1926)'s 1873 painting *Impression: Soleil Levant* (*Impression: Sunrise*); other important Impressionist artists included Édouard Manet (1832–1883), Paul Cézanne (1839–1906), Edgar Degas (1834–1917), Mary Cassatt (1844–1926), Auguste Renoir (1841–1919), and Paul Gauguin (1848–1903).

Impressionism in music similarly focused on evocation and atmosphere, often aiming to depict ancient or exotic scenes through sound:

- Phrases tend to be irregular in length, and forms are similarly ambiguous— thematic material may return, but not in the predictable manner of the classic forms.
- Orchestral colors tend to be muted, analogous to the soft, subtle colors in Impressionist art.
- Traditional harmonic progressions are often avoided—sometimes sonorities are simply shifted or transposed up and down, in a technique called **planing**.
- Unresolved dissonances are common; ninths, elevenths, and thirteenths are often added to chords for the sake of harmonic color, rather than as melodic dissonances to be resolved.
- Exotic scales are also often used, such as whole-tone scales, pentatonic and octatonic scales, and modes (see Chapter 2).

Impressionistic music often has a tonal center but does not follow common-practice harmonic syntax. Rather than creating a tonic through functional harmony, such music may project a tonic through repeated assertion, for example through the use of an ostinato or pedal point. Often dissonances are left unresolved, allowing the listener to hear those added dissonances as color tones within the chord. For example, the first of the *Three Gymnopédies* by Erik Satie uses unresolved major-major sevenths in a placid IV^7–I^7 ostinato (Example 28.4). The static accompaniment contributes to the overall languid mood (the title refers to a slow athletic dance performed by youth in ancient Greece).

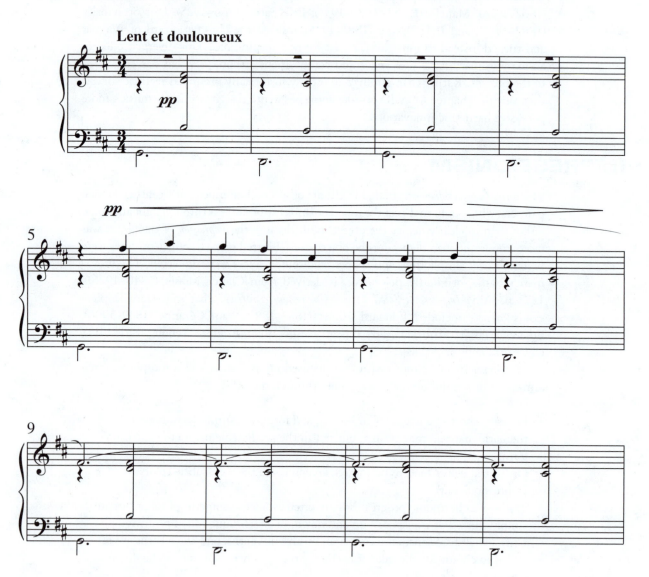

Example 28.4. Satie, "Premiere Gymnopédie," mm. 1–12.

PLANING

In Impressionist music, one will often encounter chords that are treated as stacked "blocks" of sound, shifting position as a unit. This technique is called **planing**. In **diatonic** (or **free**) **planing**, the entire passage makes use of the diatonic pitch collection (see Chapter 2); the chords themselves, however, are not always of the same quality (Example 28.5). In **chromatic** (or **strict**) **planing**, by contrast, the chords are all of the same quality; in Example 28.6, for instance, all of the chords are major-minor-major (MmM) ninth chords, and certain pitches are chromatically changed over the course of the planing (for example, both A♭ and A♮ occur in the passage). Thus, the passage is not limited to the diatonic pitch collection.

Example 28.5. Diatonic (free) planing.

Example 28.6. Chromatic (strict) planing.

Example 28.7, the opening of Debussy's "La Cathédrale Engloutie" ("The Engulfed Cathedral"), shows an example of the G major pentatonic pitch-class collection, employed in the context of planing sonorities made up of perfect harmonic intervals (octaves, fifths, and fourths). (Note that the F1–C2–F2 sonority in the left hand at measures 3 and 4 does not belong to this pitch-class collection; it could thus be interpreted as having a "passing" function between the G1–D2–G2 sonority in the left hand at measure 1 and the E1–B1–E2 in the left hand at measure 5. The bass descent is also achieved by planing.)

Profondément calme (Dans une brume doucement sonore)

Pentatonic collection
(G, A, B, D, E)

Example 28.7. Debussy, "La Cathédrale Engloutie," from *Preludes*, Book 1, mm. 1–6.

In another passage from "La Cathédrale Engloutie" (Example 28.8), diatonic planing and a reiterated C pedal tone evoke the sound of medieval choral *organum* and a large tolling bell. Note that the passage begins with the C Ionian mode (or major scale) pitch collection, but changes to Mixolydian mode when B♮ is replaced by B♭.

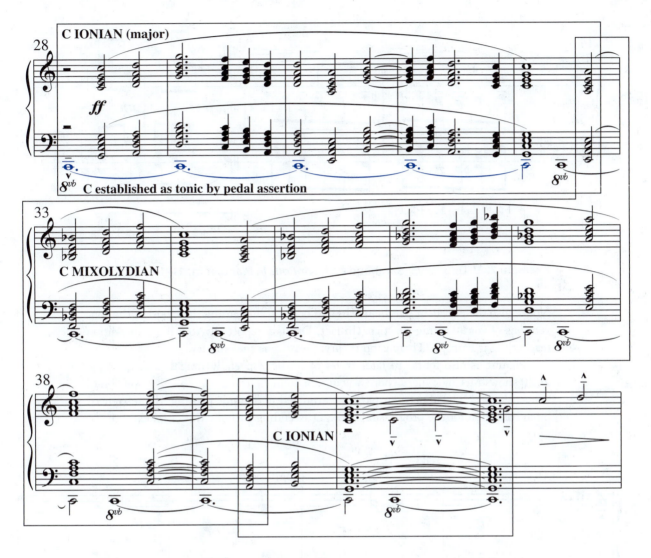

Example 28.8. Debussy, "La Cathédrale Engloutie," from *Preludes*, Book 1, mm. 28–41.

Example 28.9 contains a number of major-minor ("dominant") seventh chords in sequence; however, none of these chords function as seventh chords (in which the chord seventh resolves downward by step in progressing to the next chord). Instead, the overall *sonority* of the dominant seventh chord shifts up and down by chromatic planing.

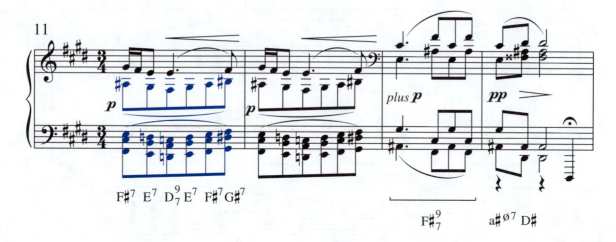

Example 28.9. Debussy, "Sarabande," from *Pour le Piano*, mm. 11–14.

Notice also the prevalent parallel fifths and octaves, in seeming disregard of the conventions of voice-leading practice. (In fact, Debussy reportedly told his composition teacher César Franck, "There is no theory; pleasure is the only law.")

Planing is also found in later styles of music, especially modal jazz. Example 28.10 shows McCoy Tyner's chord voicing for John Coltrane's (1926–1967) version of "Greensleeves." The upper four parts are arranged in diatonic planing; the referential pitch collection for the progression is the D ascending melodic minor scale.

Example 28.10. McCoy Tyner's chord voicings in the introductory vamp to "Greensleeves."

LEVEL MASTERY 28.1

1. Given the complete sonority for the first chord and the bass note for each subsequent chord, complete the progressions using strict (chromatic) planing. Be sure to use naturals to cancel out any previous chromatic alterations.

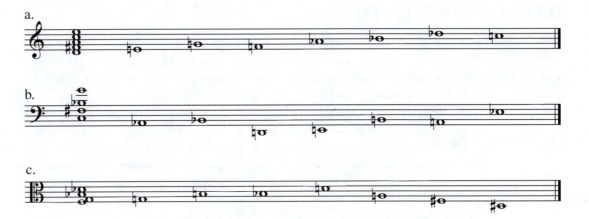

a.

b.

c.

2. Given the pitch collection implicit in the key signature of each example, the completed sonority for the first chord, and the bass note for each subsequent chord, complete the progressions using free (diatonic) planing. For the first two examples, identify the resultant chord qualities in the blanks above the staff. (Example c. is quartal-quintal, i.e. made up of fourths and fifths rather than thirds.)

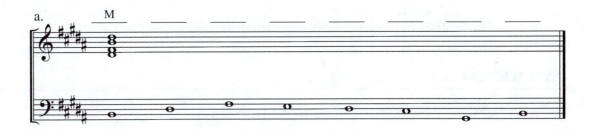

a.   M _____ _____ _____ _____ _____ _____ _____

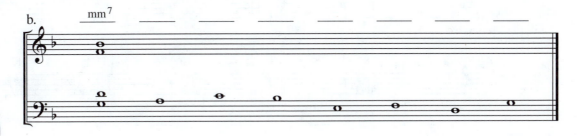

b.   mm⁷ _____ _____ _____ _____ _____ _____

For more on extended tertian chords and planing in a piece by Maurice Ravel, see Web Feature 28.1 at this time.

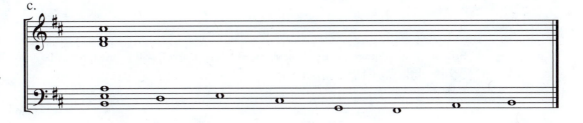

c.

INTEGER NOTATION

In much of the music of this period, functional tonality no longer strictly applies. Whereas in the Classic and Romantic eras the spelling of a pitch-class name would communicate very different things about the note's function (chromatically raised notes would resolve upward while chromatically lowered notes would resolve downward, for example), in so-called "post-tonal" styles these distinctions are irrelevant. Instead, pitches are often labeled primarily for notational convenience (ease of reading).

Since the functional distinction implied by enharmonic labels no longer applies, it is often convenient to label pitch classes by **integer notation**; designating C as zero (0), each half step upward is assigned a number between 1 and 9, as shown in Example 28.11; because 10 and 11 are double-digit numbers, they are designated as either (arbitrarily) A and B or as T (for "ten") and E (or "eleven").[1]

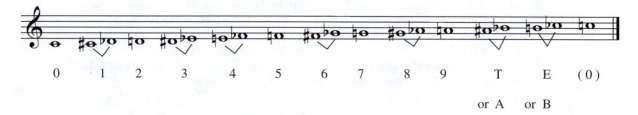

Example 28.11. Integer notation for pitch classes.

LEVEL MASTERY 28.2

Provide the integer label for each of the pitches below.

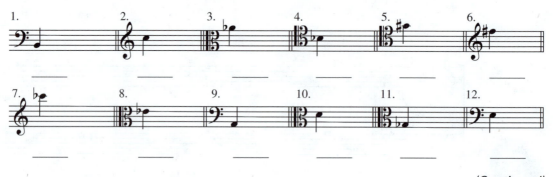

(Continued)

---

[1]Because of the arbitrary nature of the A and B labels, T and E will be used in this book to signify pcs "ten" and "eleven."

(Continued)

Workbook
Exercise 28.1
may be done
at this time.

SYNTHETIC SCALES

Equal temperament and the expansion of chromaticism also led some composers to formulate new scales. For example, Debussy and other composers made use of the **whole-tone scale**, made up entirely of whole steps (mostly major seconds, though at some point in the scale a diminished third—as an enharmonic equivalent—is unavoidable). There are only two possible whole-tone collections: WT_0 (including C) and WT_1 (including C♯ or D♭), shown in Example 28.12a. If we take either of these two scales and transpose it up or down a whole step, the result is a rotation of the original scale. Notice also that, using the whole-tone system, the only triad available is the augmented triad, a triad that also has symmetrical properties (Example 28.12b). A famous instance of Debussy's use of the whole-tone pitch-class collection is shown in Example 28.13.

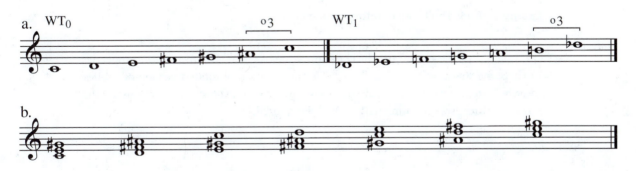

Example 28.12. a. The two whole-tone pitch-class collections. b. Augmented triads constructed from the WT_0 collection.

Modéré (♪ = 88)
(Dans un rythme sans rigueur et caressant.)

Example 28.13. Debussy, "Voiles," from *Preludes*, Book 1, mm. 1–6.

Debussy also turned to the past for other scalar resources, such as modes and the pentatonic scale.

Other composers, notably Nikolai Rimsky-Korsakov (1844–1908), Rimsky-Korsakov's pupil Igor Stravinsky, and Béla Bartók, made use of the **octatonic scale**, constructed of alternating half and whole steps. There are three types of octatonic collections, shown in Example 28.14. These are sometimes given the labels $OCT_{0,1}$, $OCT_{1,2}$, and $OCT_{2,3}$, referring respectively to the presence of their distinctive dyads C–D♭, C♯–D, or D–E♭ (or their enharmonic equivalents).[2]

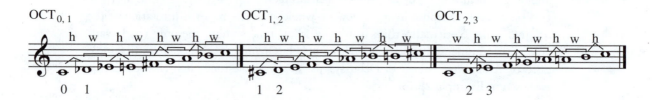

Example 28.14. The three octatonic scale collections.

Like the whole-tone scale, the octatonic scale has its own symmetrical properties. In the same way that the whole-tone scale transposes to a rotated version of itself at the whole step, the octatonic scale transposes to a rotated version of itself when transposed by three, six, and nine half steps (Example 28.15).

---

[2] Some theorists refer to the $OCT_{2,3}$ collection as $OCT_{0,2}$. This label, however, does not maintain the half-step interval used to identify the other two collections.

PART 4: Advanced Chromatic Harmony and Contemporary Techniques

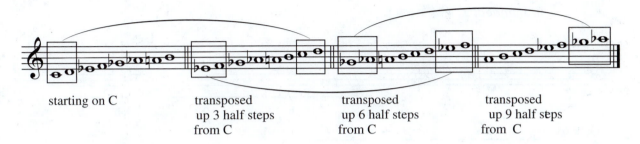

starting on C

transposed
up 3 half steps
from C

transposed
up 6 half steps
from C

transposed
up 9 half steps
from C

Example 28.15. Rotations of the OCT$_{2,3}$ collection.

The symmetrical properties of the whole-tone and octatonic scales inspired the French composer Olivier Messiaen (1908–1992) to devise other scales with similar properties. He called these scales **modes of limited transposition,** because they were capable of only a small number of transpositions before mapping onto a rotated version of their original state. Messiaen's modes of limited transposition are shown in Example 28.16; note that his Modes 1 and 2 correspond with the whole-tone and OCT$_{0,1}$ octatonic collections, respectively. The brackets show the scale segments subjected to symmetrical transformations, mostly transposition. There are, for example, three possible transpositions of Mode 3, each separated by four semitones (a major third or its enharmonic equivalent). Mode 5 possesses both transpositional symmetry (at the tritone) and mirror symmetry, in that the same order of intervals (h–w–h) is palindromic.

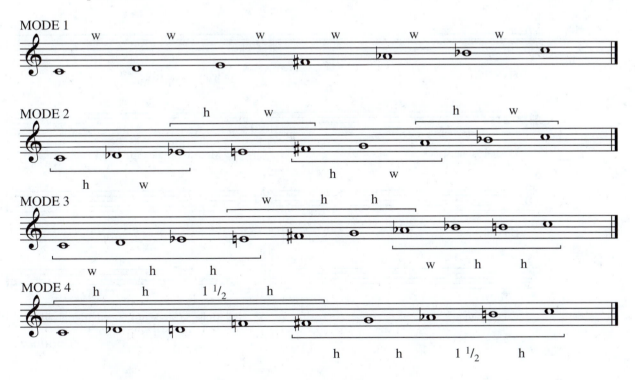

Example 28.16. Messiaen's modes of limited transposition. *(Continued)*

(Continued)

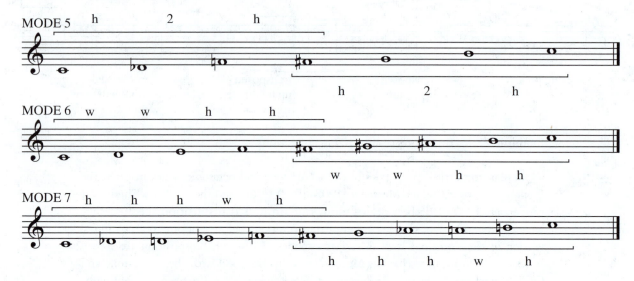

LEVEL MASTERY 28.3.

Complete the indicated scales, given the initial pitch. Some of the scales are modes introduced in Chapter 2, here for review.

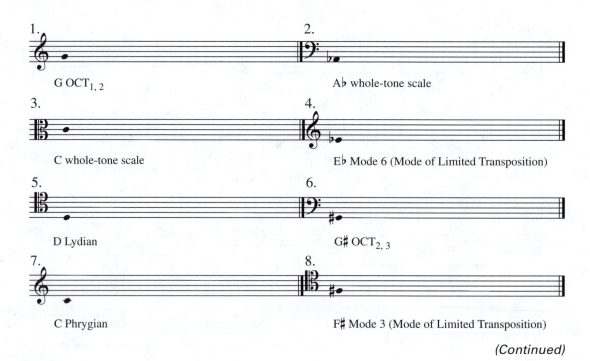

(Continued)

(Continued)

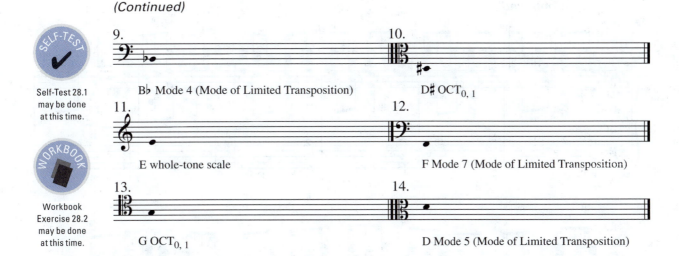

9.

B♭ Mode 4 (Mode of Limited Transposition)

10.

D♯ $OCT_{0, 1}$

11.

E whole-tone scale

12.

F Mode 7 (Mode of Limited Transposition)

13.

G $OCT_{0, 1}$

14.

D Mode 5 (Mode of Limited Transposition)

POLYTONALITY

Polytonality refers to the juxtaposition of two or more functional tonalities in a piece of music (usually two keys are involved, and so the term **bitonality** is also commonly used). We have already encountered polytonality in the interlude sections of Ives's *Variations on America* (Chapter 23); Stravinsky also famously juxtaposed C major and F♯ major arpeggios in *Petrouchka* (1911). In both of these examples the effect is rather jarring. The technique can also be used more subtly, however, with an effect akin to extended tertian sonorities in jazz, as in *Saudades do Brasil* (1920) by Darius Milhaud (1892–1974) (Example 28.17). The outer layers of the texture (lowest and highest registers) are in G major; the middle, accompanying layer is in B major. Although these keys are distantly related (chromatic mediant), they share the pitch class B (and the pitch class F♯, found in B major, is present in a G major-major seventh chord). Note also the circle-of-fifths sequence present in both keys simultaneously, from measure 30 to the end of the excerpt.

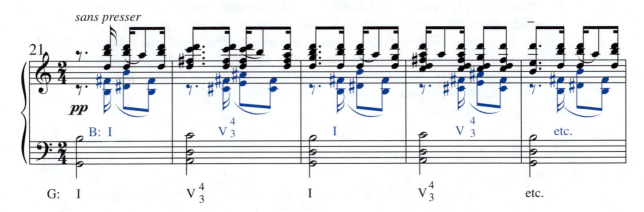

Example 28.17. Milhaud, "Copacabana" (from *Saudades do Brasil*), mm. 21–37a.

(Continued)

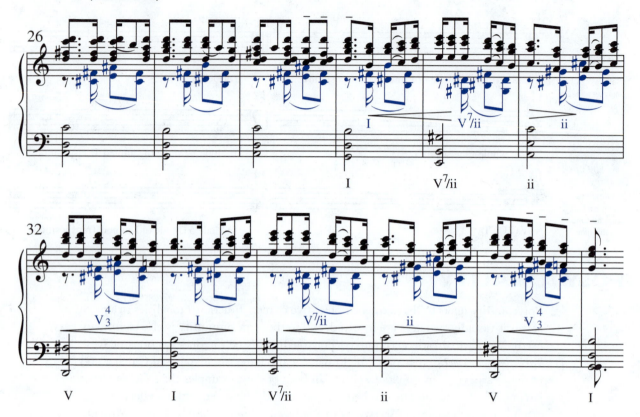

(Continued)

SECUNDAL AND QUARTAL-QUINTAL CHORDS

Composers also explored alternatives to tertian harmony, building harmonies on intervals such as seconds (**secundal harmony**, sometimes called **tone clusters**), or fourths and fifths (**quartal-quintal harmony**).[3] Examples of both of these harmonic techniques can be found in the Charles Ives song "Majority," composed in 1921; two excerpts are found in Example 28.18. In the first excerpt, the secundal chords in the bass are **diatonic clusters**—that is, they are constructed from the C major diatonic pitch class collection. Other composers, notably Henry Cowell (1897–1965), used **chromatic clusters** that involved all twelve pitch classes. The right-hand chords in measures 8–10 are quartal-quintal chords; measures 18–20 contain a number of strictly quartal chords.

---

[3] The term **quartal** refers to chords built up exclusively of stacked fourths; **quintal** refers to chords built up exclusively of stacked fifths. However, because fourths invert to fifths, the two intervals usually coexist in the same sonority (when, for example, a member of the chord is doubled at the octave). In such instances it is best to use the hybrid label.

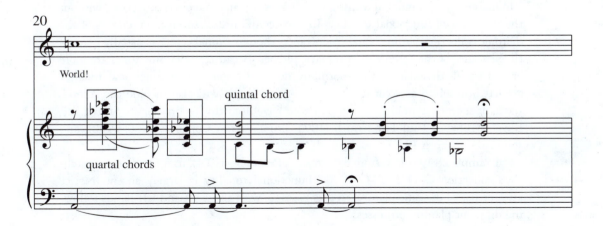

Example 28.18. Ives, "Majority," mm. 8–10 and 18–20.

For another example of quartal-quintal chords, see Example 28.7.

Label the following chords as quartal (QT), quintal (QN), or quartal-quintal (QT-QN).

Workbook
Exercise 28.3
may be done
at this time.

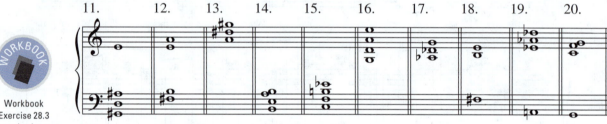

PANDIATONICISM

Pandiatonicism is a musical technique that uses the diatonic pitch collection, without the strictures of functional tonality. In this technique, all seven pitch classes of the diatonic collection assume equal importance, though a tonal center is usually perceptible because of the absence of chromatic pitches. Because all diatonic tones are more or less equal, dissonances that normally demand resolution in functional tonality are left unresolved as color tones; "added-note" triads will also include the second, sixth, or seventh. Among the composers to have used this technique are Stravinsky, Ravel, Milhaud, Paul Hindemith (1895–1963), Aaron Copland (1900–1990), and John Adams (born 1947).

Workbook
Exercise 28.4
may be done
at this time.

Example 28.19 below, from Stravinsky's *Petrouchka* (1911), uses the diatonic pitch-class collection C–D–E–F–G–A–B♭. Functional tonality is largely absent. Notice also the use of diatonic planing in this passage, with the right and left hands following different planing processes.

Example 28.19. Example of pandiatonicism in Stravinsky, *Petrouchka*, "A group of drunken revelers passes, dancing," rehearsal number 5 (piano reduction).

CONCLUSION

The music of the twentieth century exhibits a wide range of compositional approaches. Many of the techniques described in this chapter were explored concurrently, and some composers employed more than one of them. As a result, the chronological style-based approach to music history breaks down as we reach the twentieth century; thus, the next few chapters will present these techniques in a "survey" fashion. In this chapter we considered some of the pitch-based innovations: scales and harmonic techniques. In the next chapter we will continue in the pitch realm, but moving beyond tonality into atonal and serial music. Finally, in Chapter 30, we will survey time-based innovations—new approaches to form.

Terms to Know

bitonality

integer notation

leitmotif

modes of limited
    transposition

octatonic scale

pandiatonicism

planing (diatonic vs.
    chromatic)

polytonality

quartal harmony

quartal-quintal harmony

quintal harmony

secundal harmony
    (tone clusters)

whole-tone scale

Self-Test

28.1. Given the first pitch, complete each indicated scale.

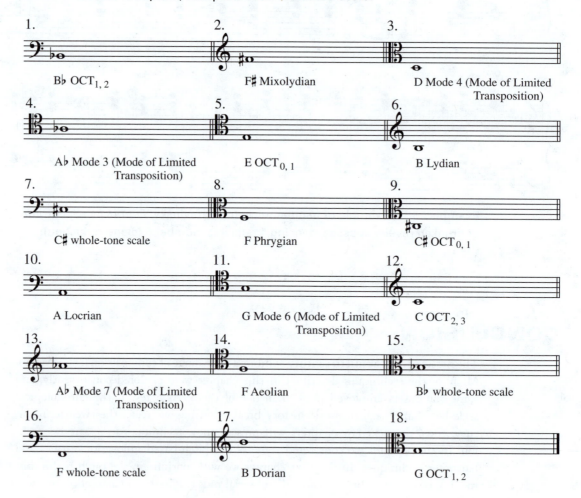

1. $B\flat$ OCT$_{1, 2}$

2. $F\sharp$ Mixolydian

3. D Mode 4 (Mode of Limited Transposition)

4. $A\flat$ Mode 3 (Mode of Limited Transposition)

5. E OCT$_{0, 1}$

6. B Lydian

7. $C\sharp$ whole-tone scale

8. F Phrygian

9. $C\sharp$ OCT$_{0, 1}$

10. A Locrian

11. G Mode 6 (Mode of Limited Transposition)

12. C OCT$_{2, 3}$

13. $A\flat$ Mode 7 (Mode of Limited Transposition)

14. F Aeolian

15. $B\flat$ whole-tone scale

16. F whole-tone scale

17. B Dorian

18. G OCT$_{1, 2}$

Apply This!

28.1. Composition.

a. A composition in the style of Debussy. Write a composition for piano, 55 measures in length, following the formal diagram below. Be sure to include performance details such as dynamics, phrasing, and pedal markings.

	m. 1	m. 8	m. 13	m. 21	m. 34
Form:	A	A′	B	A″	A
Tonal center / mode:	C major / minor (chromatic)	Whole-tone scale	A modal	Whole-tone scale	C major / minor (chromatic)
Harmony:	Planing V⁷ chords; triads with added tones	Whole-tone scale	Quartal, Quintal harmonies	Whole-tone scale	Planing V⁷ chords; triads with added tones
Phrases:	4 + 3 or 3 + 4	2 + 3 or 3 + 2	$\frac{4}{4}$ meter, 4 + 4	3 + 5 + 5 or 5 + 5 + 3 or 5 + 3 + 5	8 + 8 + 5 or 5 + 8 + 8 or 8 + 5 + 8
Melody:	based on tritone(s)	based on tritone(s)	contrast to tritone(s)	based on tritone(s)	based on tritone(s)
Rhythm:	long values	medium values	short values	medium values	long values

CHAPTER 29

CONTEMPORARY TECHNIQUES 2

OVERVIEW

The late-nineteenth-century trend toward ever-expanding chromaticism led to what Arnold Schoenberg called "the emancipation of the dissonance" and ultimately to the dissolution of tonality. Schoenberg's early efforts in this style were highly motivic, using constant transformations of small musical cells or sets to generate material. This proved less useful for larger forms, and so ultimately Schoenberg derived a method of composition using rows constructed of all twelve pitch classes. It is with that later, more controlled application of free atonality that this chapter begins.

CHAPTER OUTLINE

AUDIO LIST

Arnold Schoenberg, "Mässige Viertel," from   Pierre Boulez, *Structures 1a*
Three Piano Pieces, op. 11 no. 1

INTRODUCTION

We saw in the previous chapter that in the early twentieth century, some composers responded to the chromatic impasse presented by Richard Wagner by striking out in new directions: new scales (and newly rediscovered modes), chords created from intervals other than the third, or alternatives to functional tonal progressions such as "planing" harmonic sonorities or connecting chords with chromatic mediant relationships. Other composers extended the emphasis on chromaticism and motivic development found in the earlier music of composers such as Wagner and Gustav Mahler. The Austrian composer Arnold Schoenberg (1874–1951) began composing in a post-Wagnerian style, but he ultimately abandoned tonality altogether, searching for other means of organizing harmonic and melodic material. The result is often described as **atonal** music, or **atonality** (that is, music without a tonal center), but Schoenberg preferred the label "pantonal" (implying that all tones are of equal importance). Schoenberg, along with his best-known pupils Alban Berg (1885–1935) and Anton Webern (1883–1945), are sometimes referred to as the **Second Viennese School** (the "first Viennese School" being Haydn, Mozart, and Beethoven).

In the absence of a governing key structure, Schoenberg relied on motivic transformations to give his earliest atonal works coherence—short ideas are manipulated, inverted, and transposed. Without tonality's hierarchical system to control large-scale forms, however, Schoenberg encountered a compositional dilemma. His solution was to organize all twelve pitch classes into an ordered set, called a **row** or **series**, which would be used as material for development and variation across the composition. It is with Schoenberg's technique of "composition with twelve tones" that we begin our study, even if it came later in his career, because the concepts behind twelve-tone technique are easier to understand and they can be used to better understand his earlier free-atonal style.

TWELVE-TONE TECHNIQUE

Schoenberg's first composition to employ the twelve-tone row technique, the *Suite for Piano*, Opus 25, was composed between 1921 and 1923; he is generally credited with inventing the technique although others (such as Josef Matthias Hauer [1883–1959]) were experimenting with similar methods at around the same time. The row for the *Suite for Piano* is shown in Example 29.1. The numbers below the pitches are **ordinal numbers**, indicating a pc's position in the row. Note that ordinal numbers usually start with 0 rather than 1.

Example 29.1. Schoenberg, *Suite for Piano*, op. 25, row.

This original appearance of the row is called the **prime** (P) form of the row. Other forms of the row include **retrograde** (R)—the pitch classes of the prime form in reverse order; **inversion** (I)—the intervallic contour of the row reversed so that the row appears "upside down"; and **retrograde inversion** (RI)—the pitch classes of the inversion form in reverse order. Any of these row forms, of course, may appear in transposition as well, so that ultimately forty-eight different versions of the row are at the composer's disposal. Example 29.2 shows sample retrograde, inversion, and retrograde inversion forms of the opus 25 row, compared with the prime form.

Example 29.2. The row from Example 29.1 in prime (P), retrograde (R), inversion (I), and retrograde inversion (RI) forms.

It is customary to arrange the various row forms on a twelve-by-twelve **matrix**. The original prime version of the row goes on the top row; this is labeled P_4 (the subscript number, called an **index number**, denotes the first pc in prime and inversion forms and the last pc in retrograde and retrograde inversion forms; here the 4 designates the first pitch of the row).[1] The inversion of this row, using the first pitch class as the axis of symmetry, becomes the first (leftmost) column. This results in the matrix below for the row in Example 29.1:

	I_4	I_5	I_7	I_1	I_6	I_3	I_8	I_2	I_{11}	I_0	I_9	I_{10}	
P_4	4	5	7	1	6	3	8	2	E	0	9	T	R_4
P_3	3	4	6	0	5	2	7	1	T	E	8	9	R_3
P_1	1	2	4	T	3	0	5	E	8	9	6	7	R_1
P_7	7	8	T	4	9	6	E	5	2	3	0	1	R_7
P_2	2	3	5	E	4	1	6	0	9	T	7	8	R_2
P_5	5	6	8	2	7	4	9	3	0	1	T	E	R_5
P_0	0	1	3	9	2	E	4	T	7	8	5	6	R_0
P_6	6	7	9	3	8	5	T	4	1	2	E	0	R_6
P_9	9	T	0	6	E	8	1	7	4	5	2	3	R_9
P_8	8	9	E	5	T	7	0	6	3	4	1	2	R_8
P_{11}	E	0	2	8	1	T	3	9	6	7	4	5	R_{11}
P_{10}	T	E	1	7	0	9	2	8	5	6	3	4	R_{10}
	RI_4	RI_5	RI_7	RI_1	RI_6	RI_3	RI_8	RI_2	RI_{11}	RI_0	RI_9	RI_{10}	

Notice that the subscript numbers for a row and its retrograde are the same. In other words, for example, RI_4 means "the R of I_4," and R_4 is similarly shorthand for "the R of P_4."

---

[1] An alternative means of numbering row forms assigns "0" to the first appearance of the row in a composition, ascribing to it the status of the "original" row. Thus, the first appearance of Schoenberg's row would be labeled P_0 even though the first pc is 4.

a. Using the matrix provided in this chapter for Schoenberg's Opus 25 row, identify the row forms in Example 29.2.

R: I: RI:

b. On a separate piece of paper, construct a matrix for the following P_0 row:

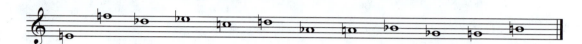

Using that matrix as a guide, identify the following row forms.

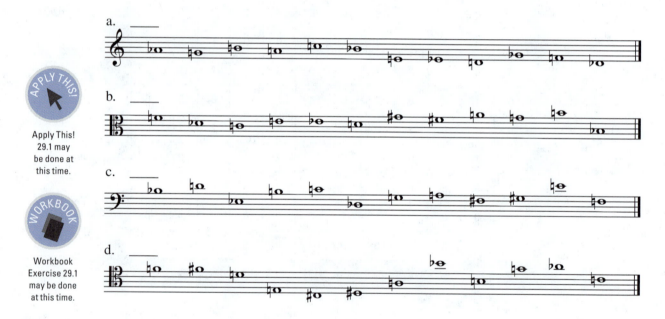

APPLY THIS!

Apply This!
29.1 may
be done at
this time.

WORKBOOK

Workbook
Exercise 29.1
may be done
at this time.

EXTENSIONS OF TWELVE-TONE TECHNIQUE: INTEGRAL SERIALISM

It was not long before composers began to apply the principles of twelve-tone technique, which serialized pitch, to other parameters of music such as rhythm, dynamics, and articulation. Some of Anton Webern's later compositions, especially his *Symphony*, Opus 21, and *Variations for Orchestra*, Opus 30, hinted at the serialization of rhythm with their symmetrical treatments of rhythmic motives, and in the second movement of Webern's *Variations for Piano*, Opus 27, each tone of the row appears in its own distinctive octave, serializing register along with pitch as a result.

The earliest known example of **integral serialism** in music—in which elements of music other than pitch are serialized—is Milton Babbitt's (1916–2011) *Three Compositions for Piano*, composed in 1947. However, Olivier Messiaen's *Modes de Valeurs et d'Intensités*, from his *Quatre Études de Rhythme* (1949)—while not strictly serial—was of arguably greater influence, inspiring two of Messiaen's students—Pierre Boulez (1925–2016) and Karlheinz Stockhausen (1928–2007)—to pursue integral serialism more rigorously. In this piece, Messiaen divided a thirty-six-note series into three twelve-note segments allocated to three different registers of the piano, along with seven dynamic levels (*ppp* to *fff*) and twelve types of articulation.

The influence of *Modes de Valeurs* is discernible in Boulez's *Structures 1a* for two pianos, composed in 1952. The beginning of this work is shown in Example 29.3. Piano I begins with the P_0 form of the series, while piano II presents the I_0 form. Boulez also derived a **duration series** and **articulation series** for the work from the first of the three series divisions used by Messiaen in his *Modes de Valeurs* (Example 29.4).

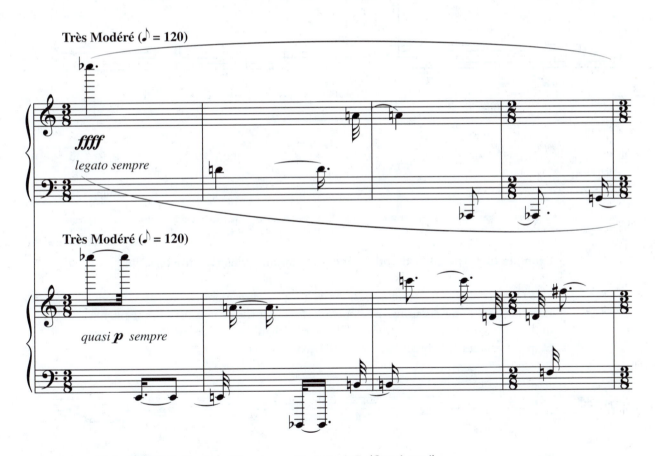

Example 29.3. Boulez, *Structures 1a*, mm. 1–7. *(Continued)*

(Continued)

Ordinal number	0	1	2	3	4	5	6	7	8	9	10	11
Pitch class	3	2	9	8	7	6	4	1	0	T	5	E
Duration (in 32nd notes)	1	2	3	4	5	6	7	8	9	10	11	12

Articulation series: 1. accent; 2. staccato-accent; 3. staccato; 4. (blank); 5. normal; 6. portamento (staccato-slur); 7. staccatissimo (wedge); 8. sforzando or staccato-marcato; 9. staccatissimo-accent; 10. (blank); 11. portamento (staccato-tenuto); 12. slur

Example 29.4. The pitch, duration, and articulation series for *Structures 1a*.

There is also a **dynamic series**, derived by an even more circumspect means. First, devise a **T-matrix** using the *ordinal numbers* (not the pc numbers) of the pitches in the pitch series, numbered from 1 to 12 (rather than the customary 0 to 11), so that E♭ (pc3) becomes 1, D becomes 2, A (pc9) becomes 3, etc.:

The above row—and set of ordinal numbers—becomes the top row of the T-matrix. The matrix is then filled in for each subsequent row, beginning on each note in turn

and keeping the original relationships. Since the second note of the series is D, for example, the second row of the matrix begins on D and is generated as shown below. See how the numbers in this row are derived from the ordinal numbers in the first row above:

The third note of the series is A, so the third row of the matrix begins on A and looks like this:

The complete matrix looks like this (notice that the leftmost column and top row are identical):

1	2	3	4	5	6	7	8	9	10	11	12
2	8	4	5	6	11	1	9	12	3	7	10
3	4	1	2	8	9	10	5	6	7	12	11
4	5	2	8	9	12	3	6	11	1	10	7
5	6	8	9	12	10	4	11	7	2	3	1
6	11	9	12	10	3	5	7	1	8	4	2
7	1	10	3	4	5	11	2	8	12	6	9
8	9	5	6	11	7	2	12	10	4	1	3
9	12	6	11	7	1	8	10	3	5	2	4
10	3	7	1	2	8	12	4	5	11	9	6
11	7	12	10	3	4	6	1	2	9	5	8
12	10	11	7	1	2	9	3	4	6	8	5

An **I-matrix** can be constructed the same way, using the ordinal numbers of the pcs in the I0 form of the row to derive the leftmost column and top row.

1	7	3	10	12	9	2	11	6	4	8	5
7	11	10	12	9	8	1	6	5	3	2	4
3	10	1	7	11	6	4	12	9	2	5	8
10	12	7	11	6	5	3	9	8	1	4	2
12	9	11	6	5	4	10	8	2	7	3	1
9	8	6	5	4	3	12	2	1	8	10	7
2	1	4	3	10	12	8	7	11	5	9	6
11	6	12	9	8	2	7	5	4	10	1	3
6	5	9	8	2	1	11	4	3	12	7	10
4	3	2	1	7	8	5	10	12	8	6	9
8	2	5	4	3	10	9	1	7	6	12	11
5	4	8	2	1	7	6	3	10	9	11	12

Upon perusing these matrices it can be seen that the retrograde of the lowest row in the T-matrix gives us the first duration series in Piano II, and the retrograde of the lowest row in the I-matrix gives us the first duration series in Piano I. In other words, Piano I's duration series is based on the RI$_4$ form of the pitch series, while Piano II's duration series is based on the R$_8$ form.

To find the dynamic series, one must start with Boulez's "dynamic scale," which has twelve elements just like the chromatic scale: <*pppp*, *ppp*, *pp*, *p*, quasi *p*, *mp*, *mf*, quasi *f*, *f*, *ff*, *fff*, *ffff*>. The **dynamic series** for each piano, shown incompletely in Example 29.15, is determined by reading each matrix diagonally from the upper-right corner to the lower-left corner. Thus, Piano I's dynamic series, read from the T-matrix, is <12, 7, 11, 5, 11, 7, 12>, or <*fff*, *mf*, *fff*, quasi *p*, *fff*, *mf*, *ffff*>; Piano II's dynamic series, similarly read from the I-matrix, is <5, 2, 8, 12, 8, 2, 5>, or <quasi *p*, *ppp*, quasi *f*, *ffff*, quasi *f*, *ppp*, quasi *p*>.

This discussion of *Structures 1a* provides only one example of how composers attempted to organize musical parameters other than pitch. Milton Babbitt's *Semi-Simple Variations* (1956) uses a rhythmic series based on the sixteen different ways of parsing a quarter-note pulse using a sixteenth-note subdivision into sound or silence (like binary code). This series is shown in Example 29.5. The "inversion" of such a series can be found by substituting sounds for silences and vice versa.

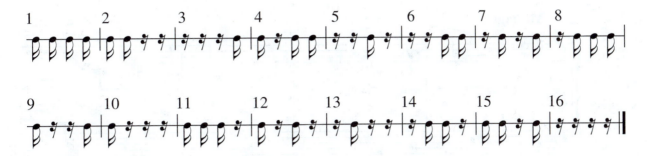

Example 29.5. Babbitt, *Semi-Simple Variations*, rhythmic series.

One criticism that is often raised against integral serialism is that its intricate structures are not perceptible to the listener, leading to the supposition that the composer is indifferent to the audience. The apparent divorce between structure and perceptibility might instead be likened to the ancient Platonic philosophy distinguishing between idealized "forms" and their "shadows" as perceived by the senses. Seen this way, Boulez's various series and scales governing each parameter stand as examples of idealized form, manifested in their "shadow" form through the "filter" of, for example, the T- and I-matrices.

In the 1950s and 1960s, serialism came to be associated especially with a number of European composers active in the Darmstadt International Summer Courses for New Music held every year in Germany; the composer Luigi Nono coined the term **Darmstadt School** in 1957 to describe the serial music being composed there. To this day, the term "Darmstadt School" is often used to refer to music in a serialist style, whether or not its composer had ever studied at Darmstadt.

See Web Feature 29.1 for a look at some examples of twelve-tone technique in jazz.

FREE ATONALITY AND SET THEORY

Examine Example 29.6, the opening of an early atonal work by Schoenberg (op. 11, no. 1) composed in 1909. There appear to be several vestigial references to tonality here. We might perceive G to be a tonal center of sorts, or at least an important pitch in the melodic line. The E4–G4 motive with its accompanying ascending eighth note figure first heard at measures 4–5 might be heard as having a cadential quality, an impression reinforced by its repetition in measures 5–6 and 7–8. However, even with the seeming importance of G, traditional harmonic analysis tells us little about how the work is held together. Instead, we need new analytical tools. The most commonly used method for analyzing atonal music, devised from mathematical set theory, was devised by Allen Forte and published in his book *The Structure of Atonal Music*[2]; for this reason this methodology is sometimes called **Forte analysis**, but it is more commonly called **atonal theory** or **set theory**.

---

[2] Allen Forte, *The Structure of Atonal Music* (New Haven, CT: Yale University Press, 1973).

Example 29.6. Schoenberg, Piano Piece, op. 11 no. 1, mm. 1–8.

Before we go further, we first need to understand the tools of set theory and how to apply them. Analyzing a piece of atonal music begins with a process of **segmentation**—locating and identifying meaningful groups of three or more pitch classes called **sets** or **pcsets** (where **pc** stands for pitch class). Pitches in a set may belong together based on (1) being close together in time (as in a succession of notes in a melody, or simultaneously in a chord), (2) similar in register, or (3) sharing a given dynamic or timbre. Here a quote from Schoenberg's writings is instructive:

> [T]he unity of musical space demands an absolute and unitary perception. *In this space . . . there is no absolute down, no right or left, forward or backward. Every musical configuration, every movement of tones has to be comprehended primarily as a mutual relation of sounds, of oscillatory vibrations, appearing at different places and times.* [emphasis in original][3]

[3] Arnold Schoenberg, "Composition with Twelve Tones," in *Style and Idea: Selected Writings of Arnold Schoenberg*, edited by Leonard Stein, translations by Leo Black (Berkeley, CA: University of California Press, 1975), p. 223.

We could isolate the first three notes of Schoenberg's Opus 11, Number 1, as a set, shown in Example 29.7a. This would be an example of an **ordered set**—the notes are in a fixed order, as a melody. On the other hand, if those three pitches appear in a chord (or if we wanted to discuss those three pitches out of their melodic order), they would comprise an **unordered set** (Example 29.7b). Set theory's "mathematical" aspects and terminology may appear to be abstract at first, but its concepts are rooted in such musical truisms as enharmonic equivalence, octave equivalence, transposition, and interval inversion. We consider enharmonic equivalence and octave equivalence first, consulting Example 29.7 as we do so.

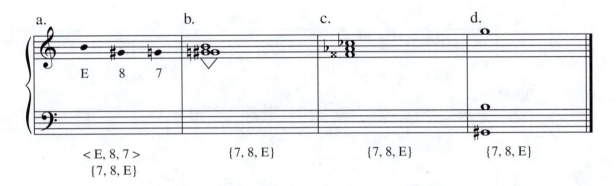

Example 29.7. Properties and labels of a set.

Brackets are used to designate sets. If the set is an ordered set, as in Example 29.7a, angle brackets are used; thus the melodic line is designated as <E, 8, 7>. If the set is an unordered set, curly brackets are used, and the pitches are usually listed in ascending order; thus the chord in Example 29.7b would be labeled as {7, 8 E}. It may help to think of the angle brackets as being like sergeant stripes, representing something strictly regimented, whereas curly brackets are rather like a cloud, representing something rather amorphous (since the order of an unordered set can be variable, like the shape of a cloud).

OCTAVE EQUIVALENCE AND MOD 12. We have already learned the difference between pitch and pitch class, understanding that pitches an octave apart from one another are considered to be members of the same pitch class. Thus, if any of the pitches in the sets in Example 29.7 were to appear in other octaves, this would not change the pcset label. Similarly, because of enharmonic equivalence, the chords in Example 29.7c and d would also have the same pcset label. Remember also that upon arrival at C an octave higher, the integer label reverts back to zero. This is because the integer naming for pitches in atonal music follows a **modulo 12**, or **mod 12**, system—an integer cycle in which the numbers "wrap around" after the twelfth element in the integer system, since the **aggregate**—the complete chromatic pitch collection—contains twelve pitch classes. It may be helpful to think of a clock face, where the numbers start with 1 and wrap around after 12. Thus, just as pitches an octave apart are perceived as congruent due to octave equivalence, so too are their integer labels.

LEVEL MASTERY 29.2.

Provide labels using integer notation for the following sets. Enclose your integers in the appropriate brackets for unordered sets (chords) or ordered sets (melodic fragments). Integers in unordered sets should be arranged in ascending order.

Workbook Exercise 29.2 may be done at this time.

NORMAL ORDER. In order to facilitate comparing sets, it is useful to have them in the simplest and most compact arrangement possible. Considering the first set in Example 29.8a below, if we simply list the pitch classes from lowest to highest we would have {8, E, 7}. Cyclically (through mod 12), the distance from 8 to 7, ascending, is eleven semitones. We can reorder this more compactly. Starting on E and ascending cyclically, our set would be E, 7, 8. Here the distance from first to last pc is nine semitones—better, but still not ideal. Starting on 7 and ascending cyclically, our set is 7, 8, E. Because here the distance from first to last pc, ascending, is only four semitones, this is the **normal order** for the set. A set in normal order is enclosed in square brackets, thus [7, 8, E]. With larger sets, a kind of shortcut can be devised by simply comparing each integer in a set (listed in ascending order) with the integer to its immediate left and considering the difference between those two numbers in ascending cyclical order. Example 29.8b shows how to do this, using a harmonic minor scale as our set.

a.

11 semitones   9 semitones   4 semitones
                                            (normal order)

b.

| 10 sts ← | 11 sts ← | 10 sts ← | 10 sts ← | 11 sts ← | **9 sts** ← | 11 sts ← |

C	D	E♭	F	G	A♭	B♮	C
0	2	3	5	7	8	E	

sts = semitones

[E, 0, 2, 3, 5, 7, 8]

(9 semitones)

Example 29.8. Finding normal order for a set.

Keep in mind that occasionally sets may be in normal order in two different rotations. For example, the set {C, F, G} occupies a registral space of seven semitones when arranged as {C, F, G} *and* when arranged as {F, G, C}. In this scenario, {F, G, C} gives us the **best normal order**, since—assigning the lowest pitch the value 0—the numbers add up to a lower sum:

C		F		G				F		G		C		
0	+	5	+	7	=	12		0	+	2	+	7	=	9

Another useful observation in comparing these two arrangements is that, if a set is in best normal order, the smallest intervals will be "packed to the left" reading left to right (compare the interval <0, 5> with <0, 2> within the arrangements above).

LEVEL MASTERY 29.3.

Arrange the following sets in normal order and provide their integer labels as unordered sets.

1.   2.   3.   4.   5.

_____   _____   _____   _____   _____

(Continued)

(Continued)

TRANSPOSITIONAL EQUIVALENCE:
THE TRANSPOSITION (T*n*) OPERATION

Two pitch-class sets can be related through transposition, in the same way that a C minor triad [0, 3, 7] transposed up a perfect fifth is still recognizable as a minor triad (G minor, or [7, T, 2]). The transposition operation, or **T*n***, is done by taking two pc sets in normal order and finding the difference between the integer labels of the corresponding members of each set.

Take another look at Example 29.6. Consider the first three notes of the melodic line (<E, 8, 7>) and compare them with the accompanying chord in measure 3, [9, T, 1]:

$$
\begin{array}{r}
[7, 8, E] \\
+ \quad 2\ 2\ 2 \\
\hline
9, T, 13 \\
\end{array}
$$

(equals, through mod 12)   [9, T, 1].

Thus the distance from [7, 8, E] to [9, T, 1] is two semitones, or, T_2 of [7, 8, E] results in [9, T, 1] (Example 29.9). T-values are always expressed in positive terms; thus, even though the later set in our comparison is lower in register ("minus 10 semi-tones," if the B♭2 in the measure 3 is transposed up an octave), through octave equivalence the T-value is nevertheless expressed as *up* two semitones. With the exception of the tritone transposition (T_6) and the trivial instance of transposing by 0 (the "identity operation"), the transposition operation is not commutable or reversible. "Undoing" T_2 to arrive at the first set, for example, would require a T_{10} (10 being the complement of 2 within mod 12—that is, 10 is the difference between 2 and 12; consider for example how a major second interval inverts to a minor seventh).

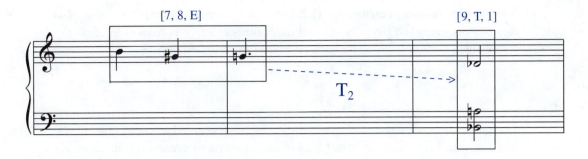

Example 29.9. The transpositional relation.

INVERSIONAL EQUIVALENCE—THE INVERSION (*Tn*I) OPERATION

In Chapter 2 you learned about inversion of intervals—how, for example, a minor third inverts to a major sixth by moving the lower note of the interval up an octave or moving the upper note of the interval down an octave. Within an atonal context it should be clear that doing so provides us with the interval's complement within a mod 12 system. For example, if a minor third is equivalent to 3 semitones, its inversion—the major sixth—is equivalent to 9 semitones, the difference between 12 and 3.

Recall Schoenberg's quote regarding the unity of musical space. In the same way that we can categorize pitches through octave equivalence as belonging to one of twelve pitch classes, through octave equivalence we can also isolate six **interval classes (ics)**, defined as the shortest distance from one pitch class to another within an octave. Thus, there are six interval classes, ranging in size from 1 (a semitone) to 6 (a tritone). Any interval larger than a tritone is the same interval class as its inversion (thus, a major sixth is of interval class 3, or ic3).

Schoenberg's quote also leads us to the idea that two sets can be related through inversion. Consider the two sets in Example 29.10, which are taken from the first three notes of Schoenberg's Opus 11, Number 1 (<B, G♯, G>) and the boundary tones (or framing tones—highest and lowest pitches that "frame" the gesture) that accompany the cadence at measures 4–5: the <E, G> melodic line and the G♯ bass note. Thus, isolating the boundary tones we have the unordered set {G♯, E, G}, arranged from lowest to highest. Arranging this second set in normal order gives us [E, G, G♯] or [4, 7, 8], and we can see that this set is an intervallic mirror image of the first.

Example 29.10. Inversion of a set about zero (C).

The **inversion operation**, or **T*n*I**, between two sets is almost always a two-step process. Once you have determined that both sets are in normal order, find the complement (within mod 12) for each pc integer in your first set:

	7	8	E
complement:	5	4	1

The set made up of integer complements is the **inversion about zero** (T_0I) of the first set, which is to say that 0, or C, represents the **axis of symmetry** about which the set is "reflected." This is shown above in Example 29.10; the second set is given without changing registers for octave equivalence.

If the relation you are finding happens to invert around C, you have finished, and the resulting relation is T_0I (T_0, or the identity operation, applied to I); eleven times out of twelve, however, transposition will be the next step. Once the inversion about zero has been found, transpose that result to arrive at the desired set being compared.

	5	4	1		
(transpose)	3	3	3		
	8	7	4	=	[4, 7, 8]

Thus, the T*n*I relation between [7, 8, E] and [4, 7, 8] is T_3I (invert first, *then* transpose).

Unlike the transposition operation, the inversion operation *is* commutable. In the same way that turning an object upside down and then turning it upside down again restores it to its original position, we can reverse the T*n*I operation above:

	4	7	8		
complement:	8	5	4		
transpose:	3	3	3		
	E	8	7	=	[7, 8, E]

LEVEL MASTERY 29.4.

a. Provide the set at the indicated Tn or TnI relation to the sets below. Provide your answers in the form of unordered sets in normal order.

1.	{8, 9, 1}	← T_6I →
2.	{2, 5, 6, T}	T_2 →
3.	{2, 3, 6, 8}	← T_7I →
4.	{3, 4, 7}	← T_0I →
5.	{1, 2, 5, 9}	T_7 →
6.	{4, 6, E}	T_6 →
7.	{4, 5, 8}	← T_6I →
8.	{0, 2, 4, 6, 8}	T_3 →
9.	{0, 1, 3, 4, 6}	T_5 →
10.	{1, 3, 7}	← T_3I →

b. Determine the *Tn* or *TnI* relation of the sets below. Be sure to connect your sets with single-headed arrows for transposition or double-headed (two-way) arrows for inversion, as appropriate.

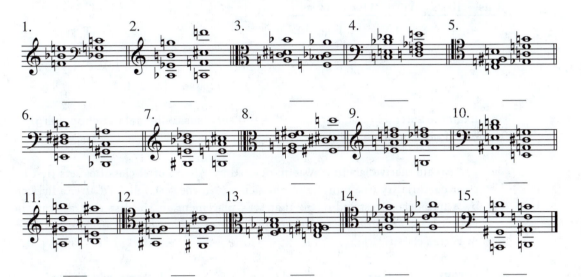

SET CLASS, INTERVAL VECTOR, AND Z-RELATION

Ultimately, it is fair to say that in much atonal music the intervallic relations between pitches are at least as important as the pitches themselves. The integer labels given to specific pitches or sets are useful only inasmuch as we wish to refer to a specific element in a piece of music. To get a broader picture of a piece's coherence we will need other analytical tools.

SET CLASS. One of the most useful concepts is the **set class** (or **set type**), a set of integers, starting with 0, representing the intervallic structure of *all sets that are related by transposition and/or inversion*. Set classes are usually denoted by parentheses (as opposed to the angle brackets for ordered sets and curly brackets for unordered sets).

To find the set class for a given set, begin with the set in best normal order. Consider the accompaniment in measures 4–5 of Schoenberg's op. 11 no. 1 (Example 29.6). The pitch classes are (in ascending integer order) {2, 6, 8, 9, T, E}. Rotating this to normal order the set is [6, 8, 9, T, E, 2] (Example 29.11). Next, assign the value 0 to the lowest integer, and "count up" in semitones from 0; then, do the same from the top down (assign 0 to the *highest* pitch in the set and "count down" in semitones). Recall that for the set to be in best normal order, the smallest intervals should be "packed to the left," so the lowest integer sum will give prime form. Since the interval from 6 to 8 (2 semitones) is smaller than from E to 2 (3 semitones), we "count up" from the lowest pitch and determine the set class to be (023458). Similarly, the three-note sets we were comparing earlier are all of set class (014).

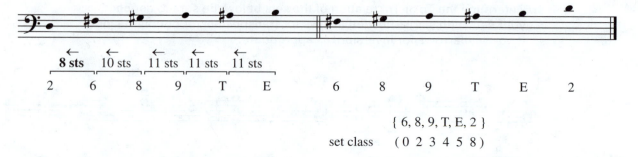

$\{ 6, 8, 9, T, E, 2 \}$

set class   (0 2 3 4 5 8)

Example 29.11. Finding normal order and set class of the set in Schoenberg, op. 11 no. 1, mm. 4–5.

An alternative labeling system, devised by Allen Forte, classifies sets first by their **cardinality** (the number of pitch classes in the set), followed after a hyphen by a number corresponding to that set's placement in the list that appears in Forte's book *The Structure of Atonal Music*. For example, set class (014) is also 3–3 in Forte's classification.

INTERVAL VECTOR. It is also useful to find a set's **interval vector**, which is an inventory of the interval classes present within a given set. The interval vector consists of six numbers, the digits left to right representing the number of interval classes from ic1 (semitones) to ic6 (tritones). The interval vector for the set class (014) is 101100: There are one each of ic1, ic3, and ic4, and the other interval classes are not found. The interval vector for (023458) is 333321. These are demonstrated in Example 29.12.

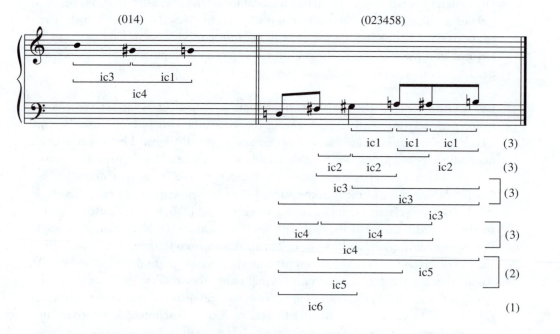

Example 29.12. Demonstrating the interval vector for set classes (014) and (023458), using the examples from Schoenberg's op. 11 no. 1.

Z-RELATION. Some sets—especially hexachords (those with six pitch classes)—may have identical intervallic content *without* being related by transposition or inversion. These sets are **Z-related** (the term is Forte's, "Z" being an arbitrary designation). For example, set class (023458) has the Forte label 6-Z39, indicating that it has a **Z-correspondent** (another set class sharing the same interval vector). The Z-correspondent of set class (023458) is 6-Z10 (013457).

An excellent example of Z-related sets can be found in Alban Berg's song "Dem Schmerz sein Recht" (op. 2 no. 1). An important sonority for much of this piece is the chord shown in Example 29.13a, which belongs to set class (0146). This is one of two **all-interval tetrachords**, meaning that the interval vector for the set class is 111111 (one of each interval class). This special property is shared by only one other tetrachord, set class (0137). (0137) has several appearances in the song as well, and at the singer's final cadence we find both sets adjacent to one another (Example 29.13b).

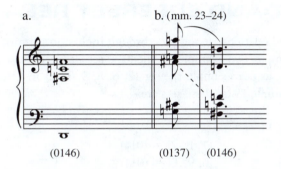

a.   b. (mm. 23–24)

(0146)   (0137) (0146)

Example 29.13. a. The set {0, 2, 5, 6}, set class (0146).   b. Cadence involving Z-related set classes (0137) and (0146), from Berg's "Dem Schmerz sein Recht," op. 2 no. 1.

LEVEL MASTERY 29.5.

Determine the set class (SC) for the following sets, and provide the interval vector (IV) for each set.

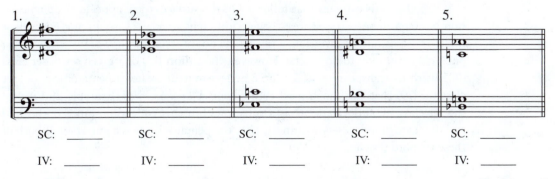

1.   2.   3.   4.   5.

SC: _____   SC: _____   SC: _____   SC: _____   SC: _____

IV: _____   IV: _____   IV: _____   IV: _____   IV: _____

(Continued)

(Continued)

Self-Tests
29.1 and 29.2
may be done
at this time.

Workbook
Exercises
29.3, 29.4,
and 29.5 may
be done at
this time.

Apply This!
29.3 may
be done at
this time.

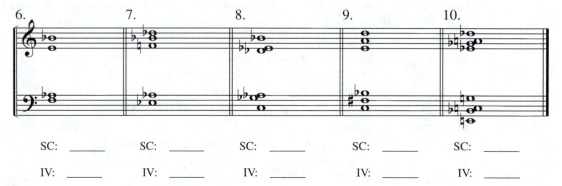

SC: _____ SC: _____ SC: _____ SC: _____ SC: _____

IV: _____ IV: _____ IV: _____ IV: _____ IV: _____

SUBSET AND SUPERSET RELATIONS

We can also find relations among sets through **inclusion**, **union**, and **complementation**. For example, two examples of the (014) set class are found as **subsets** within (023458). Using as our example the set {2, 6, 8, 9, T, E} in Schoenberg's Opus 11 Number 1 (Example 29.6), these sets are:

$$\{2, 6, 8, 9, T, E\}$$

2	T, E	{T, E, 2} = (014)
6,	9, T	{6, 9, T} = (014)

The sets {2, T, E} and {6, 9, T} are **included** (or **embedded**) within the set {2, 6, 8, 9, T, E}; another way of describing this is to say that {2, T, E} and {6, 9, T} are **subsets** of {2, 6, 8, 9, T, E}. The **union** (∪) of {2, T, E} and {6, 9, T} results in the set {2, 6, 8, 9, T, E}. Finally, because {2, T, E} and {6, 9, T} are included within {2, 6, 8, 9, T, E}, {2, 6, 8, 9, T, E} is a **superset** of both {2, T, E} and {6, 9, T}. The set comprising the remaining pitches of the aggregate—{0, 1, 3, 4, 5, 7}—makes up the **complement** of {2, 6, 8, 9, T, E}.

For an example from a quite different repertoire, consider the two sets shown in Example 29.14. The first, set class (027), is the opening sonority from the "Acknowledgement" section of John Coltrane's *A Love Supreme*; the second, set class (025), is the <5, 8, 5, T> bass ostinato that follows. On the surface, there appears to be no relation between these two gestures; they are different set classes, so are not equivalent under transposition or inversion, and there is no **intersection** (∩) between them (no pitch class common to both sets). However, the **union** (∪) of a given set of set class (025) with its transposition at T5 (up a perfect fourth) creates a pentatonic scale, set class (02479) that was much used throughout *A Love Supreme* (Example 29.15), and the set class (027) does appear as a subset within this collection. Since both (025) and (027) are found as sets within (02479), the pentatonic set is a **superset** of both of these trichord set classes.

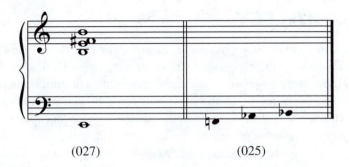

(027)   (025)

Example 29.14. Two sets from John Coltrane's *A Love Supreme*.

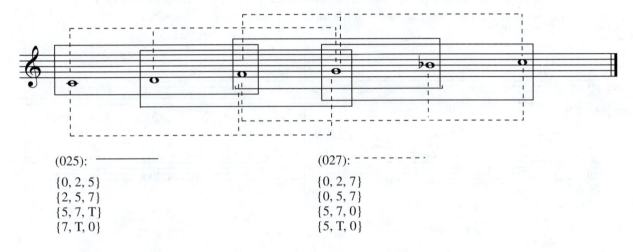

(025): ————————   (027): - - - - - - - -

{0, 2, 5}   {0, 2, 7}
{2, 5, 7}   {0, 5, 7}
{5, 7, T}   {5, 7, 0}
{7, T, 0}   {5, T, 0}

Example 29.15. A pentatonic collection, (02479), created through the union of transposed sets of set class (025).

As our last example demonstrates, set theory has potential for application in other music beyond the early twentieth-century atonal repertoire with which it is often associated. It works well with any music that is motivic in character. We have only touched on its very basic elements here.[4] It is also important to remember that Forte's methodology for applying principles of set theory to so-called "freely atonal" music was not devised until the 1960s. Schoenberg himself did not use such techniques as a conscientious means of predetermining his composition—such concepts as "sets" were thought of only intuitively and as a means for motivic development.

---

[4] For further study, the following titles are recommended: Joseph N. Straus, *Introduction to Post-Tonal Theory*, 3rd edition (Upper Saddle River, NJ: Pearson-Prentice Hall, 2005); Allen Forte, *The Structure of Atonal Music* (New Haven, CT: Yale University Press, 1973); and George Perle, *Serial Composition and Atonality*, 6th revised edition (Berkeley: University of California Press, 1991).

COMBINATORIALITY

Returning now to twelve-tone technique, examine the row forms below in Example 29.16, which are used in Schoenberg's *Suite for Piano*, Opus 33. The pairing of these row forms illustrates Schoenberg's solution to the problem of combining different row forms simultaneously, such that the row forms could be perceived as closely related to one another without creating unwanted note doublings. Schoenberg found that in combining two row forms related to one another as P_0 to I_5, the first hexachord of both rows would contain completely different pitch classes; this also means that the second hexachord of the first row would contain the same pitch classes as the first hexachord of the second row, albeit in a different order. This property was given the label **combinatoriality** by Milton Babbitt (1916–2011), who exploited this type of relationship between row forms in his own compositions.

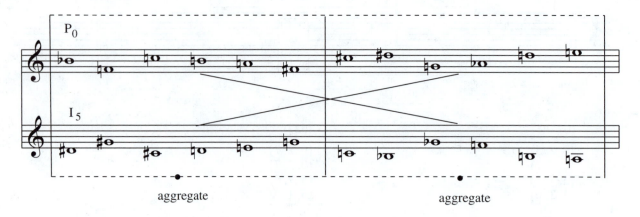

Example 29.16. Schoenberg, *Suite for Piano*, op. 33, P_0 and I_5.

A hexachord is combinatorial if:

1. Transposing the hexachord yields its complement (the first hexachord **maps** onto the second by transposition)—this is **prime combinatoriality**. (For a trivial example, consider the first six scale degrees of C major—0, 2, 4, 5, 7, 9 or C, D, E, F, G, A—and their complement yielded under T_6—6, 8, t, e, 1, 3 or F♯, G♯, A♯, B, C♯, D♯.)

2. Inverting the hexachord yields its complement (the first hexachord maps onto the second by inversion)—this is **inversion combinatoriality**.

Ordered hexachords may also be combinatorial under retrograde or retrograde inversion.

A hexachordal set that is combinatorial under one of the four row operations—transposition, inversion, retrograde, or retrograde inversion—is called **semi-combinatorial**. A select few rows are **all-combinatorial**. For example, the first hexachord of the prime row form in Example 29.17 maps onto its complement at R_0, T_6, I_9, and RI_3. Compare the first hexachord of P_0 with the first hexachord of the other three rows; then do the same with the second hexachord).

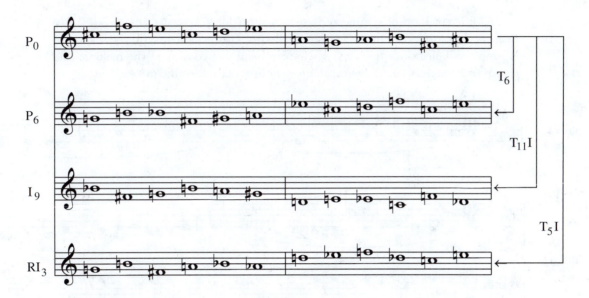

Example 29.17. An all-combinatorial row with its self-mapping transformations.

SYMMETRY

Riemann's theory of tonality (examined in Chapter 26) is but one way in which symmetry became a topic of interest in twentieth-century composition. Composers such as Alban Berg and Béla Bartók made use of symmetrical sets and scales in their compositions. Example 29.18 shows the beginning of Bartók's piece "From the Island of Bali," a miniature from his set of pedagogical pieces *Mikrokosmos*. Notice that the first two measures are set as a kind of mirror canon, the right-hand *comes* a strict melodic inversion of the left-hand *dux* (at measure 3 the nature of the canon changes). What is the axis of symmetry in the first two measures? Notice also that the pitch content in each staff is mutually exclusive; the pitch content in each staff is also symmetrical, forming the set class (0167). (This set class is also interesting for its transpositional symmetry, as its pitch-class content maps onto itself when transposed by a tritone.) When both hands are put together, the result is the octatonic scale, also a symmetrical pitch-class collection.

Example 29.18. Bartók, "From the Island of Bali," no. 109 from *Mikrokosmos*, vol. 4, mm. 1–4.

A different kind of symmetry is seen here in John Tavener's (1944–2013) *The Protecting Veil*, composed in 1987 (Example 29.19). The melodic line (in the solo cello) is simple and chant-like; the orchestral accompaniment consists of the melodic line transposed a perfect fourth below, along with its strict intervallic mirror.

Example 29.19. Tavener, "The Dormition of the Mother of God," from *The Protecting Veil*, rehearsal letter BB excerpt.

LEVEL MASTERY 29.6.

Self-Test 29.3 may be done at this time.

Apply This! 29.2 may be done at this time.

Workbook Exercise 29.6 may be done at this time.

Comment on Berg's use of symmetry in this passage. Locate symmetrical chords and explore their symmetrical properties (you may need to transfer pitches to other octaves). What vestiges of tonality do you see in this excerpt?

Berg, "Schlafend trägt man mich," op. 2 no. 2, mm. 1–4.

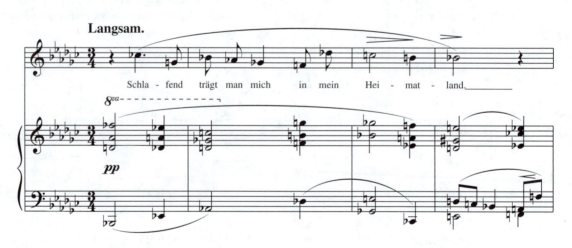

CONCLUSION

The terminology associated with atonal music can seem dauntingly "mathematical," but its concepts are rooted in basic musical principles such as octave equivalence and enharmonic equivalence. It is also important to remember that atonality is a logical extension from the extended chromaticism of late-nineteenth-century Romanticism; Schoenberg saw himself as a traditionalist, continuing in the path of Mahler and Brahms. Analysis through set theory reveals that much atonal music has a motivic character, establishing its place in a historical thread extending back to Beethoven and Bach.

Schoenberg developed his twelve-tone method out of a compositional need; he found that "free" atonality was difficult to use over large-scale forms. Remember, however, that twelve-tone technique is not a "style"; in fact, it has been used to compose music in a wide variety of styles. Much of Alban Berg's twelve-tone music, for example, is richly expressive and sounds like a continuation of the Romantic idiom. By contrast, Anton Webern's music possesses a cool, almost Baroque formalism, a quality developed (and expanded to parameters other than pitch) in the integral serial compositions of Milton Babbitt, Pierre Boulez, Karlheinz Stockhausen, and others. Meanwhile, the Italian composer Luigi Dallapiccola (1904–1975) freely adapted the twelve-tone method to almost tonal-sounding ends. Even Stravinsky (in his late works) and John Cage (1912–1992) (in his earliest works) adapted serial techniques with rows shorter or longer than twelve notes.

Terms to Know

aggregate
all-interval tetrachord
atonality
axis of symmetry
best normal order
cardinality
combinatoriality
complement
Darmstadt School
Forte analysis (set theory)
index number
integer notation
integral serialism

intersection ($\cap$)
interval class (ic)
interval vector
inversion (I_0)
matrix
modulo 12 (mod 12)
normal order
ordered set
ordinal number
pc (pitch class)
prime (P_0)
retrograde (R_0)
retrograde inversion (RI_0)

row (series)
Second Viennese School
segmentation
set (pcset)
set class (set type)
subset
superset
Tn
TnI
union ($\cup$)
unordered set
Z-correspondent
Z-relation

Self-Test

29.1. Identify the set class (SC) and interval vector (IV) of each set below.

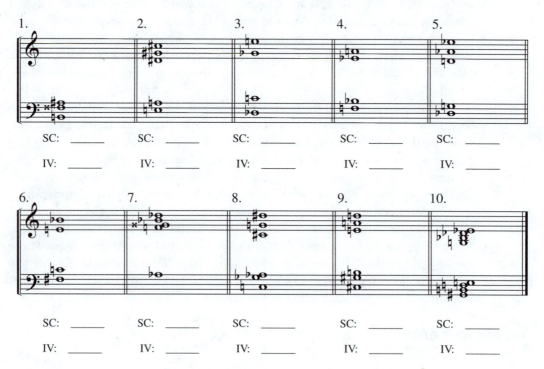

SC: _____   SC: _____   SC: _____   SC: _____   SC: _____

IV: _____   IV: _____   IV: _____   IV: _____   IV: _____

SC: _____   SC: _____   SC: _____   SC: _____   SC: _____

IV: _____   IV: _____   IV: _____   IV: _____   IV: _____

29.2. Determine the T*n* (transposition) or T*n*I (inversion) relation between each of the pairs of sets below. Be sure to use single-sided arrows for T*n* and double-sided arrows for T*n*I.

(Continued)

(Continued)

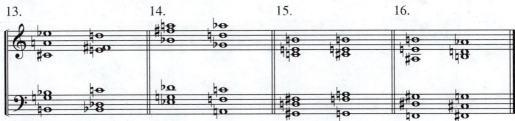

29.3. Find the pitch that is the axis of symmetry in the passage below. Identify the set class for each staff, and determine the T*n*I relation between the two parts.

Holm-Hudson, "Humoreske"

Apply This!

29.1. Analysis. Given the following series, <0, 8, 7, 6, E, 1, 5, 4, 3, 9, T, 2>, prepare a matrix on a separate sheet of paper. Then, identify and label the row forms used in the composition below.

Holm-Hudson, "Waltz"

29.2. Composition.

a. A composition in free-atonal style. Write a fifty-quarter-note-beat composition for voice and piano, based on the formal diagram below:

$$\| \quad A \quad | \quad B \quad | \quad A' \quad \|$$
$$\text{(contrasting section)}$$

| beats | 1–18 | 19–31 | 32–50 |

All pitches in the *A* section must be derived from set classes (014) and (026). All pitches in the *B* section must be derived from set classes (048) and (016). Mark all trichords on your score. All trichords within each section must be connected by intersecting pitches (common tones).

The form should be articulated by means of contrasting materials (dynamics, texture, etc.) in the *B* section. The final section should not be a literal restatement of *A*, but rather a reinterpretation of the first *A* section.

You may use the following text, or choose a text of your own, but the song must have a text.

Colors' five hues from the eyes their sight will take;
Music's five notes the ears as deaf can make;
The flavors five deprive the mouth of taste;
The chariot course, and the wild hunting waste
Make mad the mind; and objects rare and strange,
Sought for, men's conduct will to evil change.
{from Tao Te Ching, *translated by James Legge}*

Finish your composition by adding performance details such as dynamics, phrasing, and pedal markings.

b. A composition using twelve-tone technique.

1. Compose a twelve-note row in which the first pitch is C. Construct a matrix from this row, designating your original row as P_0.

2. Write a 16-measure composition for piano solo in which the time signature is $\frac{4}{4}$ and the form is ABA'; the sets should be segmented to articulate the structure (for instance, use tetrachords in the A sections and trichords in the contrasting B section). All four row forms (P, R, I, RI) should appear at least once. Two row forms should appear simultaneously at least twice (for example, P in the right hand and I in the left hand). No harmonic octaves should occur in the entire composition. Mark all row forms on your score, and add performance details such as dynamics, phrasing, and pedal markings.

29.3. Ear training. With practice, it is possible to tell the difference between and to identify set classes by ear, particularly trichords. Play and carefully listen to each of the trichords in the first row of Apply This! 29.3a and 29.3b below. Then, have a friend play for you the trichords in the subsequent rows, and identify the set class for each one. In each example, your choices will be limited to the six trichord types listed in the first row.

a.

BONUS ROUND involving inversions of non-symmetrical sets above:

b.

(play:)

BONUS ROUND involving inversions of non-symmetrical sets above:

CHAPTER 30

CONTEMPORARY TECHNIQUES 3

OVERVIEW

The stylistic development of Western music in the seventeenth through nineteenth centuries may be compared to a stream that, over time, broadened into a wide river. By the beginning of the twentieth century this musical river had widened into a delta, with numerous tributaries flowing outward. As the twentieth century progressed, this mighty river finally flowed out into a vast ocean. In this chapter we examine some of that musical ocean's more powerful currents.

CHAPTER OUTLINE

AUDIO LIST

Igor Stravinsky, *Three Pieces for String Quartet*, i

Roxy Music, "Re-Make/Re-Model"

INTRODUCTION

As we have learned from previous chapters, reaction to Wagner's music led to a split in aesthetic goals and musical styles. The split between those who pursued further chromaticism (Mahler, Reger, Schoenberg) and those who instead sought other techniques as a reaction against the perceived excesses in Wagner's style (Debussy, Stravinsky, Bartók) ultimately led to the profusion of styles that characterized music in the twentieth century. In this chapter we investigate some of the important formal and stylistic concerns of the twentieth century.

NEW APPROACHES TO FORM

As some composers continued to find inspiration in Baroque and Classic-era forms (see Web Feature 28.1 for an example), other composers reached even farther back into the past for inspiration. Igor Stravinsky's *Le Sacre du Printemps* (*The Rite of Spring*) (1913), for example, has the subtitle "pictures of pagan Russia" (an excerpt from this work was featured in Web Feature 3.5). In this work and others from Stravinsky's early "primitive" period (which include *Petrouchka* and *Les Noces*), material is not "developed" so much as juxtaposed and recombined in various ways. For example, in the first of his *Trois Pièces pour Quatuor à Cordes* (*Three Pieces for String Quartet*) (1914), each instrument has a largely static role (Example 30.1). The first violin has a four-note pitch collection (G4, A4, B4, C5) arranged in a melody that repeats every twenty-three beats. This melody is heard four times before "winding down" in the middle of the fifth time. Against the first violin's part, the second violin makes brusque and irregular entrances of a descending line made up of the pitches F♯4, E4, D♯4, and C♯4 (sharing no pitches in common with the first violin). The cello, meanwhile, plays a seven beat (3+2+2) ostinato comprised of the pitches C2, D♭3, and E♭3, while the viola provides a hurdy-gurdy-like drone on D4 (with "ghost notes" of C♯3 heard at the beginning and end of the piece). There seems to be little interaction among parts; this "layering" effect is called **stratification**. Example 30.2 shows these overlapping motives in the first eighteen measures of the score.

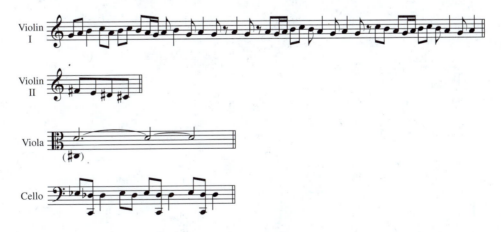

Example 30.1. Stravinsky, No. 1 from *Trois Pièces pour Quatuor à Cordes*, textural layers.

Example 30.2. Stravinsky, No. 1 from *Trois Pièces pour Quatuor à Cordes*, mm. 1–18. *(Continued)*

(Continued)

The music of Olivier Messiaen (first introduced in Chapter 28) is full of idiosyncratic techniques such as the use of transcribed birdsong, Hindu rhythmic formulas, so-called "non-retrogradeable" (palindromic) rhythms, and harmonic and rhythmic "pedals" (cycles or ostinati of different lengths), all of which convey a sense of timelessness or eternity in his music. Example 30.3, "Regard du Fils sur le Fils" ("Contemplation of the Son upon the Son") from the 1944 piano suite *Vingt Regards sur L'Enfant-Jésus*, provides an example of Messiaen's use of rhythmic augmentation canon between the upper and middle staves; there are three such augmentation canons in this movement, each of differing lengths but all beginning from the same point of synchronization, suggesting a "starting over" of the process with each canon. This example also shows harmonic and rhythmic pedals; the top staff has a harmonic pedal of seventeen chords and a rhythmic pedal of seventeen durations (shown in Example 30.4), while the middle staff does the same with different chords and durations that are 50 percent longer. Finally, the excerpt shows polymodality—the use of multiple "modes of limited transposition" discussed in Chapter 28. The top staff uses the third transposition of Messiaen's Mode 6, the middle staff uses the fourth transposition of Mode 4, and the lower staff—featuring Messiaen's "Theme of God"—uses Mode 2 (the $OCT_{0,1}$ collection) for the first eleven measures, followed by the second transposition of Mode 2 (the $OCT_{1,2}$ collection) beginning in measure 12. Careful study of the example will reveal these details.

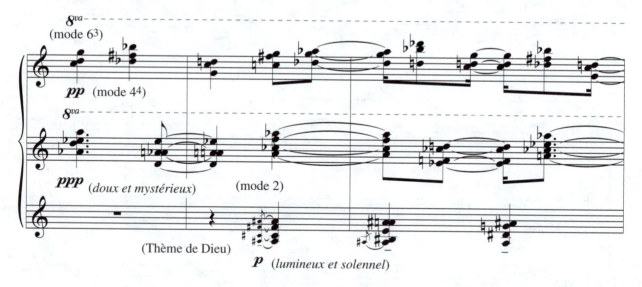

Example 30.3. Olivier Messiaen, "Regard du Fils sur le Fils," no. 5 from *Vingt Regards de l'Enfant-Jesus*, mm. 1–21. *(Continued)*

PART 4: Advanced Chromatic Harmony and Contemporary Techniques

(Continued)

(Continued)

(Continued)

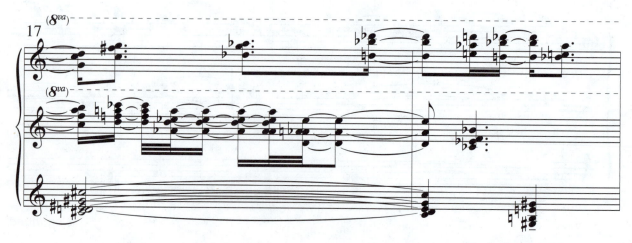

(Continued)

PART 4: Advanced Chromatic Harmony and Contemporary Techniques

(Continued)

Example 30.4. The rhythmic pedal for the upper staff in "Regard du Fils sur le Fils."

INDETERMINACY

Indeterminacy refers to music that involves some element of chance or randomness. Although Classic-era composers occasionally wrote "dice game" pieces (*Würfelspielen*) in which rolls of dice would determine the content and order of measures in a simple composition (see Workbook Exercise 20.2), the term is most often associated with the works of the American composer John Cage (1912–1992). Cage began using the Chinese oracle *I Ching* ("Book of Changes") as a compositional tool in the early 1950s in an effort to distance his compositional ego or "personality" from the work. The *I Ching* consists of 64 hexagrams, patterns made up of six stacked solid or broken lines; it is traditionally consulted by tossing yarrow stalks, although one can also use three coins.

Depending on how chance methods are used, an aleatoric work can be *indeterminate* with regard to *composition, performance,* or *both.* Cage's *Music of Changes* (1951–52) is a meticulously notated piece composed entirely by chance procedures—every detail, including pedaling, was determined by tosses of the *I Ching.* Later Cage pieces were constructed from imperfections in paper (the *Music for Piano* series), star charts (*Atlas Eclipticalis,* 1961–62), the music of other composers (*Cheap Imitation,* 1969, based on Erik Satie's *Socrate*), and silence itself (the famous *4'33″,* written in 1952, which consisted of an indeterminately-generated duration of "silence" within which any sounds in the environment became the "performance"). In the last five years of his life Cage wrote various "number pieces," in which sounds were to be performed within time brackets. An excerpt from one such piece, *One⁴* for solo percussionist, composed in 1990 (the superscript number indicates that this was the fourth solo composition among the "number" pieces), is shown in Example 30.5. In this excerpt, the sound is to begin at some point in the first minute of the piece, and the sound is to stop somewhere between forty seconds and one minute and forty seconds into the performance. The number 8 on the staff refers to the designated percussion instrument (one of ten) chosen by the performer. Cage's instructions indicate that the sound should be either "long (a tremolo with individual attacks that are not noticeable)" or "very short (without resonance, completely stopped)." Thus, for example, depending on whether the instrument chosen was, for example, a wood block or a marimba, the sound could be as varied as a single short wood block stroke or a rolled note or chord on marimba lasting for as long as a minute and forty seconds. (However, subsequent sound events overlap in time with this event, which can complicate matters for the performer.) Dynamics are also indeterminate, left to the performer.

Example 30.5. Cage, *One⁴*, first sonic event.

Other well-known composers of aleatoric music include Morton Feldman (1926–1987), Earle Brown (1926–2002), and Christian Wolff (born 1934). These composers, along with Cage, are sometimes referred to as the **New York School**.

MINIMALISM

John Cage once remarked, "In Zen they say: If something is boring after two minutes, try it for four. If still boring, try it for eight, sixteen, thirty-two, and so on. Eventually one discovers that it's not boring at all but very interesting."[1] Perhaps taking Cage at his word, **minimalism** is characterized by its repetitive nature—in many minimalist pieces a short cell or motive is repeated a number of times, to be followed by another cell that is a slight variant of the first, so that over time the smallest changes become magnified. Minimalist music also tends to have an asserted tonal center, and much of it is also strongly rhythmic or pulse-oriented in character. Composers most often associated with minimalism include the Americans Philip Glass (born 1937), Steve Reich (born 1936), Terry Riley (born 1935), and La Monte Young (born 1935). Later composers that have drawn upon minimalism include Henryk Górecki (1933–2010), Arvo Pärt (born 1935), Louis Andriessen (born 1939), John Tavener (1944–2013), John Adams (born 1947), and Wim Mertens (born 1953).

---

[1] John Cage, *Silence: Lectures and Writings* (Middletown, CT: Wesleyan University Press, 1961), p. 93.

Example 30.6 shows the first two "cells" of an early Philip Glass piece, *Music in Contrary Motion* (1969). Certain elements of this piece—its duration, tempo, dynamics, the number of repetitions for each cell, and its instrumentation—are indeterminate in regard to performance. (Early performances of this piece were usually given by Glass's own ensemble, which had variable personnel and instrumentation but usually involved a number of electric keyboards, saxophones, and flute; Glass himself would usually cue the change from one cell to the next by a nod of the head.) Note that the rhythm is a constant stream of eighth notes, and the pitch content is extremely limited. These two parameters do not change for the entire composition. However, closer examination of these two cells reveals that they differ in melodic contour and rhythmic *grouping*; listening to this music, we might even hear the pitch-classes A and E as having contour accents, creating eighth-note groupings in ever-shifting sizes. Also, as the composition proceeds, the cells get longer, so that eventually even the most attentive listener loses track of where the beginnings and endings of cells are.

Example 30.6. Glass, *Music in Contrary Motion*, first two cells.

POSTMODERNISM AND STYLISTIC PLURALISM

Much twentieth-century music, for all its stylistic diversity, still held to the tenets of **modernism** that dated back to the Romantic era—the notion that cultural progress was possible through a self-conscious break with earlier tradition. While composers such as Schoenberg, for example, respected tradition (Schoenberg saw his atonal music as a continuation of both the chromatic language of Wagner and Mahler and the developing motivic variation of Brahms), they saw no point in self-consciously quoting or replicating those traditions (unlike Stravinsky in his neo-classic period, for instance, who often cited specific composers and even compositions as "raw material" for his own works). By the 1960s, however, composers began to use music from the past in a curiously detached way; Luciano Berio (1925–2003), for example, grafted quotations from Mahler's "Resurrection" Symphony and Debussy's *La Mer* into his composition *Sinfonia* (1968–69), and George Crumb (born 1929) inserted a quotation from Chopin's "Fantasie-Impromptu," op. 66 (posthumous), into the "Dream-Images (Gemini)" movement of *Makrokosmos, Volume I* (1972). Rock musicians during the same period, from Frank Zappa to the Beatles, were drawing upon the styles of (and sometimes quoting) common-practice art music and employing avant-garde techniques. Rather than continue to belabor the notion of modernist "progress," the task was now to recombine fragments of the past in new and ironic ways. Thus, **postmodernism** was a reaction to the modernist emphasis on progress, by emphasizing stylistic eclecticism (including juxtapositions of "high" art and "low" popular genres) and irony.

The song "Re-Make/Re-Model" by Roxy Music (1972) serves as a good example of postmodernism in music. The lyrics convey a sense of post-historical detachment, as vocalist Bryan Ferry sings "looking back all I did was look away. . . . If there is no next time, where to go?" (Even the song's refrain is merely a license plate number.) The extended coda, starting at [3:12], conveys a kind of jumbled mini-history of Western music in its solo breaks. The drum break at [3:17] seems ordinary enough— such drum fills are common in rock music, though the practice here can also be traced to "trading fours" in jazz, in which passages involving the full combo alternate with brief drum solos. The next break, a bass solo at [3:24], partially quotes from the Beatles' 1965 hit "Day Tripper." At [3:30] we are presented with a burst of random synthesizer noise, perhaps a 1970s version of "futuristic music" (the use of electronic music to denote a "music of the future" goes back at least as far as the 1956 science-fiction film *Forbidden Planet*). Next, at [3:37], is a saxophone quote from Richard Wagner's "Ride of the Valkyries," followed by a guitar riff at [3:45] that quotes from Eddie Cochran's 1958 hit "Summertime Blues." Finally, the random volley of secundal piano chords at [3:52] perhaps suggests free jazz, or even an effort to "wipe out" or obliterate the previous musical-historical references.

Apply This!
30.1 and 30.2
may be done
at this time.

CONCLUSION

The twentieth century was a time of unprecedented social, political, technological, and cultural change, and music naturally reflected (or responded to) all of these changes. The enormous influence of Wagner in the late nineteenth century led some composers—notably Debussy, Ravel, Satie, Stravinsky and Bartók—to react against his style and seek alternatives.

Sometimes music develops in response to cultural changes. For example, minimalism was impacted from composers' contact with non-Western music, especially north Indian art music (as performed by musicians such as Ravi Shankar) and African music (the Nigerian drummer Babtunde Olatunji (1927–2003) was an important influence on many musicians of the 1960s, from John Coltrane to the Grateful Dead's drummer Mickey Hart). The 1960s youth counterculture also played a role, as did developments in the visual arts (the repetition of visual images in much of Andy Warhol's work, for instance, and the "minimalist" art of painters such as Sol LeWitt).

Musical change also follows sociopolitical upheavals. Especially after the two world wars, there was a perception that new music and art must emerge from the ashes of war-torn Europe; thus, the objectivity of Stravinsky's neo-classic style can be seen as a response to the horrors of World War I, and the integral serialism of the Darmstadt School and the indeterminacy of the New York School both emerged within a few years of the end of World War II.

The cultural "gray-out" of high and low as seen in the later music of the Beatles as well as a number of other artists and bands in the 1960s and 1970s, as well as the openness of "classical" musicians to those trends, helped give rise to the postmodern tendencies of the 1970s and beyond (it should be pointed out that many of these "postmodern" composers grew up on the cartoon soundtracks of composers like Carl Stalling [1891–1972], perhaps the first musical postmodernist). Technological innovations such as the mp3 player will likely accelerate this trend; already the old mode of listening to entire albums or CDs has given way to more atomistic, even randomly generated playlists of songs that can be of staggering diversity. How will the randomness of an mp3 in shuffle mode and the easy access of all types of music and video on YouTube affect the next generation of composers? What might a theory for this future music look like?

Terms to Know

indeterminacy   modernism   postmodernism (in music)
minimalism   New York School   stratification

Apply This!

30.1. Composition.

An indeterminate composition. For this exercise you will compose a piece that is indeterminate in regard to composition and performance.

Begin with four random numbers between 2 million and 3 million (you might use on online random number generator, such as www.random.org, to do this, ensuring a true random selection). These random numbers will be used to locate materials (as call numbers, for example) in your local university or public library, which you will use as "found" source material for your composition. Four numbers are given to avoid potential problems, such as: 1) nothing available under that call number; 2) the item is checked out; 3) the item is missing; or 4) the item is restricted in access—for example, it is on reserve, is a media item (such as a DVD or microfiche, etc.), or is a rare book not accessible to the general user.

If all four random numbers do not produce any source materials, generate additional random numbers or change the last digit of one of your original numbers until an item is found.

Your composition should be a four-minute performance piece based on your source material. Create a random sampling of the source "text" by using dice, cards, computer, etc., to determine which page, which sentence, which word is to be used, how it is to be presented (spoken, sung, screamed, whispered, written, recorded, etc.), and in what order it is to be presented. Prepare a "score" for your materials and perform it in class if possible.

30.2. Improvisation. A number of twentieth- (and twenty-first-) century compositions involve improvisation guided by written instructions or graphic scores (scores that use lines, shapes, or pictures to denote sound events rather than conventional musical notation). Try to locate, and perform, the following pieces:

Earle Brown, *December 1952*
Cornelius Cardew, *People-Influenced Music*
Cornelius Cardew, *Treatise*
Pauline Oliveros, *Sonic Meditations*
Tom Phillips, *Postcard Pieces*
Christian Wolff, *For 1, 2, or 3 People*
Christian Wolff, *Stones*
La Monte Young, *Composition 1960 no. 10*

Alternatively, try a "silent movie accompanist" improvisation to a video found on YouTube, such as an old black-and-white movie excerpt or a cartoon. Do not watch the video beforehand, and turn the sound off. Your improvisation should be a reaction/accompaniment to what you are seeing, ideally for the first time.

CHAPTER 31

THE STORIES WE COULD TELL
Musical Narrativity and Intertextuality

OVERVIEW

We all know that music is expressive, but what does it express? "Absolute" music expresses its own structure. Program music is said to tell a story—but how exactly does it do this? Are there elements of music that can be isolated as having narrative qualities?

We also know that some pieces of music sound like or refer to other pieces. These shared "family resemblances" are an important element of musical style, and its development. In this chapter we explore how music can tell a story even if a story is not specified, and how music can refer to other pieces of music in an increasingly media-aware culture.

CHAPTER OUTLINE

AUDIO LIST

Fréderic Chopin, Ballade No. 1 in G minor, op. 23

Emmylou Harris, "Goodbye"

Janet Jackson, "Someone to Call My Lover"

The Orb, "Little Fluffy Clouds"

Pink Floyd, "Comfortably Numb"

Erik Satie, "d'Edriophtalma"

Franz Schubert, "Erlkönig"

U2, "Where the Streets Have No Name"

INTRODUCTION

Sometimes even casual listening can reveal new insights about the music that is all around us. For example, consider the following scenario: Two young children are engaged in deep imaginative play with little doll figures, and one of their characters "dies," prompting one child to sing the following melodic snippet:

Upon hearing this, the other child immediately responds as follows:

You probably realize that these two melodic excerpts (both transposed here to the same key) come from very different pieces. The first is from Fréderic Chopin's Sonata no. 2 in B♭ minor, op. 35 no. 2; the second, the "Imperial March" from John Williams's score to *The Empire Strikes Back*, associated with *Star Wars* villain Darth Vader. We might ask what connects the second melodic fragment to the first. One notable similarity is that both melodic fragments begin with a single pitch repeated on the first three beats. Another similarity is the pervasive dotted rhythms. Finally, each phrase ends on the tonic. You might notice other similarities.

In scoring appropriate dramatic music to portray the menace of Darth Vader, Williams drew upon models from "classical" music that conveyed death and destruction. Chopin's "Funeral March" melody is one of the best known melodies in the common-practice literature. As Chopin gave the movement the label *Marche Funèbre*, there is no doubt that it is meant to be associated with death and funeral processions. (The accompaniment to Williams's "Imperial March" has a different "classical" model—the insistent, intensely rhythmic string ostinato bears some similarity to Gustav Holst's "Mars, the Bringer of War" from his orchestral suite *The Planets*.)

HOCKED HOOKS AND RECYCLED RIFFS: MUSICAL INTERTEXTUALITY

The term **intertextuality** originates from the poststructuralist author and philosopher Julia Kristeva, who introduced the term in her 1969 essay "Word, Dialogue and Novel."[1] The concept is that no "text" (verbal, visual, aural) is "original" in and

---

[1] Julia Kristeva, "Word, Dialogue and Novel," in *The Kristeva Reader*, ed. Toril Moi (New York: Columbia University Press, 1986), 34–61.

of itself, existing in a vacuum, but instead every text draws upon an ever-expanding web of inevitable (and often unintentional) references to or quotations from other texts. Thus, for example, John Williams's "Imperial March" draws upon part of its meaning from references to Holst's "Mars" as well as Chopin's "Funeral March"; each of those pieces in turn bring in references of their own. Chopin's piece, for instance, can call to mind references to other famous funeral marches (such as Beethoven's, in the second movement to his Third Symphony) as well as to other instances of its use in popular culture (such as old cartoons, Monty Python, and the death of Pac Man in video games). The rhythmic figure of Holst's "Mars" is alluded to (but not directly quoted) at the beginning of the classic rock song "White Room" by Cream (1968). The "Imperial March" itself has become so well known that it has spun off resonances of its own, from *The Simpsons* to National Hockey League games. These are just a few of the musical reference points that can be traced out of this single example.

We can distinguish between **stylistic** and **strategic intertextuality**.[2] In stylistic intertextuality, certain musical features are used to evoke traits of a particular musical style. For example, an Alberti bass accompaniment (Example 31.1a) is often used to evoke music of the Classical era (we hear it in the beginning of Styx's "Come Sail Away" [1977], for example). On the other hand, an accompaniment figure such as that shown in Example 31.1b may suggest the 1950s rock 'n' roll style of Chuck Berry as exemplified by songs such as "Johnny B. Goode" (especially if this figure is played on guitar).

Example 31.1a. An Alberti bass figure from Classic-era music.

Example 31.1b. A "Chuck Berry" guitar figure from 1950s rock 'n' roll.

These are two examples of **genre synecdoches**.[3] A *synecdoche* is a grammatical term that refers to the type of metaphor in which a single part is used to symbolize something much more general. For example, when a sea captain calls out "all hands on deck," it is evident that the captain is not referring merely to hands but to the entire person—the term "hand" is thus a synecdoche. Similarly, the musical gestures shown in Example 31.1 refer not merely to a single specific piece (such as, for

---

[2] These terms were coined by the music theorist Robert Hatten. See his article "The Place of Intertextuality in Music Studies," *American Journal of Semiotics* 3, no. 4 (1985): 69–82.

[3] This term was introduced by the popular music scholar Philip Tagg. See his *Introductory Notes to the Semiotics of Music*, pp. 26–27. On the Internet: http://www.tagg.org/xpdfs/semiotug.pdf.

example, Mozart's Piano Sonata in C major, K.545 or Berry's "Johnny B. Goode") but by extension to an entire body of work ("classical piano music," "Chuck Berry's style") by evoking the common and distinctive features of that repertoire. In this way, genre synecdoches can be powerful carriers of intertextual reference.

Because "texts" involve other domains besides musical sound, stylistic intertextuality in music can also apply to notational elements. For example, doubled rhythmic values (half notes in place of quarter notes, in a meter such as $\frac{4}{2}$, etc.) were common features of Renaissance music, and in later eras became known as *stile antico* ("old style"), usually implying music of a more solemn or serious nature. Accordingly, in Debussy's piano prelude "La Cathédrale Engloutie" ("The Engulfed Cathedral"), certain passages of Gregorian-chant-like melodies are notated in *stile antico*, so that the prelude bears the unusual metric signature $\frac{6}{4} = \frac{3}{2}$. Example 31.2a shows the first two measures of the piece, in $\frac{6}{4}$ (note the tie treating the third bass note in measure 2 as a syncopation rather than the second half-note beat in $\frac{3}{2}$); Example 31.2b shows one of the "chant" passages, notated in $\frac{3}{2}$ (the second half note in measures 33 and 35 would be "broken" as two tied quarter notes to show the syncopation if this passage were in $\frac{6}{4}$).

Example 31.2. Debussy, "La Cathédrale Engloutie," mm. 1–2 and 32–35.

In strategic intertextuality, a *specific* text is referenced within another text. Musical quotation is nothing new, of course—composers in the late Middle Ages and the Renaissance frequently used fragments of Gregorian chant as a *cantus firmus* in polyphonic works, and sometimes entire tunes are fitted with different words to become new tunes (the melody of the American national anthem "The Star Spangled Banner," for example, is borrowed from a British drinking song, "To Anacreon in Heaven"). Carl Stalling wove references to classical pieces, folk songs, and old "Tin Pan Alley" pop tunes throughout his soundtracks to hundreds of Warner Brothers "Looney Tunes" cartoons throughout the 1940s and 1950s. Rock musician Frank Zappa inserted quotations from music as diverse as Stravinsky's *Rite of Spring* and the rock song "Louie Louie" into his music. The use of recorded samples in hip hop, R&B, and electronic dance music would also qualify as strategic intertextuality.

However, strategic intertextuality does not need to directly *quote* from a work in order to *refer* to it. We often find references by *allusion*, in which certain musical features enable us to associate one musical work with another. This is the case with John Williams's references to Chopin and Holst in the "Imperial March"—neither work is directly quoted, but the similarities are close enough that we recognize the melody as based specifically on Chopin's "Funeral March" (as opposed to something merely "in the style of Chopin").

Intertextuality might seem like an academic game of "Name That Tune." There's more to it than that, however; the real interest lies in what happens when references to multiple texts of different styles are found simultaneously—when "information brushes against information," as the media theorist Marshall McLuhan once put it. For example, Janet Jackson's "Someone to Call My Lover" (2001) begins with a two-chord acoustic guitar loop sampled from the 1972 song "Ventura Highway" by the soft-rock group America; the order of the chords is reversed, however, so that instead of a GMaj7–DMaj7 progression (IV^7–I^7 in D major) the progression is DMaj7–Gmaj7 (I^7–IV^7). Nevertheless, for those who recognize the connection with the America song and its associations of wanderlust ("Chewing on a piece of grass / Walking down the road . . ."), the Jackson song expresses a similar sentiment ("Back on the road again / Feeling kinda lonely and . . ."). A new layer of intertextual reference is introduced during the chorus, which is first heard beginning at [0:47]; a bell-like keyboard playing the opening melody from the first of Erik Satie's *Trois Gynopédies* for piano (1888). Interestingly, Satie's piano piece, a slow, languid work in $\frac{3}{4}$ meter, begins with the same two-chord progression heard at the beginning of America's "Ventura Highway"; here, then, the melody is also heard with a different harmonic backdrop (the chords being reversed) as well as rhythmically altered to fit the $\frac{4}{4}$ meter.

The harmonic content of the Orb's "Little Fluffy Clouds," which we briefly considered in our discussion of binary form in Chapter 20, is derived entirely from a two-chord excerpt from Steve Reich's composition *Electric Counterpoint*, as performed by jazz guitarist Pat Metheny (the sample comes from the third movement of that work, measures 120–123). The sample can be heard at [1:12–1:31] and elsewhere throughout the song; in its first appearance it accompanies the spoken-word sample "layering different sounds on top of each other," an apt description of the Orb's compositional process (as is the phrase "electric counterpoint"). Like Jackson's use of Satie's *Gymnopédie*, the sample has been metrically altered—in this case the last beat of each of Reich's $\frac{3}{4}$ measures is simply copied and pasted an extra beat to fit the $\frac{4}{4}$ meter of "Little Fluffy Clouds." Most of the spoken-word elements—including the phrase that gives the song its title—come from an interview with singer Rickie Lee Jones,

For an
example of
how a "riff"
in popular
music changes
context over
time through
intertextuality,
see Web
Feature 31.1.

in which she described her memories of the colorful skies at her Arizona childhood home. The "lonesome" harmonica sound heard at the beginning of the song and elsewhere is taken from "The Harmonica Man" from Ennio Morricone's soundtrack to the film *Once Upon a Time in the West*. The inclusion of this sample provides an additional layer of intertextual reference, for Jones's childhood recollections of the Arizona skies tell her own story of "once upon a time in the west."

Another kind of intertextual reference occurs in the popular-music practice of recording a **cover version** (or **cover**) of a well known song—a new version by a different artist. There are antecedents of this in "classical" music as well. For example, anytime a composer composes a set of variations "on a theme" by another composer—as in Johannes Brahms's famous variations on themes of Haydn or Handel, or Brahms's or Clara Schumann's variations on a theme by Robert Schumann—the original is an implicit reference point. Arrangements of previous compositions by other composers may also be regarded as a kind of "cover version," as we can see from William Schumann's orchestration of Ives's *Variations on America* or Bach's numerous adaptations of concerti by Vivaldi and other composers. In jazz, the many versions of a "standard" refer to some idealized original even as they reflect the imprint of the performer's improvising personality; Monk's version of "Well You Needn't," for example, is the unheard-yet-remembered point of reference for versions such as the walking shuffle of Miles Davis's version, the frenetic Latin jazz of pianist Gonzalo Rubalcaba, or the deconstructive skronk of the "fake jazz" group the Lounge Lizards.[4] There is something of a "primacy effect" at work here, as some covers become better known than the originals that inspired them (Jimi Hendrix's version of Bob Dylan's "All Along the Watchtower," for example, is better known than Dylan's original); in general, however, hearing a cover of a song usually brings up the original version by association (provided, of course, that one has heard the original).

Thus far, we have focused on examples of intertextuality in popular music, but it can also be found in common-practice Western art music. The first movement of Clara Schumann's Trio in G minor, op. 17 (i), provides a good example. Clara Schumann was married to the composer Robert Schumann; she was a piano virtuoso as well as a gifted composer in her own right, and like most concert pianists of her generation she was intimately familiar with the piano sonatas and chamber literature of Ludwig van Beethoven. Not surprisingly, this piece contains several specific references to Beethoven's sonatas, particularly his eighth (op. 13, the "Pathétique") and tenth (op. 14 no. 2) sonatas.

The primary theme of Schumann's work is exchanged between violin and piano in a manner reminiscent of Beethoven's chamber music, such as his "Spring" sonata for violin and piano (op. 24). The Beethoven references are more notable, however, in the transition between the primary and secondary themes, shown in Example 31.3.

---

[4] Monk himself recorded "Well You Needn't" many times, of course, with different line-ups of supporting musicians. This is why the rather philosophical term "idealized original" is used here; the "original" version, as such, is a rather fluid construct.

The assertive dotted-rhythm gesture shared by violin and piano in measures 22–23 and 26–27 is strongly evocative of the opening to the first movement of Beethoven's "Pathétique" sonata, shown in Example 31.4. This gesture is answered by a gracefully arcing descending figure in the violin (see measures 24–25 of Example 22.5); this figure is reminiscent of the first movement of Beethoven's Sonata in G major, op. 14, no. 2, which we examined in detail in Chapter 21. Example 21.2 showed the primary theme of that work—the rhythmic figure Schumann uses in the violin at this point resembles the rhythm of measures 6–8 in Example 21.2. In addition, Schumann develops her material in this transitional passage in a manner strikingly similar to Beethoven. Examining measures 70–72 in Example 21.6, for example, shows Beethoven's imitative treatment of the primary theme's motive; compare this with measures 34–38 in Example 31.3 below. The effect of this transition section in Clara Schumann's Trio, then, might be likened to a "call and response" between two different Beethoven sonatas.

Example 31.3. Clara Schumann, Trio in G minor, op. 17 (i), mm. 22–45a.

(Continued)

(Continued)

(Continued)

(Continued)

Grave.

Example 31.4. Beethoven, Sonata in C minor, op. 13 ("Pathétique") (i), mm. 1–2.

It is easy to interpret the references to Beethoven in Clara Schumann's Trio as a kind of homage. Quotation and allusion can also, however, be used as a form of parody, and it increasingly serves this function in music of the twentieth century. The music of composers as diverse as Charles Ives, Erik Satie, and Frank Zappa all tend to use quotation and stylistic reference with an air of parody or irony. In Chapter 28 we encountered Satie's gentler, more "impressionist" side in his *Trois Gymnopédies*; Satie was also known, however, for writing bizarre piano miniatures with outlandish titles (such as "Veritable Flabby Preludes for a Dog"), often with written commentary provided throughout the piece for the performer's amusement (in at least one work Satie expressly forbade the sharing of these commentaries with the audience). One such work is *Embryons Desséchés* ("Dried Up Embryos"), published in 1913. Given that many piano miniatures of the late nineteenth and early twentieth centuries were "character" pieces portraying something or someone in sound (as in the childhood topics of Schumann's *Kinderszenen* or Mussorgsky's *Pictures at an Exhibition*, for example), Satie rather whimsically (if grotesquely) named each of the suite's three pieces for some obscure biological specimen. The second piece, "d'Edriophtalma," thus attempts to convey the solitary, melancholy life of the sea cucumber.

"d'Edriophtalma" is in ternary form. The outer sections of the piece begin with gently rolled, ascending open-fifth sonorities very similar to those that begin his friend Debussy's "La Cathédrale Engloutie," which had been published just three years before (Example 31.5).

Sombre

pp   *Ils sont tous réunis

*They are all reunited

Example 31.5. Satie, "d'Edriophtalma," introduction.

The contrasting middle section features a substantial quotation from the second theme of Chopin's "Funeral March," transposed to C major and with the commentary that the passage is "a citation from the famous mazurka of Schubert" (Example 31.6). A mazurka is a rather stately Polish dance in $\frac{3}{4}$ meter; even without the barlines here (another of Satie's "jokes," no doubt), it is obvious that this passage is not in triple meter. Furthermore, Schubert, an Austrian composer, was not a composer of mazurkas. Satie's text, even as it aims to distract the performer from the true source of this musical passage by providing incorrect information, thus ironically adds other layers of reference—to mazurkas and the piano works of Franz Schubert as well as the specific Chopin reference that we hear.

*Ils se mettent tous à pleurer

(*Citation de la célèbre mazurka de SCHUBERT*)

*They are all put to crying

Example 31.6. Satie, "d'Edriophtalma," Chopin quote in middle section.

Even before the specific quotation is heard, however, Satie has introduced *stylistic* references to funeral marches as a *genre* (Chopin's and others) in the dotted rhythms, low register, and plodding quarter-note accompaniment of the outer sections (just after the rolled-chord "Debussy" reference). Such musical elements that evoke an entire musical genre are genre synecdoches.

An audience member in Clara Schumann's day may well have recognized the Beethoven references in her Trio; likewise, a listener attending a performance of Satie's piece in pre–World War I Paris may also have recognized the references to Chopin and Debussy. Concertgoers in our day, however, would likely not understand these references unless they have a thorough grounding in a wide range of the common-practice repertoire (and that, admittedly, would not likely be the case, since "classical" music occupies an increasingly smaller slice of our modern media culture). In the same way, discerning fans of electronica or hip-hop will recognize certain famous samples or rhythmic patterns—such as the James Brown "Funky Drummer" break—while these would likely be meaningless to someone whose tastes inclined to country or big-band jazz. This is because such gestures depend on the **stylistic competence** of the listener—the ability to recognize meaningful genre references through prior exposure to examples of that genre. Someone who watches a lot of movies would be more likely to spot the references to the original *Star Wars* trilogy or to the Arnold Schwartzenegger action film *True Lies* in the animated film *Toy Story 2*. A saxophonist who listens to (and plays) a great deal of jazz will be more likely to recognize the

Self-Test 31.1 may be done at this time.

stylistic differences in the playing style of different musicians—comparing John Coltrane, Cannonball Adderly, and Coleman Hawkins, for example—and to incorporate references to those players' distinctive styles in his or her own playing.

NARRATIVITY AND MUSICAL MEANING

The idea that music is a "universal language" is a well-worn adage. One of the enduring "unanswerable questions" about music is whether or not it communicates, and if so, what exactly is communicated. At one extreme, Igor Stravinsky famously argued that music was not capable of communicating specific emotions; at the other extreme, Leonard Bernstein not only advocated for music's communicative power but went as far as to theorize about musical grammatical structure, in his famous Harvard lectures which became a book (and television miniseries) called *The Unanswered Question*. British musicologist Deryck Cooke even compiled a number of musical gestures with allegedly specific "meanings" into a book called *The Language of Music*.[5]

As we have seen, the harmony of Western art music (and much Western jazz and popular music) does employ a hierarchical structure of predominant, dominant, and tonic functions, which are customarily arranged according to a syntax that moves from dissonance to consonance. A one-to-one mapping of grammar from linguistics to music, however, does not hold up to closer scrutiny; although it is possible to think of some chords as having an "adjectival" function (the use of a borrowed iv chord instead of a IV, for example), what chords would function as nouns or verbs?

Nevertheless, we can point to certain "generic" musical elements that have common functions in Western music, and generalize them into a kind of typology.[6] We have already noted the importance of genre synecdoches in our examination of stylistic intertextuality; they may be contrasted with **style indicators**. If genre synecdoches are those musical elements that refer to musical genres and repertories *outside* the norms of the piece in question, style indicators are those musical elements that are compositional norms *within* the style of the piece. Thus, for example, an Alberti-bass piano texture would be a style indicator in eighteenth-century Viennese classical piano music, but it becomes a genre synecdoche when used in Styx's "Come Sail Away."

Similarly, the third movement of Mozart's Piano Sonata in A Major, K.331 is sometimes referred to as the "Rondo alla Turca" for its stylistic incursions of Turkish janissary march rhythms. In Example 31.7a, Mozart's use of grace-note rolls in the bass brings out this rhythmic pattern as it also evokes snare-drum ruffs. In the stylistic context of Mozart's music, this functions as a genre synecdoche; as Example 31.7b shows, the pattern is still a style indicator for the "left, right, left" call of military march cadences.

---

[5] Deryck Cooke, *The Language of Music* (New York: Oxford University Press, 1959).
[6] This section on a typology of musical elements is heavily indebted to the work of Philip Tagg. See especially his *Introductory Notes to the Semiotics of Music*, pp. 23–28.

Example 31.7a. Mozart, Piano Sonata No. 11 in A major, K.331 (iii), mm. 24b–32a.

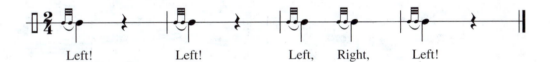

Left!   Left!   Left,   Right,   Left!

Example 31.7b. A military march cadence.

ANAPHONES

On a more emotive level, much of music's communicative power derives from what Philip Tagg has called **anaphones**—gestures that function symbolically for sounds in the same way that an analogy does for words. Anaphones may be sonic, tactile, or kinetic.

A **sonic anaphone** involves the direct, onomatopoeia-like process of using one (often non-musical) sound as the model for a musical sound. Examples include the use of timpani to suggest distant thunder in Beethoven's Pastorale Symphony and Berlioz's Symphone Fantastique, the periodic, heavy low-C pedal point throughout the midsection of Debussy's "La Cathédrale Engloutie" to evoke the sound of a huge tolling bell, and the "whinnying" trumpet solo imitating a horse at the end of Leroy Anderson's "Sleigh Ride." As Tagg points out, the success of a sonic anaphone depends on the listener's comprehension of the original sound's properties and connotations. Thus, for example, for the trumpet in "Sleigh Ride" to be recognized as a "horse," one must know what a horse's whinny sounds like, and recognize in the context of its use here that the horse is playful (perhaps shaking off snow!) and is not spooked or charging violently.

Maurice Ravel's *Jeux d'Eau* ("Fountains," "Playing Water," or literally "Water Games") is, in the composer's words, "inspired by the noise of water and by musical sounds which make one hear the sprays of water, the waterfalls and the brooks."[7] The idea of "musical sounds *which make one hear* the sprays of water" suggests the arpeggios throughout this piece function as sonic anaphones for the rippling and spraying sound of water (Example 31.8).

Example 31.8. Ravel, *Jeux d'Eau*, mm. 1–6. *(Continued)*

---

[7] Maurice Hinson, *At the Piano with Ravel* (Los Angeles: Alfred Publishing Co., 1986), 5. For a slightly different translation, see Ian Bradley, *Water Music: Music Making in the Spas of Europe and North America* (New York: Oxford University Press, 2010), 25.

PART 4: Advanced Chromatic Harmony and Contemporary Techniques

(Continued)

Tactile anaphones, as their name implies, use sound to evoke textures, thus using one sensory stimulus to suggest another. We may refer to the "gauzy" harmonies of Enya, for example, the "cold" robotic precision of Kraftwerk or Daft Punk, or the "grunge-y" guitar sound of Nirvana. Composers of TV and film music often use "pads"—slowly changing sonorities with a lack of sharp attack and decay that are often used to "pad" holes in a musical texture. Such pads are often described as "lush," "smooth," "warm," and so on.[8] As the above examples demonstrate, this type of anaphone is mainly associated with timbre.

Emmylou Harris's rendition of Steve Earle's "Goodbye," from her 1995 album *Wrecking Ball*, provides a vivid example of a musical texture dominated by tactile anaphones. Harris's producer, Daniel Lanois (who has also worked with U2, Peter Gabriel, and Bob Dylan), is known for his productions that are usually quite atmospheric, creatively using reverberation and sound processing to dramatically alter the timbre and texture of a song. Here, the instrumentation of "Goodbye" consists of two acoustic guitars, electric guitar, mandolin, piano, bass, and percussion. Can you hear the roles that each of these instruments play in the texture?

The song fades in [0:00–0:08] from the right channel, with acoustic guitar and shaker in the right channel joined by a hand drum at left-center and occasional reinforcing strums on a second acoustic guitar in the left channel. The sound is already warm and reverberant. At 0:08 the instruments pause for a count-off from the guitarist in the right channel, reinforcing the impression that this is an intimate gathering; perhaps the musicians are seated close to one another around a circle (you can even hear someone clear their throat quietly in the left channel at 0:10). When the players come back in at 0:14, the texture is hazy; there is some spatial separation between the two acoustic guitars, but there is also considerable reverberation, enhanced by the sustained bell-like piano chords that seem to emerge from the texture between the chord changes. Occasional guitar and piano notes seem to echo from the right to the left channel. A drum kit enters at 0:28; the snare sound seems dry and taut compared to the other instruments.

---

[8] Tagg, *Introductory Notes to the Semiotics of Music*, p. 25.

The overall "haze" of the introduction is even carried over into the harmonic domain. The harmony of the song is simple and diatonic, mostly comprising I, IV, and V; there is no modulation. However, the tonic A major chord seems to persistently be "clouded" by a suspended fourth; this can be heard at 0:35–0:40, for example, and even the very last chord of the song.

The first verse begins at 0:40; it is in an AABA form, with the contrasting bridge beginning at 1:29. During the bridge [1:29–1:55], the piano emerges somewhat in the mix. Following the first verse, from 2:14 to 2:45 there is an electric guitar solo, distorted and with noticeable echo in addition to the reverberation, beginning in the left channel; the electric guitar recedes somewhat into the mix when Harris returns for the second verse at 2:45, but it remains, offering a series of background counter-melodies behind the vocals. As the song reaches its end with the repetition of the last line and a deceptive cadence (4:29–4:33), the electric guitar soars into its highest register yet for the song.

Harris's vocals are front and center throughout. It is evident that the recording level for her vocal was fairly high—breaths are audible before phrases, for example, and her vocal lines tend to trail off into the mix quietly (without printed lyrics, it can be hard to discern exactly how some lines end). This also adds to the overall "hazy" feel of the song, perhaps illustrating the druggy haziness of memory portrayed by the song ("were we just too high / but I can't remember if we said goodbye").

Kinetic anaphones imply motion. The movement of a sound from one speaker to the other in a stereo recording—a technique called **panning**—implies movement of the object producing that sound. Bernard Herrmann's staccato high-register cluster chords used in the shower scene from *Psycho* (see Chapter 2, Example 2.8) are memorable evocations of the rhythmic motions of repeated stabbing. March rhythms (see Example 31.7a and b), dance rhythms such as the tango, mambo, and samba, the "walking bass" pattern of jazz, and the similarly "walking" repeated "tonic–fifth" bass pattern heard in bluegrass music (as well as Igor Stravinsky's *L'Histoire du Soldat*) are also examples of kinetic anaphones. As the variety of potential human motion is vast—walking, dancing, running, jumping—so is the variety of possible kinetic ana-phones. One should also consider the possible motions of animals (horses galloping, insects swarming, fish swimming, birds soaring or swooping from the sky) as well as the motions of technology (factory machines, trains, automobiles, planes)—all can be portrayed with particular sonic gestures.

In "Marche du Soldat" ("Soldier's March"), the first movement in Igor Stravin-sky's 1918 suite *L'Histoire du Soldat*, the bass accompaniment functions as a kinetic anaphone for the steady pace of a marching soldier—obstinately so, against the changes of meter in measures 14–17 (Example 31.9).

Example 31.9. Stravinsky, "Marche du Soldat" (from *L'Histoire du Soldat*), mm. 5–19.

U2's "Where the Streets Have No Name" presents a number of kinetic anaphones in a field of considerable depth and stereophonic richness. The introduction—a stately and swirling blend of organ-like synthesizer chords, drenched in reverberation—emerges out of silence evidently *in medias res*, as the first chord of the progression is missing. At 0:30 the progression repeats (beginning with the tonic chord, which is how we know the song faded in mid-progression), this time with a slightly more prominent melodic line; a bright, cycling 6-beat guitar pattern fades in, also *in medias res*, at 0:40, a kinetic anaphone providing the first indicators of the pulse stream that will propel the song (Example 31.10).

original guitar pattern:

time interval: 3♪

perceived pattern resulting from union of guitar pattern with its delayed version:

Example 31.10. "Where the Streets Have No Name": cycling guitar figure, guitar figure displaced by three sixteenth-notes value, and the perceived union of both patterns.

The lack of a strong pulse to this point and the minimalist patterning of the guitar convey a feeling of vastness, or perhaps eternity. Soon, however, the cycling pattern turns to vigorous strumming at 1:06; a few seconds later bass and drums enter with an energetic $\frac{4}{4}$ groove. Here's what musicologist Allan Moore has to say about the song:

> {T}he texture remains the same throughout, but seemingly by design rather than thoughtlessness, creating a texture of great energy. Anything that could disturb this is seemingly removed. The guitar is present throughout, covering a small range in a single register, with fast, intricate movement. The stable bass (keeping to the root of harmonies rather than constructing an independent line) gives great firmness to the texture while, of the kit, only the ride cymbal is allowed to threaten this equilibrium. The guitar remaining above the voice sets up a perfect platform for the voice to dominate as the only sound source that really moves.[9]

Although it is true that the song's texture and instrumental roles remain largely static for most of the song (until 4:51, when the song's coda brings back a reprise of the introduction), the surface is loaded with kinetic anaphones in its propulsive drumming, the steady-eighth-note bass line, and the chiming guitar ostinato which might be described as "spiraling" or "circling." The impression is one of contained, pent-up energy, building until it is finally released when the drums and bass cease at 4:51.

---

[9] Allan Moore, *Rock: The Primary Text—Developing a Musicology of Rock* (Burlington, VT: Ashgate, 2001), p. 124.

Musical gestures often embody a combination of these different anaphonic qualities; these are called **composite anaphones**. For example, the quick anapestic rhythm of Rossini's overture from *William Tell* evokes for many listeners the rhythm of galloping hoofbeats, largely through its inspired use as a theme for *The Lone Ranger*. The sound, however, is both a sonic anaphone (because of the anapestic rhythm's resemblance to the pattern made by galloping hoofbeats) and a kinetic anaphone (because of the repetitive nature of the pattern, suggesting ongoing motion).

Other musical gestures are used to signal an imminent change from one state or section to another. For example, Classic-era composers often used a lead-in—a short scalar melodic passage—to "lead" the listener into the next phrase or section. This is an example of an **episodic marker**—a musical event that signals a one-way change from one section to another. The change may be sectional (moving from verse to chorus in a pop song, for example, or the retransition from episode to refrain in a rondo), dynamic (a crescendo or decrescendo), harmonic (as in a sudden key change), or textural (in pop music and jazz, for example, sectional changes are prepared by a drum fill—a brief flourish that departs from the usual groove). In each case, the change is *one-way*: A crescendo followed by a decrescendo, for example, results in no net change, and a tonicization—though it may be considered a very brief modulation—is not the same as a change of key. In Phil Collins's "In the Air Tonight," the abrupt drum entrance heralds a new, more violent version of the chorus; once the drums have entered, the mood of the song has altogether changed and it would be anti-climactic for them to disappear again as suddenly as they entered. Episodic markers are also usually short, although there are instances—the famous atonal orchestral glissando and crescendo in the middle of the Beatles' "A Day in the Life," for example—where an episodic marker can be longer. (Similarly, the Prelude to Richard Wagner's opera *Das Rheingold*—an extended crescendo over a single E♭ harmony that lasts for several minutes—is a kind of episodic marker, leading the listener into the mythic world of Wagner's *Ring* cycle.)

Self-Tests 31.2 and 31.3 may be done at this time.

An Analysis of Anaphones: Pink Floyd, "Comfortably Numb" (*The Wall*, 1979)

The Wall is one of the most famous classic rock albums of the 1970s, and it is one of Pink Floyd's most richly textured productions. Its storyline concerns an individual (named "Pink" in the 1980 movie based on the album) who builds a psychological "wall" as a defense against various childhood traumas; the protagonist's isolation is made worse by substance abuse. Various elements of the storyline are loosely autobiographical, including the scenario depicted in "Comfortably Numb." In the song, Pink has reached a catatonic state shortly before a performance, and a doctor has been dispatched to give him some medication and make him (somewhat) able to perform. The lyrics are structured as a dialogue between the doctor's examination and Pink's (internal) response; contrasting musical elements are used to enhance the separation between the two characters. The most noticeable contrasts involve changes of key (between B minor and its relative major, D major), vocal timbre and register, and orchestration.

The song opens with a brief (seven-second) introduction; an upward slide guitar glissando with copious echo and reverberation at 0:03 acts as an episodic marker into the vocal entry, coinciding with the first verse. The first section of the song (the Doctor's first dialogue), which lasts from 0:07 to 0:52, is actually three verses, each cycling through a harmonic progression of i–VII–VI–iv–i in B minor. The Doctor's verses are sung in lower register (mostly between B2 and A3) by bassist Roger Waters; echo is selectively applied to certain words (e.g., "Hello . . .," "Relax . . ."). The echo, along with some of the lyrics ("Is there anybody in there?") conveys the psychological distance between the doctor and his catatonic rock-star patient. Echo can also be heard on discreet guitar tones that bounce back and forth between the left and right channels with each reiteration. An orchestra provides a tactile-anaphone "cushion" of somber, lower-register wind and brass chords toward the rear of the mix.

Pink's response (presumably not spoken out loud to the Doctor) occurs at 0:53–2:04. A quickly rolled chord on an acoustic guitar (which had not been prominent in the mix before this point) functions as an abrupt episodic marker into the chorus. There is also a direct modulation to the relative major, D major, at this point, along with a different timbre to the vocals (sung in this section by guitarist David Gilmour). Gilmour's vocals are in a higher register, mostly falling in the range between A3 and E4—thus, there is almost no overlap between the two vocal ranges. The vocals also lack the echo that had been applied to Waters's vocals. The orchestra, meanwhile, also changes to the brighter timbre of strings and treble woodwinds; in the left channel the strings and winds sustain chords, while in the right channel strings play a more active repeating pattern of descending sixteenth notes.[10] The harmonic progression is sequential, a I–V progression answered a step lower by ♭VII–IV.

In the second half of the chorus the orchestration thickens slightly and Gilmour's vocal is joined by a harmony part. A simple but direct drum fill acts as an episodic marker for the concluding refrain line (sung in unison), "I have become comfortably numb." On the word "numb," a subtle sweep of a bell tree at 2:01 sets up the orchestral crescendo that acts as an episodic marker into the first guitar solo (set to an instrumental version of the chorus). Thus, the chorus is neatly framed by two "sweeping" gestures—the acoustic guitar strum at 0:53 and the bell tree at 2:01.

The first guitar solo, set to the music of Pink's chorus, begins at 2:04, lasting until 2:46 (overlapping with the return of the voice on the refrain line at 2:35). The solo has a lyrical, soaring quality, in which sustained high notes are usually followed by gracefully descending lines (for example, 2:04–2:13, 2:15–2:19, 2:20–2:26, and 2:29–2:35). The orchestration becomes richer in this section as well, the sustained chords occupying an expanded range beginning at 2:20. Significantly, there are no episodic markers (for example, a drum fill) to lead us into the next (Doctor's) verse.

The Doctor's next section begins at 2:46, lasting to 3:16 and this time comprising two verses. The orchestra momentarily fades away (replaced by a low flute-like keyboard) from 2:46 to 2:59, when bass clarinet and English horn fade in to bring back the woodwinds and horns (strings are absent from this section). The suddenly

---

[10] Interestingly, producer/arranger Bob Ezrin had used an almost identical string arrangement in a song by Lou Reed, "Sad Song," from the album *Berlin*, released in 1973.

PART 4: Advanced Chromatic Harmony and Contemporary Techniques

thinner texture—there are also strategic rests in the bass line—helps to emphasize the climax or turning point in the narrative, the moment when the Doctor gives Pink his shot. The shot—musically illustrated by a high electric-piano "pin prick" arpeggio [2:50–2:52]—is a tactile anaphone. Pink's responsive scream of pain at 2:54–2:57 is more toward the right channel and is unusually quiet for a scream; the change in vocal perspective could represent a physical recoiling from the pain, since up to this point the vocals have been front and center.

Pink's second chorus begins at 3:16, again led off by the acoustic guitar strum. Musically it is quite similar to the first chorus, although there is less spatial separation between the orchestral sustained chords and the strings' sixteenth-note figurations. The orchestration dramatically increases in range at 4:10, as the violins take on a soaring high line (the horns also suddenly move to a higher register). This brings the orchestra to a climax at the refrain line [4:17] with an abrupt drop off at 4:23, leaving the line "comfortably numb" relatively exposed.

The song ends with a second, longer and more blues-inflected guitar solo, this time over the B minor verse progression. The solo is set up with the longest episode marker yet [4:28–4:32], during which there is not only a crescendo but also the introduction of distortion in a low D2 guitar tone. Just before the guitar solo at 4:32 there is also a "spark" of feedback noise that hints at the drama of the solo to come. The solo lasts for seven verse progressions—nearly 30 percent of the total song—and the orchestra is mostly absent as it appears the rock band has taken over; even the low brass lines are played here on distorted guitars. The cymbals become more active as the solo progresses, with hits on beats 2 and 4 on the fifth chorus [5:33–5:48] and on each quarter-note beat on the sixth chorus [5:48–6:03]. The sixth chorus is also where the guitar reaches the peak of its register (D6), just before the song begins to fade out.

MUSIC AND NARRATIVE

Although we may be no closer to a specific, invariable "dictionary" of musical meaning, there has been a consensus through the ages that music has some direct effect on the emotions. The Old Testament tells us that David soothed King Saul with his harp playing: "David took an harp, and played with his hand: so Saul was refreshed, and was well, and the evil spirit departed from him" (1 Samuel 16:23 KJV). Plato, writing in *The Republic* around 360 B.C.E., warned of the political power of music: "when modes of music change, [those] of the State always change with them" (Book IV). In the Baroque era, composers believed in a "doctrine of the affections" in which certain melodic motions or chord progressions were thought to embody particular emotions or philosophical concepts that could be imparted, through such gestures, to the listener. Today, it would be difficult to think of a film that has no musical soundtrack whatsoever; composers such as Aaron Copland, John Williams, and Philip Glass have been drawn to the possibilities of the medium.

Beyond this more generalized approach of acting upon the listener's emotions, some composers aimed to give their music a more specific meaning. **Program music**—music that aimed to tell a story—became commonplace in the nineteenth century; one notable example was Hector Berlioz's *Symphonie Fantastique* (1828–30). As discussed in Chapter 28, Richard Wagner made effective use of **leitmotifs**—short motives or themes that symbolized particular characters, emotions, or concepts—in his operas. These could effectively be used to convey motivations or feelings deeper than those expressed on the surface; for example, a character's line could use a theme meant to convey noble sacrifice, while a countermelody or harmonic progression in the orchestra might convey duplicity or treachery, indicating to the attentive listener that things are not what they seem.

Music as Narrative

We have seen that in the case of program music, a composition can reportedly serve as a kind of "musical narrative," portraying key points in the story. Schubert's "Erlkönig" (Web Feature 31.2) further demonstrates how certain musical elements can enhance the meaning of the text, often hinting at emotions or motivations beyond a simple reading of the text. What happens when the music *becomes* the narrative, "telling a story" in an metaphorical sense?

CONCLUSION

In the web features accompanying this chapter, we have applied a narrative interpretation to music of Schubert and Chopin. The classical sonata form of the late eighteenth and early nineteenth centuries, discussed in Chapter 21, maps particularly well to the three-part Classical narrative model proposed by Aristotle. The exposition section was seen as the section in which "characters" (themes) were introduced or "exposed," during which the listener learned something of their character (heroic, tragic, tender, melancholy). The development section corresponded to the "rising action," ultimately leading to the climax just before the recapitulation; here is where the characters encountered all sorts of challenges, adventures, and obstacles, manifested in such musical details as motivic transformation, modulations, and key relationships to the tonic. The recapitulation presented the denouement in the narrative; any lingering conflicts from the development section left unresolved were often resolved in the coda, if there was one. Such a "dramatic" conception of the sonata left its mark on later compositions, such as Chopin's Ballade in G minor—the degree of dramatic detail merely became more elaborate, in the same way that Freitag's five-part model of narrative structure was an elaboration of Aristotle's three-part model.

With this chapter we have admittedly entered rather unexplored territory in the field of music theory. Narrativity and **semiotics** (the study of signs and symbols) in music are rather new and still-developing areas of study, lacking the uniformly accepted symbols and terms that we find in, for example, harmonic analysis. Of course, harmonic analysis also has an established tradition of practice dating back a couple of centuries.

When considering questions of musical meaning, it is easy to say "this means X to me," simply based on how we respond to the music emotionally. However,

For an example of how music can provide a deeper "program" behind the text, see the study of Franz Schubert's "Erlkönig" in Web Feature 31.2.

To see how music can provide a narrative in the *absence* of a text, see the analysis of Chopin's Ballade no. 1 in G minor, op. 23, in Web Feature 31.3.

Apply This! 31.1 may be done at this time.

Workbook Exercise 31.1 may be done at this time.

one must be careful not to let an analysis slip into solipsism; any interpretations must be logically supported by evidence in the music. For example, certain narrative aspects can be linked to musical patterning and the degree to which the musical flow matches our culturally ingrained expectations. If we hear a V^7, we expect a tonic chord to follow; we would expect a four-bar antecedent phrase to be followed by a four-bar consequent phrase. If the V^7 goes instead to a vi or iii, or if the four-bar antecedent phrase is followed by a massively extended consequent phrase of twenty-one measures, then such thwarting of musical expectations might be interpreted as analogous to a "twist in the plot." We would have musical evidence for such a conclusion.

Throughout this book, you have been given a rich variety of analytical tools for the study of musical structure: musical notation, harmony, phrase structure, hierarchical musical structure and syntax, musical forms, and finally aspects of music's symbolic structure—narrativity, anaphones, genre synecdoches, episodic markers, and different types of intertextuality. Analytic listening does not diminish our sensory or emotional enjoyment of the listening experience; rather, it *adds to* our enjoyment of music at those other levels. As you get older, you will find that you will continue to respond to, enjoy, and understand music in new and deeper ways—even music you know well and have enjoyed for many years. This is why performers as varied as Herbert von Karajan, Vladimir Horowitz, Glenn Gould, and Thelonious Monk returned to and rerecorded the same music much later in their lives, and why people continue to enjoy Miles Davis's *Kind of Blue* or The Beatles's *Sgt. Pepper's Lonely Hearts Club Band* decades after their release (and why entire books continue to be written about such recordings). The enjoyment of music never ends.

Terms to Know

anaphone
catastrophe (in Web Feature 31.3)
climax (in Web Feature 31.3)
composite anaphone
cover version (cover)
denouement (in Web Feature 31.3)
episodic marker
exposition (in Web Feature 31.3)
falling action (in Web Feature 31.3)
genre synecdoche
intertextuality
kinetic anaphone

panning
program music
reversal (peripeteia) (in Web Feature 31.3)
rising action (complication) (in Web Feature 31.3)
semiotics
sonic anaphone
strategic intertextuality
style indicators
stylistic competence
stylistic intertextuality
tactile anaphone

Self-Test

31.1. What is the difference between stylistic and strategic intertextuality? Provide an example of each type.

31.2. How are style indicators different from genre synecdoches?

31.3. Examine the boxed gesture within each musical excerpt below. Then, choose the multiple-choice option that best describes the expressive function of the gesture.

    a. Mozart, Piano Sonata K.333 (iii), mm. 105–120a. (Both boxed gestures are of the same type.)

(Continued)

PART 4: Advanced Chromatic Harmony and Contemporary Techniques

(Continued)

(a) sonic anaphone   (b) tactile anaphone   (c) episodic marker

b. Chopin, Prelude in C♯ minor, op. 28 no. 10, mm. 1–4.

(a) genre synecdoche   (b) episodic marker   (c) kinetic anaphone

c. Beethoven, Piano Sonata, op. 81a ("Les Adieux") (iii), mm. 1–16.

* - Farewell

(a) kinetic anaphone   (b) genre synecdoche   (c) tactile anaphone

Apply This!

31.1. Analysis. Provide an analysis of the narrative elements in Chopin's Ballade no. 2 in F major (op. 38), found on the following pages. Remember that in analyzing narrative elements you are not inventing or providing a story line to go with the music—rather, focus on elements that function as anaphones in the manner discussed in the text, as well as episodic markers that signal one-way changes into a new section of music and genre synecdoches that refer to bodies of work outside this musical text. The first genre synecdoche is provided for you: The *Siciliano* is a pastoral genre characterized by a dotted rhythm in $\frac{6}{8}$ meter and a pedal point that evokes drone instruments such as the hurdy-gurdy. What do these elements, found in the opening of the piece, lead us to expect in what follows?

(Continued)

(Continued)

(Continued)

PART 4: Advanced Chromatic Harmony and Contemporary Techniques

Presto con fuoco.

(Continued)

(Continued)

PART 4: Advanced Chromatic Harmony and Contemporary Techniques

(Continued)

(Continued)

(Continued)

(Continued)

(Continued)

PART 4: Advanced Chromatic Harmony and Contemporary Techniques

Tempo I.

(Continued)

(Continued)

(Continued)

(Continued)

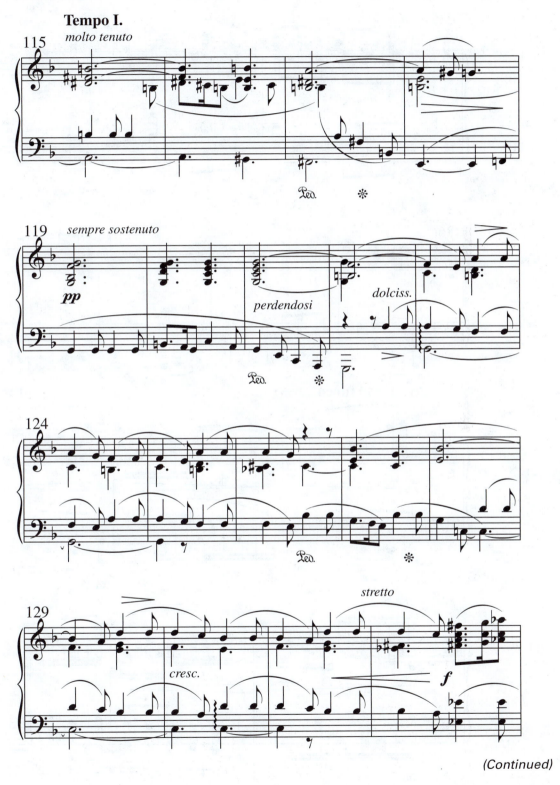

PART 4: Advanced Chromatic Harmony and Contemporary Techniques

(Continued)

(Continued)

(Continued)

PART 4: Advanced Chromatic Harmony and Contemporary Techniques

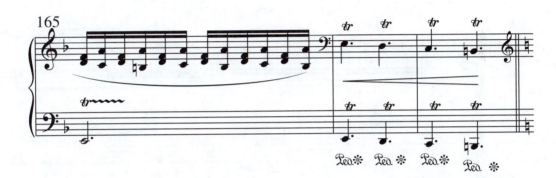

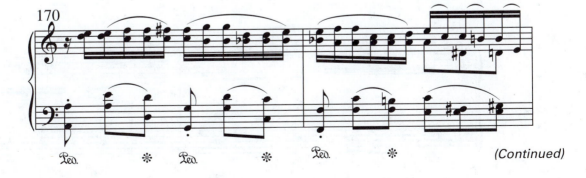

(Continued)

(Continued)

PART 4: Advanced Chromatic Harmony and Contemporary Techniques

(Continued)

(Continued)

(Continued)

PART 4: Advanced Chromatic Harmony and Contemporary Techniques

Tempo I.

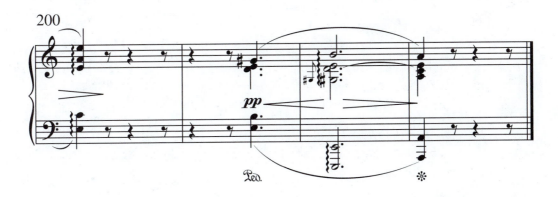

31.2. Composition. Compose a short piece of program music based on one of the Brothers Grimm's fairy tales. Allow the form of your piece to be determined somewhat by the nature of your story—in other words, do not write a piece in ternary form, for example, unless the story provides for some sort of homecoming or return to circumstances as they were before dramatic conflict was introduced in the story. Arrange to have your piece performed.

31.3. Improvisation. Choose a widely familiar story (such as, for example, Noah's Ark and the Flood) and improvise a piece of music that conveys the narrative. Try to structure your improvisation according to the narrative stages of exposition–rising action–climax–falling action–denouement, and also try to incorporate specific anaphone or genre synecdoche gestures into your playing. Play before an audience if possible, informing them of your narrative before your improvisation, and ask for their feedback regarding how successfully you conveyed the narrative in sound.

Apply This 2.3: "Geübtes Herz," Op. 3, no. 5 by Arnold Schoenberg. Used by permission of Belmont Music Publishers, Los Angeles.

Example 5.13: "What's Going On" by Al Cleveland, Marvin Gaye and Renaldo Benson. © 1971 Jobete Music Co., Inc. (BMI).

Example 7.6: "Well You Needn't" by Thelonious Monk. © 1944 (Renewed) Regent Music Corporation (BMI).

Example 7.8c: "If You Leave Me Now," words and music by Peter Cetera. © 1976 by Universal Music—MGB Songs and Big Elk Music.

Level Mastery 7.3f: "Don't Stop Me Now" by Freddie Mercury. © 1979 Queen Music Ltd/EMI Music Publishing Ltd.

Example 7.19b: "March of the Witch Hunters" words and music by Stephen Schwartz. © 2004 GraydogMusic/Williamson Music Company.

Level Mastery 11.3: "The Hours" by Philip Glass. Famous Music Corporation/BMG Music.

Level Mastery 12.1d: "This Jesus Must Die" by Andrew Lloyd Webber and Tim Rice. Universal/MCA Music Ltd.

Example 14.14: "Autumn Leaves" music by Joseph Kosma. © 1947, 1950 Enochet CIE, © renewed 1975, 1978 Enochet CIE.

Example 15.9: "Sweet Georgia Brown" words and music by Ben Bernie, Maceo Pinkard, and Kenneth Casey. © 1925 Warner Bros. Inc. (Renewed)

Example 16.7: "Once You Had Gold," music by Enya and Nicky Ryan; lyrics by Roma Ryan. © 1995 EMI Songs, Ltd.

Level Mastery 17.1, no. 2a: "S.O.S.," by Benny Anderson, Bjorn Ulvaeus and Stig Anderson. © 1975 Union Songs AB Stockholm.

Apply This 27.1: "Wreck of the Hesperus" by Matthew Fisher and Keith Reid. © 1969 (Renewed) Onward Music Ltd. and Headphone Publishing, London, England. TRO—Essex Music International, Inc., New York control all publication rights for the U.S.A. and Canada. Used by Permission.

Example 29.3: *Structures 1a* by Pierre Boulez. Universal Edition/European American Music Distributors LLC.

Example 29.6: Piano Piece Op. 11, no. 1 by Arnold Schoenberg. Used by permission of Belmont Music Publishers, Los Angeles.

Example 29.18: "From the Island of Bali," by Béla Bartók. Boosey and Hawkes Music Publishers, Ltd.

Example 30.3: "Regard du Fils sur le Fils," by Olivier Messiaen. Editions Durand Durand-Salabert-Eschig/Universal Music Publishing.

Example 30.6: "Music in Contrary Motion" by Philip Glass. Dunvagen Music Publishers (ASCAP)/Chester Music.

INDEX OF MUSICAL EXAMPLES